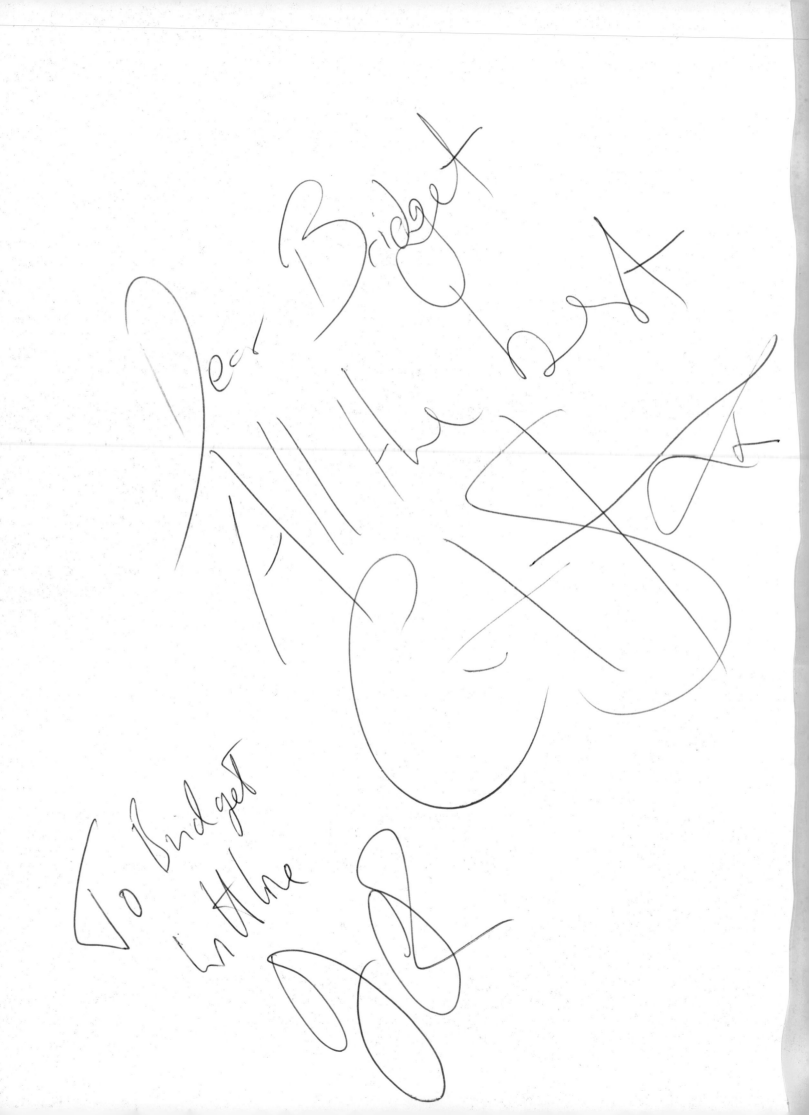

Dear Bridget x

All the best

To Bridget
with love

Foreword

AUSTRALIAN WINE
A Pictorial Guide

The creation of this new book has been a revelation. Publisher, Peter Simic and I, began with the thought of producing a book on Australia's wonderful wineries; a book estimated to be of 250 pages, with 200 detailed features. The depth and breadth of Australian wine and the many new exciting regions and their wineries has meant that the book has grown to 352 pages, incorporating more than 300 detailed features.

Not only has Australian wine, in a pure quality sense, developed in the last decade, with its complexity and balance of the myriad of different wine styles, but it is now being taken to the world. Australia's wine is receiving unanimous support in all parts of the globe. The importance of wine to Australia, both economically and as a "cultural ambassador" for the nation, cannot be denied. Even more exciting and important times are ahead!

The development of wine tourism in Australia and the investment in this field by wineries and associated tourism and hospitality operators has been astounding. More than all this, the welcoming attitude towards visitors by all in our great industry has undergone a revolutionary change.

The support of the individual wineries of Australia and the great and developing cheese industry of our nation has made this comprehensive publication possible. We salute them all.

Also, to our sponsors, Kodak, Ansett Airlines and Cathay Pacific, in addition to

Left to right:
Peter Simic, Editor and Publisher
Milan Roden, Photographer
Tom Hardy, Author

the hospitality houses which have looked after us on our travels our most sincere thanks.

Before letting you loose on the discovery trail that this book offers, I would like to pay homage to a very special human being, Milan Roden, whose talents and ability to inspire are a true gift, no more so than his grace in putting up with my driving and

desire to pack as much into each day as is humanly possible. I trust your journey through the pages that follow will give you some of the pleasure we experienced in creating it.

Cheers,

TK Hardy

Introduction

Sir James Hardy

"In my many nautical miles as a seafarer, a great companion on board the yacht has always been the "Pilot Book". This publication describes in detail the bays, headlands and harbours of any particular coastline. It is, however, the accompanying pictures and drawings which give the visiting mariner the confidence to explorethese waterways.

So it will be with this magnificent volume, authored and enriched by my nephew, Tom Hardy, with sensational photographs by renowned artist Milan Roden, and bringing them together, Peter Simic, Editor/Publisher of Australia's national wine magazine, Winestate.

Local and/or overseas visitors, whether they be experienced wine connoisseurs or not, can now chart their course through the highways and by-ways of Australia's fascinating wine districts."

Sir James Hardy O.B.E.

Robert Mondavi

"For many years I have advocated the philosophy that truly fine wines can be produced throughout the world, where one could bring together all the necessary elements; climate, soil, grape varieties, skilled viticulturists and winemakers.

As in North America, Australia is blessed with many regions that present these ideal conditions.

My own involvement with Australian wine goes back many decades to the early 1970's, when I assisted in the establishment of the beautiful Leeuwin Estate, in Western Australia. We ran many experiments with varieties, then little known in Australia, such as chardonnay and pinot noir as well as other classic grape types.

The innovative nature of the Australian people and the increasing sophistication and superb balance of the wines has brought Australia into the company of the world's premium winemaking countries.

With Milan Roden's sensitive and artistic photography evoking the variety and the spirit of wine, along with Tom Hardy's heartfelt words and the publishing expertise of Peter Simic, another great wine book has been created.

Australia is blessed with many top winemakers, many of whom I count as my friends. Through the pages of this book you will get to meet them and see their lives' work. I wish you a rich and rewarding journey."

Robert Mondavi, Napa, California.

Kodak

"At first glance, the participation of Kodak's Professional and Printing imaging division in the Australian Pictorial Wine Guide seems an unusual collaboration. Yet, we are proud to help sponsor this volume, for its colorful photographs which support the rich descriptions admirably.

In some ways there is an interesting connection between professional photography and wine making. Aside from the the enjoyment of wines, photographers share with vignerons a craftsmanship that is based on tradition, yet, like wine making, is finely tuned to the latest developments in technology.

Both wine making and professional photography require excellent techical expertise as well as devotion and artistic nurturing throughout the process. The artist, whether professional photographer or vigneron, brings his product alive after much creative input.

Through Kodak professional products, we are pleased to bring together Milan Roden's craftsmanship and Thomas Hardy's prose.

This book will capture the attention of wine lovers everywhere!"

Dr Andy Sierakowski,
Kodak,
Manager Professional and Printing
Imaging, Australia and New Zealand.

The history of Australian wine begins with the first settlers. Vine cuttings were brought into the country by Captain Arthur Phillip when he landed at Sydney Cove in 1788. Planted where Sydney's Botanic Gardens now stand, the cuttings, mainly because of unsuitable soil, did not thrive.

It wasn't long, however, before others such as the great pastoralist and grazier John Macarthur moved on to more suitable areas around Parramatta. From there, the vineyards extended to the rich, volcanic soils of the Hunter Valley, around the towns of Pokolbin and Cessnock. All southern mainland states had vineyards established within a few years of their founding.

Ethnic groups were a major influence in establishing the various vineyard areas. The Lutherans, having fled religious persecution in Germany, pioneered the Barossa Valley in South Australia. Their influence is still very obvious today. It can be seen in the picturesque churches and local townships, along with the classic Germanic-style rieslings and the unique German mettwursts which are showcased in the Barossa's colourful and exuberant wine festival. This is a traditional German celebration which was imported to the Barossa Valley to become the first of its kind in Australia, and is now held every two years.

Victoria's strong beginnings in the industry date back to the Swiss settlers who were encouraged to come to Australia by the first Governor, Charles LaTrobe and his wife, who was Swiss. Victoria went on to become the premier wine state, having three quarters of the country's total production until the 1980s. Unfortunately, wine in Australia has always been subject to fashion, changes in taste and economic conditions. Only in the last couple of decades, when wine has become an integral part of the Australian way of life, has some sort of stability and steady growth taken place. Of course stability is also dependent on the forces of nature. The worldwide plague phylloxera swept through most of Australia's vineyards in the 1890s. This tiny vine louse eats into and eventually kills the root of the vine. South Australia was, fortunately, spared this threat and remains one of the very few areas in the world not devastated by this plague. Nevertheless, it still remains a threat.

In the early days winemaking, even at its very best, was a 'hit or miss' affair. With little knowledge worldwide as to the very nature of the process of fermentation from grape juice to wine, many wines were unsound. Some exceptional wines however, which are now making a comeback, were made in the cooler areas such as the Yarra Valley in Victoria.

Heavy fortified wines became increasingly popular as they were refined by blending with higher quality grape spirit, thus ensuring their integrity. They could be produced in the warmer and often irrigated areas where crops were often of greater size per hectare than in the cooler, high quality table wine areas. The Great Depression of the 1930s reinforced the drinking of fortified wines. Not only was it the most affordable beverage, but it was also very palatable in its rich, sweet style.

The dominance of fortified wines lasted some 70 to 80 years, only being reversed in the early 1970s when table wines eventually rose to above 50 percent of wine consumed. Many factors were at work. The heavy post-war immigration of Europeans brought to Australia the century-old tradition of drinking table wine with meals. This influence, along with the growing affluence of the average Australian, brought more leisure time, overseas travel and an interest in the finer things of life, and thus there was an upsurge in wine drinking. The industry accommodated this change with a reasonable price structure, and the introduction of bulk containers such as the flagon, which culminated in the ingenious Australian invention, the 'bag in the box' wine cask. People were now able to enjoy table wine whenever they so desired, without fear of the wine 'going off'.

White wines improved dramatically in the mid-70s. With technological advances in winemaking and wine becoming a part of our everyday life, the preference for chilled wine in our generally warm climate meant that the whites took off, leaving the reds in their wake. There may also have been other factors involved in the downturn of the red wine market. Red wines, which had started the table wine boom in the '60s, had failed to keep up with demand, had run short and in order to stretch diminishing stocks, been thinned by blending with lighter grape varieties.

Red wines have certainly made a resurgence in the late 1980s and 1990s and the richness in colour, flavour and the complexity and balance winemakers today are achieving with their reds is indeed marvellous. The best Australian reds are easily on the top rung of the world's great wines. Much credit for this and the overall outstanding quality of Australian wines goes right back to the vineyard. Soil selection, the aspect of the new plantings, micro-climates carefully chosen, the clonal selections of grape varieties now available, vine spacing, innovative trellising and pruning are all contributing to better and better grapes and consequently wine.

Since the '60s, interest and investment have grown in the wine industry, particularly from the multi-national companies, and lately rationalisation has occurred among the ownership of the bigger wine companies. Alongside this has been the enormous growth in 'boutique vineyards' and the expansion into new viticultural areas. We now have vineyards in all states of Australia and undoubtedly world-class wines.

Australia is the best-performed by far in any world wine competitions. During the last decade, to 1995, Australian wines have taken the wine world by storm. Wine exports have increased more than 10-fold, wine is now one of Australia's main exports, and a very prestigious one at that. To cope with this demand and future plans - among others, a billion dollar Australian wine export goal around the turn of the century - huge plantings are under way. Some 15,000 hectares of vines are going into the ground as I write this introduction, which in several years will produce about an extra $150 million in export revenue.

Exciting times and challenges are ahead for Australian wines. The Australian wine industry has really come of age. In this book, we look forward to guiding you to wineries and vineyards, large and small; a comprehensive tour which not only provides readily identifiable wine labels, up to the minute maps and sensitive photography, but also experiences that you, the traveller, should seek out.

AUSTRALIAN WINE PRODUCING AREAS

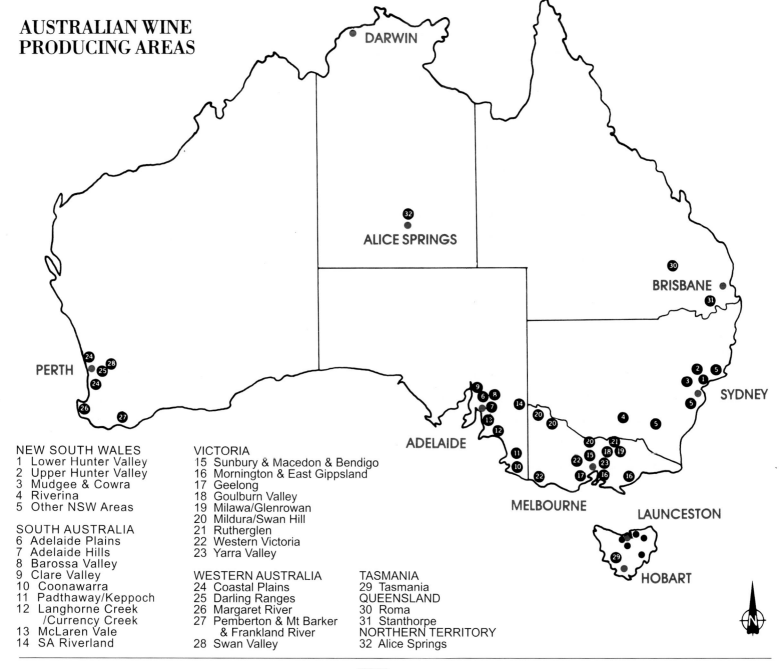

NEW SOUTH WALES
1 Lower Hunter Valley
2 Upper Hunter Valley
3 Mudgee & Cowra
4 Riverina
5 Other NSW Areas

SOUTH AUSTRALIA
6 Adelaide Plains
7 Adelaide Hills
8 Barossa Valley
9 Clare Valley
10 Coonawarra
11 Padthaway/Keppoch
12 Langhorne Creek
   /Currency Creek
13 McLaren Vale
14 SA Riverland

VICTORIA
15 Sunbury & Macedon & Bendigo
16 Mornington & East Gippsland
17 Geelong
18 Goulburn Valley
19 Milawa/Glenrowan
20 Mildura/Swan Hill
21 Rutherglen
22 Western Victoria
23 Yarra Valley

WESTERN AUSTRALIA
24 Coastal Plains
25 Darling Ranges
26 Margaret River
27 Pemberton & Mt Barker
   & Frankland River
28 Swan Valley

TASMANIA
29 Tasmania
QUEENSLAND
30 Roma
31 Stanthorpe
NORTHERN TERRITORY
32 Alice Springs

Contents

New South Wales 7
Lower Hunter Valley 8
Upper Hunter Valley 32
Mudgee 41
The Riverina 48
Cowra 58
Other wine producing areas of NSW 61

South Australia 68
Adelaide Plains and Environs 70
Adelaide Hills 74
Barossa Valley 86
Clare Valley 116
Coonawarra 129
Padthaway/Keppoch 148
Langhorne Creek 151
McLaren Vale - South Australia 155
Riverland 197
Currency Creek/Middleton Beach 208

Victoria 211
Bendigo Region 212
Macedon Ranges 216
Sunbury 221
East Gippsland 224
Mornington Peninsula 227
Geelong 238
Goulburn Valley 240
Milawa/Glenrowan 247
Mildura/Swan Hill 249
Rutherglen 255
Western Victoria 262
Yarra Valley 276

Western Australia 293
Coastal Plains of WA 294
Margaret River 300
Great Southern 316
Swan Valley 321
Pemberton 326

Tasmania 330
Northern Tasmania 332

Queensland 344

Northern Territory 346

Classic Blends 347

SPONSORS:

Our thanks to national sponsors
Kodak
Ansett Airlines
and
Cathay Pacific

*- their help has been
most valuable in the
success of this book.*

Written By: Thomas K Hardy in
conjunction with the participating wineries
and associated companies.

Photography: Milan Roden

Editor/Publisher: Peter Simic

Project Co-ordinator: Jenny Baker

Project Assistant: Julie Idema

Production: Chris Loft
Tim Bannister
Margaret Lemac

Finished Art/Film: Tony Witcher
Kerrie Feirclough

Printed by: Griffin Press

Published by: Pictorial Wine Publishers,
81 King William Road
Unley SA 5061
Copyright 1995

*No part of this publication
may be reproduced by any
process or means without the
prior written permission
of the publishers*

ISBN 1-876082-00-3

New South Wales was the first state to plant vines; in fact, the first vine cuttings arrived with Governor Phillip and the first fleet in 1788. The vines were planted at Farm Cove which is now part of Sydney's Botanic Gardens. These vines unfortunately did not fare well due to poor soil conditions.

Vineyards soon sprang up in many areas around Sydney. The first commercial wine came from Gregory Blaxland, a member of the famous pioneering family, from his vineyard at Brush Farm on the Parramatta River, which is now part of metropolitan Sydney. Another included the Robby Hill 'Minchinbury' Vineyard of Penfolds. None survive today.

Other vineyards sprang up around the State but it was not until vines were planted in the Hunter Valley in the late 1820s that the New South Wales wine industry became firmly established. The first vines in the Hunter were planted in the Branxton/Singleton area. This is 20 kilometres north of the current main grape-growing area around Cessnock, referred to as the Lower Hunter Valley, although Wyndham Estate have a large and very successful vineyard at Branxton. The main pioneers were George Wyndham at Dalwood near Branxton, and James Busby at Kirkton. George Wyndham's classic old home, 'Dalwood House', was built in 1828 and had fallen into disrepair. It was restored in a joint project by Wyndham Estate and the National Trust of Australia for the Australian Bicentenary in 1988. George Wyndham also planted some 10 hectares of vines at Inverell in 1850. This vineyard produced until 1890. (No further vines were planted in the region until the mid 1960s when Gilgai Vineyard was established). James Busby established his vineyard at Kirkton between Branxton and Singleton in 1825.

Mudgee, situated in the northern part of the Great Dividing Range, 300 kilometres north west of Sydney, was the next wine region to be opened up. It was pioneered in 1858 by Arthur Roth, a vineyard worker from Germany. He named his property Rothweir and his family were still involved in viticulture a century later. He was followed by other Germans, namely Andreas Kurtz and Frederick Buchultz. As in the Barossa Valley in South Australia, there was a notable German wine growing influence.

Other areas of New South Wales planted in the latter part of the 19th century were Junee, Wellington, Molong, Bathurst and Young on the slopes of the Great Dividing Range. Today this area is enjoying a renaissance, with huge areas of vines being planted at Cowra, and other large vineyards such as McWilliam's Barwang property near Young.

By far the largest wine region in New South Wales is the Riverina area, first planted to vines in 1912, and centred around the towns of Griffith and Leeton. This area produces almost 100,000 tonnes of grapes from nearly 5,000 hectares of vines, representing approximately one-fifth of Australia's total wine production. Some very high quality table wines come from this region, particularly from the two oldest family companies, McWilliam's and De Bortoli. McWilliam's crush 25,000 tonnes at their two Riverina Wineries and De Bortoli crushes 35,000 tonnes. Until the late 1950's the majority of wine produced in the region was fortified, but since the wine boom of the mid-60s table wine production has risen dramatically in both quantity and quality.

New South Wales is an important producer. Viticulture and winemaking are bound to expand in this populous state. The search for cooler regions with abundant water is continuing. A notably successful vineyard and winery is Cassegrain in the Hastings Valley, in the sub-tropic Port Macquarie area, which supported some 60 wineries in the last century, against all odds. Cassegrain is producing outstanding wines, once again proving the adaptability of the vine in the right hands. There are now 16 wine regions in New South Wales, some well established as described here, others just emerging and establishing their individual indentities.

An introduction to the Lower Hunter Valley

The Lower Hunter Valley was the first wine region to really cater for the wine-lover with properly turned out tasting areas, personal service by proprietors and a framework of restaurants, galleries, art and craft outlets and other venues of interest to attract visitors. Probably it was its proximity to Sydney and the fact that Australia's first boutique wineries sprang up here that the Hunter led the way.

The development of these small but very attractive wineries occurred in the early 1960s and their reputation for beauty and quality of produce has spread worldwide. The first such operation was Dr Max Lake's 'Lake's Folly', established in 1963. Today the Lower Hunter boasts more than 50 wineries and many more vineyards. Nearly all are very keen to open their doors and offer hospitality to the visitor.

The larger companies such as McWilliam's, Lindemans, Hungerford Hill, Wyndham Estate, Tyrrell's, McGuigan and others have responded by upgrading their facilities and staff, resulting in improved conditions for the visitor. Progress in this area over the last decade has been remarkable and has been augmented by the establishment of some great restaurants and accommodation houses which are fine-tuned to the wine traveller's needs. Peppers, the McGuigan Wine Village and Vineyard Resort, Robert and Sally Molines at the Pepper Tree complex and the Casuarina Restaurant are just a few.

If there was an area in Australia that outwardly seemed totally unsuited to viticulture, it would be the Lower Hunter. The climate is very hot. Many vineyards are on poor soil, and the sub-tropical climate can bring rain exactly when it isn't needed, at vintage time. Why then does the Hunter produce some outstanding table wines? After talking to that great district identity Murray Tyrrell, I believe part of the answer lies with the cool, afternoon sea breezes that seem to concentrate around the vineyard area and then die along the magnificent Brokenback Range, the backdrop to the whole region. This often prevents excessive temperatures, and when coupled with afternoon cloud in summer, results in protecting the grapes from direct heat, thereby conserving flavour components.

There is much feeling within Australia that only areas with cool climates can produce really top quality wines. The Lower Hunter is one of several regions that are certainly exceptions to this rule. After all it is the wine in the bottle that people enjoy (even the wine judges) and this is the real proof of the pudding! I am sure it is the great beauty of the region that has attracted many of the winery proprietors to the Hunter despite its difficult climate and low yields from the vineyards. There are now approximately 3,000 hectares of vines planted. The wines that originally put the Hunter on the map were whites made from semillon (or Hunter River riesling as it was known in the area), and the dry reds from shiraz, often referred to as hermitage. Both are distinctive styles.

The semillon, particularly, has come back into vogue after spending some years languishing in the shadows of the more 'trendy' varieties such as chardonnay and sauvignon blanc. Hunter semillons age exceptionally well, developing deep golden colour and rich toasty, nutty and honey-like flavours. There is too, a delightful crisp lemon-citrus finish which stays with them all their life. The older wines of Lindeman, McWilliam, Tulloch, Tyrrell, Drayton and Elliot often show these sought-after characteristics which make Hunter semillons such good food wines.

The late 1960s and early 1970s saw the Australian wine boom at its peak and there was a veritable rush from Sydney to invest in the Hunter Valley. Many co-operative ventures started, including the Pokolbin Winemakers Co-operative, which bought Draytons Happy Valley, the Rothbury Estate, brain-child of Len Evans, and Brokenwood where James Halliday and other notables were involved.

The Rothbury Estate has endured tough times but is now firmly established with its solid 30,000 strong membership and mail order business which sells more than 100,000 cases of wine each year. The winery is magnificent with its banquet hall regularly used, and the light delicatessen-style luncheon you can enjoy daily on the lawns is excellent. Many co-operative ventures such as Pokolbin Winemakers and McPhersons have failed, but others such as Rothbury, Brokenwood and Terrace Vale are now well and truly on the right road. The Lower Hunter is rich in natural beauty, history, wonderful wines and beautiful wineries. A great place for a visit.

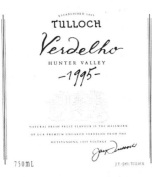

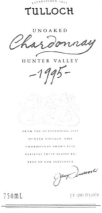

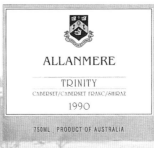

The Lower Hunter Valley

Lower Hunter - Nsw

1	Allandale Winery	32	Moorebank
2	Allanmere	33	Mount View Estate
3	Belbourie Wines	34	Oakvale Winery
4	Blaxland's Wine Sales	35	Parker Wines
5	Briar Ridge	36	Pendarves Estate
6	Brokenwood	37	Pepper Tree Wines
7	Calais Estate	38	Peppers Creek Winery
8	Chateau Francois	39	Peterson's Champagne House
9	Dawson Estate	40	Peterson's Vineyard
10	Draytons Family Wines	41	Pokolbin Estate
11	Evans Family Wines	42	Rothbury Estate
12	Farrell's Limestone Creek	43	Reg Drayton Wines
13	Fraser Winery	44	Saddlers Creek
14	Golden Grape Estate	45	Sandalyn Wilderness Estate
15	Hollyclare Vineyard	46	Scarborough Wine Company
16	Honeytree Estate	47	Simon Whitlam
17	Hunter Estate	48	Small Winemakers Centre/
18	Hunter Valley Wine Society		Verona Vineyard
19	Jacksons Hill Vineyard	49	Sutherland Wines
20	Kevin Sobels Wines	50	Tamburlaine
21	Kindred's Lochleven	51	Terrace Vale Vineyard
22	Lake's Folly Vineyards	52	Thalgara Estate
23	Lesnick Wines	53	Tullochs
24	Lindemans Hunter River	54	Tyrrells Vineyards
25	Little's Winery	55	Van De Sheur Wines
26	Marsh Estate	56	Wandin Valley Estate
27	Mcguigan Bros Cellars	57	Wyndham Estate
28	Mcguigan Hunter Ridge		
29	Mcguigan Hunter Village Hunter Cellars Hunter Valley Cheese Co Vineyard Resort		
30	Mcwilliams Mount Pleasant		
31	Molly Morgan Vineyard		

Drayton's Family Wines

DRAYTON'S FAMILY WINES
Address: Oakey Creek Road, Pokolbin NSW 2321
Phone: (049) 98 7513
Fax: (049) 98 7743
Established: 1853
Winemaker: Trevor Drayton
Principal varieties grown: Semillon, chardonnay, verdelho, shiraz, cabernet, merlot
Ha under vine: 65
Average no. cases produced: 80,000

Principal wines & brands	Cellar potential
Bin 5555	2-5 years
Verdelho	2-5 years
Chardonnay	2-5 years
Cabernet Merlot	2-5 years
Chardonnay Semillon	2-5 years
Semillon	5-10 years

Public & trade tours: By appointment only
Cellar door & mail order sales: Yes
Hours open to public: 8 am-5 pm Mon-Fri; 10 am-5 pm Sat/Sun

Drayton is a famous family wine name in the Hunter Valley with the winery being a real family affair. Max Drayton, a fourth generation member, owns and runs the business with his three sons. Trevor, who graduated from Roseworthy Agricultural College as dux of the course in 1977, is winemaker. Eldest son, John, a giant of a man, returned to the fold in 1989 after tracking around NSW for some 14 years.

Youngest son Greg is vineyard manager, helped along by his father, Max. Greg has an agricultural diploma from Tocal Agricultural College where he passed all subjects with distinction.

The Drayton story started when Joseph Drayton, in his early twenties, set sail from England in 1852 with his wife Anna and two sons. Tragically, during the voyage, he lost his wife, newborn daughter and one of his sons. Undaunted, he and his surviving son Frederick purchased a property in the Hunter in 1853. The dynasty, I am sure retains this solid commitment. The Draytons are not flashy people - they go about their business producing great wines which they figure do the talking, and more power to them.

Hunter Valley Wine Society

The Hunter Valley Wine Society was founded over a decade ago to give members Australia-wide instant access to world class, but often difficult to get wines, unique to the Hunter Valley region of New South Wales.

The society now has many thousands of members, who, for only $20 a year receive many benefits. Every three months they receive a magazine, a total update of happenings in the Hunter and its wines. They also receive a dozen of their choice, white, red or mixed, of prestige wines at exceptionally good prices - delivered to their door.

The society's superbly appointed tasting rooms at Pokolbin are conveniently located to act as a starting point for members' visits to the wineries. We found the enthusiastic and knowledgeable staff most helpful in making the Hunter wine pilgrimage a total success. The society also organises a number of events each year for members. These include gourmet dinners, where one can meet and talk to the winemakers. The Hunter Valley Wine Society is a welcome addition to the Hunter Valley and reinforces the progress this great wine region has made in recent times.

Address: 107 Griffith Road, Lambton, NSW 2299
Phone: (049) 56 2800 fax: (049) 52 8474

LAKES FOLLY VINEYARDS
Address: Broke Road, Pokolbin, NSW 2321
Direction: 10 minutes north of Cessnock
Phone: (049) 98 7507
Fax: (049) 98 7322
Year of establishment: 1963
Owner: The Lake family
Winemaker: Stephen Lake

Principal varieties grown: Cabernet sauvignon, chardonnay, merlot, shiraz
Ha under vine: 12
Average annual crush: 50-60 tonnes
Average no. cases produced: 4,000

Principal wines & brands	Cellar potential
Cabernet	5-15 years
Chardonnay	2-5 years

Public & trade tours: By appointment only
Cellar door & mail order sales: Yes
Hours open to public: 10 am-4 pm Mon-Sat; closed Sun.
Points of interest: Lakes Folly was the first new vineyard in the Hunter Valley this century
Retail distribution: De Bono Wholesale, Sydney, but basically mail order plus cellar door @ $22 per bottle vs. RRP of $30.

Allanmere

The Hunter Valley seems to attract the cream of medical practitioners like a magnet. Dr Newton Potter gained his medical degree from the University of Durham in England and migrated to Australia with a view to becoming a 'country GP.' He began a practice in South Australia but moved to the Royal Newcastle Hospital, where he gained a further degree in anaesthetics, and later finished at the Crown Street Women's Hospital in Sydney.

His interest in wine saw him move to live in the Hunter Valley and after a few years he decided to venture into the wine industry. His first fully-fledged vintage of two reds, a cabernet and a hermitage in 1985, both won gold medals at that year's Hunter Wine Show.

Allanmere has been extremely successful at wine shows with more than 200 medals and many trophies in just 10 years, unbelievable for a small maker. In 1987, Allanmere introduced their "Trinity White" a blend of chardonnay, semillon and sauvignon blanc. In 1988 "Trinity Red" a blend of cabernet, merlot and shiraz, was released; both have been highly successful on the show circuit and with wine drinkers. The 'Durham' chardonnay is the top of the range white, and the 'Gold Label' chardonnay is also a big success. Allanmere takes the 'mere' part of the name from its 10 acre lake and 'Allan' from the sub-region's name Allandale. Those who enjoy the chardonnay known as Endless Summer and the Fisherman's dry white at world-renowned Doyle's Restaurant in Sydney have a taste of Allanmere's skill - they make them.

ALLANMERE WINERY
Address: Lovedale Road, Pokolbin NSW 2321
Direction: 10 km from Cessnock
Phone: (049) 30 7387
Fax: (049) 30 7387
Established: 1985
Owner: Dr Newton Potter
Winemaker: N. Potter
Average annual crush: 40-60 tonnes
Average no. cases produced: 3,500-4,000

Principal wines & brands	Cellar potential
Allanmere	
Durham Chardonnay	2-5 years
Gold Label Chardonnay	2-5 years
Trinity White	2-5 years
Trinity Red	5-10 years

Cellar door & mail order sales: Yes
Hours open to public: 11 am-4 pm Mon-Fri. (closed Wed); 9.30 am-5 pm Sat/Sun
Points of interest: Picnic area available, local inter-winery horse-drawn carriage trips
Retail distribution: Selected cellars only, restaurant & Liquorland Fine Wine Outlets, Sydney metropolitan area; export, Switzerland & Japan

---

Briar Ridge

The Mount View sub-region at the south end of the valley is really in the foothills of the Brokenwood Ranges and quite a deal cooler than the vineyard area in the valley proper. Briar Ridge has won the most successful small wine trophy at the annual Hunter Valley Wine Show several times.

The vineyard and winery was started by the enigmatic but charming Murray Robson back in 1971 and he built a pretty cottage which was available for visitor accommodation. Today, Briar Ridge is run by the energetic and enthusiastic Neil McGuigan, younger brother of the human dynamo Brian. Neil still retains an interest in McGuigan Brothers but was keen to make his own statement.

The charming rustic winery is built from local timbers and other materials and retains a lovely country boutique nature. The wines are excellent and largely snapped up by the 'Briar Ridge Vintage Club' which is certainly worth joining. Briar Ridge is a good place to start your tour of the Hunter if you're coming from Sydney.

BRIAR RIDGE VINEYARD
Address: Mount View Road, Mount View, via Cessnock NSW 2325
Direction: 5 km west of Cessnock
Phone: (049) 90 3671
Fax: (049) 90 7802
Established: 1972
Owner: John Davis and Neil McGuigan
Winemaker: Neil McGuigan and Karl Stockhausen
Principal varieties grown: Chardonnay, semillon, hermitage, cabernet sauvignon, verdelho
Ha under vine: 15
Average annual crush: 200 tonnes
Average no. cases produced: 10,000

Principal wines & brands	Cellar potential
Briar Ridge	
Semillon	5-10 years
Chardonnay	2-5 years
Stockhausen Semillon	5-10 years
Stockhausen Hermitage	5-10 years

Public & trade tours: By appointment only
Cellar door & mail order sales: Yes
Hours open to public: 10 am-4.30 pm seven days a week
Points of interest: The winery is tucked away amidst some of the most picturesque scenery in the lower Hunter region
Retail distribution: Estate Wine Distributors, Sydney, Three Ridge Wine Co., Nth NSW

Brokenwood

One of the highest profile and most respected wineries in the Hunter Valley is Brokenwood, which was born in 1970 as a joint venture between three prominent Sydney solicitors and wine lovers - James Halliday, Tony Albert and John Beeston. This trio managed to seduce their friends into helping perform the necessary vineyard and winemaking tasks with invitations for a relaxed weekend in the country.

The initial hectares were expanded in 1978, when the partnership grew to nine, and they purchased the property next door and planted a further vineyard. They named it 'The Graveyard' as it was designated by the town planners of Pokolbin in the last century, but never used as such. No doubt they buried plenty of money planting the vineyard. In 1982, winemaker and managing director Iain Riggs became a fulltime employee and Brokenwood took on a fully professional feel. The winery was insulated and airconditioned and refrigeration for the fermentations also installed.

The Graveyard label is used for the domain-sourced wines. These include a cabernet sauvignon first released in 1983, a hermitage (shiraz) and a chardonnay . Brokenwood also make a selection of regionally-sourced wines including a Yarra Valley Pinot Noir. Two blended wines under the 'Cricket Pitch' label are regionally sourced and of excellent quality. They take their name from the other Brokenwood Vineyard which the town planners originally designated a 'cricket pitch'. Iain Riggs is still in charge, highly regarded by all his peers, as are the Brokenwood wines.

BROKENWOOD WINES PTY LTD
Address: McDonalds Road, Pokolbin NSW 2321
Direction: West of township of Cessnock
Phone: (049) 98 7559
Fax: (049) 98 7893
Owner: Brokenwood Wines Pty Ltd
Winemaker: Iain Riggs
Principal varieties grown: Chardonnay, shiraz
Ha under vine: 15
Average annual crush: 500 tonnes
Average no. cases produced: 32,000

Principal wines & brands	Cellar potential
Cricket Pitch Sauvignon	
Blanc-Semillon	0-2 years
Semillon	2-7 years
Chardonnay	2-4 years
Shiraz	5-10 years
Cabernet Sauvignon	5-10 years

Trade tours: By appointment only
Cellar door & mail order sales: Yes
Hours open to public: 10 am-5 pm seven days a week
Retail distribution: All states

Hungerford Hill

A product of the wine boom of the 1960s, Hungerford Hill's first vines were planted in 1967. Over a period of five years, the original area expanded to well over 200 hectares, much of which was shiraz grapes. By the time the first Hungerford Hill reds came onto the market, red wine popularity was in a dramatic decline. A drastic rationalisation program followed, which is now seeing Hungerford Hill wines back on the rails to success.

In 1990 Hungerford Hill was bought by Seppelt, already part of S.A. Brewing which later became Southcorp. The good reputation of Hungerford Hill, particularly the chardonnay with its rich buttery style and with good stone fruit flavours, the pinot noir and the cabernet sauvignon, is now being extended through the winemaking and marketing skills of Southcorp. Hungerford Hill is one of the prestige labels of Southcorp and can be relied upon to give you a consistent and enjoyable experience.

Calais Estates

As one enters the driveway of Calais Estate the impressive winery buildings come into view over the vines. The huge convict-hewn stones, the wide two-storied verandahs with their intricate iron lacework trimmings all give a feeling of the Victorian colonial charm of yesteryear.

The winery started off in the 1970s under the name Wololundry Estate which was later changed when Colin Peterson from the dynamic Peterson wine clan became involved. The cellar door also has much charm inside with huge wooden beams coming from early colonial buildings, giving it a warm solid atmosphere. Calais Estates also runs a corporate wine club and should you wish, would be delighted to send you the details. The cellar door also caters for functions, private dinners and wine tasting functions.

The award-winning Calais range includes semillon, chardonnay, pinot noir, shiraz, cabernet sauvignon and a sauternes. Specially selected reserve wines are also available. Why not taste a glass or two while enjoying the splendid views.

Petersons

The name Mount View is most applicable as a location for one of the Hunter Valley's most revered wineries, Petersons. The cottage-style tasting room in front of the winery opens out to a delightful garden which has elevated views in all directions over the orderly vines and the rich fertile valleys surrounding them. As a backdrop the steep slopes of the impressive mountains not only add a grandeur to the whole scene, but give a sheltered yet surprisingly cool micro-climate.

Petersons was founded in 1971 and quickly began to collect awards at the Hunter Valley Wine Show, particularly with its chardonnay, and forging an enviable reputation for all the wines in a very short time.

The family is very involved in the operation and are modest, open and friendly people. Son Colin has a definite entrepreneurial flair and is also co-proprietor of the Calais Winery with the assistance of his father and the rest of the family, is working on the completion of the exciting Petersons Champagne House, a publicly-floated venture to produce outstanding methode champenoise in the French tradition, from a superb 'maison', prominently located on the corner of Branxton and Broke Roads. I am sure they will have every reason to toast its success. The Petersons are a credit to the Hunter Valley.

Allandale

Allandale is located in the Lovedale area near the Cessnock Airport which during the last century, boasted many vineyards and wineries, including the Hunter's largest, 'Daisy Hill'.

This is the home of 'the friendly boutique winery', of which Allandale was one of the first, established in 1978. Allandale is situated on a hill with commanding views of

its seven hectares of vines and the Brokenback Ranges. The tasting area is in the winery itself and you are surrounded by French and American oak barrels quietly maturing the wines.

Enthusiastic and knowledgeable winemaker, Bill Sneddon, a graduate of Charles Sturt University's wine course at Wagga Wagga, has been in charge for the last 10 years and makes an excellent range of wines, including a semillon, chardonnay and shiraz which go under the Allandale label.

Bill's chardonnay has made a real name for itself and sells out each year. Whilst a number of chardonnay labels were produced by the winery each year, Bill is now concentrating on just one, which is a superb, no expense spared wine, fermented in new french oak and aged "sur-lie" giving a rich opulent distinctive wine of which Allandale can be justly proud.

Bill also produces a top class sparkling wine from pinot noir which carries the name "William" on the label.

ALLANDALE WINERY
Address: Lovedale Road, Pokolbin NSW 2321
Direction: Via Maitland
Phone: (049) 90 4526
Fax: (049) 90 1714
Established: 1978
Owner: Villa Villetri (Wines) Pty Ltd
Winemaker: Bill Sneddon & Peter Orr
Principal varieties grown: Pinot noir, chardonnay, semillon
Ha under vine: 7
Average annual crush: 200 tonnes
Average no. cases produced: 12,000

Principal wines & brands	Cellar potential
Chardonnay	2-5 years
Semillon	5-10 years
Matthew Shiraz	5-10 years

Trade tours: Yes
Cellar door & mail order sales: Yes
Hours open to public: 9 am-5 pm Mon-Sat; 10 am-5 pm Sun
Retail distribution: Restaurants & bottle shops

Little's Winery

The Little family purchased the vineyard established by the late Dr. Quentin Taperell on Palmers Lane. That was back in 1983. Ian Little studied biochemistry in England and worked at Tooth's Brewery in Sydney on arriving in Australia.

Ian took the wine course at what is now the Charles Sturt University at Wagga Wagga and worked with Geoff Merrill at Chateau Reynella during the 1981 and 1982 vintages. Ian also had some experience at Penfolds, working in their champagne cellars. After buying the vineyard, the Littles quickly established a winery on the property.

I well remember visiting the winery during its early days. I was, and still am, very impressed by their wines and the quiet no-nonsense way they go about producing and promoting them. Ian is meticulous with his picking, and chills all the fruit in his large cool room before crushing; he also shows great care in his wood maturation. The striking Little's label has won a packaging award and is not easily missed. I was most impressed by the Little's Vintage Port, along with their warm hospitality.

LITTLE'S WINERY
Address: Lot 3, Palmers Lane, Pokolbin NSW 2320
Phone: (049) 98 7626
Fax: (049) 98 7867
Established: 1983
Owner: Michael Little & family
Winemaker: Ian Little
Principal varieties grown: Chardonnay, pinot noir
Ha under vine: 5
Average annual crush: 80 tonnes
Average no. cases produced: 3,500-5,000

Principal wines & brands	Cellar potential
Chardonnay	2-5 years
Semillon - Dry F.O.M.	2-5 years
Semillon Sauvignon Blanc	2-5 years
Gewurztraminer	2-5 years
Shiraz	5-10 years
Cabernet Sauvignon	5-10 years
Vintage Port	10+ years

Public & trade tours: By appointment only
Cellar door & mail order sales: Yes
Hours open to public: 10 am-4.30 pm seven days a week
Points of interest: Craft products, wine accessories, picnic area, wine club/mail order
Retail distribution: Cellar door, mail order & wine club

McWilliam's Mount Pleasant Winery

There are probably very few family-owned companies as proud or as conscious of their heritage as McWilliam's Wines, who are well into their second century of winemaking. In addition to being one of Australia's largest wine producers, the company is entirely family-owned and controlled.

The McWilliams are a close-knit family, and members of the last three generations can be found throughout the company. While most of those involved are working in the managerial area, or the running of one of their huge wineries in the Riverina or at Robinvale, the McWilliams are not above a hard day's work in whatever field demands their attention.

Both the winery itself and the wines from Mount Pleasant are close to the heart of the McWilliam family, not surprising given the outstanding show record of Mount Pleasant's wines over many decades. In what must be an expensive exercise, Mount Pleasant is one of the few remaining wine producers to cellar-age commercial quantities of bottled table wines until they are at their peak. This enlightened policy allows wine lovers to enjoy fully mature, five year old whites and reds at very reasonable prices. There is also a regular release of even older wines. This conscious policy by McWilliam's is to be applauded.

The birth of the winery and vineyards at Mount Pleasant began in 1880 when Charles King planted vines on some of the best red volcanic soil in the region. Exciting things started to happen when the property was purchased by the O'Shea family. The young Maurice O'Shea was sent to study winemaking at Montpelier in France and upon his return in 1921 quickly established a reputation for himself as perhaps the greatest and most celebrated winemaker of his time. During the most dismal period of the Great Depression in 1932, O'Shea was forced to sell half of the property at Mount Pleasant to the McWilliams, who later completed the purchase by buying the remaining half while allowing Maurice O'Shea to stay on as winemaker and winery manager until his death in 1956.

The wines made by Maurice O'Shea are legendary and their longevity is astonishing, with some wines of more than 40 years of age still drinking magnificently. It was O'Shea who started a tradition, now adopted by McWilliam's, of naming his wines after friends of the family. Some well-known examples are their 'Elizabeth', formerly called 'Elizabeth Riesling' but in fact made from semillon (often referred to in days gone

by as Hunter River Riesling), and 'Philip' (formerly 'Philip Hermitage') made from shiraz. Another wine named after a friend was 'Ann Riesling', an excellent aged Hunter semillon with its intense, toasty, honey and lemon flavours from Mount

Pleasant's historic Lovedale Vineyard. The name 'Ann' was in fact dropped with the latest release of this wine, the 1984 Mount Pleasant Lovedale Semillon which now gives due recognition to the vineyard of its origin. This is a wine now regarded as one of

Australia's, and indeed the world's best.

Other great wines in Mount Pleasant's Individual Vineyard range are a shiraz from the Rosehill Vineyard and another from the Old Paddock and Old Hill Vneyards. Keep an eye out too for regular re-releases of some of the older vintages of Mount Pleasant Elizabeth under the 'Museum Release Label'.

The current long-serving winemaker at Mount Pleasant is Phil Ryan, a quiet, astute man who is also a terrific host - if you can track him down. Phil was one of the first graduates from the new winemaking course at Charles Sturt University, and has been with McWilliam's for many years - like the winery name, he is a very pleasant chap. The cellar door has been rebuilt and is delightful.

I well remember a tasting at the winery some 10 years ago; I'm not sure if Milan remembers it so well as he kept asking me how I could spit out the exquisite wines. After 23 wines, all more than 15 years old, finishing with a 1946 Maurice O'Shea Sauternes of which McWilliam's at that stage still had over 1,000 dozen, Milan found out why I do spit them out. As we exited the tasting room, the moon was rising. That was our first day working together and I had to help him put the camera on the tripod. He took one of his greatest photos ever. In an incredible stroke of luck, the moon again rose at sunset on our visit there for the research and photography of this book. To Phil Ryan and all his team, and to the great Mount Pleasant Wines, thanks for the memories.

Lindemans Hunter Valley Winery

This famous winery is a vital part of the Southcorp wine empire. Formerly known as the Ben Ean Winery, it was purchased to become Lindemans, from John MacDonald in 1912. The company of Lindemans was started at a much earlier date, however, by the famous Dr Henry Lindeman, a Royal Navy surgeon who settled in the Hunter Valley in 1842. With his three sons, Dr Lindeman bought and established vineyards at Cawarra, Coolalta, Catawba, Warrawee and Kirkton.

The Lindemans also purchased the name of 'Porphyry' along with all remaining stock of the wine (the vineyard had ceased to exist) from the Carmichael family. Porphyry had an enviable reputation and had been served to Queen Victoria in 1851. Lindemans still produce Porphyry Sauternes, of which the Carmichael family would have been proud, improving as it does with every year in the bottle.

Lindemans Hunter River Wines are probably Australia's best-known wine 'family', with their simple but bold label and distinctive four figure bin classification. The Hunter Valley whites are made mainly from semillon and chardonnay grapes. The major wines marketed under this label are the Lindemans Hunter River Semillon and the Hunter River Chardonnay. These wines are produced each year and the four figure bin numbers change each vintage. They age exceptionally well and develop into classic and unique wines of world class, which dominate Australian wine shows.

When young, Lindemans Hunter Valley semillons are pleasant, but often simple and uninteresting. They usually have a grassy, herbaceous character both in the aroma and on the palate, with a distinct lemon-citrus flavour in the aftertaste. As they approach 10 years of age however, marvellous things begin to happen. Flavours develop which include toast, honey and nuts and the finish is enhanced by the beautiful lemon-citrus character. The colour too, develops into a bright yellow gold, but does not tarnish. The Hunter River Chardonnay has also shown this marvellous ageing potential.

Until 1978, Lindemans chardonnays wines were not aged in new imported oak casks, as is the trend today, and so the wines exhibited pure, although complex fruit flavours. Since then, however, some wood ageing has become part of the style. This procedure, combined with temperature control and modern white winemaking techniques, has produced wines with more fruit and vanilla oak characters. Grape selection has also changed with the times; fruit now comes to Lindemans from various parts of the Hunter Valley, including vineyards in the Broke Region. These changes were brought about by Karl Stockhausen who made the wines from 1960 until the late 1980s.

The red wines from the Hunter Valley winery have nothing to fear from the reputation of the whites. They are Steven Vineyard Hermitage and various Hunter River Burgundies with different bin numbers every year. The Hunter River Burgundy is made from shiraz grapes and develops a silky feel in the mouth as it ages. This wine does not necessarily have a deep colour or heavy body, but it does always have long and interesting flavours combining Hunter River 'leather' and an earthy character. The wine is well-balanced, has a soft silky finish and is usually reasonable buying when young. Although it is good drinking

Lindemans Hunter Valley Winery

while young, this wine improves further with ageing. The 'Steven Hermitage' is a firmer wine with light acid and occasionally more body than the burgundy. This is a wine to put down for some years.

Early in 1986, Karl Stockhausen took up a senior marketing position with

Lindemans. His winemaking position was filled by Gerry Sissingh, who had assisted Len Evans in establishing Rothbury Estate. The current winemaker is Pat Auld, from a famous South Australian winemaking family, who in 1995 completed his twenty second Hunter vintage. Today the

Southcorp team are carrying on a fine tradition. Lindemans jealously guard their reputation for premium wines. For as long as the wine's unique quality is maintained, Dr Lindeman will be making us smile.

Pendarves Estate

Dr Philip Norrie is a general practitioner in a northern beaches suburb of Sydney. He is also president of the 'Australian Medical Friends of Wine Society' and with his wife Belinda is the owner of the premium wine producer, Pendarves Estate, which they founded in 1986. Philip is one of a long line of doctors, going right back to Dr Henry Lindeman, who have been prime movers in the Hunter Valley wine industry. The roll-call of doctors who have started wineries in Australia is now up to at least 150, way in excess of what would be a representative sample, proving beyond doubt that medical practitioners at large believe in the medicinal value of wine.

Recently, with the aid of a McWilliam's Wines grant, Dr Norrie has published a booklet entitled 'Wine and Health.' This most informative booklet quotes the world's leading epidemiologist and Oxford professor, Sir Richard Doll, who states, 'The positive effect of wine consumption in moderation has been conclusively proved.' If you wish to obtain this booklet, contact Pendarves or McWilliam's Wines, PO Box 80, Greenacre NSW 2190, Australia. When in the Hunter on a weekend, why not drop in on the good doctor and imbibe a little of his beloved cabernet blend verdelho or chambourcin - for your health's sake.

PENDARVES ESTATE
Address: Lot 12, Old North Road, Belford, NSW
Phone: (065) 74 7222
Established: 1986
Owner: Dr P.A. & Mrs B.J. Norrie
Winemaker: Tamburlaine
Principal varieties grown: Verdelho, sauvignon blanc, chardonnay, pinot noir, merlot, malbec, chambourcin, pinot meunier shiraz

Ha under vine: 22
Average annual crush: 150-200 tonnes
Average no. cases produced: 3,200

Principal wines & brands	Cellar potential
Cabernet-Merlot-Malbec	5-10 years
Shiraz	5-10 years
Pinot Noir	2-5 years
Chambourcin	2-5 years
Chardonnay	2-5 years
Verdelho	2-5 years
Sauvignon Blanc-Semillon	2-5 years
Semillon	2-5 years

Public & trade tours: By appointment only
Cellar door & mail order sales: Yes
Hours open to public: 11 am-5 pm Sat/Sun
Points of interest: Picnic area, BBQ, petanque (French bowls) played
Retail distribution: Cellar door, Premier Vineyards, agent in Sydney

Simon Whitlam

In 1982, two of Sydney's top businessmen, one of whom was prominent banker Nicholas Whitlam, formed a partnership based on their love of wine and purchased Yellow Rock Estate - situated at the western end of the Brokenback Ranges. The vineyard is located at the foot of Yellow Rock, a precipitous outcrop whose peak is the highest point in the ranges, only a few kilometres from the township of Broke.

Nicholas renamed the property Wollombi Brook, and planted eight hectares of vines. Now operated by Arrowfield Wines, of which Nicholas Whitlam is chairman, the wines are made by prominent Winemaker Don Buchanan. The Simon Whitlam label continues to have a very devoted following around Australia, where the boutique label is often found in leading restaurants. A top spot to stop and take in this quiet, untouched setting amongst the increasingly commercialised Hunter district.

SIMON WHITLAM & CO.
Address: Wollombi Road, Broke, NSW 2330
Direction: 2.5 km from Broke
Phone: (065) 76 4041
Fax: (065) 76 4144
Established: 1983
Owner: Arrowfield Wines Pty Ltd
Winemakers: Don Buchanan, Elizabeth Radcliffe
Principal varieties grown: Chardonnay, cabernet sauvignon, semillon
Ha under vine: 9
Average annual crush: 90 tonnes
Average no. cases produced: 7,200

Principal wines & brands Simon Whitlam	Cellar potential
Chardonnay	2-5 years
Semillon	2-5 years
Semillon Chardonnay	0-1 years
Cabernet Sauvignon	2-5 years
Shiraz	5-10 years
Late Picked Semillon	0-2 years

Cellar door & mail order sales: Yes
Hours open to public: 10 am-4 pm Sat, Sun, PH
Retail distribution: Arrowfield distribution

Sutherland Wines

Neil and Caroline Sutherland have established a thoroughly professional vineyard and winery, and a beautiful home, overlooking the Brokenback Range. To sit on their verandah with a glass of their fine wine, enjoying their excellent company, is a delightful experience.

Once managing director of a Hong Kong chemical company, Neil became disenchanted with the corporate rat-race. He maintained a consulting position, but began a search for a small vineyard in the Hunter to develop into a lifetime concern and to make his family's home.

Both Neil and Caroline already had a love of wine and were members of Rothbury Estate. In 1977, they purchased part of the McPherson Co-operative vineyard which was badly in need of some attention. For the first few years of production, grapes were sold and bottled under the Allandale label. The Sutherland's built, by hand, their lovely colonial-style home and the winery (commercially built) is both smart and functional, with a beautiful wood-panelled tasting area on a raised mezzanine. This raised area promotes the feeling of being part of the winemaking process.

The first vintage was produced in the new winery in 1983. As winemaker, Neil draws on his science degree and a number of courses he has completed at the Charles Sturt University at Wagga. Neil is a positive, assertive sort of fellow and his wines definitely echo these characteristics, being full of positive fruit flavours and rich varietal character. Neil invests heavily in new French oak but uses it with admirable restraint to enhance the wine's character, not dominate. The early chardonnays were a revolution in the Hunter and won a number of awards and trophies. Sutherlands winery is an invigorating place to visit and seeing people leave with armloads of wine must be a just reward for Neil and Caroline's hard work.

SUTHERLAND WINES PTY LTD
Address: Deaseys Road, Pokolbin, NSW 2321
Phone: (049) 98 7650
Fax: (049) 98 7603
Established: 1979
Winemaker: Neil G Sutherland
Principal varieties grown: Chardonnay, semillon, chenin blanc, pinot noir, cabernet sauvignon, shiraz
Ha under vine: 22
Average annual crush: 100 tonnes
Average no. cases produced: 8,000

Principal wines & brands	Cellar potential
Semillon	5-10 years
Chardonnay	5-10 years
Chenin Blanc	2-5 years
Shiraz	5-10 years
Cabernet Sauvignon	5-10 years

Trade tours: By appointment only
Cellar door & mail order sales: Yes
Hours open to public: 10 am-4.30 pm seven days a week
Retail distribution: Ex winery

Brian McGuigan

Brian McGuigan and his wife Fay are two of the loveliest people you'll ever meet. Even with the breakneck pace of their super busy lives, their achievements and the wealth they have created, they have time for everyone and for the simple pleasures and family values of life.

This was brought home to me strongly on a recent visit to the winery. Milan and I arrived just as a most beautiful glowing Hunter sunset was starting. We tore Brian away from his business papers spread across his large dining room table and raced up into the vineyards surrounding his Hunter Ridge winery and home. Milan was thrilled with the conditions and Brian was in his best ebullient form, it was an

cheeses. On the contrary, a passionate cheese lover, he had given up this passion for Lent. I couldn't believe it - another side to McGuigan had surfaced. As I was explaining that my mother had always done the same thing, my mobile phone rang and my mother in Adelaide and Brian had a great conversation.

When you're around the McGuigans magic things happen. I am sure they have a positive psychic power and it definitely transfers into their wines. At this moment Fay arrived home from a promotion in Sydney in time to pick up wine and food for a Hunter Valley Wine Club meeting. She should have been absolutely stressed out, but no, as she got it all together, she chatted and shared the time she didn't

long time winemaker and manager for Penfolds at their Dalwood Winery in the northern part of the Lower Hunter Valley, a winery established in 1827 by George Wyndham. Brian and his father bought the run-down winery from Penfolds in 1971. By the mid '80s Brian, who had taken over from his father, owned three other Hunter wineries, Hunter Estate, Saxondale and Richmond Grove. Shortly after, he bought Montrose and Craigmoor, the two biggest wineries in Mudgee.

In 1991, Brian who had formed a public company, although unlisted, sold his entire wine empire to the Orlando Wine Group, then owned by the giant French Pernod Ricard Company. Being idle is not Brian McGuigan's favourite pastime and

adrenalin-packed half hour.

On arriving back at his home, he proudly made us a platter of the cheeses from his new Hunter Valley Cheese Company. They were sensational and we enjoyed washing them down with a glass or two of the McGuigan wines. I noticed Brian was not eating any cheese and I jibed at him that he couldn't stand his own

have with us, even enjoying a glass of the sparkling methode traditional named after their equally dynamic daughter Lisa. Lisa runs the Hunter Valley McGuigan Wine Village in front of their other winery, the rejuvenated ex-Hungerford Hill property.

The McGuigan family have long been involved in the wine industry of the Hunter Valley. Brian's father Perc was the

he quickly formed a vineyard investment company. He could see the coming need for more grape supply with export sales booming and the certainty that domestic sales would recover from their slight decline due to the recession of the late '80s and early '90s.

Brian was itching to get back into the mainstream of winemaking and

marketing, which saw the formation in 1992 of McGuigan Brothers with his two brothers Neil and Ross, and of course his dynamic wife Fay. The company made a public float and Brian in his usual way took the show on the road. I ran into him one day in a leading Melbourne broker's office where he was delivering an address to their leading clients, followed naturally by a wine tasting.

Brian and Fay chose a most unusual symbol for their label, inspired, I am sure, by their deep religious convictions. Many of their labels have carried the likeness of St. Francis Xavier, the patron saint of Australia, carrying his shepherd's crook. After forming the company, Brian and Fay took off to live and work in America for six months. They say St. Francis was working hard for them also, particularly in the very religious southern states. At the 1994 'New World Wine Competition' in Los Angeles, the McGuigan modestly-priced 'Bin 2000' Shiraz won the accolade of 'best shiraz wine in the world' and their 'Bin 7000' chardonnay won a gold medal. At Intervin in New York several months later, their 'Shareholders Reserve Chardonnay' also won a gold medal.

The McGuigan wines are made for easy drinking by the widest range of people world-wide. For my mind, this is a noble goal and one which is making McGuigan liquid sunshine in the bottle, the flavour of Australia

McGuigan Hunter Village

Nestled under the Brokenback Ranges and set amongst the vineyards of the Lower Hunter is the McGuigan Hunter Village, a mecca of wine, food, craft and culture that brings together many individual businesses that offer the visitor and wine-lover a rich interesting experience and an opportunity to buy produce and crafts that are entirely unique.

There are even activities such as aqua golf and importantly that rare commodity in a wine region, activities for the children which include a miniature steam train and a playground.

The complex backs onto the 'Vineyard Resort' accommodation, function and seminar centre and has its own individual conference centre. The very well set up Hunter Cellars features a huge range of Hunter Wines and is run most capably by Brian McGuigan's vivacious daughter Lisa.

A great number of restaurants and food outlets abound, all with their individual character. These include The Vineyard Restaurant, The Cellar Restaurant, The Pavilion Restaurant, AlFresco in the Hunter and The Vineyard Kitchen Coffee and Burger Shop. There is even a picturesque barbecue area if you want to cook your own. The antique and bric-a-brac boutique and Pokolbin Gallery and Gifts both have loads of great things to tempt the tourist and if you are really feeling a little frisky, there's a bush dance every Saturday night.

Behind the McGuigan Hunter Village is the main McGuigan Brothers Wines production facility, where, in 1995, Brian McGuigan has inaugurated technical winery tours for wine enthusiasts. These educational tours help people discover how a winery operates and gain a valuable insight into the winemaking process. In Brian McGuigan's words, 'Everyone loves a glass of wine, but very few people really understand what makes one wine stand out from another.' During vintage, visitors to the winery will see how the grapes are crushed, taste the juice straight out of the tanks and emerge well-informed about different varieties of wine as well as their production processes. These expert tours are conducted by the actual cellarmasters at McGuigan Brothers.

Hunter Valley Cheese Company

In early 1995 a joint venture was agreed to between dynamic wine producer and gourmet cheese lover, Brian McGuigan, and pioneer specialty cheese maker, David Brown, from the Milawa Cheese Company, just down the road from Brown Brothers Wines in Victoria.

In quick time, a cheese factory was built as part of the McGuigan Hunter Village at Pokolbin, next door to the main Hunter Valley production winery of McGuigan Brothers. This cottage factory is now producing a range of fine cheeses, taking their names from the region: Branxton Brie and Busby Blue, an assertive gorgonzola style; Pokolbin White, a fresh acid cheese with a soft texture (great with a McGuigan 'Lisa' Brut Sparkling) a Cessnock Cheddar and a multi-facet Pokolbin Club Blue. Hunter Valley Gold is a washed rind cheese and the Fromage Blanc a farmhouse cheese. Added to this impressive list are three goat's milk cheeses, Hunter Valley Chevre, Hunter Valley Table Chevre in a pyramid - delicate and white moulded - and the Hunter Valley Aged Ashed Chevre - dusted with grape vine ash - a cheese which ages well.

A visit to the Hunter Valley Cheese Company is a great learning experience. It will help you to get to know one of wine's great accompaniments.

Vineyard Resort

The Vineyard Resort & Convention Centre is situated in the beautiful Hunter Valley, Australia's oldest commercial wine growing area, less than 2 hours drive north of Sydney offering the perfect setting for any occasion.

Some of the Resort's facilities include; 52 well appointed rooms - interconnecting rooms, disabled rooms and family rooms available - heated swimming pool, spa, sauna, tennis court, on site cheese and wine tasting, air conditioned rooms, lounge with open fire place and many more modern conveniences.

Nestled in the shadow of the Brokenback Range, the Hunter Valley has a rich history spanning over 150 years. Today more than 40 wineries, a diverse range of tourist attractions and facilities, plus some of the most scenic countryside in Australia, make it an ideal venue for a holiday, convention or short break.

The Resort is part of McGuigan's Hunter Village and is situated in the heart of the Lower Hunter Valley wine growing area and surrounded by panoramic views of vineyards.

The Village houses McGuigan brothers tasting cellars, eateries, gift shop, a unique aqua golf driving range and children's adventure playground. Something to interest all ages.

We are adjacent to McGuigan's working winery and the Hunter Valley Cheese Company, within walking distance of 5 local wineries and next door to Cypress Lakes Golf Course.

VINEYARD RESORT

Tamburlaine

Tamburlaine has developed an enviable reputation as one of the most innovative and quality-conscious of the Hunter's boutique wineries.

The wines are made from the 30 year old vines on the Estate and small parcels of selected vineyards and carry the one distinctive blue, gold and white label.

The winery location, in the rolling foothills of the Brokenback range opposite Cypress Lakes Country Club, is one of the prettiest in the valley. The verdant grounds and iron bark clad tasting area surrounded by pergolas is open seven days a week.

A consistently successful exhibitor at the Hunter Valley Wine Show, Tamburlaine has seen top results for semillon, chardonnay, verdelho and their stylish red blends. Liqueur muscat and a raspberry "Framboise" liqueur are also available for the visitors to sample. The range is only available from the winery itself.

TAMBURLAINE
Address: McDonalds Road, Pokolbin, NSW 2321
Phone: (049) 98 7570
Fax: (049) 98 7763
Established: 1966
Winemaker: Greg Silkman, Mark Davidson
Principal varieties grown: Syrah, cabernet sauvignon, semillon, chardonnay
Ha under vine: 10
Average no. cases produced: 15,000

Principal wines & brands	Cellar potential
The Chapel Reserve Dry Red	10+ years
Cabernet Merlot Malbec	5-10 years
Chardonnay	2-5 years
Sauvignon Blanc	2-5 years
Semillon	5-10 years
Verdelho	5-10 years
Petite Fleur Blanc de Noir	2-5 years

Public & trade tours: By appointment only
Cellar door & mail order sales: Yes
Hours open to public: 9 am-5 pm seven days a week
Points of interest: Private tasting room, BBQs

Terrace Vale

It was a syndicate of 20 Sydney businessmen and their families who started Terrace Vale. Most remain, and other than winemaker Alain Leprince and some administrative staff, the rest of the 'workers' are the syndicate members and families. Work, including cellar door sales, is handled on a roster basis and the result of this extraordinary co-operation is a congenial 'family' atmosphere.

The Terrace Vale vineyard was planted in 1971 and the first vintage was produced in 1974 at Tyrrell's Winery. The first vintage to be made in the new winery at Terrace Vale was in 1976. As his name suggests, winemaker Alain Le Prince is French and from the Touraine region of the Loire Valley. Alain is a gentle person who cares deeply for his wines.

The Bin 2 Chardonnay was an early success story for the winery when the 1979 vintage won many medals and trophies. Terrace Vale reds are often big, fruity wines as is the shiraz which will improve with several years' cellaring. The pinot noir is usually a lighter style wine with pronounced fruit, while the cabernet sauvignon is a more elegant wine which develops well in the bottle. There is a stunning view of the Brokenback Ranges from Terrace Vale and this, combined with lovely wines and warm hospitality, makes it a must for the visitor.

TERRACE VALE WINES PTY LTD
Address: Deasy Road, Pokolbin, NSW 2320
Direction: Off Hermitage Road
Phone: (049) 98 7517
Fax: (049) 98 7814
Established: 1971
Winemaker: Alain Leprince
Principal varieties grown: Semillon, chardonnay, shiraz, cabernet, pinot noir, gewurztraminer, sauvignon blanc
Ha under vine: 36.69
Average annual crush: 100 tonnes

Average no. cases produced: 7,000-8,000

Principal wines & brands	Cellar potential
Semillon	2-5 years
Chardonnay	2-5 years
Chardonnay Semillon	2-5 years
Gewurztraminer	0-2 years
Cabernet Sauvignon	2-5 years
Shiraz	2-5 years

Public & trade tours: By appointment only
Cellar door & mail order sales: Yes
Hours open to public: 10 am-5 pm seven days a week
Retail distribution: NSW, Tyrrells

J. Y. Tulloch and Sons

The year 1996 marks 160 years since the arrival of the first member of the Tulloch family in Australia. It was not until 1883, however, that John Younie Tulloch became the slightly reluctant owner of a vineyard. In settlement of a debt to his store at Branxton, he accepted a 17 hectare property around the corner from Lindemans. Although a devout Methodist, John obviously saw no sin in developing nature's gift of the grape.

After rejuvenating the small shiraz vineyard, Tulloch made his first wine in 1895. By the 1920s, he had bought much surrounding property and had more land under vine than any other local winemaker. Tullochs, like many other winemakers, sold their wine in bulk to large wine merchants in the capital cities, including Rhinecastle with Johnnie Walker and Leo Buring.

John Younie's son Hector succeeded him in 1940 and established the first Tulloch label in the early 1950s. Later, Tulloch was bought out by the Reed Paper Group, but the family were left in control and upgraded production and cellar door facilities. There was a confusing period for Tullochs with many changes of ownership.

The company is now owned by the Southcorp Group and is still managed by Jay Tulloch, who is re-establishing the Tulloch name on the market. Tulloch wines are consistently excellent. They are individual in style and the verdelho is particularly good each year. Tullochs have a reputation for their white wines, which have managed to remain consistently good throughout the company's tumultuous history.

Tullochs also make an excellent Vintage Sparkling wine from chardonnay and semillon under the label "Hunter Cuvee" which was recently named Budget Sparkling Wine of the Year in the Penguin Wine Guide. Their Glen Elgin Estate is a pretty place with vineyards planted over the undulating countryside and now has a very settled happy feeling about it, which is reflected in the characterful wines of recent years.

Tyrrell's Vineyard

Murray covers the promotional trail for Tyrrells, Bruce astutely handles the marketing and business side of the company. As well as their excellent still wines, Tyrrells produce some wonderful methode champenoise wines from semillon, pinot noir and chardonnay grapes.

Left: Bruce Tyrrell

Murray Tyrrell is, without doubt, the character of the Hunter Valley. He has been awarded the Order of Australia for his services to the wine industry, and is very outspoken about Australian wine, in particular that of the Hunter Valley.

When Murray took over Tyrrells in 1959, the company sold only bulk wine to other wine companies, such as McWilliams, where Maurice O'Shea blended them with his own. O'Shea also bottled some of Tyrrell's wines and sold them under the 'Richard' label. As soon as he had taken charge, Murray Tyrrell instigated some major changes. He developed a label and began exhibiting wines successfully in many shows. Visitors soon flocked to the winery's cellar door and sales boomed. From only several hundred tonnes in the 1960s, Tyrrell's now crush many thousands of tonnes and are investing in vineyards in other regions such as McLaren Vale and Coonawarra in South Australia.

Tyrrells have a number of traditional labels such as their top selling 'Long Flat' wines and the 'Old Winery' label. The Tyrrell's Vat 47 Chardonnay was really the first commercial chardonnay in Australia and has just celebrated 25 successful vintages, regularly winning gold medals and trophies in wine shows. This 'Vat' series, which includes a number of white and red wines, really put Tyrrells on the map when they were launched by Murray in the mid-1960s, at the start of the wine boom.

Tyrrells also made some of the first pinot noirs in Australia. Their pinot noir vineyard is planted in rich, red volcanic soil over shale and limestone on the Brokenback Range to the rear of the winery. This is an ideal location for this grape variety and Tyrrells have produced some incredible wines. Their 1976 Pinot Noir won an international wine show award in France as the top pinot exhibited. This led to world-wide publicity and acclaim for Tyrrells, which was further enhanced by Murray's own distinctive way of passing on good news.

The history of Tyrrell's Hunter Valley Winery is the longest and most continuous progression of any of the winemakers in the district. In 1993, they celebrated 135 years of operation. The business was begun by Edward Tyrrell who was granted 330 acres of land at Pokolbin in 1858. This property was ideally suited to the vine with its rich volcanic soils on well drained slopes. A slab hut (which is still preserved by the family) was built and vines planted, with the first vintage occurring in 1864. Edward's son Dan took over winemaking in 1885 at the age of 15, and proceeded to make 75 vintages, surely a world record. It was not until a fall from a ladder in 1958 that Edward was forced into retirement.

Murray took the helm in 1959 and his son Bruce is now general manager. While

---

TYRRELL'S VINEYARD
Address: Broke Road, Pokolbin NSW 2320
Phone: (049) 98 7509
Fax: (049) 98 7723
Established: 1858
Winemaker: Andrew Spinaze
Principal varieties grown: Semillon, chardonnay, pinot noir, shiraz
Ha under vine: 300
Average annual crush: 2,193 tonnes
Average no. cases produced: 540,000

Principal wines & brands	Cellar potential
Vat 47 Pinot Chardonnay	5-10 years
Vat 9 Shiraz	5-10 years
Vat 1 Semillon	5-10 years
Shee-oak Chardonnay	5-10 years
Stevens Semillon	5-10 years
Old Winery Chardonnay	2-5 years
Old Winery Cabernet Merlot	5-10 years

Public tours: Yes (buses by appointment only)
Cellar door & mail order sales: Yes
Hours open to public: 8 am-5 pm Mon-Sat
Retail distribution: Liquor stores

Wyndham Estate

Located on the banks of the Hunter River, Wyndham Estate was founded by one of the earliest pioneers in the region, George Wyndham, who planted his first vines in 1828 on a property called "Dalwood". The classic old homestead, Dalwood House is being restored as an official Australian Bicentennial Project as an important part of Australia's Heritage.

Vines and winemaking were a large part of George Wyndham's rural interests, however he is also credited with introducing the first Hereford cattle to mainland Australia.

George Wyndham purchased property throughout New South Wales and planted vines as far north as Inverell near the Queensland border. Under careful handling by his son, the wine business grew until it was the second largest wine company in the State. Unfortunately with the great 1890s depression and the death of both Wyndhams by 1870, the Wyndham company was reduced to bankruptcy, to be bought by H. Wilkinson in 1901. The vineyards, winery and related interests were later bought by Penfolds who kept

the Dalwood name and gave it great circulation, with their "Dalwood" series of table wines. The winery was sold to their winemaker Perc McGuigan, whose son Brian began Wyndham Estate Pty Ltd in 1971, and in late 1989 early 1990, was sold to current owners Orlando Wyndham. Wyndham Estate is now the largest and perhaps most widely-known winery in the Hunter Valley, with its wines also well known on the international market through the marketing prowess of parent company, Orlando Wyndham.

Wyndham Estate wines reflect the vibrant team that produces them, and always seem to have a liveliness and zest to

them along with rich fruit flavours. The Bin TR2 and Bin 222 Chardonnay are amongst Australia's market leaders in their price range and are superb fruit driven wines. In fact, Bin TR2 is a favourite to many consumers being one of the top selling white wines in New South Wales. The Oak Cask Chardonnay is extremely good, and benefits from a few years' bottle ageing. The Wyndham range also includes a verdelho, the grape of the Island of Madeira. On tasting the verdelho at the winery, I was most impressed with its lifted apricot, pear and tropical fruit flavours. The Bin 555 Selected Hermitage made from shiraz

grapes, is a wine of great drinkability, ideal as a lunchtime red. Bin 444 Cabernet Sauvignon is a rich, round wine, full-bodied, but with typical Wyndham approachability.

The historic winery has been broght back to its former glory, with extensive refurbishment and now houses a wonderful cellar door, restaurant, function facilities, wine education centre and caters for daily tours. The gardens at Wyndham are also superb, with riverside barbecue and picnic grounds, in fact the whole estate is wonderfully turned out and a must for a visit on your Hunter pilgrimage.

An introduction to the Upper Hunter Valley

The area loosely called the Upper Hunter Valley surrounds the Hunter and Goulburn Rivers and their tributaries, and the towns of Denman, Muswellbrook, Sandy Hollow and Scone. The landscape is striking and diverse with both rich alluvial plains and steep mountain ranges. It is rich country with deep red and black soils over many coal deposits, this being one of the region's major industries.

Vines have been grown in the Upper Hunter since early in the 19th century. One of the first wine growers was George Bowman who established Arrowfield and other properties, and made wine at his property, Archerfield. Other wines in the area were made mostly as a hobby. In 1960, Penfolds bought a large property at Wybong (just north of Sandy Hollow), where they planted several hundreds of hectares of vines of great variety. A winery and dam was constructed on the property, but there was only limited supplies of water available at times. This property was sold to Rosemount in 1977.

The period of real growth for the Upper Hunter started in 1969 when Arrowfield began a huge development at Jerry's Plains. This became the largest single vineyard in Australia consisting of more than 800,000 vines by 1977. Also in 1969, Bob Oatley bought a large tract of land at the junction of Wybong Creek and Goulburn River which became Rosemount Estate. The period saw other beginnings for the Upper Hunter with David Hordern beginning a vineyard at Wybong.

Winemaker Simon Gilbert has become a stalwart of the area, first making wines for Arrowfield and in 1995, when three weeks before vintage he took over the old Oak Factory at Muswellbrook and converted it to a winery which crushed several hundred tonnes on behalf of clients during the 1995 vintage.

Although the Upper Hunter receives less rain than the Lower Hunter, there is an abundant water supply in the local rivers and nearly all new vineyards rely on drip irrigation to become established. The mature vines in the area seem to be producing better fruit each vintage. The area seems to produce white grape varieties more successfully than red and it was the Rosemount rieslings and traminers, produced in the ''70's by John Ellis, that first brought the area wide acclaim. Since then, the Upper Hunter has become best known for its chardonnays with Phillip Shaw of Rosemount winning accolades worldwide. Other whites such as wood-aged semillons and sauvignon blancs have also brought credit to Rosemount as well as Richmond Grove and others.

Red wines in the region are now getting their stripes, particularly those produced from Rosemount's Roxburgh vineyard and red wine specialist Cruickshanks Callatoota. Like most areas, the Upper Hunter has had its teething problems, but these appear to have subsided and the area now produces some very high quality wines, many of which are just right for drinking now.

Arrowfield Vineyard

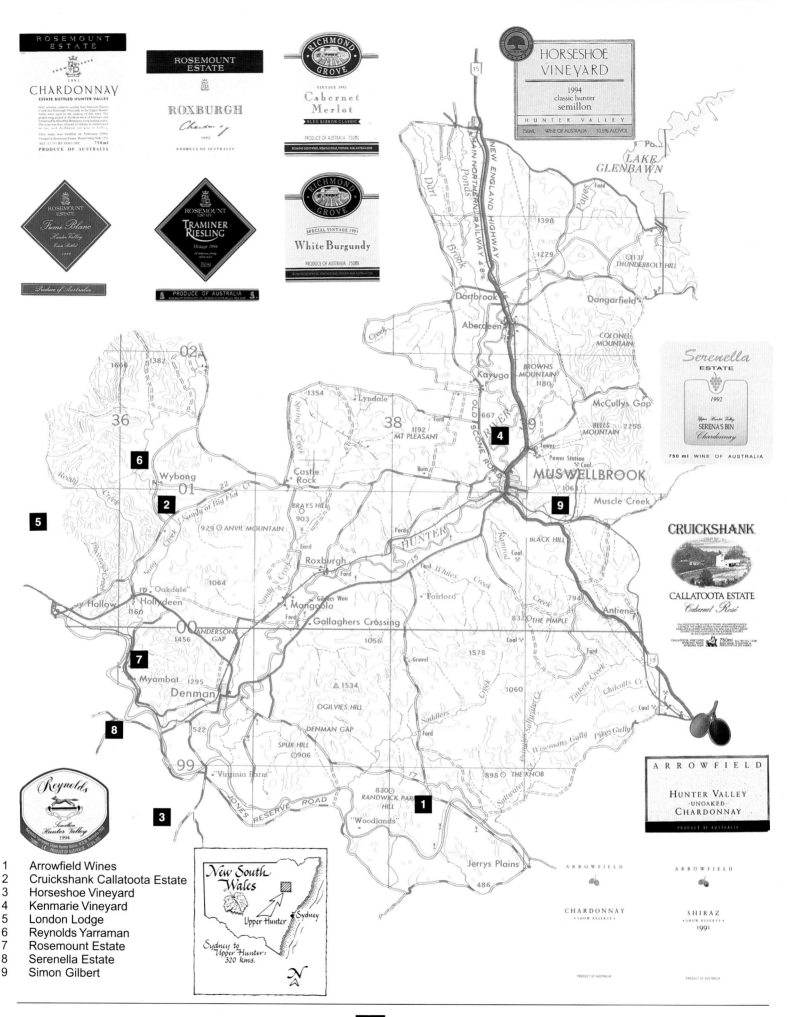

1   Arrowfield Wines
2   Cruickshank Callatoota Estate
3   Horseshoe Vineyard
4   Kenmarie Vineyard
5   London Lodge
6   Reynolds Yarraman
7   Rosemount Estate
8   Serenella Estate
9   Simon Gilbert

Arrowfield

ARROWFIELD WINES PTY LTD
Address: Denman Road, Jerrys Plains, Upper Hunter NSW 2330
Direction: 10 km from Jerrys Plains, 30 km from Denman
Phone: (065) 76 4041
Fax: (065) 76 4144
Established: 1969
Owner: Arrowfield Wines Pty Ltd
Winemakers: Don Buchanan,Elizabeth Radcliffe
Principal varieties grown: Chardonnay,semillon, shiraz, cabernet sauvignon, merlot
Ha under vine: 65
Average annual crush: 1,500 tonnes
Average no. cases produced: 120,000

Principal wines & brands	Cellar potential
Arrowfield Show Reserve	
Chardonnay	2-5 years
Shiraz	5-10 years
Cabernet Sauvignon	5-10 years
Semillon	2-5 years
Late Harvest Rhine Riesling	2-5 years
Arrowfield Cowra Range	
Chardonnay	2-5 years
Sauvignon Blanc	2-5 years
Cabernets	2-5 years
Late Harvest Gewurztraminer	5-10 years
Arrowfield Range	
Chardonnay	2-5 years
Semillon/Chardonnay	2-5 years
Sauvignon Blanc	2-5 years
Shiraz Cabernet	2-5 years
Cabernet Merlot	2-5 years
Arrowfield Hunter Valley Range	
Unoaked Chardonnay	2-5 years
Unoaked Semillon	2-5 years
Shiraz	5-10 years

Public & trade tours: Yes
Cellar door & mail order sales: Yes
Hours open to public: 10 am-5 pm seven days a week
Points of interest: BBQs, picnic areas, children's playground, croquet lawn, function and tour facilities, restaurant
Retail distribution: Arrowfield distribution

Arrowfield's history dates from 1824 when George Bowman, one of the first settlers in the Upper Hunter region, received several large land grants from Governor Macquarie. A vineyard was planted and a horse stud and grazing property developed.

In 1969, new owners established a large vineyard and winery and by 1977 it was the largest single vineyard in Australia with 1,200 acres of vines. The collapse of the red wine market in the late 1970's saw a rationalisation of the vineyard keeping only the best plantings on the best soil types and aspects.

The nucleus of Arrowfield Wines now consists of the best 300 acres of this most picturesque valley with the remainder of its grapes being sourced from other premium regions around Australia - semillon from the Barossa Valley, shiraz from McLaren Vale, cabernet sauvignon from the Goulburn Valley and chardonnay from the Cowra region. The Cowra Chardonnay is acknowledged as the best of the region and a leader in the premium chardonnay market.

More than 50% of Arrowfield's sales are from premium wine exports to markets in USA, Germany, Singapore, Japan and New Zealand. The growth in these markets is driven by their "new world" wine styles made in the high tech winery. The artistry of the winemaking team is led by Chief Winemaker Don Buchanan. In the search for quality and innovation Arrowfield believe there is no finishing line.

Horseshoe Vineyard

This small vineyard, owned and operated by the Hordern family, was established in the late 1960s. However, it was not until 1987 that the first commercial Horseshoe wines were released onto the market.

John Hordern is one of the few locals in the Upper Hunter who was raised in the region, developing his interest in wine from his father, who first planted semillon and shiraz on the family property in the '60s.

John's philosophy that 'specialisation is one of the most important elements for success in the wine industry' has certainly proven very successful for Horseshoe. Aside from a swag of gold medals for their semillon and chardonnay, the 1987 Horseshoe Vineyard Chardonnay was selected by wine writer James Halliday as one of the top wines released in 1988. Small amounts of Horseshoe wines have been exported to the United Kingdom, USA and Japan. In 1993 the Horseshoe Vineyard 1991 Chardonnay Semillon was awarded the UK Critics Choice for the best imported dry white wine. The Horseshoe wines are full flavoured with both elegance and complexity

and will age gracefully with cellaring. Try these delightful wines for yourself during your next visit to the Upper Hunter.

HORSESHOE VINEYARD
Address: Horseshoe Valley, Denman NSW 2328
Direction: 16 km south of Denman
Phone: (065) 47 3528
Fax: (065) 47 3548
Established: 1967
Owner: R.C. Hordern
Winemaker: John Hordern
Principal varieties grown: Semillon, chardonnay, shiraz
Ha under vine: 10
Average annual crush: 35 tonnes
Average no. cases produced: 3,000 dozen

Principal wines & brands	Cellar potential
Horseshoe Vineyard Classic Hunter Semillon	5-10 years
Horseshoe Vineyard	5-10 years
Horseshoe Vineyard Cabernet/Sauvignon	5-10 years
Horseshoe Vineyard Cabernet/Shiraz	10+ years

Public & trade tours: By appointment only
Cellar door & mail order sales: Yes
Hours open to public: 10 am-4 pm Sat, Sun & PH; weekdays by arrangement ((065) 47 3528)
Retail distribution: Fine Wine Specialist (NSW distributor), Sydney, Canberra, Brisbane

---

Simon Gilbert

Simon Gilbert, a fifth generation winemaker, could have been baptised with wine when he was christened in the chapel at the Pewsey Vale Vineyard in the Barossa Ranges. This vineyard was first planted by his great-great-grandfather Joseph Gilbert, a well respected Adelaide identity in the 1840s.

Joseph also established other vineyards, the grapes of which was sold to Leo Buring until 1950. Ironically, it was there that Simon later had his first hands-on winemaking experience during his studies in winemaking at Roseworthy Agricultural College, from which he graduated in 1977.

Subsequently he worked for the Lindemans Group at Karadoc, the Hunter and Coonawarra and in 1985 he became chief winemaker at Arrowfield in the Upper Hunter. In January 1994 Simon established his own Winemaking Services company in time for the 1994 vintage crushing 295 tonnes. A year later an opportunity to lease the huge Oak Factory at Muswellbrook arose and in several weeks Simon whipped the place into gear, together with the assistance of John Hordern and many others, Simon crushed almost 500 tonnes. Previously a

milk factory with stainless steel equipment, tanks and refrigeration, Simon recognised the natural transition and changes required to turn it into a winery. Simon is to be commended for this courage and endeavour in making it all happen.

Since commencing Consulting Operations in the Hunter Simon has won 4 Trophies, 17 Gold medals, 36 Silver and 122 Bronze at International and National Wine

Shows on behalf of his clients, an impressive performance. His clients include Inglewood, Kenmarie, Broke Estate, Verona and Dunsinane in the Hunter Valley, Andrew Harris in Mudgee, Cowra Wines, Brangayne Vineyards in Orange and Bald Mountain in Stanthorpe. Simon has plans in the distant future to launch his own label with a selection of premium varietals from selected regions in Australia.

Rosemount Estate stands out as one of the great success stories of the modern Australian wine industry. During a recent visit to their head office in Sydney, I posed the question, "What does the Latin expression under your crest mean?" Founder Bob Oatley's son Ian replied, "We always land on our feet."

Certainly the family was blessed by a great premonition when they chose these words. Under the watchful eye of general manager Chris Hancock, Rosemount Estates has excelled in all areas. They have managed to select the best areas of the Upper Hunter for planting and obtain very good grape yields of exceptional quality.

Although John Ellis was young and without great experience when he was appointed as Rosemount's winemaker, he proved himself more than capable and produced some white wines of extraordinary quality which excited the wine drinking public and got Rosemount off to a flying start. His use of modern equipment and techniques saw these early rieslings, traminer and chardonnay capture instant market acclaim.

The vineyard began as a small and successful operation planted by Carl Brecht in the 1860s. It was bought by Bob Oatley in 1969 and a winery was built in 1975. The first vintage made in the winery was by John Ellis. His wines were very successful on the show circuit which generated great publicity for Rosemount, and in combination with a powerful advertising campaign brought the wines to the Australian wine-drinker.

Spurred on by this success, Rosemount expanded its home vineyard, planted vines at Roseglen on the banks of the Goulburn and planted 15 hectares at the Edinglaissie homestead. With a greater amount of fruit each vintage and demand for its wines exceeding supply, the Rosemount winery was soon bursting its seams. In 1977 the Penfolds winery and vineyard were

The wine has a full feel derived from a combination of glycerol compounds in the grapes, strong vanilla character and some tannin from the wood ageing and intense peach apricot flavours inherent in the Roxburgh fruit. The wine is not as soft as some people suggest, but it does have quite high acid levels which help to balance its weight and flavour. It is an extraordinary wine. Rosemount also produces other chardonnays. The Show Reserve has achieved world-wide acclaim as the best wine of its variety, both in price and quality. The yellow label chardonnay is also of a similar rich style and as such is incredibly popular with wine drinkers.

Although John Ellis got the wines at Rosemount off to a flying start, the winemaker from 1979-81 was Mark Turnbull. He had assisted John since 1977, and developed many of the techniques which led to Rosemount's phenomenal success. Rosemount Wines, however really came of age under current winemaker Philip Shaw, who has made the wines at Rosemount for the last 14 vintages. Philip is definitely one of the three or four most gifted winemakers in Australia. After graduating from Roseworthy College he spent two years working for Lindemans where he was in charge of developing their range of premium wines. He is a laconic character who takes his position very seriously.

Philip also makes the wine from Rosemount's various vineyard interests in Victoria and Coonawarra as well as other NSW regions, a challenging job which he takes in his stride. He also has overall responsibility for the Ryecroft winery in McLaren Vale, now owned by Rosemount and producing a good deal of red wine for the Rosemount label as well as its own full range of Ryecroft wines. The Rosemount Black Label Shiraz has been a huge success, several times being awarded the World's Best Shiraz accolade by the American Wine Spectator Magazine, beating wines at many times its modest price. Philip also consults for a Chinese wine venture and at Rosemount at vintage time there are often a few Chinese winemakers in the vintage team along with Californian and French winemakers.

Rosemount has created a truly great international feel to its whole operation. The great success of Rosemount on the export market, particularly in the USA, has been hard won. Rosemount has taken tough and expensive individual initiatives that other wine exporters would do well to note, but in the long run, it is the consistently high quality of its whole wine range that has gained it fame and outstanding sales results. At Rosemount, they always land on their feet and keep running!

purchased and the pressure was alleviated. In 1983, Rosemount purchased a further 400 hectares at Mt. Danger, where now more that 100 hectares are under vine.

The prize purchase by Rosemount has proved to be their Roxburgh vineyard. Bought from Denman Estate as a small planting of chardonnay with some cabernet sauvignon, semillon and rhine riesling, the company have also added shiraz, pinot noir and sauvignon blanc. The wines produced from Roxburgh grapes all exhibit rich varietal fruit characters, and the chardonnay is fermented in wood and left to mature on its lees for three months.

The Roxburgh chardonnay is the top of the company's range and is the richest style of chardonnay produced in Australia.

ROSEMOUNT ESTATE

Address: Rosemount Road, Denman NSW 2328
Phone: (065) 47 2467
Fax: (065) 47 2742
Established: 1969
Owner: Mr Robert Oatley
Winemaker: Philip Shaw
Principal varieties grown: Chardonnay, semillon, shiraz, cabernet sauvignon, merlot
Ha under vine: 700
Average no. cases produced: 700,000

Principal wines & brands	Cellar potential
Roxburgh Chardonnay	10+ years
Show Reserve Hunter Valley Chardonnay	10+ years
Show Reserve Coonawarra Cabernet Sauvignon	5-10 years
Rosemount Estate Hunter Valley Chardonnay	2-5 years
Rosemount Estate Hunter Valley Sauvignon Blanc	2-5 years
Rosemount Estate McLaren Vale Shiraz	2-5 years
Rosemount Estate Cabernet Sauvignon	2-5 years

Public & trade tours: By appointment only
Cellar door & mail order sales: Yes
Hours open to public: 10 am-4 pm Mon-Sat; 10 am-4 pm Sun (summer) 12-4 pm Sun (Winter) (closed Christmas Day & Easter Friday)
Points of interest: Rosemount Vineyard Brasserie open Tuesday to Sunday for lunches. Tuesday to Saturday for dinners.
Retail distribution: National distribution

Cruickshank Callatoota Estate

A true individualist, John Cruickshank has his vineyard planted with only two grape varieties, cabernet sauvignon and cabernet franc. From this unique vineyard only four wines are produced. Two are cabernet sauvignons, one a lighter style than the other, the third a blend of cabernets sauvignon and franc. The fourth wine is a very good cabernet rose.

A very logical approach was taken to set up this vineyard. The location chosen is ideal, with deep red alluvial soil and good water access. The vines chosen were specially selected clones that have grown beautifully on their high trellises (which seem to be found in all the best vineyards these days). These trellises, which ensure an open canopy essential for high quality fruit, are also helpful in preventing diseases of the vines which can attack in humid weather.

The first four hectares were planted in 1974, but the winery itself was not built until 1981 after a study of small wineries both in Australia and overseas. The most modern equipment was purchased to give total control of fermentation. This is necessary for the production of a top rose and for the full herbaceous berry fruit style of cabernet sauvignon. John and his son Andrew use American Oak and the resulting wines are of a high quality that will age very well in the bottle. After completion of the winery a further 4 hectares of vines were planted, three to cabernet sauvignon and one to cabernet franc. The cabernet franc is released as a straight varietal wine in some years and in others blended with the cabernet sauvignon.

John Cruickshank has been involved in engineering and management consulting. His approach to the vineyard was to look at it as a factory producing the best possible material for the finished product - the wine.

The management has seen the industrial designed trellises presenting the strong vines in the form of a giant glass with four arms holding the bowl. This gives great exposure to the leaves and fruit as well as benefits explained previously.

Two eagles protect the vineyard from small grape-eating birds, and if that's not

enough, Andrew sprays the vines with a natural garlic oil solution. Naturally, the only garlic that gets near the finished wine will be what you put on the prime steak you enjoy with the big, generous and complex Callatoota Cabernet. Bon appetit!

Footnote: The Cruickshanks pride themselves on their winery visitor's centre and were recently rewarded by winning the 1995 Hunter Tourism Award For Excellence as "The Most Significant Local Tourism Attraction" for the entire region, a fine achievement and yet another reason to visit this haven of natural beauty and great wine.

CRUICKSHANK CALLATOOTA ESTATE
Address: Wybong Road, Wybong NSW 2333
Direction: 18 km north of Denman
Phone: (065) 47 8149
Fax: (065) 47 8144
Established: 1974
Winemaker: Andrew Cruickshank
Principal varieties grown: Cabernet sauvignon, cabernet franc
Ha under vine: 8.2
Average annual crush: 100 tonnes
Average no. cases produced: 6,500

Principal wines & brands	Cellar potential
Cabernet Sauvignon Pressings	10+ years
Cabernet Sauvignon/Cab. Franc	10+ years
Cabernet Franc	10+ years
Cabernet Sauvignon Vat 2	10+ years
Cabernet Sauvignon Cask 12	5-10 years
Cabernet Rose	2-5 years

Public & trade tours: Yes
Cellar door & mail order sales: Yes
Hours open to public: 9 am-5 pm seven days a week (winter); 9 am-6 pm seven days a week (summer)
Points of interest: BBQ area, camping area, children's playground - all adjacent to the vineyard & winery. Winery sells some of its young wine in 27 litre drums and helps people bottle it in the winery using the short-run equipment.
Retail distribution: Sydney Area: Estate Wine Distributors, 8/40-76 William Street, Leichhardt 2040 Ph (02) 550 0300

Reynolds Yarraman

Jon Reynolds is a consummate winemaker who has had long experience making wines for some of Australia's largest, most progressive and dynamic companies. Although originally from the Maitland area in the Lower Hunter, he began his winemaking career in South Australia. This was followed by a stint of eight years in Western Australia, where he oversaw a renaissance of the wines at the famous Houghton Winery.

Jon then returned to the Hunter and became chief winemaker for the Wyndham empire of Brian McGuigan. Jon and his wife Jane were looking for their own domain where they could put their joint talents to work. Good fortune smiled on them. They bought a property at Wybong on a sandstone ridge with majestic views over the valley, now planted with their vines and with the Yarraman Range

in the background. A beautiful old sandstone building that was part of the Bengala Homestead near Muswellbrook, built in 1837, was dismantled in the mid-1970s and rebuilt at Yarraman.

The winery is housed in the building and a cellar is dug into the hillside underneath, which gives ideal cool conditions. The massive ironbark beams came from the old Dalgety Woolstores at Darling Harbour, the rafters from the old Resch's Brewery, and the ceiling is old red cedar. Reynolds have created an

extraordinary open plan house on the top floor. Jon and Jane's wines are hand-crafted masterpieces with fabulous varietal fruit flavours and amongst the truly top echelon of Australia's wine offerings.

REYNOLDS YARRAMAN
Address: Yarraman Road, Wybong NSW 2333
Direction: Between Muswellbrook and Denman
Phone: (065) 47 8127
Fax: (065) 47 8013
Established: 1967
Winemaker: Jon Reynolds
Principal varieties grown: Semillon, chardonnay, merlot, shiraz
Ha under vine: 16
Average no. cases produced: 8,000

Principal wines & brands	Cellar potential
Semillon	5-10 years
Cabernet/Merlot	5-10 years
Chardonnay	2-5 years
Cabernet Sauvignon	10-15 years
Shiraz	5-10 years
Botrytised Sweet Semillon	5-10 years

Public & trade tours: By appointment only
Cellar door & mail order sales: Yes
Hours open to public: 10 am-4 pm Mon-Sat; 11 am-4 pm Sun & PH
Points of interest: Historic building constructed of convict-hewn sandstone in 1837. Visitors are welcome to walk through the winery
Retail distribution: Sydney, Fesq Dorado & Co; Queensland, Eureka Wine Co.; Western Australia, MLM Wholesalers; Victoria, Harbury Wine Consulting; ACT, Fesq Dorado & Co

---

Serenella Estate

Serenella is a new and exciting wine venture of the Cecchini Family in the Upper Hunter. They make nine wines, including blends with sylvaner grapes. The property was etablished by Giancarlo Cecchini. I think these heartfelt notes from his daughter Tish say it all!

"Serenella Estate 1993 Bin GCC Chardonnay is our most special wine, grown and bottled on this estate. Bin GCC is named after Giancarlo Cecchini. Giancarlo founded and established Serenella Estate, his dream come true. He purchased this remote acreage with his wife, Maria, in 1968. He worked the land from a bushy aspect to a fine pastoral property, at Baerami in the Uppermost Hunter Valley.

"A highly regarded engineer, he 'retired' in 1990 to finally realise his most special dream, to establish his own family winery, alongside his family. A winery which has become highly regarded within the wine industry as first rate in construction, technology, wine quality and integrity. He

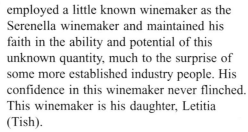

employed a little known winemaker as the Serenella winemaker and maintained his faith in the ability and potential of this unknown quantity, much to the surprise of some more established industry people. His confidence in this winemaker never flinched. This winemaker is his daughter, Letitia (Tish).

"Giancarlo died suddenly and quietly at Serenella Winery early on a Tuesday morning, 23 March, 1993 vintage. He worked full-time and over-time during vintage, he operated the crane, did varied cellar work, helped run cellar door wine-tastings and most importantly, put his winemaker constantly in her place! Some of his old workmates came along to lend a hand at vintage; he left them with many wonderful and amusing memories.

"Bin GCC Chardonnay was Serenella estate bottled, with the help of a few of these old workmates and of course his winemaker, in late December '93. So, what makes this Chardonnay so special is quite simple. Aside

from the outstanding quality and flavour of this 100% Hunter chardonnay, the strength of this wine lies in the enthusiasm, skill and optimism with which it was created."

SERENELLA ESTATE
Address: Mudgee Road, via Denman, Baerami NSW 2333
Direction: 20 km south west of Denman
Phone: (065) 47 5168
Fax: (065) 47 5164
Established: 1989
Owner: Cecchini family
Winemaker: Letitia 'Tish' Cecchini
Principal varieties grown: Cabernet sauvignon, shiraz, chardonnay, merlot, sylvaner, pinot noir
Ha under vine: 32
Average annual crush: 150 tonnes
Average no. cases produced: 10,000

Principal wines & brands	Cellar potential
Bin GCC Chardonnay	5-10 years
Semillon Sauvignon Blanc	5-10 years
Semillon Chardonnay	5-10 years
Shiraz	5-10 years
Cabernet Sauvignon	5-10 years
Chardonnay Bin GCC	5-10 years

Public & trade tours: By appointment only
Cellar door & mail order sales: Yes
Hours open to public: 10 am-4 pm Sat/Sun/PH
Points of interest: BBQ facilities, lunches and functions can be organised with bookings only
Retail distribution: Serenella Pastoral Co. Pty Ltd, Sydney, Queensland & Victoria

Richmond Grove - Upper Hunter

Richmond Grove has become one of the best known and respected wines in Australia in a relatively short time. In 1977, John Muddle decided a change of lifestyle was necessary and bought a large property on a bend in the Goulburn River; he had no aspirations to grow vines or produce wine.

As his interest in wine slowly grew, he approached his friend Brian McGuigan to survey his property with a view to planting vines. The verdict was positive and 15 hectares of vines were planted on the rich alluvial river plain. The grapes were sold to Penfolds until 1977 when Wyndham Estate formed a partnership with Muddle, buying 50 percent of the property and forming the present company Richmond Grove. Planting was commenced on a large scale. The vineyards of Richmond Grove now cover more than 100 hectares of mainly chardonnay and sauvignon blanc, but also some cabernet sauvignon, merlot and traminer.

In the early 1990s the great Orlando Group took over Richmond Grove, along with Wyndham Estate and its other related wineries. In a period of investment and consolidation, as well as expansion, the Richmond Grove banner now flies over a huge vineyard at Cowra and the old Leo Buring Winery in the Barossa Valley, but the original vineyards in the Upper Hunter are still producing great wines. Try the French Cask Chardonnay and the Cabernet Merlot. They are both world beaters.

An introduction to Mudgee

Like the Barossa Valley in South Australia, the viticultural roots of the Mudgee area were planted by German immigrants. In the case of Mudgee, the Germans were invited to Australia by William Macarthur to tend his vineyard at Camden, now part of outer Sydney.

Vines were first planted at Mudgee by one of these 'vine dressers,' Adam Roth, who was given a grant of 37 hectares in 1858. Although gold was discovered in the area in 1872, Roth was not tempted to change his interests. By 1880, six out of the 13 wineries in the area were operated by Roth and his sons.

Andreas Kurtz, another of the German immigrants, planted the second vineyard in the area. The largest vineyard of 80 hectares was planted by Fredrich Bucholz, and later bought by the Roth family. The Australian Surgeon General of the time, Thomas Fiaschi, purchased the Augusine vineyard from the Roth family in 1917. By 1930, Jack Roth had bought out his brother at Rothview, the original winery, and was the only surviving winemaker in the area, although several growers remained. He also consolidated winemaking at the Craigmoor winery and there made a dry white wine containing a nameless grape variety. The wine fared very well. The same nameless variety was planted by a descendant of Andreas Kurtz, with great success. Eventually, it was identified by a French viticulturist as a chardonnay, one of the best disease-free clones he had seen. In this way, Mudgee became the first wine-growing area in Australia to grow chardonnay, and other areas used this stock to start their own chardonnay vineyards.

Two more wineries were established in Mudgee in 1969, the Botobolar Winery by Gil Wahlquist and Huntington Estate by Bob Roberts. The 1970s saw a number of new wineries open, including the characterful Burnbrae Winery, Miramar, Pieter Van Gent and Platts Wines. There are now more than 20 wineries in the region; outside of the large Montrose and Craigmoor operations now under the Orlando Wyndham banner, all the other wineries are small individual boutiques.

The sense of the 1960s and 1970s wine renaissance is strong in Mudgee. Many locals are pioneering organic grape-growing and winemaking, learning every day the wonderful balance in nature, who's whose natural predator and who's whose friend. I am sure this work will reap its rewards as our world becomes ever more conscious of our fragile, precious environment, our own health and the health of future generations.

Mudgee grapes are much sought-after due to their rich flavours, and most existing wineries are expanding. Although on the same latitude as the Hunter Valley, vintage in Mudgee is almost a month later. The district is 500-1,000 metres above sea level and therefore has some cold nights from spring through to early summer whilst the vines are flowering. This extends the growing season and, in combination with the warm climate and rich soil, the grapes have a long ripening period. As a result, local table wines average 13, 14 and even 15 per cent alcohol.

The well-made wines of the area, particularly the whites, exhibit well-defined varietal flavours. It is a beautiful district in Australia to introduce a wine appellation scheme. This occurred in 1979, and all wines are guaranteed free of defects and of 100 percent Mudgee fruit. This is no guarantee of enjoyment but the wines I have tasted from the area, which carry the appellation approval, are of a very high standard.

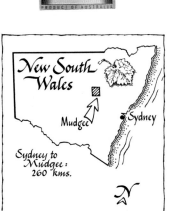

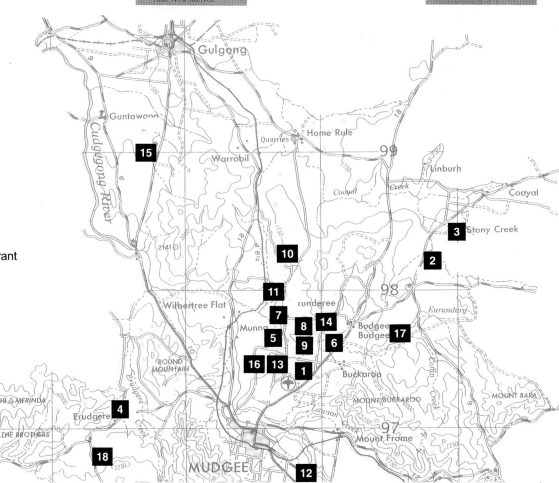

Mudgee - NSW

1 Augustine Vineyard & Restaurant
2 Botobolar Vineyard
3 Britten's Vineyard
4 Burnbrae Wines
5 Craigmoor Winery
6 Huntington Estate
7 Knight's Vines
8 Lawson Hill Estate
9 Mansfield Wines
10 Miramar Wines
11 Montrose Wines
12 Mount Vincent Mead & Wines
13 Mudgee Wines
14 Pieter Van Gent Winery
15 Platt's Winery
16 Seldom Seen Vineyard
17 Stein's Wines
18 Thistle Hill Vineyard

Botobolar Vineyard

Botobolar was the pioneer of the organic vineyard management concept in Australia. In 1971 journalist Gil Wahlquist planted this extraordinary vineyard using a mixture of specially chosen cover crops to attract vine-friendly insects, and to ward off vine predators and diseases. Along with the use of some natural substances and the absence of chemicals, Botobolar have managed to grow grapes successfully in a perfectly natural way, and make excellent wines.

Botobolar is the aboriginal Kouri tribe's word for the black native pine prevalent on the property. On our trip through the region, we met Chicago-born Kevin Karstrom, the new proprietor at Botobolar who recently purchased the winery and vineyard from the Wahlquist family. Kevin and Trina are totally devoted to the organic vineyard principal and his love for the property is obvious.

The 1995 vintage will be seriously affected quantity-wise by the drought, but the quality of the just-fermented wines I tried was great. Kevin is in the process of putting

BOTOBOLAR VINEYARD
Address: Mudgee NSW 2850
Phone: (063) 73 3840
Fax: (063) 73 3789
Established: 1971
Owners: Kevin & Trina Karstrom
Winemaker: Kevin Karstrom
Principal varieties grown: Riesling, chardonnay, shiraz, cabernet sauvignon, mataro, crouchen, marsanne, traminer, pinot noir
Ha under vine: 23
Average annual crush: 150 tonnes
Public & trade tours: Yes
Cellar door & mail order sales: Yes
Hours open to public: 10 am-5 pm seven days a week
Retail distribution: Fine Wine Specialist, NSW.

in a large dam to help the vines through such a situation next time. The vineyard produces a very good marsanne, the honeysuckle-like style of wine native to the French Rhone Valley. The chardonnay is a full- flavoured style in the Californian mould. The reds are also powerful wines. Apart from losing my poloshirt off my back in the typical 'American trade', I vote this winery in Australia's top 10. Keep up the good work, Kevin.

Burnbrae Wines

Robert and Pamela Mace are a cultured and interesting couple who run a vineyard and winery full of the charm one expects from a true family cottage operation. Everything is made from natural materials and tastefully decorated with Pamela's paintings and other creative artwork and photography. This pretty country cottage looks out over the vineyards towards the picturesque McDonald's Creek at the foot of the property and the winery is built under and around an ancient pepper tree which one must climb to get to the top of the fermenting and draining tank. The vineyard is run on organic principles and the wines, like the proprietors, are full of interest and character.

BURNBRAE VINEYARD & WINERY
Address: Hargraves Road, Mudgee NSW 2850
Direction: 12 km from Mudgee Centre, close to Gulgong, Mudgee & Hill End
Phone: (063) 73 3504
Fax: (063) 73 3601
Established: 1969
Owner: Robert & Pamela Mace
Winemaker: Robert Bassel Mace
Principal varieties grown: Shiraz, cabernet, malbec, chardonnay, semillon, riseling, black muscat, traminer
Ha under vine: 8
Average annual crush: 20 tonnes
Average no. cases produced: 2,600

Principal wines & brands	Cellar potential
Cabernet Sauvignon/Malbec	10+ years
Shiraz	10+ years
Vintage Port	10+ years
Liqueur Muscat	10+ years
Pinot Noir	5-10 years
Sauvignon Blanc	5-10 years
Chardonnay/Semillon	2-5 years
Traminer/Riesling	5-10 years
Pinot Noir Rose	2-5 years

Public tours: By appointment only
Cellar door & mail order sales: Yes
Hours open to public: 9 am-5 pm seven days a week
Points of interest: Surrounded by picturesque undulating hills. A small personalised vineyard, with a relaxed and friendly atmosphere, without irrigation and practising organic methods.
Retail distribution: At present, due to the drought, only Mudgee, Gulgong, Mount Victoria, North Ryde and Port Macquarie. Will expand when drought has broken.

Huntington Estate

HUNTINGTON ESTATE
Address: Cassilis Road, Mudgee, NSW 2850
Phone: (063) 73 3825
Fax: (063) 73 3730
Owner: Bob & Wendy Roberts
Winemaker: Susie Roberts
Principal varieties grown: Shiraz, cabernet sauvignon, merlot, pinot noir, semillon, chardonnay
Ha under vine: 43
Average annual crush: 300 tonnes
Average no. cases produced: 20,000

Principal wines & brands	Cellar potential
Cabernet Sauvignon	5-10 years
Cabernet Merlot	5-10 years
Shiraz	5-10 years
Semillon Chardonnay	2-5 years
Chardonnay	2-5 years
Semillon	2-5 years
Rose (Pinot Noir)	0-2 years
Bulk Red	

Public & trade tours: By appointment only
Cellar door & mail order sales: Yes
Hours open to public: 9 am-5 pm Mon-Fri; 10 am-5 pm Sat; 10 am-3 pm Sun.
Points of interest: Home of the Huntington Chamber Music Festival
Retail distribution: Very limited, basically cellar door and mailing list.

Bob Roberts is one of the modern-day pioneers of the Mudgee region. Huntington is a total estate concept with a large 40 hectare vineyard. In the words of wine critic James Halliday, 'rated absolutely tops for both quality and value for money. One of the most impressive family operations in Australia.'

Bob and Wendy set up the whole operation on a long term basis. The large well-integrated winery also hosts an annual chamber music festival with five days of recitals, which fills the winery's intimate atmosphere and marvellous acoustics with magic music. The Roberts also age their reds an unusual length of time, a real plus in these days of cash flow considerations. The substantial Huntington Estate reds spend a full two years in oak and two years in the bottle before release.

Huntington also offers wine for home bottling, a rarity these days, and dozen purchases attract a most attractive price. The wines include one of Mudgee's rare pinot noirs, along with shiraz, cabernet sauvignon, merlot, semillon, chardonnay and sauvignon blanc.

Pieter van Gent

Pieter van Gent is one of the strong characters of the Mudgee region. He arrived in the area in 1970 to work for Craigmoor Wines, after previously spending 11 years at Penfolds working with champagne and fortified wines.

Fortified wines are a favourite of Pieter's and he is the only winemaker in Mudgee to make them consistently. His Pipeclay Port is a rich, unique style with intense flavours and a smooth quality. It is a hit with visitors to the winery.

The winery is charming with wide verandahs, wooden vats and casks and a warm friendly atmosphere. There is an earthen floor and the furnishings include pews from an old church. Pieter was one of the first chardonnay makers in Australia, producing award winners for Craigmoor. He now makes his own, the best known wine being Mudgee White Port along with a range of unusual wine varieties.

Pieter van Gent and his family are delightful hosts and at the time of writing are busy expanding and redecorating the winery and tasting area. Their approach to winemaking and visitors is a sincere, honest and no-fuss one, which makes you feel right at home. Pieter has many fans in his own Dutch homeland and some of his wine finds its way there too.

PIETER VAN GENT WINERY & VINEYARD
Address: 141 Black Springs Road, Mudgee NSW 2850
Phone: (063) 73 3807
Fax: (063) 73 3910
Established: 1979
Winemaker: Pieter van Gent
Principal varieties grown: Cabernet sauvignon, shiraz, chardonnay, muller thurgau
Ha under vine: 10
Average annual crush: 60 tonnes
Average no. cases produced: 4,500

Points of interest: 20 x 1,000 gallon oval shaped wine casks; and 100 year old choir stalls from the Nun's Chancel at Singleton. Lot of atmosphere.
Retail distribution: McLaren Vale Cellars, Fyshwick, ACT

Principal wines & brands Mudgee	Cellar potential
Chardonnay	2-5 years
Muller Thurgau	2-3 years
Cabernet Merlot	5-8 years
Pipeclay Port	8-12 years
White Port	2-5 years
Cornelius Port	10+ years
Pipeclay Vermouth (Herbs & Spices)	3-5 years

Cellar door & mail order sales: Yes
Hours open to public: 9 am-5 pm Mon-Sat; 11 am-4 pm Sun.

Craigmoor

Craigmoor is the oldest established winery in Mudgee and planted its first vineyards over 135 years ago, by the then owners, the Roth family who ran the winery for 100 years.

From these historic origins Craigmoor is also known as the birthplace of chardonnay in Australia as it was Jack Roth who planted cuttings of a particularly fine clone of chardonnay given to him indirectly from either William Busby or William MacArthur. This small planting was to become the sourceblock for much of Australia's chardonnay. Craigmoor released a chardonnay from the 1971 vintage making it a pioneer of the variety in Australia. This great wine is still the flagship of the Craigmoor range.

Orlando Wyndham took over the Craigmoor winery in late 1989 early 1990, happily supporting capital and quality investments in both the vineyards and the winery and producing fantastic varietal wines under chief winemaker Robert Paul, who maintains their traditional full-bodied style.

The facilities for visitors are first class with a rustic ambience including an excellent restaurant, banquet hall, new tasting area, museum containing old winemaking and viticultural equipment, a picnic area and even a newly laid cricket pitch.

Craigmoor has a delightful unspoiled historic Australiana feel about it, with sweeping lawns and a picnic area going down to the creek in front of the winery and the ranges in the distance.

Montrose

The Montrose Winery, overlooking the picturesque Cudgegong Valley, is situated in an area that has long been a source of inspiration.

Located on the central western tablelands of New South Wales, aproximately 260 kilometres north west of Sydney, the setting inspired aboriginals to name it Mudgee, "nest in the hills".

It is a region that inspired the poet Henry Lawson. Today it has also inspired a range of premium Montrose table wines. The winery was established in 1974 and upgraded in 1989 to incorporate the latest technology in winemaking practices.

At Montrose, under the guidance of the extremely talented wine craftsman, Robert Paul, the philosophy is to produce wines with well defined varietal characters and freshness of fruit. The wines are subtle and show finesse, exhibiting elegance and restraint, especially when young. The emphasis is on fruit flavour but superbly complemented by high quality oak treatment and varietal integrity.

Australia's greatest "poet of the bush", Henry Lawson spent much of his life near the site of Montrose winery. Local mythology tells how the tranquil beauty of the landscape here inspired some of this greatest works. The popular Poet's Corner wines were named in his honour.

These wines have carved out a nice niche in the value for money premium market and are consistently amongst the better wines I see in masked line-ups.

The cellar door at Montrose is extensive and often features wines from older vintages. The winery exudes an atmosphere of quiet strength and stability and this must reflect the confidence the management places in their recent releases and successes.

Stein's

STEINS WINES

Address: Pipeclay Lane, Mudgee NSW 2850
Phone: (063) 73 3991
Fax: (063) 73 3709
Established: 1976
Owner: R.S. & L.M. Stein
Winemaker: R. Stein
Principal varieties grown: Chardonnay, shiraz, cabernet sauvignon, semillon, rhine riesling, traminer, black muscat
Ha under vine: 7
Average annual crush: 70 tonnes
Average no. cases produced: 5,000

Principal wines & brands	Cellar potential
Shiraz	5-10 years
Chardonnay	2-5 years
Semillon Chardonnay	2-3 years
Semillon Riesling	2-3 years
Cabernet Sauvignon	2-5 years
Rum Cask Port	10+ years
Liqueur Muscat	10+ years

Public & trade tours: By appointment only
Cellar door & mail order sales: Yes
Hours open to public: 10 am-4 pm seven days a week
Points of interest: Free gas BBQ, permanent vintage bike displays

Bob Stein is a descendant of the family of vignerons who brought the first riesling cuttings from Germany to Australia last century. Bob was tempted by his family's 30 acres of land at Mudgee and planted shiraz. Later he planted a further 6 more varieties, all the vines are trickle irrigated.

The Stein label has not been long on the market; its art deco style caught my eye the day before we visited the vineyard, and on trying this semillon I was most impressed. Stein's have just received an award at the 1995 International Wine Challenge, London, a well deserved honour. The winery, which is now processing a solid vintage, has a colonial-inspired tasting room surrounded by large, healthy, well-manicured vines. This is an impressive newcomer to the Mudgee region.

Thistle Hill

David and Lesley Robertson have changed their lives completely from the high tech computer business in Sydney they were both involved in, to a very rural lifestyle in the Mudgee region. The Robertson's both enjoy growing things and vegetables and fruit trees are planted on the property as well as vines.

The vineyard is certified 'A' organic by NASAA, the National Association for Sustainable Agriculture in Australia. This is the association's top classification and reflects credit on the Robertsons. As I write this story it is coincidentally World Environment Day!

Both David and Lesley are perfectionists and their wines are excellent; they include a shiraz port and a fortified black muscat. The vineyard has picnic and barbecue facilities and a charming tasting room. Thistle Hill also has a fully self-contained three bedroom cottage available for bed and breakfast accommodation, which I highly recommend. The vineyard is a member of the Appellation Society of Mudgee and the wines have won many awards. Don't go

THISTLE HILL VINEYARD
Address: 74 McDonalds Road, Mudgee NSW 2850
Direction: 10 km west of Mudgee
Phone: (063) 73 3546
Fax: (063) 73 3540
Established: 1976
Winemaker: David Robertson
Principal varieties grown: Cabernet sauvignon, chardonnay, riesling, pinot noir
Ha under vine: 10
Average annual crush: 60 tonnes
Average no. cases produced: 4,000

Principal wines & brands	Cellar potential
Thistle Hill	
Cabernet Sauvignon	8-12 years
Chardonnay	4-8 years
Pinot Noir	5-10 years
Riesling	2-5 years

Public & trade tours: By appointment only
Cellar door & mail order sales: Yes
Hours open to public: 9 am-5 pm seven days a week
Points of interest: B & B cottage for rent, Grade A NASAA-certified organic vineyard
Retail distribution: Limited bottleshops and restaurants. Some export to UK, USA & NZ.

An introduction to the Riverina

Centred on the thriving towns of Griffith and Leeton in the Murrumbidgee Irrigation Area, the Riverina is the largest winemaking region in NSW and one of the largest in Australia. With more than 100,000 tonnes of grapes produced by 500 growers in a normal year, the region has the highest proportion of premium varietal fruit of any of the major inland grapegrowing regions. In 1994 the region produced almost 30,000 tonnes of semillon, or approximately two-thirds of Australia's production, while its 16,000 tonnes of shiraz represents 20% of Australia's production. As well, there are large plantings of chardonnay, cabernet sauvignon, sauvignon blanc, while newer varieties such as merlot, marsanne and verdelho represent an increasing proportion of the Riverina's varietal portfolio.

Being an efficient, low cost producer, the Riverina's grapes are now keenly sought for Australia's burgeoning export market, and in the past five years there has been considerable investment in new broad acre viticulture on the adjacent rice farms.

There are a dozen wineries in the region ranging from the large scale of De Bortoli and McWilliams to the tiny LillyPilly in Leeton. While in the past the area was dominated by McWilliams and Penfolds, the Riverina is the home of Australia's remaining family wine companies including De Bortoli, Miranda, Rossetto and Toorak, with the growing enterprises of Riverina Wines, Cranswick Estate, Wilton Estate, LillyPilly, West End and the new enterprise of Casella.

While in the past much of the wine produced was bulk white and red destined for the cask market, increased interest in Australian wine overseas over the past decade now sees much of the region's wine exported. Improved viticultural and winemaking techniques have seen the overall quality of bottled varietal wine improve dramatically, with the region's semillon - chardonnay blends prominent.

By far the region's star is the botrytised semillons which have swept the world by storm taking award after award in international contests. Pioneered by the De Bortoli family with the 1982 vintage, there are now more thana dozen different botrytised wines produced locally.

Founded in 1912 when John James McWilliam planted his first vines in Hanwood (some of these have been retained at Hanwood and still bear fruit!), the area now produces almost every style of wine from the more than 40 grape varieties. Following the First World War the area became the new home for returned soldiers, followed in the 1920s by many Italian immigrants who contributed greatly to the wine industry's development. The Riverina's cultural heritage is still prominent today.

The area is probably the most efficient wine producer in Australia, with its large yields approaching an average of 20 tonnes of grapes per hectare. The area pioneered the use of mechanical harvesting which enables picking of fruit at optimum ripeness and in the cool of the night, thus enhancing wine quality. The Riverina was also in the forefront of the development of mechanical pruning. A sense of purpose and a desire to meet the challenges of modern viticulture and winemaking pervades the Riverina - it's an exciting, positive feeling.

For further information on the Riverina write to the Winemakers of the Riverina Promotions Committee, PO Box 2401, Griffith 2680.

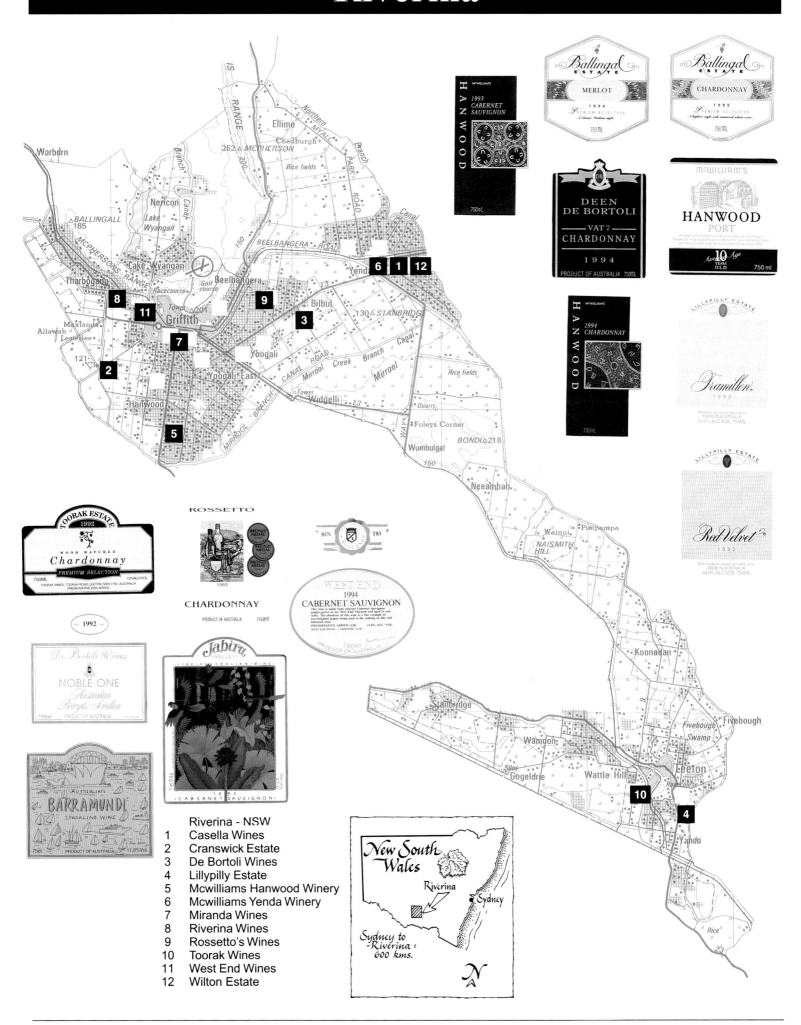

Riverina - NSW
1   Casella Wines
2   Cranswick Estate
3   De Bortoli Wines
4   Lillypilly Estate
5   Mcwilliams Hanwood Winery
6   Mcwilliams Yenda Winery
7   Miranda Wines
8   Riverina Wines
9   Rossetto's Wines
10 Toorak Wines
11 West End Wines
12 Wilton Estate

Casella

and the winemaking centre was still in frantic progress. The massive stainless steel tanks holding hundreds of thousands of litres of wine are now full and John can breathe a sigh of relief knowing his dream and vision are fast becoming a reality. Tucked away in the corner of the old family shed is the first fermenting tank of his father's, proudly shown to us by John.

The Casella wine label is shortly to be launched and if the wines shape up as well as they looked still fermenting at vintage time, they will be good indeed. The Riverina wines John has made for the Sergi family have been excellent, so the wine drinker can look forward to the Casella release with enthusiasm.

John Casella's parents arrived as Italian immigrants in the 1950s, settling on a small fruit block near Yenda in the Riverina. The Casellas didn't take long to set up a small winery on their vineyard to make the traditional family wine each year. Gradually many of the family friends started to come by to replenish their wine cellars. The family grape and fruit growing business remained the main focus.

Then son John became a trained winemaker and today is in charge of the winemaking at the giant Riverina Wine Company, the other side of Griffith. Things began to change rapidly in 1994, when John commissioned a huge modern building to house a large winemaking operation. As the 1995 vintage started, work on the building

CASELLA WINES
Address: Farm 1471, Wakely Road, Yenda NSW 2681
Phone: (069) 681346
Fax: (069) 681196
Established: 1969
Winemaker: John Casella
Principal varieties grown: Chardonnay, semillon, shiraz, colombard, marsanne, verdelho, merlot
Ha under vine: 100
Average annual crush: 5,000 tonnes
Principal wines & brands
Casella, Yenda Estate
Public & trade tours: No
Hours open to public: Not open currently

West End Wines

On the western outskirts of Griffith lies the West End Winery, established in 1945 by Francisco Calabria and his wife Elizabeth. Today their son William carries on the tradition. Bill has his own non-irrigated vineyards and uses small parcels of these intensely flavoured grapes to blend with his other selected fruit.

The winemaking process at West End is very personal and Bill oversees every step of the process. The whites are fruit-driven and go through a long temperature-controlled fermentation, they are bottled young and are great drinking. The red wines go through an extended fermentation to extract maximum colour and character, and to keep some elegance in the wines. Bill uses minimum filtration techniques to preserve as much flavour as possible in his reds, so a little precipitation in the wines with a small 'crust' may appear. If anything, this is just a statement of quality and ageing potential, so don't be worried.

West End, like many wineries established more than 30 years ago, produces a large range of table, fortified and sparkling wines, along with some Italian styles, lambrusco (red and white) and spumantes.

WEST END WINES
Address: 1283 Brayne Road, Griffith, NSW 2680
Phone: (069) 64 1506
Fax: (069) 62 1673
Established: 1945
Winemaker: William Calabria
Principal varieties grown: Shiraz, semillon, chardonnay, chenin blanc, cabernet sauvignon, merlot
Ha under vine: 21
Average annual crush: 1,400 tonnes
Average no. cases produced: 5,000

Principal wines & brands	Cellar potential
Hermitage	5-10 years
Chardonnay	5-10 years
Chablis	2-5 years
Colombard Chardonnay	5-10 years

Public & trade tours: Mon-Fri
Cellar door & mail order sales: Yes
Hours open to public: 8.30 am-5 pm Mon-Fri
Retail distribution: Mailing list, phone orders, cellar door, throughout Riverina and other major metropolitan areas

The Cranswick Estate

One of Australia's most progressive and successful wine companies, professionally crafting wines for specific market needs in Australia and overseas, is The Cranswick Estate. They are in the top 10 in size, being Australia's seventh largest wine exporter with sales of $A9.6 million overseas in 1994, almost doubling their 1993 performance.

The Cranswick Estate is a totally professional operation - its history dates back to 1931 when the Cinzano family of Italian vermouth fame began winemaking in Australia. In 1974, they built one of Australia's most modern and best-equipped wineries and began making table wines under contract, as well as their own vermouths. In 1991 the management team, led by dynamic managing director Graham Cranswick Smith, bought out the business. Their immediate focus was on fine- tuning the winemaking and establishing exciting brands to attack the premium bottled wine export market.

Their success speaks volumes for their courage and foresight. One might also say "well done, Ken Done" - his uniquely Australian Barramundi design wine labels have flooded the export market. In four short years, sales overseas have rocketed from nothing to 200,000 cases. Barramundi is Australia's second fastest growing major export wine label.

The other success story for exports is the Jabiru Valley label, designed by talented Queensland artist Jo-Anne Hook, which has won several prestigious international design and packaging awards, one at the San Francisco Fair International Wine Label Competition and another at the American Graphic Arts Competition in Virginia. Both Jabiru and Barramundi have a distinct Australian feel with their design, and carry graphically the message 'Australian wine - sunshine in the bottle.'

Cranswick also has a more traditional range of varietal wines under the Cranswick Estate label. The 1993 Botrytis Semillon has carried all before it on the wine show scene "Autumn Gold" - awarded the highest score for any wine at the 1995 International Wine & Spirit Competition, and awarded the "Top Gold" in its class at the 1994 Canberra National Wine Show.

Cranswick grower Pat Zirilli worked hand in hand with winemaking team of production director Andrew Schulz and Ian Hongell, both wine graduates from Roseworthy, to get his botrytised (noble rot) grapes to perfect condition, a risky business in which he could have lost everything, but this sense of trust and teamwork typifies the Cranswick operation. In 1993, Cranswick spent $2 million on a 400 hectare property on the slopes (a rarity in the Riverina) near Scenic Hill. The property has been named Cocoparra, aboriginal for Kookaburra. More than 100 hectares have been planted with another 160 hectares to follow shortly. This massive investment on this vineyard of perfect soils and good well-drained slopes and drip irrigation, also a rarity in the Riverina, has already shown great results. Expansion at the winery has seen the ability to give the reds long fermentation, adding to body, flavour and quality.

The Cranswick Estate's managing director, Graham Cranswick Smith, is also a keen private pilot, a suitable pastime for his high flying style of taking Cranswick to the top. The company also supports local charities and recent endeavours include a $5,000 dollar donation to the Police Citizens Youth Club of Griffith each year, saving it from extinction. The Cranswick Estate is a credit to the Australian Wine Industry.

THE CRANSWICK ESTATE
Address: Walla Avenue, Griffith NSW 2680
Direction: South-west of city centre
Phone: (069) 62 4133
Fax: (069) 62 2888
Established: 1931
Owner: Graham Cranswick Smith
Winemaker: Ian Hongell
Principal varieties grown: Chardonnay, shiraz, merlot, cabernet sauvignon, marsanne
Ha under vine: 150
Average annual crush: 12,000 tonnes
Average no. cases produced: 700,000

Principal wines & brands	Cellar potential
Autumn Gold Botrytis Semillon	10+ years
The Cranswick Pinot Noir Chardonnay	5-10 years
Cranswick Estate	
Semillon	5-10 years
Semillon Chardonnay	0-3 years
Sauvignon Blanc	0-3 years
Chardonnay	0-3 years
Shiraz Cabernet	5-10 years
Shiraz Merlot	5-10 years
Cabernet Sauvignon	5-10 years
Barramundi (White & Red Table Wine & Sparkling)	0-3 years

Trade tours: By appointment only
Cellar door & mail order sales: Yes
Hours open to public: 10 am-4.30 pm Mon-Fri.
Retail distribution: Cellar door, mail order, local restaurants

De Bortoli Wines

Vittorio De Bortoli arrived in Australia in 1924 and began working at Beelbangera Winery. In 1927 he purchased land, now the site of his winery. His son Deen joined him in the 1950s and has since taken over the management of the company. Deen expanded the winery, increasing its capacity, and developed a bulk sparkling wine system. This system produced the De Bortoli 'Vittorio Spumante' which was an instant success in the market place. In 1982 the third generation of the De Bortoli family took its place in the company ranks, as Deen's son Darren graduated from Roseworthy College in South Australia.

Darren made his mark on the industry fairly quickly by experimenting with semillon grapes which had been left on the vines until two months after vintage and were heavily infected with mould. Unsure as to whether the grapes contained the 'noble rot' (botrytis cinerea) he had to make the wine before he could be sure. The result has passed into Australian wine history. The 1982 De Bortoli Semillon Sauternes has won more gold medals within a relatively short period of time than any other Australian wine, and is sold worldwide. The family have also been successful with a bottle-fermented sparkling wine, using mainly chardonnay grapes.

Today the giant winery at Bilbul has a storage capacity of more than 30 million litres, producing the equivalent of three million cases of wine annually. More than 100 people are now employed in production, marketing and distribution through branches in Sydney, Melbourne and Brisbane and Darren De Bortoli is in charge of a team of five winemakers. Because of the large varietal mix and the long growing season, the vintage lasts from early February to late May with the picking of the botrytised grapes for the now legendary 'Noble One' Botrytis Semillon.

In 1987 De Bortoli purchased Miller's Chateau Yarrinya in the Yarra Valley of Victoria. This adventurous move has been totally successful and the Yarra operation (which is covered in the relevant chapter of this book) makes its own range of wines and has an award winning restaurant and hospitality complex on site. The 'Montage' label is a blended series of Southern Victorian and Yarra Valley wine. The 'Sacred Hill' value for money range from the Bilbul winery is of outstanding quality and like everything De Bortoli do, reflects great credit on the family and the Australian wine industry.

DE BORTOLI WINES PTY LTD
Address: De Bortoli Road, Bilbul, NSW 2680
Phone: (069) 64 9444
Fax: (069) 64 9400
Established: 1928
Winemaker: Darren De Bortoli
Principal varieties grown: Shiraz, cabernet sauvignon, pinot noir, semillon, chardonnay, traminer, riesling, colombard, trebbiano, sauvignon blanc
Ha under vine: 200
Average annual crush: 35,000 tonnes

Principal wines & brands	Cellar potential
Noble One Botrytis Semillon	10+ years
Rare Dry Botrytis Semillon	10+ years
Deen De Bortoli range	
Chardonnay, Sauvignon Blanc, Emeri (sparkling)	2-5 years
Cabernet Sauvignon, Shiraz, Late Semillon	5-10 years
Sacred Hill Range	
Chablis, Colombard Riesling, Rhine Riesling, Traminer Riesling	2-3 years
Semillon Chardonnay, Shiraz Cabernet, 5 Year Old Port	2-5 years
Black Label Fortified Range	
8 Year Old Port	
10 Year Old Liqueur Muscat	

Public & trade tours: By appointment only
Cellar door & mail order sales: Yes
Hours open to public: 9 am-5.30 pm Mon-Sat; 9 am-4 pm Sun.
Retail distribution: Available through most fine wine stores

McWilliam's Hanwood Winery

In 1912, shortly after the completion of the Murrumbidgee Irrigation Scheme, J. J. McWilliam arrived with his bullock waggon loaded down with 40,000 cuttings from the family's vineyard at "Markview", near Junee, and planted the area's first vines. The Hanwood winery was built in 1917 and is the centre of McWilliam's operations in the Riverina. They also have large wineries at Yenda and Beelbangera.

The Hanwood winery is enormous and its entrance is modelled to appear like a huge barrel. This is the tasting and visitors' entertainment area. Alongside the barrel is a giant bottle on its side, about 25 metres in length. This houses a museum, which details the history of McWilliam's. The winery itself produces mainly white and red varietal table wines but is also the wood maturation centre for McWilliam's range of sherries and ports.

Perhaps the best known of these is 10 year old Hanwood Port, one of Australia's most popular and finest tawny ports - a wine that still contains a drop of the original blend of 1926. McWilliam's also make an excellent vintage port at Hanwood. Total storage capacity at Hanwood is a massive 22 million litres, about seven per cent of Australia's annual wine consumption.

The genius behind this modern setup is Glen McWilliam who foresaw the swing in popularity away from fortified to table wines, and changed the emphasis in production at McWilliam's accordingly. He was also responsible for building the Robinvale Winery on the Murray River in Victoria in 1961. Glen McWilliam refurbished and expanded the local McWilliam's wineries with equipment of his own design in the 1950s and my family had many dealings with him. After graduating from an engineering course at Adelaide University in 1948, my father went to work for Glen at Hanwood, where he picked up valuable information and experience. This was later utilised when he designed all of Hardy's new winery equipment and additions, over the next few decades.

Glen's contribution to McWilliam's Wines and the Australian wine industry cannot be underestimated; he is a typical member of an extraordinary family who are not surprisingly well into their second century of winemaking. McWilliam's was one of the first wine companies in the Riverina and Australia, for that matter, to market varietal table wines some 30 years ago. The focus today is on vibrant wines with young fresh obvious varietal character. The Hanwood Range - a chardonnay, semillon/chardonnay, shiraz and cabernet sauvignon, have been re-dressed in a distinctively Australian style with labels featuring Aboriginal dot art from the artists living on the Napperey Station, 200 kms north-west of Alice Springs. These wines at great value prices have already gained a good slice of the export market. Production director in charge of all of McWilliam's wineries is Doug McWilliam, a graduate from the famous Davis University's oenology course in California. Day to day management of the Hanwood Winery itself is in the very capable hands of his cousin, the genial, Brian McWilliam.

Lillypilly Estate

Picture: Pasquale Fiumara

LILLYPILLY ESTATE WINES
Address: Lillypilly Road, Leeton, NSW 2705
Direction: Between Yanco and Leeton
Phone: (069) 53 4069
Fax: (069) 53 4980
Established: 1982
Winemaker: Robert Fiumara
Principal varieties grown: Chardonnay, cabernet sauvignon, traminer, semillon, muscat of Alexandria, riesling, shiraz, sauvignon blanc
Ha under vine: 17
Average annual crush: 180 tonnes
Average no. cases produced: 8,000 dozen

Principal wines & brands	Cellar potential
Tramillon	2-5 years
Red Velvet	0-2 years
Chardonnay	2-5 years
Fume Blanc	2-5 years
Cabernet Sauvignon	5-10 years
Shiraz	5-10 years
Vintage Port	10+ years
Noble Muscat of Alexandria	

Public & trade tours: By appointment only
Cellar door & mail order sales: Yes
Hours open to public: 10 am-5 pm Mon-Sat (some long weekends);Sunday by appointment
Points of interest: Vineyard - winery grows all its own grapes
Retail distribution: From the winery

Post-war immigrant to Australia Pasquale Fiumara brought to his new homeland the expertise of thousands of years of viticultural and winemaking heritage. He also followed many of his countrymen in starting a retail fruit and vegetable business as well as a general store.

Vines were planted on Pasquale's property in 1972 and the grapes sold to wineries in the region. With seven sons to keep busy, a winery was the logical choice. Son Robert, a giant of a man, went to Charles Sturt University as one of the first students under wine guru Brian Croser's instruction. The first vintage was made at Lillypilly in the new winery in 1982. Robert coined a name - during his first vintage he made a wine from traminer and semillon, calling it 'Tramillon.' It was an instant hit not only with the wine-drinking public but with the wine judges, winning a trophy at the 1983 Royal Sydney Easter Show. This wine shows lifted aromatic, spicy cloves and cinnamon with lemon, pineapple and melons on the palate, and just a hint of sweetness. It has also proven to age well.

Lillypilly has won more than 300 awards since this first success. Robert has definite skill in making the late harvest and botrytised dessert wines. I tried his Noble Semillon, Noble Riesling, Noble Traminer and Noble Muscat of Alexandria. All have similar luscious characters with divine richness and complexity. Often, the grapes are not picked until June or July, several months after the normal vintage - a risky business, but the rewards to the drinker are high. Lillypilly also wins many awards for its chardonnay, sauvignon blanc, shiraz cabernet sauvignon, spatlese lexia and vintage port. It also makes a spatlese lexia and a vintage port. I am certain if you visit Lillypilly and enjoy its charming atmosphere, you will also fall in love with at least one of the Fiumaras' fine wines.

Miranda

Our trip through Griffith in 1995 had a slightly sad note to it. The Miranda family was still mourning the passing of Francesco, the Miranda family's wine business founder, affectionately known to all as 'Pop', just a few days short of his 84th birthday. Pop came to Australia with his new bride Caterina in 1938, following in his brother's footsteps. Although a professor of languages in his homeland, he and Caterina bought a half share in a general store in Kooyoo Street, Griffith, buying out their partners a year later.

Frank was unfortunately interned during World War II at the Loveday Camp in Barmera, but not before making his first vintage, three tonnes of grapes trodden with his feet in the old Italian tradition. The wine was not a total success, most of it finding its way to the McWilliam's distillation plant.

Frank's winemaking career took an unusual turn. He was sent to the prison camp in Katherine, an unlikely place to make wine as you could imagine, but not for the innovative Pop. With dried sultanas, re-hydrated, and many winemaking books in his hand, he became a very popular individual indeed. Two years after his release in 1944, with the store going well, he began building a small winery. Four years later he bought vineyards at Bilbul, and in 1954 the Mirandas sold the store to invest further in the wine business. In the early '50s, Frank employed equally innovative winemaker Ron Potter, inventor of much of Australia's winemaking equipment.

Pop was totally devoted to his family and friends, and in his life built

Miranda with the help of his three sons and their families into the seventh biggest wine business in Australia. In 1991, Miranda, under the control of Sam, Jim and Lou, expanded considerably with the purchase of Rovalley Wines in the Barossa Valley, which is now managed by Lou Miranda. The Rovalley Wines have since won a score of medals and trophies. In 1995, the Rovalley Ridge Show Reserve Chardonnay, Shiraz and Shiraz Cabernet Sauvignon have been highly successful at both national and international wine shows.

Winemaker at Miranda's Griffith Winery is Californian Shayne Cunningham, who spent 14 years with the famous Christian Brothers in the Napa Valley. Shayne really has a feel for chardonnay production and has the winery really humming. The hospitality flows freely at Miranda and the generously flavoured wines follow this theme. 'Mirrool Creek' and 'Somerton' Riverina Wine ranges represent excellent value for money. Pop can justly be proud of his family's achievements.

MIRANDA WINES
Address: 57 Jondaryan Avenue, Griffith, NSW 2680
Phone: (069) 62 4033
Fax: (069) 62 6941
Established: 1939
Winemaker: Shayne Cunningham
Principal varieties grown: Semillon, shiraz, chardonnay, cabernet sauvignon, rhine riesling, sauvignon blanc
Ha under vine: 25
Average annual crush: 23,000 tonnes
Average no. cases produced: 1 million cases annually

Principal wines & brands	Cellar potential
Mirrool Creek Chardonnay	2-5 years
Mirrool Creek Cabernets Shiraz	2-5 years
Rovalley Ridge Chardonnay	5-10 years
Somerton Semillon Chardonnay	2-5 years
Somerton Shiraz Cabernets	2-5 years

Public & trade tours: Coach tours by appointment only
Cellar door & mail order sales: Yes
Hours open to public: Seven days a week
Points of interest: Tours are conducted every Wednesday at 2.15 pm. Function room available for light meals on request. Extensive lawn area and BBQ facilities.
Retail distribution: Extensive wine, beer & spirit selection. Walking distance from Main Street. Coaches welcome.

Riverina Wines

Tony Sergi is a hardworking, down-to-earth man, reflecting his solid Italian roots. He is happiest when working with his men out in his large vineyard holdings and he's much happier at the wheel of his four wheel drive than behind his seldom used desk. Tony's father, Joe, who has just turned 85, migrated from his native Italy to the Riverina; he had nine children - eight daughters and one son.

From small beginnings, Riverina now rates as the eighth biggest winery in Australia. At present, the Sergis have 140 hectares of vines bearing, but a massive 480 hectares planted, which will ensure they have the varieties and quantities needed for their ambitious expansion program. The spread of varieties planted includes a substantial quantity of chardonnay, but also 40 hectares of verdelho, the famous variety from the island of Madeira which also makes an exciting, fruity, full- bodied white wine and is ideally suited to a warm climate like the Riverina. There are also substantial plantings of sauvignon blanc.

Tony Sergi also runs a number of vineyards for other members of his family, and Riverina is one of the most self-sufficient wineries in the region which also gives them good quality control over the grapes they process. The winemaker is Sam Trimboli and the main brand, Ballingal, has an impressive range of wines. At a recent masked tasting I conducted, all the judges agreed that the Ballingal wines shone out, often out-pointing much more expensive wines. The sparkling burgundy made mainly from shiraz recently impressed all the judges.

The hardworking and professional manager is David Hammond, formerly with Hungerford Hill Wines. The winery has just gone through a $1.2 million upgrade and expansion, with the accent on winemaking equipment to enhance quality, and a further expansion and bottling hall is on the drawing board. The Riverina Winery has a large and attractively appointed tasting area and a pleasant, leafy, covered outdoor alfresco area. It is a pleasant place indeed to while away a few moments while tasting the impressive range of wines.

RIVERINA WINES PTY LTD
Address: Farm 1305 Hillston Road, Griffith, NSW 2680
Phone: (069) 62 4122
Fax: (069) 62 4628
Established: 1969
Owner: Tony & Angela Sergi
Winemaker: Sam Trimboli
Principal varieties grown: Chardonnay, semillon, sauvignon blanc, merlot, verdelho, shiraz, cabernet sauvignon
Ha under vine: 484
Average annual crush: 24,000 tonnes

Principal wines & brands	Cellar potential
Ballingal	
Chardonnay	2-5 years
Semillon	2-5 years
Semillon Sauvignon Blanc	2-5 years
Shiraz	5-10 years
Cabernet Sauvignon	5-10 years
Merlot	5-10 years

Public & trade tours: By appointment only
Cellar door & mail order sales: Yes
Hours open to public: 9 am-5.30 pm seven days a week
Points of interest: BBQ area
Retail distribution: Retail outlets/restaurants

Rossetto Wines

The Rossetto winery was founded in 1930; today the third generation of the family runs the vastly expanded business, crushing an average of 12,000 tonnes of grapes each vintage. The family has its own vineyards, known as Beelgara Estate, which adjoins the winery in the Beelbangera district of the Riverina.

The three Rossetto brothers, Garry, Brian and Kevin, run the enterprise and control everything, from the viticulture, through their modern well-equipped winery, to their own bottling line, making the most of the richly flavoured, ripe grapes the fertile soils of their region produce. The Rossettos, like many long-established wineries, make a large range of wines - table, fortified, sparkling and even cocktail styles - and all represent excellent value for money. At a recent line-up of chardonnays I tasted at Winestate Magazine - masked - the Rossetto Chardonnay was one of the best in its class. Its rich, peachy fruit flavours shone through. The Rossetto motto 'From the heart of the grape' rings true.

ROSSETTO WINES

Address: Farm 576, Beelbangera, NSW 2680
Direction: 7 km from Griffith
Phone: (069) 63 5214
Fax: (069) 63 5542
Established: 1930
Winemaker: John Schwartzkopf
Principal varieties grown: Semillon, chardonnay, gordo, colombard, trebbiano, shiraz, mataro
Ha under vine: 15
Average annual crush: 10,000 tonnes

Principal wines & brands	Cellar potential
Shiraz Bin 332	2-5 years
Cabernet Sauvignon	2-5 years
Chardonnay	2-5 years
Semillon	2-5 years
Rhine Riesling	2-5 years
Mount Bingar Tawny Port	10+ years
Liqueur Muscat Old Anniversary	10+ years

Cellar door & mail order sales: Yes
Hours open to public: 8.30 am-5.30 pm Mon-Sat;
Points of interest: BBQ facilities, picnic area
Retail distribution: Cellar door sales at the winery, also retail outlets through Australia.

Toorak Wines

Francesco Bruno Snr migrated from Sicily in 1950. Three years later he purchased a small 18 hectare property which was then planted with fruit trees. In 1963, together with his two sons, Frank Jnr and Vincent, he decided to expand into winegrape growing and in 1965 established a small winery and produced local and regional wines. The winery has expanded during the last 30 years to produce approximately 3 million litres of mainly table wines. These wines are sold under contract to various customers throughout Australia. Some 80,000 cases of mixed varietal wines, such as chardonnay, semillon, cabernet, shiraz and traminer, are sold under the Toorak Estate Label. As well, the Company produces a secondary label for the 4 litre wine cask market. Frank Jnr looks after the winemaking productions and Vincent the administration. They have plans to expand the Packaging Plant in the near future to produce wines for the export

market.

Toorak wines over the years have won several awards at major Australian Shows and continue to produce wines of exceptional character and flavour from the Riverina District of NSW.

The Toorak Estate Chardonnay, Semillon Chardonnay, as well as Cabernet Sauvignon, display excellent varietal character and are made from 100% Riverina fruit. Also, Frank Snr Port and Liqueur Muscat are well regarded by consumes and the trade.

Frank Snr has now retired and the business is run by brothers Frank Jnr and Vincent Bruno. Cellar door sales are handled by sister Nina and Frank Jnr's son Robert, who is studying at Charles Sturt University for his Bachelor of Applied Science in Winemaking.

TOORAK WINES PTY LTD

Address: Toorak Road, Leeton, NSW 2705
Phone: (069) 53 2333
Fax: (069) 53 4454
Established: 1965
Winemaker: Frank Bruno Jnr.
Principal varieties grown: Semillon, chardonnay, traminer, shiraz, cabernet sauvignon, colombard, sauvignon blanc
Ha under vine: 20
Average annual crush: 4,000 tonnes
Average no. cases produced: 20,000

Principal wines & brands	Cellar potential
Chardonnay	4-6 years
Semillon	4-6 years
Shiraz	4-8 years
Cabernet Sauvignon	4-8 years

Public & trade tours: Yes
Cellar door & mail order sales: Yes
Hours open to public: 9 am-5 pm Mon-Sat.
Points of interest: Wine tasting and tours
Retail distribution: Victoria, New South Wales, Queensland.

An introduction to Cowra

Situated in the heart of New South Wales, not far from Orange and the National Capital, Canberra, Cowra is probably best known for the infamous 'Cowra Breakout' of Japanese prisoners from the Cowra Prison Camp during the Second World War. Cowra is a pretty town and features a Japanese War Cemetery Garden and Cultural Centre. The town is built around a hill of huge granite rock; a nesting place for wedgetail eagles. From this lofty viewpoint, the vine rows seem to stretch into eternity.

The vineyard expansion in recent years has been astounding. Richmond Grove's vineyard alone now covers more than 250 hectares, the largest vineyard venture ever undertaken in Australia in one year. More than 600 hectares are now covered with vines on the fertile soils. These are made up of broken down granite and basalt, with alluvial loam brought down by the Lachlan River, which also provides supplementary irrigation during the rather dry summers.

Three main vineyards dominate the region - Cowra Estate was the first established vineyard in 1973, followed by Rothbury and Richmond Grove. Arrowfield has had a long association with the region and long-term contracts with some of the few independent growers. Several small wine producers have also sprung up over recent years, whilst Brokenwood and McGuigan Wines have just established vineyard operations adjacent to Windowrie's vineyards at Billimari, 15 kms north-west of Cowra.

Cowra is fast becoming the chardonnay capital of Australia. Rothbury has made a strong statement with this variety in recent years, as have Arrowfield, Cowra Estate, and now, Richmond Grove. The chardonnays are ripe, rich and fleshy with strong stone fruit peach-nectarine characters often with some nuttiness in the background, finishing with easy-drinking acids. (Brian Croser helped launch chardonnay from Cowra in his days as lecturer at Wagga Wagga's then Riverina College, now Charles Sturt University). Other varieties, both red and white, seem to thrive in this climate with its good soils and water. Undoubtedly further expansion will see this region as a major player in the Australian wine scene by the turn of the century.

14. Benfield Estate
15. Cartobe Vineyard
16. Cassegrain Vineyards
17. Clonakilla Wines
18. Connellans Wines
19. Cowra Wines
20. Cullarin Cellars
21. Doonkuna Estate
22. Giribaldi Brothers
23. Glenswood Wines
24. Lachlan Valley Wines
25. Markeita Cellars
26. McArthur Estate Winery
27. R. Medway
28. Mountilford Vineyard
29. Murrumbidgee Wines

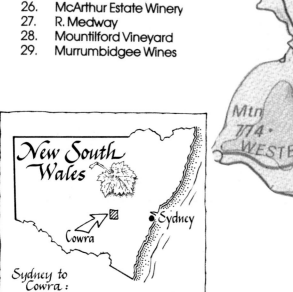

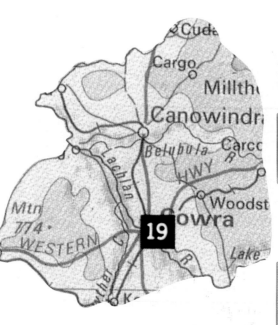

Cowra Estate

Food and beverage entrepreneur John Geber took over Cowra Estate in 1995 after an association making and marketing wines from the vineyard, mainly in Europe under the 'Naturally Australian' label. Exciting times surely lie ahead for this well set up operation. The vineyard, the first in the region, was pioneered by Tony Gray in 1973 with the help of viticulturist John Brocksopp, now at Leeuwin Estate in Western Australia.

In 1979 Greg Johnston moved in to manage the vineyard after being vineyard manager for Rothbury in the Lower Hunter Valley. In his own words, "I came to town with a view to retaining my sanity after the constant viticultural battle of the Hunter". Liz, his wife, had a top restaurant in Sydney and the Johnstons have a superb entertaining area in the beautiful home they have built in the middle of the vines. Liz also started the excellent Quarry Restaurant and the Vineyard Motel. These days, you can taste the Cowra Estate and other Cowra wines at the Quarry's tasting room.

The Eagle on the Rock, symbol of the

region, features on Cowra's excellent range of wines, from the now 73 hectares of vines. There are two chardonnays, including a Director's Reserve, a riesling, gewurztraminer and a sauvignon blanc in the whites. The reds include a cabernet sauvignon with a touch of cabernet franc and a straight merlot as well as a pinot noir. The new Cabernet Franc Rose is indicative of what a truly good rose should be and is most timely for Australian Consumers. Watch out for these excellent wines made by Simon Gilbert at Scone. The Eagle has landed!

COWRA ESTATE/COWRA WINES
Address: Boorowa Road, Cowra NSW
Direction: 4 km from Cowra on Boorowa/ Yass Road
Phone: (02) 905 4613, (063) 42 1136
Fax: (02) 9054613, (063) 42 4286
Established: 1983
Owner: Cowra Wines, John Geber
Winemaker: Simon Gilbert
Principal varieties grown: Chardonnay, pinot noir, merlot, sauvignon blanc, merlot, cabernet sauvignon, cabernet franc
Ha under vine: 75
Average annual crush: 1,100 tonnes
Average no. cases produced: 20,000

Principal wines & brands	Cellar potential
Cowra Estate	
Chardonnay & Directors Res.	2-5 years
Merlot & Directors Reserve	5-10 years
Cabernet Sauvignon	5-10 years
Cabernet Franc Rose	2-5 years
Chardonnay Directors Reserve	5-10 years

Trade tours: By appointment only
Cellar door & mail order sales: Yes
Hours open to public: 10 am-4 pm Tues-Sun (sales/tasting)
Points of interest: Quarry Restaurant, Tues-Sun, Lunch at the Vineyard; Thurs, Fri & Sat nights from 7 pm
Retail distribution: PO Box 363, Harbord NSW 2096, 02 905 4613

Richmond Grove - Cowra

Richmond Grove is in the leading bunch of Australia's best-selling varietal table wines. After an auspicious start in the '70s, with wine wizards Brian McGuigan and Mark Cashmore calling the tune, Orlando purchased Richmond Grove along with the Wyndham Estate wine interests.

Orlando's owners, the giant Agro-Alimentaire (food-beverage) company, Pernod Ricard, had seen the Richmond Grove potential and were looking for a reliable quality vineyard site to produce the prodigious quantities of premium wine they needed. They chose Cowra, in 1989, and I am absolutely certain they have made a wise choice. In 12 months they have planted some 240 hectares to add to the existing vineyard in one of the largest vineyard developments ever undertaken in Australia.

On our visit to the vineyard, we were awestruck by its enormous size, accentuated by the rich red colour of the soils and the impressive slopes and aspects of the vineyard. When you pull the cork on any of the Richmond Grove 'great value' Cowra wines, you can take part in the celebration of this vast vineyard venture.

Being the first Australian state, and the first wine-producing state, established in Australia with the arrival of vines on the first fleet, New South Wales has vineyards in all areas, including the far west. As well as the main wine-producing regions, excellent wines are found in the cool south near Bega, with Grevillea Estate, and on the mid-south coast near Shoalhaven Heads and Nowra.

The cool and hilly regions around Yass and Young produce excellent table and sparkling wines. Nearby the Canberra district has vineyards and wineries sited in both NSW and the ACT, where the traditional cabernet-merlot blend has become a hallmark of the region.

Emerging regions, with wine quality reputation growing faster than their plantings, demonstrate the potential of NSW wines from regions with higher altitudes or with cooling breezes. Along the ridges surrounding Young, the appropriately named Hilltops, originally planted to vines almost 100 years ago, is reclaiming its reputation with cabernet sauvignon, shiraz and riesling. It includes McWilliams Barwang vineyards and the Woodonga Hills Winery. Further north around Orange, in a newly planted wine region at altitudes between 600 and 1,000 metres above sea level, wines are already highly sought after for unique and full-flavoured varietal characteristics.

Vineyards stretch to the north through Port Macquarie, where one of the state's most heralded wine producers, Cassegrain, has a large winery and restaurant complex, right up to Tenterfield on the Queensland border. One can only admire the intrepid souls who have so diligently sought out the regional conditions and mini-climates and who prove that, with attention to site and variety, and in caring hands, the vine is a marvellous plant, always able to produce fine wines with the right management.

Other Wine Producing Areas.

Other Wine Producing Areas - NSW

1   Afleck Winery
2   Barwang Wines
3   Benfield Estate
4   Bloodwood Estate
5   Brindabella Hills Winery
6   Broken Bago Winery
7   Brooks Creek Vineyard
8   Canobolas-Smith
9   Cargo Road Winery
10 Cassegrain Vineyards

11 Charles Sturt University Winery
12 Charley Brothers Winery
13 Clonakilla
14 Cobbitty Wines
15 Doonkuna Estate

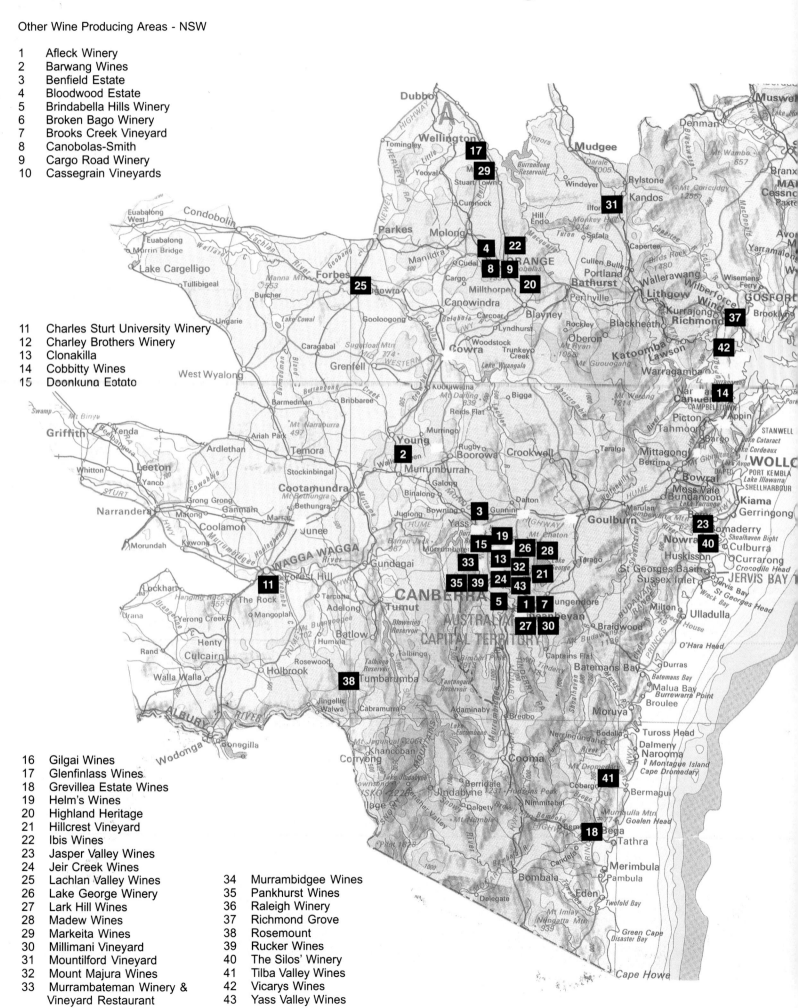

16 Gilgai Wines
17 Glenfinlass Wines
18 Grevillea Estate Wines
19 Helm's Wines
20 Highland Heritage
21 Hillcrest Vineyard
22 Ibis Wines
23 Jasper Valley Wines
24 Jeir Creek Wines
25 Lachlan Valley Wines
26 Lake George Winery
27 Lark Hill Wines
28 Madew Wines
29 Markeita Wines
30 Millimani Vineyard
31 Mountilford Vineyard
32 Mount Majura Wines
33 Murrambateman Winery &
     Vineyard Restaurant

34 Murrambidgee Wines
35 Pankhurst Wines
36 Raleigh Winery
37 Richmond Grove
38 Rosemount
39 Rucker Wines
40 The Silos' Winery
41 Tilba Valley Wines
42 Vicarys Wines
43 Yass Valley Wines

Other Wine Producing Areas.

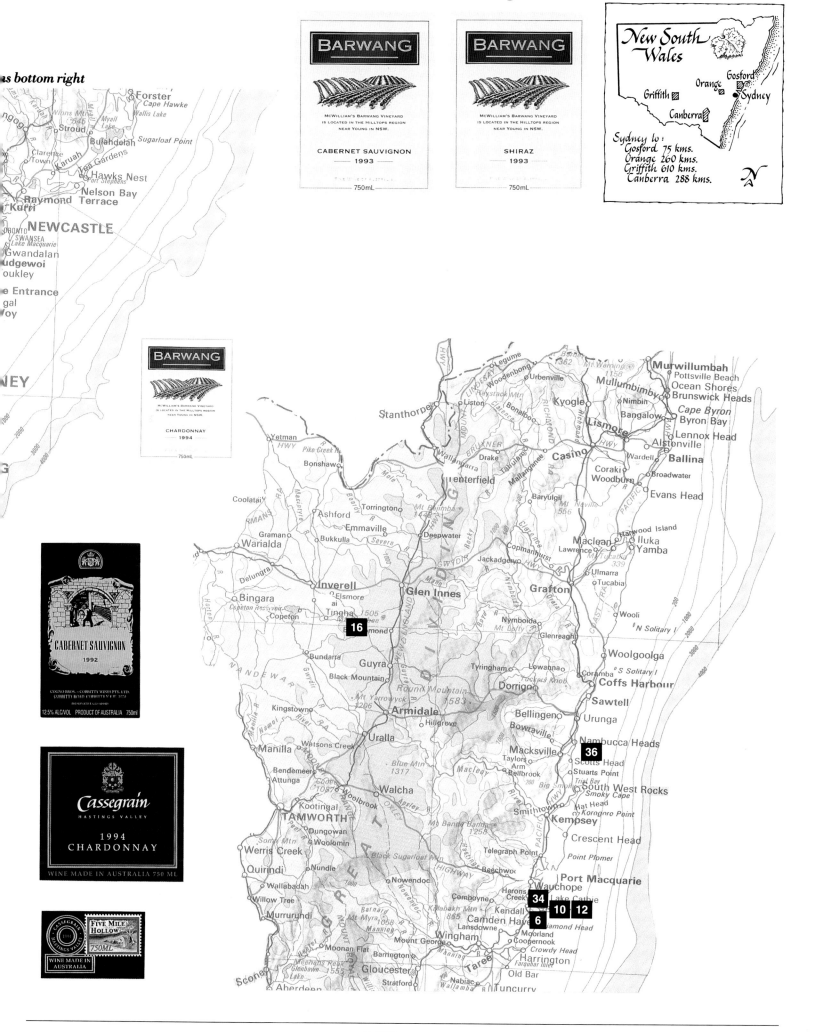

as bottom right

BARWANG

McWilliam's Barwang Vineyard
is located in the Hilltops region
near Young in NSW.

CABERNET SAUVIGNON
— 1993 —

750mL

BARWANG

McWilliam's Barwang Vineyard
is located in the Hilltops region
near Young in NSW.

SHIRAZ
— 1993 —

750mL

New South Wales

*Griffith   Orange   Gosford
                              Sydney
        Canberra*

*Sydney to:
Gosford 75 kms.
Orange 260 kms.
Griffith 610 kms.
Canberra 288 kms.*

BARWANG

McWilliam's Barwang Vineyard
is located in the Hilltops region
near Young in NSW.

CHARDONNAY
— 1994 —

750mL

CABERNET SAUVIGNON
1992

COGNO BROS. - COBBITTY WINES PTY. LTD.
COBBITTY ROAD, COBBITTY N.S.W. 2570

12.5% ALC/VOL   PRODUCT OF AUSTRALIA   750ml

Cassegrain
HASTINGS VALLEY

1994
CHARDONNAY

WINE MADE IN AUSTRALIA 750 ML

CASSEGRAIN
HASTINGS VALLEY

FIVE MILE
HOLLOW
750ML

WINE MADE IN
AUSTRALIA

McWilliam's Barwang

On the south-western slopes of the Great Dividing Range some 25 kilometres east of Young, at an average height above sea level of 600 metres, is the impressive McWilliam's Barwang Vineyard. The vineyards cover 100 hectares of rolling hills of the 400 hectare property and the view over the patchwork quilt of vines from the furthest hill is quite something. The soils are deep red decomposed granite impregnated with basalt, and I'm sure this comes through in the strength and complexity of the red wines.

This remote cool climate location was first planted back in 1969, 13 hectares along the high ridges to avoid the worst of the frosts that are common in the area. McWilliam's bought the vineyard in 1989 from the founders, the Robertson family, whom McWilliam's had been supplying with vine cuttings since the vineyard's founding. McWilliam's immediately planted a further 87 hectares, and today it is all bearing. The grapes are crushed on site and then make the three-hour journey to the McWilliam's Hanwood Winery as chilled 'must' (grape juice).

The vineyard is chiefly planted to cabernet sauvignon, shiraz and chardonnay with smaller quantities of merlot, pinot noir, semillon, sauvignon blanc and riesling. The wines from Barwang have been spectacularly successful in wine shows and are often confused with those from Coonawarra. The first vintage shiraz, a 1989, has already won five gold medals and the 1991 Cabernet Sauvignon has won two trophies and two gold medals. In all, the McWilliam's Barwang wines have won more than 100 medals in only five short years. Qantas and a number of prestigious 5-star hotels have already included Barwang on their wine lists, along with other Australian classics, proving McWilliam's aim of developing fruit-driven wines from the excellent viticultural conditions to be absolutely correct.

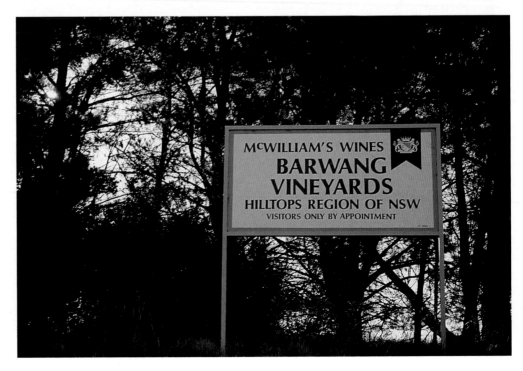

Cassegrain

The Hastings River was a viticultural paradise in the last century. During the 1860s there were no fewer than 33 wineries, mainly producing wine from the native North American grape variety isabella, which is resistant to the vine diseases that can occur in this maritime climate of the mid-north coast of New South Wales. Modern viticultural research and practices mean the understanding and ability to cope with these conditions is not a problem. John Cassegrain even has an organically-run vineyard which is doing fine.

John's background has more than prepared him for a career in the wine industry. His mother was Countess Francoise de Solere from a winemaking family in Burgundy, and his uncle, Count Barignot de Varenne, is the head of France's oldest cognac-producing company, Augier Freres & Co. John is a graduate of Roseworthy College in South Australia, who has already worked for Tyrrell's Wines for 10 years and had a hand in producing such great wines as their 1976 Pinot Noir. He has planted this variety in his own vineyard along with chardonnay, sauvignon blanc, merlot, cabernet sauvignon, chambourcin, semillon, verdelho and shiraz. John was encouraged to plant chambourcin, an unusual French hybrid, by viticultural guru Dr. Antcliff who also bred tarango, now planted by Brown Brothers in Victoria.

John's own family came from the wheat district around Orleans, south of Paris. The name Cassegrain means literally 'breaking the grain.' His father came to Port Macquarie, and from nothing built a huge construction business of which the headquarters are still across the road from the winery. He was affectionately known as 'Frog' and well loved by the locals. The trees, parks and gardens he planted around all his properties pay tribute to his caring good taste. John, together with his brother, has developed 'Le Clos Estates' a French custom where investors get a beautiful building block among the trees surrounding the vineyards, plus a share of the vineyard, a yearly return on their investment and some wine, of course. Many well-known Australians have their own 'Clos Estate'. The vineyards now cover 170 hectares and the annual crush of 750 tonnes is set to rise to about 1,500 tonnes by the turn of the century, producing more than 100,000 cases of wine. The 'fromenteau' - an old French term for chardonnay, is a very good wine indeed. The chambourcin has a rich dark cherry character - soft, with mouth-filling flavours. Also look out for the 'Cassae', a version of the famous Pineau-des-Charentes of Cognac, literally grape juice fortified with brandy. It comes in a small frosted cognac-type bottle and, chilled, it makes a delicious pre- or after-dinner drink.

Cassegrain has a splendid Terrace Cafe in the French tradition, looking out on the vineyards and the gardens which boast 2,500 roses. If any winery has a claim to paradise in Australia, it's Cassegrain.

CASSEGRAIN HASTINGS RIVER WINERY
Address: Fernbank Creek Road, Port Macquarie NSW 2444
Direction: 400 km north of Sydney, just off Pacific Highway
Phone: (065) 83 7777
Fax: (065) 84 0354
Established: 1980
Owners: John & Eva Cassegrain
Winemakers: John Cassegrain & Drew Noon
Principal varieties grown: Chardonnay, semillon, verdelho, sauvignon blanc, pinot noir, chambourcin, merlot, shiraz, cabernet sauvignon, cabernet franc
Ha under vine: 170
Average annual crush: 700 tonnes
Average no. cases produced: 35,000

Principal wines & brands	Cellar potential
Fromenteau Chardonnay	3-7 years
Hastings River Chardonnay	2-5 years
Hastings River Semillon	5-10 years
Hastings River Chambourcin	2-5 years
Hastings River Pinot Noir	2-5 years
Hastings River Shiraz	5-10 years
Hastings River Merlot	5-10 years
Five Mile Hollow White	1-2 years
Five Mile Hollow Red	1-2 years

Public & trade tours: By appointment only
Cellar door & mail order sales: Yes
Hours open to public: 9 am-5 pm seven days a week (except Christmas Day & Good Friday)
Points of interest: Restaurant (verandah), rose gardens, children's play area, picnic & BBQ facilities, annual Discovery Concert
Retail distribution: New South Wales, Queensland, South Australia, ACT, Western Australia, Victoria.

Charles Sturt University Winery

Australia's first degree course in winemaking, Bachelor of Applied Science (Wine), was introduced by the Riverina College of Advanced Education, (now the Charles Sturt University) at Wagga Wagga in 1975. The course can be studied either full-time or by external studies and there are currently 400 students enrolled.

The winery has since been expanded and now processes approximately 300 tonnes each vintage.

Brian Croser was the first winery director and the first crush was in 1977. On our visit, we tasted a superb pinot noir from a mountain vineyard at Tumut, and a great shiraz from Forbes. The winery enterprise demonstrates an accountable commercial operation and provides stimulating training for those students fortunate enough to be employed (winery scholarship). In association with the formal teaching, the practical experience the students obtain will prepare them for challenging careers in the wine industry.

CHARLES STURT UNIVERSITY WINERY
Address: McKeown Drive, Wagga Wagga NSW 2678
Phone: (069) 33 2435
Fax: (069) 33 2107
Winemaker: Rodney Hooper
Principal varieties grown: Chardonnay, cabernet sauvignon, merlot, cabernet franc, traminer, semillon, shiraz
Ha under vine: 15
Average annual crush: 300 tonnes
Average no. cases produced: 10,000

Principal wines & brands	Cellar potential
Chardonnay	2-5 years
Cabernet Sauvignon	2-5 years
Limited Release Chardonnay	2-5 years
Limited Release Red	5-10 years
Limited Release Botrytis Semillon	2-5 years

Public & trade tours: By appointment only
Cellar door & mail order sales: Yes
Hours open to public: 10 am-4 pm Mon-Fri; 11 am-4 pm Sat-Sun
Points of interest: Charles Sturt University Wagga Wagga is one of only two wine science schools in Australasia; experimental vineyards
Retail distribution: Cellar door; Sydney, Melbourne, Adelaide, Brisbane

Cobbitty Wines (Cogno Brothers)

The Cogno family winery is situated at Camden, near where pioneer Captain John Macarthur planted vines shortly after the settlement of New South Wales. This area is now part of outer Sydney.

The Cogno's arrived in Australia in 1950 and planted their 5.6 hectare vineyard at Cobbitty in 1964. The Cobbitty vineyard is planted with barbera, shiraz, trebbiano, grenache and muscat with the remainder of grapes purchased from South Australia. John's son Joseph Cogno takes care of the premium end of the market producing wines under the new found Cogno Brothers label.

The company has now diversified into the manufacturing of Wine Base Liqueurs which are produced on premise for substitutes of imported Liqueurs. The majority of all wines produced are for exclusive sale through cellar door and local bottle shops

" . . . where pioneer Captain John Macarthur planted vines shortly after the settlement of New South Wales"

including restaurants. This amount signifies approximately 90,000 cases per year.

Cobbitty Wines is open everyday for tasting and there are BBQ and picnic facilities with a wide range of wines as the family motto states "The best wine is the one you like".

COBBITTY WINES PTY LTD
Address: 40 Cobbitty Road, Cobbitty NSW 2570
Direction: 60 km south-west of Sydney
Phone: (046) 51 2281
Fax: (046) 51 2671
Year of establishment: 1964
Owner: Cogno Bros.
Winemaker: John Cogno
Principal varieties grown: Trebbiano, grenache, muscat, barbera, shiraz
Ha under vine: 5
Average annual crush: 25-30 tonnes
Average no. cases sold: 80,000

Principal wines & brands	Cellar potential
Cabernet Sauvignon	5-10 years
Chardonnay	2-5 years
Shiraz	5-10years
Mama Port	10+ years
Lambrusco Rosso & Bianco	0-1 years
Barbera	2-5 years

Cellar door & mail order sales: Yes
Hours open to public: 9 am-5.30 pm Mon-Sat; 12-5.30 pm Sun.
Points of interest: Picnic grounds, large selection of fortified wines and liqueurs, free wine tasting
Retail distribution: Cellar door and mail orders

Grevillea Estate

revillea is a real family affair. Jim and Moira Collins pioneered the venture back in 1954. They have a 440 hectare property chiefly devoted to milk production for the Bega Cheese Factory. Son Michael is in charge of a dairy herd of 600, which produce some 3 million litres of milk a year.

In the early 1980s Jim and Moira planted vines; today the seven hectare vineyard on rich basalt and granitic soils produces a range of classy wines. Daughter Nicola, Proprietor, is vineyard manager and winemaker, while her sister Jennie runs 'Bails' restaurant in the old 1860s slab hut that was the 'Kirby' milking bails.

Visitors can view the milking on the rotary dairy at 3 pm, children can even hug the calves.

There's a nature walk around the lagoon for those interested in nature bird life. Grevillea is a real gem, on the Sapphire Coast squeezed in between the mountains and the sea.

GREVILLEA ESTATE WINES
Address: Buckajo Road, Bega, NSW 2550
Phone: (064) 92 3006
Fax: (064) 92 3006
Established: 1980
Owner: Nicola Collins
Winemaker: Nicola Collins
Principal varieties grown: Chardonnay, sauvignon blanc, traminer, rhine riesling, merlot, cabernet sauvignon
Ha under vine: 6.4
Average annual crush: 60 tonnes
Average no. cases produced: 4,000

Principal wines & brands	Cellar potential
Chardonnay	2-8 years
Sauvignon Blanc	2-5 years
Rhine Riesling	2-5 years
Traminer Riesling	2-5 years
Spatlese Rhine	2-5 years
Merlot	2-5 years
Cabernet Sauvignon	5-10 years

Trade tours: By appointment only
Cellar door & mail order sales: Yes
Hours open to public: 9 am-5 pm seven days a week (except Christmas Day)
Points of interest: Restaurant, lunches Sun-Fri; wetland walk; calf rearing; milking 3 pm
Retail distribution: Restaurants throughout the south-east region, some outlets in Canberra

Glenfinlass Wines

ituated near Wellington, the second oldest settlement west of the Blue Mountains, is the unique Glenfinlass Winery and its 'Elysian Farm' vineyard. This completely organically-grown vineyard is nestled among 400 hectares of natural forest and bushland, retained as a wildlife refuge.

Natural vineyard management is carried through into the winemaking, using traditional methods of open fermentation, natural yeast and hand-operated presses, with the final fermentation in oak barrels and storage in oak puncheons for up to three years before bottling. Glenfinlass produces a sauvignon blanc with typical fume dry finish, and large, full-bodied red wines with unique fruit character and natural balance, which are only available from the cellar door or by mail order.

GLENFINLASS WINES
Address: Elysian Farm, Parkes Road, Wellington NSW 2820
Direction: 8 km from Wellington on the road to Parkes
Phone: (068) 45 2221
Fax: (068) 45 3329
Established: 1972
Owner: Brian & Nyasa Holmes
Winemaker: Brian Holmes
Principal varieties grown: Shiraz, cabernet sauvignon, sauvignon blanc
Ha under vine: 2
Average annual crush: 10 tonnes
Average no. cases produced: 500

Principal wines & brands	Cellar potential
Shiraz	5-10 years
Cabernet Sauvignon	5-10 years
Sauvignon Blanc	2-5 years

Cellar door & mail order sales: Yes
Hours open to public: 9 am-5 pm Sat.
Retail distribution: Cellar door sales & mail order

An introduction to South Australia

Beautiful Barossa Valley from the Yaldara Inn lookout.

Although one of the last settled states in Australia, by 1887 South Australia was leading Australian wine production.

In 1837, only one year after the state's founding, J.B. Hach and George Stevenson planted vine cuttings from Tasmania in North Adelaide. Later that same year Richard Hamilton planted his Ewell vineyards in what is now the suburb of Marion. Shortly afterwards, John Reynell planted his first vines at Reynella.

In 1844 Dr Christopher Rawson Penfold established his Grange vineyard at Magill. The

1840s was the period when the German Lutheran immigrants began arriving in the Barossa Valley and Johann Gramp planted his Jacob's Creek Vineyard. English immigrant and brewer Samuel Smith established Yalumba in 1849.

During the 1850s, the wake of the gold rush saw a flurry of new vineyards. Thomas Hardy, Jesse Norman and the Holbrook family all commenced winemaking and established vineyards in what are now inner suburbs of Adelaide; Woodley's vineyard was established at Glen Osmond in 1858.

Back to the Barossa, where Joseph Seppelt

commenced planting in 1851 and Samuel Hoffmann even earlier in 1847. The names of the early pioneers of wine in South Australia have lived on and continue to dominate the wine scene in the state. One of these early pioneers, like many others, was a medical practitioner, Dr Alexander Kelly, who planted his Trinity Vineyard at Morphett Vale in 1843. An entrepreneur at heart, he later formed the Tintara Vineyard Company and planted extensive vineyards at McLaren Vale, later to be bought out of bankruptcy by Thomas Hardy.

Petaluma pickers from Piccadilly.

We must not forget Clare, where John Horrocks put his first vines in the ground in 1840; he was only 22 years of age, but managed to convince many others to plant vines in this beautiful valley. By the 1860s more than 6,000 acres of vines covered many areas of the state. In fact, the first wine surplus was at hand and the vignerons of the state made their first assault on the English market. The logistics and time involved meant this push had a very limited effect, thus many growers and suppliers to the larger wineries were forced to make their own wine or see their grapes go to waste. Unfortunately there was a flood of cheap, poorly-made wine which affected the industry's reputation badly for a period; however, the earlier established companies and well known names today such as Hardy, Seppelt, Penfold, Orlando and Yalumba continued to focus on quality and grew stronger through the period, although overall production decreased dramatically.

South Australian wine began to secure markets in the other states; this progress was halted somewhat late in the century with tariffs being imposed by NSW and Victoria on South Australian wine, by then the nation's leading producer. At this time the dreaded vine louse phylloxera struck the vineyards in Victoria and to a degree, New South Wales. South Australia, being more remote and on lighter soils, escaped this blight which destroyed other states' vineyards. In fact, South Australia remains one of the few producing regions of the world where phylloxera has never struck, vine quarantine regulations are understandably strict.

It was with great interest that I read a collection of contemporary "letters to the editor" contained in a scrapbook kept by my great-great-grandfather at Bankside in Adelaide. Dated 1869-1870 they chronicled the differences of opinion in certain matters pertaining to wine and vines between Messrs Hardy and Seppelt of South Australia and Messrs Morris and Chambers of Victoria. By the outbreak of World War I, South Australia was producing 18 million litres of wine, more than half the nations output. Fortified wines had started to make in-roads in the market; they were easier to keep pure and in good condition and during the next 50 years dominated the wine scene in South Australia.

It was the influx of European immigrants after the World War II that began to tip the scales back in favour of table wines and changed our drinking habits; it was only in 1970 when table wine production actually exceeded that of fortified wines, and the culture of nearly universal enjoyment of table wines with meals began. Development over the last two decades in the South East of the state started with Coonawarra in the early 1950's with Samuel Wynn and also Ron Haselgrove from Mildara reviving Coonawarra as a wine region, almost 100 years after John Riddoch had founded the regions' wine industry as part of his "Penola Fruit Colony". Padthaway and now many other parts of this region, from Bordertown down to Mt. Gambier and across to Robe, promise that this Limestone coast is set to be a huge world-renowned quality wine region.

Langhorne Creek near the mouth of the mighty Murray River has a cool but mild climate and has had vineyards since the last century. Stonyfell with their Metala and Wolf Blass have shown in the last few decades the capabilities of the the region. Huge vineyard plantings are now underway.

The resurgence of wine-growing in the Adelaide Hills has been quite remarkable with modern day pioneers such as Brian Croser, Stephen Henschke and Tim Knappstein forging the way. South Australia richly deserves its title of The Wine State, producing more than 60% of Australia's wines. With suitable land and climate, water is really the only problem in the driest state on the world's driest continent.

South Australians are determined, inventive and proud of the impact their wines are having on the world market. In 1995 $250 million in export income was earned by the state's wine industry, with 70% of the nation's wine exports. The South Australian Government is understandably very supportive of its wine industry and the burgeoning wine tourism industry.

An introduction to the Adelaide Plains

Although this area saw the birth of South Australia's wine industry, Adelaide's urban sprawl has all but wiped out viticulture within the greater metropolitan area, however vineyards and wineries still remain.

Tolley's Hope Valley still has an operating winery and vineyard. The Magill Cellars and Vineyards, spiritual home of Grange Hermitage, along with the original home of founder Dr. Christopher Rawson Penfold, remain an active part of Australian wine and are protected by National Trust classification.

Richard Hamilton's original Ewell Vineyards, planted in 1837, a year after the state's settlement, have fallen to housing and a transport depot, but Patrittis in Dover Gardens are still going strong along with Crestview, Hardy's Chateau Reynella and Mt. Hurtle in the Happy Valley regional area, plus Torresans at Flagstaff Hill.

Many changes have occurred in the consolidation of the wine industry of South Australia. Hamiltons moved to the Eden Valley and were taken over by Mildara, Woodleys went to the Barossa and were taken over by Seppelts, and Normans have expanded by moving to Angle Vale as well as buying the Coolawin Winery at Clarendon in the Adelaide Hills. Hardys moved from their Bankside Winery after it was destroyed by fire in 1904. They established Mile End Cellars close to the city, and champagne cellars in Currie Street in the city.

In 1983 Hardys moved lock, stock and barrel to Reynella and the former property of early settler, Walter Reynell. The wonderful old homestead and Chateau were restored and a new winery, bottling and storage facilities were constructed. So far $6 million has been spent on these improvements, and further developments are planned.

Angoves had extensive vineyards and a winery at Tea Tree Gully, a north-eastern Adelaide suburb. Their Tregrehan vineyard was famed for its red wine but unfortunately, and much to the disgust of the Angove family, it was compulsorily acquired by the State Housing Commission. Douglas A. Tolley of Pedare fame still has an operating winery in the area but no longer holds any local vineyards.

The significant vineyards of the Adelaide Plains area are now found around Angle Vale near Gawler, and around the entrance to the Barossa Valley. There have been grapes grown in this area since the first days of the industry. Expansion began in 1969, when the Angle Vale winery was built as a consortium venture. However, the business foundered and equipment was virtually sold off piecemeal until a co-operative was formed with the assistance of the Berri-Renmano Consolidated Co-operative.

The new Valley Growers Co-op Ltd took over the winery in 1984, employing Colin Glaetzer who is producing some great wines, stylishly packaged. This operation is now named Barossa Estates.

Norman's also have a large vineyard at Angle Vale called Evanston Estate, where many grape varieties are planted, and in 1973 in the same area the Grilli family established Primo Estate.

The region is very warm, but with the moderating effects of sea breezes from St. Vincents Gulf the climate is not too harsh. The soil is the result of a rich alluvial flood plain and fruit picked at the right time, and handled well, produces award-winning wines. However, with the heat and low rainfall, irrigation is essential. Adelaide Plains is renowned for producing high quality wines. At the northern end of the region lies the famous Roseworthy Agricultural College where so many of Australia's great winemakers have trained.

Barossa Valley Estates

Barossa Valley Estate winery is located on Heaslip Road at Angle Vale. Barossa Valley Estate Wines was formed in 1985 by Valley Growers Co-operative. As the name suggests the Co-operative is a group of Barossa Valley growers who joined together to purchase the winery and produce wines from this famous region. Under the name of Barossa Valley Estate - The Pick of the Barossa - business has flourished and Barossa Valley Estate Wines now produce various ranges of exceptional quality wines. All the fruit that goes into the Barossa Valley Estate wines is sourced from within the Co-operative therefore making all the wines 100% Barossa.

The labels include the E & E Black Pepper Shiraz and E & E Sparkling Shiraz as well as the Ebenezer range, all of which have been bestowed with awards both nationally and internationally. This gives great testament to the quality of wines made from this premium grape growing area. The other ranges that come under the umbrella of Barossa Valley Estate are the Moculta range of premium selection reds and whites as well as the Barossa Valley Estate Dry White and Barossa Valley Estate Dry Red.

The winery crushes approximately 3,000 tonnes of fruit over the vintage and is situated at Angle Vale on the Adelaide Plains amidst extensive lawned parkland and majestic Gawler River gums. Picnic and barbecue facilities are available on the grounds for gatherings with friends and family with the Cellar Door Sales located at the winery and open daily for tastings.

BAROSSA VALLEY ESTATE WINERY
Address: Heaslip Road, Angle Vale SA 5117
Phone: (08) 284 7000
Fax: (08) 284 7219
Established: 1984
Winemaker: Colin Glaetzer
Average annual crush: 2,500 tonnes
Average no. cases produced: 90,000

Principal wines & brands	Cellar potential
E + E Black Pepper Shiraz	10+ years
E + E Sparkling Shiraz	2-5 years
Ebenezer Shiraz	5-10 years
Ebenezer Chardonnay	2-5 years
Ebenezer Cabernet Malbec Merlot	10+ years
Ebenezer Pinot Noir	N.V.

Public & trade tours: By appointment only
Cellar door & mail order sales: Yes
Hours open to public: 9am-5 pm Mon-Fri; 11 am-5 pm Sat; 1-5 pm Sun.
Points of interest: Picnic srea & BBQs.

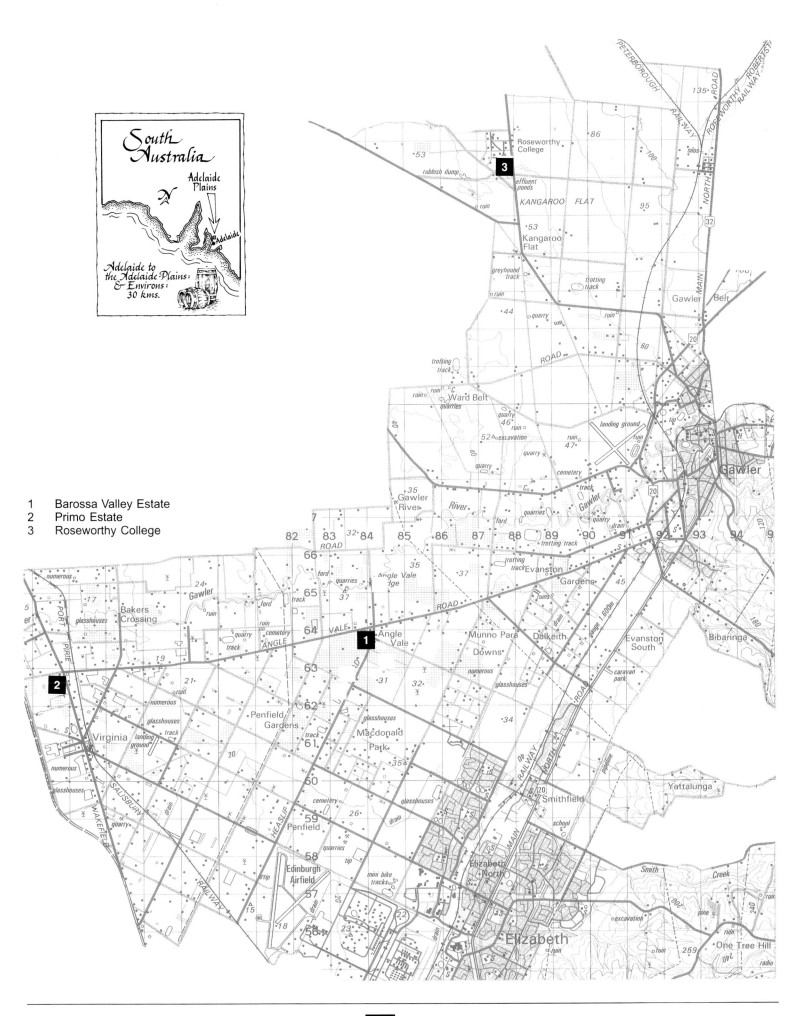

1   Barossa Valley Estate
2   Primo Estate
3   Roseworthy College

Adelaide Hills and Eden Valley

Kuitpo Vineyards

Adelaide Hills region stretches from Mount Pleasant in the north to Mount Compass in the south. Together with Eden Valley it forms Australia's largest cool climate viticultural region, outside of Coonawarra/Padthaway in the south east of South Australia, with vineyards at a height of more than 400 metres above sea level.

The region is quickly forging a strong reputation worldwide with high profile winemakers such as Brian Croser at Piccadilly, Tim Knappstein, Stephen and Prue Henschke and Geoff Weaver at Lenswood.

Pinot noir is becoming a shining star for the Hills with Henschke and Knappstein being pressed for supremacy by some great pinots from the super small wineries of Ashton Hills, Pibbin and Hillstowe. In the southern Adelaide Hills, Geoff Hardy's large Kuitpo Vineyard is a showpiece vineyard of Australian viticulture, supplying the likes of exclusive wine producer Shaw and Smith along with the large companies. Geoff keeps his favourite little patches of the vineyard to make his stunning Geoff Hardy Kuitpo varietal wines.

Eden Valley Region stretching from Moculta to Mount Pleasant is the historic home of the famous names of Henschke, Yalumba and Mountadam. The diverse hills regions are certainly at the forefront of the quality wine development of Australia. The sky is the limit so to speak. Perhaps one day we'll see the hundreds of vineyards in the Hills that the last century boasted.

Gumeracha Cellars - Chain of Ponds Wines

Caj Amadio is a legend in his own time. Following many years of entrepreneurial ventures attacked with remarkable success, he has finally launched his own wine label, Chain of Ponds, named after the township in the headwaters of the Torrens River in the beautiful Adelaide Hills.

Caj and his family established the first vineyard in the Gumeracha area, one of the modern day pioneers in the region. Several years later he established a commercial vineyard around his pilot vineyard, together with his brothers-in-law and their families. Most of the grapes from the commercial vineyard are supplied to Penfolds, and although they will continue to do so Caj selects a few of his favourite batches from both vineyards to produce his own wines. The quality is outstanding.

Gumeracha is fast developing as the premium red wine sub-region in the Adelaide Hills. The Cellar Door is an easy picnic drive from Adelaide, in fact one of the closest of all to the city, set within the picturesque countryside.

Caj also has vineyard interests on Kangaroo Island and for the last few years has released a red wine from Michael and Rosie Florence's vineyard, which is situated at Cygnet River. It is the only commercial wine from the island and is a magnificent Bordeaux blend that is worth seeking out.

The first release Chain of Ponds wines includes, a 93 semillon, 93 chardonnay, 94 riesling, 93 pinot noir and 93 cabernet sauvignon; all have intense aromatic fruit qualities from the cool climate of Gumeracha, some 425 metres above sea level. The 93 cabernet sauvignon was released in September 95, a wine of great power and ageing potential.

Also released in September 95 is a vibrant young grenache/sangiovese, called Novello Rosso. This wine is made partly by the maceration carbonique technique, like French Beaujolais. Its fresh fruit flavours and lighter body make it ideal to be served chilled with an alfresco-style lunch or picnic. The Novello Rosso will be released each spring. In fact, why not visit the gorgeous Gumeracha Cellars, it's only a stone's throw from Adelaide. Grab a bottle of the Novello Rosso and enjoy a picnic in this beautiful part of the hills.

Caj Amadio and Genn

Adelaide Hills

1 Angoves Tea Tree Gully Winery	12 Hill Smith Estates
2 Ashbourne Stafford Ridge Vineyards	13 Hillstowe Wines
3 Bridgewater Mill	14 Irvine
4 Craneford Wine Co.	15 Leo Buring High Eden Estate
5 Glenara Winery	16 Mountadam
6 Grand Cru	17 Penfold's Magill
7 Gumeracha Cellars Chain of Ponds Winery	18 Petaluma
8 Hamilton's Springton Winery	19 Pewsey Vale Vineyards
9 Heggies Vineyard	20 Pibbin
10 Henschke Cellars - Kayneton	21 Seppelt's Partalunga Vineyard
11 Henschke Cellars - Lenswood	22 Stonyfell Winery
	23 Tollana Woodbury Vineyard
	24 Tolleys Hope Valley

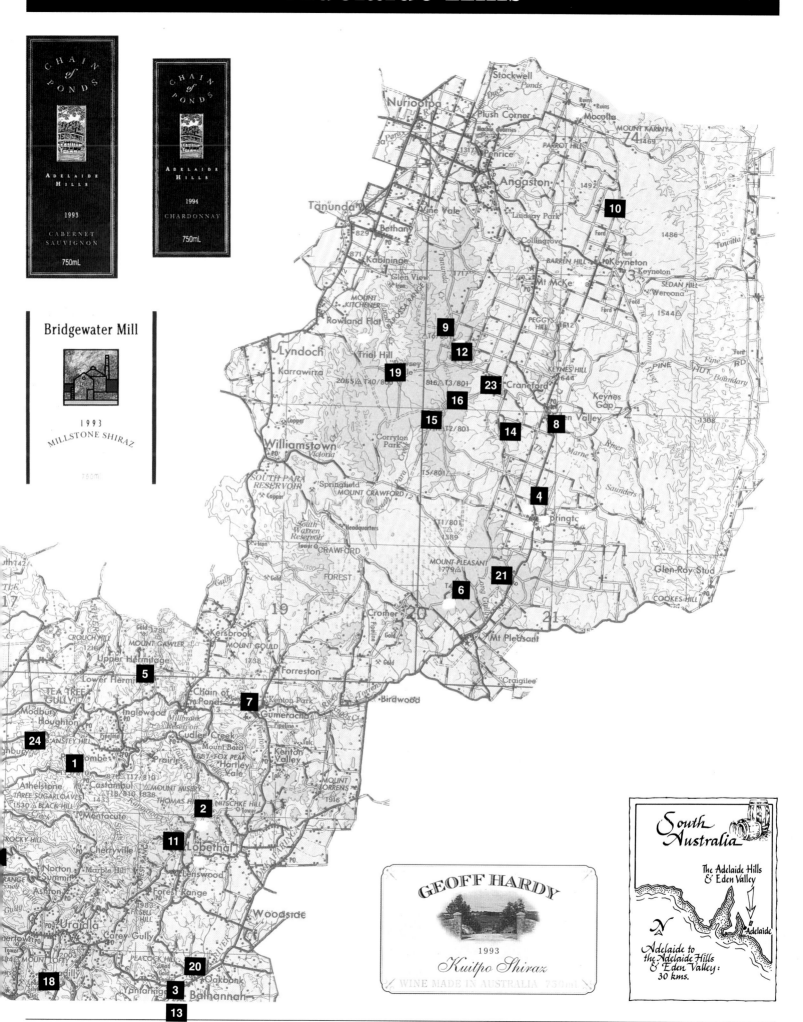

Hillstowe

Back in 1970, Dr. Chris Laurie, a successful medical practitioner, purchased a steep, yet picturesque property in the cool climes high in the Adelaide Hills at Carey Gully.

After the success of the McLaren Vale vineyard, Chris saw a future for further vineyards in the Hills. Demand for top quality, cool climate grapes, particularly chardonnay and pinot noir by the larger companies such as Petaluma for their Croser label, reinforced the decicision for planting at this site. Chris was also involved in the development of the Hoddles Creek vineyard in the Yarra Valley of Victoria, and in 191

decided to launch the Hillstowe label featuring regional wines from Carey Gully, McLaren Vale and Hoddles Creek. Hoddles Creek has since been sold to BRL Hardy, however, the other vineyards at Hillstowe are forging ahead.

A problem, or might I say opportunity, vexed Chris and his son, Hamish, his marketing chief, for many months in where to locate the home and winery for Hillstow. The decision came in early 1995 with a unique site in the turist hamlet of Hahndorf in the Adelaide Hills. A series of beautifully constructed stone buildings, on the main road as it enters the heart of Hahndorf, is now the permanent residence of Hillstowe. The street level building is a gallery with arts and crafts, the second stone residence is now a restaurant, the third a beautiful cellar door and the last and largest, a winery and maturation cellars for the great wines of Hillstowe.

Already, the location has proved a real success and a perfect place to visit on a lazy weekend in the picturesque Adelaide Hills. Hillstowe produces fine elegant wines with informative art deco inspired labels which reflect wines an impeccable pedigree.

Petaluma

The pursuit of excellence is becoming a well-worn phrase, but when used in reference to Petaluma it is most appropriate.

Petaluma is the brainchild of the brilliant Brian Croser. Brian graduated with honours from Adelaide University in 1972, and joined the winemaking team at Thomas Hardy and Sons, where he assessed the entire winemaking, bottling and vineyard production areas. In 1973, he was sent to Davis University in California for further study and returned in 1974 in time to take over the year's white wine production.

Brian did his best to introduce his philosophy and technique of oxygen exclusion from the time grapes arrive in the winery to the time of bottling. Unfortunately the winemaking equipment at Hardys was not fit for this procedure. Whilst working with Brian, I well remember dragging cylinders of carbon dioxide around the winery at Waikerie at 4 am, attempting to cover and protect wine being loaded for transport to Adelaide for bottling.

In 1975, Croser convinced Hardys to invest in new equipment, refrigeration and improved storage facilities. He helped introduce oxygen exclusion, cold settling of wines, filtering before fermentation, careful yeast choice and long slow fermentation at Hardys, and the rest is history. The 1975 white wines took the industry and market by storm. They dominated the rhine riesling, dry white hock and sweet white wine classes in every wine show in Australia, and overnight Brian Croser became a legend.

Despite an offer of chief winemaker's position, Brian left Hardys in 1976 and joined the staff at the Riverina College of Advanced Education at Wagga Wagga in New South Wales. The first Petaluma wine, a spaetlese rhine, was made at the college winery in 1976 from Mitchelton fruit.

By 1978, Brian had left the college and begun a wine consultancy business, where he instantly amassed a huge group of clients. In the same year, he constructed a winery and planted a vineyard for champagne at Piccadilly. Brian brings in his grapes from selected regions which he believes have the potential to best produce the varietal characteristics he is looking for. Petaluma have large vineyards in the Clare Region specialising in riesling in the high cool Polish Hill river Region. The reds largely come from Petaluma's Coonawarra and Sharefarmers vineyards in the cool southeast of South Australia, rich in the famed terra rossa soils. The chardonnay and sparkling wines under the Petaluma and Croser labels largely come from the Adelaide Hills, as does the

Bridgewater Mill Sauvignon Blanc.

Petaluma recently became a public company and now also owns Tim Knappstein Wines of Clare and Lenswood and the Mitchelton Winery in Victoria. Brian is now immersed in the maximisation of wine quality and production efficiency of these two additions to Petaluma's wine stable.

The Bridgewater Mill is a beautiful

PETALUMA LIMITED

Address: Spring Gully Road, Piccadilly SA 5151
Phone: (08) 339 4122
Fax: (08) 339 5253
Established: 1976; public company 1993
Winemaker: Brian Croser

Principal varieties grown: Riesling, chardonnay, cabernet sauvignon, merlot, pinot noir
Ha under vine: 120
Average No. Cases Produced: 150,000

Principal Wines & Brands	Cellar Potential
Croser sparkling wine	5-10years
Petaluma Coonararra	2-5yrs
" Chardonnay	2-5yrs
" Riesling	2-5yrs
Sharefarmers Blend	5-10yrs
Bridgewater Mill Range	

Trade Tours: By appointment
Retail Distribution: Tucker Seabrook in NSW, VIC QLD, WA, David Ridge in South Australia

historic mill nearby to Petaluma in the hills. It was a derelict shell when Brian took it over in the early 1980s; today it is a splendid restaurant and gallery which also holds concerts. It is also a successful cellar door for Petaluma as well as marketing a Bridgewater Mill Label, encompassing some exciting and different fresh fruit driven wine styles.

Brian Croser has been a true crusader for the wine industry in its fight against the huge increases in wine taxes proposed in the 1993 Federal Budget. Over two years, at least half his working life has been devoted to fighting for the industry, creating a plan and blueprint for the Australian wine and grape industry as we approach the 21st century. One can only hope commonsense prevails, and the industry gets the government support and understanding it so richly deserves, considering its employment, export success and tourism multiplier efforts. Petaluma and Brian Croser are a credit to wine in Australia.

Bridgewater Mill

In between Aldgate and Mount Barker in the pretty Adelaide Hills lies one of the gems of the wine industry and a monument to good taste and cultural living. The Bridgewater Mill is fully restored with even its giant wheel quietly ticking over as the tranquil stream flows by.

Brian Croser was searching the hills to find a suitable location for a cellar for his methode champenoise; solid, cool and somewhat humid were the basic demands.

In the Bridgewater Mill, he found all those things plus a handsome historic building. The cellars hold some of his beloved Croser Sparkling, whilst the internal structure now holds a multi level gallery and restaurant. When Brian and long time friend Len Evans were giving the Mill the once-over, Len remarked it would make a marvellous theatre. The cleverly designed internal roof of the tasting area and bar is actually on a hydraulic system and towers to form a genuine stage.

Like the wine, the ambience at the Mill is a real treat. The Bridgewater Mill Sauvignon Blanc is fresh and fruity with a keen exotic oriental edge to its flavour and the

finish is a winner. The Riesling Methode Champenoise is superb and the reds very fruity and balanced. Put a lunch at the Bridgewater Mill on your must-do list now.

BRIDGEWATER MILL
Address: Mt Barker Road, Bridgewater SA 5155
Phone: (08) 339 3422
Fax: (08) 339 5311
Established: 1976; public company 1993
Winemaker: Brian Croser

Principal wines & brands	Cellar potential
Bridgewater Mill Sauvignon Blanc	2-5 years
Bridgewater Mill Chardonnay	2-5 years
Bridgewater Mill Millstone Shiraz	10+ years

Public & trade tours: By appointment
Cellar door & mail order sales: Yes
Hours open to public: 10.30 am-5 pm daily
Points of interest: Restaurant, cellar door facility for Petaluma, function centre, historical flour mill houses sparkling wine cellar
Retail distribution: Tucker Seabrook in NSW, Vic, Qld & WA David Ridge in SA

Irvine

High up in the Eden Valley is the Springhill Manor of Jim and Marjorie Irvine, built in 1860. Jim is a real gentleman and without doubt Australia's busiest and most sought-after winemaking consultant.

Over the years Jim has made wine on a consulting basis for some 43 different wineries, all of whom speak highly of his professionalism and ability.

In 1993, he achieved the ultimate accolade when a wine made by him for the Elderton Winery won the Jimmy Watson Trophy.

For his own label, Jim has chosen the high ground; he makes an absolute stunner of a merlot. Many years ago when consulting for Normans, at a lunch with the Horlin-Smiths he tasted Chateau Petrus, the world's most expensive red wine - a 100% merlot from the Pomerol district near Bordeaux.

Jim has attempted to make his own version of the taste he fell in love with that

---

IRVINE
Address: Basil Roeslers Road, Eden Valley SA 5235
Phone: (085) 64 1046
Fax: (085) 64 1046
Established: 1980
Owner: J.G. & M.J. Irvine
Winemaker: James Irvine
Principal varieties grown: Merlot, meslier, chardonnay
Ha under vine: 8
Average annual crush: 90 tonnes
Average no. cases produced: 6,000

Principal wines & brands	Cellar potential
Irvine Grand Merlot	5-10 years
Irvine Edencrest Merlot/Cabernet	5-10 years
Irvine Brut Royale Blanc De Blanc	5-10 years
Irvine Edencrest Meslier Brut	2-5 years
Irvine Edencrest Chardonnay	2-5 years

Public & trade tours: No
Hours open to public: Not open
Points of interest: Only meslier vineyard in Australia
Retail distribution: United Kingdom, Switzerland, New Zealand, Victoria, South Australia

---

day. The merlot spends almost four years in wood and yet is still fresh, but so silky smooth and complex. It earns every bit of its regal name 'Grand Merlot,' dressed in its regal robes - probably Australia's best packaged wine. The 1988 Merlot won the World Merlot Competition from hundreds of entrants.

Jim also makes several superb methode champenoise wines including a straight meslier, an unusual variety used in the Champagne region of France to help the acidity in the base wines during warm years; its zesty fruit makes it the ideal aperitif drink.

The Irvine Blanc de Blanc Chardonnay normally spends 4-5 years on yeast lees but often longer, his merlot methode champenoise is exquisite.

For almost 46 years since his first job in the laboratory at Glenloth as a sixteen year old, Jim Irvine has weaved his creative magic with wine, never losing his enthusiasm and zest for life, shared wholeheartedly by his wife Marjorie and their two daughters. The elder, Joanne, has just traded in her nursing theatre sister's degree to study winemaking. The Irvine wines of the future look assured.

Mountadam

MOUNTADAM
Address: High Eden Ridge, Eden Valley SA 5235
Phone: (085) 64 1101
Fax: (085) 64 1064
Established: 1972
Winemaker: Adam Wynn
Principal varieties grown: Chardonnay, pinot noir, cabernet sauvignon, merlot
Average annual crush: 250 tonnes
Average No. cases produced: 40,000

Principal wines & brands	Cellar potential
Mountadam Chardonnay	2-5 years
David Wynn Chardonnay	2-5 years
Mountadam Pinot Noir	5-10 years
David Wynn Patriarch Shiraz	5-10 years
Eden Ridge Cabernet	5-10 years

Public & trade tours: By appointment only
Cellar door & mail order sales: Yes
Hours open to public: 10 am-4 pm Mon-Fri; 11am-4 pm w/e and PH
Points of interest:
Excellent views of the Eden Valley
Retail distribution:
Bottle shops and restaurants Australia-wide

Adam Wynn is a real winner, focused, positive and urbane; his technical skills rank with the world's best, but his creative flair and love of music and art give extra dimensions to his wines that are truly exciting.

His family's achievements in Australian wine have been extraordinary, however, he is one of the most likeable and natural people you would be likely to meet.

The Wynn wine saga commenced in Poland just after the turn of the century. Samuel Wynn made a yearly pilgrimage to the Black Sea and returned to Poland with dried raisins which he reconstituted and turned into wine. At 21 years of age he arrived in Australia keen to pursue a career in wine; this began with a wine bar in Bourke Street Melbourne, where he came up with the classic barrel-design Wynns 2 litre flagon. Samuel lived until 90 years of age, a testament to a life tempered by good wine.

Adam's father David truly put the Wynn family on the wine map. In 1950 he purchased the rundown old Coonawarra Estate, featuring its famous three-gabled roof on his Wynn's Coonawarra label. The world recognition of this region bears testament to David's greatness, but he did much more. A very talented artist, he was chairman of the Adelaide Festival Trust for many years and created the concept of the highly successful Barossa Music Festival which he served until his death as its founding chairman.

David had enormous vision, his search for the top viticultural region in Australia ended 600 metres above the Barossa and Eden Valleys. A visit to Mountadam is a rare treat, set high on Eden Ridge in rugged rocky country, habitat of the majestic wedgetail eagle, the symbol of the winery, and prominently displayed in the huge granite sculptures on the impressive stone pillared entrance to the vineyard. The setting just on the lee side of the ridge gives protection to the vines from harsh winds, and provides an ideal frost-free microclimate; the resultant outstanding fruit is the cornerstone of Adam's wines.

Adam followed a degree in agricultural science with a postgraduate degree in oenology from Bordeaux in France, where he was dux of the course in 1981.

Rarely have I seen so many expensive French oak barrels in any winery, let alone the modestly-sized Mountadam. Adam follows a no expense spared philosophy, using French Troncais oak, tight-grained and with subtle but distinct flavour characteristics. Barrel fermentation, careful selection and individual treatment of the many hundreds of barrels for the chardonnay and the reds produces complex wines that shine at the top of Australia's wine tree.

Adam produces a 50/50 merlot cabernet wine simply called 'The Red', which is simply superb. The cornerstone of the product range is the Mountadam Chardonnay. The David Wynn range of quality Eden Valley varietals and the Eden Ridge organic range complement the domain-grown Mountadam wines. Adam Wynn has literally taken the high ground of Australian wine.

Tollana - Woodbury Vineyard

Tollana's Woodbury Vineyard is situated down the road from Mountadam in the rugged Barossa Ranges. It was established in the 1960s when Tolley, Scott & Tolley decided to branch out from distilling into the premium wine market.

The grape varieties already planted in the Barossa Valley were for fortified wine production and thus were unsuitable for premium wine production. New land was required to facilitate the company's expansion and Woodbury Vineyard was the result. The vines planted along certain lines cover a massive area, even more impressive because from the road you can see over the entire rolling hillsides of vines; it's the largest contour-planted vineyard in Australia and an awesome sight in autumn.

The varieties include riesling, chardonnay, semillon, sauvignon blanc, shiraz and cabernet sauvignon. The rhine riesling has proved to be the consistent medal winner and the 'TR' series of red wines have had a distinguished show career, including several trophies and many gold medals.

The Woodbury roll call of winemakers is also impressive. Wolf Blass, winemaker from 1968-1973, was followed and ultimately joined by John Glaetzer. Alan Hoey gave the Tollana Woodbury whites their real boost and was capably followed by Pat Tocaciu. Today the devoted winemaker and ambassador for Tollana is Neville Falkenberg who has 'Toll' in one eye and 'ana' in the other.

The Tollana range with their bold black labels are all marvellous wines. If you want one of Australia's finest botrytised rieslings for that special dessert, you just cannot go past the Tollana which is also sold at a most reasonable price. Considering the expense involved in making this unique style, search it out!

Henschke - Eden Valley/Keyneton

The Henschke family have a long and rich winemaking history in Australia. They are dignified and private people, who are purposeful and enthusiastic in their desire to produce individual and exceptional wines.

Johann Christian Henschke arrived in South Australia in 1841, initially settled in the Barossa Valley at Bethany, and moved to Keyneton in the Barossa Ranges in 1862. Henschke's is now the only winery in the immediate area but it was once one of many established by German and English settlers in the last century.

The first wine was made at Henschke in 1868 and Johann's grandson Paul Alfred helped his father build substantial cellars at the turn of the century, which include storage vats that can hold up to 10,000 litres. The wine was sold in bulk until 1951 when Cyril Henschke took over the business, and began bottling and labelling Henschke wine. In 1970 he received a Churchill Fellowship and travelled the world studying winemaking.

Henschke wines are now made and managed by Stephen Henschke who was educated at Adelaide Univeresity and at the Geisenheim Wine Institute in Germany. He has updated and restored much of the winery, and the cellar door area is superb. The winery exudes an air of history and the wonderful 130-year-old Henschke home next door is set in a beautiful garden.

Stephen Henschke's white wines are exciting. The improvements to the winery and his study have paid off, producing a range of excellent white varietal wines including a chardonnay, semillon, riesling, sauvignon blanc, gewürztraminer and a magnificent noble riesling. The Henschke reds are living up to their big reputation with Mount Edelstone and Hill of Grace (from a vineyard near the Church of the same name) being outstanding. The Henschkes are a real team with research viticulturist Prue Henschke providing Stephen with fantastic grapes for his great wines, which easily rank the winery in the top ten of Australia's best.

HENSCHKE
Address: Keyneton
Phone: (085) 64 8223
Fax: (085) 64 8294
Established: 1868
Winemaker: Stephen Henschke
Principal varieties grown: riesling, semillon, shiraz, cabernet sauvignon, chardonnay
Ha under vine: 75
Average annual crush: 510 tonnes
Average no. cases produced: 35,000

Principal wines & brands	Cellar potential
Hill Of Grace	10+ years
Cyril Henschke	
Cabernet Sauvignon	5-10 years
Mount Edelstone	5-10 years
Keyneton Estate	5-10 years
Julius Eden Valley Riesling	5-10 years
Eden Valley Semillon	5-10 years
Tilly's Vineyard	2-5 years

Public & trade tours: By appointment only
Cellar door & mail order sales: Yes
Hours open to public: 9 am-4.30 pm Mon-Fri; 9 am - 12 noon Sat; 10 am - 3 pm public holidays
Retail distribution: Nationally through Tucker Seabrook

Henschke - Lenswood

During the 1980s the Henschke's conducted a search to find vineyard land to produce the highest quality table wines. Their search led them to the heart of the Adelaide Hills, where they purchased an existing 40 acre apple orchard and began establishing a picture book vineyard at Lenswood, which is 50 km south of their Keyneton vineyards.

Prue and Stephen Henschke met during their studies at Adelaide University in the 1970s, where Prue was then majoring in botany and zoology. After marrying they took off to Germany, where they both studied at the famous Geisenheim Wine Institute. Prue worked closely with the world-renowned viticulturist and oenologist Dr Helmut Becker for two years, learning German's meticulous and rigorous approach to viticulture in particular.

The quality of the grapes Prue is producing is truly world class and one wonders just how good the Henschke wines of the future will be. I for one await them with keen anticipation.

HENSCHKE
Address: Lenswood
Phone: (085) 64 8223
Fax: (085) 64 8294
Established: 1981
Winemaker: Stephen Henschke
Principal varieties grown: chardonnay, riesling, pinot noir, merlot, cabernet sauvignon
Ha under vine: 12
Average annual crush: 65 tonnes
Average no. cases produced: 4,500

Principal wines & brands	Cellar potential
Lenswood	
Abbotts Prayer	5-10 years
Greens's Hill Riesling	2-5 years
Giles Pinot Noir	2-5 years
Croft Chardonnay	2-5 years

Retail distribution: Nationally through Tucker Seabrook

Penfolds Magill Estate

The first Penfold to reach Australia was Dr. Christopher Rawson Penfold. He and his wife Mary arrived in Adelaide in 1844. Being a great believer in the healing powers of red wine (especially when treating anaemia), Dr Penfold planted vine cuttings he had obtained from the south of France. He built a solid stone cottage which he called The Grange, and which is today classified by the National Trust.

The soil at the Magill Estate is rich and red and Dr Penfold's vines thrived. After his death in 1870 his wife, daughter Georgina and son-in-law Thomas Francis Hyland took over the company, opening offices in Melbourne and Sydney.

Penfolds wines were increasingly successful and by 1913 the company had purchased Wyndham's Dalwood vineyards in the Hunter Valley, Pridmore's Southern Vales winery south of Adelaide, the Minchinbury winery and cellars on the outskirts of Sydney, and established the Nuriootpa Cellars in the Barossa Valley.

In order to process the large crops of grapes being produced by returned soldiers, Penfolds also established a winery at Griffith in New South Wales in 1921.

Over the next 40 years the company purchased further properties in the Hunter Valley, Coonawarra and next door to their own winery at Magill, the latter being the old Auldana Cellars and future home of Penfolds' famous St. Henri Claret.

By 1950, 95 per cent of Penfolds production was based on fortified wines. The management decided to change the company's direction and develop a range of table wines. The man chosen to head this project was Max Schubert, who had been with Penfolds since his youth. As a youngster, Max had worked each night after school, mucking out stables and priming gas lanterns, for the princely sum of 2 shillings and sixpence (25 cents)a week.

Max was sent to Europe to study winemaking and while in France met one of the Bordeaux region's most famous winemakers, Christian Cruse. After observing his winemaking techniques and tasting some very old Bordeaux wines, Max was determined to create a new style of Australian red wine, one that would age well for decades. The wine he produced in 1951 was the first vintage of Australia's most famous wine, Grange Hermitage.

Very few people recognised the quality or potential of the wine and it received some aggressive criticism. Today, however, Granges of the early 50s sell for thousands of dollars a bottle at auction.

Sensitive to the criticism, Penfolds revoked their support of the wine, but were forced to capitulate as it grew in popularity and acclaim during the 1960s.

Like Grange Hermitage, Penfolds St. Henri Claret was not instantly accepted by the public. This wine was originally made at the Auldana Winery and is of a rich, full bodied style, being aged only in old oak casks.

As with Grange, St. Henri was considerably ahead of its time. So were Penfolds Bin 389, a cabernet shiraz blend aged in the previous Grange hogshead, Bin 28, a soft, full, Kalimna shiraz and Bin 128, an elegant, Coonawarra shiraz. Koonunga Hill is a similar style of wine, although more commercial and excellent value for money.

In 1985, Penfolds released its 1983 Magill Estate. This special wine was made entirely from the remaining 5 ha shiraz vines at the famous Grange Vineyards. Originally covering 77 ha, the vineyard has been reduced to 5 ha by Adelaide's suburban sprawl.

The wine is made in the old Grange fermenting cellar and aged in new American and French oak hogsheads.

Even in his retirement, Max spent much of his time in his laboratory office which was always open to anyone who wanted to bring in their old Penfolds wines for "Dr"

Max to check over and if necessary restore to good health with a top-up or a new cork. Max was ever-generous, a true gentleman, and he is sadly missed by all since his death in early 1994.

John Duval, the chief winemaker for Penfolds, is a protege of Max Schubert and is doing an excellent job with all the Penfolds wines, which cover the whole gambit of styles - reds, whites, the fortifieds - up to the great Grandfather Port and many excellent sparkling wines.

Magill Estate, with Dr Rawson Penfold's old cottage and its vineyards remains the spiritual home of Penfolds and has undergone a major restoration, to make it a splendid showpiece of the wine industry, doing justice to its true heritage.

The modern day winemaking hub of Penfolds is now the Nuriootpa Cellars which is one of the world's most technically advanced wineries.

"Dr." Max and his baby
"Grange-Schubert's Unfinished Symphony"

Hill Smith Estate

ill Smith Estate is across the road from Heggies Vineyard and is part of the S. Smith and Son vineyard development, producing premium fruit for reasonably priced varietal table wines.

These wines are exported and have already achieved considerable success. An important part of the viticultural plan of this winery is the development of the best possible clones of each grape variety. Although these grapes must embody the maximum possible varietal flavours, they are less subject to disease and should bear well with good yields.

The varieties currently planted at Hill Smith Estate are cabernet, shiraz, chardonnay and sauvignon blanc. Expensive research by the winery seems to have paid off, as wines made from these grapes exhibit

the distinct flavours and characteristics of each fruit variety.

The 50 hectare Hill Smith Estate vineyard is in the Western section of Eden Valley, 520 metres above sea level. The vineyard has produced premium wines which to date have been actively exported, but are now being gradually marketed in Australia.The wines are selected and blended each year by the Hill Smith family and

represent rich and distinctive Australian styles of the highest quality.

HILL SMITH ESTATE
Address: Flaxmans Valley Road, Eden Valley SA 5235
Phone: (085) 61 3200
Established: 1972
Owner: Hill Smith family
Winemaker: Paul Boulden
Principal varieties grown: Sauvignon blanc, chardonnay, cabernet sauvignon, shiraz
Ha under vine: 33
Average annual crush: 150 tonnes
Average No. cases produced: 10,000

Principal wines & brands	Cellar potential
'Hill Smith Estate'	
Sauvignon Blanc	2-5 years
Chardonnay	2-5 years
Cabernet/Shiraz	5-10 years

Trade tours: By appointment only
Retail distribution: All states, Samuel Smith & Son Pty Ltd

Heggies Vineyard

he large grazing property that stretches along the Western edge of the Eden Valley hills was purchased by the Hill Smith family in 1971 from grazier Colin Heggie. The distinctive Heggies label features a likeness of Colin astride his horse, Jack, riding on the property.

This is truly majestic country and the colours and grandeur of the countryside as we drove through in the premature autumn of 1995 were magic. Viticulturally speaking, the land and climate are ideal and the wines, reflecting this, are extremely long living.

The Hill Smith family, are justifiably proud of their Heggies Vineyard wines and give them extra barrel and bottle maturation before release. The Heggies Botrytis Riesling, in particular, is a wine you must try. Colin Heggie on his solid steed would be proud to see what his beloved land has produced.

HEGGIES VINEYARD
Address: Heggies Range Road, Eden Valley SA 5235
Phone: (085) 61 3200   **Established**: 1971
Owner: Hill Smith family   **Winemaker**: Simon Adams
Principal varieties grown: Merlot, chardonnay, riesling
Ha under vine: 40
Average annual crush: 200 tonnes
Average No. cases produced: 12,500

Principal wines & brands	Cellar potential
Cabernets	5-10 years
Riesling	2-5 years
Chardonnay	2-5 years
Viognier	2-5 years

Trade tours: By appointment only
Points of interest: A beautiful, picturesque vineyard
Retail distribution: All states - Samuel Smith & Son Pty Ltd

Pewsey Vale

he panorama of Pewsey Vale is awesome. Contoured vines wind their way into the distant hills, a very Australian viticultural statement.

Located in a remote and rugged part of the Eden Valley hills, it was originally planted by Joseph Gilbert in 1847. The new terrain presented Gilbert with many problems, but his willingness to abandon one system of grape cultivation for another, as nature necessitated, ensured his reputation as a vigneron.

Despite his efforts, however, the turn of the century saw a swing in popular taste, to fortified wines and as a result, the winery faded from existence.

The resurrection of this winery occurred in 1961 when Geoffrey Parsons, owner of Pewsey Vale Station, entered into a partnership with S. Smith and Son, the managing family of Yalumba wines. Their decision to replant the vineyard has, in

retrospect, proved to be well-founded. The vineyard now produces an exceptional riesling and cabernet sauvignon, and more recently a stunning sauvignon blanc.

The Yalumba feature covers the illustrious history of S. Smith and Son, but certain of their strategies are relevant here. A decision was made years ago to concentrate on quality grape production in the areas most suited to individual grape varieties. For example, riesling grapes were planted in areas best suited to their needs, that is, high altitudes and cooler climates.

The company created a huge vine nursery and recruited a small staff of experts who could assist in the development of small premium vineyards such as Pewsey Vale.

S. Smith and Son are now reaping the rewards of their foresight. The several vineyards they own in the Eden Valley hills are excellent working examples of their program. In particular Pewsey Vale, in line

with the climatic conditions it enjoys, is one of the latest picked vineyards in Australia and this brings to the wines an extra dimension of flavour.

PEWSEY VALE
Address: Browns Road, Eden Valley SA 5235
Phone: (085) 61 3200
Established: 1961
Owner: Hill Smith family
Winemaker: Alan Hoey
Principal varieties grown: Riesling, cabernet sauvignon, sauvignon blanc
Ha under vine: 52
Average annual crush: 350 tonnes
Average no. cases produced: 25,000

Principal wines & brands	Cellar potential
'Pewsey Vale'	
Riesling	2-5 years
Cabernet Sauvignon	5-10 years
Sauvignon Blanc	2-5 years

Trade tours: By appointment only
Points of interest: A picturesque vineyard
Retail distribution: All States, Samuel Smith & Son Pty Ltd

An introduction to the Barossa Valley

Without doubt the most famous of Australia's wine regions is the Barossa Valley. Something of an institution with Australian wine lovers, the area has a personality all its own.

This character is mainly due to the Barossa's large German population who began to arrive in 1842. Having sought a new start in a new land, not possible in their homeland, many hundreds of German Lutherans were settled on the huge properties of George Fife Angas. Many of these immigrants had already been involved in viticulture in Germany and soon planted vine cuttings they had brought with them to Australia.

Significant amongst these first commercial plantings were those made by Johann Gramp at Rowland Flat, which saw the beginning of the Orlando Company and that of Samuel Smith at Angaston which became Yalumba. The Seppelt family company was established with Joseph Seppelt's plantings in 1851.

The first wines produced in the Barossa were table wines, but as fortifieds gained in popularity by the turn of the century, winemakers were forced to alter the emphasis of their production. This transition was easy due to the valley's temperate climate, rich soils and sheltered environment, which enabled new grape varieties, such as Grenache and Pedro to reach production relatively quickly. Over the last ten years however, popular tastes have reverted to premium table wines. As a result, the area under vine in the Barossa is currently less than at its peak, as many vignerons are replanting their vineyards with grapes more suitable for table wine.

Companies such as Peter Lehmann, Basedow, St. Hallett, Rockford and others are producing excellent premium table wines and have recently been joined by newcomers on the boutique arena such as Jenke, Burge Family, Bethany, Twin Valley Estate, Charles Melton, Charles Cimicky, Willows, Turkey Flat, Grant Burge and others. The Barossa Valley is also home to many large companies such as Penfold's and Kaiser Stuhl, Orlando, Seppelts, Yalumba, Wolf Blass, Tollana, Krondorf and Leo Buring.

All these wineries are totally committed to Barossa fruit exclusively and have a full recognition of the Barossa's solid viticultural base. Many vineyards have been in the same families and worked by them for five - six generations.

Many vineyards of shiraz, grenache and semillon have 50 year old vines and some over 100 years old, whilst other regions have changed dramatically viticulturally.

There has also been a renaissance of quality bottled table wines such as Chateau Yaldara and Rovalley Estate. The growing emphasis on wine tourism has led to the establishment of the likes of Kaesler Wines with its restaurant, conference and seminar facilities and recently completed cottage accommodation.

Others in this ilk are Chateau Dorrien & Vintners.

The list goes on, with many fine restaurants and Bed and Breakfast Inns being established during the last decade.

Every two years the Barossa Valley is the setting for a wonderful Vintage Festival. Commencing on Easter Monday, the festival runs for a week and is centred around the Tanunda oval. There is a giant fair and all the local wine companies set up marquees for public tastings. A colourful parade passes through the streets and a Vintage Festival Queen is crowned.

The highlights of this celebration are the huge banquets, held in Tanunda's enormous hall, consisting of a sit down Barossa feast for 2,000 people at a time. The entertainment provided at these functions is excellent, particularly from the comedian - who is the local undertaker. In addition, the Ledertahl Choir and Tanunda Brass Band usually perform to delighted crowds who, by the end of the evening are usually standing on their tables clapping to the music.

The Festival wine auction is also worth attending and must be the best of its kind held in Australia.

The Spring Barossa Music Festival features two weeks of outstanding concerts at wineries, the valley's beautiful churches and other venues. This event is not only of National but International significance and is already a major South Australian Tourism attraction. Another event, the Annual Barossa Classic Gourmet Weekend in August, where most wineries participate and team up with a leading restaurant and provide live entertainment, is hugely successful. This weekend welcomes more than 30,000 happy visitors each year. The Valley also boasts some of the best bakeries and smallgoods makers in Australia. Put a trip to the Barossa on your travel agenda. Until then, why not enjoy some of her fine wines.

St Hallett
POACHER'S BLEND
1994
ST. HALLETT WINES
BAROSSA SOUTH AUSTRALIA 5352
PRODUCE OF AUSTRALIA 750mL

TWIN VALLEY ESTATE
1991
QC
WINES OF QUALITY AND CONSISTENCY
CABERNET-MERLOT
TWIN VALLEY WINES
Produce of Australia 750 ml

ROCKFORD
BASKET PRESS
Shiraz
BAROSSA VALLEY
750ml

MIRANDA
ROVALLEY
RIDGE
BAROSSA VALLEY
1991
Cabernets
Shiraz
PRODUCT OF AUSTRALIA
12.5%ALC/VOL. 750mL

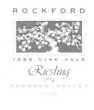

ROCKFORD
1886 VINE VALE
Riesling
BAROSSA VALLEY
750ml

BAROSSA
ROVALLEY RIDGE
SHOW RESERVE
1991
Eden Valley
Shiraz Cabernet
Winner of 20 Trophies & Show Medals
750ml

Bethany

1990
DORRIEN
CABERNET
SAUVIGNON
CNR. BAROSSA VALLEY WAY & SEPPELTSFIELD RD.
DORRIEN, BAROSSA VALLEY SOUTH AUSTRALIA
PRODUCE OF AUSTRALIA 750ML Alc. Vol. 12%

KIES
LYNDOCH HILLS
CABERNET
SAUVIGNON
1% MERLOT
1992

1991
OLD VINE
SHIRAZ
KAESLER WINES
750 mL

St Hallett
OLD BLOCK
SHIRAZ
1992
ST HALLETT WINES
BAROSSA
SOUTH AUSTRALIA 5352
PRODUCE OF AUSTRALIA 750mL

CHARLES CIMICKY
SIGNATURE SHIRAZ
BAROSSA VALLEY
1993

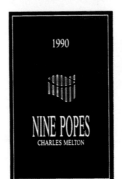

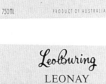

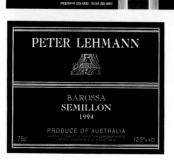

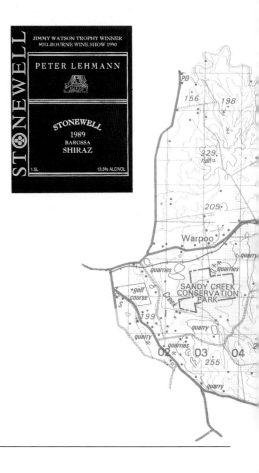

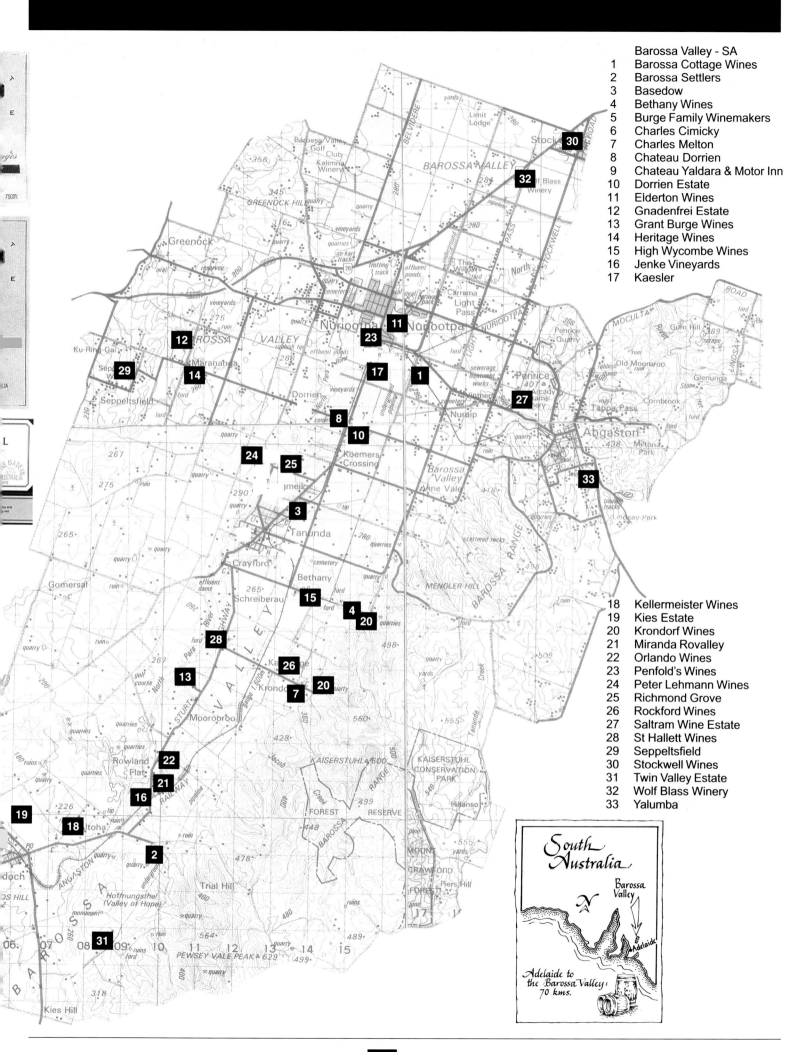

Barossa Valley - SA

1 Barossa Cottage Wines
2 Barossa Settlers
3 Basedow
4 Bethany Wines
5 Burge Family Winemakers
6 Charles Cimicky
7 Charles Melton
8 Chateau Dorrien
9 Chateau Yaldara & Motor Inn
10 Dorrien Estate
11 Elderton Wines
12 Gnadenfrei Estate
13 Grant Burge Wines
14 Heritage Wines
15 High Wycombe Wines
16 Jenke Vineyards
17 Kaesler

18 Kellermeister Wines
19 Kies Estate
20 Krondorf Wines
21 Miranda Rovalley
22 Orlando Wines
23 Penfold's Wines
24 Peter Lehmann Wines
25 Richmond Grove
26 Rockford Wines
27 Saltram Wine Estate
28 St Hallett Wines
29 Seppeltsfield
30 Stockwell Wines
31 Twin Valley Estate
32 Wolf Blass Winery
33 Yalumba

South Australia

N

Barossa Valley

Adelaide

Adelaide to
the Barossa Valley:
70 kms.

Bethany Wines

The Schrapel family, with Robert as winemaker and Geoff as marketing/ sales/viticulturist, represent one of the oldest grape-growing families in the region, going back to the German pioneers of the last century.

In 1977 they set up a beautiful winery, with a stunning panoramic view over the entire valley, by building into an old disused quarry. The natural cellar and insulation this has provided at minimal expense shows their good sense. Like many Barossa wineries, they first made a mark with their riesling and today make a fine range of premium table and fortified wines including the aptly-named The Old Quarry Port. In November 1994, at the Canberra National Wine Show, Bethany Wines won the trophy for the best dry red table wine, shiraz predominant, with its 1992 Bethany Shiraz.

If you are ever in the Valley for the Barossa Gourmet Weekend, don't miss Bethany. The folk there always put on a great show with food, wine and dancing and the location is a knock-out.

BETHANY WINES PTY. LTD.
SCHRAPEL FAMILY VINEYARDS
Address: Bethany Road, Tanunda SA 5352
Direction: 4 km east of Tanunda
Phone: (085) 63 2086
Fax: (085) 63 0046
Established: Vineyard, 1850; Winery, 1981
Owners: Robert & Geoffrey Schrapel
Winemakers: Rob & Geoff Schrapel
Principal varieties grown: riesling, chardonnay, shiraz, semillon, cabernet sauvignon, grenache
Ha under vine: 25
Average annual crush: 200-250 tonnes
Average no. cases produced: 18,000

Principal wines & brands	Cellar potential
Bethany Reserve Riesling	2-5 years
Bethany Chardonnay	2-5 years
Bethany Semillon	2-5 years
Bethany Shiraz	5-10 years
Bethany Cabernet/Merlot	5-10 years
Bethany Grenache Pressing	2-5 years
Vintage Brut Chardonnay	2-5 years
Select Late Harvest Cut	2-5 years

Trade tours: By appointment.
Cellar door & mail order sales:
Hours open to public: 10 am-5 pm Mon-Sat; 1-5 pm Sun.
Points of interest: Tasting area, picnic area and great view overlooking the Barossa Valley.
Retail distribution: S. & V. Wine Merchants, SA; Westwood Wine Agencies Vic; Carol-Ann Martin Classic Wines, NSW; WAZA Wines, WA; FNQ Wine Merchants, N.Qld; Allied Vitners, ACT; Tasmanian Fine Wines, Tas; Newmarket Wine & Spirits Ltd, New Zealand; The Wine Shopper, Sheffield, England.

Burge Family Winemakers

Back in 1928 the Burge family founded Wilsford Wines. Today carrying on that fine tradition is Rick Burge, a big genial fellow with both winemaking and hospitality skills at his fingertips.

I first ran into Rick in Rutherglen some 10 years ago when Milan and I were researching our first book. He was running the Poachers Paradise, an excellent restaurant and tavern in the main street. Rick did a stint as winemaker at St. Leonards but decided home in the Barossa Valley and the family wine business was for him.

Rick has built a beautiful winery on the family's property at Lyndoch, just as you enter the town. Functionally and aesthetically, it is very well done. Rick has also phased in the new name Burge Family Winemakers and runs the Wilsford

label for his fortified wines.

The Burge family run a number of wine , food and music events, always innovative, informative, interesting and lots of fun. During the last Barossa Vintage Festival, Rick ran shiraz and Rhone-style tasting luncheons, showing a range of French, Californian and Australian Rhone-style wines featured by the glass with a provincial meal and they were an unqualified success. The Burge Family's wines have nothing to fear from competition.

BURGE FAMILY WINEMAKERS
Address: Barossa Highway, Lyndoch SA 5351
Direction: Outskirts of the Lyndoch township towards Adelaide
Phone: (085) 24 4644
Fax: (085) 24 4444
Established: 1928
Owner: Rick & Bronwyn Burge
Winemaker: Rick Burge
Principal varieties grown: shiraz, cabernet sauvignon, merlot, grenache, touriga, cabernet franc, riesling, muscat blanc
Ha under vine: 12
Average annual crush: 60 tonnes
Average no. cases produced: 3,300

Principal wines & brands	Cellar potential
Draycott Shiraz	5-10 years
Draycott Homestead Blend	5-10 years
Draycott Merlot	2-5 years
"Old Vines" Grenache	2-5 years
Olive Hill Riesling	2-5 years
Muscat Blanc Late Harvest	2-5 years
"Wilsford" Tawny Port	(20 YO)

Cellar door & mail order sales:
Hours open to public: 10 am-5 pm daily except Christmas and Good Friday
Points of interest: Magnificent views of the Barossa Ranges. Stylish architecturally designed cellar sales & tasting room.
Retail distribution: All wine sold direct ex-cellars & by vineyard (mailing list) newsletters.

Charles Cimicky

Charles Cimicky's family came from Czechoslovakia where they had a background in winemaking and grape-growing. The family had also been involved in the building trade.

In 1972, Charles built a winery in the Lyndoch region of the Barossa Valley and crushed his first vintage in 1973. Somehow, in between establishing a business and making wine he found time to study winemaking at the Charles Sturt University in Wagga Wagga in New South Wales. The Charles Cimicky winery is a grand-looking building with the air of a European castle, perched on top of a ridge surrounded by a sea of vines.

CHARLES CIMICKY PREMIUM WINES
Address: Gomersal Road, Lyndoch SA 5351
Phone: (085) 24 4025
Fax: (085) 24 4772
Established: 1973
Owner: Charles and Jennie Cimicky
Winemaker: Charles Cimicky
Principal varieties grown: Sauvignon blanc, chardonnay, shiraz, cabernet sauvignon, merlot
Average no. cases produced: 4,000

Principal wines & brands	Cellar potential
Sauvignon Blanc	2-5 years
Shiraz	5-10 years

Trade tours: By appointment only
Cellar door & mail order sales: Yes
Hours open to public: 10.30 am-4.30 pm seven days

The Charles Cimicky wines are all from their own vines, as well as a small quantity from two neighbouring vineyards. The reds of recent times have impressed me considerably. The cabernet sauvignon is a big opulent style, with a little merlot and cabernet franc blended into it in some years when Charles feels it needs it.

The other wines are a shiraz, a very herbaceous, crisp sauvignon blanc and a chardonnay. Occasionally a semillon or a semillon chardonnay are produced, depending on the season. Aided by the cooler climate of the southern Barossa and their own carefully tended vineyard, the Charles Cimicky wines are indeed impressive. Charles purposely keeps the range small to help him in his quest for quality.

Charles Melton

Charlie Melton is not your everyday winemaker - he makes an extraordinarily good sparkling red wine, but is most famous for his "Nine Popes" a satirical little story based around the French Chateauneuf-du-Pape.

The French word for new and nine (masculine) is the same, neuf. Some say Charlie was confused, others that it's just a joke, but there is nothing to laugh about in the 'Nine Popes.' It's a really excellent full-bodied yet complex and warm style of wine,

Charles Melton Wines
Address: Krondorf Road, Tanuda 5352
Phone: (085) 63 3606
Fax: (085) 63 3422
Established: 1984
Winemaker: Charlie Melton
Principal varieties grown: Shiraz, grenache, cabernet
Ha under vine. 10
Average annual crush: 120 tonnes
Average no. cases produced: 7,000

Principal wines & brands	Cellar potential
Nine Popes	10+ years
Shiraz	5-10 years

Cellar door & mail order sales: Yes
Hours open to public: 11am - 5 pm 7days a week
Retail distribution:Fine Wine Stores/Restaurants - Sydney, Melbourne, Adelaide, London, Auckland

very much along the lines of a good French Cote du Rhone wine that Charlie likes so much. In fact, in the Chateauneuf-du-Pape region they use up to 13 grape varieties to make their red so nine is not out of the question.

Charlie's wine is mainly grenache and shiraz (becoming more widely popular in France) . Charlie is part of the Krondorf Road 'gang' of St. Halletts, Rockford, Bethany and Krondorf, not to forget Grant Burge. This is a great way to spend a day with these characterful winemakers, but be careful - you may not see any of the rest of the Valley - they hope!

Chateau Yaldara

From the visitor's point of view, Chateau Yaldara must be the most impressive winery in Australia. Originally an old flour mill, the building was little more than ruins when purchased and rebuilt along the lines of a European chateau by Hermann Thumm.

Work started in the late 1940s and in addition to the chateau, Yaldara have since built a stone distillery and a large stone reception and convention centre, seating up to 300 people. The whole complex is surrounded by beautiful gardens and two large lakes.

Hermann arrived in Australia just after the Second World War. He had studied winemaking in his native land and on arrival in the Barossa found a job working in a winery. A year or so after his arrival, he bought the old flour mill near Lyndoch and began creating Chateau Yaldara.

The chateau building proper is filled with European and Australian antiques and works of art. A strong wine theme goes through the whole collection which has been completed with great care and style.

During the 1970s, Hermann was joined in the business by his two sons, Robert and Dieter. Robert graduated from the

Hermann Thumm

Geisenheim College of Oenology in Germany and has made wine at Chateau Yaldara. Dieter is Managing Director of Chateau Yaldara and takes a keen interest in every aspect of this diverse company.

Chateau Yaldara also sports a seminar, convention and motel complex - the famous Barossa Motel was completed in 1969.

Over the years Chateau Yaldara have gained a reputation for producing many high quality, value for money wine styles, not only table and fortified but also sparkling, being the pioneers of the "Charmat" bulk natural fermentation method. They also produce a range of non-alcoholic grape beverages.

The Chateau Yaldara fortified wines include a number of very old, fine tawny ports and to top everything off they also produce brandy and a range of liqueurs. Visitors to Chateau Yaldara can certainly stock their cellar without a problem.

When Yaldara's distillery was built in 1974, the Australian brandy industry was in a real slump due to a 1972 tax slug. Always innovative, Hermann Thumm developed a revolutionary vacuum distillation method which is not only economical and energy-saving, but imparts more fruit flavour to the brandy due to its lower temperature operation.

In 1985 Chateau Yaldara went through a real revolution with the introduction of the Lakewood range of premium table wines. The name was inspired by the many lakes and wooded gardens on the property.

Ace wine consultant Jim Irvine works with the Thumm family to create some extraordinary wines, concentrating on whites, particularly chardonnay as an initial focus.

The wines were released at ludicrously low prices considering their quality. The wine-drinking public were quick to react and today a range of some half a dozen Lakewood wines have carved a very substantial niche in the wine market. The recently released Whitmore Old Vineyard grenache, brought on to the market in the same year of its vintage, is an absolute stunner.

Chateau Yaldara expanded their vineyard holdings substantially in the early 1990s. Among other purchases they have bought a property known as The Farms right next to the winery. This vineyard is blessed with terra rossa soil and produces red wine grapes of extraordinary quality. Chateau Yaldara recently released a super-super premium range of wines in very, very limited

quantities called The Farms (at Grange Hermitage-like prices). The straight merlot made by world merlot champion Jim Irvine is a revelation. The merlot/cabernet is exquisite and the tawny port, probably the oldest commercial port released in Australia, is liquid gold.

The overall impression one receives from a visit to Chateau Yaldara is that of orderly elegance and prosperity. The Thumms have come a long way with their energy and hard work and Australian wine is the beneficiary.

CHATEAU YALDARA PTY LTD
Address: Gomersal Road, Lyndoch SA 5351
Phone: (085) 24 4200
Fax: (085) 24 4678
Established 1947
Owner: Thumm Family
Winemaker: James Irvine
Principal varieties grown: Cabernet sauvignon, merlot, shiraz, chardonnay, semillon, sauvignon blanc, pinot noir, grenache
Ha under vine: 65
Average annual crush: 6,500 tonnes
Average no. cases produced: 550,000

Principal wines & brands	Cellar potential
The Farms	
Merlot	2-5 years
Cabernet	5-10 years
Semillon	2-5 years
Lakewood	
Chardonnay	2-5 years
Shiraz	5-10 years
Sauvignon Blanc Semillon	2-5 years
Sparkling Acacia Hill	
Shiraz Cabernet	5-10 years
Semillon Chardonnay	2-5 years
Ducks Flat	2-5 years
Great Barossa Champagne	
Fine Old Tawny Port	10+ years

Public & trade tours: Yes
Cellar door & mail order sales: Yes
Hours open to public: 8.30 am-5 pm Mon-Friday; 9 am - 5 pm w/e
Points of interest: Winery bistro, Flag Motor Inn, reception hall for weddings, conferences, etc; picnic areas
Retail distribution: Every state, export to United Kingdom, Canada, New Zealand

Kies Estate - Lyndoch Hills Cellars

KIES ESTATES - KARRAWIRRA, REDGUM TM
Address: Barossa Way, Lyndoch SA 5351
Direction: 1 km south of the township
Phone: (085) 24 4110
Established: vineyard, 1880; winery, 1969
Owner: Ken Kies
Winemaker: James Irvine
Principal varieties grown: Semillon, sauvignon blanc, riesling, muscat, chardonnay, shiraz, cabernet, merlot, grenache, chenin, cabernet franc, traminer
Ha under vine: 16 ha Lyndoch, 65 ha Hoffnung Valley, Stahl
Average annual crush: 100 tonnes (balance sold)
Average no. cases produced: 1,000

Principal wines & brands	Cellar potential
Semillon/Sauvignon Blanc	2-5 years
Chardonnay (Barrel Ferment)	2-5 years
Semillon	2-5 years
Cabernet/Merlot	5-10 years
Shiraz	5-10 years
Champenoise Chardonnay	Vintage
Champenoise Chardonnay	Non-Vintage
Tawny Ports	10+ years
Kies Estate Karrawirra	
Kies Estate Redgum	

Public & trade tours: No
Cellar door & mail order sales: Yes
Hours open to public: 10 am-4.30 pm seven days a week
Points of interest: Children's playground, picnic area & gazebo; tourist information centre for Barossa District Council
Retail Distribution: Cellar door and mailing list only

As one enters the small hamlet of Lyndoch on the main road into the Barossa Valley the attractive stone cellars of Kies Estate, behind expansive lawns and neatly tended gardens, beckons one to stop off for the first visit of the day, or as a farewell to the beautiful valley on departure.

Ken Kies is a long-time grower and began making table and fortified wines back in 1969. I first met Ken in 1970 when he was looking for some good brandy spirit for his fortified winemaking. I must say he is one of nature's real gentlemen and his wines reflect his honest and open character.

For a number of years, he traded as Karrawirra and he used the name Red Gum Vineyard for sometime also.

Helen Napier-Kies, who runs the cellar door where most of the wine is sold, is an experienced wine merchant employing qualified staff, and a visit to Kies Estate is not only enjoyable but very informative. Premium wines are produced from traditional varieties. You can also try Kies' excellent sparkling and fortified wines.

Chateau Yaldara Motor Inn

Chateau Dorrien

Seppelts Dorrien Winery was built just after the turn of the century to make and store more wine for the expanding House of Seppelt, then the largest winemaker in Australia.

The winery with its turreted tanks, a signature of Seppelt, is right in the heart of the Barossa on the main road between Tanunda and Nuriootpa.

The tiny township of Dorrien started its life as Siegersdorf, so named by the Silesian settlers. During World War I the name, like many other Germanic names, was changed. The winery's attractive style and location were not lost on Fernando Martin, a visionary restaurateur who had created Adelaide's first wine bar taverns in the sixties. The turreted tanks have been opened up and are now turreted towers. Inside the winery is an excellent bistro and a fascinating tasting area where murals depicting the history of the Barossa settlement are painted on a row of original 80 year old concrete wine vats.

Chateau Dorrien has the only Barossa Meadery. It produces honey mead, mans oldest drink. Exotic gran miele, scarlet, spicy mead, sweet mead and the newest quandong liqueur mead, made from the native quandong and bush honey.

The Black Label Cabernet Sauvignon and Black Label Shiraz produced from a small patch of old vines from the Dorrien vineyards are Fernando's pride and joy and should not be missed.

Twin Valley Wines

High in the foothills under the awesome peaks of the Eden Hills, some eight kilometres south of Lyndoch, lies "Fernando's Hideaway" — Twin Valley.

Fernando Martin is a dynamic and innovative man who was the true pioneer of the modern wine bars in Adelaide in the 1960s. After many years as a prominent restaurateur in Adelaide, he decided to go right to the source, and over the last decade or so, he has bought two wineries. Chateau Dorrien in the heart of the valley was previously the Dorrien Winery of Seppelts. The turreted tanks now contain the history of wine, rather than the wine itself and it has a top bistro.

Fernando's winemaking headquarters is his Twin Valley Estate, aptly named as it is hidden in between these valleys which rise to the Eden Hills. Fernando's partner and wife Jeanette is as equally dynamic as Fernando. Together they produce a large range of table wines, fortifieds and liqueurs. Fernando also utilises his winery year-round to produce Australia's best cider, Cobbley's, including the premium, Eden Gold. His entrepreneurial spirit has seen the fresh surplus apples from the growers in the Adelaide Hills at Ashton turned into great cider instead of going to waste. This is not an easy market to tackle but Fernando can be proud of his cider, it's light years ahead of the competition.

The Twin Valley table wines are very successful in wine shows. Proudly stamped on the labels are the large letters QC, standing for quality and consistency and the wines reflect this philosophy in every way. The cabernet merlot and the cabernet sauvignon/cabernet franc blends are among the best in the Barossa and real bargains.

Fernando sources much of his grape supply in the cool Eden Valley region above him and his Light Pass Sauvignon Blanc and his St. Beth Rhine Riesling show the cool climate aromatic qualities to perfection. The QC Chardonnay is rich and full and the Barossa Spatlaese Frontignac has a loyal following.

Why not take the adventure, gather a posse and search out Fernando's Hideaway in the hidden valley - they have a large cool tasting room hidden under the winery. Don't forget to try the Cobbley's Apple Nectar Liqueur, it's sensational. If by chance you don't have time for this adventure, all the wines and ciders are at Chateau Dorrien.

Grant Burge Wines

Grant Burge comes from a family long involved in grape-growing in the Barossa Valley. I first met Grant some 25 years ago when, as young lads, we used to travel to wine shows together. Grant was working as a winemaker for the Southern Vales Co-operative in McLaren Vale just across the road from Hardy's where for a couple of years I prepared the show wines for the company.

Grant then, as now, was a quiet but happy sort of fellow, very committed to his quality winemaking. Some years later, he formed a partnership with colleague Ian Wilson -

Burge and Wilson. They created a label and made wine together using their good contacts in both McLaren Vale and the Barossa to source very high quality grapes.

The partnership purchased the Krondorf Winery in the Barossa from the Seagram Wine Estates Group. Ironically it was right next door to the old Burge winery, Wilsford.

Grant and Ian were highly successful and had been using the winery since 1976, a few years before purchasing it. In 1983, Krondorf went public to help with capital expenditure and expansion and two years later, Mildara purchased it, retaining Burge and Wilson as consultant winemakers.

In 1988, Grant decided to go out on his own and bought the beautiful cellars at Jacobs Creek, which were restored by Colin Gramp in the 1970s and run as a restaurant and wine cellars as Gramps Winekeller. This base gave Grant the chance to develop a high profile for his excellent wines. His many talents and the help of his wife Helen in the marketing area has seen Grant Burge wines through a period of explosive growth. Grant won the Telecom South Australian Small

Business of the Year Award in 1993, not only the under 30 employees category, but also the overall award.

Grant Burge has quietly amassed large vineyard holdings around the Barossa Valley and Barossa Ranges. At present, 450 acres are planted in strategic locations and planting is underway to bring this up to 750 acres by 1997. Grant's total land holdings are around 2,000 acres, so he has further potential to expand his vineyards. He is already in fact, one of the largest grape-growers in the valley.

This control of the vineyards is what gives Grant the opportunity to make the styles of wine he wants. For many years Grant used the Basedow winery for his making and in 1993 he purchased the winery which is currently being expanded and brought up to the absolute state of the art technically speaking.

Grant pays great credit to all his staff who have pulled together in this remarkable success story. Grant's wines have won many awards and are all very approachable in their rich fruit-driven style.

GRANT BURGE WINES PTY LTD
Address: Barossa Way, Jacob's Creek, Tanunda SA 5352
Phone: (085) 63 3700
Fax: (085) 63 2807
Owner: Grant Burge
Winemaker: Grant Burge
Principal varieties grown: Riesling, semillon, chardonnay, sauvignon blanc, shiraz, frontignac, traminer, sylvaner, merlot cabernet franc
Ha under vine: 140
Average annual crush: 1,000 tonnes
Public & trade tours: Yes
Cellar door & mail order sales: Yes
Hours open to public: 10-5 daily

Dorrien Estate - Cellarmaster Wines

This impressively large facility is home to Cellarmaster Wines, Australia's leading mail-order wine merchant. The complex includes a vast temperature-controlled cellar, with capacity for over 300,000 cases, and a purpose-built barrel hall for extended oak-ageing of selected wines. One hundred per cent Australian owned, Cellarmaster Wines have over 220,000 members in Australia and New Zealand, and ship around 800,000 cases a year direct to members' homes, making them the largest merchant of home-delivered wine in the world.

If you haven't got time to get around to the wine regions, or even if you do, the wine club offers a convenient and competitive alternative to traditional retail outlets. I've heard nothing but good reports of this organisation. They are definitely one of the look-ahead players in the wine industry. If you would like more information, Cellarmaster's toll free phone number is 1-800 500 260.

Leo Buring

Leo Buring was born in 1876 into the winemaking family involved in the Quelltaler Winery in Clare and certainly made his own distinctive mark in the Australian wine industry.

Somehow his innovative style and entrepreneurial spirit always seems to show through in the exciting quality and good-value prices the Buring label has become known for.

Leo graduated at the top of his class from Roseworthy Agricultural College; he was then privileged to travel to Europe and during his extensive travels through the wine regions he visited the respected wine colleges of Geisenheim in Germany and Montpellier in France.

On his return in 1898 he worked several vintages in Quelltaler before joining Minchinburg Cellars in 1902, later to become Penfolds in 1912. During his 17 years there he pioneered many winemaking techniques, including producing the first Penfolds Minchinbury Champagne. In 1919 Leo struck out on his own as one of Australia's first winemaking consultants and advisors. It was in this capacity that he was called into Lindemans in 1923 at a time they were beset by serious financial problems. Unfortunately these could not be solved, but Buring went on

to other successful consulting jobs until forming a partnership, Leo Buring and Company with Reg Mowat from Great Western. They quickly developed Australia's first universally accepted table wine, the famous Burings Rinegold (from the German for pure gold). This semi-sweet wine from Hunter Valley semillon was enormously successful, packaged in its unique squat bottle.

Sales soared and Burings took over the Melbourne wine merchant Matthew Lang in

the 1930s. By 1945 Burings were looking for a permanent home and purchased a small winery in the heart of the Barossa Valley, established in 1897 by Gottleib Hoffman. The property became known as Chateau Leonay and became famous for its unusual round tower and attractive style.

Leo Buring died at 85 in 1961. Ironically, the following year the winery was bought by Lindemans. Even more ironically, Leo Buring came under the Penfolds wing with the Southcorp purchase of Lindemans in the late 1980s. The winemaker extraordinaire who put the Leo Buring white wines at the pinnacle of their class in the 1950s and 60s was John Vickery, whose innovations such as skin cooling and the dedicated attention to detail created so many classic wines, often from Clare and Eden Valley.

Under Southcorp's direction, Leo Buring continues to make fabulous quality and great value wines which are very successful on the local and overseas markets.

If you are looking for some of Australia's best value premium wines, take a look at the Leo Buring label and muse over the incredible exploits of the great Leo Buring and the rich wine heritage he has left us.

Basedow

In 1996, Basedow celebrate their centenary. The winery, built beside a creek in the centre of Tanunda by brothers Martin and Johann Basedow, was eventually taken over by Martin's son Oscar and renamed O. Basedow and Sons.

Basedow's history and reputation had been forged with fortified wines, although John Basedow won the coveted Jimmy Watson Trophy in 1970 with his dry red. The real transformation for Basedow came during the mid-seventies when Peter Lehmann's son Doug took over the reins, restoring the lovely old sandstone buildings, upgrading the facilities and expanding the winery's capacity considerably.

Doug began contract crushing for the likes of Wolf Blass as well as upgrading the Basedow wines. The Basedow White Burgundy was the real pioneer for wood-aged semillons and remains a success story today. In 1993, Grant Burge, who had been using the Basedow winery for most of his fast-growing production, took over the winery, upgrading even further.

The Basedow wines and label today represent a quality boutique style wine at

O. BASEDOW WINES PTY LTD
Address: 161-165 Murray Street, Tanunda SA 5352
Phone: (085) 63 3666
Fax: (085) 63 2597
Established: 1896
Winemaker: Craig Stansborough
Principal varieties grown: chardonnay, semillon, shiraz, cabernet sauvignon, grenache
Ha under vine: 50
Average annual crush:
Average no. cases produced: 40,000

Principal wines & brands	Cellar potential
Oscars Brut	
Oscars Traditional	
White Burgundy	2-5 years
Oscar's Heritage	5-10 years
Chardonnay	5-10 years
Barossa Shiraz	5-10 years
Fine Old Tawny Port	10+ years

Public & trade tours: By appointment only
Cellar door & mail order sales: Yes
Hours open to public: 10 am-5 pm Mon-Fri; 11 am-5 pm w/e
Retail distribution: National Liquor Co., Queensland & WA; Hill International, Victoria & Queensland; Harry Williams & Co., ACT; Chace Agencies, SA, Australian Liquor Marketers, Tasmania.

bargain prices. The underground tasting cellar is one of the best in the valley. Drop in while you are in Tanunda - it's easy to find.

Jenke Vineyards

Kym Jenke is a sixth generation Barossa winemaker full of enthusiasm and life, just like his wines. Kym has travelled the world of wine extensively and has made wine in California.

The Jenke winery, cellars and tasting room are housed in an historic old building built in 1850 by Kym's great-great-great-grandfather who had arrived from Germany only two years earlier. The moss-covered roof hides a really special and lovingly restored part of Australia's wine history and the old slate walls have withstood the test of time superbly.

All of Kym Jenke's wines have very forward fruit flavours. I found the straight varietal cabernet franc and the chardonnay to be easy gold medal standard wines and the Jenke semillon has traditional Barossa flavours and style. Jenke is one of the most exciting winemakers in the valley. Try their wines, or better still, drop in and say g'day to Kym and his best friend Jazz (the dog). You'll have a great time.

JENKE VINEYARDS
Address: Jenke Road, Rowland Flat SA 5352
Direction: Barossa Valley Way
Phone: (085) 24 4154
Fax: (085) 24 4154
Established: 1989
Winemaker: Kym Jenke
Principal varieties grown: Cabernet sauvignon, grenache, shiraz, semillon, merlot, chardonnay, cabernet franc, riesling
Ha under vine: 45
Average annual crush: 60 tonnes
Average no. cases produced: 4000

Principal wines & brands	Cellar potential
Chardonnay	2-5 years
Semillon	2-5 years
Shiraz	5-10 years
Cabernet Sauvignon	5-10 years
Cabernet Franc	2-5 years

Public & trade tours: By appointment only
Cellar door & mail order sales: Yes
Hours open to public: 10 am-5 pm seven days
Points of interest: Cellar door is a restored 1850 settler's cottage
Retail distribution:
Pinnacle Wine Merchants, NSW;
J Harvey Long Wine Co., Victoria;
Regional Liquor Merchants, South Australia.

Jacobs Creek

Johann Gramp, one of the early German settlers in the Barossa Valley, planted the first grapes back in 1847 at Jacob's Creek, just past the massive Orlando Winery at Rowland Flat.

Orlando remained small until the 1920s when the production of popular fortified wines greatly expanded the business.

During the early 1950s, Colin Gramp went to Germany and brought back with him some German pressure controlled stainless steel fermenting tanks, which started the most significant technological breakthrough yet in the history of the Australian wine industry. The control of the rate, temperature and length of the fermentation produced white wines with much more aromatic floral and fruit flavours and naturally being sealed, prevented oxidisation of the wines. These radically different and improved white wines quickly gained popularity and set the stage for the white wine boom of the early 1970s.

Colin Gramp also brought to Australia German winemaking genius Gunter Prass. Gunter spent more than 30 years with Orlando, finishing as managing director and overseeing the remarkable development of Orlando into one of the largest and most respected wine companies in Australia. Orlando was taken over by Reckitt and Coleman in 1971 but the late 1980s saw a well-orchestrated employee buyout supported by the South Australian Government. After a successful few years, capital demands and the need to build an international distribution network led to a buyout by world wine and spirit giant, the French Pernod Ricard company.

Along the way, Orlando has been at the forefront of many winemaking developments, none more so than Barossa Pearl in its unique pear-shaped bottle, introduced as Australia's first bulk fermented sparkling wine and at a never before seen

affordable price. It became de rigeur when courting a young lady to crack a bottle or two of this exciting new wine. Orlando produced Australia's first commercial chardonnay in the late 1970s and this first affordable chardonnay became the forerunner of what is now Australia's biggest selling premium white variety.

In the mid-70s Orlando released four premium wines in the popular price bracket, Lyndale Riesling, Moorooroo White Burgundy, Fromm's Spaetlese and Jacob's Creek Claret. Although most of the advertising and promotion was directed at Lyndale, it was the Jacob's Creek Claret, named after the site of Johann Gramp's original vineyard, which stole the show.

Jacob's Creek is an incredible success story; today the red wine, a blend of cabernet shiraz and malbec, is Australia's biggest-selling bottled wine in England. The trickle of the creek has turned into a river which is

flowing around the world. Jacob's Creek Chardonnay has also had great success, winning a number of trophies and awards, including a top French honour, quite a feat for a wine which sells at well under $10 Australian.

Orlando R.F. Chardonnay, the R.F. standing for Rowland Flat, has been most successful in the affordable semi-premium category. Old stalwarts such as the Steingarten Riesling from the "Garden of Stones" vineyard, high on Trial Hill behind the valley, produces incredibly small crops of exceptional wines have captured wine lovers' imagination.

The Orlando Saints - St. Helga Eden Valley Riesling, St. Hugo Coonawarra Cabernet Sauvignon and the more recently released St. Hilary Chardonnay from

Padthaway - are all rich in flavour and truly great wine bargains in their price bracket.

In the super premium area, Orlando has two individual vineyard red wines, the Lawsons Shiraz from Padthaway and the Jacaranda Ridge Coonawarra Cabernet Sauvignon. These are in the top few of consistently great Australian red wines.

The Russet Ridge Cabernet blend from Coonawarra, first released in 1993, is already a success in the medium-priced area.

Orlando has a very well-balanced and well-rounded range of wines. Their winery and its state of the art packaging centre is world class. One would be remiss not to mention the great sparkling wines - Trilogy, a pinot noir, chardonnay and pinot meunier cuvee and Carrington. Why not toast their success with these fine sparklers?

Krondorf

O ne of the older traditional wineries in the valley, Krondorf has had a rich and varied history. The Barossa Valley was settled in the mid 1800's by German Immigrants who brought with them vine cuttings from their homeland. The Krondorf Winery was established by one of these pioneering families - although it was not called

In 1976, a strong partnership emerged between two young and dynamic winemakers, Grant Burge and Ian Wilson. They began their Burge and Wilson label and made their first wines at the Krondorf Winery, which they later purchased. The wine quality, the elegant packaging and good promotion saw Krondorf's reputation and sales soar.

In 1983 the company went public and two years later was purchased by Mildara. Burge and Wilson stayed on and continued to create their magic, which was cemented when they won the 1980 Jimmy Watson Memorial Trophy with a 1979 McLaren Vale, Barossa and Coonawarra cabernet sauvignon.

Burge and Wilson went their separate
ways, but Krondorf continued upward.
Krondorf's main focus, under Mildara's
wing now for more than 10 years, is to
regionally select grapes available and
make top quality consistent styles that
remain true to label from year to year.
Krondorf is a label to be relied upon
always.

Kaesler Wines

Toby and Treena Hueppauff are a delightful down to earth couple who have worked very hard indeed to create the charming and multi-faceted Kaesler Estate on the main road through the Barossa Valley, just before the township of Nuriootpa.

The whole complex has a real feel of old Australiana, with its corrugated iron roofs and verandahs; indeed some of the buildings were German pioneers' cottages.

The property was purchased in 1986 to expand Toby's landscaping business, but the potential was soon realised and the restoration process began. In 1990 came the tasting area and the delightful vine and pergola-covered courtyard, then the lake with its mini bridges and landings.

The initial development was followed by an alfresco style restaurant and then a conference and seminar area. In 1994 Toby and Treena decided to convert some of the older buildings into high class bed and breakfast accommodation with a superb central lounge area where one can gaze out over the vineyards to the Barossa Ranges beyond.

The Kaesler wines cover the main table wine styles along with some excellent old fortifieds. The flagship is the Old Vine Shiraz with its distinctive oval shaped black and gold label. The vines this wine comes from celebrated their centenary in 1992; it's a wine well worth seeking out. The Kaesler semillon is also a great traditional Barossa white.

Kaesler's laid-back style, its cosy atmosphere and the Hueppauffs' hospitality make a visit here one to look forward to.

KAESLER WINES
Address: Barossa Valley Way, Nuriootpa SA 5355
Direction: Between Tanunda & Nuriootpa
Phone: (085) 62 2711
Fax: (085) 62 2788
Established: 1990
Owner: T.C. & T.K. Hueppauff
Winemaker: Roger Harbord
Principal varieties grown: Shiraz, semillon, grenache, mataro, cabernet sauvignon
Ha under vine: 11
Average annual crush: 30 tonnes
Average no. cases produced: 2000

Principal wines & brands	Cellar potential
Old Vine Shiraz	5-10 years
Prestige Semillon	2-5 years
Late Harvest Semillon	2-5 years
Bush Vine Grenache	2-5 years
Beerenauslese	2-5 years
Ruby Port	10+ years
Tawny Port	10+ years

Public & trade tours: No
Cellar door & mail order Sales: Yes
Hours open to public: 10 am-5 pm seven days
Points of interest: A la carte restaurant (indoor/outdoor dining), cottage accommodation for three couples
Retail distribution: Parker Evans Agencies, Adelaide

Peter Lehmann

Peter Lehmann is a legend - his long and rich winemaking career has spanned many decades and many moods of the Australian wine industry.

Peter is staunchly Barossa, he eats, drinks and breathes the Barossa. Peter began his career at Yalumba where he worked for 13 years before joining Saltram where he spent 20 vintages creating wine history through wonderful wines, some classics of Australian wines which occasionally surface today.

The Mamre Brook Red won the Jimmy Watson in 1967. In 1979, Peter was so disgusted with the big companies in the valley who were refusing to buy grapes from the stalwart growers of the Barossa he began his own wine company. Masterson Barossa Vignerons Pty Ltd was a saviour for the growers. Even today, Peter Lehmann's favourite spot is in his cosy little weighbridge where there's always a warm welcome, a cold drink, a glass of wine, a stick of Barossa metwurst, all personally dispensed by Peter. The growers have a chat with Peter and he inspects their grapes and directs them on to their ideal destination in the winery.

Peter Lehmann is like the captain on the bridge, steering his winery in the right direction. Each year approaching Christmas, Peter Lehmann puts on a splendid picnic day for his growers and hundreds turn up with their families to enjoy the day on the lawn of the winery. Top marks to the Lehmanns. Peter's wife Margaret is very active in the company's affairs and recently she and Peter finished off their magnificent stone home above the winery with its panoramic views over the valley.

Not long ago I enjoyed one of the best wine releases ever held, when the 1989 Peter Lehmann Stonewell Shiraz, winner of the 1990 Jimmy Watson Memorial Trophy was released. More than 70 guests arrived at the winery at midday to be greeted by the growers themselves. We all chatted on, enjoying a glass of wine or even beer and nibbling on the delicious Barossa tidbits prepared by incomparable chef Maggie Beer of Pheasant Farm fame. Then a casual stroll up the hill to the Lehmann home, a beautiful blend of Australian colonial architecture and French provincial style. Along their sunroom at the rear a long table for 75 had been set and the meal that followed was superb.

Peter Lehmann has a great team around him - his son Doug is C.E.O, and winemaker Andrew Wigan joined Peter in 1976. Peter threw a few good-natured barbs at some of his local mates, but generously set the stage for his winemaker extraordinaire Wigan.

The 1989 Stonewell Shiraz has been bottled only in magnums; they looked impressive, like a row of soldiers down the table. The 1989 is not the only Stonewell to succeed - this premium shiraz (always Peter's preferred variety) was launched with the 1987 vintage and leads a Peter Lehmann range of extraordinary wines.

PETER LEHMANN WINES

Address: Para Road, Tanunda SA 5352
Phone: (085) 63 2500
Fax: (085) 63 3140
Established: 1979
Owner: Peter and Margaret Lehmann
B: Peter Lehmann, Andrew Wigan

Principal wines & brands	Cellar potential
1989 Cellar Collection Stonewell Shiraz	20+ years
1991 Mentor (Cabernet blend)	20+ years
1992 Cellar Collection Chardonnay	10+years
1991 Cellar Collection Riesling	8+ years
1993 Peter Lehmann Barossa Cabernet	5-10years
1992 Peter Lehmann Barossa Shiraz	5-8+years
1992 Clancy's Gold Preference	8+years
1994 Peter Lehmann Barossa Semillon	5 years
1994 Peter Lehmann Barossa Chardonnay	5years
1994 Peter Lehmann Barossa/ Eden Valley Riesling	8 years
1994 Peter Lehmann Noble Semillon	8+ years
1990 Vintage Bin AD2011	21+ years

Public & trade tours: Yes
Cellar door & mail order sales: Yes
Hours open to public: 9.30 am-5 pm Mon-Fri; 10.30 am-4.30 pm w/e and PH
Points of interest: Picnic grounds
Retail distribution: Negociants Australia, all states

Several weeks previously, the Stonewells had absolutely blitzed the other reds at the Royal Adelaide Show. The 1990 won the Montgomery Trophy for the best full bodied red as well as the trophy for the best red in the show. The 1989 added to its illustrious reputation with the Wally Ware Trophy for the best medium bodied red.

Andrew Wigan spoke eloquently and showed his great depth of knowledge and respect for his mentor. It's been a long way for him since his youth, growing up in another great wine region, Great Western in Victoria, where family friend and legendary winemaker Colin Preece kindled Andrew's interest in wine. For the 1995 Barossa Valley Vintage Festival launch the Lehmanns, along with their neighbours at the Richmond Grove Winery, helped organise a banquet to remember with the bounty of the Barossa, washed down by the best wines of the Valley. This glorious Barossa evening on the lawns at Lehmanns featured "the winemaker, the chef, the butcher, the baker, and yes, even a candlestick maker."

Even Grange Hermitage was opened along with the 1989 Stonewell and a host of other great wines. What a night, with music and hospitality you dream about. A toast to a great winemaking team and a very special family!

Richmond Grove - Barossa

Housed in the old Leo Buring Winery, right across the lawns from the Peter Lehmann Winery, is the Richmond Grove Barossa Winery.

This leading Australian wine label which had its beginnings in the Upper Hunter in New South Wales was taken over some years ago by the Orlando Wyndham Group, who started looking for a home in the Barossa for Richmond Grove. The giant Southcorp conglomerate owned the Leo Buring label and winery but with a number of large, efficient, quality wineries in the region handling their winemaking needs,

the beautiful old Chateau Leonay Winery, built around the turn of the century complete with its turreted tower, lay idle.

Today the winery is a buzzing beehive of activity. John Vickery, the living legend of Australian white winemaking, who put Burings on the map in the 1960s and '70s, is back at his beloved Chateau Leonay after a long absence.

The cellar door area has been enlarged and beautifully styled. John's first "back home" vintage in 1994 produced some great wines, including two exquisite rieslings, one from The Barossa and another from Watervale.

Richmond Grove's success and expansion has breathed life into a great winery. Why not check it out for yourself?

Richmond Grove has played host to some great cultural events and has been a major sponsor of the Barossa Music Festival and a popular venue during the Barossa Gourmet Weekend.

Its flemish charm, roomy facilities and beautiful grounds make it an ideal venue for a variety of wine-related events.

Rockford

Robert O'Callaghan has built a winery that captures the spirit of the traditional Barossa. This is also clearly reflected in the attitude of those who grow the grapes and the wines made from them.

The original 1850's stone buildings have been restored and extended in the same style by Robert and his good friend Michael Waugh. This retains the feel of a Barossan farm yard and winery while the thick stone walls provide insulation that makes these buildings ideal for maturing wine in wood.

In 1965 Robert left school to take a 5 year position as an apprentice winemaker with B. Seppelt & Sons at Rutherglen. This was the last period before modern technology started to change Australian winemaking forever. This winery was full of equipment, procedure and attitudes that had not changed for a very long time. Robert's winemaking career with Sepptelts took him through their wineries at Rutherglen, Chateau Tanunda, Dorrien and Seppeltsfield. Even though he left Seppelts to work for other winemakers and was part of this modernisation of the Australian wine industry, his grapegrowing background and the impressions instilled by his time with Seppelts are at the heart of what Rockford is today.

The "coup de grace" of the Rockford range is their Black Shiraz, a sparkling red methode champenoise that is well-named, inky black in colour, with a kaleidoscope of flavours, rich and superb. I know quite a few people who would "kill" to get some; it is swallowed up literally straight away when the small batches are released.

The sales emphasis has always been at the Cellar Door to encourage people to visit the winery, taste the wines and understand what they represent. To this end the majority of sales are made in South Australia, there is no interstate wholesale distribution so all interstate sales are direct from the winery via a mailing list with a newsletter once a year to keep those customers informed. Rockford value tradition, there is a real sense of family and belonging to all who work there and you get a really good feeling when you walk through the gates into this domain where wine is respected and enjoyed.

<table>
<tr><td colspan="2">ROCKFORD WINES</td></tr>
<tr><td>Address:</td><td>Krondorf Road, Tanunda SA 5352</td></tr>
<tr><td>Phone:</td><td>(085) 63 2720</td></tr>
<tr><td>Fax:</td><td>(085) 63 3787</td></tr>
<tr><td>Established:</td><td>1984</td></tr>
<tr><td>Winemaker:</td><td>R. O'Callaghan & Chris Ringland</td></tr>
<tr><td colspan="2">Principal varieties grown: Grenache, riesling, shiraz, cabernet sauvignon, semillon</td></tr>
<tr><td colspan="2">Average annual crush: 350 tonnes</td></tr>
<tr><td colspan="2">Average no. cases produced: 15,000</td></tr>
<tr><td colspan="2">Cellar door & mail order sales: Yes</td></tr>
<tr><td colspan="2">Hours open to public: 11 am-5 pm seven days</td></tr>
</table>

Low yielding vineyards, hand pruned and picked, open fermenters, wooden crushers and basket presses are combined with handed down knowledge to produce the rich earthy complex red and white wines for which Rockford are renowned. The Basket Press Shiraz represents all of this and was one of the first to establish a traditional style that is now an important part of Australia's premium wines.

Miranda Rovalley Wines

Like most Italian families who have migrated to Australia, the Mirandas are very close and hardworking. The family's patron, Frank Miranda, affectionately called "Pop" by his youngest son Lou who now runs the Rovalley winery, came to Australia in 1939.

Pop loved his adopted land, even despite four years' internment during the Second World War. He didn't waste his time, honing his winemaking skills in of all places, Katherine in the Northern Territory, making wine from dried sultanas and raisins.

On returning to Griffith to the general store in Kooyoo Street his wife Caterina had been running in his absence, he began making wine commercially. Today, Miranda is Australia's seventh largest winery and becoming a bigger and bigger player in the premium wine market every year.

In 1991, the Mirandas took over the Rovalley Winery from the Leibich family who had founded it in 1919. Likeable Lou Miranda and his wife Val moved over from Griffith to run the winery. Lou has overseen a rejuvenation of the winery in terms of equipment, new oak barrels and a whole new attitude.

Lou is very much hands on and works hand in hand with winemaker Mos Kaesler and David Norman. For three years running, 1993 - 1995, they have won the top Gold Medal in the Royal Sydney Easter Show for their Rovalley Ridge Show Reserve Chardonnay. The 1991 Rovalley Ridge Show Reserve Shiraz Cabernet won the trophy at the 1994 Royal Perth Show for the best red wine. The "Old Vine Shiraz" has had considerable success. The 1991 won a trophy in London, with the 1992 vintage winning a gold the following year. The often overlooked Variety Riesling has also been a great success for the Miranda's in the Barossa the 1992, 1993 and 1994 all winning gold medals at Australian Wine Shows.

Rovalley is fast forging a reputation for top quality wines at very affordable prices. The old winery is undergoing a facelift to provide a cellar door and restaurant where the Mirandas can suitably disperse their warm hospitality and give their exceptional wines the environment they deserve.

Seppeltsfield

Joseph Seppelt arrived in Australia in 1849. Purchasing a large area of land near Tanunda in 1852, he built a homestead which is known as Seppeltsfield.

In addition to planting vines, Joseph originally attempted to establish corn, wheat and tobacco as well as grazing cattle. Initially wine facilities were not a priority as is evident in the fact that the first vintage was made in the dairy.

With the exception of tobacco, all Joseph's endeavours were successful but the emergence of wine as his main interest can be seen in the encouragement he gave to other landowners to plant vines. In 1867, Joseph started work on the magnificent stone buildings which make up Seppeltsfield and by the turn of the century, the company was the largest wine producer in Australia with two million litres of wine being produced annually.

Seppelt purchased another large winery in 1916, Chateau Tanunda. Built in 1890, this impressive stone construction was equal to Seppeltsfield in its grandeur. During the early 1900s much of its large output was dedicated to brandy production and so, Seppelt on the purchase of the property not only acquired an historic landmark, but also inherited large stocks of brandy. The early years of this century saw Seppelt also purchase wineries and vineyards at Great Western in Victoria and Dorrien near Tanunda, both of which were later furnished with the characteristic Seppelt turrets.

Throughout the difficult 1930s the Seppelts were most considerate to their staff. Although on reduced wages, the employees not only kept their jobs but also were provided with food and shelter, if necessary. In return, employees were requested to plant date seeds to a set pattern at each of their wineries. This elegant feature has become another distinguishing characteristic of Seppelt wineries. Seppeltsfield is no exception. The impressive family mausoleum stands on a hill overlooking a valley of palm lined avenues, magnificent stone buildings and turreted tanks. This picture is completed by the rolling greens and golds of Australia's first contoured vineyard.

James Godfrey is in charge of the Seppelt range of old fortified wines and in fact of all the fortified wines of the huge Southcorp wine conglomerate that purchased Seppelt several years ago. James is a Roseworthy graduate who worked previously with Wynns at Coonawarra, Tolleys Pedare and Saxonvale. Having judged fortified wines with James a few times, I can attest to the fact he is as skilled and knowledgeable about fortified wines as any person could be. The Winery and the ageing fortified wines are in the capable hands of Dean Kraehenbuhl who began his wine career in 1958 and whose family have been in the valley for four generations.

Seppelt winemakers have always been master blenders and their long and successful show record confirms their skills in this area. Recently, the company purchased an historic property near Eden

Valley named Partalunga. A huge vineyard development that stretches over the hills, it is managed by Alan Jenkins whose fine work is also evident at the Tollana Woodbury Vineyard in the Eden Valley. Rhine riesling, chardonnay, sauvignon blanc and cabernet sauvignon from Partalunga have all shown real class.

Seppeltsfield has always stored huge quantities of ageing top class fortified wines which in the case of the old Seppelt Para Liqueurs go back to the 1878 vintage. Occasionally, these old Paras are bottled for special occasions - they are almost liquid gold, the essence of wine and history in a glass. The Seppelt fortified wines are all superb, right down to the commercial sherries, ports and muscats. The Mt. Rufus and Old Trafford ports are particularly good value. The DP 90, a drier style tawny is superb, as is the richer Para Liqueur.

The Seppelt old fortified sherries in the DP series, the fino, amontillado and oloroso are a must in the aperitif cabinet or to add that classy zest to a soup or casserole. It's a real myth that you can use old opened or oxidised wine in cooking. Wine is a food and an ingredient when you cook - you wouldn't use limp vegetables or meat that's on the turn so why handicap your cooking with spoiled wine? Anyway, back to the wine; the secret with good fortified wines is to have old stocks in a solero system (ironically the name of the Seppelt range of sherries) where new wine is added to old in a gradual process each year. With more than 15 million litres of old fortifieds in their Seppeltsfield stronghold, Seppelt has this unique asset.

The Seppeltsfield buildings are some of the finest and best-kept Australian colonial architecture and a must for a visit whilst in the Barossa. The palm-lined avenues, the mausoleum, the peaceful grandeur of the place have a special spiritual feel to it. Seppeltsfield is a winery with soul - I'm certain your's will be enriched by visiting there.

Wolf Blass

In a very short space of time, Wolf Blass built one of Australia's most successful wine companies. The company was founded in 1973 and went public in 1984 to help fund expansion; two years later it was worth some $22 million, a reflection of the strength and drive of its founder.

Wolf was born in East Germany and worked as an apprentice on his grandfather's vineyard. He graduated from university as the youngest ever holder of the Kellermeister Diploma (Master degree) in Oenology. Wolf studied champagne production in France and worked in England for a time before coming to Australia at the invitation of Kaiser Stuhl. He arrived in 1960 to become sparkling wine manager for Kaiser Stuhl and it was not long before the industry was sitting up and taking notice of this outspoken new winemaker.

However, three years at Kaiser Stuhl found Wolf Blass' ambitions and ideas without an outlet and this frustration led to his departure from the company to become Australia's first freelance winemaker since Leo Buring made a similar move in 1919. Earning $2.50 per hour, Wolf drove from winery to winery, seven days a week, in his old Volkswagen. Many small wineries were eased into table wine production with his assistance. Wolf became winemaker for Tolley, Scott and Tolley's new Tollana Winery, whilst continuing to a lesser degree with his own winemaking.

In the course of his time spent at Tollana, which ended in 1973, Wolf purchased a couple of hectares on the Sturt Highway north of Nuriootpa. There, he built a large shed which became his winemaking headquarters. Today, it is a magnificent complex, set among gardens and fountains, much of which was created by Wolf himself. The public relations/entertainment area of the winery is opulent in its decor, indicating the priority given to wine-drinkers on all levels. Although Wolf was trained in white and sparkling wine production, the first Wolf Blass wine was a red; a shiraz made in 1966. The grapes were brought from Langhorne Creek, an area that has supplied much of the red fruit he has used over the years. The contacts he established as a consultant with small wineries enabled him to utilise their facilities for his own winemaking.

By the mid-1970s, Wolf Blass' domination of the wine shows was widespread and consistent. In 1975, Wolf Blass became the first company ever to win the Jimmy Watson Trophy at the Melbourne Show for three consecutive years. The company also won the Montgomery Trophy

for the best commercially available red wine at the Adelaide Show six years running, and the best red wine in the Sydney Show for the years 1981 to 1983. Needless to say, the wine industry could only marvel at such a success story.

Throughout this period, Wolf produced only red wines, but this was to change during a visit to Singapore when he tasted a well-

known Australian wine, popular at the time. He found the white wine too acidic and hard, and decided it was time for a new well-balanced Aussie white. Determined to bring about the necessary changes for a new wine, Wolf immediately rang his bewildered winemaker, John Glaetzer, who was at that time bottling one of the first vintages of the Wolf Blass Rhine Riesling and told him to

wines starting with the Yellow Label Rhine Riesling which contains fruit from the Wolf Blass vineyards in Clare, the Classic Dry White; a predominantly wood-aged chardonnay blend; and the Green Label Frontignac Traminer. Wolf Blass also produce a full flavoured chardonnay cuvee (blend) champagne which is excellent. This wine spends some time lying on its lees, ensuring maximum flavour development and is therefore, capable of favourably "taking on" the French sparkling wines. In 1987 Wolf took over the old Quelltaler winery in Clare and launched his Eaglehawk brand, utilising the Eagle hawk symbol so prominent on his own distinctive labels. In 1991 Wolf's growing interest in tourism, horse racing and a desire to step back a little from his stressful lifestyle led him into a merger with Mildara Wines, also a dynamic company and fast expanding. The synergy of the move was perfect and today the Wolf Blass wines continue to please the palates of an ever growing wine

halt production. On his return, Wolf added grape juice concentrate giving greater balance and fruit to the wine. The key to Wolf's success is simple - not only is he a master winemaker, blender and marketer, but he produces wines that people want to drink. Constantly questioning the people with whom he comes in contact, Wolf has been able, because of this feed back to ascertain popular taste and through his skill as a winemaker to produce wines that people enjoy. The Wolf Blass range of red wines are nearly all blends, these include the Black Label, which is mainly cabernet sauvignon with some shiraz and the Grey Label which is 100% Langhorne Creek cabernet sauvignon. There is also a range of white drinking public around the world. The Mildara Blass team of winemakers and marketers have built the most successful public wine company, and Wolf Blass Wines are a real cornerstone in this success story. Ein Prosit Wolfie!!

St Hallett Wines

In 1988, a small band of Barossa producers joined Carl Lindner at the St Hallett winery. A partnership developed to create a bolder image and style for St Hallett, while pursuing their love of the industry.

Carl commenced the "revival" through vineyard acquisitions and development with winemaker Stuart Blackwell assigned to upgrading the winery and equipment. He then set out to produce wines that would meet the approval of the Australian public.

The third in this partnership, Bob McLean, was an electrician by trade and a part-time bouncer by build, he found his niche as 'marketer'. Applying a very simplistic approach to St Hallett's marketing he criticises others in the industry by saying "too many people lose sight of the fact they are in the business of producing 26 ounces of happiness". How basic it all is.

St Hallett believes the Barossa is one of the most unique wine producing regions of Australia. The valley extends over many boundaries, from the extreme heights of the Barossa Ranges to the hot flat plains of the Valley floor. Soils differ from dark clay to river loam to sandy, and varying micro-climates enable enormous diversity in the wine styles produced.

There are now more premium quality 'appellation' wines being made by individual winemakers than ever before in the Valley's 150 year history. St Halletts is in an enviable position sourcing fruit from its own vineyard

Bob McLean

and purchasing fruit from growers, this enables greater flexibility and access to some of the best fruit of the Barossa region.

The Old Block Shiraz, was the forerunner of a number of premium big Australian wines made from the grapes of very old vines. A number of traditional Barossa growers have a long-term arrangement to produce grapes for The Old Block; the vines vary from around 70 years old to over a

century. The wine was a huge success under Stuart Blackwell's skilled supervision and led to an enlarged range of St. Hallett premium bottled table wines. Other medium-priced wines of exceptional quality including The Poachers Blend, named after the old story involving poachers and the creek at the end of the winery's land, have been most successful additions to the St. Hallett stable.

ST HALLETT WINES
Address: St. Halletts Road, Hallett Valley, Tanunda SA 5352
Phone: (085) 63 2319
Fax: (085) 63 2901
Established: 1944
Winemaker: Stuart Blackwell
Principal varieties grown: Shiraz, cabernet sauvignon, semillon, chardonnay
Ha under vine: 50
Average annual crush: 950 tonnes
Average no. cases produced: 40,000

Principal wines & brands	Cellar potential
Old Block Shiraz	5-10 years
Cabernet Sauvignon	5-10 years
Cabernet Franc Merlot	2-5 years
Gamekeeper's Reserve	2-5 years
Chardonnay	2-5 years
Semillon-Sauvignon Blanc	2-5 years
Poacher's Blend	2-5 years

Public & trade tours: By appointment only
Cellar door & mail order sales: Yes
Hours open to public: 10 am-5 pm Mon-Sat; 10 am-5 pm Sun (summer)
11 am-5 pm Sun (winter)
Points of interest: Function facility, large lawns around dam and vineyard. State of the art winemaking facility.
Retail distribution: National, Inchcape Liquor Marketing; export, UK, France, Germany, Canada, USA, New Zealand.

Yalumba

Yalumba is at the forefront of premium wine production in Australia. It is managed by S. Smith and Sons Pty Ltd and 100% family owned. The Hill-Smith family manage their business in an innovative way, encouraging open communication and a team spirit. The relationship between staff and management is also excellent and this overall co-operation has contributed markedly to their success.

Unlike the majority of Barossa Valley Wine companies which were established by German immigrants, Yalumba was founded by an Englishman, Samuel Smith, who was a Dorset brewer whose first work in Australia was for George Fife Angas at Angaston. Whilst employed for George Fife Angas, Smith purchased 12 hectares of land on the lower slopes of the Barossa Ranges, which he planted with vines. He called his property "Yalumba" which is Aboriginal for "all the country around". This was ultimately an auspicious choice as the Yalumba empire grew to cover just that.

In 1852, Smith, like many others headed to the goldfields and with singular luck, struck gold. He returned to the Barossa, purchased a further 32 hectares and established a winery. Although he did not live long enough to see it, by the turn of the century Yalumba was one of the largest and most successful wine companies in Australia.

Robert Hill-Smith is now managing director, having guided a family buy-out along with his late father, Wyndham. They purchased the business from many cousins including Mark, Michael and Matthew Hill Smith.

Yalumba and the S. Smith & Son family have ongoing projects aimed at producing the best possible grapes for their winemaking team to work with. Now, under the eye of their viticulturist Robin Nettelbeck, S. Smith & Son have established a substantial vine nursery and viticultural research unit. Their good work is obvious when you visit any of their vineyards in the Eden Valley or "The Menzies" Vineyard at Coonawarra; these vines are a joy to behold. Needless to say, the Yalumba wine stable since the late 1980s is flawless - each year the wines just keep getting better. Clonal selection, fruit evaluation trials and grafting techniques might all sound a bit obscure and highbrow, but their relevance comes through loud and clear in the finished wines.

S. Smith and Sons choose the best possible and most suitable micro-climates for each grape variety they wish to plant. They have developed three areas in the Eden Valley hills with Pewsey Vale, Heggies, and Hill Smith Estate. All three vineyards are separate, self sufficient concerns, with wines appearing under their respective names. Common resources are shared at Yalumba's winery, however, where all the fruit is processed.

Yalumba owns additional vineyards at Oxford Landing in the Riverland. "The Menzies" and "The Hawthorn's" vineyards in the Coonawarra and vineyards in the emerging winegrowing region of Koppamurra.

Yalumba have a unique way of honouring those family members, friends or business associates who have in some way assisted or been very dear to the company. The idea occurred to Wyndham Hill Smith when Sir Robert Menzies described a 1961 Yalumba Special Reserve Stock Galway claret as "the finest Australian wine I have every tasted". Yalumba began holding back the best red each year and releasing it only when they felt the wine had achieved sufficient maturation both in wood and bottle. The flagship wine series became known as "The Signature".

I recently had the privilege and pleasure of tasting every Signature release going back from 1990 to 1962; what a wonderful way to imbibe Australia's wine history. From 1988 onwards the wines have become richer and more full-bodied; they would be great to put down in the cellar. My pick of The Signatures were the wines commemorating the winemakers of their eras, Rudi Kronberger (1967) and Peter Wall (1990).

Recently, Yalumba began a new red wine tradition of Barossa Shiraz with "The Octavius I" and "The Octavius II". These substantial wines are aged in Octaves, the smallest casks used commercially for wine.

The oak complexity can be infused into the wine in a shorter time with more wood contact, thus maximising the fruit character of the wine - they are indeed awesome shiraz wines.

Yalumba have also entered into a unique arrangement with Mildara Blass whereby Mildara have purchased all the lovely old fortified brands like Galway Pipe Port and directors Special Tawny Port. Yalumba continue to make them and age them and Mildara Blass distribute them nationally.

If reflects sensible and admirable wine industry co-operation and enabled Yalumba to get the necessary capital injection for future development.

YALUMBA WINERY
Address: Eden Valley Road, Angaston SA 5353
Phone: (085) 61 3200
Fax: (085) 61 3393
Established: 1849
Owner: Hill Smith family
Winemaker: (Chief) Brian W. Walsh
Principal varieties grown: Riesling, chardonnay, cabernet sauvignon, shiraz
Ha under vine: 572
Average annual crush: 20,000 tonnes
Average no. cases produced: 480,000

Principal wines & brands	Cellar potential
The Signature	10+ years
'D' Methode Champenoise	
Family Reserve Range	
Oxford Landing Range	
Angas Brut NV Cuvee	
Galway Hermitage	2-5 years
Christobels Classic Dry White	

Trade tours: By appointment only
Cellar door sales: Yes
Hours open to public: 9 am-5 pm Mon-Fri; 10 am-5 pm Sat/PH; 12-5 pm Sun.
Points of interest: Gardens, Yalumba building, catering by appointment
Retail distribution: All States - Samuel Smith & Son

The region known as the Clare Valley incorporates four main river systems and stretches for 30 - 35 kms in length and 5 - 10 kms in width. There are five sub-divisions within the valley, proceeding south from the northern end, they are the sub-regions of Clare, Sevenhill, Watervale, Polish Hill River and Auburn. Each has its own geographic and climatic characteristics. Some of the vineyards are quite elevated, and although the general climate could be described as continental, each small area is subject to its own microclimate. Many Clare wines exhibit distinct cool climate characteristics and intense varietal fruit flavours.

Compared to the Barossa Valley, the Clare Valley has a later growing period and vintage, with fruit ripening after the intense heat of summer.

John Horrocks first settled in the area very early in the state's history in 1840. He named his property Hope Farm and planted some vines there. While on a trip to England, Horrocks ordered some South African vine cuttings to be sent back to his property and planted them. Unfortunately Horrocks died in a shooting accident at the age of 28, having set the area on its viticultural course.

Another early settler, Irishman Edward Gleeson, named the valley after his home, County Clare. Gleeson brought many new vine cuttings into the area, and the industry progressed slowly until the 1890s when planting greatly increased. The Clare Valley was planted largely with red grape varieties such as shiraz, cabernet sauvignon and malbec. These

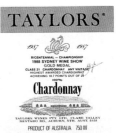

were gradually replaced with higher yielding varieties as the demand for fortified wines grew.

In 1894, the Stanley Wine Company was established and it quickly became one of the largest vignerons in the state.

The four companies still operating in Clare after the depression were Stanley, Buring & Sobels, Sevenhill and Birks Wendouree. During the 1950s, many companies re-established themselves for table wine production by planting high quality grape varieties, particularly riesling. Today, riesling has almost become synonymous with the Clare Valley and recently major wine companies such as BRL Hardy and Petaluma have planted riesling vineyards in the area. Penfolds and Taylors have extensive new vineyards near Sevenhill and Auburn respectively.

The Clare Valley has continued to attract winemakers as an exciting area for premium wine production. Some of the fruit grown in the region however is moved to wineries in other areas for processing. Clare Valley grapes, particularly riesling, are very much in demand all over Australia.

Today, there are more than 20 wineries in the region and its reputation and new plantings are both rapidly increasing.

In 1984, Clare became the first region to introduce the concept of a gourmet weekend of wine, food, music and art, a celebration of the culture of wine, and each May this most successful event reconfirms the Clare Valley's elevated position in the Australian wine industry.

Clare Valley

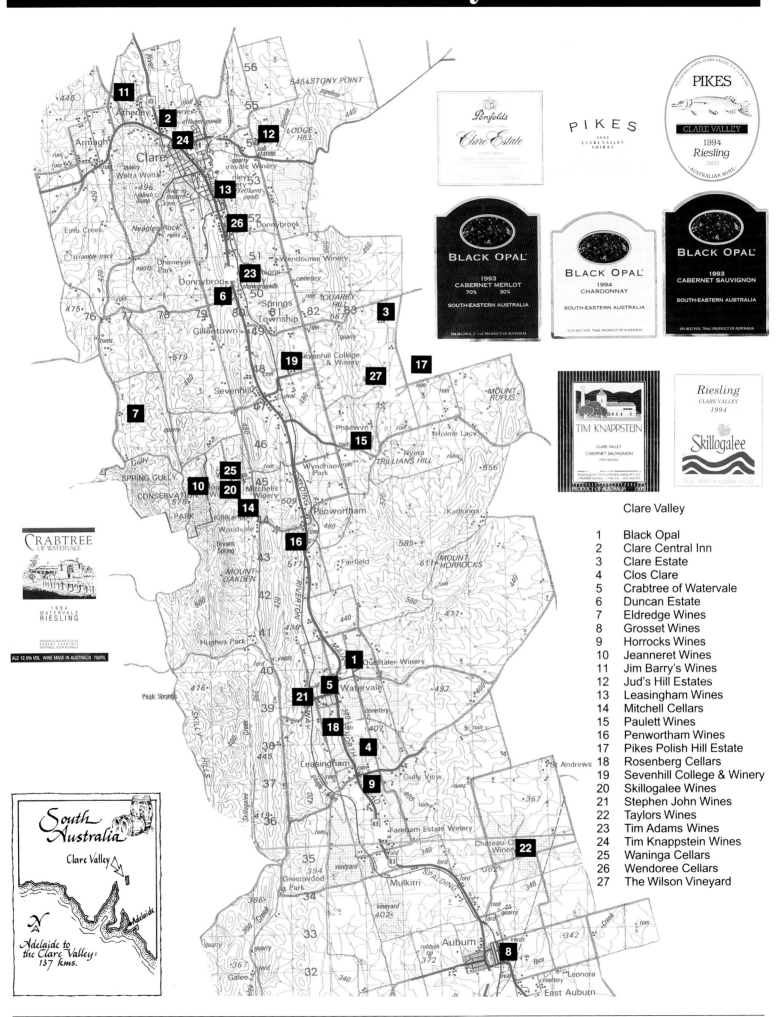

Clare Valley

1. Black Opal
2. Clare Central Inn
3. Clare Estate
4. Clos Clare
5. Crabtree of Watervale
6. Duncan Estate
7. Eldredge Wines
8. Grosset Wines
9. Horrocks Wines
10. Jeanneret Wines
11. Jim Barry's Wines
12. Jud's Hill Estates
13. Leasingham Wines
14. Mitchell Cellars
15. Paulett Wines
16. Penwortham Wines
17. Pikes Polish Hill Estate
18. Rosenberg Cellars
19. Sevenhill College & Winery
20. Skillogalee Wines
21. Stephen John Wines
22. Taylors Wines
23. Tim Adams Wines
24. Tim Knappstein Wines
25. Waninga Cellars
26. Wendoree Cellars
27. The Wilson Vineyard

Black Opal

Through many changes of name and many great winemakers, this beautiful old winery in the centre of the Clare Valley at Watervale remains as a reminder of the grandeur of days gone by.

Of recent years, the winery has been thoughtfully and thoroughly restored by the Mildara Blass Company and now sports the new name of Black Opal. It is true to its name, a real gem in the crown of Australian wine and it has been a hugely successful export brand for Mildara, particularly in the USA.

Black Opal's history goes back to 1860 when Walter Hughes purchased the property. Vines had already been planted by a previous owner and as these came to bear fruit, Hughes hired Carl Sobels to supervise winemaking and the construction of a winery. After his employer's death, Sobels formed a partnership with Herman Buring and they bought the property in 1890.

By this stage the number of hectares under vine had increased to more than 30, and wine production was increasingly

successful. To formalise the establishment of this new business, the property was renamed Quelltaler which is derived from the German translation of 'Spring Vale.' Leaving Sobels and his sons to manage the winery and vineyard, Buring supervised the company's distribution from Adelaide. The stone houses built at Quelltaler to accommodate Carl Sobels' growing family are still lived in and beautifully maintained.

The most popular wines made by Quelltaler during the first years of this

century were their hock (made from rhine riesling), sauternes and San Carlo Claret. The Quelltaler Hock was probably the first wine of its style to be made in Australia and many companies attempted to emulate it for decades without success. As well, the Granfiesta Flor Sherry was both acclaimed and very popular during the 1930s. The Sobels family remained with Quelltaler until the 1960s.

The winery is now owned by the progressive Mildara Blass Company, who apart from their sensitive restoration of the classic old winery and its magnificent museum have invested heavily in the vineyards and re-equipped the winery with the latest state of the art winemaking technology.

In a real coup in 1995, Black Opal has lured the renowned and respected winemaker David O'Leary from BRL Hardy. David, winner of the 1988 Jimmy Watson Trophy, has wasted no time in re-commissioning the classic old open fermenting tanks to create some of his classic reds. On the day of our visit, it was the first day of the vintage and the dark rich red shiraz grapes and skins were already bubbling away in the old fermenters, filling the winery with that indescribable scent of vintage; the whole place had a happy feel as if it was rediscovering its soul and destiny. Watch out for the gems from Black Opal who will surely add to the reputation of Australian wine around the world.

Penfolds Clare Estate

In line with their policy of investing heavily in top quality viticultural regions, Penfolds in 1980 began establishing a large vineyard in the highly respected Polish Hill River Valley, next door to The Wilson Vineyard.

For a number of years, Penfolds have released a truly great red wine, made in the Bordeaux style from the varieties of cabernet sauvignon, merlot, malbec and cabernet franc. The wine has been very quietly promoted and remains a true hidden gem for the lover of big opulent reds, yet with some elegance and complexity.

Penfolds started their move into Clare with the purchase of the old Clarevale Co-op. This was consolidated by Southcorp's (Penfolds' parent company) buyout of Lindemans and Leo Buring, who had produced some extraordinary white wines in the region.

As one stands on the hill above the new plantings in the vineyard and gazes at the vine posts stretching over the hills into the distance, one feels anticipation for the great wines that are surely just over the horizon.

Clare Central Inn and Treloars Restaurant

Right next door to Tim Knappstein's beautiful winery in the old stone buildings of the former Enterprise Brewery is the Clare Central Motor Inn.

Hosts Barry and Phyl O'Connor are warmly hospitable and go about their work at this very well-appointed inn with real professionalism. Barry's up every morning cooking breakfast and Phyl has everything in tip-top order.

Treloars restaurant is decorated in simple good taste and the meals are well known by the local winemakers as the best in town, an innovative blend of French and Asian cuisines. The wine list offers a carefully thought out representation of the region's wines, both in style and price.

The rooms are spacious and tastefully decorated; each features a long bench where the light breakfast supplied can be prepared. Families are made welcome in spacious two-bedroom family suites. Many of the rooms are equipped with spas for the ultimate, relaxing treat at the end of the day's adventure around the region's wineries.

I'm sure you will feel very much at home in the Clare Central, one of the best and certainly best value wine regional accommodation and eating houses.

Jim Barry

Jim Barry is a legendary Clare identity. After graduating from the first post-war Roseworthy course in 1946 he became the first Roseworthy graduate to work in the valley in 1947 and brought with him the first pH (acid meter) used in Clare winemaking when he began his 22 years with the Clarevale Co-operative Winery, many of these as its general manager.

In 1959 Jim began to plant his own vineyards with a view to beginning a family wine business involving his children. Gradually, Jim bought land around the Valley and with his children's assistance planted vines. Their cellar door operations began in 1974 and today four of Jim's six children are directly involved in the business. Peter is general manager, Mark is winemaker, with Julie and John both toiling hard in various areas of the wine business.

Jim Barry and his family now have over 100 hectares of their own vines planted throughout the valley - from the northern flats on the edge of town to the high, cool ranges in the east, and the famous 'Florita' vineyard at Watervale where the Jim Barry Watervale Riesling is produced.

With their 1985 vintage the Barry's started a great tradition with The Armagh, a shiraz of mammoth proportions from their extremely low-yielding Armagh vineyard on the western flats of Clare, planted by Jim back in 1968. The name Armagh, which was given circa 1859, to a settlement 4 kilometres west of Clare, dates back to

County Armagh and was bestowed by the Irish settlers of the region.

Jim Barry has also released a second shiraz from the 1992 vintage called McCrae Wood, named after a vineyard planted on land bought by Jim from an old friend,

Duncan McCrae Wood. It is like a junior version of the opulent Armagh; both are huge wines, yet balanced, flavoursome and approachable even when young.

The Barry family have also restored to original, a classic FJ Holden. Bought new in Clare in 1956 by Jim's father, Frederick James Barry, it has travelled only 63,000 miles and is in mint condition. Jim Barry has enjoyed a prosperous career making wine in Clare, a tradition which will be continued by his children.

JIM BARRY WINES
Address: Main North Road, Clare SA 5453
Direction: 3 km north of post office
Phone: (08) 8842 2261
Fax: (08) 8842 3752
Established: 1959
Owner: Jim Barry
Winemaker: Mark Barry (eldest son)
Principal varieties grown: Riesling, sauvignon blanc, chardonnay, cabernet sauvignon
Ha under vine: 100
Average no. cases produced: 40,000

Principal wines & brands	Cellar potential
The Armagh	5-10 years
McCrae Wood Shiraz	5-10 years
Watervale Riesling	2-5 years
Personal Selection	
Cabernet Sauvignon	5-10 years
Personal Selection Chardonnay	2-5 years
Sentimental Bloke Port	10+ years

Trade tours: By appointment only
Cellar door & mail order sales: Yes
Hours open to public: 9 am-5 pm Mon-Fri; 9 am-4 pm w/e and PH
Points of interest: Excellent view, well balanced range of wines, sparkling wine, table wine, dessert wine, port
Retail distribution: Negociants Australia, SA, WA, Vic, NSW, Qld; Australian Liquor Marketers, Launceston & Hobart, Northern Territory

---

DUNCAN ESTATE
Address: PO Box 5003, Clare SA 5453
Direction: West of Clare Caravan Park along Spring Gully Road
Phone: (08) 884 34335
Fax: (08) 884 34335
Established: 1968
Owner: Jim and Nancy Barry
Winemaker: John Duncan
Principal varieties grown: Riesling, chardonnay, sauvignon blanc, traminer, semillon, grenache, cabernet sauvignon, shiraz, merlot, malbec, pinot noir, petit verdot
Ha under vine: 6.5
Average annual crush: 25-30 tonnes
Average no. cases produced: 2,000

Principal wines & brands	Cellar potential
Clare Valley Riesling	2-5 years
Cabernet Sauvignon/ Merlot/Shiraz	10+ years
Shiraz	10+ years
Clare Valley Chardonnay	2-5 years

Public & trade tours: By appointment only
Cellar door & mail order sales: Yes
Hours open to public: 10 am-4 pm daily
Retail distribution: Clare Valley Discount Liquor Store, SA; Aust Liqor marketers, Tas; Toorak, Vic; Nick Stores, Doncaster, Malvern & City, Vic.

MITCHELL WINES
Address: Hughes Park Road, Sevenhill via Clare SA 5450
Phone: (08) 8843 4258
Fax: (08) 8843 4340
Established: 1975
Winemaker: Andrew Mitchell
Principal varieties grown: Riesling, shiraz, semillon, cabernet sauvignon
Average no. cases produced: 18,000

Principal wines & brands	Cellar potential
Watervale Riesling	2-5 years
Semillon	2-5 years
Peppertree Vineyard Shiraz	5-10 years
Cabernet Sauvignon	5-10 years
Growers Grenache	2-5 years

Trade tours: By appointment only
Cellar door & mail order sales: Yes
Hours open to public: 10 am-4 pm seven days
Retail distribution: All states of Australia, United Kingdom, USA (limited), New Zealand, Switzerland

Leasingham

Towards the end of last century, the Clare Valley saw an enormous growth in viticulture. The wine market had been very healthy and many Australian wines were exported, particularly to England.

With so many new vines a grape surplus looked imminent. A syndicate was formed, made up of the valley's leading industry members, including J H Knappstein, the area's largest grower. The new syndicate was called the Stanley Wine Company and purchased the Clare jam factory for conversion into a winery. Stanley's first vintage was in 1895, their first winemaker being Alfred Basedow, of the famous winemaking family. Alfred had studied at Montpellier in France and after only a few years at Stanley, he was presiding over one of the largest wineries in South Australia.

Due to trouble on the export market however, wine stocks began to build up. By 1911 Knappstein had bought out his partners and owned the company. After much hard work in re-establishing overseas markets, Knappstein left the company in good shape when he died in 1919.

By the mid 1940s, under new management, Stanley were selling bulk wine to most major companies, particularly Lindemans. Five years later the company began developing their vineyards at Leasingham, near Watervale. Rhine riesling and cabernet sauvignon were the major grape varieties planted. Stanley developed a unique system with their vineyard employees, who were paid with a share of the value of the crop. In this way, enthusiasm was generated, and the vineyards were developed quickly and successfully.

Stanley began marketing bottled wine under their own label during the 1960s. New equipment was acquired for the winery and Leasingham grew in stature. In 1970 the first vintage of the multi-award winning Leasingham Bin 56 Cabernet Malbec was released.

In 1971 the winery was taken over by H J Heinz. The Leasingham Bin wines grew in stature and in the mid 70's were one of the highest regarded labels in Australia. In 1984 H J Heinz moved the Stanley cask operation to Buronga in NSW, across the border from Mildura in the Sunraysia region. The Sunraysia was a source of good quality cheaper grapes perfect for the Stanley wine casks. The premium side of the business - Leasingham remained in the Clare Valley.

Thomas Hardy & Sons purchased both Leasingham and Stanley in 1988. Hardy's

recognised the potential of the Clare Valley and spent considerable capital on up-grading the winery and vineyards.

Because of rampant discounting by H J Heinz in the 80's the image of the Bin range label had been badly mauled and was deleted from the Leasingham portfolio. In 1990 the Domain label was launched to replace the Bin's.

Consumers never forgot the Bin wines and in 1993 the winery's centenary saw the re-introduction of the Bin 56 Cabernet Malbec and Bin 37 Chardonnay. A premium limited release range - Classic Clare was also introduced featuring a shiraz and a cabernet sauvignon and more recently a rhine riesling.

Since 1993 the Bin wines have been awarded many accolades, including the 1995 Jimmy Watson Trophy, and have rightfully regained their prestige position, demand has outstripped supply. Bin 61 Shiraz and Bin 42 Semillon Sauvignon Blanc have been added to the portfolio.

After 100 years of winemaking Leasingham has survived the test of time and is firmly established as one of Australia's leading wine producers.

Crabtree of Watervale

Robert Crabtree is a graduate in law from Oxford University. Having practised in the UK for several years, he felt the desire to travel and pursue his interest in wine/viticulture. Robert worked in vineyards and wineries in the Dordogne, Bordeaux in France and in New Zealand. In the late seventies he visited Australia and decided to emigrate and purchase land in the Clare Valley. He studied Oenology at Roseworthy at that time.

Robert now has extensive vineyards in Watervale and lives with his wife Elizabeth and family in a heritage listed stone homestead which has panoramic views of the surrounding district. The winery is modern, having been newly built in 1986. The tasting area is in the original cellars of the homestead. The wines are the classic styles of the region and are excellent examples of Watervale at its best.

Pikes Polish Hill River Estate

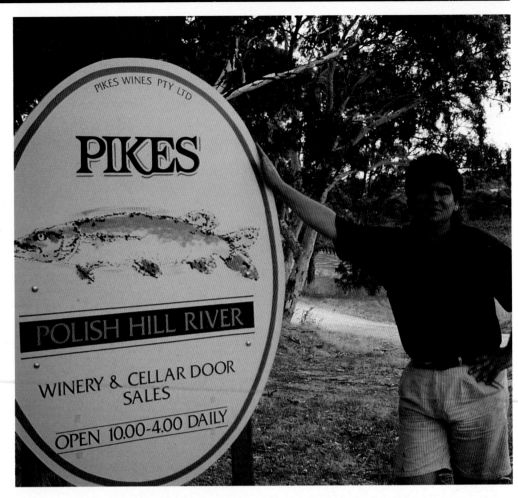

Neil Pike is a gregarious, happy young man with a very positive attitude to life. His family has long been heavily involved in the beverage industry.

Henry Pike, Neil's great-great-grandfather arrived in South Australia in 1878. He settled in the pretty town of Oakbank in the Adelaide Hills and established a brewing and soft drink business, the symbol of which was the distinctive English pike fish.

In 1972, the business was sold; however by this time Edgar Pike, Neil's father, was vineyard manager for a large wine company and dabbling in his own private winemaking. Neil and his brother Andrew both studied viticulture and winemaking at Roseworthy Agricultural College. Andrew is involved in viticulture and management, whilst Neil handles the winemaking and marketing and they are a great team.

Their vineyard was established in 1984 and they made wine from the region the following year. The cool Polish Hill River is a genuine sub-region of the Clare Valley, ripening several weeks after most of the valley, giving the wines that extra depth of flavour and keen cool climate edge. All the Pikes wines will age well; the only problem is they just haven't been able to keep up with demand, particularly from the restaurant trade. The riesling led the way and runs out each year, as does their succulent shiraz with its approachable Rhone Valley character.

Pikes have just released a reserve shiraz, a rigorously selected wine from the best few barrels of the year. The first wine is a 1992 vintage, the next will be a 1994. The 1993, although excellent, didn't rate a reserve selection. Neil and Andrew have dedicated the first reserve to their hardworking and inspirational parents, Edgar and Merle.

Look for the pike fish and make sure he's not the one that got away and was served on someone else's table! After the shiraz and riesling, try the sauvignon blanc and the cabernet with a touch of merlot and cabernet franc.

PIKES WINES PTY LTD
Address: Polish Hill River Road, Sevenhill, Clare SA 5453
Phone: (08) 8843 4370
Fax: (08) 8843 4353
Winemaker: Neil Pike
Principal varieties grown: Riesling, sauvignon blanc, chardonnay, shiraz, cabernet sauvignon, merlot, cabernet franc
Ha under vine: 20
Average annual crush: 200
Average no. cases produced: 15,000

Principal wines & brands/Cellar potential

Riesling	5-10 years
Sauvignon Blanc	0-2 years
Chardonnay	2-5 years
Shiraz	5-10 years
Cabernet sauvignon	5-10 years
Shiraz Reserve	10+ years

Public & trade tours: By appointment
Cellar door & Mail order sales: Yes
Hours open to public: 10-4 daily
Retail distribution: National distribution by Tucker Seabroook Classic Group

Taylors Wines

The Taylor Family established their vineyard and winery at Auburn in the Clare Valley in 1969. The site was carefully chosen for the red brown loam over limestone soils and the cool climate of the Clare Valley. The initial planting consisted of 178 hectares of which 149 hectares were cabernet sauvignon. Today the vineyard has grown to 500 hectares with the addition of three white varieties riesling, chardonnay and crouchen and two red varieties shiraz and pinot noir. In 1973 the first Taylors Estate grown and bottled cabernet sauvignon received a gold medal in every National Wine Show in Australia. Since then every vintage has won awards at National and International Wine Shows. This is reflected by the long list of medals on each Taylors label.

The unique feature of Taylors is that all the wine is made from the single vineyard at the Winery Estate. This provides the solid base of excellent fruit that produces some of the finest and most consistent wines in Australia. The vineyard is well managed by George Finn and Ken Noack and the winemaking is in the capable hands of Andrew Tolley. Bill Taylor, who was one of the founding Directors of the company, is the present Managing Director. His son Mitchell is the Export Director and also assists in the winemaking.

The philosohy at Taylors is to make soft, easy drinking wines and to hold them back from the market until they are ready to drink. This fact together with an obsession for quality, sparing no expense, make Taylors one of the best value wines in the country.

TAYLORS WINES PTY LTD
Address: Mintaro Road, Auburn SA 5451
Direction: 110 kms north of Adelaide (Clare Valley)
Phone: (08) 8849 2008
Fax: (08) 8849 2240
Established: 1969
Owner: Taylor family
Winemaker: Andrew Tolley
Principal varieties grown: Chardonnay, cabernet sauvignon, shiraz, riesling, crouchen, pinot noir
Ha under vine: 500
Average annual crush: 3,000 tonnes
Average no. cases produced: 250,000

Principal wines & brands	Cellar potential
Taylors Cabernet Sauvignon	5-10 years
Taylors Chardonnay	2-5 years
Taylors Shiraz	5-10 years
Taylors White Clare	2-5 years
Taylors Clare Riesling	2-5 years
Taylors Pinot Noir	2-5 years

Public & trade tours: By appointment only
Cellar door & mail order sales: Yes
Hours open to public: 9 am-5 pm Mon-Fri; 10am -5 pm Saturday
Retail distribution: Australia, New Zealand, Malaysia, Hong Kong, Singapore

Wakefield Wines

Wakefield Wines is the export label of Taylor Wines from the Clare Valley which was created due to the restrictions of international trade marks held by Taylor's Port of Portugal and the Taylor Wine Company of the U.S.A. The Wakefield River passes through the vineyards at Auburn and finishes at Port Wakefield where it flows into South Australia's Gulf of St. Vincent.

The Wakefield River was named after Edward Gibbon Wakefield who proposed a system to encourage emigration from Britain by "free" men and women to colonise South Australia as the first free state.

It is the "terra rossa" soils of the Wakefield River that produce cabernet sauvignon, chardonnay and white clare (a unique blend of chardonnay and crouchen) some of the most exciting and interesting wines of the New World.

WAKEFIELD WINES PTY LTD
Address: Mintaro Road, Auburn SA 5451
Phone: (08) 8849 2008
Fax: (08) 8849 2240
Established: 1969
Winemaker: Andrew Tolley

Principal varieties grown: Chardonnay, cabernet sauvignon, shiraz, riesling, crouchen
Principal wines & brands — **Cellar potential**

White Clare	2-5 years
Chardonnay	2-5 years
Cabernet Sauvignon	5-10 years

Retail distribution: England, Ireland, Germany.

Skillogalee Wines

Skillogalee is located in a cool valley, several kilometres west of the main road near the township of Penwortham. Its elevation of some 475 metres and the east-facing slopes of the 48 acre vineyard mean it is one of the latest ripening vineyards in the Clare region.

These factors contribute to fruit ideal for premium table wines which are all 'domaine grown'. Skillogalee is named after a creek running through the bottom corner of the property, so called by explorer John Horrocks in the 1840s. Horrocks had just returned from an exploration into the Flinders Ranges. Running short of food, his party survived on a version of a celtic dish called 'skillogalee' a thin porridge of grass seeds and water and on returning to Penwortham, Horrocks named the creek to commemorate the event.

The property was first settled in the 1850's by John Trestrail, a Cornish miner who certainly had no lack of family help on his farm with 13 surviving children. The property was planted to vines in 1969 by Spencer and Margaret George and in 1989 management consultant Dave Palmer and his wife Diana, a former school teacher who had studied as a chef, bought the property, upgrading the vineyard and opening a restaurant in the 140-year-old stone cottage built by the Trestrail family.

Today the property is a picture, and the

SKILLOGALEE WINES
Address: Hughes Park Road, Sevenhill, Clare SA 5453
Phone: (08) 8843 4311
Fax: (08) 8843 4343
Established: 1970
Winemaker: Dave Palmer
Principal varieties grown: Riesling, shiraz, cabernet sauvignon, cabernet franc, muscat, malbec, traminer
Ha under vine: 22
Average no. cases produced: 7,000
Cellar door & mail order sales: Yes
Hours open to public: 10 am-5 pm seven days a week
Retail distribution: Porter & Co., SA; Domaine Wine Shippers, Victoria; D. Johnstone, Tasmania; Fine Wine Specialist, New South Wales; FNQ Winemerchants, N Qld.

wines are of extremely high quality. These include an excellent spicy gewurztraminer, a sparkling riesling, a vintage port in the dry Portuguese style, as well as a liqueur muscat and more traditional styles.

The restaurant started in 1990 as a casual adjunct to the cellar door operation, but now enjoys an enviable reputation in its own right. It is open for lunch seven days a week and serves morning and afternoon teas. Why not drop in on the Palmers for a very pleasant lunch and tasting?

The Wilson Vineyard

When John Wilson went looking for his vineyard site in 1973, he had a soil map and a sampling auger. These led him to an obscure little hollow aside the main valley of Clare, that was known as Polish Hill River. It was grazing country, and well-meaning locals were quite generous in their advice about the unsuitability of the area for vineyards. The locals were wrong. The Wilson vines thrived and the wines were beyond expectations. Soon others followed, and today, as John Wilson savours his wines and success, he looks down over a small valley system with hundreds of hectares of young vines. He is certainly a deep thinking person who has a great eye for detail and is passionately involved with all he does. His love of trains is evident, as a huge rail car which is still under renovation adorns the vineyard.

Recently completed is a large semi-underground cellar with a hill of earth piled over it, much like the classic old cellar at Chateau Reynella. This of course provides an ideal maturation cellar for the Wilson Vineyard wines.

John is fascinated by the history of the region and has a wealth of information on the Polish immigrants who settled this unique area of South Australia. These religiously persecuted Poles arrived in South Australia in 1856. Thirty five families settled along the upper reaches of the Hill River, which in time became known as Polish Hill River. They spoke an ancient dialect of the Posen region of Western

THE WILSON VINEYARD
Address: Polish Hill River Road, Sevenhill SA 5453
Phone: (08) 8843 4310
Established: 1974
Owner: The Wilson family
Winemaker: John Wilson
Principal varieties grown: Riesling, cabernet sauvignon, chardonnay, shiraz, merlot, viognier, zinfandel, gewurztraminer
Ha under vine: 13
Average annual crush: 60 tonnes
Average no. cases produced: 4,000

Principal wines & brands	Cellar potential
Gallery Series Riesling	2 5 years
Gallery Series Cabernet Sauvignon	5-10 years
Hippocrene (Sparkling Red)	5-10 years
Chardonnay	2-5 years
Zinfandel (375ml only)	10+ years
Liqueur Gewurztraminer (375ml only)	10+ years

Public & trade tours: By appointment only
Cellar door & mail order sales: Yes
Hours open to public: 10 am-4.30 pm w/e (subject to stock being available)
Points of interest: 1928 ex-South Australian Railways railcar being restored available for club tastings or lunch groups of 15-30
Retail distribution: Adelaide, Sydney, Melbourne.

Poland, a dialect that continued with the second, and even third generations, well into this century. Their dialect in fact died out in Poland, amazing some Polish linguists who discovered it still being spoken in the Clare Valley. The Poles moved on when their growing families outgrew the land in the region. Today many of their descendants are farming the plains to the west and north of Clare.

John Wilson began planting his property in 1974 and the winery was licensed in 1980. Today about 30 acres of the 150 acre property are planted to vines, like many in the region, The Wilson Vineyard specialises in riesling. The labels for the cabernet sauvignon since the 1988 vintage have featured a painting of the regional landscape

by a different local artist each year. This tradition has continued with the 1995 riesling, which is an excellent wine showing the typical fruit characters of the region, tropical guava and lychee overtones. I am sure it will develop splendidly with bottle ageing.

Fortunately for those without the patience to bottle-age their rieslings, The Wilson Vineyard usually has a 5-6 year old wine still available in limited quantities.

John Wilson is a really genuine vigneron who wants to share the joy and health-giving aspects of wine with as many appreciative people as possible. Also look out for his excellent cabernet sauvignon and the Hippocrene Sparkling Burgundy to toast The Wilson Vineyard's continued success.

Tim Knappstein

The Knappstein name has been involved wine business in Clare in the since 1895 when the local brewer, the local doctor, a solicitor and J H Knappstein began the Stanley Wine Company in the premises of the Clare Jam Factory.

When Heinz, of "fifty seven varieties" bought the Stanley Wine Company from the Knappstein family in 1971, they sowed the seeds of a new Knappstein wine business in Clare. At the time the youthful Tim Knappstein was the Chief Winemaker of the Stanley Wine Company and had achieved wine show and chimerical success records second to none, in this early era of the modern premium Australian wine business in Clare, Tim Knappstein began Enterprise Wines in the old brewery building originally owned by the brewer, who was a founding partner in the Stanley Wine Company. Enterprise Wines was later to change its name to Tim Knappstein Wines.

Before leaving the Stanley Wine Company and founding his own wine business in 1976, Tim Knappstein selected land high up against the slate hills to the east of Clare on the edge of the Hill River Station. Here he planted 30 hectares of vineyard, mainly cabernet sauvignon, riesling, merlot sauvignon blanc and chardonnay.

Planted in 1972, the Knappstein Vineyard adjoins Petaluma's Hanlin Hill Vineyard and the 45 hectare Yertabulti Vineyard currently being planted with premium red varieties to supply Tim Knappstein Wines.

Tim Knappstein Vineyard on Spring Farm Road, Clare, supplied the core fruit for the development of the Tim Knappstein brand during the 1980s. Tim Knappstein riesling, fume blanc and carbernet merlot owe their commercial success to the qualities of the concentrated grapes grown on the Knappstein Vineyard and to Tim Knappstein's dedication and skills as a quality winemaker.

In the early 1980s Tim knappstein began a vineyard at Lenswood in the Adelaide Hills to grow cool area varieties for the development of a different style of wine to the ripe fruit traditional wines of Clare.

Coveting the quality of the Clare Knappstein Vineyard across the fences from their own and respecting the quality image of the Tim Knappstein brand, Petaluma Limited purchased the Tim Knappstein Winery in 1992 and the vineyards in 1995.

Tim Knappstein left Clare and turned to the Adelaide Hills to develop his Lenswood Vineyard Brand, leaving Petaluma's Chief Winemaker of seven years, Andrew Hardy, to take over the reins as manager and winemaker. Although owned by Petaluma Limited, Tim Knappstein Wines operates as a small independent premium quality winery.

Andrew Hardy is the manager and winemaker of Tim Knappstein Wines, having spent the previous seven years as Chief Winemaker and Viticulturist at Petaluma.

Andrew Hardy and Tim Knappstein Wines are dedicated to producing "essence of Clare" and most especially the world renowned dry riesling and full bodied ripe fruit reds.

The 40 hectare Yertabulti Vineyard, adjacent to Knappstein Vineyards, is being planted to supply shiraz, cabernet sauvignon, merlot, malbec and riesling to Tim Knappstein wines

under Andrew Hardy's watchful eye. Adjacent to the Knappstein Vineyards, Yertabulti is on vibrant red earth over limestone as is much of the Clare and Watervale region. In fact, it is argued by some that there is more terra rossa in the Clare Valley than there is in the Coonawarra.

Whatever, one thin is clear! The historically renowned ability of the high perched Clare Valley to produce intense flavoured stone fruits and wine grapes is now supporting a Clare regional renaissance in which Andrew Hardy is dedicated to make Tim Knappstein Wines a leader.

After making a fortune selling supplies to gold prospectors and running stores in Ballarat and Geelong, John Riddoch and his family moved to Coonawarra in 1861. Riddoch purchased 200 acres (80 ha), but within 20 years he owned the extensive property, Yallum Park, which covered tens of thousands of hectares.

On the advice of a local gardener, Riddoch subdivided much of the land into 25-75 ha blocks, forming the Penola Fruit Colony. This land was bought by 'blockers' as they came to be known, who planted and later sold grapes to Riddoch. Until the bank crash in 1893, the Fruit Colony prospered, due to the magic 'terra rossa' soil of the area. This soil covers about 4,800 ha of land in a strip about 1.6 km wide and 14.5 km long.

With 140 ha under vine at Yallum Park, Riddoch built substantial cellars in which to store the wines made from the blockers' fruit. These were largely shiraz, cabernet sauvignon, malbec and some pinot noir. The cellars were built with three distinct gables and have come to be very well known as the building on the Wynns Coonawarra Estate woodcut labels. The cellars were designed to store 340,000 litres of wine but with the depressed market and large vintages, they soon became inadequate. The Yallum shearing sheds at Katnook provided further storage space for Riddoch's wine.

John Riddoch died in 1901 at a time when fortified wines were becoming increasingly popular. The property was taken over by trustees, who gradually disposed of the land, vineyards and wine. Bill Redman arrived in Coonawarra in the year of Riddoch's death and began at Yallum Park. By 1907, at 20 years of age, he had reached the position of head cellarman and was able to purchase a 16 ha block from Riddoch's estate. Redman's first wine was made using an old cheese press and was fermented in hogsheads purchased from Douglas A. Tolley who had agreed to buy the wine for one shilling per gallon (4.5 litres).

After Yallum Park was purchased by Chateau Tanunda in 1919, Redman became the only winemaker in the area, as the wine remaining from Riddoch's estate was distilled into fortifying spirit and brandy - a shocking waste of excellent reds.

In 1945 Woodleys purhased the Yallum Estate, winery, distillery and vineyards and renamed the property Chateau Comaum. Bill Redman and family were commissioned to manage the winery. Wynns purhased the property in 1951, renaming it Wynns

Coonawarra Estate. There are now more than 20 wineries in the region and many more wine companies around Australia either own vines or purchase grapes or wine from the region.

The climate in Coonawarra is cool and occasionally frosts and ripening are problems. There is a constant underground water supply , but there is limestone between it and the terra rossa. This makes establishing vines both difficult and expensive, as the limestone must be ripped through under each row of vines to enable

their roots to reach the water source. Once established, vines are protected from the vagaries of annual rainfall by a constant water supply.

Internationally, Coonawarra is the first region in Australia to have a reputation for its wines and their style as distinct from just being an Australian wine. The south east of South Australia now has wines growing far and wide, new multi-million dollar wine planting schemes seem a dime a dozen, but the name Coonawarra still has the magic which has been hard- earned and deserved.

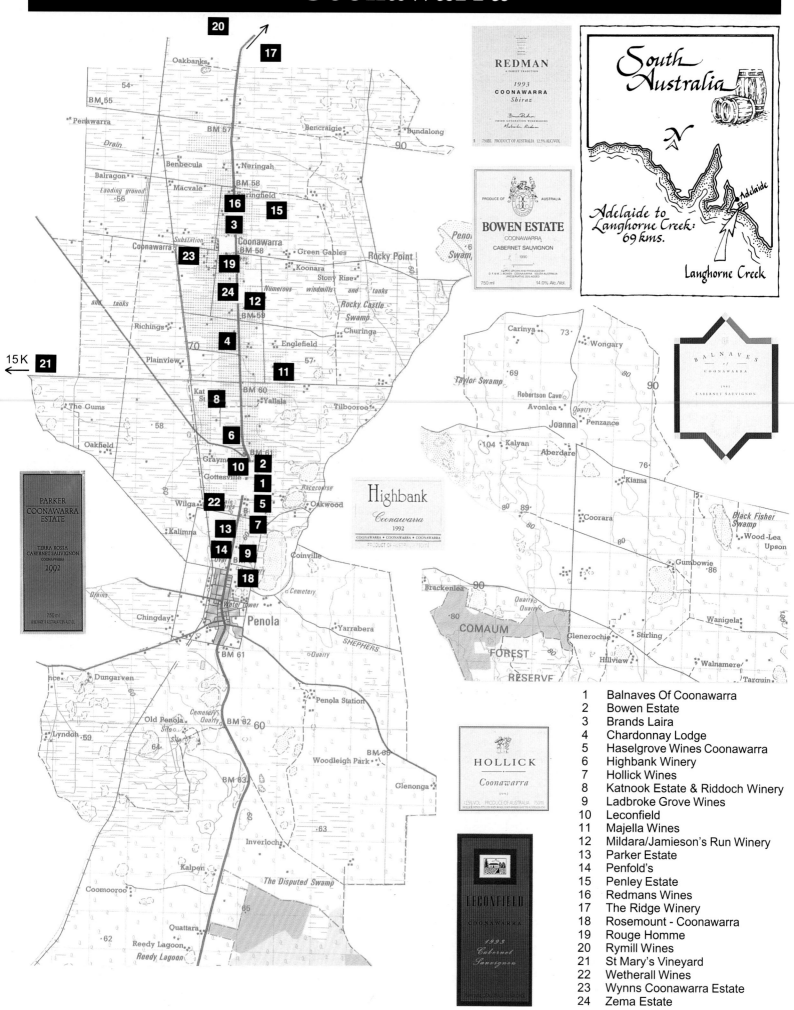

1   Balnaves Of Coonawarra
2   Bowen Estate
3   Brands Laira
4   Chardonnay Lodge
5   Haselgrove Wines Coonawarra
6   Highbank Winery
7   Hollick Wines
8   Katnook Estate & Riddoch Winery
9   Ladbroke Grove Wines
10   Leconfield
11   Majella Wines
12   Mildara/Jamieson's Run Winery
13   Parker Estate
14   Penfold's
15   Penley Estate
16   Redmans Wines
17   The Ridge Winery
18   Rosemount - Coonawarra
19   Rouge Homme
20   Rymill Wines
21   St Mary's Vineyard
22   Wetherall Wines
23   Wynns Coonawarra Estate
24   Zema Estate

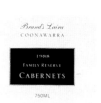

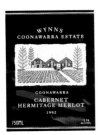

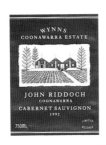

Balnaves of Coonawarra

Doug Balnaves commenced his carreer in the Wine Industry when he developed and managed the Hungerford Hill Vineyards in Coonawarra. In 1975, the family began planting their own vineyards and today they have a magnificent 100 acre vineyard at the southern end of the cigar shaped terra rossa strip, in the heart of Coonawarra.

The predominant variety at Balnaves is cabernet sauvignon, but other varieties include shiraz, merlot, cabernet franc and chardonnay. In 1991 the Balnaves launched their own wine label and opened a state of the art-tasting and cellar door sales area over looking a small lake, always resplendent with native bird life. Doug's wife, Annette, is a great photographer and the Cellar Door sales features some of her excellent work.

Balnaves of Coonawarra uses only about 20% of the grapes for their own wines. The wines include the flagship cabernet sauvignon, a wine called The Blend, a superb merlot/cabernet franc blend, shiraz, chardonnay and a sparkling burgundy made from cabernet sauvignon.

Kirsty Balnaves is responsible for the office administration, and Cellar Door sales and Peter Balnaves manages the vineyards. Balnaves is a high quality family wine business and a great addition to Coonawarra.

BALNAVES OF COONAWARRA
Address: Main Road, Coonawarra SA 5263
Phone: (087) 37 2946
Fax: (087) 37 2945
Established: 1975
Winemaker: Peter Bissell
Principal varieties grown: Cabernet sauvignon, shiraz, chardonnay, merlot, cabernet franc
Ha under vine: 40
Average no. cases produced: 3,000

Principal wines & brands	Cellar potential
Cabernet Sauvignon	5-10 years
Sparkling Burgundy	2-5 years
Chardonnay	2-5 years
Merlot/Cabernet Franc	5-10 years
Shiraz	5-10 years
Cabernet Merlot	5-10 years

Public & trade tours: By appointment only
Cellar door & mail order sales: Yes
Hours open to public: 9 am-5 pm Mon-Fri; 10 am-5 pm w/e & PH
Retail distribution: Cellar door sales only

Bowen Estate

Doug Bowen's nonchalant manner is deceptive; he is actually a very dedicated, talented winemaker and viticulturist.

His love for the Coonawarra region grew out of his student days at Roseworthy, when he wrote his thesis on the area. At the first opportunity Doug and Joy purchased 16 ha of land at the region's southern end and began planting immediately. The winery, a grand looking yet, very functional building of local Mount Gambier stone, was built in 1980 and is now being extended. The establishment of this winery was achieved in less than a decade, an indication of the dedication of the Bowen family.

On completion of his studies in 1971, Doug began work at Lindemans Rouge Homme winery and remained there until his own winery's first vintage in 1975. Since then, Bowen's reds have become among the best and most consistent in the region. Mechanisation now dominates the pruning of vines in Coonawarra but the traditional hand pruning at Bowen Estate has created a style of wines being consistently richer and more opulent and with greater depth of flavour and body. The shiraz exhibits the peppery and spicy cassis flavours much

sought after in this variety. The cabernet sauvignon is a little more intense and in addition shows a herbaceous cool climate character, an effect produced by the cooler conditions experienced in this area. Vintage here is usually a week or two later, a delay which only increases the superb flavours of the wine.

Bowen Estate Chardonnay is a blend of stainless steel and barrel fermented fruit to encapsulate the positive aspects of both

fermentation styles. The rich peach/melon flavours of chardonnay combined with the subtle french oak flavours make for a very strong complex style. Doug spends much of his time in the vineyard and winery, and it is not an easy task to drag him out of either

---

BOWEN ESTATE
Address: Main Road, Coonawarra SA 5263
Phone: (087) 37 2229
Fax: (087) 37 2173
Established: 1972
Owner: D.F. & M.J. Bowen
Winemaker: Doug Bowen
Principal varieties grown: Cabernet sauvignon, shiraz, chardonnay, merlot, cabernet franc, petit verdot
Average annual crush: 160 tonnes

Principal wines & brands	Cellar potential
Cabernet Sauvignon	5-10 years
Shiraz	5-10 years
Cabernet Sauvignon/ Merlot/Cabernet Franc	5-10 years
Chardonnay	2-5 years

Tours: By appointment only
Cellar door & mail order sales: Yes
Hours open to public: 9 am-5 pm Mon-Sat; Open Sunday of long weekends & school holidays
Retail distribution: Tucker, Seabrook Pty Ltd, NSW, Victoria, Queensland; Tucker Seabrook Classic Wines, SA; David Johnstone & Associates, Tasmania; David Mullen Wine Agency, WA

Brand's Laira Wines

Eric Brand married into the wine industry in 1950 when he wed Nancy Redman, Owen's sister. He purchased a small property from Redman, which was mostly orchards, but which also included several hectares of vines, some of which were amongst the first planted in Coonawarra in 1896.

There are still walnut trees along the drive and visitors can buy pickled walnuts from the cellar door. Also, the Original Vineyard, with its one hundred year old vines, continues to produce outstanding red wines, but the early fruit orchards have long since given way to Brand's expanding vineyards.

Eric Brand sold his grapes to local winemakers for many years but began making his own wine in 1966. After many meetings with Hardy's winemaker Dick Heath, Brands were supplied with a crusher and other necessary equipment. The resulting wine was sold to Hardys directly after vintage. Redman's also made wine at Brand's winery before completion of their own.

During the late '60s, Brand's began bottling and selling some wine under the "Laira" label, from their cellar door. "Laira" was the ship owned by Captain Stentiford, the first owner of Brand's property. The red wines released under this label have developed a legendary reputation, and since Eric's sons Bill and Jim have joined the company, some interesting new wines and styles have evolved. Brand's made steady progress in the market place and in fact were innovators in some areas - they produced Coonawarra's first pinot noir in 1982, and were one of Australia's first wineries to produce straight merlot.

The demand for cash for expansion and the challenge of marketing and distributing their wines needed more capital input if Brand's were to reach all their goals. This led to an arrangement with McWilliam's, the strong family wine company from New South Wales. The balance was perfect; McWilliam's were looking to expand into a number of premium table wine regions, Brand's fitted the bill, so in 1990 they took a half share in the company.

Brand's Wines leapt ahead and in 1994 McWilliam's purchased the remaining half of the company. At the same time McWilliam's purchased an additional 200 hectares immediately adjacent to Brand's existing vineyards making it one of the largest landholders in the Coonawarra area. Sensibly McWilliam's have let Jim and Bill Brand stay on and manage things in their very thorough, diligent style. The Brand's wines are consistently among the best in Coonawarra and remain great value for money.

Chardonnay Lodge

S et mong the vines bordering the main road in the heart of Coonawarra is the impressive Chardonnay Lodge. It was built in 1984 by the Yates, Coop and Giles families.

Approaching the main arched doorway, visitors are impressed by the magnificent leadlight glass panelled entrance produced by Barry and Glenys Mulligan of the district's St Mary's vineyard.

The classic Victorian inspired complex spreads out comfortably, surrounded by the poplar trees traditionally used in Coonawarra as windbreaks. The rooms are spacious with high timber ceilings; a family can happily spread out here. Partners James and Anne Yates have managed the establishment for more than ten years and managed it most efficiently. The food in the restaurant is creative and uses many local ingredients and the seminar and function facilities are large and beautifully appointed. Chardonnay Lodge was a pioneer in terms of offering the wine traveller a truly wine integrated experience. Open every day of the year, Chardonnay Lodge provides an ideal stopover for visitors to Coonawarra.

Haselgrove Wines Coonawarra

The Haselgrove connection goes back to the rebirth of the region, in the early 1950s, when Mildara's Ron Haselgrove began planting vineyards.

One of Ron's sons, James, formed his own wine company back in 1981 and opened up a facility on the main road in a substantial old home. The wines were made at the best wineries in the region from James Haselgrove's already established vineyards.

In 1987, the bubbly Di Blok joined the business, astute and filled with an effervescent enthusiasm to make sure the visitor's experience at Haselgrove was both informative and thoroughly enjoyable. In 1992, Di managed the Haselgrove Coonawarra operation on a lease basis and are 1994 puirchased the freehold. The large old home with rambling rooms have a cosy atmosphere and is an ideal environment to enjoy the excellent Haselgrove wines.

Haselgrove also have a winery and vineyard in McLaren Vale. The Coonawarra grapes are sent to the McLaren Vale operation, where expert winemaker Nick Haselgrove makes some fine wines. The Haselgrove Futures Shiraz is one of Australia's best wines and a certain

percentage is sold prior to release. Drop in and see Di, she'll put you on the list for next year's. Try the Haselgrove Botrytis while you are there - it's one of their great array of wines.

HASELGROVE WINES COONAWARRA
Address: PO Box 14, Coonawarra SA 5263
Direction: Main Penola-Naracoorte Road SA 5263
Phone: (087) 37 2734
Fax: (087) 37 2994
Established: 1991 - 1981
Owner: Di & John Blok
Winemaker: Nick Haselgrove
Principal varieties grown: Cabernet sauvignon, shiraz, chardonnay, merlot
Ha under vine: 17
Average annual crush: 400 tonnes
Average no. cases produced: 17,500

Principal wines & brands	Cellar potential
Coonawarra Reserve Cabernet	5-10 years
Cabernet Sauvignon	5-10 years
Coonawarra Chardonnay	2-5 years
All Haselgrove McLaren Vale lines	

Cellar door & mail order sales: Yes
Hours open to public: 10 am-4 pm seven days
Points of Interest: Large lawn area available for b.y.o. picnic lunches, tables and chairs can be arranged also
Retail distribution: Sydney, Melbourne, Adelaide

Highbank

Right in the heart of Coonawarra is the pretty two storey house of Highbank, whose gardens and glowing ambience drags one from the long straight road like a magnet.

Highbank is the creation of the most charming, warm and enthusiastic couple, Dennis and Bonnie Vice, where mi casa is certainly su casa (their house is your house). Dennis is a tall American hailing from San Diego.

Dennis' work brought him often to Australia and he and Bonnie saw it as a great place to settle down and raise their family. Dennis grew great chemical-free grapes and wanted them to be made into the best possible wine. Many times each vintage he made the three-hour drive to Trevor Mast's winery at Langhi Giran near Ararat in Victoria. Trevor is a true master winemaker and the Highbank cabernet sauvignon and chardonnay, now made by Trevor, rank in the top flight of Australian wine.

Beside the winery, under an enormous red gum, is the Highbank Honeysuckle Rise Cottage, a stunning country stone building with a high vaulted ceiling and open plan

living, one of the nicest vineyard bed and breakfasts you could find, with an open log fire to keep you cosy in winter. Above the winery, with the same romantic decor of old colonial times, is the 'Room with a View' with its expansive views over the vineyards. In both venues the fridge is stocked with goodies, from bacon and eggs to foie gras –

HIGHBANK VINEYARDS
Address: Main Penola Road, Warners Corner
Phone: (087) 36 3311 Free Call 1800 653 311
Established: 1986
Winemaker: Dennis Vice, Trevor Mast
Principal varieties grown: Cabernet sauvignon, merlot, cabernet franc, chardonnay
Ha under vine: 4
Average annual crush: 30 tonnes
Average no. cases produced: 700

Principal wines & brands	Cellar potential
Highbank Coonawarra Cabernet Sauvignon	2-10 years
Highbank Chardonnay	2-5 years

Trade tours: By appointment only
Cellar door & mail order sales: Yes
Hours open to public: Weekends/holiday periods, other times by special appointment
Points of interest: Guest Cottages - Honeysuckle Rise or Room with a View
Retail distribution: Dieter Going, Adelaide; Select Vineyards, Melbourne

---

most on the free list.

You can call the free number to book and find out more details on 1800 653 311. Highbank Honeysuckle Rise hospitality is second to none.

Hollick Wines

Ian and Wendy Hollick purchased 40 acres of land at the southern end of Coonawarra in 1974. At the time, Ian was employed by one of the larger Coonawarra wine companies, and in their spare time the couple began developing a vineyard.

Cabernet sauvignon, riesling, merlot, chardonnay and pinot noir were planted during the following six years, until in 1983 the decision was made to build a winery. The winning of the Jimmy Watson Trophy in 1985, with only their third vintage, gave the Hollicks further incentive to expand and in 1987 they purchased the nearby 'Wilgha' vineyard, which is connected to their original property by Ravenswood Lane, a name used for their super premium cabernet sauvignon.

In 1989, Pat and Jenny Tocaciu (ex Penfolds) joined in partnership with the Hollick winemaking team to share the workload. Both Ian Hollick and Pat Tocaciu have a wealth of experience in the wine industry, having worked for many years for larger companies, Ian in the viticulture field and Pat in winemaking. Hands-on winemaking and a personal expression in the

styles of wine produced has attracted these two personalities to the smaller operation, and led to a merger of expertise unmatched in Australia in such a small winery.

The Hollicks have a most beautiful home and tasting area for their wines right in front of the winery, in the form of a cottage that was the home of the poet, John Shaw Nielson. The cottage has been lovingly

restored and the Hollicks take delight in dispensing their warm hospitality along with their wines. A recent addition to their fine stable of reds is 'Terra,' a great Coonawarra blend at a real value price, its name alluding to the rich terra rossa soils that nurtured it.

HOLLICK WINES PTY LTD
Address: Main Road/Racecourse Road, Coonawarra SA 5263
Phone: (087) 37 2318
Fax: (087) 37 2952
Established: 1983
Winemaker: Pag Tocaciu and Ian Hollick
Principal varieties grown: Cabernet sauvignon, cabernet franc, merlot, shiraz, pinot noir, petit verdot, chardonnay, sauvignon blanc, riesling, semillon
Ha under vine: 50
Average annual crush: 400 tonnes
Average no. cases produced:

Principal wines & brands	Cellar potential
Coonawarra	8-10 years
Chardonnay	4-5 years
Sparkling merlot	6-8 years
Cornel	5-10 years

Trade tours: By appointment
Cellar door & mail order sales: Yes
Hours open to public: 9-5 daily
Points of interest: Historic cottage, birthplace of John Shaw Nielson (lyric poet) has been restored for cellar sales area.

Leconfield

The Leconfield vineyard was planted in 1974 and the winery built in 1975 by Sydney Hamilton at the age of 76. Syd was a fourth generation descendant of Richard Hamilton, South Australia's first vigneron ca. 1837.

After retiring from Hamilton Ewelll in the mdi 50s, Syd searched the Australian continent for the site to make the classic Australian Red table wine. He decided on Coonawarra to achieve this ambition. In 1974 Syd planted the vineyard of 12 hectares mainly to Cabernet Sauvignon and the following year used his engineering skills to build the Leconfield winery. Syd created a legend with his early vintages, the 1978 and 1980 Leconfield Cabernets.

In 1981 Leconfield was purchased by Syd's nephew, Dr Richard Hamilton, a plastic surgeon. Dr Hamilton also has a winery and vineyards at McLaren Vale established in 1972.

The Leconfield Cabernets have all been superb wines. The inclusion of merlot and petit verdot into the cabernet blend by respected winemaker, Ralph Fowler, has made Leconfield Cabernet arguably one of Australia's great red wines.

Leconfield, an imposing Romanesque style building constructed of local limestone, is situated right on the main road. It strikes me as some other Coonawarra vineyards do, with its similarity to a Bordeaux chateau. Certainly its cabernets are in the mould of the very best Bordeaux.

LECONFIELD
Address: Penola Road, Coonawarra SA 5263
Direction: 3 km north of Penola
Phone: (087) 37 2326
Fax: (087) 372285
Establishmented: 1974
Owner: Dr Richard Hamilton
Winemaker: Ralph Fowler
Principal Varieties Grown: Cabernet Sauvignon, Merlot, Petit Verdot, Cabernet Franc, Shiraz, Chardonnay, Riesling
Ha under Vine: 25
Average Annual Crush: 400 tonnes
Average No. Cases Produced: N/A

Principal Wines & Brands	Cellar Potential
Cabernet	10+ years
Merlot	10+ years
Cabernet Franc	5+ years
Shiraz	5-10 years
Chardonnay	3-5 years
Riesling	2-5 years

Public & Trade Tours: Yes (By Appointment Only for buses or large groups)
Cellar Door & Mail Order Sales: Yes
Hours open to Public: 10am-5pm Monday - Saturday 11am-5pm Sunday & Public Holidays
Points of Interest: Established by Richard Hamilton, an early pioneer of the wine industry
Retail Distribution: Fine Wine Stores & Premium Restaurants

Mildara - Jamieson's Run Winery

Jamieson's Run has taken the wine world by storm. Mildara launched the name with an exciting new red wine, back in 1987. The wine, a 1985 vintage, was a blend of cabernet sauvignon, shiraz, merlot and cabernet franc and in some years a little malbec is added for balance. The aim with Jamieson's Run is to produce a rich smooth style that is consistent and recognisable year after year.

The choice of the name Jamieson's Run is particularly apt as it was the name of the property at Mildura where the Chaffey Brothers built their original winery, Chateau Mildura, back in 1888. This became the forerunner of Mildara Wines. The connection is even more appropriate because of Mildara's investment in the early 1950s through long time technical and

managing director, Ron Haselgrove who, along with David Wynn, rediscovered Coonawarra and really put it on the wine map.

For many years, one of my favourite red wines was the Mildara Coonawarra CSM (cabernet/shiraz/malbec). I am sure it was this wine, its success and style which influenced Jamieson's Run. The proof of the pudding came in 1989 when the 1988 Jamieson's won the golden urn in the form of the Jimmy Watson Memorial Trophy, the grand prix of Australian wines. After this victory, Jamieson's Run became a truly recognised Australian wine.

Mildara is absolutely committed to the Coonawarra and sees it as the best and most consistent wine region in Australia for red wines. They are extremely well served in the

viticultural area by the experienced Vic Patrick, a dynamic character who was vineyard manager for Wynns Coonawarra for many years.

Mildara's main plantings are red varieties, which are all planted on the red terra rossa soil. The grey and other soil types are reserved for the white wine varieties and pinot noir. Some of the chardonnay and pinot noir is made into base wine for the Yellowglen sparkling wines.

Jamieson's Run chardonnay is no slouch either, a very drinkable wine showing good barrel fermented complexity. In fact any wine bearing the Mildara Coonawarra label is a guarantee of real enjoyment; long-time winemaker Gavin Hogg has got it right.

Katnook Estate and Riddoch Winery

Katnook is a winery with a history that goes back to the early settlement of Coonawarra. John Riddoch was lured to Australia in the early 1850s by the prospect of gold. He did make his fortune, but as a trader, finally arriving in the Coonawarra in 1861. He named his first Coonawarra property Yallum Park, Yallum being derived from an aboriginal word meaning grassy.

Riddoch began by constructing a magnificent sandstone mansion surrounded by splendid gardens and a deer park. He was elected to the South Australian Parliament in 1865 and his land holdings quickly grew to 250 square kilometres. Riddoch became known as the 'Squire of Penola' and his restored home, Yallum Park, can be visited when you are in Coonawarra. Riddoch's first enterprises in Coonawarra were grazing and wool and to this end, he built a woolshed, calling it Katnook. Today, it is an historic monument and the winery for Katnook wines.

In 1890 Riddoch decided Katnook could support closer settlement and horticulture, and he formed the Coonawarra Fruit Colony at Katnook and from the office set up there sold off 10 acre blocks at 10 pounds per acre, a considerable sum in those days. Twenty six colonists began planting fruit and vines on their blocks. The second vintage in 1896 was made at Katnook in the woolshed.

During the 1960s, Melbourne businessman, Peter Yunghaans, purchased the property, replanting vines and building a high-tech, state-of-the-art winery, within the historic old woolshed. The first Katnook wines, made with the help of oenology's dynamic duo, Brian Croser and Dr. Tony Jordan, were sensational and the reds, particularly, gained instant acceptance in the premium wine market. Katnook today is vastly expanded and a further 250 acres of wines are being planted in 1995 and 1996.

Wayne Stephens is the capable, affable winemaker, and his lovely wife ,Michelle, manages promotion and the cellar door sales. Katnook also produce a second label, Riddoch; these wines and the leading label, Katnook, are great examples of the best Coonawarra can produce. Katnook produces Coonawarra's best sauvignon blanc, which has won many gold medals and trophies. John Riddoch would indeed be proud to see the way his old woolshed winery has been restored and the great wines it is producing.

KATNOOK ESTATE	Principal wines & brands	Cellar potential
Address: Penola-Naracoorte Road, Coonawarra SA 5263	Katnook Estate	
	Cabernet Sauvignon	10+ years
Direction: 4 km north of Penola	Chardonnay & Merlot	10+ years
Phone: (087) 37 2394	Sauvignon Blanc	5-10 years
Fax: (087) 37 2397	Chardonnay Brut	5-10 years
Established: 1967	Riesling	10+ years
Owner: Wingara Wine Group	Riddoch	
Winemaker: Wayne Stehbens	Shiraz	5-10 years
Principal varieties grown: Cabernet sauvignon,	Cabernet Shiraz	5-10 years
merlot, shiraz, pinot noir, chardonnay, riesling,	Chardonnay	2-5 years
sauvignon blanc, cabernet franc	Sauvignon Blanc	2-5 years
Ha under vine: 200	Riesling	2-5 years
Average annual crush: 1,100 tonnes	**Public & trade tours**: By appointment only	
Average no. cases produced: 50,000	**Cellar door sales**: Yes	
	Hours open to public: 10 am-4.30 pm seven days	
	Retail distribution: Inchcape Liquor Marketing	

Rouge Homme

Right in the heart of Coonawarra are the Rouge Homme vineyards. Their history dates back to 1908 when the Redman family purchased part of John Riddoch's Penola Fruit Colony.

For half a century, Rouge Homme winemakers supplied wine to other companies and merchants which brought great fame to Coonawarra. But it was not until the release of the 1954 Cabernet Sauvignon, wearing the first Rouge Homme label, that the brand itself began to attract some of that fame.

The translation of the name 'Rouge Homme' - French for 'red man' - signified the similarity of the wines to the red wines of Bordeaux. The 'Richardson's' label was introduced with the 1992 vintage and named in honour of Henry Richardson - one of Coonawarra's pioneer settlers. In 1892 Richardson purchased land offered for sale by Riddoch's Coonawarra Fruit Colony and established a vineyard and winery on the property.

In 1965 the Redman family sold the vineyards and winery which, with the original Richardson property, became Rouge Homme as it is today. Occupying about 60 hectares, the vineyards are planted to classic varieties including shiraz, cabernet sauvignon, cabernet franc, merlot and pinot noir, with a small amount of chardonnay. The Rouge Homme winery is now one of the most modern and sophisticated in Coonawarra. A climate of cold, wet winters and mild to warm, dry summers, allows slow ripening of the grapes, with excellent development of sugar levels and flavour, and the retention of good acidity. Because of the cold winters and springs, the vines at Rouge Homme are trained over especially high trellises, with overhead mist sprinklers to protect them from frosts during spring.

Five Rouge Homme wines are produced today in contemporary labels reflecting the earthy colours of the Coonawarra. The original claret which forged Rouge Homme's early reputation is still made but is today varietally labelled as a shiraz cabernet. This was followed by the straight cabernet sauvignon, a wine of power and presence. Later, Rouge Homme began to produce a pinot noir which consistently exhibits good colour and varietal character. "Richardsons Red Block" is a blend of the classic Bordeaux varieties of cabernet sauvignon, malbec, merlot and cabernet franc. The chardonnay also shines in the white arena.

Winemaker, Paul Gordon, has been with Rouge Homme since 1989. As custodian of the winery's great Coonawarra tradition he continues to produce a range of distinctive, approachable wines which have the potential to develop great complexity with bottle ageing over many years. With a considerable reputation as classic Coonawarras, Rouge Homme wines are frequent gold medal winners - particularly the reds. In 1994, Rouge Homme received what is regarded by many to be the wine industry's greatest accolade - the Jimmy Watson Memorial Trophy.

Lindemans - St George

During the early 1970s the wine boom struck Australia with force, red wine consumption rocketed and names and places become the catchcry of the new devotees to quality wine.

Lindemans, the master blenders of years gone by, decided to attack this market and appeal to its desire for individual and boutique style wines. What better way than to pick out the best parcels of its large Coonawarra holdings and give them individual names, somehow relating to their own history or that of the region. Thus were born the vineyards of Limestone Ridge, St Cedd's, The Nursery Vineyard and the pride of them all, St George. It is a regal name, its origin stemming from a famous viticulturist of years gone by, Surgeon Major-General Hinton St George, an early settler in the region.

This 'vineyard designation' philosophy, as they call it in California, was well before its time and is more and more relevant as Australia's wine industry matures - well done, Lindemans!

The St George vines are, as you can imagine, huge and imposing, producing myriads of small bunches of flavoursome berries. The resulting wines are always full-bodied with broad cabernet character, a leafy herbaceousness and a chewy meaty texture.

The 1980 vintage won the Jimmy Watson Trophy. If you can get some today, you are a very lucky person indeed; it's one of the finest wines I have ever tasted.

Majella

Brian and Anthony Lynn began planting vines back in 1969 when modern day Coonawarra was in its infancy. The two brothers are third generation farmers whose main specialisation was wool; their father named the property Majella after Saint Gerard Majella, a Spanish saint and the patron saint of motherhood. All the produce of the large property goes out under the brand of Majella.

Up until 1991 all the crop from their 85 acres of vines was sold to winemakers in the region. In 1991, they decided to produce a Majella red wine made at Brand's Wines by

MAJELLA WINES
Address: Lynn Road, Coonawarra SA 5263
Phone: (087) 36 3293
Fax: (087) 36 3293
Owner: Brian & Anthony Lynn
Winemaker: Bruce Gregory
Principal varieties grown: Shiraz, cabernet sauvignon
Ha under vine: 35
Average annual crush:
Average no. cases produced: 650

Principal wines & brands	Cellar potential
Majella Shiraz	5-10 years

Mail order sales: Yes
Retail distribution: Limited

Bruce Gregory. At present the vineyard is being expanded to 100 acres, all red grape varieties, about one half cabernet sauvignon and one half shiraz.

The Lynns are a gregarious family and along with their lifelong friend, Bill Brand, and their respective wives, they opened up a great little restaurant in the tiny Coonawarra township, penning for it the name 'Nibs' after the school next door where they all went as kids.

At Nibs you make yourself at home and cook your own food on the large open grill, choosing from a stunning selection of delicacies, accompanied by a creative salad bar. It's become a local success story, so drop in when you are in the region and try out your cooking skills; why not wash it down with a Majella red, with its striking label and great flavour.

Parker Coonawarra Estate

Parker Coonawarra Estate, a 50 acre vineyard property on the main road in the heart of the famous terra rossa strip, is a totally professional operation conceived by three very experienced wine industry identities.

In only a few years it has risen to the very top level of Australian wine. John Parker, who in the late 1960s was founding chairman and chief executive of Hungerford Hill Ltd, had long desired to produce a truly great red wine without normal commercial constraints.

To achieve this aim, he recruited two total professionals with whom he had worked for many years - fifth generation Coonawarra viticulturist, Doug Balnaves, and highly respected winemaker, Ralph Fowler.

Together they produce two red wines both made without regard to cost.

Their flagship wine flies proudly on the label the words 'Terra Rossa First Growth' and is ranked year after year both in Australia and overseas as one of our nation's best red wines. Chiefly cabernet sauvignon, with some merlot and cabernet franc, the exact blend and amount of oak maturation it receives is dependent on the particular vintage. The second wine is simply called Terra Rossa Cabernet Sauvignon, again, an opulent wine which can be enjoyed a little younger than the First Growth.

PARKER ESTATES
Address: Coonawarra SA 5263
Phone: (02) 357 3376
Fax: (02) 358 1517
Established: 1988
Winemaker: Ralph Fowler
Principal varieties grown: Cabernet sauvignon, cabernet franc, merlot
Ha under vine: 21 approx.
Average no. cases produced: 2,000

Principal wines & brands	Cellar potential
Parker Coonawarra Estate first growth	10+ years
Parker Coonawarra Estate Cabernet Sauvignon	2-5 years

Retail distribution: NSW, Young & Rashleigh; SA, Options Fine Wines (08) 223 7554; Qld, J Addley (07) 391 5519; Vic, Domaine Wine Shippers (03) 84 22499.

Rosemount - Coonawarra

In line with the Oatley family philosophy of estate production and the growing of their own grapes in each region, Rosemount established their Kirri Billi vineyard at Coonawarra in 1980.

Rosemount specialise in what they believe Coonawarra does best - cabernet sauvignon. After crushing, the wine is made at the main winery in the Upper Hunter Valley.

Hand pruning and hand picking of Rosemount's premium fruit, a rarity in Coonawarra, shows Rosemount's determination to make a no expense spared classic Coonawarra Cabernet.

The concern that the Oatley family takes in the selection, planting and management of this vineyard is at the heart of this remarkable company's rapid success.

Rosemount, have for their size been the most successful exporter and ambassador for Australian wines overseas, particularly in North America. With Coonawarra's growing reputation far from our shores, Rosemount have put their Coonawarra Show Reserve Cabernet Sauvignon well and truly on the world wine map.

Penley Estate

Kym Tolley is steeped in wine history. His father is Reg Tolley, chairman of the traditional old Tolley Wine Company, his mother was a Penfold Hyland, niece of Jeffrey Penfold Hyland, and in fact his great great great grandfather was Penfold's founder, Dr Christopher Rawson Penfold.

Kym, a Roseworthy graduate winemaker, worked for 17 years at Penfolds before striking out alone and forming Penley Wines in 1988.

In only ten years, Penley Estate have won nine trophies, 50 gold, 61 silver and 121 bronze medals in Australian and international wine shows.

Penley's Vineyard occupies less that half the property, at present, and the 68 hectares of vines comprise cabernet sauvignon, pinot noir, shiraz, chardonnay, merlot, cabernet franc and pinot meunier.

Variable canopy management and a sophisticated water management scheme for each variety and each soil has given Penley the best possible fruit to work with.

Penley Estate utilise the very best 20% of the grapes, the rest are sold to other premium winemakers.

Kym's winemaking philosophy is "Every wine must be the best I can produce". Creating a perfect balance between fruit, tannin and acid to give balance and length of flavour, great fruit, good wood, time, attention to detail and a dose of luck are Kym's well-managed ingredients. Kym's wines must reflect what he feels, in his own words — "My objective has always been to produce the best wines I can, and I will continue to do so in years to come. If something is worth doing, it's worth doing well".

Penley's packaging is a revolution, Kym has spared no effort or expense to package the wines he is so proud of in the most beautiful way. His Coonawarra Cabernet Sauvignon has already won a stack of trophies and gold medals, the Shiraz Cabernet is a very good wine at a reasonable price and the recently-released Hyland shiraz is another superb drop. Kym has just released a 100% Coonawarra Methode Champenoise, 90% pinot noir and 10% chardonnay and soon pinot meunier will be added; it's already won a trophy in the 1994 Perth Show.

Kym oversees every part of the Penley operation and has added even more lustre to the reputation of Coonawarra as a world class wine region.

PENLEY ESTATE

Address: McLeans Road, Coonawarra SA 5263
Phone: (08) 231 2400
Fax: (08) 231 0589
Established: 1988
Owner: Kym Tolley
Winemaker: Kym Tolley
Principal varieties grown: Cabernet sauvignon, pinot noir, shiraz, chardonnay, merlot, cabernet franc, pinot meunier
Ha under vine: 68
Average no. cases produced: 15,000

Principal wines & brands	Cellar potential
Shiraz Cabernet	5-7 years
Cabernet Sauvignon	5-10 years
Hyland Shiraz	3-5 years
Chardonnay	2-5 years
Penley pinot Sparkling	Now

Public & trade tours: By appointment only
Hours open to the public:
Mail order sales: Yes
Retail distribution: Australia-wide, United Kingdom, Switzerland, Holland, Austria

Redman Winery

Fourteen year old Bill Redman arrived in Coonawarra in 1901 and began working for Riddoch's winery, thus beginning a long and distinguished career in the wine industry. In 1908, having gained experience in winemaking and cellar management, Bill gained his independence by forming a partnership with his family in the acquisition of established vineyards, later known as Rouge Homme. After 1910, when winemaking all but ceased in Coonawarra, he remained the area's only producing winemaker for many decades.

During the 1940s, Bill was joined in the business by his son, Owen, and this alliance lasted until the sale of Rouge Homme to Lindemans in 1965. Owen then decided to establish his own winery. He purchased a vineyard as well as extra land where he mainly grew shiraz vines. Until his winery was built in 1969, Owen's first wines were made at Brand's Laira Winery. Today, Redman's winery is very well set up with the tasting area having picturesque views of the

Bruce Redman

vineyard and the winery.

Bill Redman died in 1979 at 92 years of age, having presided over 65 vintages. His contribution to the wine industry was enormous and he can be truly called one of the fathers of Coonawarra. His grandsons

Bruce and Malcolm Redman are continuing this heritage, having not only taken over the management of their father's winery, but also expanding its size and reputation.

Redman Wines had traditionally produced only two wines, a shiraz and a cabernet sauvignon (they're real red men); recently they have introduced a third wine, a cabernet merlot. I tried several vintages at the cellar door and can confirm it is a lovely wine, showing some lifted floral characters and soft plummy flavours; a certain percentage of the wine is barrel fermented.

For many years, Bruce and Malcolm persisted in the lighter claret style their father made famous, but in recent years they have beefed up the colour and body in their wines and used more small oak. The Redman's vineyards, some of which date back to before the turn of the century, produce superb fruit. The wines I have seen in recent years are certainly doing these fine vineyards justice.

Wynns Coonawarra Estate

Late last century, orchardists in the far south east of South Australia noticed the particular fertility of the soil around Penola. The Wynns Coonawarra Estate story began in 1890 when John Riddoch, who had vast landholdings in the area, developed the Coonawarra Fruit Colony, selling off 10 acre blocks of this land to hopeful farmers.

Riddoch himself planted vines and built a large stone winery, which was completed in 1895. It is the facade of this building that has adorned Wynns Coonawarra Estate wine labels since the 1950s.

Riddoch's venture failed to prosper and Coonawarra languished for the first half of the 1900s. Were it not for David Wynn, who purchased the estate in 1951, the winery would almost certainly have become a woolshed and the vineyards a sheep run.

One of the two flagship reds of today's Wynns Coonawarra Estate is John Riddoch Cabernet Sauvignon, a majestic wine that wins trophies and gold medals in Australian and International Wine shows with monotonous regularity.

The first John Riddoch was the 1982, a wine of such incredible richness, mouthfeel and velvet-like texture that it almost defied description.

I first encountered it in a lineup of the celebrated 1982 Bordeaux first and second growth wines. All were masked and to my mind it was at the top of the class. If anything, the John Riddochs of the 1990s are even better.

If John Riddoch Cabernet commemorates the founder of Coonawarra, the second Wynns Coonawarra Estate flagship red links us with the family that re-established

Coonawarra in our own time.

Michael Hermitage, a best-of-vintage Shiraz, takes its name from the legendary wine of 1955, created by David Wynn as a memorial to his young son who had died suddenly the previous year.

This wine was introduced - or reintroduced - with the 1990 vintage and has quickly become one of Australia's most talked-about wines.

Wynns' most widely-available reds are the black label Coonawarra Estate Cabernet Sauvignon, the white label Coonawarra Estate Shiraz and the Coonawarra Estate Cabernet-Shiraz-Merlot blend with its black and single red-striped label.

All are fine-textured, full-flavoured wines of the region. Often displaying a minty, herbaceous character over the fruit flavours, they have great appeal to the wine lover and

have grown in stature both domestically and internationally through the 1980s and 90s. They are, as a group, widely regarded as pre-eminent among Coonawarra reds.

The estate also produces whites of great quality.

Wynns Coonawarra Estate Riesling is exceptional value and always exhibits very good floral and fruity aromas and flavours.

In recent years the Wynns Coonawarra Estate Chardonnay has also consolidated its following. This buff-labelled wine shows excellent peach/apricot flavours, beautifully integrated with subtle oak. It explodes in the mouth and is ideal with poultry and other white meats.

The 1990s perspective makes it difficult to imagine that the name Coonawarra was virtually unknown when David Wynn set himself the task of rebuilding the estate.

From their beginnings as Melbourne wine merchants, the Wynns had gained much experience in wine marketing. Their advertising campaigns stressed the Coonawarra origins of the wines and one of David Wynn's first steps was to commission a new label. Simple and striking, it soon became the best-known in Australia.

During the 1960s the popularity of red wine and the establishment of the label's image was consolidated, with the result that Wynns Coonawarra Estate and "claret" became synonymous.

Some of the top names in Australian wine helped raise Coonawarra's stocks. Ian Hickinbotham was the first winemaker to work under Wynns' management and his early efforts to improve facilities laid a firm foundation for success. Another who contributed to the credibility of the estate

was John Wade. Winemaker from 1978 to 1985, he introduced new techniques and created that first John Riddoch Cabernet.

The winemaker since 1985 has been Peter Douglas, under whose leadership the estate's reputation has continued to grow.

Both the underground cellars at Wynns, and the newer, air-conditioned, ground-level facilities, are brimming with great wines in a forest of the world's finest oak; it's one of the great liquid assets in Australia.

John Riddoch's vision has finally been fulfilled, a century after its beginnings, but sadly, David Wynn, who masterminded this red wine revolution in Australia, died early in 1995.

If they could, I'm sure both would happily raise a glass of John Riddoch, or Michael, to toast Wynns Coonawarra Estate's hard-won success.

The Ridge Vineyard

Sid and Susan Kidman have one of the most characteristic cellar doors in Coonawarra, on the northern fringes of the region. It is in former stables on their property, built in the 1860s.

Their lovely sprawling old colonial Australian home behind the winery dates back even further, to the 1840s. The 'paradise lost' garden behind the homestead would do the magazine *Home and Garden* proud and is lovingly tended by Susie.

The Kidmans have been landowners and farmers in the region since pioneering days. Even during his school years, Sid used to love jumping on the tractor to do some work on the property and, in fact, he still occasionally drives the old 1960 tractor he learnt on. Sid helped his father establish a large vineyard across the road from The Ridge in partnership with Melbourne wine merchant, Dan Murphy, in the 1970s. In 1984 Susie and Sid went their own way, changing their vineyard from grape production to wine production.

The Ridge rieslings are excellent, often showing fruit flavours in the mandarin fruit spectrum and are quite full-bodied. Sid has planted more shiraz and has been very successful with the variety, with complex and characterful wines that live on for many years. Why not drop in to The Ridge and share the history and warm hospitality of the Kidmans.

THE RIDGE WINERY
Address: Naracoorte Road, Coonawarra SA 5263
Direction: 12 km north of Coonawarra store
Phone: (087) 36 5071
Fax: (087) 36 5070
Established: 1984
Owner: Sid & Susie Kidman
Winemaker: Sid Kidman
Principal varieties grown: Cabernet sauvignon, shiraz, sauvignon blanc, riesling
Ha under vine: 12
Average annual crush: 100 tonnes

Principal wines & brands	Cellar potential
The Ridge	
Cabernet Sauvignon	5-10 yrs
Shiraz	5-10 yrs
Sauvignon Blanc	2-5 yrs
Riesling	2-5 yrs

Public & trade tours: Yes
Cellar door & mail order Sales: Yes
Hours open to public: 9 am - 5 pm daily

RYMILL COONAWARRA WINERY
Address: The Riddoch Run Vineyards, Coonawarra SA 5263
Direction: Turn into Clayfield Road, approx. 4 km north of Coonawarra township
Phone: (087) 36 5001
Fax: (087) 36 5040
Established: 1974
Owner: Peter Riddoch Rymill
Winemaker: John Innes
Principal varieties grown: Cabernet sauvignon, chardonnay, shiraz, sauvignon blanc, cabernet franc, merlot, gewurztraminer
Ha under vine: 120
Average annual crush: 1,000 tonnes
Average no. cases produced: 40,000

Principal wines & brands	Cellar potential
Rymill	
Cabernet Sauvignon	5-10 years
Chardonnay	2-5 years
Shiraz	5-10 years
Sauvignon Blanc	2-5 years
Methode Champenoise	2-5 years
June Traminer	2-5 years
Cabernet/Cabernet Franc/Merlot	2-5 years

Public & trade tours: Yes
Mail order sales: Yes
Hours open to public: 10 am-5 pm daily
Points of interest: Facilities for exhibitions, small functions (up to 100 people)
Retail distribution: Negociants Australia, all states and ACT; Tim Seats Pty Ltd, NT.

Sid Kidman

Mildara were keen to expand their vineyard holdings in the general south eastern South Australian wine regions, which led them to purchase and some 15 km north of the tiny township of Coonawarra. They have planted a large vineyard here mainly to cabernet sauvignon. The property borders the main road from Penola to Naracoorte, a couple of kilometres north of the impressive old Victorian inspired homestead, Struan.

Now converted into a centre for the Department of Agriculture, Struan was built for the Robertson family, wealthy Scottish immigrants, who arrived in the region via Portland in Victoria. They

brought with them from their homeland their servants, shepherds and all. Robertson purchased a huge tract of land north of Coonawarra, becoming the neighbour of John Riddoch, the only other large landholder in the region.

Mildara chose the site because its terra rossa soil and the north-westerly aspect of the long ridge supporting the vineyard is ideal in its soil structure aspect and drainage to grow absolutely first class cabernet.

Ironically, the Robertson's Well Vineyard is not in the defined Coonawarra region. Mildara, however, have released a cabernet sauvignon featuring the old windmill and tank from the vineyard on

the label. The wine however is entirely made from fruit grown in the best vineyards of the Coonawarra region and is the premier cabernet sauvignon to be produced each year by Mildara. Their aim, in the words of their astute and knowledgeable marketing chief Hugh Cuthbertson, "is to make a cabernet sauvignon so chock-full of fruit, rich cassis flavours with the mintiness and herbaceous characters so typical of Coonawarra that even a Martian landing on earth could pick up a glass and recognise it. " I'm no Martian, but I love a good cabernet and Robertson's Well has got the depth I like. Why not choose it for yourself?

An introduction to Padthaway/Keppoch

When land in Coonawarra became increasingly scarce and expensive, many of Australia's major wine companies were forced to search for an alternative area to develop for the production of premium wine.

The Padthaway/Keppoch region, 80 kilometres north of Coonawarra, proved to be the most suitable. Made up of a similar terra rossa soil over limestone, the strip of rich, red soil is 16 km long and 1 to 1.5 km wide. The area has a slightly warmer climate, providing a stability that produces less variation in vintages.

Rainfall is lower, but like Coonawarra, there is a good supply of underground water, and, once established, the vines grow very well. Before Seppelts established the vines in 1963, the region was divided into seven large grazing-oriented properties, the most famous being Padthaway House, home of the Lawson family, descendants of Henry Lawson. Padthaway House was refurbished in the late 1920s; it is one of the most beautiful old colonial homes where you can stay in Australia.

Padthaway has been developed largely by the bigger companies such as Seppelts, Hardy's, Lindemans, Wynns and Orlando, but with others such as the Brown family, who opened a winery in 1994, after many years as a major grape grower in the region. Andrew Garrett and Tolleys moved in in more recent years, along with the Padthaway Estate vineyards and winery.

Although originally envisaged as a red wine area, this region has proved to be extremely versatile, producing white wines of many styles. Rhine riesling, chardonnay and sauvignon blanc along with pinot noir have been successful grape varieties, producing excellent results. Padthaway now has a comparable area under vine to Coonawarra.

The intense varietal character found in the high grade fruit of the area will certainly see Padthaway/Keppoch become of increasing importance to the industry. New areas further south and east of Naracoorte in the hundreds (an old land measure - 10 miles x 10 miles) of Joanna and Jessie are being planted at present, mainly by the large companies. Along with the existing Koppamurra Vineyard, this will provide a huge resource of top quality grapes for the future of wine in Australia, particularly for export.

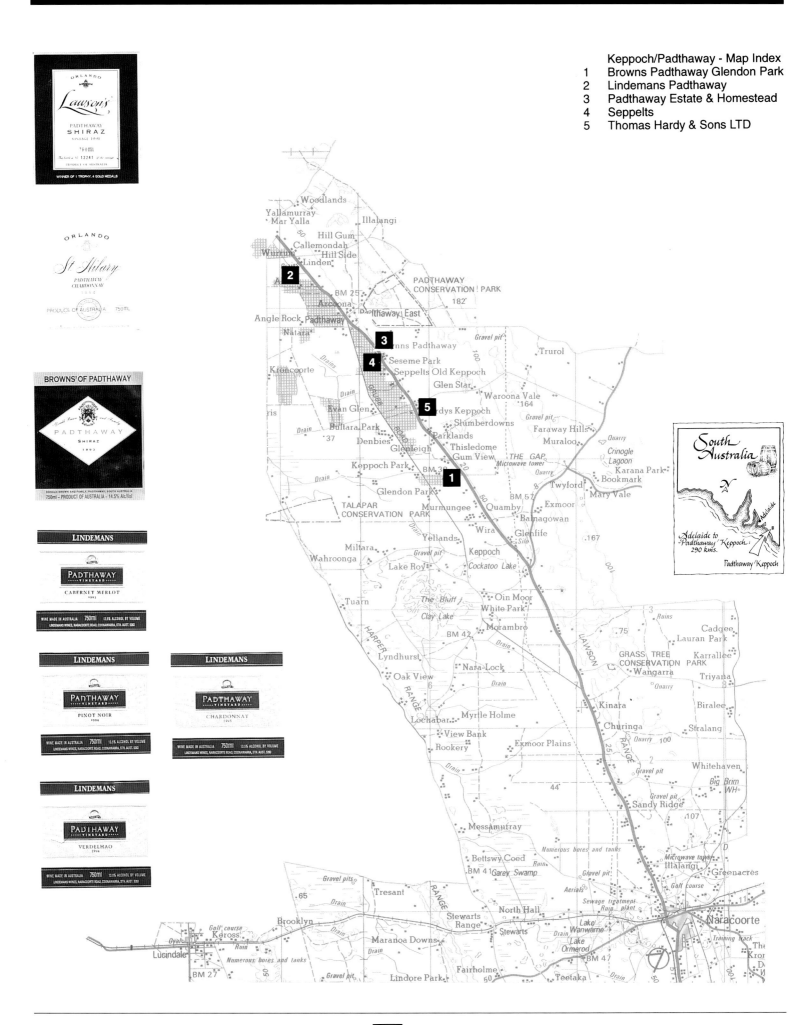

Keppoch/Padthaway - Map Index

1   Browns Padthaway Glendon Park
2   Lindemans Padthaway
3   Padthaway Estate & Homestead
4   Seppelts
5   Thomas Hardy & Sons LTD

Lindemans Padthaway

Vying for the title of Australia's largest vineyard, Lindemans have set up a picture book vineyard which saw the first vines planted in 1968.

Colin Kidd, then the viticulturist under his brother and general manager, Ray Kidd, purchased a 1,000 acre property from grazier Bill Smith, subsequently adding the two adjoining properties and building the total holding up to nearly 2,750 acres. Today, much of this is under vine and the track record of the wines in shows and the market place has been impeccable.

The old standby wines that have been so successful for Lindemans, Cawarra Claret, Nyrang Hermitage, Ben Ean Moselle and Bin 65, and so on, benefited greatly from the fine wines coming out of the Padthaway vineyards.

The Padthaway Vineyard is immaculate with its high trellises and sturdy vines, established to be mechanically harvested, an absolute necessity for such a large vineyard to harvest each variety quickly at optimum ripeness. In any case, the hundreds of grape-pickers needed to do anything like this amount of work were just not available in the region. Picking is carried on during the cool of the night and early morning, maximising the quality of the fruit.

The Lindemans Padthaway Chardonnay has amassed an impressive number of trophies and gold medals, but the pinot noir and riesling are most impressive wines as well. The Lindemans Auslese Riesling made using the technique of cutting the vine canes, to shrivel the grapes and concentrate the sugar and flavours, have all been stunning wines. Any time you see a Lindemans wine made from Padthaway fruit, it's bound to be good.

Browns' of Padthaway

In 1959, fourth generation Yorke Peninsula farmer, Don Brown, purchased a 290 hectare property at Padthaway. Yorke Peninsula is very dry and famous for its barley, much of it ending up in beer and in some instances, Scotch whisky.

The Browns were looking for land which could be irrigated for their Border Leicester and Southdown stud sheep. Padthaway is actually derived from an Aboriginal word for 'good water'. Don and his wife Glenda named the property Glendon Park and gradually they have expanded it to more than 2,500 hectares. The original 4 hectares of irrigation has been expanded drastically.

During the 1960s Don developed his 'small seed production' business before planting vines in 1970. Today the vineyard has expanded to 150 hectares. Don also began a contracting company specialising in grape harvesting and transportation.

For many years his eagerly sought after grapes were purchased by large companies such as Orlando, then in 1993, the Browns launched their own label beginning with a riesling and a non-wooded chardonnay; plans are afoot to increase the range. Certainly they have more than enough vines to supply their needs.

Their three children all live and work on the property. Andrew and David both have degrees in farm management from Roseworthy, whilst daughter Sue has the Roseworthy wine marketing diploma. Daughter-in-law, Lisa, has a business degree and son-in-law, Michael, an agricultural degree. All in all it's a pretty formidable team at Browns' and the wines so far have reflected this. Expect great things from Browns' of Padthaway, I'm sure they won't let you down.

**BROWNS' OF PADTHAWAY
GLENDON PARK VINEYARDS**
Address: PMB Naracoorte SA 5271
Direction: 15 km south of Padthaway
Phone: (087) 65 6063
Fax: (087) 65 6083
Year of establishment: 1970
Owner: Donald Brown & Co
Winemaker: John Innes, Rymill Winery
Principal varieties grown: Chardonnay, rhine riesling, cabernet, shiraz, malbec
Ha under vine: 150
Average annual crush: 200 tonnes
Average no. cases produced: 12,000

Principal wines & brands	Cellar potential
Browns' of Padthaway	
Rhine Riesling	2-5 years
Chardonnay	2-5 years
Shiraz	2-5 years

Retail distribution:
Hill International Wines (02) 630 5429

An introduction to Langhorne Creek

Situated some 80 kilometres south-east of Adelaide, along the banks of the River Bremer, lies the grapegrowing region of Langhorne Creek.

The rich alluvial plain is periodically flooded by the Bremer River, an event that the local growers look forward to each year, as it brings much-needed water and fertile silt to the vineyards.

Planting of vines on Langhorne Creek began in the middle of last century. The oldest and largest winery in the region is Bleasdale, established by Frank Potts back in 1850. Today the Potts family still manage this historic winery.

Many of the great winemakers from around Australia have used Langhorne Creek grapes in their winemaking. The first wine to acknowledge this on the label was the famous Stonyfell Metala with its distinctive label explaining its origins. During the late 60s and early 70s Wolf Blass relied heavily on Langhorne Creek fruit, a significant ingredient of his trio of Jimmy Watson trophies. Today, four excellent wineries share the region with many grape-growers, including a recent influx of larger companies. Orlando Wyndham are in the process of establishing a huge $15 million vineyard development. The wine industry and the State Government have just implemented a massive irrigation scheme, bringing water in a large pipeline from Lake Alexandrina; this sense of cooperation in South Australia's future is welcome. Why not visit the region and see the historic Bleasdale and the fast-developing family wineries, Lake Breeze, Temple Bruer and the delightful Bremerton Lodge with its excellent restaurant?

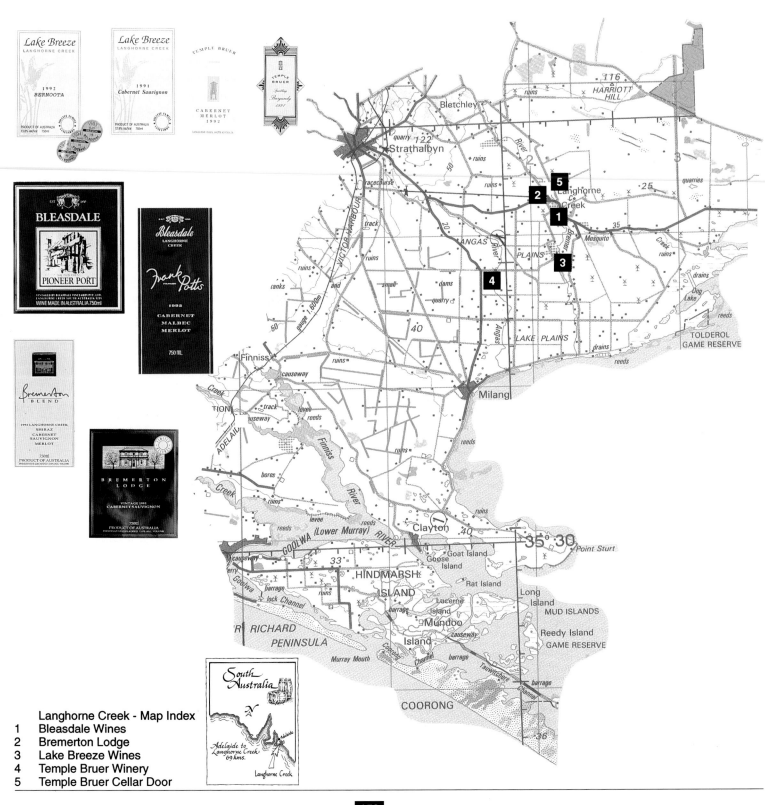

Langhorne Creek - Map Index
1 Bleasdale Wines
2 Bremerton Lodge
3 Lake Breeze Wines
4 Temple Bruer Winery
5 Temple Bruer Cellar Door

Bleasdale

Bleasdale is one of Australia's oldest family owned and operated wineries. Little has changed in parts of the winery since it was established by Frank Potts in 1850. Potts was one of the State's original settlers, landing in Adelaide from H.M.S. Buffalo in 1836. An energetic and entrepreneurial chap, he also built 3 large paddle steamers which plied the Murray River for many years. The old part of the winery is on the National Trust and National Heritage register and makes a fascinating visit; the huge old redgum lever press is truly incredible.

Until the late 1950s, Bleasdale produced only fortified wines, including a number of ports and sherries and a madeira, still produced, made from the rare grape variety, verdelho. Bleasdale still makes great fortifieds but today their table wines form the greater part of their business.

Winemaker is Roseworthy graduate and family member, Michael Potts. Michael has continued installing modern winemaking equipment and increased oak barrel storage. The reds, the chardonnay and the verdelho (table wine) have really shown the benefit of this investment and Michael's skill,

combined with the superb fruit from the Langhorne Creek vineyards, has seen some sensational wines produced.

The winery's tasting room is full of old

photographs by family member, Diddy Potts, and paintings by his brother, A.B. Potts. Drop in to Bleasdale and immerse yourself in our wine history.

BLEASDALE VINEYARDS PTY LTD
Address: Wellington Road, Langhorne Creek SA 5255
Phone: (085) 37 3001
Fax: (085) 37 3224
Established: 1850
Winemaker: Michael Potts
Principal varieties grown: Cabernet sauvignon, shiraz, malbec, verdelho
Ha under vine: 45
Average annual crush: 1,000 tonnes
Average no. cases produced: 60,000

Principal wines & brands	Cellar potential
Cabernet/Malbec/Merlot	5-10 years
Cabernet Sauvignon	5-10 years
Shiraz	5-10 years
Verdelho	2-5 years
Pioneer Port (Tawny Port)	10+ years
Madeira (Verdelho)	10+ years

Public & trade tours: Yes
Cellar door & mail order sales: Yes
Hours open to public: 9 am-5 pm Mon-Sat; 11 am-5 Sun
Points of interest: Historic winery (redgum lever press, redgum vats etc.), picnic area nearby
Retail distribution: National distribution, Carlton Special Beverages; fortifieds ex winery.

Bremerton Lodge

Craig Willson and his delightful wife, Mignonne, (it's French for cute) have restored a beautiful century-old stone building on their property and turned it into a showplace of good taste as a winery and charming restaurant, where Mignonne serves her mood food for lunch, at weekends.

The tasting area of Bremerton Lodge features many historic items from the region and opens out to an outdoor entrance patio which is delightful on a summer's day.

The sweeping circular driveway adds to the beautifully-balanced overall impression. In the winery, with its high roof, the eating area is on a mezzanine above the wine store where the wine quietly ages.

The care and aesthetic understanding of the Willsons shows through in their wines which are beautifully balanced and good examples of the top quality that Langhorne Creek is famous for; their presentation quality Mignonne! Why not wend your way around Langhorne Creek one weekend and then breeze into Bremerton Lodge. I'm sure Mignonne's mood food will suit yours!

BREMERTON LODGE WINES
Address: Strathalbyn Road, Langhorne Creek SA 5255
Direction: 15 km from Strathalbyn
Phone: (085) 37 3093
Fax: (085) 37 3109
Established: 1991
Owner: C.H. & M. Willson
Winemaker: Craig Willson & Andrew Mitchell
Principal varieties grown: Cabernet sauvignon, shiraz, merlot
Ha under vine: 44
Average annual crush: 40 tonne
Average no. cases produced: 2,500

Principal wines & brands	Cellar potential
Bremerton Lodge 'Old Adam' Shiraz	5-10 Years
Bremerton Lodge Cabernet Sauvignon	5-10 Years
Bremerton Blend Cabernet/Shiraz/Merlot	5-10 Years
Bremerton Lodge Sauvignon Blanc/Semillon	0-2 Years
Bremerton 'Watervale' Riesling	2-5 Years

Cellar door & mail order sales: Yes
Hours open to public: 10 am-5 pm Thurs-Mon.
Points of interest: Light food on weekends. Quality cheese platters every day. Cellar door in magnificently restored 1866 ex-horse stables/barn.
Retail distribution: SA only and Melbourne.

Lake Breeze

Like their wines, the Follett family are youthful, exuberant and dynamic. Father Ken still hasn't hung up his Aussie Rules footy boots and is one of the fittest men of his age you're ever likely to meet. Quietly-spoken Ken is a fastidious, hard-toiling farmer, whose superb vineyard and the wonderful fruit it produces is respected by winemakers from near and far.

After many years supplying grapes to Australia's leading winemakers, Ken decided to start a small winery to put his growing family to work. His three sons are the driving force of the winery - Roger is a viticulturist and assists his father in the vineyard, Tim helps in the vineyard and Greg is the highly successful winemaker. Greg and Ken also handle the marketing. Lake Breeze uses only the top 10 per cent of their crop for their own wines and sell the rest.

Greg in his short winemaking career has won a truckload of wine show trophies. His lightning rise to fame began when he graduated from Roseworthy in 1991. He followed this with a vintage at Hardy's, and then a vintage at Geyser Peak winery in

Right: Ken and Greg Follett

California. Then he worked in France at Domaine du Vaissiere for the world famous winemaking Lurton family in the Minervois region south of Bordeaux.

Ken Follett is the epitome of a truly supportive parent and his sons are doing him proud.

LAKE BREEZE WINES
Address: C/o Post Office, Langhorne Creek SA 5255
Phone: (085) 37 3017
Fax: (085) 37 3267
Established: 1991
Winemaker: Greg Follett
Principal varieties grown: Cabernet sauvignon, shiraz, chardonnay, small amounts white frontignac and grenache
Ha under vine: 60
Average annual crush: 60 tonnes
Average no. cases produced: 3,000-4,000

Principal wines & brands	cellar potential
1992 cabernet sauvignon	5-10 years
'Bernoota'	5-10 years
1994 Chardonnay	2-5 years
White Frontignac	2-5 years

Trade tours: By appointment only
Cellar door & mail order sales: Yes
Hours open to public: 10 am-5 pm seven days
Points of interest: Friendly family atmosphere, panoramic views

---

Temple Bruer

TEMPLE BRUER WINES
Address: Milang Road via Strathalbyn, SA 5255
Phone: (085) 37 0203
Fax: (085) 37 0131
Established: 1980
Winemaker: David Bruer
Principal varieties grown: cabernet sauvignon, shiraz, merlot, malbec, verdelho
Ha under vine: 12
Average annual crush: 140 tonnes
Average no. cases produced: 8,000

Principal wines & brands	Cellar potential
Cabernet Merlot	2-5 years
Shiraz Malbec	5-10 years
Cornilopia Grenache	0-2 years
Riesling	2-5 years
Botrytis Riesling	5-10 years
Sparkling	5-10 years

Cellar door sales: at Wine Vat Restaurant, Langhorne Creek, 10.30 am-4.30 pm Tues-Sun and public holidays.
Mail order sales: Yes

David Bruer is a very talented winemaker. For 13 years he lectured in chemistry and microbiology at the famous Roseworthy College Diploma (now degree) course in winemaking.

He left in 1982 to establish Temple Bruer Winery, some 7 - 8 km south-west of the township of Langhorne Creek and marginally cooler than the other vineyards in the region.

The vineyard at Temple Bruer was established by David in 1973. Geoff Joppich, is now the vineyard manager and David Haeusler the production manager. David Bruer gives credit to Langhorne Creek's climate, one of the coolest in Australia in summer, and the mildest in winter, for the fruit flavour packed wines he produces.

Temple Bruer houses some of the finest winemaking equipment featuring 100 percent stainless steel, from picking bins to the final storage. David also utilises some of the best imported oak barrels I've seen in Australia. David Bruer is a man on a mission in his temple to good wine.

McLaren Vale - South Australia

The McLaren Vale wine region stretches from the southern suburbs of Adelaide including Reynella in the north, to Aldinga and Willunga in the south. The region is bordered by the Adelaide Hills to the east and the Gulf of St Vincent to the west.

John Reynell planted the first vines of the region at Reynella in 1838. He was followed by Dr Alexander Kelly, who founded the Tintara Vineyard Company and developed a considerable property covering 285 hectares.

The first vines planted by Dr Kelly are still bearing fruit, which has traditionally been used in a fortified dessert wine. In 1850 George Manning established the Hope Farm Vineyard, which is now Seaview. By late 1880 wine industry development was booming throughout Australia.

In McLaren Vale, new businesses were founded by J.G. Kelly with the Tatachilla Vineyard, the Kay family with their Amery winery, the Johnstons' Pirramimma Wines and Robert Wigley with Wirra Wirra. Much of the wine produced in McLaren Vale/Reynella was exported to England. The area was subject to export market vagaries and grew slowly until the table wine boom of the 1960s

Larger companies such as Lindemans and Penfolds started purchasing McLaren Vale red wines for blending and many existing local companies began to bottle and market their own wine. Towards the end of the decade and through the early 70s new companies blossomed throughout McLaren Vale. There are now more than 50 wineries in the area and the 1980s and 1990s have seen the area under vines expand dramatically. More importantly, the awareness of McLaren Vale wines and their reputation for quality has grown even more dramatically.

I can well imagine how the beauty of the region would have captured the heart of my own great-grandfather, Thomas Hardy, as he drove his horse and buggy over the final rise of the southern Adelaide Hills and saw the peaceful valley spread out before him, the time-worn fingers of the hills holding its final exit into St. Vincents Gulf (by coincidence, St. Vincent is the patron saint of winemakers). The gently undulating hills have traditionally supported vines, olives and almonds. The almonds in blossom around the first week or so in August gives the Valley a special glow.

During the 1870s, the area had fallen on hard times, the over-cropping of cereals and over-grazing leading to diminishing rural returns. Thomas Hardy set about promoting the vine and educating farmers in its cultivation. He also bought the grand, but bankrupt, Tintara Vineyard Company and

the disused flour mill, soon having the region well on its feet, with his own flourishing enterprise.

McLaren Vale is one of the world's best-placed wine regions, being only 45 minutes' drive south of the Adelaide city centre. This, combined with its physical beauty, has led to a boom in tourism through which, fortunately, the region has lost none of its charm or individual character of its winemakers.

Forerunner among this development was David Hardy, great-grandson of pioneer Thomas, along with renowned artist, David Dridan. They set up the wine-inspired restaurant, The Barn, in 1970 with its vine-

Thomas Hardy

covered courtyard and 'choose your own' wine cellar. It was an innovative and welcome addition to Australia, let alone McLaren Vale.

David also founded the Wine Bushing Festival in 1974, based on the old Elizabethan tradition of hanging a bush outside the inn when the new wine was ready. In October each year, this tradition continues. The makers of the best commercially available McLaren Vale wine are crowned "Bushing King and Queen" at the annual Winemakers' Luncheon. The month kicks off with the McLaren Vale Continuous Picnic on the October long weekend, a Sunday and Monday celebration of wine and food. Some 30 wineries all have a guest restaurant cooking, and all manner of entertainment.

Bushing Week usually starts with the crowning McLaren Vale Wine Show, a varietal workshop and the Winemakers' Luncheion which showcases the show's award winning wines, complemented by regional produce from the Fleurieu Peninsula. All awards from the wine whow are presented during the luncheon, the

highlight being the crowning of the "Bushing King and Queen".

The festival culminates with the Bushing Festival Street Procession and Fair Day when the whole town stops, and stalls and entertainment reign supreme. In between, wineries have dinners, concerts, theatre pieces and all manner of other music, art and cultural experiences.

McLaren Vale has long been known for its full-bodied red wines, aided by the complex soils and mild temperate climate. These rich round generous wines can really warm the soul. The region also produces great whites and although its chardonnays led the way, they have latterly been joined by sauvignon blancs, which are becoming a regional speciality and highly regarded by the wine cognoscenti.

Much of the industry's success originally was based on fortified ports and sherries and while sherry making has ceased, the ports of the region are outstanding; both the vintage and tawny styles excel. The number of winery restaurants, bed and breakfasts and regional eating houses is growing daily and they are superb. The Barn has been joined by The Salopian Inn at the other end of town and the McLarens on the Lake Restaurant, function and accommodation centre is splendid, indeed. Woodstock has a superb large restaurant and function centre, The Coterie, and a Sunday lunch here is compulsory. Middlebrook has two restaurants and a David Dridan-run gallery and art and craft showcase.

Chapel Hill has a splendid gallery in its old chapel and outdoor eating facilities. Wirilda Creek features a casual restaurant and great bed and breakfast, while closer to town St. Francis has accommodation and a restaurant and conference centre at Reynella. Geoff Merrill's historic Mt. Hurtle Winery also has a restaurant and function area and the Cellar Bistro at Haselgrove is famous for its vineyard platter.

"Magnums" at the Hotel McLaren and Pipkins BYO restaurant are located near the Almond Train at the entrance to Hardy's Tintara Winery in McLaren Vale's main street.

The McLaren Vale Regional Visitor Centre (to open mid-1996) is located near the McLaren Vale township's western entrance. The centre offers visitors a glimpse of what they can discover in the McLaren Vale region and beyond the Fleurieu Peninsula.

Any visitors to Adelaide with an interest in wine should spend a day or two exploring the magnificent scenery, beaches, wines and food of the McLaren Vale Wine Region - Adelaide's playground.

McLaren Vale - South Australia

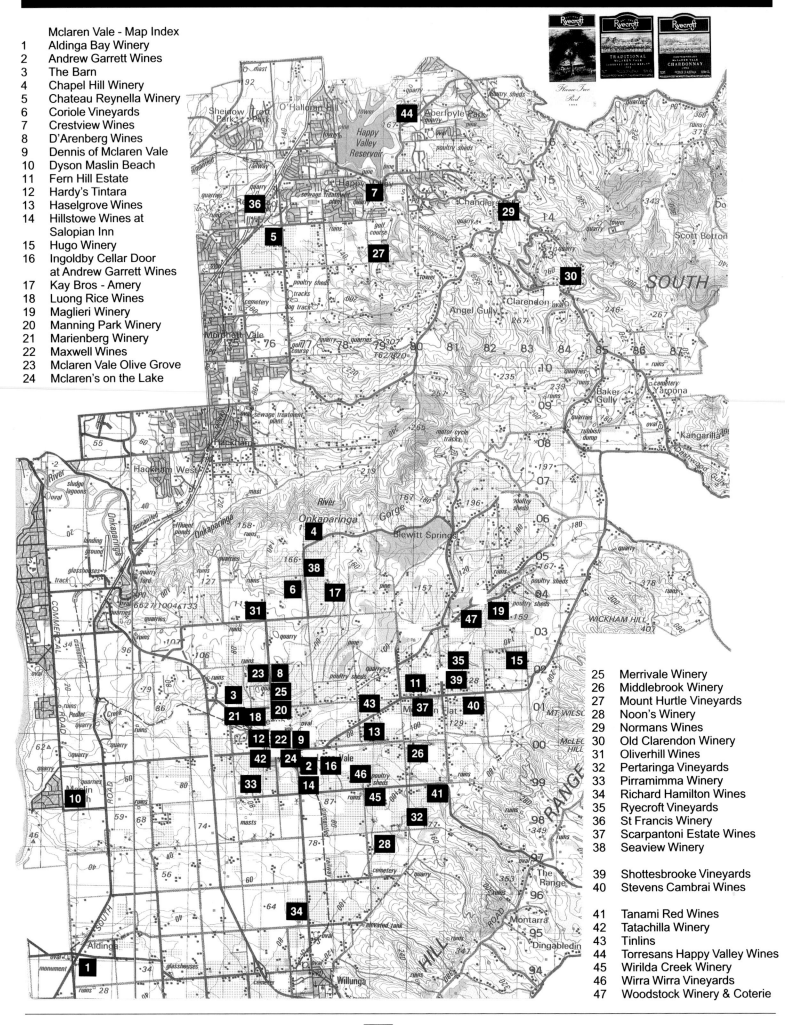

Mclaren Vale - Map Index
1 Aldinga Bay Winery
2 Andrew Garrett Wines
3 The Barn
4 Chapel Hill Winery
5 Chateau Reynella Winery
6 Coriole Vineyards
7 Crestview Wines
8 D'Arenberg Wines
9 Dennis of Mclaren Vale
10 Dyson Maslin Beach
11 Fern Hill Estate
12 Hardy's Tintara
13 Haselgrove Wines
14 Hillstowe Wines at
   Salopian Inn
15 Hugo Winery
16 Ingoldby Cellar Door
   at Andrew Garrett Wines
17 Kay Bros - Amery
18 Luong Rice Wines
19 Maglieri Winery
20 Manning Park Winery
21 Marienberg Winery
22 Maxwell Wines
23 Mclaren Vale Olive Grove
24 Mclaren's on the Lake

25 Merrivale Winery
26 Middlebrook Winery
27 Mount Hurtle Vineyards
28 Noon's Winery
29 Normans Wines
30 Old Clarendon Winery
31 Oliverhill Wines
32 Pertaringa Vineyards
33 Pirramimma Winery
34 Richard Hamilton Wines
35 Ryecroft Vineyards
36 St Francis Winery
37 Scarpantoni Estate Wines
38 Seaview Winery

39 Shottesbrooke Vineyards
40 Stevens Cambrai Wines

41 Tanami Red Wines
42 Tatachilla Winery
43 Tinlins
44 Torresans Happy Valley Wines
45 Wirilda Creek Winery
46 Wirra Wirra Vineyards
47 Woodstock Winery & Coterie

ANDREW GARRETT
1994 Riesling
DRY STYLE

ANDREW GARRETT
1993 Cabernet Merlot
FRENCH OAK MATURED

MAGLIERI
McLAREN VALE
1992 SHIRAZ

MAGLIERI
INGLEBURNE ESTATE
McLAREN VALE
1992 CABERNET SAUVIGNON

FERN HILL ESTATE
Semillon 1994

FERN HILL ESTATE
Chardonnay 1994

FERN HILL ESTATE
Cabernet Sauvignon 1992

FERN HILL ESTATE
Shiraz 1992

INGOLDBY
Shiraz

INGOLDBY
COLOMBARD

Haselgrove
1995 McLAREN VALE
SAUVIGNON BLANC

MARIENBERG
OF McLaren Vale
1991
CABERNET SAUVIGNON

MARIENBERG
McLaren Vale
1993
Chardonnay

MARIENBERG
OF McLaren Vale
1992
Lavinia
CLASSIC DRY WHITE

MARIENBERG
OF McLaren Vale
1992
SEMILLON CHARDONNAY

Maxwell
1993
Ellen Street Shiraz
McLaren Vale

WIRRA WIRRA VINEYARDS
1993
McLaren Vale
Church Block
Cabernet - Shiraz - Merlot

WIRRA WIRRA VINEYARDS
1994
HAND PICKED
Riesling

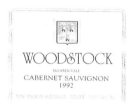

WOODSTOCK
McLAREN VALE
CABERNET SAUVIGNON
1992

WOODSTOCK
McLAREN VALE
BOTRYTIS SWEET WHITE
1994

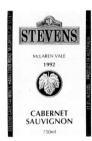

STEVENS
McLAREN VALE
1992
CABERNET SAUVIGNON

RICHARD HAMILTON
McLAREN VALE
CHARDONNAY
1994

RICHARD HAMILTON
McLAREN VALE
OLD VINES SHIRAZ
1993

wirilda creek
SHIRAZ

CHATEAU REYNELLA
Basket Pressed
CABERNET MERLOT
McLAREN VALE

CHATEAU REYNELLA
CHARDONNAY
McLAREN VALE

KAY BROTHERS
Centenary
BLOCK 6
SHIRAZ
VINTAGE 1992

HILLSTOWE
McLAREN VALE
CABERNET MERLOT
Buxton
1992

MANNING PARK

Great White
1994

MANNING PARK

Savage Grenache
1994

HARDYS
Nottage Hill
1994
CHARDONNAY

HARDYS
Nottage Hill
CABERNET SHIRAZ

DYSON
1990
'Clarice'
Cabernet Sauvignon

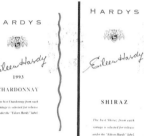

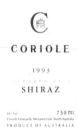

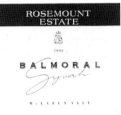

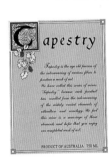

Dennis of McLaren Vale

E gerton Dennis is one of the real gentlemen of the wine industry. During the 1960s, he and Jim Ingoldby regenerated the old Ryecroft winery and vineyards -their vision in fact predated the wine boom. In 1973, the same year as Ingoldby, Dennis's Daringa Cellars was born. Egerton had by then established his own vineyards at the eastern side of the valley, although the winery is located right on the edge of town just opposite McLarens on the Lake.

The wines are all made from the family's own vineyards by Ege's son Peter, who is ably assisted by his wife Margaret.

Dennis were one of the pioneers of chardonnay in the region and their full-flavoured reds are excellent value.

DENNIS OF McLAREN VALE
Address: Kangarilla Road, McLaren Vale SA 5171
Direction: 40 km from Adelaide
Phone: (08) 323 8665
Fax: (08) 323 9121
Established: 1970
Owner: Dennis family
Winemaker: Peter Dennis
Principal varieties grown: Shiraz, cabernet sauvignon, merlot, chardonnay, sauvignon blanc
Ha under vine: 13
Average annual crush: 150 tonnes
Average no. cases produced: 5,000

Principal wines & brands	Cellar potential
Shiraz	5-10 years
Cabernet Sauvignon	5-10 years
Merlot	5-10 years
Chardonnay	2-5 years
Sauvignon Blanc	2-5 years

Public & trade tours: Yes
Cellar door & mail order sales: Yes
Hours open to public: 10 am-5 pm daily
Points of interest: Picnic grounds, historic site, natural spring
Retail distribution: NSW, National Wine Merchants; ACT, Capital Fine Wines; VIC, Westwood Wine Agencies

Noons Wines

D avid Noon bought a vineyard and began making wine as a hobby alongside his profession as a school teacher. Noon's winery is one of the smallest in McLaren Vale and a little off the beaten track.

A few years ago Noon's made the decision to specialise in red wines, using only fruit grown in the McLaren Vale region. The wines are hand-made in open fermenters, basket pressed and typify the big full-bodied, fruit-driven styles of yesteryear.

In addition to their conventional shiraz, cabernet and grenache wines, Noon's produce some unusual styles such as 'Maceration Carbonique', mulled red wine and the very popular unfiltered wines as well

as a rose and a vintage port.

David Noon and his hardworking manager Clive Simmonds creatively extract all that the great McLaren Vale red grapes have to give.

NOON'S
Address: Rifle Range Road, McLaren Vale SA 5171
Direction: 5 km south east of McLaren Vale
Phone: (08) 323 8290
Fax: (08) 323 8290
Established: 1976
Owner: David & Nerida Noon
Winemaker: David Noon
Principal varieties grown: Grenache, shiraz, cabernet
Average annual crush: 30 - 50 tonnes
Average no. cases produced: 2,500

Principal wines & brands	Cellar potential
Noon's Traditional Red (Shiraz)	5-10 years
Noon's Cabernet Sauvignon	5-10 years
Noon's Cabernet Shiraz	5-10 years
Noon's Vintage Port	10+ years

Public & trade tours: No
Cellar door & mail order sales: Yes
Hours open to public: 10am-5pm every day
Points of interest: Barbecue hut, picnic areas, children's playground
Retail distribution: Cellar door and mail order only

Kay Brothers - Amery Vineyard

I n 1890, brothers Frederick and Herbert Kay bought the Amery property perched high on the hills above McLaren Vale. Today, one of their original vineyards, Block 6, still has its original vines, 5,000 shiraz planted in 1892 from cuttings supplied by Thomas Hardy for the princely sum of 25 shillings. Colin Kay, photographed, is now in charge of the property, and his father Cud (Cuthbert) is still very active in the business, although more than 80 years of age.

The original brothers, Fred and Bert, kept a meticulous diary which survives today. Its chronicle of daily events of more than a century ago is fascinating.

KAY BROTHERS AMERY VINEYARD & WINERY
Address: Kays Road, McLaren Vale SA 5171
Direction: 6 km north of McLaren Vale
Phone: (08) 323 8211 **Fax:** (08) 323 9199
Established: 1890
Owner: Kay Brothers **Winemaker:** Colin Kay
Principal varieties grown: Shiraz, sauvignon blanc, pinot noir, merlot, cabernet sauvignon, mataro
Ha under vine: 12
Average annual crush: 100 tonnes (some grapes bought in from neighbouring growers)
Average no. cases produced: 6,000

Principal wines & brands	Cellar potential
Block 6 Shiraz	5-10 years
Cabernet Sauvignon	5-10 years
Shiraz	5-10 years
Grenache	2-5 years
Sauvignon Blanc	2-5 years
Late Harvest Frontignac	1 year
Liqueur Muscat	Fully matured
Tawny Port	Fully matured

Public & trade tours: By appointment only
Cellar door & mail order sales: Yes
Hours open to public: 9 am-5 pm Mon-Fri,12-5 pm w/e and PH
Points of interest: Heritage-listed winery, local pottery and produce sales, picnic grounds, oldest McLaren Vale winery still in original founding family's hands, best view in the south
Retail distribution: Victoria: J. Harvey Long Wine Co.; South Australia: direct to Kays; New South Wales: Broadway Liquor Distributors.

Merrivale Wines

Merrivale with its pretty name and picturesque location was always a Cinderella winery searching for the fairy godmother.

Jack Starr started up the winery in the renaissance days of the early 1970s and got off to a flying start. The winery travelled through some troubled waters until its saviour came along in the form of the innovative winemaker Brian Light and his effervescent wife Kay.

Between them, they have really rejuvenated Merrivale. Much of the 26 acres has been either revived or replanted. Brian has an illustrious winemaking background; his father Lloyd has a large, highly respected vineyard in the cool Bakers Gully near Kangarilla. Together, they began one of the new wave wineries in the region in 1974 perched on the top of Chandlers Hill near Clarendon.

Unfortunately, in calling the winery Light Wines, the connotations of the family name didn't help their splendid wines succeed, thus the name Coolawin Estates was launched. The Lights sold the winery to Norman's in 1985 but Brian remained as winemaker. In 1988 he was awarded the immense honour of becoming 'Australasian Winemaker of the Year'.

Today, he makes the wine at three wineries, 14,000 tonnes at the two Norman's establishments and his own pride and joy, Merrivale. The winery is being prettily decorated and landscaped by the bubbly Kay. They are a happy fold, laughing and smiling - the warm Lights are shining brightly.

MERRIVALE WINES
Address: Olivers Road, McLaren Vale SA 5171
Direction: 1.5 km north of McLaren Vale
Phone: (08) 323 9196
Fax: (08) 323 9746
Established: 1971
Owner: Kay & Brian Light
Winemaker: Brian Light
Principal varieties grown: Shiraz, Cabernet Sauvignon, Chardonnay
Ha under vine: 10
Average annual crush: 70-100 tonnes
Average no. cases produced: 5,000

Principal wines & brands	Cellar potential
Tapestry Rhine Riesling	2-5 years
Tapestry Chardonnay	2-5 years
Tapestry Cabernet Sauvignon	5-10 years
Tapestry Cabernet-Shiraz	5-10 years
Tapestry Spaetlese	
Muscat of Alexandria	1-3 years
Tapestry 10year Old Tawny Port	Fully matured

Public & trade tours: By appointment only
Cellar door & mail order sales: Yes
Hours open to public: 11 am-3 pm Mon-Thurs; 11 am-5 pm Fri-Sun & P/H
Points of interest: Picnic area being developed
Retail distribution: New South Wales, Victoria, South Australia, Northern Territory

Tinlins

One of the most unusual wineries in Australia is the Tinlins operation in McLaren Vale, probably Australia's busiest cellar door.

Wine lovers who like a good wine at a bargain price line up with their own containers and everything from white and red table wines to some good fortifieds are available by the litre at yester-year's prices.

The winery has just been expanded and upgraded enormously by new owners Warren Randall and Warren Ward. The quaint cellar door reminds me so much of many like it in France; its rustic charm and sincerity is refreshing. Local products such as almonds and olive oil are also available in quantity at great value prices.

The new owners have absolutely no intention of changing this unique operation which is to their credit. Their only desire is to make even better wine that will be an even greater bargain at the price.

Wine lovers rejoice, and make sure there is plenty of room in the car boot when you call in. I'm sure you will be tempted to splurge out or enjoy a joke with the Warrens or their fun-loving staff.

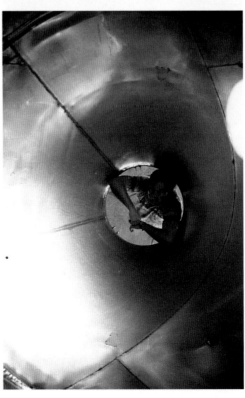

Warren Randall

TINLINS WINES
Address: Kangarilla Road, McLaren Vale SA 5171
Direction: Between McLaren Vale and McLaren Flat
Phone: (08) 323 8649
Fax: (08) 323 9747
Established: 1950
Winemaker: Warren Randall
Principal varieties grown: chardonnay, sauvignon blanc, riesling, chenin blanc, pinot noir, shiraz, cabernet sauvignon, merlot, grenache
Ha under vine: 100
Average no. cases produced: 25,000

Principal wines & brands	Cellar potential
Bulk white wines	1 year
Bulk red wines	1 year
Bulk sherries	2 years
Bulk ports	2 years
Bulk vermouth marsala	2 years
Bulk apricot, ginger, coffee wine	2 years

Public & trade tours: By appointment only
Cellar door sales: Yes
Hours open to public: 9 am-5 pm every day
Points of interest: Tinlins specialise in selling bulk wine from their cellar door outlet. They fill customers' containers with table wines and fortified wines for $1.50/litre and $3.40/litre respectively
Retail distribution: None

Pertaringa Vineyards

One of the most recently established wine companies in McLaren Vale is Pertaringa, an Aboriginal word meaning "belonging to the Hills".

The company, owned by Geoff Hardy and Ian Leask, has extensive vineyards and is one of the area's largest suppliers. Pertaringa grapes are sold to a number of leading wine companies.

The first parcel of land was purchased in 1981 and was planted mainly with shiraz grapes. Only nine hectares of shiraz still remain, other vines having been grafted with chardonnay, sauvignon blanc, white frontignac, semillon, cabernet sauvignon and cabernet franc. A further 30 hectares were purchased from Middlebrook in 1983.

In addition to selling much of their fruit, Ian and Geoffrey intend to release a range of dessert wines. Since 1981 a combination of different wines including a 1981 Fortified Muscat, 1984 Liqueur Frontignac and 1986 Brown Muscat have been blended together to form the continuing base for a Solera style. A proportion of these wines will be bottled and released each year. The first releases under the Pertaringa and Geoff Hardy labels have been an auslese style 1982 Late Picked Rhine Riesling and a special limited 1985 Trockenbeerenauslese.

The 1990 Cabernet Sauvignon and a 1991 Kuitpo Shiraz from Geoff Hardy's Adelaide Hills Vineyard have been outstanding wines, as have the 1992 and 1994 Sauvignon Blancs and an exciting 1994 Barrel Fermented Semillon. The 1993 Geoff Hardy Kuitpo Shiraz is a stunning wine currently winning high acclaim. Pertaringa won the inaugural South Australian Vineyard of the Year in 1990 and their wines have proven to be as successful as the vineyard. Geoff Hardy and Ian Leask have become a welcome and interesting addition to the winemaking fraternity.

Andrew Garrett Wines

Andrew Garrett arrived on the wine scene like a whirlwind. Not since the early days of Wolf Blass's arrival a decade earlier had Australia's wine drinkers' imagination been captured so fully.

Andrew Garrett was the new wave, a sophisticated label featuring a fresh and comforting country scene, with old world charm. His wines were exciting. A chardonnay packed full of fruit flavour, with good oak treatment, and methode champenoise of exceptional quality, lifting people's sights well above the ordinary. The Garrett reds were also lively and fruit-driven. The labels had a vibrancy and richness with dark greens and bordeaux reds embellished with gold foil.

Andrew Garrett was a man on a mission fresh from the newly inaugurated Roseworthy Agricultural College's two-year winemaking and marketing courses.

The wines were made by Andrew, much like Wolf Blass had done previously, when he travelled in his old Volkswagen Beetle, moving around, choosing great batches of grapes from leading regions, mainly in the McLaren Vale and Langhorne Creek areas, and under his careful eye, making wine under contract at the best wineries.

Andrew's flamboyant marketing style also had a Blass-like ring about it. Where next for Andrew? He bought the old Romalo Champagne Cellars at Magill, opposite Wynns, and proceeded to invest money and hard work into stylishly restoring and enhancing the historic old cellars. His business was expanding rapidly, but the

Andrew Garrett Wines

stunning Hazelmere Complex at McLaren Vale was in a little hot water. Andrew, not one to miss an opportunity, leapt in and launched McLarens on the Lake, and the Andrew Garrett banner flew over the winery. The sky was the limit.

Andrew had the right style for the eighties, backed with very high quality premium wines and a happy knack of correctly reading the consumers' fashion whims.

Andrew Garrett Wines are of absolutely the highest quality and the growth of the brand I am sure will accelerate even further, both domestically and overseas. The Andrew Garrett N.V. Pinot, a Non-Vintage Methode Champenoise Cuvee with its very faint blushing colour and delectable pinot noir nuances, is a rightful market leader.

The Garrett Red Sparkling is a truly regal rich red at the pinacle of its class. In the table wine area the quality and styles are equally well conceived and created. The chardonnay and the "bold" shiraz stand out, but all the wines are outstanding.

The enormous medal success of Andrew Garrett wines at wine shows is a tribute to their innovative approach in the search of excellence in winemaking.

One of the prettiest in the area, the setting for Andrew Garrett wines at McLarens on the Lake oasis is idyllic.

ANDREW GARRETT WINES

Address: Kangarilla Road, McLaren Vale SA 5171
Direction: Southeastern outskirts McLaren Vale
Phone: (08) 323 8853
Fax: (08) 323 8550
Established: 1983
Owner: Mildara Blass
Winemaker: Phillip Reschke
Principal varieties grown: Cabernet sauvignon, shiraz, chardonnay, pinot noir
Ha under vine: 86
Average annual crush: 2,000 tonnes
Average no. cases produced: 170,000

Principal wines & brands	Cellar potential
Pinot Noir Methode Champ.	0-2 years
Fume Blanc	2-5 years
Semillon	2-5 years
Chardonnay	2-5 years
Cabernet/Merlot	5-10 years
Cabernet Sauvignon	5-10 years
Shiraz	5-10 years

Public & trade tours: By appointment only
Cellar door & mail order sales: Yes
Hours open to public: 10 am-5 pm daily
Points of interest: McLarens on the Lake is the adjoining restaurant and functions centre, gardens and lakefront picnic area. Opal factory and Australian gift shop in the complex.
Retail distribution: Southern Cross, Australia-wide

The Barn Restaurant and Gallery

The Barn was Australia's first wine region hospitality house when it was created back in 1970 by David Dridan, one of Australia's foremost artists, and David Hardy, great-grandson of Thomas Hardy, the wine pioneer who had in fact owned what was the old stage stop for changing horses between Adelaide and Victor Harbor.

The gorgeous whitewashed thatched-roof cottage sits serenely on the Chalk Hill road corner as one enters the main street of the town, off the Main South Road.

The entrance is a quaint and characterful gallery, warmed in winter by a lovely log fire. The exhibitions are always changing and full of interest. The main restaurant opens up into a vine-covered courtyard, protected from inclement weather. Off the restaurant is the marvellous cellar, where one can wander to choose from a superb array of the region's wines, as well as sparkling and fortifieds.

As you enter, a warm welcome greets you from Brian and Rose Tierney, who have run this culinary mecca for almost 20 years. Downstairs is the cellar function room which has hosted many a fine wine and food function over the years. It's even complete with its resident spirit, a kindly soul from the last century, who has made her appearance from time to time over the years; in the most vivid, to comfort a child crying on the steps, she materialised in a beautiful Victorian Regency dress.

One could not forget Ann Lavis, the delightful hostess who has added her special sparkle to The Barn since its inception. I always look forward to my next pilgrimage to this special place.

Hugo Winery

I might start this expose on Hugo Wines with a few words of philosophy from winemaker John Hugo - "The McLaren Vale region is a region of small winemakers, people who know their craft - ply it well - I firmly believe that we have to be specialists, people who pick a path in wine production and then follow that course."

John Hugo's philosophy is basically to use his own grapes from his 30 acre vineyard, established by his father, Colin in 1950.

John is a fastidious viticulturist and the quality of his grapes are renowned in the region. He first began work in the family enterprise in 1970 and established the winery in 1982. Currently, he is planting another 18 acres of vines, which will come into bearing in about 1997. His reds, a cabernet sauvignon and a shiraz, are rich and full-bodied in the tradition of the region and there is also a dry rhine riesling, and more recently, a full-bodied chardonnay. The tawny port, 'Solero' started by John in the 1970s is worth the trip to the cellar door to find.

The winery is the highest in the McLaren Vale and has a wonderful panoramic view.

HUGO WINES PTY LTD	Average no. cases produced: 5,000	
	Principal wines & brands	**Cellar potential**
Address: Elliott Road, McLaren Flat SA 5171	Shiraz	4-6 years
Phone: (08) 383 0098	Chardonnay	3-5 years
Fax: (08) 383 0446	Cabernet Sauvignon	4-6 years
Established: 1982	Riesling	2-5 years
Owner: John Hugo	Tawny Port	10+ years
Winemaker: John Hugo		
Principal varieties grown: Shiraz, cabernet sauvignon, chardonnay, riesling, grenache, cabernet franc	**Public & trade tours:** No	
	Cellar door & mail order sales: Yes	
Ha under vine: 20	**Hours open to public:** 10.30 am-5 pm daily	
Average annual crush: 110 tonnes	**Retail distribution:** SA, NSW, Vic, New Zealand, Hong Kong	

Haselgrove Wines

Haselgrove is a winery on the move in McLaren Vale. Nick Haselgrove is the well credentialled winemaker. His grandfather, Ron Haselgrove put Mildara on the map many decades ago and his great uncle Colin was a winemaking legend at Hardy's and then Reynella.

Nick won the 'Bushing King' title in 1993 with his 1992 Futures shiraz. This is Haselgroves premium wine sourced from their own vineyard in McLaren Vale, producing about 1,200 dozen bottles per year. Since 1983 this wine has been pre-sold to the winery's mailorder customers. Basically the buyer commits and pays for three dozen bottles whilst the wine is still maturing in oak. In the past, some of the wine was reserved for retail sale from 1994 vintage onwards "Futures" will only be available this way, however plans are currently underway to release a Reserve Shiraz from the "Futures" vineyard which will be available in fine wine outlets.

Reg Wymond is principle and managing director, with the other two owners carrying quite high profiles. Mark Hastwell has various business interests in Adelaide and Martin Lightfoot is a leading light in the regional development of McLaren Vale. Mark and Martin also own a vineyard in McLaren Vale.

Haselgroves have formed a joint venture with Kay Brothers at Amery and have invested into the winery with winemaking equipment. The Haselgrove wines are certainly among the best in the region.

At the cellar door, which is situated at the "Futures" vineyard, Haselgrove run a lovely alfresco luncheon from Wednesday through to Sunday each week. During winter, a wood fire makes a warm cosy atmosphere - in the summer the conservatory overlooking the vineyard is a great place to spend a lazy lunch that could happily drift well into the afternoon.

HASELGROVE WINES
Address: Cnr. Kangarilla & Foggo Rds, McLaren Vale SA 5171
Phone: (08) 323 8706
Fax: (08) 323 8049
Winemaker: Nick Haselgrove
Principal varieties grown: Shiraz, cabernet sauvignon, chardonnay, merlot
Ha under vine: 17
Average annual crush: 400 tonnes
Average no. cases produced: 17,500

Principal wines & brands	Cellar potential
Reserve Shiraz	10+years
Futures Shiraz	10+ years
Cabernet Merlot	2-5 years
Grenache Shirz	2-5 years
Chardonnay	2-5 years
Sauvignon Blanc	2-5 years

Public & trade tours: No
Cellar door & mail order sales: Yes
Hours open to public: 9 am-5 pm weekdays, 10 am-5 pm w/e
Points of interest: Cellar door lunches Wed-Sun
Retail distribution: Sydney, Melbourne, Adelaide.

Stevens Cambrai

Graham Stevens is a down to earth man who has great skill and experience as a winemaker. After working for seven years at d'Arenberg, he became winemaker/manager for Coriole from 1969 to 1979.

In 1974 he purchased land at nearby McLaren Flat and began establishing his own vineyard and winery The property was named Cambrai and after resigning from Coriole in 1979 Graham began full time operations at his own establishment.

Graham has a reputation for his excellent wines, with many gold, silver and bronze awards, several championship awards and three 'Bushing King Festival' Awards for best wine McLaren Vale wine to his credit. The latest Bushing crown was in 1985 with his 1984 McLaren Heights Hermitage.

The Stevens wines show the cool climate characteristics of berry aroma and flavour. As the vineyard is situated in the foothills of the Mt. Lofty Ranges, southeast of McLaren Vale, the overall temperature is slightly cooler than most of the region, and vintage is a little later. The Stevens Cambrai wines have gained a reputation for quality with each vintage.

Stevens Cambrai Winery is a family business with a warm family feel. It truly reflects the renaissance of the region in the seventies and is well worth a visit.

Graham Stevens

STEVENS CAMBRAI WINES PTY LTD
Address: Hamiltons Road, McLaren Flat SA 5171
Phone: (08) 383 0251
Fax: (08) 383 0251
Established: 1975
Owner: Graham Stevens
Winemaker: Graham Stevens
Principal varieties grown: Chardonnay, müller thurgau, frontignac, shiraz, cabernet sauvignon, pinot noir, malbec, cabernet franc, zinfandel
Ha under vine: 6
Average annual crush: 80-100 tonnes
Average no. cases produced: 4-5,000
Cellar door & mail order sales: Yes
Hours open to public: 9 am-5 pm daily
Retail distribution: Queensland, Canberra, Melbourne.

Hillstowe

D r. Chris Laurie and his son Hamish form a pretty formidable team. Chris, a medical practitioner turned viticulture and long-time wine enthusiast, has now become the full-time executive in charge of this high profile and multi-faceted wine business. Hamish, who is responsible for sales and marketing, was formerly an export manager for several years with Yalumba, which followed vintages spent in both France and California.

It all started in 1970, when Chris and then partner, David Buxton, purchased an excellent, but run down vineyard at McLaren Vale. Followed by replanting with classic premium varieties were several successful vintages, Chris then looked to the Adelaide Hills for potential sites. It was on his Carey Gully property in the cooler climes of the Hills that he discovered an ideal vineyard site for early ripening varieties chardonnay and pinot noir.

Great fruit and top technical handling, hence the company motto "Better Vines - Better Wines" has led to some exceptional wines. In a relatively short time Hillstowe has achieved an impressive track record: 4 trophies, 10 gold, 13 silver and 57 bronze medals. The Hillstowe range consists of McLaren Vale chardonnay, McLaren Vale sauvignon blanc and Buxton cabernet merlot. Hillstowe wines can be tasted and purchased at the Salopian Inn at McLaren Vale daily and now also at the new Hillstowe Winery complex at Hahndorf in the Adelaide Hills - but more of that in the Adelaide Hills chapter

The Salopian Inn

T he historic old building on the corner of the main South Road and McMurtrie Road as you travel south from McLaren Vale was commissioned as an inn way back in 1856.

During the 1970s The Salopian, the name for someone born in the English county of Shropshire, was purchased by David Hardy with a view to resuscitating it as a historic inn.

The licensing laws changed, however, and David sold the property which was finally restored and turned into a restaurant and wine cellar.

The Salopian has forged a name as a high quality, friendly restaurant and deserves every bit of praise heaped upon it.

The classic old colonial windows look out on vineyards in all directions. The decor is rustic but classy and owner-mine host Pip Forrester is extremely personable. She runs a tight ship with great support from the local wineries.

Treat yourself to a meal at the Salopian, I'm sure it will be a memorable one.

Richard Hamilton Wines

Proprietor of wineries and vineyards at Willunga in McLaren Vale and Leconfield at Coonawarra, Dr Richard Hamilton is both great-great-grandson and namesake of one of the founders of South Australia's wine industry.

Richard Hamilton (1st) established the famous Ewell Vineyard at Marion, near Adelaide, in 1837, one year before John Reynell planted his first vines. Hamilton's Leconfield winery and vineyard were founded by Richard's uncle, Sydney Hamilton (the pioneer of refrigeration and quality white table winemaking in Australia) in 1974. Richard's father, Burton, affectionately known as 'Burt', was a noted vigneron and spent the later years of his long life helping young Richard make wine at his McLaren winery.

From this long family commitment to the wine industry, Dr. Hamilton has re-established the proud tradition founded by his ancestor. The vineyards at McLaren Vale date back to 1892 from cuttings sourced from the old Ewell vineyard and were acquired by the Hamiltons in 1947. The first wines released under the Richard Hamilton label were made in 1972. All the Richard Hamilton wines are made from grapes grown in the company's three vineyards in McLaren Vale, and there is a small vineyard at Coonawarra on the terra rossa strip, near Leconfield. The range consists of premium table wines, with an excellent chardonnay leading the way.

Richard Hamilton has been instrumental in the revival of grenache as a premium variety in the region from very old bush vines growing at Burton's Vineyard, one of the old family properties. The Burton's Vineyard wine includes 40 per cent old vine shiraz, a truly great drop.

Another vineyard-designated wine is the Farm Block Semillon, a rich and characterful wine that benefits from a few years in the cellar. The Hut Block is the company's ancient dry grown vineyard planted in 1892 which is the source of the Hut Block Cabernet, a substantial wine with elegance, showing McLaren Vale characteristics to perfection. It is from here too, that grapes from the 100 year Old Vine Shiraz are sourced. These ancient vines are being rejuvenated with a new trellis to keep them going for another 100 years!

The star label is Richard Hamilton Chardonnay, which was the first wine of this variety planted in McLaren Vale. Richard planted these vines in 1975. Like many of the wines, the chardonnay is aged in small oak casks, imparting it with complex flavours to match rich McLaren Vale fruit. Other whites in the range are the Noble Riesling, the Loire styled Hamilton Estate Chenin Blanc and the Hamilton Ewell Unwooded Chardonnay.

Wines are made by Ralph Fowler at Dr. Hamilton's sister winery Leconfield at Coonawarra, and ably marketed by Richard Hamilton and his team, including Brian Miller and dynamic Darren Gall.

Over the years when the demands of Richard's plastic surgery practice became too great, his father Burt lent a hand in the winery, working right up until his death in 1994, his 90th year and 71st vintage. As in times gone by, this family is keeping alive the noble traditions of the South Australian wine industry.

RICHARD HAMILTON WINES
Address: Main Road, Willunga SA 5172
Direction: South of the McLaren Vale township
Phone: (085) 56 2288
Fax: (085) 56 2868
Established: 1972
Owner: Dr Richard Hamilton
Winemaker: Ralph Fowler
Principal varieties grown: Chardonnay, cabernet sauvignon, shiraz, merlot, cabernet franc, sauvignon blanc, grenache

Principal wines & brands	Cellar potential
Chardonnay	2-5 years
Farm Block Semillon	2-5 years
Hut Block Cabernet Sauvignon	5-10 years
Old Vines Shiraz	5-10 years
Burton's Vineyard Grenache	5-10 years

Public & trade tours: Yes (by appointment only for buses or large groups)
Cellar door & mail order sales: Yes
Hours open to public: 10 am-5 pm Mon-Sat; 11 am-5 pm Sun and public holidays
Points of interest: Winery owned by Dr Richard Hamilton whose family has been making wine since 1837. Richard Hamilton Chardonnay is the winery's specialty. Other wines include semillon, cabernet sauvignon and a magnificent shiraz from 100 year-old-vines.
Retail distribution: Fine wine liquor stores and restaurants

Crestview

Crestview is housed in the old Horndale Winery, which nestles quietly into outer suburbia of southern Adelaide.

The winery was constructed in the 1890's by a Mr. Cholmondely. The buildings of beautifully faced stone cascade down the hillside, cleverly designed to use nature's force of gravity in the winemaking process. The grapes arrived at the crusher located at the top of the hill. The juice then flowed to the next level for clarification and then on to the maturation level before finally flowing down to the bottling and storage level. The distillery was then located a little further down the hill.

Today's energy conservationists would be most impressed. Crestview, an entrepreneurial wine venture, took over the disused premises in 1989 and each year they quietly crush a very large vintage, a great deal destined for the overseas market. The wine is made under the tutelage of Robert Dundon, for many years the red winemaker for Hardy's Wines. The wines are marketed under a number of brands, many of which pay homage to the winery's history, such as Bosanquet Estate and Beacon Hill, which takes its name from the original vineyard on the hill behind the winery, where a beacon for air navigation was placed.

The Crestview wines are all excellent, approachable drinking styles and good value for money. Rob Dundon also makes his Beresford Range of super premium wines at the winery. Rob has been carefully crafting these excellent varietal wines from the best

batches of the Southern Vales region for many years and they are worth seeking out.

If you are in Adelaide with an hour or so to spare pop in to Crestview — it's just past the Happy Valley Reservoir before you start to climb Chandlers Hill. Your wine cellar will be glad you made this little foray back into our wine history.

CRESTVIEW PTY LTD

Address: 49 Fraser Avenue, Happy Valley SA 5159
Phone: (08) 322 3611
Fax: (08) 322 3610
Established: 1989
Owner: Crestview Pty. Ltd.
Winemaker: Rob Dundon
Average no. cases produced: 85,000

Principal wines & brands	Cellar potential
Beresford Cabernet Merlot	5-10 years
Beresford Semillon Sauv. Blanc	2-5 years
Katherine Hills Chardonnay	2-5 years
Katherine Hills Cabernet Merlot	2-5 years
Echo Point Cabernet Sauvignon	2-5 years
Bosanquet Sem. Chardonnay	2-5 years
Bosanquet Cabernet Shiraz	2-5 years

Public & trade tours: By appointment only
Cellar door & mail order sales: Yes
Hours open to public: 11 am-5 pm Mon-Sun
Points of interest: BBQ entertaining area, century-old cellars, oldest operating gravity-feed winery.
Retail distribution: National distribution as well as New Zealand, Japan, United Kingdom, Holland, United States, Canada, Belgium and Germany.

Dyson Wines

It would be hard to find someone more happy with his lot in life than Allan Dyson. Allan started winemaking back in 1965 at Seaview, when Ben Chaffey was still at the helm, after which he travelled over to the Hunter Valley in 1970 and made wine for Hollydene for six years.

By 1977 Allan was back in McLaren Vale making wine at Middlebrook. The same year, he started planting vines on his estate near the coast, not far from Australia's first "naturalist" beach. He planted all the vines by hand himself and knows everyone of them intimately. In fact, in his own words "I've got 8,764 reasons to be happy."

Looking extremely young for his years, Allan tends his vines, makes the characterful wines, including a methode champenoise which he ferments in the cellars, and even does his own disgorging.

One would think he was too busy to say 'G'day;' not Allan - he loves people, and it shows in his wines. His lovely garden and tasting cottage also make this a memorable visit.

DYSON WINES

Address: Sherriff Road, Maslin Beach SA 5170
Direction: 7km west of McLaren Vale wine region
Phone: (08) 386 1092
Fax: (08) 327 0066
Established: 1977
Owner: Allan Dyson
Winemaker: Allan Dyson
Principal varieties grown: Cabernet sauvignon, chardonnay, sauvignon blanc, pinot noir, pinot meunier
Ha under vine: 6
Average annual crush: 30 tonnes
Average no. cases produced: 1,000 - 1,500

Principal wines & brands	Cellar potential
Clarice Cabernet Sauvignon	5-10 years
Dyson Chardonnay	2-5 years
Dyson Sauvignon Blanc	2-5 years
Dyson Methode Champenoise	2-5 years
Dyson Fortified Sauv. Blanc	10+ years

Public & trade tours: By appointment only
Cellar door & mail order sales: Yes
Hours open to public: 10 am-5 pm daily
Points of interest: Vineyard and winery located 2.5kms from coast. One of the closest vineyards to the sea in Australia.
Retail distribution: Sydney, Roger Brown Wine Agencies; South Australia, distribution from winery.

Chapel Hill

One of McLaren Vale's most exciting wineries is the beautiful Chapel Hill. The charming 19th century chapel is perched atop one of the highest hills of the region, with awesome views - the hills, the coast, the contoured vines on the surrounding slopes. On a summer's day with a picnic on the lawns outside the winery, one could indeed imagine oneself in paradise.

The chapel is now a lovely gallery and tasting centre. The winery has grown up all around, carefully contoured into the hill faces and constructed, like the chapel, in the attractive ironstone for which the region is so renowned.

The wines of Chapel Hill reflect the serene, sensitive balance of their home. Winemaker, Pam Dunsford, drives herself resolutely in her search for perfection in their creation. Fully qualified, Pam earned her spurs with the large Wynns/Seaview organisation, and went on to be one of the most sought-after wine consultants in Australia. Pam was Roseworthy College's first female graduate in winemaking some 20 years ago, and has travelled the world of wine extensively, always seeking self improvement. She spent a year in Champagne, has worked several vintages in France, and has studied in California.

Chapel Hill's show successes are already legendary. The state-of-the-art new winery

complex was completed in 1993 and is one of the most advanced in the world. The Gerard family, one of Adelaide's most innovative business successes, has invested heavily but wisely in Chapel Hill. They have some 125 acres of vineyards around the winery and nearby in the hills near Kangarilla.

Chapel Hill also source grapes from Coonawarra, Padthaway and the Eden Valley. The labelling of all their wines is precise and the choice of

fruit for each wine is painstakingly made. It is hard in fact, to imagine a better set up winery, winemaking philosophy or a more dedicated approach. Somehow, one can sense a little divine inspiration focussed through this beautiful 'Chapel on the Hill'.

CHAPEL HILL WINERY PTY LTD
Address: Chapel Hill Road, McLaren Vale SA 5171
Direction: 40 km from Adelaide, on the northern edge of the McLaren Vale region.
Phone: (08) 323 8429
Fax: (08) 323 9245
Established: 1979
Owner: Gerard Industries
Winemaker: Pam Dunsford
Principal varieties grown: Shiraz, cabernet sauvignon, chardonnay, verdelho, merlot
Ha under vine: 45
Average annual crush: 700 tonnes
Average no. cases produced: 50,000

Principal wines & brands	Cellar potential
Reserve	10+ years
Cabernet Sauvignon	10+ years
The Vicar	10+ years
McLaren Vale Shiraz	10+ years
Unwooded Chardonnay	10+ years
Reserve Chardonnay	10+ years
Eden Valley Riesling	10+ years
Tawny Port	10+ years

Public & trade tours: No
Cellar door & mail order sales: Yes
Hours open to public: 9 am-5 pm Mon-Fri, 11 am-5 pm w/e, PH
Points of interest: Art exhibitions in historic chapel built in 1865. Picnic grounds and BBQ adjacent to the winery at Chapel Hill Park.
Retail distribution: Negociants Australia, UK, USA, New Zealand, Canada, Switzerland.

Tatachilla

Tatachilla has happily just gained a new lease of life. During vintage time in 1995, the restored cellars were re-opened by the Premier of South Australia, Dean Brown, and blessed by the Archbishop of Adelaide, Ian George, and Father Paul Cleary.

The luncheon which followed, orchestrated by Pip Forrester of the Salopian Inn with her own chef, Andrew Summers and the talented Russell Jeavons, was a total success. One could not help feeling that at last, Tatachilla was sailing on the right course.

The events that were to create Tatachilla began late in the last century, when Horace Pridmore bought land at McLaren Vale and using wattle slabs built a small cellar in 1901. His brother Cyril joined him from England, they bought a property in the main street of the town and constructed stone cellars, calling the winery The Wattles. The original foundation stone was unearthed during recent renovations and has been restored to its rightful place.

In 1910, Penfolds bought the winery in an expansion program and it grew considerably over the years. In 1965 with the help of the State Government, 185 local growers bought the winery from Penfolds and renamed it The Southern Vales Co-operative. The wines were mainly sold in bulk to other wineries or overseas, but the best were sold under the Tatachilla label after the long-closed superb cellars on Tatachilla

Road, south of the town.

Local grower Vic Zerella saw an opportunity and with the assistance of experienced wine executive Keith Smith who had run Kaiser Stuhl and Wolf Blass Wines, they worked diligently and creatively to restore Tatachilla's fortunes. The annual crush of grapes has grown from 740 tonnes to 4,500 tonnes in three short years. The winemaking is in the hands of Michael Fragos who grew up nearby at Willunga, and holds both a Bachelor of Science degree and a Graduate Diploma in Wine, and 'Sparky' Marquis, the 1980 Roseworthy dux of the winemaking degree course.

The company has appointed Australian expatriot US "Winemaker of The Year" Daryl Groom as consultant winemaker. Groom will visit Australia regularly each year and Tatachilla's winemakers will work with him during the Californian vintage.

The wines I tried at their launch were all abundant in lively fruit flavours and of the highest quality.

An interesting wine amongst them was the Keystone Grenache/Shiraz, reviving the name Keystone used to sell enormous amounts of McLaren Vale Burgundy on the export market in years gone by. This lifted spicy wine, abundant in wild berry flavours, is a winner, as I am sure Tatachilla will be too following its rebirth.

TATACHILLA WINERY
Address: 151 Main Road, McLaren Vale SA 5171
Phone: (08) 323 8656
Fax: (08) 323 9096/(08) 323 9094
Established: 1901
Owner: Consortium headed by Vic Zerella & Keith Smith
Winemaker: Michael Fragos
Principal varieties grown: shiraz, sparkling margus
Average annual crush: 3925 tonnes
Average no. cases produced: 40,000

Principal wines & brands	Cellar potential
Sparkling Malbec	2-5 years
Chardonnay	2-5 years
Merlot	5-10 years
Bluestone Brut N.V.	0-1 year
Riesling	7-10 years
Semillon/Sauvignon Blanc	2-5 years
Cabernet Sauvignon	5-10 years
'Keystone' Grenache/Shiraz	5-10 years
'Growers'	2-5 years
'Partners'	2-5 years

Public & trade tours: Yes (by appointment only)
Cellar door & mail order sales: Yes
Hours open to public: 10 am-5 pm Mon-Sat; 11 am-5 pm Sun. & public holidays
Points of interest: Historic winery established in 1901 has had a chequered history and is being renovated to its former glory by the new owners. Tours include a history of McLaren Vale district and the winery and finish in the Barrel Room. In addition to tastings and sales, cellar door offers for sale a large range of regional produce, posters and corporate wear and gifts. Wine purchased in cellar door can be sent anywhere in Australia.
Retail distribution: Chace Agencies, SA; The Wine Company, NSW/Vic; David Johnstone, Tas; Harry Williams, ACT; Global Liquor, Qld; FDC, WA.

Wirilda Creek

Kerry Flanagan and Karen Shertock opened the Wirilda Creek Winery in 1993 and it is really an extension of their lives.

Kerry has a rich and varied background in the wine and hospitality areas. He graduated from Roseworthy in 1980, having spent some time in the Penfolds red wine cellars during his course. He worked at Wirra Wirra during the time Brian Croser and Petaluma were involved in the winemaking. This experience was followed by a stint in the Hunter, then he returned to McLaren Vale and assisted at Hazelmere, Coriole, Woodstock and the old Southern Vales (now Tatachilla).

Kerry has a definite flair in the hospitality side of wine, and saw the Old Salopian Inn as an ideal opportunity to combine the two. Having secured the Salopian, he proceeded to dig out the cellars and launched the McLaren Vale Wine Centre. Kerry and gifted chef Russell Jeavons created a fine reputation for this lovely venue.

Kerry sold the Salopian and took off overseas, travelling the wine regions of Europe and the USA. On returning, he and Karen set about building Wirilda Creek. The building of rammed earth fits discreetly into

the vineyards and the casual alfresco dining area is a delight. They also have several excellent rustic country style accommodation suites, all tastefully appointed with full facilities including a country kitchen.

The wines are equally as impressive. The first two reds released, the 1993 shiraz and 1993 cabernet merlot, were both trophy winners..

In the near future look out for Kerry's Kangaroo Island wines from premium grapes grown at pristine Antechamber Bay - this

vineyard is proposed to put Kangaroo Island on the map as a new wine district.

WIRILDA CREEK WINERY
Address: RSD 90 McMurtrie Road McLaren Vale SA 5171
Direction: 2 km southeast of McLaren Vale township
Phone: (08) 323 9688
Fax: (08) 323 9688
Established: 1993
Owner: Kerry Flanagan, Karen Shertock
Winemaker: Kerry Flanagan
Principal varieties grown: cabernet sauvignon, merlot, malbec, shiraz
Ha under vine: 3
Average annual crush: 25 tonnes
Average no. cases produced: 1,500-2,000

Principal wines & brands	Cellar potential
Sauvignon Blanc	2-5 years
Semillon Oak Matured	2-5 years
Cabernet Merlot	5-10 years
Shiraz "Rare"	5-15 years
Shiraz	5-15 years
Cabernet Shiraz Melbec	5-10 years

Public & trade tours: Yes
Cellar door sales: Yes
Hours open to public: 11 am-5 pm every day
Points of interest: Restaurant, accommodation (4 rooms), extra virgin olive oil, olives, wine vinegar, bike hire, bouledrome for petanque, enviro-sensitive building of earth and recycled materials
Retail distribution: Queensland, New South Wales, Victoria, South Australia, Australian Capital Territory and California. Mailing list. Internet.

St Francis Winery

ST. FRANCIS WINERY
Address: Bridge Street, Old Reynella SA 5161
Phone: (08) 381 1925
Fax: (08) 322 6655
Established: 1856
Winemaker: Various depending on variety
Average no. cases produced: 8,000

Principal wines & brands	Cellar potential
Grenache	3-5 years
Classic Dry White	3-5 years
Shiraz	5 years
Cabernet Sauvignon	10 years
Chardonnay	3 years
Late harvest frontignac	3 years
Ports	10+ years
Bulk Port	10+ years
Cleanskins	Usually 1 year

Public & trade tours: Yes
Cellar door & mail order sales: Yes
Hours open to public: 8.30 am-5 pm Mon-Fri; 10 am-5 pm w/e & P/H
Points of interest: Restaurant, recreation grounds and motel
Retail distribution: Mailing list, selected bottle shops and restaurants.

If one looks to the left as the Main South Road sweeps past Reynella, one spies the St. Francis Winery with its solid stone buildings and vine-covered pergolas.

A pretty sight indeed sitting on the shores of a lake, St. Francis heralds your entry into the wine country.

The winery is surrounded by an accommodation and restaurant complex.

Why not stop off and start your visit to the region right away?

The wines of St. Francis have been innovative in style, well presented and excellent value for money. In 1993, St. Francis launched a single vineyard grenache from bush vines over 50 years old, a wine which shows concentrated spicy flavours and vibrant colour, delicious drinking now. The wine has captured wine drinkers'

imagination and palates - look out for it.

St. Francis are also very successful with their promotion of individually labelled miniature ports, making ideal corporate and personal gifts, or for "bomboniere" at weddings.

Modern McLaren Vale is full of success stories, none more interesting than that of Scott and Anne Collett.

Scott, his brothers Ian and Stephen and their father, wine consultant Doug, established the winery in 1974. Doug bought the property, then named Woodstock, in 1973 and quickly rejuvenated the old vineyard.

Before settling down at Woodstock, Scott had some diverse training in the wine industry. He left Roseworthy with a degree, before making wine at a big Griffith winery for three years. Six months of travelling California running a mobile bottling line and other visits to winemaking areas of Italy, Germany and France broadened Scott's experience.

Returning to Woodstock in 1982, a young Scott attacked the winemaking with real enthusiasm and a great deal of vision. Scott released high quality McLaren Vale reds and whites under the Woodstock label. In 1986 he won the Wine Bushing Crown for the best wine of the region, and was named South Australian Winemaker of the Year. His wines went on to achieve national distribution as well as international sales to several overseas countries.

On the home front, Scott, his wife Anne and their three children, Max, Peter and Sophia, live in a big home overlooking the Woodstock vineyards. Anne and Scott believe wine should be enjoyed with food, so they built a magnificent restaurant and entertaining venue next to the winery, naming it The Coterie. The Coterie blends superbly into the environment; constructed of ochre-coloured rammed earth by Ian Collett, its clever design is like a giant slice of cake with the full length windows and French doors opening out to a native garden under the stately gums. Across the road, one can see kangaroos and wallabies peacefully grazing in the Douglas Scrub Sanctuary.

Chef Kay Cazzolato and her young enthusiastic staff run a really top class restaurant, generally open for lunch on Sundays and holiday Mondays. Each Easter Woodstock Coterie hosts a "Food, Wine, Music and Art Affair". The 1995 event was officially opened by HRH the Duchess of Kent, featuring an art exhibition, sculpture, glassware, music, fine crafts, furniture and a display of exotic roses, along with the food and wine — a real cultural extravaganza superbly staged. Woodstock Coterie also joins the regional food and wine events "From The Sea & The Vines" in late May and "The Continuous Picnic" in early October.

The Coterie often hosts guest chefs and their restaurant team for a month of Sundays. These restaurateurs enjoy a refreshing new kitchen and visits to McLaren Vale. The Coterie guests enjoy a varied menu from some of Adelaide's better restaurants.

For Scott and Anne Collett, the vision became a reality. They grow and make a range of premium McLaren Vale wines and offer them with superb food in delightful surroundings at Woodstock Winery & Coterie.

Set aside a lazy Sunday afternoon to enjoy Woodstock's side of the wonderful McLaren Vale Wine Region.

WOODSTOCK

Address: Douglas Gully Road, McLaren Flat SA 5171
Phone: (08) 383 0156
Fax: (08) 383 0437
Established: 1974
Winemaker: Scott Collett/John Weeks
Principal varieties grown: Cabernet sauvignon, shiraz, grenache, chardonnay, riesling, semillon
Ha under vine: 24
Average annual crush: 250 tonnes
Average no. cases produced: 15,000

Principal wines & brands	Cellar potential
Cabernet	5-10 years
Shiraz	5-10 years
Chardonnay	2-10 years
Botrytis Sweet White	2-5 years
Sauvignon Blanc	2-5 years
Semillon	2-7 years
Tawny Port	5 years

Trade tours: By appointment only
Cellar door & mail order sales: Yes
Hours open to public: 9 am-5 pm Mon-Fri; 12-5 pm weekends and public holidays
Points of interest: Woodstock Coterie - function centre for group bookings anytime. Open to public for Sunday lunch and holiday Monday lunch.
Retail Distribution: National, United Kingdom & New Zealand.

McLaren Vale Olive Groves

Where the vine grows so does the olive. In the traditional wine growing countries of France, Spain, Greece and Italy the olive groves blend happily with the vineyards.

The history of olives in McLaren Vale goes back to my own great great grandfather, Thomas Hardy, who planted olive trees on all the roads and spare land on his property, Tintara, and advised his neighbours to do likewise. The beautiful olives, olive oil and other products were not only a great adjunct to the table but added a welcome extra source of income. Some of these century-old trees can still be seen around the region.

In 1989 Guy and Adele Lloyd bought the olive groves near the Lloyd family winery, Coriole. David lloyd has taken over the management and continues to develop the 56 acres of olives so that today the McLaren Vale Olive Groves are producing over 10 different varieties of table and oil olives.

The table olives, principally the Greek Kalamata olives, are pickled slowly using a traditional method, whereby fresh water is used to remove the acid, followed by a relatively low salt brine and vinegar mixture. The Kalamata olives are also made into a pesto, and flavoured with garlic. This is now used in a number of local restaurants.

The cold pressed extra virgin olive oil is processed in the old oil press using traditional woven mats.

The olive harvest begins in April just as the grape harvest ends and it is in perfect sympathy with wine. The olive grove is now producing vinegar from locally made wines and supplies these through the beautiful Cottage on the property along with locally made jams and preserves, arts and crafts. The health benefits of olives and olive oil, especially when produced in the traditional manner used at the McLaren Vale Olive Groves, are well documented.

During the season, tours are available through the groves and the factory. In addition to selling the olives and other produce, morning and afternoon teas are also available from the Cottage, as are picnic baskets which can be taken out and enjoyed on the lush grass under the trees. If you feel like a substantial meal, barbecue packs accompanied by salads dressed with the grove's own oil and vinegar dressings are available to cook yourself or, alternatively, you can sit back whilst the pleasant staff do the cooking for you.

Why not complete your visit to McLaren Vale with this unique experience and make that magic connection between the olive and the vine. It will do you the world of good!

Shottesbrooke

Nick and Chris Holmes have just completed a splendid new home for their Shottesbrooke wines. This sensitively and cleverly conceived state-of-the-art winery fits beautifully into its vineyard setting towards the hills from McLaren Flat. This is one of the most impressive new wineries I have seen in this country.

Nick studied at Roseworthy, graduating in 1971. After five years winemaking in Clare, he took off overseas where he experienced a great deal of winemaking before returning to Australia. In 1981, he purchased a property at Myponga in the Southern Adelaide Hills, naming it after the Parish of Shottesbrooke in England, where one of his ancestors had been the vicar.

Nick planted 20 acres to vines, including cabernet sauvignon, sauvignon blanc, merlot, malbec and chardonnay. The first wines were released in 1984.

Nick was for many years the winemaker at Ryecroft, where he also made the Shottesbrooke wines. Shottesbrooke is now a true boutique winery in its new home. Why not drop in and see the Holmes and taste their great wine. Don't forget to stock up - their merlot is a knockout.

SHOTTESBROOKE

Address: 1 Bagshaws Road, McLaren Flat SA 5171
Phone: (08) 383 0002
Fax: (08) 383 0222
Established: Vineyards1981, Winery 1994
Owner: Nick Holmes
Winemaker: Nick Holmes
Principal varieties grown: Sauvignon blanc, cabernet sauvignon, merlot, chardonnay, shiraz
Ha under vine: 20

Principal wines & brands	Cellar potential
Cabernet/Merlot	5-10 years
Merlot	3-5 years
Shiraz	5-10 years
Sauvignon Blanc	2-3 years
Chardonnay	2-5 years

Cellar door & Mail order sales: Yes
Hours open to public: Closed Monday (except public holidays) 10 am-4.30 pm Tues-Fri; Sat-Sun and public holidays11-5 pm
Points of interest: creek
Retail distribution: All states, United Kingdom

Maxwell Wines

Mark and Ken Maxwell established Maxwell Wines in 1979. The winery, featuring an historic homestead, is situated on the outskirts of McLaren Vale township on the Kangarilla Road.

Ken designed and constructed much of the winemaking equipment himself, employing knowledge and skills developed over his long and prestigious winemaking career.

Winemaking responsibilities and management have been taken over by Ken's son Mark, who has displayed considerable flair in this role. Maxwell Wines are in the process of building a new winery and tasting centre opposite Manning Park on Olivers Road in an idyllic setting.

During the nine months of the year between vintages, winery equipment usually remains idle. Maxwells however, utilise their winery throughout these months for the production of mead (honey wine). A range of meads are released, including a standard mead which makes a delightful cool mixed drink; a spiced mead which can be served hot; and a liqueur mead which contains a higher degree of alcohol and is a delicious after-dinner drink.

The family's enthusiasm for their product can be experienced at the winery where visitors are very welcome.

Mark Maxwell's dynamic drive and innovative style will make Maxwell Wines' future exciting indeed.

MAXWELL WINES

Address: Olivers Road, McLaren Vale SA 5171
Phone: (08) 323 8200
Fax: (08) 323 8900
Established: 1979 at old address
Winemaker: Mark Maxwell
Principal varieties grown:
Shiraz, cabernet sauvignon, merlot, semillon, sauvignon blanc, riesling
Ha under vine: 8
Average no. cases produced: 6,000 (mead) 4,500 (wine)

Principal wines & brands	Cellar potential
Sauvignon Blanc	2-5 years
Semillon	2-5 years
Chardonnay	2-5 years
Cabernet Merlot	5-10 years
Ellen Street Shiraz	5-10 years
Lime Cave Cabernet	5-10 years
Maxwell Mead in three styles	10+ years

Trade tours: By appointment
Cellar door & mail order sales: Yes
Hours open to public: 10 am-5 pm daily
Points of interest: Function room, maze
Retail distribution: National, enquiries to (08) 323 8200

Coriole

CORIOLE VINEYARDS
Address: Chaffeys Road, McLaren Vale
Phone: (08) 323 8305
Fax: (08) 323 9136
Year of establishment: 1968
Winemaker: Stephen Hall
Principal varieties grown: Shiraz, cabernet sauvignon, chenin blanc, sangiovese, semillon
Ha under vine: 20
Average annual crush: 290 tonnes
Average no. cases produced: 20,000

Principal wines & brands	Cellar potential
Shiraz	5-10 years
Redstone Shiraz/Cab. Sauv.	5-10 years
Sangiovese	2-5 years
Cabernet Sauvignon	5-10 years
"Mary Kathleen"	
Cabernet/Merlot/Cab. Franc	10 years
Lloyd Reserve Shiraz	10+ years
Chenin Blanc	0-1 years
Semillon	2-5 years
Chardonnay	2-5 years

Public & trade tours: By appointment only
Cellar door & mail order sales: Yes
Hours open to public: 9 am-5 pm Mon-Fri, 11 am-5 pm w/e & PH
Points of interest: Tastings and sales are held in the old ironstone barn built in 1860. Casual picnics and occasional functions are held in the well-known cottage garden and original homestead of the property.
Retail distribution: South Australia, Tucker Seabrook Classic Wines, (08) 211 7599; Victoria, Winestock, (03) 646 6666; New South Wales, Haviland Wines, (02) 419 8202; ACT, Barter & Baum, (06) 254 8203; Queensland, Wine 2000, (07) 878 4586; Western Australia, Premium Merchants, (09) 291 9703 Tasmania, Johnstone & Associates, (002) 24 0653; New Zealand, Kitchener Wines, (09) 377 3264; United Kingdom, The Wine Treasury, (071) 730 6774; United States, New World Wines Washington, (202) 244 3040; Switzerland, Martel AG St. Gallen, (071) 30 9409; Denmark, Holger Frederiksen, (31) 64 0710; Netherlands, Coenecoop Wine Traders, Fax: 182 830 707; Ontario, du Chasse Wines, (416) 469 3495; British Columbia, Premium Wines, (604) 721 9355.

D r Hugh Lloyd purchased Chateau Bonne Sante (ironically French for good health) and surrounding vineyards in 1968. The property had a long history, with vines planted in 1920 and the ironstone buildings built in 1860.

Now known as Coriole, the property is set on the hill west of the Seaview vineyards and enjoys uninterrupted views of the valley below and St Vincent's Gulf.

The small viticulture region around Coriole, that includes several other wineries, is prized for its distinctive red brown loams over ironstone or limestone. These soils produce characteristically well structured red wines with good weight and intensity.

The Coriole shiraz is a consistent and impressive wine and the company's flagship. The first bottled vintage was in 1970. This wine though well aged, is still in fine condition. Shiraz is extremely well suited to McLaren Vale and in particular, the Coriole environment.

The top of the range wine produced is the Lloyd Reserve Shiraz. First produced in 1989, it is made from 70 year old vines grown at Coriole. The Lloyd Reserve is very rich with great complexity of flavour and has long cellaring potential.

Sangiovese has become a speciality of the winery. Coriole has led the way with this Italian variety in Australia, and is now selling its seventh vintage. Sangiovese is a late variety with good acidity that is well suited to McLaren Vale. The lighter bodied style with its savoury characters and gentle grip gives a wine that contrasts with the other reds.

Coriole is one of the few Australian wine companies to produce chenin blanc, which was rediscovered in the region by a French ampelographer. Coriole Chenin has become widely popular because of the depth of flavour - tropical, apple and quince characteristics abound.

There are also small quantities of other wines produced including Semillon, a Shiraz Cabernet called Redstone - named after the hill cabernet vineyard with its outcrops of red ironstone, a Semillon Sauvignon Blanc grown on a neighbours vineyard, and a top of range Cabernet blend named Mary Kathleen, after one of the founders of the company.

Mark Lloyd and winemaker Stephen Hall are producing wines at Coriole which compare favourably with the best in Australia. The wines are predominantly estate grown.

The old cottage and gardens at the winery with its long views of the surrounding countryside, makes Coriole a favourite place to visit for many travellers.

The winery is currently being expanded to cope with demand in Australia as well as about ten countries in the export market.

Seaview

In 1850, George Manning planted vines on his newly purchased Hope Farm in McLaren Vale. A winery and cellars were built 40 years later.

The name Seaview was coined by the owners Ben Chaffey and his partner Friend Henry Edwards, who found they could see St Vincents Gulf from various hill crests on the property.

The winery itself sits attractively, surrounded by vines in the centre of a bowl-shaped valley, splendidly landscaped with vines. The Penfolds group purchased Seaview in 1985, and Seaview is now in fact the biggest selling wine brand in Australia, a testimony to the value-packed wines constantly streaming out under this prestige label, now under the control of the successful and well-managed Southcorp. The Seaview Cabernet Sauvignon has developed a reputation as the value for money cabernet of Australia, and is also often awarded gold medals in Australian and international wine competitions.

The humble shiraz is also an extraordinarily good wine for its price - look out for it. The Seaview whites have also added a lustre to the wines of the company in recent times, with the chardonnay winning a prestige international award in

1994. Its rich melon and stone fruit flavours and great balance are consistent from year to year.

The hidden gem of the Seaview whites has been their White Burgundy, recently renamed Seaview Semillon Sauvignon Blanc, in anticipation of new labelling regulations. Again a wine to look out for, the Seaview Sauvignon Blanc is a definite leader in this growing varietal wine style. A

milestone in 1994 was the release of two super premium reds under the Edwards and Chaffey banner, a shiraz and a cabernet sauvignon both made by the Seaview wine team under Mike Farmilo from the best grapes available in McLaren Vale in an "absolutely no expense spared" style. They are sensational wines and have been joined by a Pinot Chardonnay Methode Champenoise Edwards & Chaffey

the pinnacle of the Seaview sparkling wine stable which contains Australia's biggest selling sparkling wines.

The Seaview range are value for money premium wines which are a credit to the Australian wine industry, assuring themselves of continued success.

Scarpantoni

Winemakers: Michael and Filippo Scarpantoni

D om Scarpantoni arrived in Australia as part of the post-war immigration movement into this country. He secured a job at the vineyards of David Hardy and sheltered in a shed in the backyard of Bob Hagley, manager of the Hardy's Tintara Winery in the middle of the township of McLaren Vale.

SCARPANTONI ESTATE WINES PTY LTD
Address: Scarpantoni Drive, McLaren Flat SA 5171
Phone: (08) 383 0186
Fax: (08) 383 0490
Established: 1979
Winemakers: Michael and Filippo Scarpantoni
Principal varieties grown: cabernet sauvignon, shiraz, chardonnay, sauvignon blanc, gamay, merlot, riesling
Ha under vine: 30
Average annual crush: 200-250 tonnes
Average no. cases produced: 15,000

Principal wines & brands	Cellar potential
Cabernet Sauvignon	6-20 years
Shiraz	6-20 years
Sauvignon Blanc	2- 3 years
Chardonnay	3- 6 years
School Block	5-15 years
Riesling	4-20 years
Gamay	2-5 years

Public & trade tours: No
Cellar door & Mail order sales: Yes
Hours open to public: 9 am-5 pm Mon-Fri; 10 am-5 pm weekends
Retail distribution: Victoria, New South Wales, Queensland, South Australia

Dom is an incredibly hard worker and blessed with a most helpful and pleasant nature. Gradually, as he established himself in his new land, he also began planting his own vineyards at McLaren Flat. During the '60s and '70s he supplied grapes to Hardy's and others but as the wheel of fortune of wine accelerated he decided to extend his own family winemaking enterprise and build his own winery which he opened in 1979.

Today Scarpantoni is an expanding premium wine business and Dom has taken a little step back, leaving the day-to-day business to his two sons Michael and Filipo and daughter Mirella, who recently graduated from the Roseworthy wine-marketing course. All fortunately have inherited the charm and hardworking nature of their parents.

While researching and photographing for this book, Milan and I had the great pleasure of joining the family for a true Italian feast on the front lawns of their splendid winery. Dom's wife Paula and daughters-in-law Pia and Louise prepared a meal to die for, and we were joined by grandchildren and all. As we talked and reminisced over the renaissance of McLaren Vale over the last few decades, there was a very special feeling and a sense we have all enjoyed something very strong in the welding of the cultures of Europe and Australia, and the richness this has brought not only to our wine industry, but to our whole nation.

Long live the Scarpantonis and all those European families who have enriched our lives in Australia so much.

Wirra Wirra

I first remember strolling into the ironstone relics, now the heart of the substantial high profile Wirra Wirra Winery, way back in 1972. I was searching for red grapes for my family's Tintara Winery and grower Greg Trott was on my hit list.

As I recounted this little bit of trivia to Greg just the other day, he filled in the details. The man has an incredible memory for detail of the distant past, but ask him what he did yesterday and he'll probably have a few problems filling you in!

Greg Trott is also an acute observer of life and one of the most visionary people I have encountered in the world of wine. Wirra Wirra is in fact a partnership between Greg and his cousin Roger and in recent years they have released a methode champenoise called 'Cousins' to celebrate this connection. This exceptional Pinot Chardonnay Cuvee spends almost four years ageing on the yeast lees in the bottle, and is one of the best sparkling wines you could find in Australia. Greg has a connection also with the Johnston family, large landholders and owners of Pirramimma wines - Greg's mother was a Johnston.

Working life for Greg in McLaren Vale began, in his own words, 'as a mixed-up farmer', growing almonds, grapes, prunes and apricots and producing dried fruits. In 1969, Greg and cousin Roger bought the old ironstone cellars of Wirra Wirra, built in 1893 by Robert Strangways Wigley and disused since his death in 1924.

A big job lay ahead of them. The first grapes were crushed in 1970. By 1979 the rhine riesling had become a mainstay of their business when Greg coined the name "hand picked" capturing the care and quality concerns always to the fore at Wirra Wirra.

The last eight vintages have been made by Ben Riggs, a gentle giant of a young man whose enthusiasm and creativity match his physical proportions. Ben deals with the estate grapes from Roger Trott's Moray Park and Greg's Bethany and Scrubby Rise vineyards, along with other premium growers in the region.

Winemaker: Ben Riggs

WIRRA WIRRA VINEYARDS
Address: McMurtrie Road, McLaren Vale SA 5171
Direction: 45 km south of GPO
Phone: (08) 323 8414
Fax: (08) 323 8596
Established: 1969
Owner: R.G. & R.T. Trott Pty. Ltd.
Winemaker: Ben Riggs
Principal varieties grown: Riesling, Sauvignon Blanc, Semillon, Chardonnay, Pinot Noir, Grenache, Cabernet Sauvignon, Shiraz, Merlot
Ha under vine: 31
Average annual crush: 748 tonnes
Average no. cases produced: 53,000

Principal wines & brands	Cellar potential
Cousins (meth. champenoise)	2-5 years
Hand Picked Riesling	2-5 years
Sauvignon Blanc	2-5 years
Semillon-Sauvignon Blanc	2-5 years
Chardonnay	2-5 years
Church block	5-10 years
Original Blend (Gren/Shiraz)	5-10 years
The Angelus Cab. Sauvignon	5-15 years
RSW Shiraz	5-15 years

Public & trade tours: By appointment only
Cellar door sales: Yes
Hours open to public: 10 am-5 pm Mon-Sat; 11 am-5 pm Sun & PH
Retail distribution: Available in most top restaurants and retail outlets (Distributor: Negociants Australia)

An outstanding success for Wirra has been their Church Block, a cabernet sauvignon, shiraz and merlot blend named after the vineyard opposite the winery which surrounds an old Methodist Church. Greg has built a large bell-tower outside the winery from which hangs the The Angelus. This enormous bell is rung each year by the winemaker to herald the first crushing of grapes from the region. Wirra Wirra have two super premium wines bottled in exceptional years, The Angelus, a cabernet sauvignon, and RSW Shiraz. Look out for them. Wirra Wirra have many dinners, concerts and exhibitions at the winery, reflecting Greg Trott's loves, along of course with his beloved Wirra Wirra wines.

Chateau Reynella

One of South Australia's first settlers, John Reynell, obtained vines in South Africa en-route to Australia and planted them in the rich soil of Reynella in 1838.

By 1845, he had completed the country's first underground cellar, now known as the 'Old Cave', which, due to its historical importance, has been classified by the National Trust.

After the death of John Reynell, the business became a family company but unfortunately, two world wars exacted a toll on the male line that resulted in the appointment, in 1953, of Colin Haselgrove as managing director of the winery. Under Colin's guidance, Reynella released some excellent red and fortified wines. The Reynella Alicante Flor Sherry, in particular, was one of Australia's best. Similarly, the vintage reserve clarets and burgundies released

during the 1950s were remarkable wines and generally drastically underpriced. Colin Haselgrove remained at Reynella after the take-over by Hungerford Hill in 1970. The following year he produced what he considered to be his best vintage and indeed the 1971 vintage port and cabernet sauvignon are today considered to be great wines.

However, in the following years, many changes were to occur in corporate management at Reynella. In 1972 Rothmans purchased a half share in the business and in 1976 became full owners.

Thomas Hardy & Sons purchased the company in 1982 and spent millions of dollars restoring the Chateau, winery and other buildings to their former glory. Having moved their head office and bottling cellars to Reynella. In 1992 Berri Renmano Limited and Hardys merged to form BRL Hardy Limited and the

old Reynell homestead houses the company's executive offices and boardroom.

In addition to the careful restoration of the buildings, the century-old botanical gardens planted by John Reynell have also been rejuvenated and this has resulted in Chateau Reynella becoming one of the most beautiful wineries in Australia.

Chateau Reynella has long been known for its exquisite long-living vintage ports and its mellow tawny port styles (Old Cave Port). These wines continue to be leaders in their styles and successfully promote the name of Reynella throughout the world.

The winery now produces wines made exclusively from McLaren Vale fruit. The "Basket Pressed" range of reds feature - Shiraz, Cabernet Merlot and Cabernet Sauvignon. The winemakers have worked closely with the

viticulturists monitoring cropping, irrigation and trellising methods to obtain the highest quality fruit. Small open fermenters and the abiity to maintain small batches of individual vineyard wine until the blending stage gives maximum flexibility in the quest for quality. The basket press is used to press the skins following fermentation, this process results in fine tannin structure without the bitterness sometimes associated with mechanical pressing. Chateau Reynella reds are big, rich, generous wines typical of McLaren Vale style.

There is also an award winning McLaren Vale Chardonnay in the range that is barrel fermented, stored on lees and a portion undergoes malolactic fermentation resulting in a rich, vanillin, buttery chardonnay style.

The Chateau Reynella renaissance has seen not only the restoration of a great winery, but also the development of an elegant new label along with the launching of an excellent range of table wines. The return to good management and proficient winemaking has seen the restitution of this winery to its well-deserved position as one of the country's leading premium wine producers. The beautiful Reynella complex is only 25 minutes' drive from the Adelaide GPO. A visit whilst you are in Adelaide is virtually obligatory.

d'Arenberg

d'Arenberg is one of the most significant wine companies in McLaren Vale. In 1912 Joseph Osborn, a teetotaller, director of Thomas Hardy and Sons, purchased the well established Milton Vineyards in the hills just north of the townships of Gloucester and Bellvue, now known as McLaren Vale.

Joseph's son Frank left medical school choosing to forsake the scalpel for pruning shears, selling the fruit from 78 hectares of vineyards to local wineries until the construction of his own cellars were completed in 1928. Dry red table and fortified wines were produced in ever increasing quantities to supply the expanding markets of the Empire.

In 1943 Frank's son d'Arry returned from school, aged 16, to help his ill father run the business, eventually assuming full management of d'Arenberg in 1957, bottling the first of the famous diagonal red stripe labelled wines the following year. d'Arry's wines of the 1960's gained immediate cult status amongst imbibers and judges. One Cabernet Sauvignon won a Jimmy Watson Trophy at the Melbourne Wine Show and another Grenache based wine was awarded 7 trophies and 29 gold medals from Australian capital city wine shows. It is understandable that by the 1970's d'Arenberg Wines had become very fashionable, having gained national and international profiles in less than 20 years.

Enter the fourth generation, d'Arry's son Chester. After graduating from Roseworthy College, visiting other Australian and European wine regions, Chester took over the reigns as chief winemaker in 1984, immediately rejuvenating the 70 year old cellars and 19th Century vineyards. Investing in new oak, lots of small stainless steel tanks and refrigeration resulting in immediate white dividends with his Dry Dam Riesling, Dryland Sauvignon/Chenin Blanc, Barrel Fermented Chardonnay and botrytis affected Noble Riesling all winning gold medals and trophies at wine shows.

In 1990 Chester was crowned McLaren Vale Bushing King for producing the best table wine in the district judged at the McLarenVale Wine Show. In 1995 d'Arry was invested as a patron of the Wine Industry of Australia, two years after completing his 50th consecutive vintage.

It is not surprising that with a "Red Stripe" in their blood, d'Arry and Chester's viticultural and oenological talents have ensured that d'Arenberg have continued to win numerous national and international medals, trophies and critical acclaim, none more so than in recent years.

d'Arenberg is continuing to produce wines that are a credit both to the winery and the region. They have just completed renovating the property's 19th Century homestead incorporating cellar door tastings and a restaurant overlooking McLaren Vale and the Willunga escarpment to the Gulf of St Vincent. d'Arenberg is a McLaren Vale tradition to be proud of.

---

d'ARENBERG WINES

Address: Osborn Road, McLaren Vale SA 5171
Direction: 3 km north of McLaren Vale
Phone: (08) 323 8206
Fax: (08) 323 8423
Established: 1912
Owner: Osborn family
Winemaker: Chester Osborn
Principal varieties grown: riesling, sauvignon blanc, chenin blanc, chardonnay, viognier, chambourcin, grenache, mataro, shiraz, cabernet sauvignon
Ha under vine: 80
Average annual crush: 1500 tonnes
Average no. cases produced: 65,000

Principal wines & brands	Cellar potential
White and Red Ochre	
Dry Dam Riesling	10+ years
The Olive Grove Chardonnay	5-10 years
Dryland Sauvignon Blanc	2-5 years
TheNoble Riesling 375ml	5-10 years
The Peppermint Paddock Chamb.	2-5 years
D'Arry's Original Shiraz/Gren.	10+ years
The High Trellis Cabernet Sauv.	5-10 years
The Old Vine Shiraz	10+ years
The Ironstone Pressings	10+ years
The Custodian Grenache	10+ years
The Dead Arm Shiraz	10+ years
Nostalgia Fine Old Tawny	0-1 years
Fine Vintage Declared Fortified	10+ years

Public & trade tours: by appointment only
Cellar door & mail order sales: Yes
Hours open to public: 10 am-5 pm daily
Points of interest: Restored 19th century homestead, Cellar Door and d'Arry's Verandah Restaurant overlooking the Willunga Escarpment, McLaren Flat, McLaren Vale and the valley floor to the Gulf of St. Vincent
Retail distribution: Each state and territory nationally and a dozen or so countries internationally.

Fern Hill

I n the heady days of the wine boom back in 1975, the gregarious Wayne Thomas and his wife Pat began a winery opposite Ryecroft and just down the road from Ingoldby. Fern Hill became a much-respected label.

Early in 1994 the Thomases sold the winery to dynamic Sydney wine entrepreneur Terry Hill, proprietor of Hill International Wines.

Small scale production, low quantities of super premium wines are being hand-crafted.

At present these include a chardonnay fermented in French oak and a semillon fermented and aged very briefly in American oak. The reds comprise a cabernet sauvignon plus a shiraz both made in a no-compromise fashion from selected vineyards in the McLaren Vale region.

The accent in the cellar door is also very much on the wine quality with a very personal and educational approach. The newly restored premises were re-opened on Christmas Eve 1994 with the elegant new labels proudly to the fore. I am sure at Fern Hill as things develop they will have much to celebrate.

FERN HILL ESTATE
Address: Ingoldby Road, McLaren Flat SA 5171
Phone: (08) 383 0167
Fax: (08) 383 0107
Established: 1976
Winemaker: Grant Burge
Principal varieties grown: Chardonnay, semillon, cabernet sauvignon, shiraz
Average annual crush: 100 tonnes
Average no. cases produced: 5,000

Principal wines & brands	Cellar potential
Chardonnay	2-5 years
Semillon	2-5 years
Shiraz	5-10 years
Cabernet Sauvignon	5-10 years

Public & trade tours: Yes
Cellar door & mail order sales: Yes
Hours open to public: 10 am-5 pm daily (except Christmas Day and Good Friday
Retail distribution: Fine wine stores and restaurants

Ingoldby

In May 1995, Mildara Blass Limited purchased Ingoldby Wines of the McLaren Vale and whilst this acquisition was primarily driven by the availability of premium quality fruit, they quickly realised that Ingoldby as a brand presented a very real sales opportunity. Much of this is to the credit of the previous owner and winemaker, Walter Clappis.

As the chief of Ingoldby, Walter was one of those characters who was truly larger than life - his infectious enthusiasm, love of life and the buzz he got from producing great wine was a joy to behold.

Walter began working with Jim Ingoldby at Ingoldby Wines in 1981. Jim Ingoldby established the winery in 1971 after working for many years with various other local wineries, and the Ingoldby name has been associated with the McLaren Vale region since the turn of the century.

In 1982, Jim was looking at a change in lifestyle and to go and live at his beloved Walker's Flat on the River Murray. For fourteen years, Jim Ingoldby was happy to remain the first mortgagee whilst Walter developed Ingoldby Wines into a success.

This success was largely due to Walter's ability to produce seriously good red wines - full, rich and round, they had his stamp all over them. Under Walter's direction, Ingoldby became the only winery in the region to win the Dan Murphy Trophy three times for the best Cabernet Sauvignon, awarded each year at the McLaren Vale Bushing Festival. His whites also tended to be rich and round, appealing to the red wine lover.

Now under the guidance of Mildara Blass

Walter Clappis

Limited, Ingoldby has been released nationally - previously Queensland and Western Australia had virtually no opportunity to buy Ingoldby Wines locally.

Ingoldby Wines will continue to be produced essentially from grapes grown on their own vineyards and in the McLaren Vale region. Its wine styles will continue to reflect the individuality and distinctiveness that were their signature under Jim Ingoldby and Walter Clappis - full, rich and round wines of distinct flavour and character - but now under the guidance of local winemaker, Phil Reschke.

INGOLDBY WINES PTY LTD
Address: Ingoldby Road, McLaren Flat SA 5171
Phone: (08) 323 8853
Fax: (08) 323 8550
Winemaker: Phil Reschke
Principal varieties grown: Cabernet, shiraz, merlot, grenache, semillon
Ha under vine: 10
Average annual crush: 260 tonnes
Average no. cases produced: 15,000

Principal wines & brands	Cellar potential
Cabernet	10+ years
Shiraz	10+ years
Grenache	5-8 years
Colombard	2-5 years
Sauvignon Blanc	2-5 years
Chardonnay	2-5 years

Public & trade tours: No
Cellar door & mail order sales: Yes
Hours open to public: 9 am-5 pm Mon-Fri; 1 pm-5 pm weekends and public holidays
Points of interest: Underground cellar and art gallery
Retail distribution: National: Southern Cross Wine Co.

Hardy's Tintara

At 20 years of age, Thomas Hardy arrived in the new colony of South Australia in 1850 with thirty pounds in his pocket. Within 40 years he had built the country's largest wine company. Along the way, he somehow found time to travel overseas several times, write a book on fruit and wine growing in California, keep extensive diaries and scrapbooks, and educate those people with whom he worked.

Within weeks of his arrival in South Australia, Thomas Hardy obtained a year's work with Walter Reynell at Reynella Farm. Later, while employed on a grazing property at Normanville he became gripped with gold fever and left for the Victorian gold fields, where he was promptly arrested for mining without a licence. Deciding there were easier ways of making money, Hardy persuaded his former employer to let him drive 400 head of cattle to the gold fields, where they were butchered and sold to the miners. This venture was so successful that Hardy was able to return to Adelaide and purchase a property on the banks of the Torrens, which he called Bankside. Vines, fruit and olive trees were planted, cellars were constructed and as soon as the vines began to bear fruit, winemaking commenced.

Hardy's wine quickly found ready markets both locally and in England, giving him the necessary assets to purchase the Tintara Vineyard Company in 1876. The cellars of this new property were full of barrels of rich burgundy, which Hardy sold in England, recouping his purchase price in one year. The company steadily expanded with additional purchases of a bottling plant at Mile End, champagne cellars at Currie Street in Adelaide and a disused flour mill in McLaren Vale.

By 1893, Thomas Hardy controlled the largest wine company in Australia. Thomas Hardy died in 1912, leaving his son Robert in charge of the company. Currently, fourth generation member Sir James Hardy OBE is on the board of directors of the parent company, the successfully merged BRL Hardy. In 1903, fire destroyed the cellars at Bankside. This fire occurred on a Sunday and as no fire brigade was available to attend, the fire was extinguished by pumping wine onto the flames. Some of the charred casks remain and are used in the maturation of fortified wines at McLaren Vale.

In 1968, Hardy's established extensive vineyards in the Padthaway area, which has become a great source of fruit for their premium table wines. The purchase of the Emu Wine Company in 1976 included the Western Australian

Houghton and Valencia wineries and a large winery at Morphett Vale. The next acquisition was Chateau Reynella in 1982 - ironically, a return of the name Hardy to the winery where Thomas Hardy began his working life in Australia more than 130 years before. In 1992 Thomas Hardy & Sons merged with Berri Renmano Linited to form Australia's second largest wine group, BRL Hardy Limited.

Currently, the flagship wine in Hardy's extensive portfolio is Eileen Hardy. Named after the widow of Tom Mayfield Hardy, the first of this wine, a 1970 McLaren Vale Shiraz, was released in 1973 to honour her 80th birthday. Eileen Hardy Chardonnay was launched in 1986 to partner the Shiraz.

In 1994 'Eileen' was joined at the Hardy's red wine pinnacle by the Thomas Hardy Coonawarra Cabernet Sauvignon. The first four

vintages have all won at least one trophy and several gold medals.

Other Hardy products that are household names in Australia are - Sir James Cuvee Brut and Brut de Brut, Siegersdorf Rhine Riesling and Chardonnay, the Nottage Hill range, Hardys RR, Whiskers Blake Tawny Port and Black Bottle Brandy.

During 1994/5 large sums of capital were spent expanding the Company's premium vineyard holdings. Hoddles Creek vineyard in the Yarra Valley of Victoria was acquired to supply sparkling wine fruit for the Sir James range including the new Sir James Vintage, a premium Australian sparkling wine. New vineyards in Padthaway, Koppamurra, Furner (towards Robe from Coonawarra in the Woak wine ranges), Coonawarra and Langhorne Creek will supply fruit for existing and planned new labels under the

Hardy banner. Consumers can also look forward to some superb new wines from these new properties.

New premiums recently introduced are the Bankside range - Shiraz, Grenache and Chardonnay and the Padthaway range of unwooded Chardonnay and Cabernet Sauvignon.

Hardy's are continuing to produce and market wines of which the company founder would be proud. The beautiful ironstone Tintara winery in the heart of McLaren Vale, incorporating the town's original mill, has been lovingly restored during the last decade and features a superb cellar door tasting area, brimming over with memorabilia from the company's long and rich history. A pilgrimage to this shrine of wine is a must for any visitor to McLaren Vale.

Maglieri

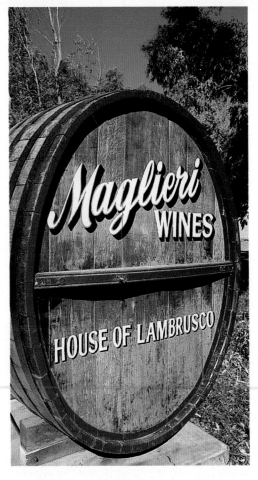

Arriving in Australia in 1964, Steve Maglieri was among the post-war influx of Italian grape growers, who did such good work in developing McLaren Vale as a premium wine region in the 1950s and 60s.

Their hard work, family values and culture, along with their community spirit has enriched the region a great deal, witnessed in many ways, such as in the impressive Italian Bocce and Function Centre alongside the McLaren Flat oval, completed in 1994.

The Maglieris expanded the plantings of premium grape varieties in McLaren Vale and by and large supplied their grapes to the bigger wineries such as Hardy's. Being Italian of course, they had to make their own vino for the casa and the multitudes of family and extended family. They couldn't resist selling some of the wines, which were of excellent quality and value, to passers-by, thus was born Gully Wines in 1972, changing its name to Maglieri Wines in 1979.

A huge success story for Maglieri has been their excellent market-leading Australian Lambrusco, made in the style of this soft fruity slightly sweet Italian red wine. Maglieri's, however, make many seriously great table wines and their highest compliment is the respect they are shown by the other winemakers of the region, both for their absolutely top quality and also for the extraordinary value they represent for the wine lover. Maglieri have won hoards of trophies and gold medals and two terms as McLaren Vale wine bushing kings for their wines, and deservedly so. The winery and vineyards are in the beautiful Blewitt Springs area of the Valley, rising up into the foothills of the Adelaide Hills and reminiscent of the rolling countryside of Tuscany, a fact not lost I am sure on the Maglieris.

John Loxton is the quiet, hardworking and highly skilled winemaker who has been toiling away in his meticulous fashion for many years. the winery is now ultramodern and crushes over 3000 tonnes of grapes and is blessed with top class oak and stainless steel storage.

The three ranges of Maglieri wines starts with two lambruscos, Amabile (red) and Bianco (white), followed by the "Ingleburne Estate" range of affordable premium table wines from the Maglieri's Ingleburne Vineyards and includes a Semillon, Shiraz and a Cabernet Sauvignon. The flagship range is under the Maglieri Label and are all award winners.

MAGLIERI WINES PTY LTD
Address: Douglas Gully Road, McLaren Flat SA 5171
Direction: 40 km south of Adelaide
Phone: (08) 383 0177
Fax: (08) 383 0136
Established: 1972
Winemaker: John Loxton
Principal varieties grown: Shiraz, cabernet sauvignon, semillon, merlot, riesling, chardonnay, traminer, sauvignon blanc, grenache
Ha under vine: 290
Average annual crush: 3000 tonnes
Average no. cases produced: 230,000

Principal wines & brands	Cellar potential
Shiraz	5-10 years
Cabernet Sauvignon	5-10 years
Ingleburne Unwooded Semillon	2-5 years
Ingleburne Cabernet	5-10 years
Chardonnay	2-5 years
Semillon	2-5 years
Cabernet Merlot	2-5 years

Trade tours: By appointment only
Cellar door & mail order sales: Yes
Hours open to public: 9.30 am-4 pm Mon-Sat; 11 am-4.30 pm Sun.
Points of interest: Large picnic area, ample parking and facilities. Wine tasting and mail order service.
Retail distribution: Maglieri Wines, Queensland and New South Wales; Tasmanian Fine Wines, Tasmania; Alexander & Paterson, Victoria; Oak Barrel Wines, ACT, Festival City, South Australia; ALM, Northern Territory.

Manning Park

George Manning constructed the classic old Australian building on the corner of Olivers road and Chalk Hill road more than a century and a half ago. In an earlier life the buildings were used as grain mill. The cellars were commissioned in 1983 and are most unusual as the foundations and long main wall actually slope down the hill rather than being constructed in the normal manner.

Recently, the winery has been taken over by the dynamic duo of Warren Randall and Warren Ward, both with loads of experience in the industry and fresh from some years working together at Andrew Garrett wines for Suntory. The Manning Park wines are being made by the Warrens at their Tinlins Winery from the top few tonnes of their extensive vineyard holdings in the region, thus they are strictly the creme de la creme of the wine crop.

At a recent visit to the newly restored winery (it is quite beautiful), I was very impressed by the quality of the wines. Typically, Warren Randall has added some flair to the wine styles and labelling. The 1994 Great White definitely hasn't got the bite of a shark, it is a semillon/sauvignon blanc blend with lovely oriental and tropical fruit highlights; the touch of herbaceousness sets it off superbly.

The Wild Shiraz is exactly that, full of spicy wild berry flavours. Probably the real stunner of the range is the Savage Grenache from old bush vines. The current number packs a real punch at 15.6 per cent alcohol. Perhaps the word 'beware' should be added to the label as its sublime flavours and freshness beckon the corkscrew to be produced again and again.

Manning Park is a name we quality wine imbibers will see a lot more of in the future, to our very good fortune.

Winemakers: Warren Randall (left)
and Warren Ward (right)

MANNING PARK WINERY

Address: Chalk Hill Road, McLaren Vale SA 5171
Phone: (08) 323 8209
Fax: (08) 323 9747
Established: 1994
Winemaker: Warren Randall
Cellar Door Manager: Mike Brown
Principal varieties grown: Sauvignon blanc, semillon, chardonnay, shiraz, cabernet sauvignon, merlot, grenache
Ha under vine: 12
Average no. cases produced: 2,000

Principal wines & brands	Cellar potential
Great White Sauvignon blanc/semillon	2-5 years
Wild Shiraz	5-10 years
Native Cabernet	5-10 years
Savage Grenache	10+ years
Chardonnay	2-5 years
Stormy Shiraz	5-10 years

Trade Tours: By appointment
Cellar door & mail order sales: Yes
Hours open to public: 10 am - 5 pm daily
Points of interest: Excellent outdoor entertaining centre and BBQ area next to historic old homestead
Retail distribution: Adelaide metropolitan and

Marienberg

Ursula Pridham became Australia's first woman winemaker back in the late 1960s when she started her own winery at Happy Valley.

After 25 years of excellent winemaking and hard work she decided to step back a little. Sydney wine dynamo, Terry Hill, saw an ideal opportunity and late in 1990 he bought the Marienberg brand.

Coinciding with this move, he also bought the old Limeburners Cottage, opposite The Barn Restaurant in McLaren Vale on the corner of Main Street and Chalk Hill Road. Wasting no time, Terry constructed another beautiful cottage and tasting centre alongside the Limeburners Cottage. The plan is to amalgamate the two into Marienberg's new home. Already, Marienberg Cottage is a very busy place, with art exhibitions and functions, often involving The Barn with the catering.

The Marienberg range has expanded, with six table wines led by a very elegant chardonnay and a rich round cabernet sauvignon. These are complemented by a non-vintage pinot noir/chardonnay methode champenoise under the name 'Nicolle' after one of Terry and Jill Hill's daughters, plus a 12 year old tawny port. The wines are from selected vineyards in the McLaren Vale area and made under the watchful eye of Grant Burge, an old school days chum of Terry's.

The Marienberg labels really stand out with their art deco inspired look. I have been singularly impressed by all the wines, particularly their very approachable style, delivering clean crisp flavours, mouthfilling but extremely well balanced. The restrained use of top quality oak in some of the wines is particularly well handled. Marienberg is back to stay. Why not make her acquaintance when you see her next, or drop into her cute cottage for a taste or two?

MARIENBERG WINE COMPANY
Address: 2 Chalk Hill Road, McLaren Vale SA 5171
Phone: (08) 323 9666
Fax: (08) 323 9600
Established: 1966
Winemaker: Grant Burge
Grapes supplied under contract: Chardonnay, cabernet sauvignon, shiraz
Average no. cases produced: 21,000

Principal wines & brands	Cellar potential
Chardonnay	2-5 years
Cabernet Sauvignon	5-10 years
Shiraz	5-10 years
Semillon/Chardonnay	2-5 years
Sauvignon Blanc/Semillon	2-5 years
Classic Riesling	2-5 years
Methode Champenoise	2-5 years
12 YO Tawny Port	2-5 years

Public & trade tours: Yes
Cellar door & mail order sales: Yes
Hours open to public: 10 am-5 pm daily (except Christmas Day & Good Friday)
Retail Distribution: Fine wine stores and restaurants.

McLarens On The Lake

In the early 1980s, entrepreneur Jack Weinart built a splendid complex on the outskirts of McLaren Vale, on the road to McLaren Flat, which he called Hazelmere Estate.

The complex included a modern winery, a la carte restaurant, function and souvenir facility along with 30 large attractive accommodation suites. The Victorian/ Australian architecture reminds me somewhat of the grand old wineries at Rutherglen, reminiscent of a bygone era.

The whole property is sensitively and beautifully landscaped around a man-made lake, all the huge old red gums have been retained and the cry of the corellas at dawn and dusk is a pleasant reminder that one is among nature in a beautiful country region.

The birdlife on the lake is multitudinous, with ducks, swans, cygnets, even seagulls happily sharing this large expanse of water as it blends more naturally into the environment each year. The name Hazelmere was changed some years ago to McLarens on the Lake. The property was taken over in the late 1980s by Andrew Garrett and exciting wines began to appear. Andrew brought in a big brother in the form of Suntory, the huge Japanese liquor conglomerate, eventually fading out of the Andrew Garrett Winery to start his own label, Garrett Family. The Andrew Garrett and Garrett Family brands have recently been taken over by Mildara Wines and I am sure they will be even more successful in the market place.

All this aside, the McLarens on the Lake complex is idyllic and runs like a well-oiled machine under its proprietors Laurie Evans and Tony Lucas, real professionals in the hospitality industry. Laurie has run international hotels and has his own wine broking business. He's a character and a half, a real showman reaching the American Chamber National Finals as the South Australian Presenter of the Year as "Sir Charles Drake M.D.", a very good impersonation of a duck, promoting McLarens on the Lake.

Tony became involved in McLaren Vale wine tourism. From 1974 to 1982 he ran the Wine Bushing Festival and the McLaren Vale Winemakers Association before helping David Hardy launch the magnificent Middlebrook Winery, restaurant and entertainment venue, which he ably ran until early 1993 when he and Laurie fired up McLarens.

McLarens on the Lake is superb, the Courtyard Conservatory Restaurant, the more formal McLarens Room Restaurant and in the seminar function area weddings abound and businesses almost queue to use the great facilities. Having often stayed in the suites, I can highly recommend them. Don't pass by McLarens whilst in the region.

Middlebrook

I n 1880 Thomas Hardy purchased a property lying between 4km east of McLaren Vale, two streams, and renamed it Glenn Hardy. Since then, the property has seen many changes of ownership and five changes of name, finishing with Middlebrook, coined ironically by David Hardy, great grandson of Thomas Hardy who, with his sons Christopher and John, restored the winery and opened it as a hospitality venue.

The winery nestles in the foothills of the Willunga Scarp and the restaurant and cellar door area look out over landscaped gardens which are ringed with stately red gums. A bandstand is the centre-point of the lawn area which sees many concerts and much activity, particularly during the wine Bushing Festival in late October. In addition, the complex includes an alfresco style restaurant, an excellent cellar door tasting area and a most interesting art gallery and The Fleurieu Showcase, an innovative and extensive display of local arts and crafts from pottery, leather goods, sculpture and painting to weaving.

David Dridan, one of Australia's leading painters, has created this mecca of good taste and a visit while in the region is compulsory. The restaurant and function centre in the skilled culinary hands of Carol Taylor can help make your visit to Middlebrook a truly enriching experience.

This must be one of the most beautiful wineries in Australia. Middlebrook wines have just reappeared on the market and Walter Clappis and his winemaking team are capable of great things. Middlebrook now has very firm foundations and the sky appears to be the limit. The complex is open every day from 10am - 5pm and the restaurant serves morning and afternoon tea aside from lunch from 12-3 daily, and dinner Friday and Saturday evenings.

Mount Hurtle - Geoff Merrill

One of the most beautiful old gravity flow wineries of the last century is Mount Hurtle which was built in 1897 by Mostyn Owen.

The winery was disused and storing hay when Geoff Merrill, then the high profile winemaker at Chateau Reynella, bought it back in the early '80s. The winery, just down the road from Reynella, was most convenient for making his own wines, then under the Stratmer banner. Later Geoff released wines under his own name and the Mount Hurtle label appeared. A later development was the Cockatoo Ridge label, inspired by the noisy corella cockatoos on the ridge behind the winery, now a joint venture between Geoff and S. Smith & Sons of Yalumba fame.

The Mount Hurtle winery is a picture. A small lake reflects the winery as one enters the tree-lined drive. The front section of the winery has been turned into a splendid function area with polished wooden floors and a balcony where one can view the working winery and barrel cellar below. Many weddings and other events now take place in this stunning setting.

Geoff is certainly not the shy and retiring type, with his huge handlebar moustache enhancing his happy smiling face, but he is a serious, fastidious winemaker and all his wines reflect this care in their great balance and sophisticated styles. The Mount Hurtle and the super premium Geoff Merrill reds are often in the more herbaceous spectrum, with fine tannins and clean varietal characteristics, not always the heaviest styles, but they age extremely well. The whites on the other hand are rich and ripe in style, showing classy wood treatments.

Geoff is a passionate cricket fan and a close friend of cricket legends Ian Botham and Bob Willis. Every year they hold a charity cricket event in England, sponsored by Geoff and Mount Hurtle, which raises hundreds of thousands of dollars for charity. Well done, Geoff Merrill!

MOUNT HURTLE WINERY/STRATMER VINEYARDS
Address: 291 Pimpala Road Woodcroft SA 5162
Phone: (08) 381 6877
Fax: (08) 322 2244
Established: 1897
Owner: Geoff Merrill
Winemaker: Geoff Merrill/Goe DiFabio
Average annual crush: 1,000 tonnes
Average no. cases produced: 80,000

Principal wines & brands	Cellar potential
Geoff Merrill Cab. Sauvignon	15+ years
Geoff Merrill Semillon Chard.	10-15 years
Mount Hurtle Sauvignon Blanc	2-5 years
Mount Hurtle Chardonnay	2-5 years
Mount Hurtle Grenache	0-2 years
Mount Hurtle Shiraz	5-8 years
Mount Hurtle Cabernet Merlot	5-8 years

Public & trade tours: By appointment only
Cellar door & mail order sales: Yes
Hours open to public: 10 am-4 pm Mon-Fri; 12-5 pm Sun
Points of interest: Elegant tasting and dining area complemented by a commercial kitchen. Extensively landscaped grounds.
Retail distribution: South Australia, Caon Tucker; Western Australia, Tucker & Co; New South Wales, Tucker & Co; Victoria, Tucker & Co; United Kingdom, Peter Lehmann Wines.

Normans

Jesse Norman arrived in Australia from England in 1853 and very soon purchased seven hectares of land near the town of Thebarton, on which he planted vines.

A winery was later established at Underdale and another vineyard planted at Sturt. Both vineyards prospered, enabling A. Norman & Sons to expand their winemaking business.

Unfortunately with the spread of Adelaide's urban areas the company's land was zoned residential by the South Australian Housing Trust, and compulsorily purchased. As a result, 52 hectares were purchased at Gawler River, and planted to vines. This vineyard still exists today, and is now known as Evanston Estate.

A. Norman & Sons Pty Ltd continued to develop slowly until 1982 when the company was bought by the Horlin-Smith family. Having had a century-long association with the hospitality industry, the Horlin-Smiths were already well acquainted with many aspects of winemaking and marketing. The company's name was changed to Normans Wine Estates and James Irvine, long-time family friend and creator of Hardys famous Siegersdorf Rhine Riesling, was asked to join the management team. Together, they decided to utilise available resources to produce the best possible table wines.

Following the modernisation of the Underdale winery a new high quality range of wines was developed which quickly won wide acclaim.

Sadly, it was soon discovered that facilities at Underdale were inadequate when coping with greater volumes of fruit and high levels of production.

Following an extensive search, Normans purchased the Coolawin winery and adjacent 3.8 hectare vineyard at Clarendon, high in the Adelaide Hills. The Underdale winery now serves as the company headquarters, sales and distribution centre, port and champagne maturation cellars.

Renamed Normans Clarendon Winery, the new property was soon fitted with the most modern winemaking equipment and ranks with the most efficient wineries in the state. All of Normans wines are now made at Clarendon. Winemaking staff is headed by the talented Brian Light.

Located near the crest of Chandlers Hill, Normans winery commands magnificent views of the nearby coastline and the rolling hills of Clarendon. High altitude and onshore winds combine to bring the cool climate ideal for the production of premium table wines. Consequently, the vineyard next to the winery is planted with classic grape varieties which will surely benefit from this site - cabernet sauvignon, shiraz and chardonnay. Additional fruit is brought in from growers at McLaren Vale and Lloyd Light's vineyard at Bakers Gully. The range includes sparkling, fortified and table wines.

All the table wines have been consistently of very high quality, and the Family Reserve Pinot Noir can be exceptional. With distinct berry fruit flavours, the Adelaide Plains Pinot is of a depth not often seen in this grape variety in Australia. The Normans Chandlers Hill range represents great value for money and the recently released exclusive Chais Clarendon range of three wines, a shiraz, a cabernet sauvignon and a chardonnay, rank on the very highest rung of Australia's wines.

Normans has just become a public company with the Horlin-Smiths still heavily involved. I am sure the influx of much-needed capital will catapult the company to even greater heights.

NORMANS WINES LTD
Address: Grants Gully Road, Clarendon SA 5342
Phone: Admin (08) 43 7011, Winery (08) 383 6138
Fax: (08) 352 1857
Established: 1853
Winemaker: Brian Light
Principal varieties grown: chardonnay, sauvignon blanc, chenin blanc, riesling, cabernet sauvignon, cabernet franc, merlot, shiraz, pinot noir, grenache
Ha under vine: 54
Average annual crush: 13,000 tonnes
Average no. cases produced: over 500,000

Principal wines & brands	Cellar potential
Normans Chais Clarendon	5-10 years
Normans Family Reserve	5-10 years
Normans Chandlers Hill	2-5 years
Langhill	5-10 years
Lukes Ridge	2-5 years

Trade tours: By appointment
Cellar door & mail order sales: Yes
Hours open to public: 10 am-5 pm Mon-Fri
Points of interest: Clarendon Winery: Great views from tasting room of coast and Onkaparinga Valley
Monash: Located close to River Murray
Retail distribution: nationally

Pirramimma

Situated on the Willunga Plains, the Pirramimma property was purchased by Mr. A.C. Johnston in 1892. Pirramimma is still wholly owned and run by the Johnston family, Alex being the general manager and Riverina College graduate Geoff, the winemaker. Pirramimma's first wine was made in 1900. The Johnston family made rapid progress with their business, both in further extending the vineyards and improving the winery.

The early success of Pirramimma was due to the company's excellent fortified wines. Their current Fine Old Liqueur Port is an excellent example of this continued quality. This port is rich in flavour and has a superb dry finish which is rarely found in Australian ports.

Most of the Johnston wines until the early 1970s were sold in bulk, a great proportion being exported to England.

Having decided to produce high quality bottled table wines, Pirramimma released their first rhine riesling in 1979 and their first chardonnay two years later. Both of these wines are full flavoured, well balanced and splendid examples of the potential of McLaren Vale fruit.

After experimenting with the various aspects of his craft, winemaker Geoff Johnston has achieved another success with his cabernet sauvignon which displays the elegant herbaceous character much sought after in this grape variety.

Pirramimma and the Johnston family have huge vineyard holdings in the region and pick the best grapes for their own label before selling the rest of the crop to other premium makers.

Just prior to the 1995 vintage, they completed a large and innovative barrel ageing cellar, cut into the hillside above the winery and constructed by the rammed earth method of building, with very thick walls offering ideal insulation for the cellaring of the wine. Some 600 tonnes of earth have gone into the building, its light ochre colour blending happily into the hillside.

Geoff has also expanded the winery considerably with the addition of ten 30 tonne fermenters, two of which incorporate white wine drainage facilities.

In a very interesting move, the family converted a number of 1,000 gallon French oak vats, built by Babidge Coopers in 1904, into 65 gallon hogsheads (the Babidges did this job too). The 1990

Shiraz, bottled to celebrate Pirramimma's centenary, went into these hogsheads. The wine is one of the best reds ever made in McLaren Vale.

Pirramimma are undoubtably on the move and we wine-drinkers are the beneficiaries.

The Johnston family have always been a strong force in the Southern Vales and their high quality wines have assured them of a place in the winemaking history of Australia.

PIRRAMIMMA

Address: Johnston Road, McLaren Vale SA 5171
Direction: 1 km south of McLaren Vale
Phone: (08) 323 8205
Fax: (08) 323 9224
Established: 1935
Owner: A.C. Johnston Pty. Ltd.
Winemaker: Geoff Johnston
Principal varieties grown: riesling, shiraz, semillon, cabernet sauvignon, chardonnay, merlot, petit verdot, grenache
Ha under vine: 170
Average annual crush: 700-750 tonnes
Average no. cases produced: 20,000

Principal wines & brands	Cellar potential
Pirramimma Shiraz	5-10 years
Pirramimma Cab. Sauvignon	5-10 years
Pirramimma Cabernet Merlot	5-10 years
Pirramimma Chardonnay	2-5 years
Pirramimma Stock's Hill Sem./Chardonnay	2-5 years
Pirramimma Stock's Hill Classic Riesling	2-5 years
Liqueur Port	10+ years

Public & trade tours: By appointment only
Cellar door & mail order sales: Yes
Hours open to public: 9 am-5 pm Mon-Fri; 10 am-5 pm Sat; 12-4 pm Sun & PH
Points of interest: Rammed stabilised earth warehouse
Retail distribution: South Australia, S & V Wine Merchants and Bulk Wine Supplies; Victoria, Vintners Pty. Ltd; New South Wales, Busby Wine Co; Western Australia, WAZA Wine Wholesaler

Ryecroft - Rosemount

Frederick Wilkinson came to South Australia in 1879 from Manchester in England to work for the Bank of South Australia. He decided banking was not for him and in 1884 he purchased 160 acres at McLaren Flat.

Planting began in 1886, with the Cellars in readiness for the 1895 vintage, including a large underground cellar where 800 gallon vats kept the temperature of the fermenting wines in check, long before the days of refrigeration.

Much of the original winery remains intact today.

Wilkinson's only son, Lewis, lost his life in the First World War and the winery was sold in 1919 to James Ingoldby, a 23 year old survivor of the war, and his father-in-law T.C. Walker, chairman of the Lion Brewery and the General Navigation Co. They expanded the vineyard area to 65 hectares, with the help of the stalwart Aubrey 'Aub' Chapman who had remained on from Wilkinson's days.

The wines, mainly full-bodied reds from the rich ironstone-riddled clay soils, went from strength to strength.

Ingoldby's eldest son tragically died in the Second World War, but his younger son, Jim, a budding artist, survived several years in the Air Force and came back to finish his arts degree, but the pull of Ryecroft was too strong.

In 1970, after building Ryecroft into a specialised premium red producer, Jim Ingoldby junior sold to Reed Consolidated, who subsequently sold to Gilbey's, neither of whom really understood the quality wine business. It was not until Rosemount Wines purchased Ryecroft in the early 1990s that the winery's direction was redefined and a programme of expansion initiated.

Today, under winemaker, Charles Whish and viticulturist, Paul Buttery, Ryecroft is growing quickly in the making and marketing of the highest possible quality table wines.

When I visited the winery with photographer Milan, I had the heady experience of seeing and smelling all that fermenting red in the traditional open fermenters. It is the most comforting and uplifting experience any human being could wish for.

RYECROFT VINEYARDS
Address: Ingoldby Road, McLaren Flat SA 5171
Phone: (08) 383 0001
Fax: (08) 383 0456
Established: 1888
Owner: Rosemount Estate
Winemaker: Charles Whish
Principal varieties grown: chardonnay, cabernet sauvignon, shiraz, merlot, sauvignon blanc, semillon
Ha under vine: 40
Average annual crush: 2,000-5,000 tonnes
Average no. cases produced: 100,000

Principal wines & brands	Cellar potential
Ryecroft Traditional	5-10 years
Ryecroft Contemporary	5-10 years
Ryecroft Flame Tree Shiraz	5-10 years
Ryecroft Flame Tree Chard.	2-5 years
Ryecroft Flame Tree White	2-5 years
Ryecroft Flame Tree Red	2-5 years

Trade tours: By appointment only
Cellar door sales: Yes
Hours open to public: 10 am-5 pm Mon-Fri; 12-5 pm w/e
Retail distribution: National distribution

The Chaffey brothers, who had pioneered many successful irrigation schemes around Victoria, were asked by the South Australian Government to examine the possibility of implementing such schemes along the course of the Murray River as it wound its way through the state.

During the late 1880s the brothers set up the scheme with canals and channels, bringing life- giving water to the rich orange-red alluvial soils. With the addition of this magic ingredient, the region began producing excellent quality crops of citrus and stone fruits. Grape-growing and winemaking spread quickly and by the beginning of the new century it was already a substantial contributor to the Australian vintage. Today it is Australia's largest winegrowing region.

The massive Berri Winery, now under the banner of BRL Hardy, and arguably Australia's largest wine producer, is complemented by its sister winery, Renmano. Angove's fast-expanding winery and distillery, producing its famous St. Agnes brandies, was the first established in the region in 1910, followed by large Australian companies such as Yalumba, Orlando and Southcorp. Tollana, Seppelt and Penfolds all have vineyards in the region.

The Riverland, however, is dominated by individual grape-growers, many of whose families took advantage of the soldier settlement program after the First World War to begin a new life planting their blocks with government assistance, a brilliantly conceived and managed scheme. The second major development in the region came with the post-Second World War European immigration flood. The newcomers with their strong link to wine and hard work developed the region quickly, inspiring others by their success. Such immigrants were the Moularadellis family whose

Kingston Estate is a premium wine success story expanding from a 60 tonne crush in 1986 to 10,000 tonnes in 1995, and winning many trophies and gold medals around the world along the way.

Viticultural developments with techniques such as minimal pruning, leading to smaller bunches of berries and increased wine quality, have been most successful. Moisture control and minimum irrigation is also contributing to increased wine quality. Winemaking methods and technology combine with top quality grapes to produce some exciting wines in this important Australian wine region whose future looks bright.

The region offers much to the visitor as it enjoys a very mild-pleasant climate all year round. The attractions of the river with its water sports, houseboat cruises and the many golf courses on its banks beckons one to come and have a break anytime.

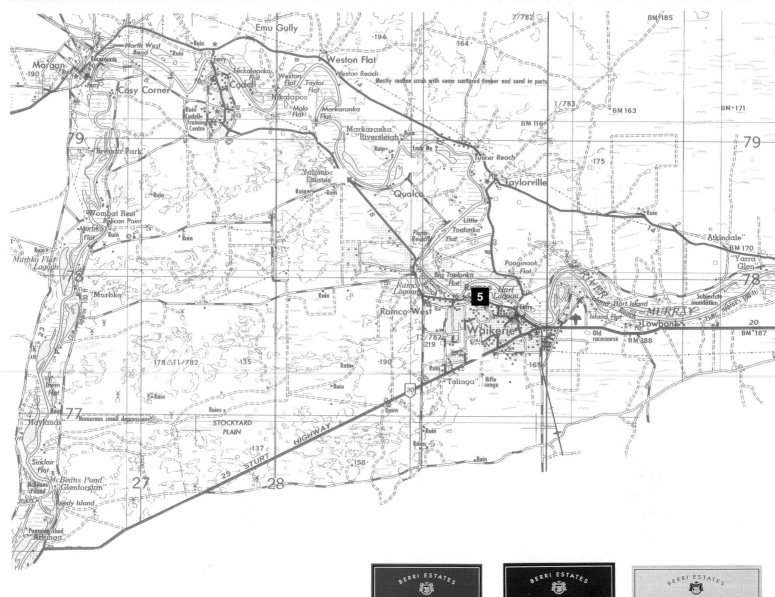

Riverland - SA

1   Angoves
2   Berri Estates
3   Bonneyview Wines
4   Kingston Estate
5   Penfolds Waikerie
6   Renmano
7   Wein Valley Estates

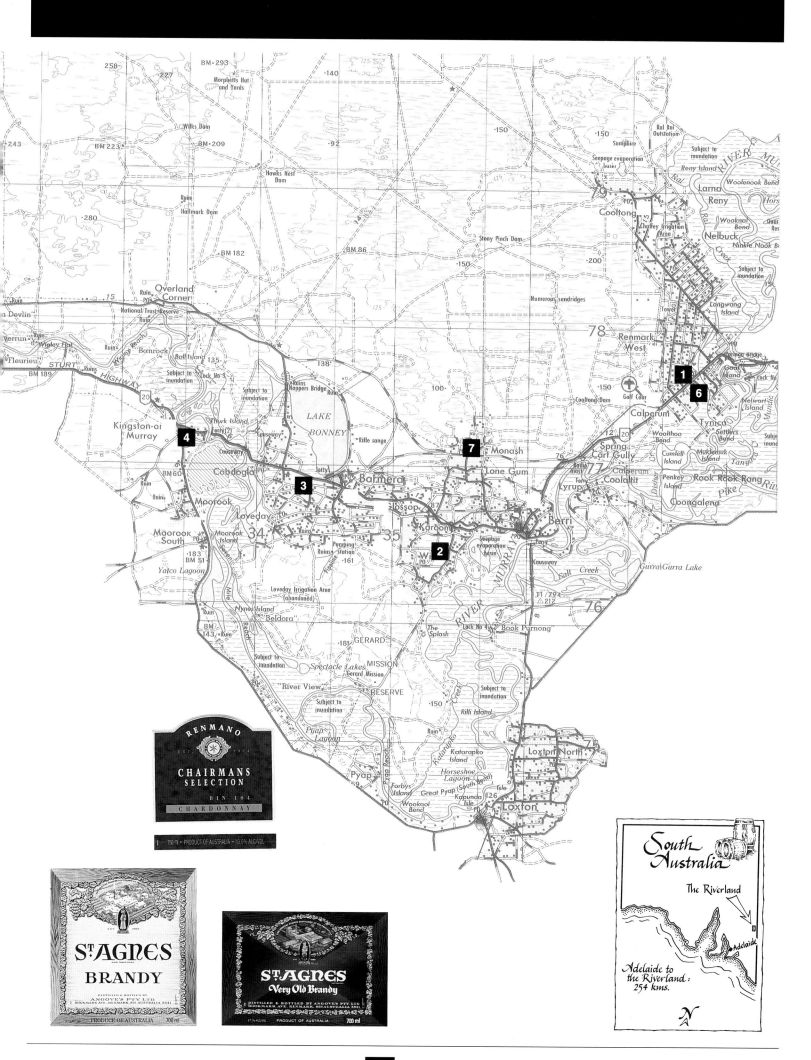

RENMANO
CHAIRMANS
SELECTION
BIN 104
CHARDONNAY

750 ml • PRODUCT OF AUSTRALIA • 13.0% ALC/VOL

St AGNES
BRANDY

DISTILLED & BOTTLED BY
ANGOVE'S PTY LTD.
1 BOOKMARK AVE • RENMARK. SS5 AUSTRALIA 5341

PRODUCE OF AUSTRALIA   700 ml

St AGNES
Very Old Brandy

DISTILLED & BOTTLED BY ANGOVE'S PTY LTD
1 BOOKMARK AVE. RENMARK, SS5 AUSTRALIA 5341

37½% ALC/VOL   PRODUCT OF AUSTRALIA   700 ml

South
Australia

The Riverland

Adelaide to
the Riverland:
254 kms.

Angove's

On July 12, 1986, Angove's celebrated 100 years of involvement in the Wine & Brandy industry. The company's first vines were planted in 1886 at Tea Tree Gully, near Adelaide, by Dr William Thomas Angove.

Dr Angove as well as being a medical practitioner was a highly successful winemaker and marketer and his business thrived. By the turn of the century his wines were well known throughout the country with many show awards to their credit. The company expanded, establishing the first winery and distillery in the Murray Valley, at Renmark, in 1910. Further developments followed, with the construction of another winery at Lyrup, south-west of Renmark in 1913, and the export of large volumes of wine to England during the 1920's.

Angove's continued to expand and consolidate their business and in 1968 plantings commenced at the Nanya Vineyard, a few kilometres east of Renmark. Now one of Australia's largest single vineyards, planted with at least 22 different varieties, the Nanya Vineyard produces a large range of varietal table wines including riesling, sauvignon blanc, chardonnay, chenin blanc, colombard and cabernet sauvignon.

The quality of the wines in the different Angove's ranges is exceptionally high and

their value extraordinary. A recent new range released by Angove's is their Classic Reserve wines, the best selections of their premium varieties which receive special treatment in the winery in small batches, and in the case of the reds and chardonnay, small barrel fermentation and ageing. The Sarnia Farm label is now the top of the range and named after one of the original Tea Tree Gully properties of Dr William Thomas Angove. The wines are all regionally selected, with the Padthaway region in SA's South East featuring prominently.

Angove's has a tremendous depth of products of the vine, producing one of Australia's finest brandies under the St. Agnes label, along with arguably Australia's best commercial fino sherry, a range of vermouths under the Marko label and the Stone's Green Ginger Wine.

Angove's wines are currently produced at Renmark in the Murray Valley. Tea Tree Gully, though originally constructed as a winery, now houses a Cellar Door sales facility as well as the state branch office. Vineyards that surrounded the Tea Tree Gully winery no longer exist, as they were compulsorily purchased by the South Australian Government to provide land for housing in the mid 70's.

Having played a major role in establishing

the Murray Valley as a wine-producing area, Angove's Pty Ltd has not only contributed to the economic welfare of the state but has also furthered the reputation of Australian wine worldwide.

ANGOVES PTY LTD
Address: Bookmark Avenue, Renmark SA 5341
Direction: 250 km north-east of Adelaide.
Phone: (085) 95 1311
Fax: (085) 95 1583
Established: 1886
Owners: Angove Family
Winemaker: Garry Wall
Principal varieties grown: Chardonnay, chenin blanc, sauvignon blanc, cabernet sauvignon, rhine riesling, shiraz, colombard, pinot noir
Ha under vine: 490
Average annual crush: 16,000 tonnes
Average no. cases produced: 800,000 (including export)

Principal wines & brands	Cellar potential
Sarnia Farm Cabernet	5-10 years
Sarnia Farm Chardonnay	2-5 years
Winemakers Limited Edition:	
Cabernet Sauvignon	2-5 years
Chardonnay	2-5 years
Classic Reserve Chardonnay	2-5 years
Classic Reserve Cabernet Sauvignon	2-5 years
Classic Reserve Sauvignon Blanc	2-5 years
Butterfly Ridge Colombard/Chardonnay	2-5 years

Trade tours: By appointment
Cellar door & mail order sales
Hours open to public 9 am-5 pm Mon-Fri
Points of interest: Largest privately owned vineyard
Retail distribution: Most major wine brands handled by key independent and group liquor stores.

Angove's – St. Agnes Brandy

John Angove

No book on Australian wine would be complete without a feature on brandy, an important beverage of the wine and grape industry. What is brandy? Brandy is the distilled spirit of wine made from fresh grapes. Australia has some of the world's strictest controls on the production and maturation of this age-old essence of wine.

The first step in the production of brandy is the fermentation of grape juice to produce wine, often referred to as brandy wash. Brandy wash is then distilled, a process that extracts the alcohol and a wide range of volatile flavour components, called congeners, from the wine. It is the mystical distillation process that gives rise to the production of brandy from wine, but before it can be called brandy is must be matured in wood for a period of not less than 2 years. This time of quiet maturation allows the spirit to mellow and soften, and to gain extra interest and complexity of flavour by interaction with the oak, wood and atmosphere. Longer maturation is not uncommon in order to produce even better quality brandy.

There are two distinct alternative methods of distillation. The first and most important is the classic "pot still" method. This technique has been utilised by the best French cognac houses for centuries. The pot still is "charged" with brandy wash or wine, which is gently heated. As boiling occurs the most volatile components vapourise first. These are called "heads" and are undesirable in the brandy and after condensation are kept separate from the heart of the distillation that follows as the boiling point temperature continues to rise. Towards the end of the distillation the heavier least volatile components are vapourised and condensed and are called "tails" and again are undesirable in the brandy. The heart of this distillation often called "Brandy Low Wine" contains about 50% alcohol by volume. The brandy low wine is returned to the pot still and distilled a second time with the heart of this second distillation being of sufficient purity to be matured in oak barrels for brandy.

A second distillation method utilises a continuous still and as the name implies is a continuous process where wine is constantly fed into the still, the alcohol in the wine is stripped from the wine by a steam and in a second column the steam alcohol mixture is

Tom Angove

successively distilled and condensed over a series of specially designed 'plates'. Spirit can be extracted from the column at up to 95% alcohol by volume. This is an excellent method for the production of fortifying spirit for addition to ports, sherries, vermouths etc., but it is not the most ideal for production of quality brandy.

St. Agnes Brandy is double distilled pot still brandy, produced by the Angove family in Renmark, South Australia. St. Agnes has been the flagship of the company for many years and has earned tophies and medals in Australia and overseas, too numerous to detail. St. Anges Very Old XO Brandy has been awarded many international honours including the Championship Trophy in France against brandies from around the world.

In the early 1970's the Federal Government severely wounded this important segment of the wine and grape industry with callous ill-conceived tax increases. At this time brandy was on a strong growth curve and Angove's were increasing the size of their distillery to accommodate a new pot still to add to the three existing stills; this space still remains vacant some 25 years later. Recent growth in St. Anges sales may herald new opportunities for expansion and the fourth pot still may yet find its way into the system.

The age of a brandy is the age in wood of the youngest component of any blend. By this rule, St. Anges 3 Star Brandy is usually between two and half and three years of age. It is a great value, superb brandy. St. Anges Old Liqueur 5 Star Brandy has a minimum

age of 10 years in wood and St. Agnes Very Old XO Brandy has a minimum age of 20 years in wood. These are superb spirits that the gods would be proud of. Older brandies are very expensive to produce with money tied up in stock for 20 years or more. Additionally, 2-3% of the volume of brandy in each barrel is lost to evaporation each year. This is called the "angel's share".

The Angove family is led by wine industry stalwart Tom Angove, with more than 60 vintages under his belt and his son John as Managing Director. This fine family company's commitment to quality wine and brandy production, always seeking to improve and give their customers extra value, is admirable. St. Agnes, the patron saint of purity, would be proud of them.

Kingston Estate

In 1994 Kingston Estate was awarded the South Australian Small Business of the year award, an accolade that could not be more deserved.

The winery and its young winemaker, Bill Moularadellis are one of the up and coming success stories of the Australian wine industry. Kingston has carved out a niche in the export market and is well on the way to repeating this success within Australia.

Although Bill's parents both came from Greece, they actually met in the Riverland. For many years they ran their fruit and vine block, selling grapes to large wine producers. As their grapes were always among the best in the region and in demand, they decided to build a small winery in 1979. By 1986 the winery was still only crushing 60 tonnes.

Bill attended Roseworthy and graduated with his winemaking credentials in 1985, followed by a vintage in the Hunter Valley. He then returned to Kingston and concentrated on creating a modern winemaking facility with state-of-the-art equipment and expanded capacity.

At the outset the Moularadellis family set quality and value-for-money as the main criteria for their wines to meet and as rapid as the growth of the winery has been, Bill has always had a clear objective to continually improve the quality of the wines being produced and refining his style of winemaking.

Bill liaises strongly with his growers assisting and encouraging in the pursuit of excellence at every level. To translate this fruit quality into wine Bill has introduced a system based on small tanks and open fermenters enabling him to isolate and personally handle those batches of grapes showing outstanding potential.

Kingston Estate produces two main wine ranges - the elegantly packaged 'Kingston Estate' and the prestige 'Kingston Reserve' range featuring rich, truly powerful wines.

In 1994, the 1991 Reserve Chardonnay won the double gold at the San Francisco International Wine Show and followed this with the Hyatt Advertiser Award for South Australia's best Chardonnay. Other whites produced are a wood-matured semillon and a semillon/sauvignon blanc blend - both classy wines full of character. Among the reds the 1991 Reserve Shiraz has won trophy and gold in International Wine Shows and the cabernet sauvignon and merlot have received rave reviews in the United States.

All Kingston wines are proudly Riverland and Bill pays tribute to the rich sandy loams of the region and the untiring efforts of his grape growers in growing ideal grapes to make great wines.

Bill Moularadellis is a 'new breed' of Winemaker, unconstrained by outmoded concepts of winemaking and marketing. Bill's view is global, and he has built a team of young professionals around him who share his passion for excellence in every area of his business. Always in the background and caring for everything, down to keeping the fermentation area clean, are his devoted and proud parents.

KINGSTON ESTATE WINERY
Address: PO Box 67 Kingston-on-Murray SA 5331
Direction: Located on Sturt Highway at turn off to Kingston-on-Murray
Phone: (085) 83 0244
Fax: (085) 83 0304
Established: 1979
Winemaker: Bill Moularadellis
Principal varieties grown: Chardonnay, semillon, sauvignon blanc, colombard, cabernet sauvignon, shiraz, merlot, grenache, pinot noir

Principal wines & brands	Cellar potential
Chardonnay	2-5 years
Shiraz	5-10 years
Cabernet Sauvignon	5-10 years
Semillon (Wood Matured)	2-5 years
Semillon/Sauvignon Blanc	2-5 years
Merlot	2-5 years
Reserve Chardonnay	2-5 years
Reserve Shiraz	5-10 years

Trade tours: By appointment only
Hours open to public: By appointment only
Retail distribution: Distributed nationally by Tucker Seabrook (Aust) Pty Ltd

Renmano

In 1915, 130 Riverland grape growers banded together to form the country's first co-operative winery. They purchased the Chateau Tanunda distillery situated just south of Renmark and produced spirit for 20 years until fortified wines became popular, and production was altered accordingly.

A range of table wines was developed during the late 1950s with Renmano's first varietal release being a cabernet sauvignon in 1962. Other varieties followed in subsequent years, although most wines were sold in bulk to other companies until the 1970s.

In addition to Renmano's cask and flagon wines, a premium range of table wines is also produced and marketed under the Chairman's Selection label. This range, cabernet sauvignon, hermitage and chardonnay represent excellent value for money and have been highly successful on the export market. The Chairman's Selection range really came into prominence when the 1988 Chardonnay won 4 trophies including the Tucker Seabrook Caon Trophy for the best show wine over the 1090 Wine Show season.

Renmano also produce a range of premium varietal 2 litre wine casks, these remain among the best and most popular wines in this field.

There is an excellent cellar door at the winery in the heart of Renmark and it makes a good visit if you are passing through the region.

Berri Estates

The largest wine producer in Australia had rather humble origins, as a grower co-operative. The co-operative's first wine, brandy spirit, was produced in a small distillery with makeshift equipment. This brandy spirit was made from a surplus of raisins and sultanas left over after the Riverland harvest of 1918. Within four years, local fruit production had greatly increased with the influx of repatriated soldier settlers to the area. This necessitated the expansion of the distillery, and the Berri Growers Co-operative was formed to manage the business.

Berri's first commercial vintage was made in 1922. The Co-operative continued to enjoy unbridled success and by 1958 a new winery/plant was constructed to cater for the swing in public tastes towards table wines. Wines were marketed in both bottles and flagons with impressive results. Sales figures skyrocketed during the early 1970s with the introduction into the market of the 'bag in the box' winecask. Berri quickly developed their five litre cask, one of the largest packaged volumes of wine on the market. The wine inside the cask is of very high quality and is great value for money. The Berri cask assured the Co-operative of a large share of the cask market which it has maintained.

Berri also developed a range of premium table wines during the 1970s. Winemakers Brian Barry and Ian McKenzie built up a range of wines that won more than 1,000 show medals over an eight-year period. These prizes include the illustrious Jimmy Watson Trophy and the 1977 Most Successful Exhibitors Trophy from the National Wine Show in Canberra. The stars of the Berri range have been their cabernet sauvignons and cabernet blends.

Today Berri Estates is part of the BRL Hardy Wine Company and quality is on a constant improvement curve, with viticultural and winemaking techniques in constant focus.

An introduction to Currency Creek/Middleton Beach

Some 30 kilometres south-west of Langhorne Creek, close to the resort towns and fishing port of Goolwa and Victor Harbor, lies a distinctive wine region. At present it supports only two wineries, but is already supplying grapes to many of South Australia's top winemakers.

The truly maritime climate is influenced by the Great Southern Ocean. In fact, it is one of South Australia's coolest climates overall, but in winter one of its mildest, both ideal for the vine, giving an exceptionally long growing season, building and retaining loads of elegant flavours in the wines.

Wally and Phillip Tonkin's Currency Creek Wines, established in 1969, produces a large range of elegant wines and has a delightful country-style restaurant for the day-tripper from Adelaide.

Likewise, Middleton Winery, under the experienced and innovative Nigel Catt, makes outstanding wines and has a most pleasant al

fresco style holiday and weekend restaurant tucked into the winery itself.

The sandy loams of the area with good drainage also help produce the unique styles this exciting new region will surely become famous for.

Currency Creek/Middleton Beach -
   Map Index
1   Currency Creek Winery
2   Middleton Winery

Currency Creek Winery

Wally Tonkin was born and raised in the region, but his bubbling energy and constant search for a new challenge to tackle led him to Adelaide where he very successfully operated a property development business and a travel business at the same time.

His main challenges met, his love for the country of his youth, and animals, led him to purchase a large rural holding on the Finniss and Currency Creeks near Goolwa. Always with a desire to be different, he "ran" a number of unusual animals and birds, from deer to ostriches and peacocks, along with his main love, horses.

He also planted a large vineyard, with most of the grapes being sold to eager winemakers further north, but he set up his own innovative little winery. Today, his son Phillip runs the successful winery, complete

with a restaurant. And planned for late 1995 are some bed and breakfast cabins.

The peacocks proudly parade, past the windows, on the expansive lawns as you sip some superb Currency Creek wines with the succulent meals in the casual and charming restaurant.

The sauvignon blanc has been particularly successful, as has their sparkling cabernet and one of Australia's finest botrytised wines, their Noble Riesling, several times the Australian Champion in the small wineries sweet white category.

Whilst Wally is busy winning many races with his self-trained stable of horses, Phillip is forging new markets for the Currency Creek wines around the world. Why not put this, one of Australia's most colourful and characterful wineries, on your next wine adventure itinerary?

TONKINS CURRENCY CREEK WINERY
Address: Winery Road, Currency Creek SA 5214
Phone: 085/554069
Fax: (085) 55 4100
Winemaker: Phillip Tonkin
Principal varieties grown: Sauvignon blanc, chardonnay, cabernet sauvignon, shiraz, gamay, pinot noir, semillon, riesling
Ha under vine: 35
Average annual crush: 162 tonnes
Average no. cases produced: 8,000

Principal wines & brands	Cellar potential
Sauvignon Blanc	2-5 years
Chardonnay	2-5 years
Fume Blanc (Semillon)	2-5 years
Seafood Dry White	0-1 years
Cabernet Sauvignon	5-10 years
Methode Traditionale N.V.	2-5 years
Sparkling Cabernet	2-5 years
Gamay	0-1 years

Trade tours:Yes
Cellar door & mail order sales: Yes
Hours open to public: 10 am-5 pm seven days a week
Points of interest: Full restaurant and function facility, relaxed country style with superb outlook. Six delightful self-contained accommodation units with breakfast (opening 1996)
Retail distribution: Australia-wide, export to various countries

Middleton Estate Winery

In 1976, surgeon Greg Markey and John Lewis planted a trial plot of vines in the V-shaped valley six kilometres north of Middleton, a surfing beach between Victor Harbor and Goolwa.

The success of the planting led them to plant a further 30 acres. For many years they sold the grapes to the likes of Orlando and Basedow, but in 1989 they took in a partner in the form of Nigel Catt, the talented winemaker of the Andrew Garrett Winery at McLaren Vale.

Middleton Estate was launched with some great wines at bargain prices and a fun label featuring a beach scene in bright colours. The wines, like the label, were fresh and full of aromatic exciting flavours. The 1990

riesling won the J.G. Kelly Trophy at the 1990 McLaren Vale Wine Bushing Festival as the region's overall best white wine.

Today the winery also supports a vibrant al

fresco bistro, open on weekends and holiday periods, featuring fresh innovative foods to match the mood of Middleton. For a refreshing change, you should try their wines.

MIDDLETON WINERY	
Address: Flagstaff Hill Road, Middleton SA 5213	
Direction: Southern Fleurieu Peninsula	
Phone: (085) 55 4136	
Fax: (085) 55 4108	
Established: 1979	
Winemaker: Nigel Catt	
Principal varieties grown: Riesling, semillon, cabernet, shiraz, merlot	
Ha under vine: 15	
Average annual crush:	
Average no. cases produced: 3,000	

Principal wines & brands	Cellar potential
Riesling	2-5 years
Semillon	2-5 years
Cabernet	5-10 years
Shiraz	5-10 years
Sauvignon Blanc	2-5 years

Tours: By appointment only
Cellar door & mail order sales: Yes
Hours open to public: 10 am-5 pm Fri-Sun; daily during school holidays
Points of interest: Restaurant on Sundays, for lunch only by chef John Marlow
Retail distribution: Parker Evans, Adelaide; Harry Williams, Canberra

Victoria has been through a wine revolution in the last decade. The number of wineries has exploded - at last count, there were more than 230 wineries in the state, the most of any state in Australia. However, Victoria accounts for less than 20 per cent of the nation's production.

One important factor is that Victoria is truly a premium wine producer. Well over 90 per cent of the wineries are small, boutique, premium bottled wine producers. No other state has such a wide spread of vineyards and virtually no region of the state is without a vineyard, showing how suitable the climate and soil are for vines.

In 1838 William Ryrie planted Victoria's first vines in the Yarra Valley at Yering Station. Within five years many vineyards had been established in Geelong, the Yarra Valley, and in and around metropolitan Melbourne. Suburban vineyards, some as large as 30 acres, were located at South Yarra, Toorak and Brighton. This development was due largely to the arrival of groups of Swiss immigrants who brought both vine cuttings and viticultural knowledge to the new colony. In particular, Paul and Hubert de Castella and the Baron Guillaume de Pury were influential in

establishing a new viticultural industry throughout the Yarra Valley. Swiss settlers also spread winemaking knowledge to Geelong where vines were first planted in 1842.

The gold rush of the late 1800s encouraged many thousands of people to travel inland in search of easy wealth. New areas were settled and towns were consequently established. Winemakers travelled also, developing vineyards in Great Western, Avoca, Ballarat, Bendigo, the Goulburn Valley and as far north as Rutherglen.

By the end of the century Victoria was producing more wine than any other colony. Unfortunately this booming industry went into decline owing to a change in public tastes and to an attack from a tiny aphix called Phylloxera Vastatrix which kills vines by eating through their roots. The louse first attacked vines in Geelong in 1875 and gradually spread north through the state. In an attempt to protect Rutherglen, Victoria's principal wine-producing area, affected winemakers were ordered to destroy all vines and chemically sterilise their soil, making replanting financially impractical. By some quirk of fate, the Yarra Valley was spared this parasite, but both here and in other unaffected areas

production soon ceased due to the growth in popularity of fortified wines and the competitive prices of interstate producers.

The only regions still producing wine by 1921 were the Goulburn Valley and Glenrowan, Great Western, Rutherglen and the North-Western Murray River. With Victoria's wine production thus affected, redevelopment did not begin until the 1960s when table wine again became popular.

A few new districts were planted to vines however, such as Drumborg in the south-western corner of the state, and the Mornington Peninsula. Each of the 11 wine-producing areas of Victoria (with many subdivisions), produces distinctly characteristic wines.

When purchasing a Victorian wine the wine-lover is now confronted with an incredible array of wine styles and varieties. Despite almost total eradication, the wine industry of Victoria has re-asserted itself across the state.

Wines currently produced cater for all tastes and compare favourably with those of other states. Generally of a very high quality, Victorian wines are finding a ready market both Australia-wide and internationally.

Bendigo Region

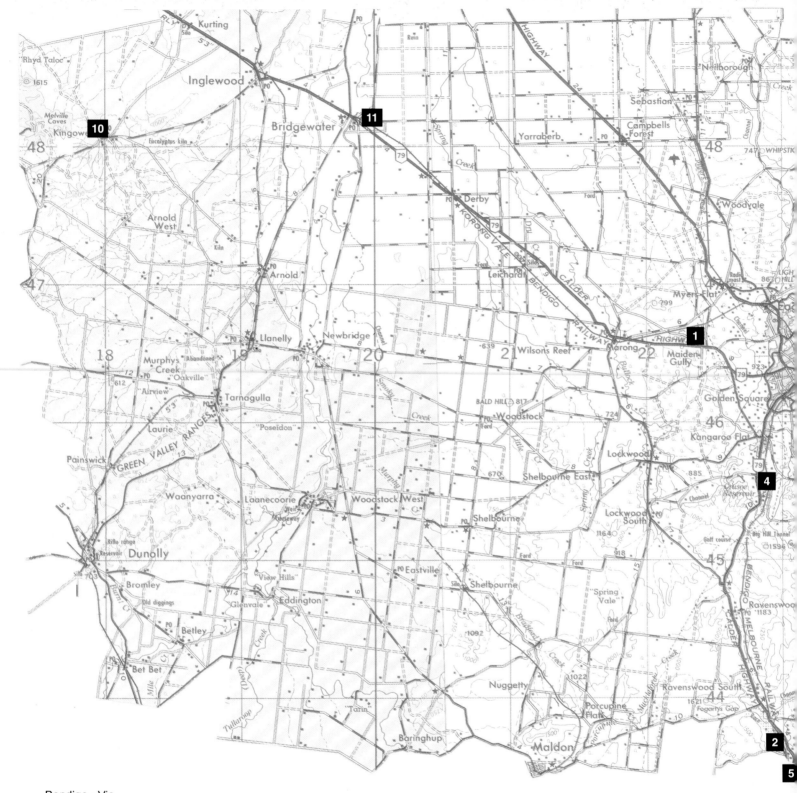

Bendigo - Vic
1   Balgownie Estate
2   Blackjack Vineyards
3   Chateau Dore
4   Chateau Leamon
5   Harcourt Valley Vineyards
6   Heathcote Winery
7   Huntleigh Vineyards
8   Jasper Hill Vineyard
9   Mount Ida
10 Passing Clouds
11 Waterwheel Vineyards
12 Wild Duck Creek Estate
13 Zuber Estate

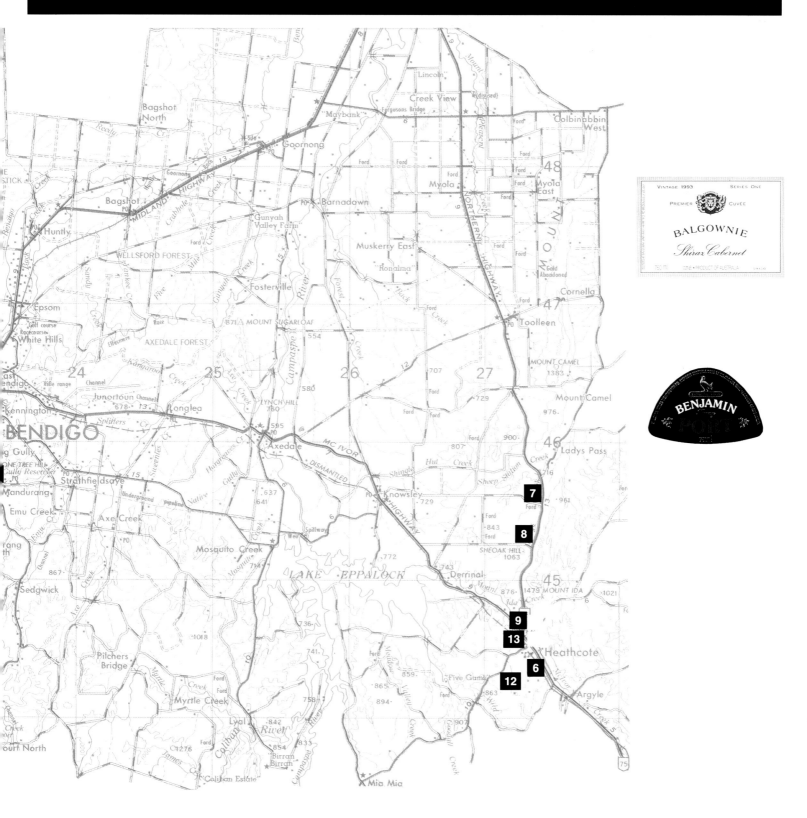

An introduction to Bendigo

Although a few vineyards existed around Bendigo during the late 1840s, the area did not fully develop until gold was discovered in 1851. Within 30 years, there were more than 100 wine producers in the region, manufacturing very high quality wines.

Phylloxera, scourge of Victoria's vignerons, was discovered in Bendigo in 1893, thus bringing a thriving industry to a grinding halt. As in the Geelong district, local winemakers were forced to destroy their vines and the area was not replanted until 1969.

In that year, Stuart Anderson established the Balgownie vineyard north-east of Bendigo. Since then, the area has once again attracted winemakers, although only a small proportion of the original number, about 12 wineries.

While the Bendigo region produces some premium wines, physical conditions of the area are far from ideal. The average annual rainfall for Bendigo is a low 500-550mm which is compensated for in various ways. Some winemakers irrigate their vineyards, others rely on an underground water supply,

while still others depend on clay subsoils to retain what rain does fall. Furthermore, the impervious nature of widespread clay soils can prove to be a problem by restricting growth of vine roots.

Once these difficulties have been overcome, however, winemakers have followed Stuart Anderson's excellent lead to produce outstanding wines from this colourful region. Innovative winemakers such as Peter Cumming from Waterwheel have done much to conquer the elements and enhance this region's reputation.

Mount Ida

In the late 1970s famous Australian artist Leonard French established a small 20 acre vineyard just north of Heathcote. He made only one wine, a shiraz cabernet of extraordinary quality from the low yielding vines. As the quality of his wines became known, they sold out virtually before they were made.

This fact did not escape the entrepreneurial Dr Peter Tisdall and his fast-expanding wine empire. Len eventually accepted an offer from the good doctor and Mt Ida's market expanded further. Tisdall fell on hard times and the vineyard was a little neglected. Mildara Blass bought the property in 1993 along with Tisdall, and the fine vines have been restored to their former glory.

Mt. Ida's reds are renowned for their lifted aromatic qualities and long life. Why not put a few of these special wines down for a decade or so - I know you'll be well repaid for your effort.

Balgownie

character similar to wines from the Rhone Valley in France.

A dozen years ago Mildara Wines saw the potential of Balgownie and with Stuart Anderson wanting to step back a little, a deal was struck. Balgownie was in fact, the first vineyard to be planted in the rebirth of the Bendigo wine region. Stuart Anderson has done far more than prove his belief in the area's ability to produce excellent wine. He led the way for other winemakers in the region, by producing a range of 100 per cent estate grown varieties. Mildara Blass are carrying on this proud tradition with Lindsay Ross now in charge of winemaking.

W hile on a visit to the Bordeaux district of France in 1950, Stuart Anderson fell in love with the region and its wines. He began a continuing association with the area and in particular, M Louis Vialard of Chateau Cissac from whom he has gained much of his considerable winemaking knowledge.

In 1969, Stuart planted approximately 30 acres of vines a short distance north-east of Bendigo. The property was named 'Balgownie' and although only 5,000-6,000 cases of wine were produced annually, these wines have always been of such high quality that they are practically sold before they are on the shelves. The Balgownie Cabernet Sauvignon is the star of the range which also includes a shiraz, formerly known as hermitage. The cabernet has great depth with berry/cassis flavours and a beautiful hint of sweet oak and is consistently one of the best wines of this variety in Australia. The Balgownie Shiraz is of a lighter style with a peppery

An introduction to the Macedon Ranges

The Macedon viticultural region, closer to Melbourne than some parts of the Yarra Valley, stretches from North of the Sunbury Region to Boynton and from Mt William, west to Malmsbury. It is really divided into two separate regions, the wineries grouped around the central Lancefield-Woodend-Macedon area and then the Boynton-Kyneton area further north.

Initial development in the region started with the gold rush in the 1850s. Within 60 years, however, due to the phylloxera plague and changes in wine drinking tastes, the industry had faded from existence.

The 1970s saw a renaissance of the area when the Knight family at Granite Hill and Tom Lazar at Virgin Hills established vineyards in the area. Other winemakers who followed were Flynn and Williams at Kyneton, Gordon and Judy Cope-Williams at Romsey, John and Ann Ellis at Hanging Rock, Keith and Lyn Brien at Cleveland Estate and many others. There are now more than 30 grape-growers in the region, supplying about a dozen wineries.

To play such a major role in the production of high quality fruit in such a short period of time is an attribute to the endeavours of all who have been involved in the re-establishment of the area as a viticultural region. The French-based champagne house, Möet and Chandon with their Australian offshoot, Domaine Chandon, have shown great interest in the potential of the central district.

Subsequently, most grape growers have planted and are planting chardonnay and pinot noir vines for the production of fruit suitable for methode champenoise wines which are an obvious strength of the region. The Northern District is also renowned for its red wines, with Virgin Hills, Knight's, Hanging Rock and many others making extremely long-living wines. Shiraz, particularly, does extremely well in the cool climate and granite soils.

Some great rieslings, sauvignon blancs and chardonnays are also made, particularly in warmer years.

Vying for the title of Australia's coolest viticultural region and with its volcanic and granite soils, the tough conditions challenge the vignerons' and viticulturists' skills to the limit, but great wines are the result. Wine tourism is fast becoming a way of life for many of the region's producers.

Cope-Williams at Romsey has an extraordinary spreadeagled, but superbly planned hospitality complex, complete with a cricket ground, pavilion and large 'Clubroom' restaurant - you can feel like a lord for the day. The beautifully restored Cleveland Mansion of Keith and Lyn Brien is an absolute gem and they also have bed and breakfast accommodation, while Hanging Rock has a casual eatery. The list continues - it's so close to Melbourne yet has a majestic isolated feel that touches the soul.

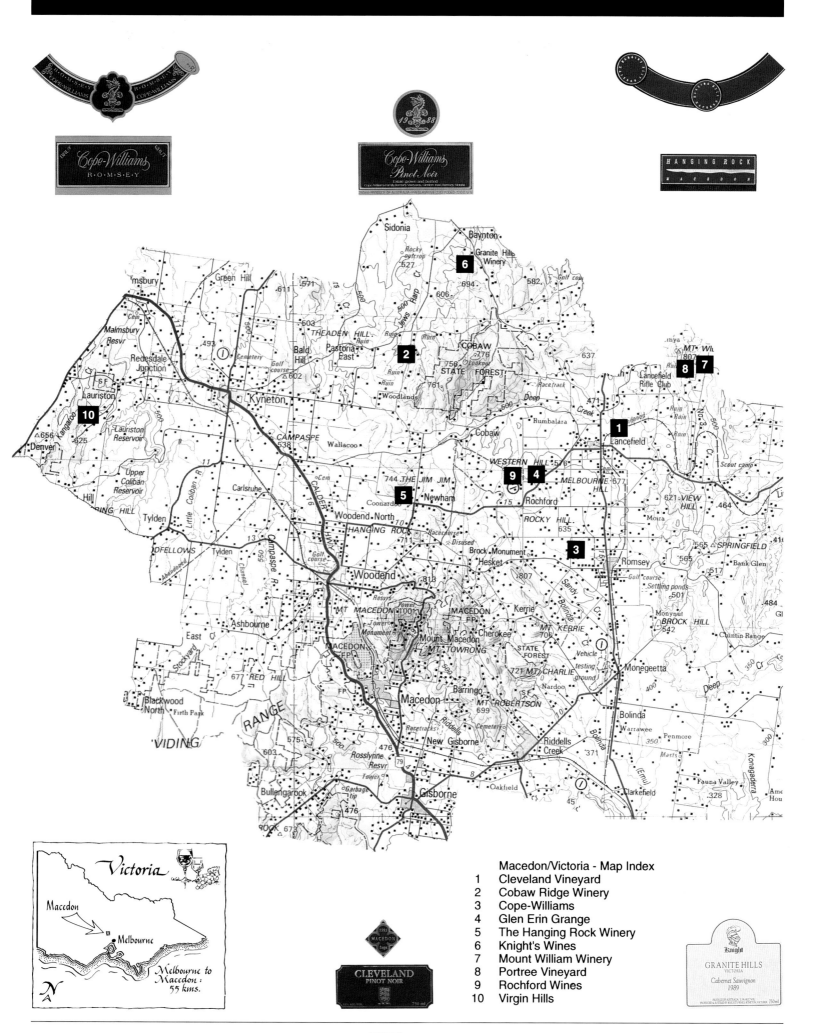

Macedon/Victoria - Map Index

1 Cleveland Vineyard
2 Cobaw Ridge Winery
3 Cope-Williams
4 Glen Erin Grange
5 The Hanging Rock Winery
6 Knight's Wines
7 Mount William Winery
8 Portree Vineyard
9 Rochford Wines
10 Virgin Hills

Cleveland

When I first met Keith Brien more than 20 years ago as a fellow member of the Shiraz Club in Melbourne, he was a keen wine connoisseur and a full-time airline pilot. he is now a full-time vigneron. Keith and his charming wife Lynette have enough energy and enthusiasm for 10 people, coupled with extraordinary good taste.

Aside from their award-winning Cleveland Brut Methode Champenoise, which won the Sommelier's Trophy at the 1994 Victorian Winemakers Exhibition on its first outing, they produce a chardonnay beginning with their first vintage in 1988. A cabernet sauvignon and a pinot noir have been added to their stable.

Alongside and above their winery the Briens have restored the historic wool shed and stables complex which now incorporates a function area for 50 people. Two delightful bed and breakfast units have panoramic views over the vineyard and ranges, as does the attic gallery room.

If you wish to celebrate a special occasion, the Briens serve dinner in the Grand Dining Room with its exquisite Victorian Gothic style and furnishings; the table setting has to be seen to be believed. The manor is surrounded by walled gardens and a number of outdoor areas can be used for summer functions. Take a trip to Cleveland and discover a world of old world grace.

CLEVELAND VINEYARD
Address: Shannons Road, Lancefield Vic. 3435
Phone: (054) 29 1449
Fax: (054) 29 2017
Established: 1984
Owner: Keith & Lyn Brien
Winemaker: Keith Brien
Principal varieties grown: Pinot noir, chardonnay, cabernet sauvignon
Ha under vine: 3.5
Average annual crush: 20-50 tonnes
Average no. cases produced: 4,000

Principal wines & brands	Cellar potential
Cleveland	
Brut	2-5 years
Pinot Noir	5-10 years
Chardonnay	5-10 years
Cabernet Sauvignon	5-10 years
Brien	
Chardonnay	2-5 years
Shiraz/Cabernet/Beverford/	
Macedon	5-10 years

Public & trade cellar tours: By appointment only
Hours open to public: 9 am-6 pm seven days
Points of interest: Historic home, underground cellars, restored 'Woolshed' Restaurant and bed and breakfast facilities
Retail distribution: Select Vineyards (wholesalers)

Knight Granite Hills

The Knight family first planted an experimental vineyard on their grazing property 'Granite Hills' in 1970. Although it is one of Australia's highest vineyards at 550 metres above sea level, and prone to occasional strong winds, the grapes ripened well and further plantings followed. Vineyards now total roughly two hectares each of cabernet sauvignon, shiraz, riesling and chardonnay. There are also smaller plantings of cabernet franc and merlot, with additional grapes bought in from neighbouring growers.

The first vintage at the Granite Hills winery was in 1979. The Granite Hills Shiraz took the wine world by storm and continues to be a benchmark for the peppery, cool climate versions of this Australian classic red. The cabernet, originally 100% cabernet, is a more generous style with the inclusion of cabernet franc and merlot - a lovely wine. Although renowned for their red wines, Knight's also produce fine white wines. The riesling exhibits pronounced floral aromas and the interesting spiciness, appraent in all Granite Hills wines. A stylish fruit driven chardonnay with soft, integrated oak is also produced.

Wines are made by Llewelyn (Lew) Knight, while the rest of the family looks after the vineyards - set amongst the rugged granite strewn hills of Victoria's central Great Divide. Like true Chevaliers of the land, the Knights battle the adversity of their climate with courage and determination, producing individual wines of character.

KNIGHT GRANITE HILLS
Address: Burke & Wills Track, Kyneton Vic. 3444
Direction: 85 km N/NW of Melbourne via Lancefield
Phone: (054) 23 7264
Fax: (054) 23 7288
Established: 1970
Owner: The Knight Family
Winemaker: Lew Knight
Principal varieties grown: Shiraz, cabernet sauvignon, chardonnay, riesling
Ha under vine: 9
Average annual crush: 100 tonnes
Average no. cases produced: 7,000

Principal wines & brands	Cellar potential
Shiraz	5-10 years
Cabernet Sauvignon	5-10 years
Riesling	2-5 years
Chardonnay	2-5 years

Public & trade tours: By appointment only
Hours open to public: 9 am-6 pm Mon-Sat; 12-6 pm Sun
Points of interest: Spectacular views of Central Victoria from the vineyard and rugged granite strewn hills surrounding.
Retail distribution: Cellar door. Regional Victoria, Melbourne, Sydney.

Cope-Williams – Romsey

Former architect Gordon Cope-Williams, a most successful designer of country houses, moved to the lush rolling Romsey countryside with his wife Judy in the early ''70's to breed Welsh mountain ponies and grow a few grapes - indulgent hobbies if you like.

The initial Rocky Hill Vineyard was planted on an exposed slope, causing considerable problems with ripening fruit. Gusty winds and a high altitude maintained lower temperatures than experienced in the more sheltered surrounding valleys and these climatic conditions resulted in very low grape yields.

Consequently, in 1982 a second vineyard was established in a more protected location close to the winery. Named the Coniston Vineyard, it was planted with pinot noir, chardonnay and small plots of cabernets and merlot.

Construction work at Romsey is on a grand scale. The towered manor is large enough to accommodate guests, as well as a magnificent music room to showcase the musical talents of Judy Cope-Williams. A beautiful walled garden amongst the vines creates a special atmosphere in the vineyard. The construction

did not stop there. Gordon, an avid cricket fan, has created an English village cricket ground, complete with charming pavilion and a large clubroom, furnished with old leather chairs, that can cater for up to 120 guests. The showpiece tasting room looks out on a traditional English rose garden adorned with sculptures and gorgeous climbing roses.

The Cope-Williams' son Michael, a Roseworthy graduate who has worked in both California and France specialising in sparkling wines, is now in charge of the winemaking, which focuses almost solely on methode champenoise. The coup de grace of the maison is their Romsey Brut. The stalwarts of their table wine range are a pinot noir and chardonnay.

The Cope-Williams Estate is surrounded by trees, mainly stately conifers which form a most pleasing-to-the-eye environment, as well as providing a necesssary windbreak for the vines and the intrepid cricketers. All in all, Cope-Williams have performed a real hat trick of wine, hospitality and cricket, not necessarily in that order.

The greatest change in recent years has been the development of Judy's catering – simple

cricket lunches have developed into first class cuisine – especially for conferences and weddings.

COPE-WILLIAMS WINERY - ROMSEY
Address: Glenfern Road, Romsey, Vic. 3434
Direction: 50 km north of Melbourne
Phone: (054) 29 5428
Fax: (054) 29 5655
Established: 1977
Owner: Judy & Gordon Cope-Williams
Winemaker: Michael Cope-Williams
Principal varieties grown: Chardonnay, pinot noir, cabernet sauvignon, merlot
Ha under vine: 14
Average annual crush: 100 tonnes

Principal wines & brands	Cellar potential
Cope-Williams Romsey Brut	5+ years
Cope-Williams Romsey Rose	5+ years
Pinot Noir	5-10 years
Chardonnay	5-10 years
Cabernet/Merlot	10+ years
Romsey Willow	5-10 years

Public & trade tours: By appointment only
Cellar door & mail order sales: Yes
Hours open to public: 11 am-5 pm seven days
Points of interest: Social cricket (mainly corporate) in village green setting, day conference centre (30 mins. north of Melbourne Airport), sparkling wine cellars under cricket pavilion/gardens/weddings/dinners & lunches
Retail distribution: Extensive in NSW & Victoria

The Hanging Rock Winery

Hanging Rock was made famous by the novel 'Picnic at Hanging Rock', adapted into a superb world-renowned film by Australian director Peter Weir. Like the heroines in this mysterious story, I'm sure you'd like to lose yourself in this truly beautiful part of Australia.

Each year, the racetrack tucked under the awesome granite boulders that form this striking landmark comes to life with that particularly Australian phenomenon, the picnic race meeting. Several kilometres away, on a slope of the opposing range, spreads the vineyards of a first class winery, Hanging Rock. The winery is also home to an extremely hospitable and well credentialled wine family.

John Ellis was the first winemaker for Rosemount Estate in the 1970s and he really put them on the map. One of the most gifted winemakers in Australia and highly regarded by his peers, he was also sought out by Dr. Peter Tisdall when he launched his wine enterprise at Echuca. John was most taken by the Mount Helen Vineyard in the cool Strathbogie Ranges. The wines he made for

Tisdall from this vineyard were sensational.

John married Ann Tyrrell, daughter of legendary Hunter Valley Winemaker, Murray Tyrrell. They were searching to put down their roots and establish their own vineyard and winery and chose their stunning site in the extremely cool Hanging Rock Valley in the centre of the Macedon Ranges Region, fast becoming one of Australia's foremost cool climate wine regions. John made wine from other vineyards' grapes until their own vineyards came into bearing, and still buys in some fruit. John also makes a good deal of wine under contract for other wineries.

The innovative winery, which incorporates the family home around it with windows looking down into the fermentation and press room, is truly amazing. The front of the winery, with its incredible view of the weathered extinct volcano that is Hanging Rock, sports a classy tasting room and hospitality area to rival anything worldwide. Why not pack your own picnic and head for Hanging Rock? John and Anne's wide range of still and sparkling wines will be the perfect accompaniment.

THE HANGING ROCK WINERY
Address: Jim Road, Newham Vic. 3442
Phone: (054) 27 0542
Fax: (054) 27 0310
Established: 1982
Owner: John & Ann Ellis
Winemaker: John Ellis
Principal varieties grown: Pinot noir, chardonnay, sauvignon blanc
Ha under vine: 6
Average annual crush: 450 tonnes
Average no. cases produced: 25,000

Principal wines & brands	Cellar potential
Hanging Rock Macedon (Sparkling) Cuvee	
Hanging Rock Jim Jim Sauvignon Blanc	2-5 years
Hanging Rock 'Victoria' Range	
Chardonnay	2-5 years
Cabernet Merlot	5-10 years
Pinot Noir	2-5 years
Riesling	2-5 years
Hanging Rock 'Picnic' Range	
Hanging Rock Heathcote Shiraz	10-20 years

Cellar door & mail order sales: Yes
Hours open to public: 10 am-5 pm seven days except Good Friday & Christmas Day
Points of interest: Close proximity to Hanging Rock with picnic grounds, cafe etc.
Retail distribution: Melbourne, country Victoria, NSW, Qld.

An introduction to Sunbury

The newest Viticultural Region in Victoria is Sunbury. It is also Melbourne's closest. Ironically it is also one of the oldest, having been first planted in the 1850s.

The renaissance of the area began in 1976 when the Carmody Family replanted the Craiglee Vineyard, first planted with vines in 1864 by James Johnston, a politician, who gained international fame for the region when he won an International Award for his 1872 "Hermitage" at an exposition in Vienna. The Carmody's have restored the old bluestone winery and cellars, which are well worth visiting.

Across the road is the impressive Goona Warra Vineyard Estate of John and Elizabeth Barnier, with its beautiful bluestone

buildings, now magnificently restored as vineyard, winery, function complex and restaurant. James Goodall Francis, an early Victorian Premier, first planted vines on the property in 1858.

These famous historic wineries have since been joined by another winery even closer to Melbourne. Under the flight path of the jets as they fly into Tullamarine Airport is the Wildwood Vineyard of surgeon, Dr Wayne Stott. The even newer Sunbury wineries of Longview Creek and Diggers Rest Vineyard now also have wines on the market.

For a day tripper or a serious wine enthusiast, Sunbury, birth place of the famous cricket ashes, is a great wine region to visit just a cricket ball throw or so from Melbourne's famous Melbourne Cricket Ground.

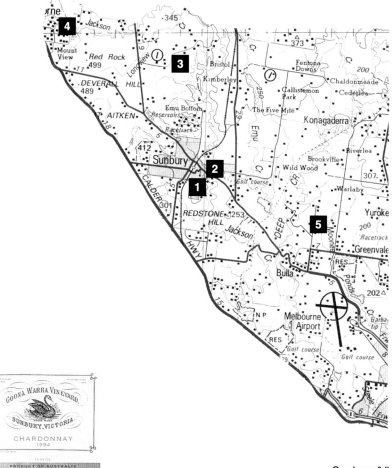

Sunbury/Victoria - Map Index
1   Craiglee
2   Goona Warra Vineyard
3   Longview Creek
4   Mount Aitken Estates
5   Wildwood

Goona Warra

Former State Premier James Goodall Francis planted vines on his property 'Goona Warra' in 1858. Shortly after the turn of the century, however, the economics of the day forced the vineyard to cease production. The vines were not re-established until John and Elizabeth Barnier purchased the land in 1983.

When the Barniers took possession of Goona Warra the original bluestone buildings, including the winery, were still standing, although sorely in need of repair. Fortunately, the Barniers were able to appreciate the historical significance of these treasures and Elizabeth's skills as an architect were well used in the restoration of the buildings which now house an excellent winery and a popular restaurant and function centre.

The first small vintage was made at Goona Warra in 1986 and the first commercial harvest occurred one year later. These wines, a cabernet franc and a chardonnay, were released in 1987, being received with acclaim by appreciative wine consumers.

Sunbury is one of Australia's most historic villages and among other things was the birthplace of the famous 'Ashes' fought for so ardently by the Australian and English cricket teams.

Sunbury is also the closest wine region to Melbourne, and by far the easiest to get to. One drives north out of the city on the Tullamarine Freeway and there are only a handful of traffic lights between the wineries and the city centre. Given reasonably easy traffic conditions, it takes little more than half an hour to get there.

Goona Warra wines are all 100 per cent estate grown. The chardonnay shows some subtle stone fruit characters with a nice citrus edge and a touch of vanilla from wood ageing. The semillon, ever in short supply, is particularly interesting with its pungent grassy-spicy flavour lifted with a mid-palate of tropical fruits; whilst the rarely grown cabernet franc is worthy of the interest the Goona Warra house style has aroused.

The beautiful bluestone buildings house, on the lower level, the cellar and tasting area, which caters for gourmet lunches and afternoon teas on Sundays. The tastefully appointed Great Hall above has become a popular venue for tying the wedding knot and for corporate dinners.

The vineyards on rich black clay soil over scoria surround the winery; their sheltered location under the Sunbury escarpment and the northerly aspect produces outstanding fruit and great wines. When in Melbourne, or anywhere near the Tullamarine airport, why not drop in on the delightful cultured couple, John and Elizabeth Barnier. It will be a visit to remember.

GOONA WARRA VINEYARD
Address: Sunbury Road, Sunbury Vic. 3429
Phone: (03) 9740 7766
Fax: (03) 9744 7648
Established: Founded 1863/Re-established 1983
Winemaker: John Barnier
Principal varieties grown: Chardonnay, semillon, cabernet franc, pinot noir, cabernet sauvignon, merlot
Ha under vine: 5
Average annual crush: 44 tonnes
Average no. cases produced: 3,000

Principal wines & brands	Cellar potential
Chardonnay	2-5 years
Semillon	2-5 years
Pinot Noir	2-5 years
Cabernet Franc	2-5 years
The Premier (Cab. Sauvignon, Merlot, Cabernet Franc)	5-10 years

Public & trade tours: By appointment only
Cellar door & mail order sales: Yes
Hours open to public: 10 am-5 pm daily
Points of interest: Grand historic Bluestone Winery now restored for functions (by appointment) plus a popular cellar lunch every Sunday
Retail distribution: Negociants Australia wholesale (fine restaurants - Melbourne, Sydney, Brisbane)

Wildwood

WILDWOOD
Address: St. Johns Lance, Wildwood Vic. 3428
Direction: Sunbury region, Victoria
Phone: (03) 307 1118
Fax: (03) 331 1590
Established: 1983
Owner: Dr. Wayne Stott
Winemaker: Wayne Stott/Peter Dredge
Principal varieties grown: Chardonnay, viognier, cabernet sauvignon, cabernet franc, merlot, shiraz, pinot noir
Ha under vine: 8
Average annual crush: 30 tonnes
Average no. cases produced: 2,000

Principal wines & brands	Cellar potential
Cabernets	5-10 years
Chardonnay	2-5 years
Shiraz	5-10 years
Pinot Noir	2-5 years

Public & trade tours: By appointment only
Cellar door & mail order sales: Yes
Hours open to public: 10 am-6 pm Mon-Sun (Sundays preferred)
Points of interest: Cellar door in century-old stables, attractive views of the Oaklands Valley
Retail distribution: Selected restaurant and retail outlets in Victoria, New South Wales and Queensland

Dr. Wayne Stott is a prominent Melbourne plastic surgeon and qualified winemaker. His winery is the closest winery to Melbourne, virtually under the flight path to the Tullamarine airport.

The cellar door is housed in century-old stables from the historic past of the property.

The wines are all of fine quality and are well priced for premium Macedon wines. They include chardonnay, pinot noir, shiraz, cabernet sauvignon/cabernet franc/merlot.

Wildwood vineyards also include the unusual French Rhone Valley white variety viognier for which Wayne has high expectations. Needless to say, the winery is ideally placed to visit and the cellar door is open daily.

Mount Aitken Estates

Travellers along the Calder Highway from Melbourne to Bendigo through the gently undulating countryside get a stunning view of the rocky craggy peak of Mount Aitken. It shelters a pretty little vineyard and charming Victorian bluestone winery and restaurant complex. Mt. Aitken specialises in port and other fortified wines which are displayed in nearly every shape and size of bottle known to man. Personalised pottery crocks, miniature bottles and oak barrels of all description form a wine mosaic that must be seen to be believed. Mt. Aitken also produces a range of table wines, including some bold red wines from its Heathcote Vineyards.

The winery restaurant has a warm and cosy feel about it, decorated in burgundy with leadlight windows and stone and timber beams adding a slightly rustic touch.

A simply wonderful venue that is ideal for a family outing and certainly the owners have created a beautiful back drop that is just perfect for weddings. Roger McLean is the innovative proprietor and winemaker. His energy and enthusiasm seems to know no bounds.

MOUNT AITKEN
Address: Calder Highway, Gisborne Vic. 3437
Phone: (03)744 6122 **Fax:** (03) 744 7854
Established: 1972
Principal varieties grown: Shiraz, cabernet, chardonnay, muscat, frontignac
Average no. cases produced: 1700 tonnes

Principal wines & brands Heathcote	Cellar potential
Shiraz	5-10 years
Cabernet Sauvignon	5-10 years
Classic Dry White & Autumn Harvest Chardonnay	5-10 years
Tawny Port	10+ years
Muscat	10+ years

Public & trade tours: yes
Cellar door & mail order sales: Yes
Hours open to public: 8.30 am-5 pm Mon-Fri; 10 am-5 pm Sat/Sun.
Points of interest: Restaurant, functions, cask-making, beautiful bluestone buildings housing historical treasures

Victoria's most isolated wine-producing area is East Gippsland in the south-eastern corner of the state. Most vineyards are small, of less than 10 hectares, and are spread over a large area which extends from Lakes Entrance in the far South East to Phillip Island in Westernport Bay. The southernmost groups of wineries in mainland Australia are the cluster in South Gippsland, between Wilsons Promontory and Phillip Island - Lyre Bird Hill, Bass Phillip, Paradise Enough, Tarwin Ridge and Windy Ridge.

There are a growing number of grape growers in the area, many aiming to make their own wine and open cellar door sales. The first vignerons to plant vines since the nineteenth century were Pauline and Dacre Stubbs at Lulgra Wines of Lakes Entrance,

now part of the Wyanga Park Estate.

Gippsland is grouped into the three subregions of South Gippsland, Central Gippsland and the Lakes District. The region covers quite a range of territory, topography and climate. Wines generally exhibit the spiciness inherent in cool climate fruit and consist of classic varieties such as pinot noir, cabernet sauvignon, shiraz, chardonnay, riesling and sauvignon blanc. Some of the best pinot noirs in the country have appeared from these tiny vineyards, notably from Lyre Bird, Bass Phillip, Parish Wines and Nicholson River Winery.

Although still largely a cottage industry, winemaking in South East Gippsland is continuing to develop and the fine wines so far produced are a credit to the far-flung pioneers who create them.

Gippsland - Vic
1 Bass Phillip
2 Coalville Vineyard
3 Lyre Bird Hill Winery
4 Nicholson River Winery
5 Paradise Enough Winery
6 Phillip Island Vineyard & Winery
7 Tarwin Ridge
8 Wa-de-lock Vineyard
9 Westernport Estate Wines
10 Wyanga Park Winery

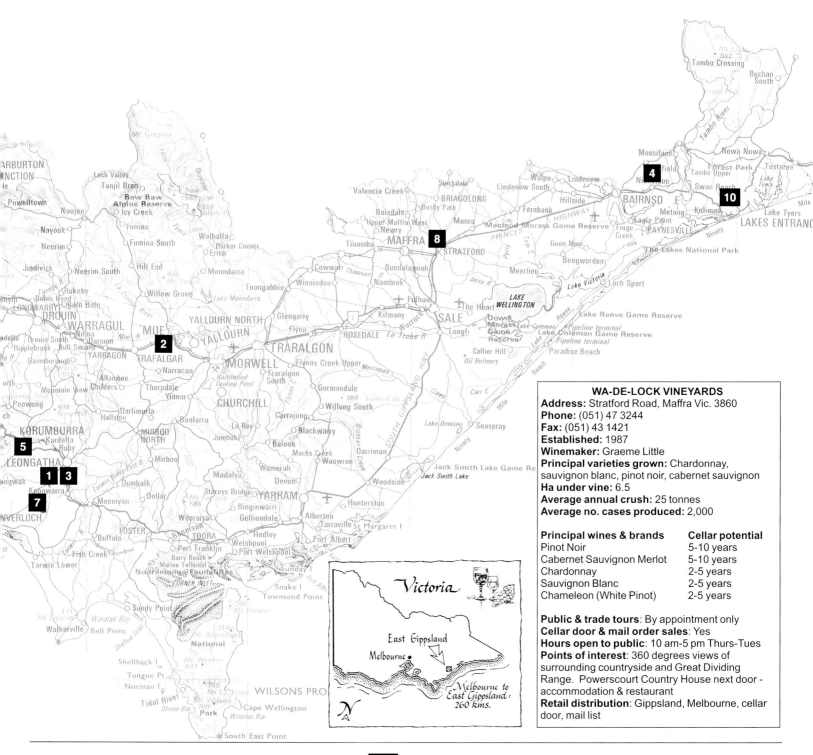

WA-DE-LOCK VINEYARDS

Address: Stratford Road, Maffra Vic. 3860
Phone: (051) 47 3244
Fax: (051) 43 1421
Established: 1987
Winemaker: Graeme Little
Principal varieties grown: Chardonnay, sauvignon blanc, pinot noir, cabernet sauvignon
Ha under vine: 6.5
Average annual crush: 25 tonnes
Average no. cases produced: 2,000

Principal wines & brands	Cellar potential
Pinot Noir	5-10 years
Cabernet Sauvignon Merlot	5-10 years
Chardonnay	2-5 years
Sauvignon Blanc	2-5 years
Chameleon (White Pinot)	2-5 years

Public & trade tours: By appointment only
Cellar door & mail order sales: Yes
Hours open to public: 10 am-5 pm Thurs-Tues
Points of interest: 360 degrees views of surrounding countryside and Great Dividing Range. Powerscourt Country House next door - accommodation & restaurant
Retail distribution: Gippsland, Melbourne, cellar door, mail list

Lyre Bird Hill

Owen and Robyn Schmidt have a deep love for their newly found lifestyle, a passion for their vines, the Lyre Bird Hill Winery and the Country House they have shaped with hard work by their own hands. The property, one of the most southerly vineyards on mainland Australia, is set in the serene beauty that is South Gippsland. Among the stately gums and ferns which once furnished the home for the exquisite, shy lyrebird, they found their little piece of paradise.

LYRE BIRD HILL
Address: Inverloch Road, Koonwarra Vic 3954
Phone: (056) 64 3204
Fax: (056) 64 3204
Established: 1993
Owner: Owen & Robyn Schmidt
Principal varieties grown: Riesling, chardonnay, traminer, pinot noir, shiraz, cabernet sauvignon
Average annual crush: 15 tonnes

Principal wines & brands	Cellar potential
Riesling	5-10 years
Chardonnay	2-5 years
Traminer	2-5 years
Pinot Noir	3-7 years
Shiraz	5-10years
Cabernet Sauvignon	5-10 years

Public & trade tours: Yes
Cellar door & mail order sales: Yes
Hours open to public: 10 am-5 pm seven days

Owen had been an accountant in the giant BHP Company. Although born in Queensland, he travelled Australia, spending a few years in South Australia. Robyn's career was in catering, mainly in the school area, spending a number of years victualling the hungry young students at Melbourne's Wesley College. They decided they would both give up their careers and set up a winery and provide a hospitality house on their weekend property near Koonwarra, south of Leongatha in South Gippsland, where they already had planted a vineyard.

Guests are welcomed into their home - the guest rooms are tastefully and practically appointed with spacious, yet cosy comfort. All rooms open onto a verandah surrounded by vines and bushland. Dinner is a table d'hote affair with Owen and Robyn showcasing their cuisine, wines and delightful company.

Lyre Bird hill is a wonderfully restorative place to recharge the batteries and get back to nature.

Tarago River Cheese Company

Hillcrest Farm is on the main road between Neerim and Neerim South, just an hour or so from Melbourne. The farm, in idyllic green grazing country, overlooks the Tarago River Lake.

In 1982, two families, the Jensens ('cheesemakers') and the Johnsons ('farmers') agreed that Australian specialist cheeses needed a shake up. The 250 acre farm and its 300 cows (mainly friesians) became suppliers to a small cheese factory built by the two families. Today the 1.5 million litres of milk convert each year to 130,000 kilograms of world class cheeses.

The first to find fame was Gippsland Blue, the first name of the enterprise. This gorgonzola grand style developed a loyal following, and Tarago River decided to expand the range of blue cheeses to include Royal Victorian Blue, a 'Stilton' style, Shadows of Blue, similar to 'Blue Castello', and Blue Orchid, a 'Roquefort' style. Tarago River now also makes Gippsland Brie, Mini Brie, Camembert, Triple Cream cheese, a hard matured cheddar-style Tarago Mature and Tarago Lavender, infused with the herb of well being. Cheeses from goats milk, and a new mild washed rind (similar to 'Port Salute') are the latest additions.

French cheese-maker, Fabrice Martin, from the Charente Maratine area, just north of Bordeaux, came to King Island several years ago and has been at Tarago for two years. He was a former neighbour of mine in France and we had a good chat on our visit. Like all Frenchmen, he is passionate about his fromage - the national accompaniment to wine. In France

the cheese is produced in a very similar way to that made by Fabrice. Tarago River is equidistant from the Yarra Valley and Mornington Peninsula. Why not pay them a visit?

The Mornington Peninsula Vineyards begin 70 kilometres south of the Melbourne C.B.D., near the Dromana area, a one hour drive south of the city. A few vineyards existed during the 19th century, but due to factors similar to those in the Yarra Valley viticulture did not continue into the 20th century.

In the late 1940s leading wine judge and Melbourne wine merchant, the late Doug Seabrook, established a vineyard on the slopes of Arthur's Seat, near Dromana. This venture petered out within 10 years however, to be followed by a re-introduction of vines to the area by several winemakers during the 1970s.

The first of these was developed by Baillieu Myer in 1972. Named 'Elgee Park', the vineyard is situated at Merricks North. A new, technically superb winery was completed in time for production of the 1984 vintage. Nat White was another vigneron to contribute to the early re-development of the Mornington Peninsula's wine industry, with the establishment of Main Ridge Estate in 1975. George and Jacquelyn Kefford followed, founding Merricks Estate in 1977 and Stoniers Merricks vineyard one year later. There are now more than 120 vineyards in the area, covering 1,000 acres, supporting 35 wineries.

By both Australian and European standards, the climate of the Peninsula is very cool, somewhat like the Bordeaux region in France. As the area is virtually surrounded by ocean, vines receive adequate rainfall throughout the growing season, and the high level of humidity in summer prevents vines from suffering stress.

Vineyards of the Mornington Peninsula produce table wines of clean, well-defined varietal characters, and crisp acidity. These features result in refreshing wines with considerable ageing potential. The predominant varieties are chardonnay and pinot noir, used in both table and sparkling wine-making. Other varieties include cabernet sauvignon, merlot, shiraz, riesling, sauvignon blanc, semillon and pinot gris. The Mornington Peninsula has produced some excellent wines since the re-establishment of viticulture in the area. Given the expertise and skill of the winemakers, this should continue and currently available wines are of a very high standard.

The physical beauty of the peninsula and its tourist pull has been well catered for by such excellent winery restaurants as Dromana Estate, where Margaret Crittenden and her family run a really fine establishment overlooking their lake and vineyards. Sir Peter and Lady Averil Derham have awesome views of Westernport Bay from their indoor/outdoor restaurant in front of the winery. Hann's Creek have a lovely French-style Sunday lunch with the strains of Piaf pumping through the winery. Fine Bed and Breakfasts abound, whilst restored mansions such as Bill and Val King's Glynt are world class. Mornington's rebirth as a wine region is a joy to behold.

Mornington Peninsula

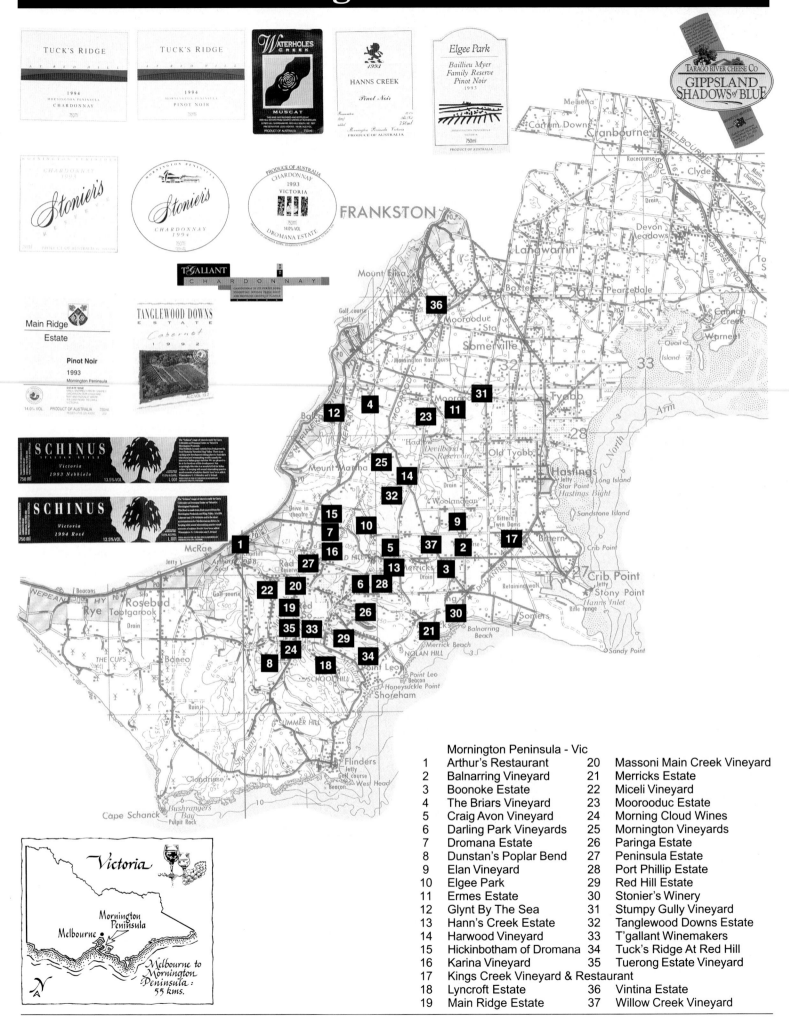

Mornington Peninsula - Vic

1	Arthur's Restaurant	20	Massoni Main Creek Vineyard
2	Balnarring Vineyard	21	Merricks Estate
3	Boonoke Estate	22	Miceli Vineyard
4	The Briars Vineyard	23	Moorooduc Estate
5	Craig Avon Vineyard	24	Morning Cloud Wines
6	Darling Park Vineyards	25	Mornington Vineyards
7	Dromana Estate	26	Paringa Estate
8	Dunstan's Poplar Bend	27	Peninsula Estate
9	Elan Vineyard	28	Port Phillip Estate
10	Elgee Park	29	Red Hill Estate
11	Ermes Estate	30	Stonier's Winery
12	Glynt By The Sea	31	Stumpy Gully Vineyard
13	Hann's Creek Estate	32	Tanglewood Downs Estate
14	Harwood Vineyard	33	T'gallant Winemakers
15	Hickinbotham of Dromana	34	Tuck's Ridge At Red Hill
16	Karina Vineyard	35	Tuerong Estate Vineyard
17	Kings Creek Vineyard & Restaurant		
18	Lyncroft Estate	36	Vintina Estate
19	Main Ridge Estate	37	Willow Creek Vineyard

Arthur's Restaurant

Perched on the pinnacle of Arthur's Seat on the Mornington Peninsula, "Arthur's" commands sweeping views of the bay and the distant City of Melbourne. Constructed in the 1930s and retaining its period charm, Arthur's offers visitors panoramic outlooks from its Peak restaurant, Vineyard Bar and Bistro and Galleria Function Room situated on three split levels.

In 1994, the operation of this establishment changed hands to the doyen of chefs in Australia, Hermann Schneider and his charming and consummate wife, Faye.

Hermann first came to Australia in 1956 as the young chef of the Swiss Olympic Team. He stayed on after the Olympics and established "Two Faces", one of the truly great restaurants of Australia's culinary history. This South Yarra food and wine mecca's reputation grew and it became the first restaurant in Australia to gain international status in the revered "Relais Et Chateaux" Guide.

Seeing the possibility to create an Australian style Relais Chateau Hospitality House, Hermann and Faye, along with several partners, entered their next venture of restoring and coverting a church run boarding school into the well known "Delgany Country House Hotel". In 1993 the Schneiders' involvement in this superbly conceived venture came to a halt. However, it was not long after that they could be found again on the Mornington Peninsula at the new location of Arthur's Seat.

Arthur's is undoubtedly in the top few restaurants in Australia, with a delightful, relaxed lack of formality, yet a reputation earned for consistent quality matched by arguably the most stunning panorama overlooking the entire Port Philip Bay.

Arthur's
Arthur's Seat Scenic Road
PO Box 145, Red Hill South 3937
telephone (059) 81 4444, fax (059 81 0651

Elgee Park

Baillieu Myer's property, 'Elgee Park', is primarily a horse and cattle stud. Vines were planted on the northern face of a naturally sheltered amphitheatre in 1972, the first vineyard on the Mornington Peninsula. The vines are closely planted and include cabernet sauvignon, merlot, chardonnay, riesling and viognier.

ELGEE PARK WINES
Address: Junction Road, Merricks North Vic. 3926
Phone: (059) 897 336
Fax: (059) 897 553
Established: 1972
Winemakers: Tod Dexter, Kevin McCarthy
Principal varieties grown: Riesling, chardonnay, viognier, pinot noir, cabernet sauvignon, cabernet franc, merlot
Ha under vine: 5
Average annual crush: 40 tonnes
Average no. cases produced: 1,200

Principal wines & brands	Cellar potential
Baillieu Myer Family Reserve	
Chardonnay	2-5 years
Riesling	2-5 years
Cuvee Brut	5-10 years
Pinot Noir	5-10 years
Cabernet Merlot	5-10 years

Public & trade tours: By appointment only
Points of interest: Open only one day of the year: Sunday of the Queen's Birthday weekend
Retail distribution: Represented by Flinders Wines; otherwise mailing list

The vineyard is very picturesque and was further enhanced in 1983 by the construction of a striking gazebo in the midst of the vines. Red gum was employed to build both the 'Vineyard Folly,' and the magnificent post and rail fences which surround the property.

The wines were either made at other wineries or under makeshift conditions at the property until 1984, when Dr. Tony Jordan of Oenotec was called on to design a winery for Baillieu Myer. Today, Elgee Park has a very close relationship with Stonier's Winery and coincidentally, winemaker Tod Dexter has a

vineyard of his own near Elgee Park.

The Elgee Park wines benefit from an excellent micro climate, sheltered from the prevailing winds by a heavily timbered ridge behind the vineyard. On a clear day, one can see the distant skyline of Melbourne from the winery. An artist's impression of this view features on the Elgee Park labels. The mature vines and first class winemaking by Tod Dexter provides complex, elegant wines with which Baillieu makes an eloquent statement for the Mornington Peninsula's winemaking potential.

Dromana Estate

Garry Crittenden is one of the Australian wine industry's most dynamic and visionary people. Garry sold a chain of plant nurseries to concentrate on his vineyard at Dromana on the Mornington Peninsula. For a number of years, he also operated a viticultural consulting business which has since been taken over by his partner, Ian Macrae.

Garry and his wife Margaret are both heavily involved in the Dromana Estate operation and have built a colonial-inspired home on the property which, like the winery, enjoys superb views over their lake and vineyard. Garry searched for a long time for the ideal vineyard site. On a trip to Tasmania a number of years ago, he tasted a Moorilla Estate wine and was most impressed. Family and business commitments prevented him from making the move to the Apple Isle, but he continued his search for a similar climate where delicate, yet intense, flavours could be produced. He found this at Dromana Estate. Protected from the cold south and south-westerly winds by Arthur's Seat, the northerly aspect and soil structure were perfect.

I have noticed on a number of visits to the Peninsula that Dromana enjoys its own special micro climate. Whereas it can be cloudy, cold and windy on the Red Hill Ridge, Dromana can be bathed in sunshine. This combination of very cool climate, coupled with loads of sunshine, really makes his wines smile, an attitude he maintains through thick and thin himself.

Garry is a horticulturist at heart and his manicured vines and the pretty gardens surrounding the winery and lake reflect this love of plants. The winery is technically state of the art, but Garry is most innovative; always experimenting, learning and seeking perfection in his wines. With the Dromana Estate Vineyard covering only some 10 acres and all the Dromana Estate wines being from the domain, Garry has introduced a second label, 'Schinus' under which he makes wines from grapes sourced in other regions. A certain fascination with Northern Italian wines and his penchant for a challenge has seen him produce both a Dolcetto from fruit sourced at the marvellous Best's Great Western Vineyard, plus a Nebbiolo from Fred Pizzini's cool climate vineyard in the King Valley. Under the Schinus label, he also produces an outstanding dry rose from cabernet sauvignon and pinot noir and a succulent chenin blanc.

The wine is only part of the Dromana Estate story. Garry's hardworking and talented wife, Margaret, also has a real

culinary flair. Garry and Margaret have built an airy tasting centre and restaurant with full-length windows and French doors opening onto a verandah above the lawns which slope down to the lake and are bordered by the vineyard. Margaret, daughter Zoe, and the friendly efficient team serve a seasonal menu or simple tasty snack platters, depending on your mood. A free tasting is offered and your selection is then available for purchase by the glass or bottle to accompany your meal, or by the bottle to take home. Margaret has fresh produce delivered daily; there is no freezer by design.

If you wish to bring your own tucker, there is a free barbecue area in front of the winery and even a trampoline for the kids. Hospitality is the keynote of the Crittendens

DROMANA ESTATE VINEYARDS
Address: Harrisons Road, Dromana Vic. 3936
Direction: 60 km or about 1 hours' drive south-east of Melbourne
Phone: (059) 87 3800
Fax: (059) 81 0714
Established: 1982
Owners: Garry & Margaret Crittenden
Winemaker: Garry Crittenden & Arthur O'Connor
Principal varieties grown: Chardonnay, pinot noir, cabernet sauvignon, merlot
Ha under vine: 4
Average annual crush: 50 tonnes local & 150 tonnes purchased.
Average no. cases produced: 3,500 off own vines for Dromana Estate label, 9,000 for the Schinus label.
Principal wines & brandsCellar potential

(as per Dromana Estate and Schinus Brochures)

Public & trade tours: By appointment
Cellar door & mail order sales: Yes
Hours open to public: 11 am-4 pm daily, except Christmas Day, Boxing Day and Good Friday
Points of interest: Tasting Centre overlooking the lake with light lunches served daily. Picnic and BBQ facilities available. Queen's Birthday and Melbourne Cup weekend festivals.
Retail distribution: Every Australian state and territory as well as throughout England, Scotland, New Zealand & Switzerland.

who see wine as a gracious adjunct to food and good company. Garry's wines are in the absolute top flight of Australia's vintage. The chardonnay and the pinot noir are extremely complex, with the judicious use of barrel fermentation, ageing and controlled malo-lactic fermentation. The cabernet merlot is a full-bodied generous wine with crystal clear fruit flavours and great balance through the use of skilful wood treatment.

Garry has been heavily involved in wine industry activities and also works with the Mornington Peninsula Tourism and Development Authorities. He sees a bright, bright future for the region and its wines and wineries, with very good reason. He and his family are an integral part of this future.

Glynt by the Sea

Inspired by a Scottish castle, Glynt was built in the early years of this century as a summer residence for a prominent Melbourne family. Entertaining was a priority and the grand manor hosted many a gracious soiree. Over the years the family's needs waned and Glynt fell into disrepair, although the superb granite and stucco building was as solid as a rock.

The rebirth of the grandeur of Glynt began when the estate and its surrounding land was purchased by Sir Peter Derham for a building development project. Ironically, Sir Peter is now a virtual full-time Mornington Peninsula vigneron at Red Hill Estate. Glynt, situated some 100 metres from Port Philip Bay at Mount Martha, was left with two and a half acres of its grounds still intact in the middle of the development.

Sir Peter, then chairman of the Australian Tourism Commission, mentioned Glynt to fellow commissioner, legendary outback tourism pioneer Bill King. Perhaps it was the glint in his eye that made Bill mention it to his wife, Val. Sir Peter suggested they have a look at it.

Bill describes their first visit, climbing through a fence, battling the brambles and head-high grass. Val was about to turn back, but once they saw the mansion cloaked in its Virginia creeper, they fell in love with it instantly. Fortunately, among their children

they had experts in all the building trades and during several years they painstakingly restored the building and grounds. To say it is a showpiece would be an understatement. The day of our visit a leading motor company was filming a television commercial at sunset -what a glorious property it is.

Bill and Val had restored Glynt as a retirement home, but their long tourism experience and gregarious natures got the better of them, so four exquisite suites have been created - each with their own drawing rooms and furnished with antiques as well as every modern convenience that would do a 5-star hotel proud. The three Garden View Suites are magnificent, but the Bay View Suite, with its own spiral staircase leading down the tower to the grand drawing room, will take your breath away.

A full English breakfast is served in the vast garden room, with arched windows overlooking Port Phillip Bay. The licensed dining room is beautifully appointed with period antiques, Royal Doulton, crystal and silver. It creates an ideal ambiance to enjoy a memorable dining experience.

Situated in the centre of the wine growing region, Glynt provides the ideal base from which to explore the peninsula wineries. Glynt by the Sea, 16 Bay Road, Mt Martha, Tel: (059) 74 1216

Hanns Creek

Denise Aubrey-Slocock has a zest for life and astounding energy - it's impossible to be around her and not feel the joy of life flowing over you. Denise's strong and most attractive French accent comes from her native Brittanny. She met her future husband, Tony while running her own little restaurant in Melbourne, earning a living to bring up her children alone Hard work is no hardship for Denise.

On my first visit to this beautiful valley, Denise was busy summer grafting shiraz, between running the cellar door and packing wine orders, always with a huge smile and a mischievous sense of humour. Tony is equally hard-working and quietly tends the vineyard and makes the wines, which have already won a number of awards.

The vineyard is in a clearing on the lee side of the prevailing winds with a northerly aspect providing a sunny sheltered environment. It produces an excellent cabernet sauvignon. The French influence is obvious, with the winery also providing a crisp rose and burgundian-style pinot noir and chardonnay.

Each Sunday, Hanns Creek comes to life

with a French-style lunch among the barrels, complete with gingham table cloths and the strains of Piaf in the air. It's a three-hour affair starting at 1 pm.

If you are in need of a little exercise between courses, Tony will instruct you in the art of petanque, the French provincial game of bowls. When on the Peninsula, head for Hanns Creek for a most uplifting experience.

HANNS CREEK ESTATE
Address: Kentucky road, Merricks North Vic. 3926
Phone: (059) 89 7266
Fax: (059) 89 7500
Establishment: 1987
Winemaker: Tony Aubrey-Slocock

Principal varieties grown: Cabernet sauvignon, pinot noir, shiraz, chardonnay
Ha under vine: 3.5
Average annual crush: 30 tonnes
Average no. cases produced: 1,800

Principal wines & brands	Cellar potential
Cabernet Sauvignon	5-10 years
Chardonnay	2-5 years
Pinot Noir	5-10 years
Cabernet Shiraz	5-10 years
Chardonnay Riesling	2-5 years
Rose	2-5 years

Public & trade tours: By appointment only

Cellar door & mail order sales: Yes

Hours open to public: 11 am-5 pm seven days

Points of interest: Restaurant for luncheon (5 course) Sundays/public holidays, Picnic facilities

Retail distribution: Numerous bottle shops and restaurants on Mornington Peninsula, Ritchies supermarkets, Phillip Murphy (Toorak), cellar door

Main Ridge Estate

Nat White, a graduate in oenology from Charles Sturt University, and his wife Rosalie, were the modern-day pioneers who began the rebirth of the Mornington Peninsula as a wine region. In the centre of the peninsula on the cool elevated Main Ridge, Nat and Rosalie cleared a sheltered hillside and planted vines more than 20 years ago. The vines today are strong, well established and producing complex wines which are full of character.

Nat's commitment to quality includes 'bunch thinning,' actually removing some of the bunches and discarding them before the ripening process begins. This lowers the crop, but the noble sacrifice results in greater flavour and colour in the wines.

The winery, sculptured into the hillside at the top of the property, has a cool underground cellar with a beautiful tasting room-gallery above. The gardens around the winery and vineyard are superb, with more than 100 species of roses planted. Nat's former occupation as a civil engineer shows through in the pleasing layout of the estate. The Whites' deep love of nature and their estate is well captured in the verse I noticed on the verandah:

"The kiss of the sun for pardon,
The song of the bird for mirth,
One is nearer God's heart in the garden
Than anywhere else on earth."

MAIN RIDGE ESTATE
Address: William Road, Red Hill Vic. 3937
Phone: Melway 190 C4 off Red Hill Arthurs Seat Road
Phone: (059) 89 2686
Fax: (059) 89 2686
Establishment: 1975
Winemaker: Nat White
Principal varieties grown: Chardonnay, pinot noir, cabernet sauvignon, merlot, cabernet franc

Hectares under vine: 2.5
Average annual crush: 7 tonnes
Average no. cases produced: 1,000

Principal wines & brands	Cellar potential
Main Ridge Estate	
Chardonnay	2-5 years
Half Acre Pinot Noir	5-10 years
Pinot Noir	5-10 years
Cabernet Merlot	5-10 years

Public & trade tours: By appointment only
Cellar door & mail order sales: Yes
Hours open to public: 12-4 pm Mon-Fri; 12-5 pm w/e and PH
Points of interest: Garden Walk, summer Sunday lunch, underground cellar, first Mornington Peninsula winery
Retail distribution: Restaurants only

Red Hill Estate

RED HILL ESTATE
Address: 53 Red Hill Shoreham Road, Red Hill South Vic. 3937
Direction: Follow Red Hill Wine Region signs
Phone: (059) 89 2838
Fax: (059) 89 2855
Established: 1989
Owner: Sir Peter and Lady Derham
Winemaker: Jenny Bright
Principal varieties grown: Chardonnay, pinot noir, cabernet sauvignon, sauvignon blanc
Ha under vine: 15
Average annual crush: 129 tonnes
Average no. cases produced: 6,000

Principal wines & brands	Cellar potential
Red Hill Estate Methode Champenoise	3-5 years
Red Hill Estate Chardonnay	3-5 years
Red Hill Estate Pinot Noir	3-5 years
Red Hill Estate Cabernet Sauvignon	3-5 years
Waterholes Creek Bass Range	

Public & trade tours: By appointment only
Hours open to public: 11am-5pm seven days
Points of interest: Panoramic views across the vineyard to Western Port to Phillip Island. Cellar door opens daily for wine tasting and sales. The restaurant serves lunch daily. Open fire, seating on terrace/lawn.
Retail distribution: Select Melbourne and Mornington Peninsula restaurants.

A successful businessman and a person of incredible vision and energy, Sir Peter Derham has turned his retirement project into a more than full-time occupation. No job on his beloved Red Hill Estate is too trivial for Sir Peter's hands to tackle.

The vineyard was established in 1989 on the virbrant red soil which so often supports the world's best pinot noirs. The hard work put in by Sir Peter and Lady Derham and their vineyard Manager, John Runting, was well repaid in 1994 when they won the coveted Department of Agriculture "Victorian Vineyard of the Year Award". The vineyard has panoramic views over Western Port and Phillip Island. To take advantage of this view, a restaurant was added to the front of the winery in 1994 and it proved instantly successful, with a focus on fresh local produce. One can also sit outdoors, although the ever changing vista can be viewed from any point in the restaurant.

The winery was completed in 1992 and talented winemaker, Jenny Bright, joined the next year. The climate at Red Hill South is ideal for methode champenoise production, and Red Hill Estate made the region's first sparkling wines. Red Hill Estate methode champenoise, chardonnay, pinot noir and cabernet sauvignon are joined in the range by a second label "Waterholes Creek", which is available exclusively at the cellar door.

Tanglewood Downs

Set among a forest of tanglewood trees lies the delightful domain of Ken and Wendy Bilham. The Bilhams planted their 7.5 acre vineyard in 1984 and two years later Ken retired from his job as a school principal.

Their home and winery blend beautifully into the rustic setting with views through the trees to Port Phillip Bay. On the first Sunday of the month they put on a superb buffet lunch. They also have a bi-monthly 'wine dinner' in the winery. Recently, the Bilhams hosted the prestigious "International Association of Culinary Professionals". More than 50 of the world's greatest chefs sat down to a Mornington Peninsula extravaganza of food and wine. Wineries, food producers and the Frankston TAFE hospitality students, under the guidance of Ken Stonehouse of Stoney's Catering, produced a fabulous feast with Ken and Wendy as the charming hosts.

Ken is serious about his wines and uses his trained and disciplined mind to make excellent styles. The gewurztraminer and chardonnay both had a spicy, slight marmalade tang to them. The cabernet merlot, cabernet franc blend showed cinnamon, cherry and cassis flavours with a slight tobacco leaf herbaceousness. The top Tanglewood wines can be enjoyed with a picnic lunch outside the winery. Nearby, hidden in the trees, is a studio where Leisa Wharington blows glass and Felicity Pope crafts her metal work. The Bilhams have created a special environment.

TANGLEWOOD DOWNS
Address: Bulldog Creek Road, Merricks North (Mornington Peninsula)
Direction: Take Mooroodue Road & Balnarring Road off freeway.
Phone: (059) 74 3325
Fax: (059) 74 4170
Established: 1984
Owner: Ken & Wendy Bilham
Winemaker: Ken Bilham
Principal varieties grown: Chardonnay, pinot noir, cabernet, riesling, traminer
Ha under vine: 2.5
Average annual crush: 12 tonnes
Average no. cases produced: 800-1,000

Principal wines & brands	Cellar potential
Tanglewood	
Chardonnay	2-5 years
Pinot Noir	5-10 years
Cabernet	5-10 years
Riesling	2-5 years

Public & trade tours: By appointment only
Cellar door & mail order sales: Yes
Hours open to public: 12-5 pm seven days
Points of interest: Lunches regularly (prior booking); vineyard tours (by arrangement)
Retail distribution: Fields of Wine, agent Lee Schleger

Stonier's Winery

S tonier's can lay claim to being Australia's most successful 'new' winemaker. In 1994, at the prestigious Royal Adelaide Show, they were awarded two trophies for their 1993 Reserve Pinot Noir, one for the best pinot noir in the show, and the other for the best varietal red table wine, against the best big reds of cabernet sauvignon, shiraz, merlot and other varieties on South Australia's home ground.

This extraordinary event marked the coming of age of the Mornington Peninsula as a wine region and continued the success story of Stonier's. In 1978, leading publisher Brian Stonier and his wife, Noel, planted 600 vines on their property at Merricks, close to the shores of Western Port Bay.

A year later, far off in the Napa Valley in California, the wine career of Tod Dexter began. Tod, a Melbourne lad and a passionate skier, had been working on the snow slopes of Colorado. He dropped into the Napa Valley to further investigate an interest that had been spawned through a family friendship with the Crittenden family in their Melbourne fine wine stores. He tried his hand at coopering (barrel-making), and ended up staying in the Napa where he worked for Cakebread Cellars across the road from the legendary Robert Mondavi Winery. Tod learnt much in five vintages at Cakebread before returning to Australia in 1985 and to join Brown Brothers. He has extended his knowledge of wines through courses at the famous Davis University in California and Australia's Roseworthy College. Tod credits the vineyards at Stonier's with producing fruit that makes his job rewarding.

His first connection with the Peninsula came when he made wine for Baillieu Myers' pioneering Elgee Park in 1987. At that time Stonier's wines were also being made at Elgee Park. Ironically Tod now makes the Elgee Park wines at Stonier's stunning 'Opera House' winery, and uses the Elgee Park winery for barrel storage.

Whilst at Elgee Park, Tod and his wife, Debbi, planted a 15 acre vineyard at Merricks North which now supplies Stonier's Winery with an important 'warmer' climate part of the vintage, adding to the 46 acre estate vineyard production. Stonier's, under the enthusiastic and capable guidance of Brian's daughter Jenny, market a wonderful chardonnay and pinot noir, both of which have won many trophies, and a 'cabernet' - a Bordeaux-style blend of cabernet sauvignon, merlot and cabernet franc. They also have a unique 'Barrique Club', a concept where you can buy a barrique - 300 bottles of wine, while it is still ageing in the winery. A brass plaque sits on the wall and your wine is bottled with your own label, adjacent to that of Stonier's. The plaques bear many famous names including many prominent wine connoiseurs.

STONIER'S WINERY
Address: 362 Frankston-Flinders Road, Merricks
Direction: Cnr Frankston-Flinders Road & Thompson Lane,
Phone: (059) 89 8300
Fax: (059) 89 8709
Established: 1978
Owner: Stonier, Yuill, Hamson & Limb Pty Ltd
Winemaker & General Manager: Tod Dexter
Principal varieties grown: Chardonnay, pinot noir, cabernet sauvignon, cabernet franc, merlot
Ha under vine: 22
Average annual crush: 175 tonnes
Average no. cases produced: 10,000

Principal wines & brands	Cellar potential
Stoniers	
Chardonnay	2-5 years
Pinot Noir	2-5 years
Cabernet	3-5 years
Stoniers Reserve	
Chardonnay	3-8 years
Pinot Noir	2-6 years
Cabernet Sauvignon	5-10 years

Public & trade tours: Yes
Cellar door & mail order sales: Yes
Hours open to public: 12-5 pm seven days (except Christmas, Good Friday, Boxing Day)
Points of interest: Lunch by prior arrangement, functions catered for, children's playground, cheese platter available every day. Festivals: Easter, Queen's Birthday and Melbourne Cup Weekend.
Retail distribution: Negociants Australia in every State.

Tuck's Ridge

Mornington Peninsula's largest vineyard, of almost 60 acres, covers the hills of Tuck's Ridge in manicured rows of vines. It is an impressive site, with Westernport Bay clearly visible only a few kilometres away. Delyse Graham is the vibrant and vivacious manager and makes visiting the winery an uplifting experience.

The project began in 1987 with a group of owners under the project management of co-owner Peter Hollick, from the renowned viticultural family. In the middle of the valley, surrounded by vines, is a wetlands sanctuary classified as a "Land for Wildlife". It was virtually impossible to build a winery on site as planned, so winemaker Daniel Green, formerly of Elgee Park, works out of a winery in a converted warehouse on an industrial estate at Dromana.

Tuck's Ridge wines are exciting, indeed. Picked late, they all have high strength combined with crisp acid from the cool climate and are loaded with fruit and varietal character. I was very impressed with the semillon - most exotic, with hints of passionfruit, kiwifruit and capsicum. The rich mellow riesling was superb and the apricot stone fruit character of the chardonnay most attractive. The Tuck's Ridge red wines are equally impressive and worth seeking out.

The vineyard has been planted and trained onto a low maintenance single wire which is lifted during the growing season. Work is aided by plenty of state of the art viticultural machinery. The vineyard provides one of the most impressive vine vistas you could see anywhere in the world. It is clearly visible from the Red Hill-Shoreham Road as one approaches the winery.

Peter Hollick hails from the famous Hollick Wine Family, being cousin to Ian Hollick of Coonawarra fame. Peter's innovative style and the affordable pricing of the classy Tuck's Ridge Wines adds greatly to the depth of this new premium wine region.

Delyse Graham came to the Peninsula in 1990. She took on a job as director of the local wine association and was talked into the management of Tuck's Ridge by the then executive director, Ian Horne (of Yellowglen fame). Production is rising fast and I'm sure you'll find the Tuck's Ridge wines without too much trouble. They are well worth snapping up!

TUCK'S RIDGE
Address: 37 Red Hill Shoreham Road, Red Hill South Vic 3937
Direction: Between Red Hill Village & Ashcombe Maze
Phone: (059) 89 8660
Fax: (059) 89 8579
Established: 1986
Owner: Peter Hollick
Winemaker: Daniel Greene
Principal varieties grown: Chardonnay, pinot noir, semillon, riesling
Ha under vine: 24
Average no. cases produced: 8,000

Principal wines & brands	Cellar potential
Riesling	2-5 years
Semillon	2-5 years
Chardonnay	2-5 years
Pinot Noir	5-10 years

Public & trade tours: By appointment only
Cellar door sales: Yes
Hours open to public: 12-5 pm seven days a week
Retail distribution: Fine wine shops & good restaurants

T'Gallant

I first met Kathleen Quealy some 10 years ago when she was making wine at the obscure Bungawarra Vineyards in Queensland's Granite Belt as a young enthusiastic Wagga graduate. Her wines shone out in a difficult environment.

At that stage she was engaged to Kevin McCarthy. Today, they are married with children and very happy indeed on their Mornington Peninsula property. Kathleen has lost none of her enthusiasm and she and her trained winemaker husband Kevin make a formidable combination. T'Gallant takes its name from the classic old four-masted barques that made voyages of discovery around Australia's coastline.

Kevin and Kathleen are keen to make an individual statement with their wines. Their love is pinot gris, a white mutation of pinot noir which needs a very cool climate to produce its rich, yet crystal clean character that in Kathleen's words "reminds you of oceans and crashing waves, yet holding back a little like a yacht before the line, with unbelievable richness and fatness, length and finesse."

This love affair has led them to plant another four hectares in their 16 hectare property on Mornington Flinders Road, where they will be building a new winery shortly. The winery crushed a remarkable 250 tonnes in 1995 for T'Gallant and other small wineries.

T'Gallant produces a white with a rosy glow from pinot noir, called Holystone, a chardonnay, a big red called Crosstrees and a late harvest dessert wine called Demi Vache from sauvignon blanc as well as their prized Pinot Grigio.

T'GALLANT WINERY & VINEYARD
Address: Mornington Flinders Road, Main Ridge Vic. 3928
Direction: Near corner of Mornington Flinders Road & Shands Road, Main Ridge
Phone: (059) 89 6565
Fax: (059) 89 6577
Established: 1990
Owner: Kevin McCarthy & Kathleen Quealy
Winemaker: Kevin McCarthy & Kathleen Quealy
Principal varieties grown: Pinot gris, Chardonnay, Pinot noir, Muscat, Tramineu
Ha under vine: 10
Average no. cases produced: 12,000

Principal wines & brands T'Gallant	Cellar potential
Chardonnay	2-5 years
Holystone	2-5 years
Pinot Gris	5-10 years
Pinot Grigio	2-5 years
Ceclia's White Pinot	2-5 years
Demi-Vache	5-10 years

Public tours: Yes
Hours open to public: 11 am-5 pm Mon-Fri; 12- 5 pm w/e
Points of interest: T'Gallant are at the cutting edge of winemaking. Introducing new winemaking and styles and grape varieties to the Mornington Peninsula & Australia
Retail distribution: Throughout Sydney, Melbourne, Queensland

An introduction to Geelong

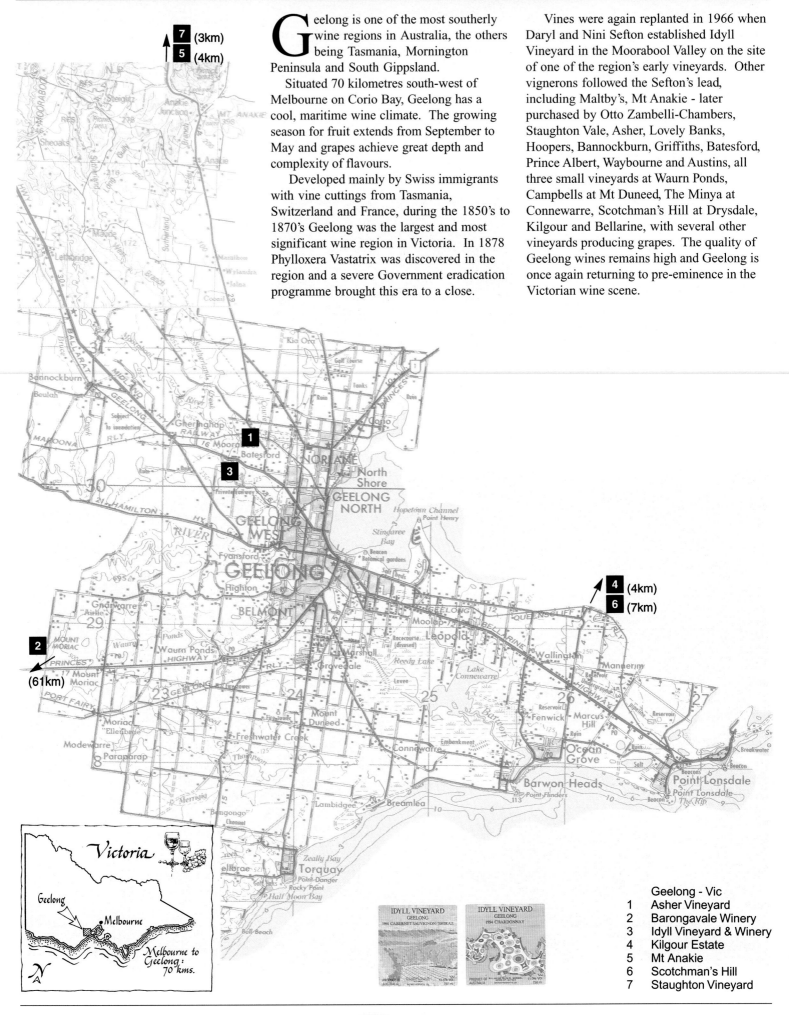

Geelong is one of the most southerly wine regions in Australia, the others being Tasmania, Mornington Peninsula and South Gippsland.

Situated 70 kilometres south-west of Melbourne on Corio Bay, Geelong has a cool, maritime wine climate. The growing season for fruit extends from September to May and grapes achieve great depth and complexity of flavours.

Developed mainly by Swiss immigrants with vine cuttings from Tasmania, Switzerland and France, during the 1850's to 1870's Geelong was the largest and most significant wine region in Victoria. In 1878 Phylloxera Vastatrix was discovered in the region and a severe Government eradication programme brought this era to a close.

Vines were again replanted in 1966 when Daryl and Nini Sefton established Idyll Vineyard in the Moorabool Valley on the site of one of the region's early vineyards. Other vignerons followed the Sefton's lead, including Maltby's, Mt Anakie - later purchased by Otto Zambelli-Chambers, Staughton Vale, Asher, Lovely Banks, Hoopers, Bannockburn, Griffiths, Batesford, Prince Albert, Waybourne and Austins, all three small vineyards at Waurn Ponds, Campbells at Mt Duneed, The Minya at Connewarre, Scotchman's Hill at Drysdale, Kilgour and Bellarine, with several other vineyards producing grapes. The quality of Geelong wines remains high and Geelong is once again returning to pre-eminence in the Victorian wine scene.

7 (3km)
5 (4km)

4 (4km)
6 (7km)

2
(61km)

Victoria
Geelong
Melbourne
Melbourne to Geelong : 70 kms.

IDYLL VINEYARD
GEELONG
1991 CABERNET SAUVIGNON/SHIRAZ
PRODUCT OF AUSTRALIA

IDYLL VINEYARD
GEELONG
1994 CHARDONNAY
PRODUCT OF AUSTRALIA

Geelong - Vic

1	Asher Vineyard
2	Barongavale Winery
3	Idyll Vineyard & Winery
4	Kilgour Estate
5	Mt Anakie
6	Scotchman's Hill
7	Staughton Vineyard

Idyll Vineyard

As one of Australia's most beautiful vineyards, Idyll is aptly named. Immaculate rows of vines extend down the valley to the Moorabool River, over gentle green undulations. The site had been planted to vines during the mid 1800s and was chosen by Daryl and Nini Sefton because of family association with the area. Daryl's great-grandparents, Jacob and Rosina Just, had been among the original Swiss settlers of the district and had also made wines.

The Seftons started planting their 20 hectare vineyard in 1966 and Daryl designed and constructed the winery and much of the wine-making equipment. Idyll's winery is undoubtedly one of the most efficient and competent small wineries in the country.

Daryl's wife and partner, Nini, has also made considerable contributions to the winery. A tireless promoter of Idyll, Geelong and Australian Wines, Nini is also an accomplished artist who has designed and painted Idyll's Painter's Series of labels.

Almost 30% of Idyll wine is exported overseas. Wines are also available through better retail outlets and cellar door. In fact, cellar door is the only point of sale for the Sefton's excellent wood-matured gewurztraminer, which is one of the best wines of this variety in Australia. Idyll wines include a delightful rose called "Idyll Blush", usually made from shiraz, gewurztraminer, chardonnay, "Bone Idyll", shiraz and cabernet/shiraz. The vivacious congeniality of the Seftons, combined with the winery's superb location and the promise of some fine wines results in Idyll being one of Australia's most popular stops for the wine-lover.

IDYLL VINEYARD & WINERY
Address: 265 Ballan Road, Moorabool Vic. 3221
Direction: 10 km from Geelong, 75 km from Melbourne, 80 km from Ballarat
Phone: (052) 76 1280
Fax: (052) 76 1537
Established: 1966
Owner: D.R. & E.M. Sefton
Winemaker: Dr Daryl Sefton
Principal varieties grown: Chardonnay, gewurztraminer, shiraz, cabernet sauvignon
Ha under vine: 20
Average annual crush: 60-100 tonnes
Average no. cases produced: 4,000

Principal wines & brands	Cellar potential
Idyll Cabernet Sauvignon/Shiraz	10-15 years
Idyll Oak Aged Shiraz	10-15 years
Bone Idyll (Lighter Style Shiraz)	5-10 years
Idyll Chardonnay	5-10 years
Idyll Gewurztraminer	5-10 years
Idyll Blush (Rose)	2-5 years
Sefton Estate Shiraz/Cabernet	5-10 years
Sefton Estate Classic Dry White	2-5 years

Cellar door & mail order sales: Yes
Hours open to public: 10 am-5 pm Tues-Sun & public holidays
Points of interest: Vineyard platters served at weekends, wine by the glass for sale
Retail distribution: Cellar door, ex-vineyard; Melbourne: Sullivan Wine Agencies

An introduction to Goulburn Valley

The area known as the Goulburn Valley was first explored and deemed suitable for development by Major Thomas Mitchell in 1836. Many graziers settled the area and despite the emphasis on farming vines were first planted as early as the 1850s.

In 1860 a successful group of landowners and merchants formed the consortium Tabilk Vineyard Proprietary. Purchasing 260 hectares of land for the purpose of establishing a vineyard and winery, the group, and in particular Mr. John Pinney Bear, energetically set about creating favourable conditions for making good wines. Mr. John Pinney Bear prompted rapid growth of the vineyard by advertising Australia-wide for vine cuttings.

Chateau Tahbilk prospered, not only because of the dedication of all those involved, but also because of innovative marketing, a kind climate and ideal topography. Today it is the most significant winery in the area and is the only winery to have remained continuously in production. Although hit by the phylloxera scourge at the turn of the century, some of the company's vineyards survived unharmed, allowing the manufacture of wines to continue. Chateau Tahbilk is now run by the Purbrick family who have utilised the original winery buildings and facilities and thus preserved the heritage of the property.

The architectural elegance of the winery coupled with the graceful layout of the surrounding grounds make Tahbilk one of the most beautiful wineries in Australia. Within the last 20 years many other winemakers have planted vines in the Goulburn Valley. In addition to Chateau Tahbilk the largest concerns are the Mitchelton Winery and Vineyards and Tisdalls Mt. Helen Vineyard.

Mitchelton's 500-acre property is bordered on one side by the Goulburn River and is widely recognised by its distinctive tower which became a part of the landscape in the early 1970s. In comparison to Chateau Tahbilk, Mitchelton has a more contemporary appearance, but it too is one of the country's most striking wineries.

The Delatite Vineyard, because of its close proximity to Goulburn Valley, has been included in this chapter. In total, there are some dozen or so wineries in the region, as well as many small growers who supply high quality fruit, both throughout this area and elsewhere. As the region includes diverse microclimates, soils and altitudes, wine styles of the Goulburn Valley are many and varied. Both red and white wines are produced and although there are some discrepancies in quality, most are highly regarded.

Goulburn Valley

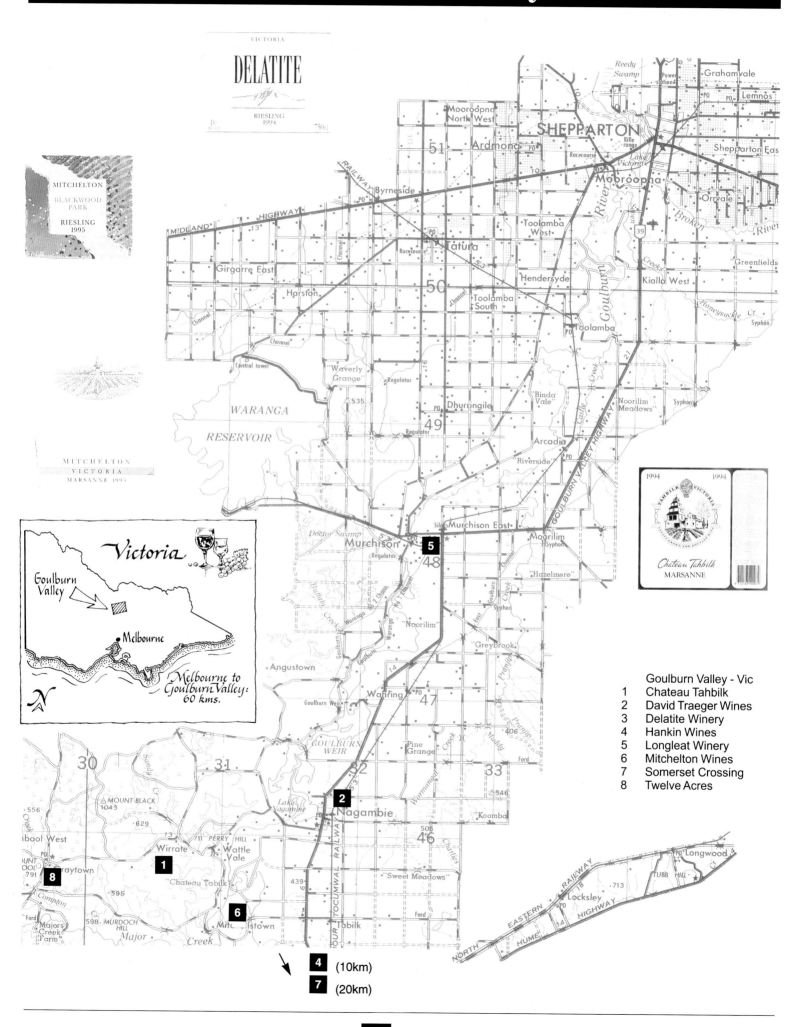

Goulburn Valley - Vic

1. Chateau Tahbilk
2. David Traeger Wines
3. Delatite Winery
4. Hankin Wines
5. Longleat Winery
6. Mitchelton Wines
7. Somerset Crossing
8. Twelve Acres

Chateau Tahbilk

Established in 1860, Chateau Tahbilk Estate is one of Victoria's most beautiful and historic properties. Situated 122 kilometres north of Melbourne, on the east bank of the Goulburn River, at a site the Aboriginals call "tabilk-tabilk", meaning "place of many waterholes".

The property comprises some 1,214 hectares of the richest river flats in the Goulburn Valley, with a frontage of 11 kilometres to the river and approximately 8 kilometres of permanent running back waters and creeks.

One of the most interesting and picturesque features of the Estate is the cellars, the main part of which is underground and eminently suitable for the maturation of high-quality table wines. The original cellar and storage, built in 1860, (and surmounted by a tower) which is classified by the National Trust, is 92 metres in length, whereas the "New Cellar", constructed in 1875 and running at right angles, is 60.5 metres long. An idea of the size of the cellars may be obtained from the fact that the roof area alone covers 1 hectare.

Throughout its career, Chateau Tahbilk has obtained over 1000 awards for wines produced on the Estate at all the world's principal exhibitions. These awards include the Diploma of Honour, the highest award obtainable at the Greater London Exhibition of 1899. Also First Order of Merit and Medals in London, Philadelphia, Paris,

Bordeaux, Calcutta, Brussels, Amsterdam, Melbourne, Adelaide and Dunedin. More than 60 firsts have been obtained at the Royal Shows of Melbourne, Adelaide, Sydney and Brisbane, and since the introduction of the medal awards in 1965, 4 Trophies, 7 Gold, 130 Silver and 365 Bronze medals have been awarded.

The Estate was purchased by Reginald Purbrick in 1925 and by 1931 his son, Eric, had taken over management and winemaking responsibilities at Chateau Tahbilk. Eric was joined by his son, John, in 1955 and John's son Alister, a graduate of the Winemaking course at Roseworthy College, took over the role as winemaker and manager in 1978.

The vineyard comprises 130 hectares of vines with classical varieties such as cabernet sauvignon, cabernet franc, shiraz, merlot, malbec, riesling, marsanne, roussanne, viognier, chenin blanc, sauvignon blanc, chardonnay, semillon and white hermitage grown.

The process of vinification at Tahbilk unites traditional winemaking methods with modern, up to date technology. The exquisitely made whites exhibit intense, varietal fruit flavours when young and with bottle age, develop marvellous complexity and character.

The reds are produced with a commitment to the traditional winemaking values held at Tahbilk for over 130 years. As young wines they show a remarkable balance of complex

Alister (left) and John Purbrick

fruit flavours and natural grape tannins which evolve with considerable bottle age into wines of great power and distinction.

CHATEAU TAHBILK WINES

Address: Tabilk, Vic. 3608
Direction: 8 km south-west of Nagambie, Central Victoria
Phone: (057) 94 2555
Fax: (057) 94 2360
Established: 1860
Owner: Purbrick Family
Winemaker: Alister Purbrick
Principal varieties grown: Cabernet sauvignon, shiraz, chardonnay, marsanne, riesling
Ha under vine: 130

Principal wines & brands	Cellar potential
Chateau Tahbilk 1860 Vines Shiraz	15+ years
Chateau Tahbilk Cabernet Sauvignon Reserve	20+ years
Chateau Tahbilk Chardonnay	5-10 years
Chateau Tahbilk Cabernet Sauv.	15+ years
Chateau Tahbilk Shiraz	10+ years
Chateau Tahbilk Marsanne	5-10 years
Chateau Tahbilk Riesling	5-10 years

Cellar door & mail order sales: Yes
Hours open to public: 9 am-5 pm Mon-Sat; 11 am-5 pm Sun. and all public holidays except Christmas Day.
Points of interest: Cellars built in 1860 are mainly underground and are classified by the National Trust. Picnic areas set aside for visitors.
Retail distribution: Tucker Seabrook Caon & Co. Pty. Ltd, all states.

Mitchelton Winery

Winemaker: Don Lewis

The late Ross Shelmerdine, an imaginative and ingenious man, made his mark on the Australian wine industry by creating one of the country's most exciting and unusual winery complexes. In 1969, having purchased a 200 hectare property on a bend in the Goulburn River, he hired Colin Preece, one of Australia's most celebrated winemakers, to assist in planning and planting vineyards. Preece was also retained as a consultant for the first few vintages, giving the winery a solid foundation on which to develop.

In late 1972 work began on the winery complex which now includes extensive underground cellars. The complex was named after Mitchellstown, the site where Major Thomas Mitchell set up camp during his exploration of the area in 1836.

The first small vintage was processed at Brown Brothers Winery in 1972. The vines originally planted by Colin Preece continued to bear excellent fruit for the production of high quality wines by winemaker, Don

Lewis, who has now made 24 vintages at the winery.

Mitchelton relies on its own vineyards for about half of its grapes and has contracts with cool climate growers in central Victoria for the rest. Don Lewis's first vintage back in 1973 was only 73 tonnes; in 1995 this was approaching 3,000 tonnes. A unique wine in the Mitchelton range is the Wood Matured Marsanne with its distinctive honeysuckle character. It also ages remarkably well.

Mitchelton has an award winning restaurant which focuses on regional produce, an art galllery and an accredited nature reserve. In fact, the level of quality afforded to the visitor by Mitchelton gained recognition in 1994 and again in 1995 with the Victorian Tourism Award for in the Wineries section. This is a show piece winery which also holds occasional concerts and hosts cultural events of various kinds. Things are well in balance at Mitchelton so why not drop in and absorb its great ambience?

MITCHELTON WINES

Address: Mitchellstown via Nagambie, Vic 3608
Phone: (057) 94 2710
Fax: (057) 94 2615
Established: 1974
Winemaker: Don Lewis
Principal varieties grown: Cabernet sauvignon, shiraz, riesling, marsanne, merlot, chardonnay
Ha under vine: 130
Average annual crush: 3,000 tonnes
Average no. cases produced: 200,000

Principal wines & brands	Cellar potential
Victorian Shiraz	10 +years
Victorian Marsanne	10+ years
Victorian Cabernet Sauvignon	10 +years
Victorian Chardonnay	10+ years
Mitchelton III	5-10 years
Blackwood Park Riesling	10-15 years
Preece	5-10 years

Public & trade tours: By appointment only
Cellar door & mail order sales: Yes
Hours open to public: 9 am-5 pm seven days
Points of interest: Restaurant, picnic area, swimming pool, observation deck, nature reserve
Retail distribution: National distribution, Fesq Dorado & Co.

DELATITE WINERY

Address: Stoney's Road, Mansfield Vic.
Direction: Take Mt Buller Road due east of Mansfield, after 8 km turn right into Stoney's Road
Phone: (057) 75 2922
Fax: (057) 75 2911
Established: 1982 (Winery) 1968 (Vineyard)
Owner: The Ritchie family
Winemaker: Rosalind Ritchie
Principal varieties grown: riesling, gewurztraminer, sauvignon blanc, chardonnay, pinot noir, cabernet sauvignon, merlot, malbec
Ha under vine: 26
Average annual crush: 200-220 tonnes
Average no. cases produced: 12,000-14,000

Principal wines & brands	Cellar potential
Riesling	12 years
Gewurztraminer	6-10 years
Sauvignon Blanc	3 years
Unoaked Chardonnay	2 years
Chardonnay	10 years
Rose	3 years
Dungeon Gully (Malbec Merlot)	4 years
Pinot Noir	10 years
Merlot	12 years
Malbec	6 years
Shiraz	12 years
Cabernet Sauvignon	12 years
Devil's River (Cab. Sav/Merlot Malbec Cab. Franc blend)	12 years
Demelza Sparkling Wine (Methode Champenoise)	6 years

Public & trade tours: By appointment only
Cellar door & mail order sales: Yes
Hours open to public: 10 am - 5 pm 7 days a week; closed Christmas Eve, Christmas Day, Good Friday, morning of Anzac Day
Points of interest: Perched on a rocky ridge under snow-capped Mount Buller. Electric barbecues and children's playground provided.
Retail distribution: Victoria, Domaine Wine Shippers; New South Wales, Premier Vineyards; Queensland, Wine Partners; ACT, Oak Barrel Wines; Tasmania, Tasmanian Fine Wines, South Australia, Barrique Wines, Western Australia, Western Wines, U.K., Australian wine Agencies, John Armit Wines, Switzerland, Veni Vino Vici, Canada, Snowy Mountains enterprises.

Robert and Vivienne Ritchie first planted vines on their cattle property, Delatite, in 1968. They sold the grapes to Brown Brothers from 1972-1981 and completed the winery at Delatite in time for the 1982 vintage. Their daughter Rosalind returned home to be the family's winemaker in 1982, having completed a degree in oenology at Roseworthy in South Australia.

Her brother David manages the vineyards, with his father Robert looking after the large farming enterprise. Vivienne is the dynamic and vivacious promoter and marketer of Delatite and makes sure the world knows about these exciting, clean and complex wines which keep winning trophies and awards from every vintage.

As well as the famous Delatite Riesling and Gewurztraminer there is also a sensational sauvignon blanc which sells within weeks of its release and an unwooded chardonnay. The Devil's River, a Bordeaux style red of cabernet sauvignon blended with merlot, malbec and cabernet franc, is a top class wine with minty and conserve-like fruit intensity plus lovely cassis fruit characters.

Delatite also has a small range of intensely flavoured red varietals - shiraz, malbec, merlot and cabernet sauvignon on their Limited Release range.

The pinot noir and chardonnay - 100% varietal wines - are aged in superb new Alliers, Vosges and Troncais (French) oak and the Demelza is a lovely pinot noir dominated sparkling wine, only available at the cellar door.

The winery has a tasting room with sensational views over Mount Buller and Mount Stirling, underlining its cool mountain location.

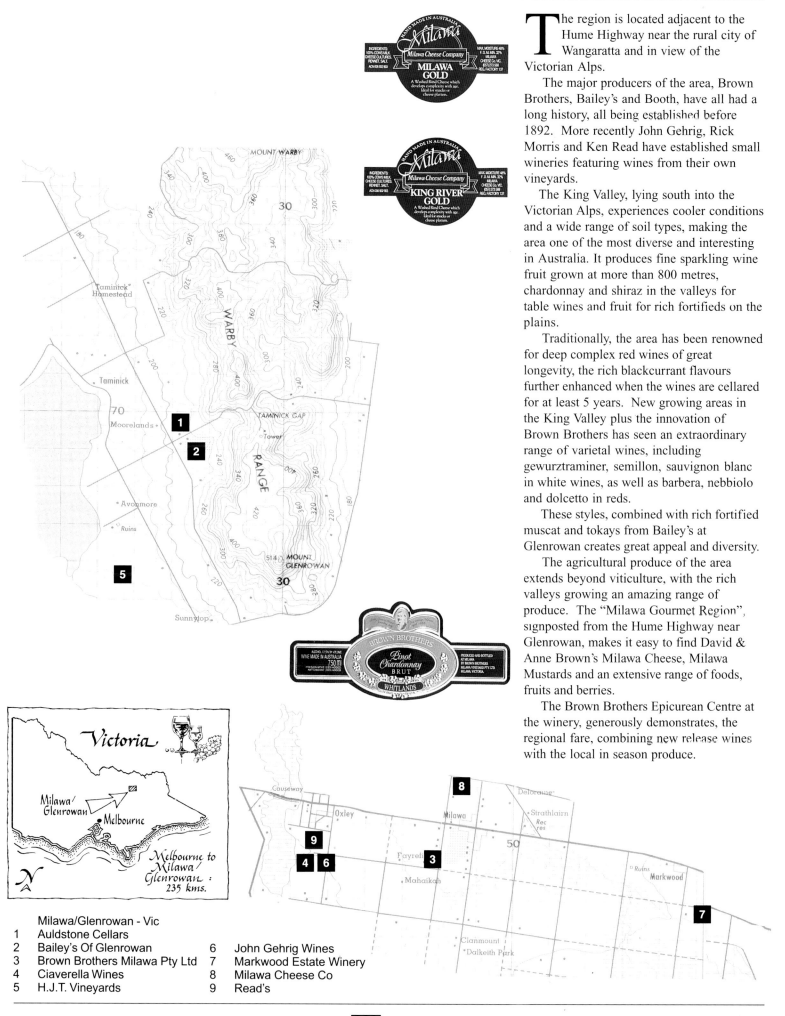

The region is located adjacent to the Hume Highway near the rural city of Wangaratta and in view of the Victorian Alps.

The major producers of the area, Brown Brothers, Bailey's and Booth, have all had a long history, all being established before 1892. More recently John Gehrig, Rick Morris and Ken Read have established small wineries featuring wines from their own vineyards.

The King Valley, lying south into the Victorian Alps, experiences cooler conditions and a wide range of soil types, making the area one of the most diverse and interesting in Australia. It produces fine sparkling wine fruit grown at more than 800 metres, chardonnay and shiraz in the valleys for table wines and fruit for rich fortifieds on the plains.

Traditionally, the area has been renowned for deep complex red wines of great longevity, the rich blackcurrant flavours further enhanced when the wines are cellared for at least 5 years. New growing areas in the King Valley plus the innovation of Brown Brothers has seen an extraordinary range of varietal wines, including gewurztraminer, semillon, sauvignon blanc in white wines, as well as barbera, nebbiolo and dolcetto in reds.

These styles, combined with rich fortified muscat and tokays from Bailey's at Glenrowan creates great appeal and diversity.

The agricultural produce of the area extends beyond viticulture, with the rich valleys growing an amazing range of produce. The "Milawa Gourmet Region", signposted from the Hume Highway near Glenrowan, makes it easy to find David & Anne Brown's Milawa Cheese, Milawa Mustards and an extensive range of foods, fruits and berries.

The Brown Brothers Epicurean Centre at the winery, generously demonstrates, the regional fare, combining new release wines with the local in season produce.

Milawa/Glenrowan - Vic

1 Auldstone Cellars
2 Bailey's Of Glenrowan
3 Brown Brothers Milawa Pty Ltd
4 Ciaverella Wines
5 H.J.T. Vineyards
6 John Gehrig Wines
7 Markwood Estate Winery
8 Milawa Cheese Co
9 Read's

Brown Brothers

The first member of the Brown Family to plant grapes for winemaking at Milawa was John Francis Brown. He made his first planting in 1885. In 1889 he produced the first vintage.

The original property is still in use. The Canadian style barn built in 1860 and used as the first winery, is today used to age fortified wines in wood.

The enterprise flourished. By 1900, a larger winery was needed to accommodate the increase in production. And then, in 1915, disaster struck. The phylloxera infection that swept through the district all but wiped out John Francis Brown, but he hung on, and replanted with phylloxera resistant American rootstock. By 1920, the vineyard was again flourishing.

The area had always been renowned for its fortified wines. Yet, John Francis Brown decided the future of the Milawa vineyard lay in the production of table wines.

His foresight and willingness to experiment with new grape varieties was inherited by his only son, John Charles Brown, who joined his father in 1934.

John Brown Senior, as he is known today, was one of the first winemakers in the area to recognise the potential of the area's quite remarkable climatic diversity for the cultivation of more varieties of grapes than had previously been thought possible.

From sun drenched river plains through the rich, rolling hills of the King Valley, to Whitlands, one of the highest and coolest vineyards in Australia, these areas produce climatic and soil conditions so diverse that Brown Brothers now produce the largest selection of grape varieties grown in any Australian vineyards.

John Brown Senior and his wife, Pat, raised four sons. John Graham, Peter, Ross, and, Roger until his early tragic death in 1990, the youngest, Roger. All have been a part of the family's enterprise and dedication to the development of varietal winemaking.

Their questioning and testing of the boundaries of winemaking has resulted in the creation, alongside the main winery, of a mini winery called the Kindergarten. Within this state of the art environment, small batches of wines can be assessed under different wine making techniques.

In 1995, John Brown Senior celebrated his sixty second vintage. It was also the year that the next generation, John Andrew Brown, joined the family enterprise to continue the traditions built up over 100 vintages by Brown Brothers of Milawa.

They extend a warm welcome to visitors to call in and to taste the fruits of their labours.

John Brown Senior

BROWN BROTHERS MILAWA VINEYARD
Address: Milawa, Vic.
Direction: North-east Victoria
Phone: (057) 20 5500
Fax: (057) 20 5511
Established: 1885
Public & trade tours: Public and trade welcome
Hours open to public: 9 am-5 pm seven days a week (not open Christmas Day or Good Friday)
Points of interest: Epicurean Centre featuring food matched to a selection of national and cellar door releases.
Retail distribution: National

Milawa Cheese Company

David and Anne Brown are pioneers of the modern gourmet Australian cheese industry. Inspired by cheese they had experienced in France and Northern Italy they sought out the abandoned butter factory at Milawa. Its location close to the famous Brown Brothers Winery, the Snow Road and the tourist attractions of North East Victoria was perfect. Cow's milk was available from the Ovens and Kiewa Valleys and a new industry of milking sheep and goats was about to begin.

The first cheeses made were based on European models, Milawa Blue derived from Delcelatte from Northern Italy and the pungent Milawa Gold from the washed rind cheeses of France.

Using these foundation stones David Brown has developed a range of uniquely Australian styles, ranging from delicate fresh curd cheeses of sheep and goat's milk to the authoritative blue styles, Milawa Roc (sheep's milk) and Mt Buffalo Blue (goat milk). The washed rind range has grown to include the delicate King River Gold as well as washed rind goat and sheep cheeses.

The complete range is available for tasting at the factory shop and espresso coffee and ploughman's luncheons are available all day.

Milawa Cheese Company
Address: Factory Road, Milawa, Vic.
Direction: North-east Victoria
Phone: (057) 27 3589
Fax: (057) 27 3590
Established: 1988
Public & trade tours: Bus groups by appointment
Hours open to public: 9 am-5 pm seven days a week (closed Christmas Day)
Points of interest: Factory shop features the largest range of hand-made specialty cheeses in Australia.
Retail distribution: National

Most of the wine grapes processed in Victoria are grown in the north-western corner of the state, along the Murray River. The region stretches from Mildura to the east, along the state border to Echuca. Irrigation is necessary as rainfall is very low.

The area was originally developed by the men who initiated the local channel irrigation, the Chaffey brothers. George Chaffey purchased Mildura Station after his arrival from California in 1886. The name 'Mildura' is appropriate to the rich burnt-coloured landscape along the Murray, being aboriginal for 'red rock'. However, even though the soil was fertile, lack of water made the area barren.

The South Australian government, realising the potential of their Murray River region, and the Chaffey brothers' irrigation successes in California, hired George and his newly arrived brother William to open up the Renmark area. The ensuing success of this project saw the Victorian government hire the pair for a repeat operation in the dry north-western corner of that state. The region quickly became a major fruit-growing area. Although many grape-growers sold their fruit to wine companies, the greater proportion of grapes were used in dried fruit production.

Wine companies were naturally drawn to the Murray Valley. The huge scale of production underway, particularly after the Soldier Settlement Scheme produced a glut of grapes on the market made for attractive development potential. The Murray Valley, concentrating mainly on the production of spirits, prospered during the fortified wine boom.

While much fortified wine is still manufactured in the area, the Mildura region now provides some 25 percent of Australia's wine, involving production in three states - Victoria and several enormous wineries just across the river in NSW at Buronga and grapes which are trucked into South Australia.

Viticultural techniques such as minimal pruning, which sees huge bushy vines producing many small bunches with small berries, has seen wine quality soar. The percentage of excellent bottled premium table wines from the region has grown enormously. Trentham Estate, Alambie, Lindemans, Matthew Lang and the Sunnycliff Wines of Wingara typify this revolution. Further down river, Best's at Lake Boga, Bullers at Beverford and Tisdall at Echuca make excellent premium wines.

Australia's competitive position on the world wine market is benefiting greatly from this innovative region. The large Simeon Wine Company had a successful public float and supplies many of Australia's premium wine producers. A trip along the river by riverboat to the lovely Trentham Winery Restaurant is a must when you visit.

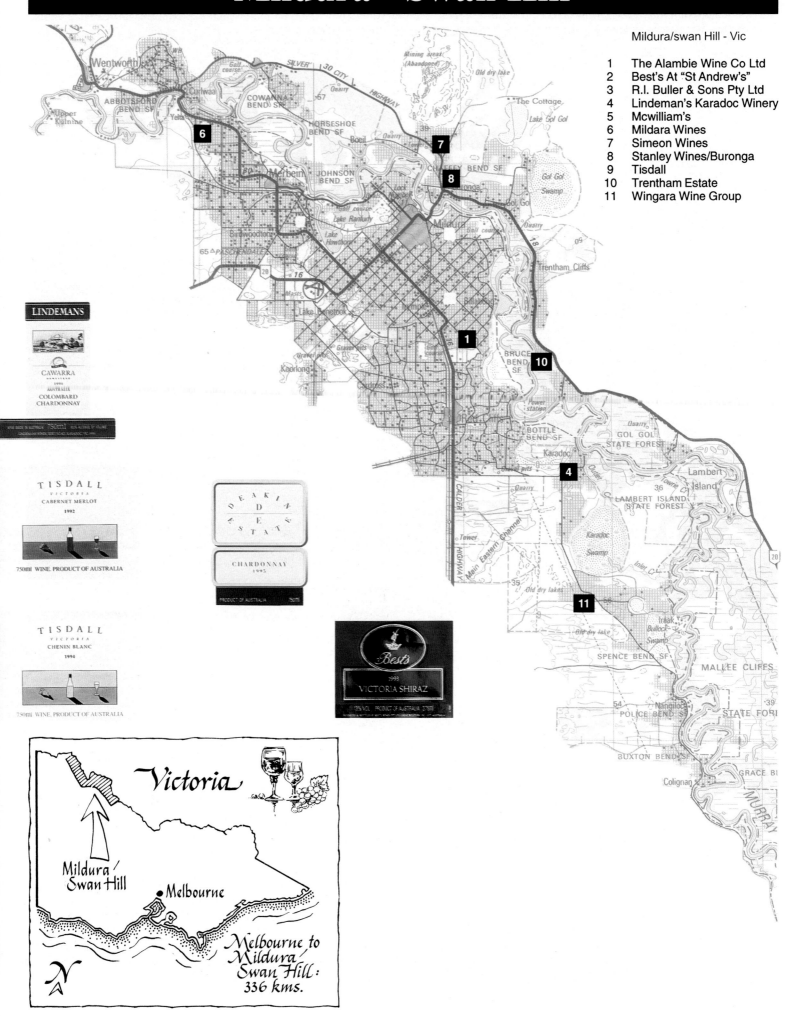

Mildura/swan Hill - Vic

1   The Alambie Wine Co Ltd
2   Best's At "St Andrew's"
3   R.I. Buller & Sons Pty Ltd
4   Lindeman's Karadoc Winery
5   Mcwilliam's
6   Mildara Wines
7   Simeon Wines
8   Stanley Wines/Buronga
9   Tisdall
10 Trentham Estate
11 Wingara Wine Group

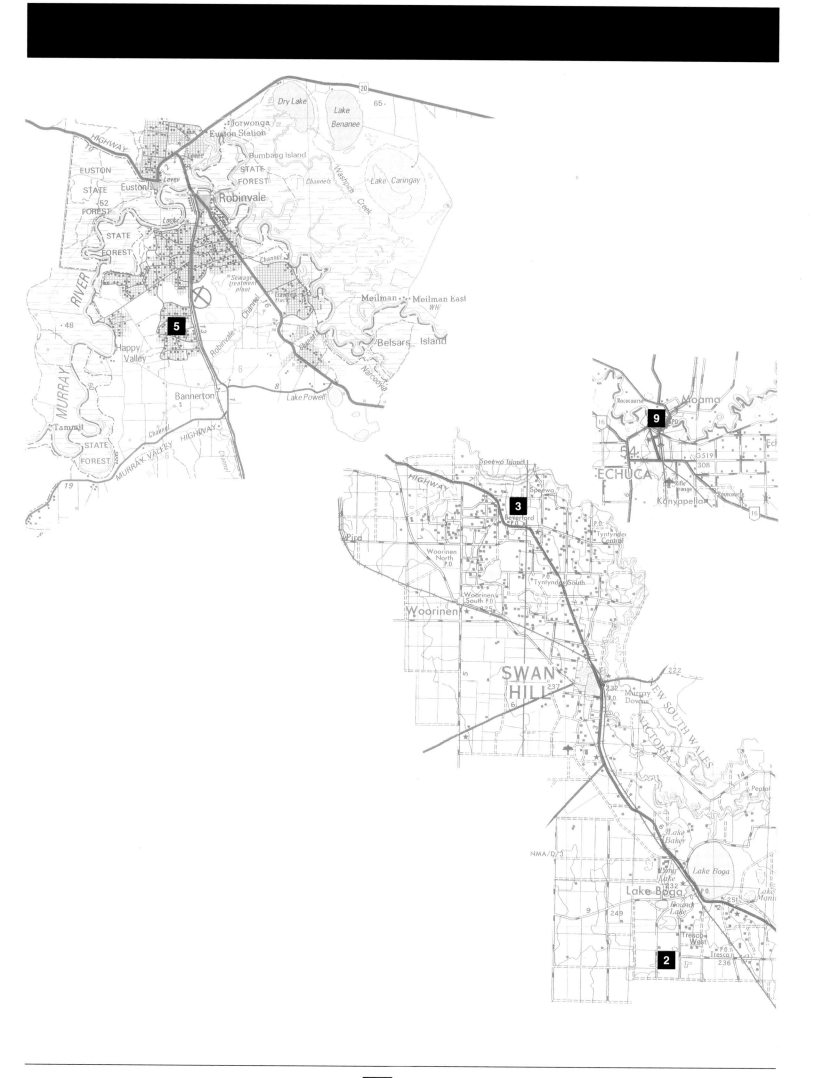

Alambie Wine Co Ltd

Rising rapidly through Australian wine industry ranks, this dynamic company now stands among the nation's top ten wine producers with its Milburn Park, Salisbury Estate and Castle Crossing red and white table wine brands.

Established 25 years ago by agricultural scientist, Peter McLaren, Alambie now boasts extensive vineyard areas as well as a large horticultural holding growing premium export quality avocados, citrus and almonds.

From origins as a small concern processing grapes to add to its rural value, Alambie today produces premium wines at vintage at its Irymple winery for national and export markets. Company controlled vineyards mean that quality of production is supervised by Alambie's winemaking team from vineyad to bottle. The popularity of Alambie's bottled wine brands is fast outstripping the company's respected reputation as a supplier to the nation's inter-winery business.

Chief winemaker, Bob Shields worked previously with Lindemans. At Alambie, he credits the viticultural techniques of minimal pruning to the creation of strong, disease and drought-resistant vines that produce grapes in small berried bunches yielding concentrated flavour. Alambie recently restructured as an unlisted public company. Technological developments have continued each year since the company's inception, assisting in producing critically acclaimed wines. In value-for-money and quality terms, all the Alambie wines are outstanding.

ALAMBIE WINE CO LTD
Address: Campbell Avenue, Irymple Vic. 3498
Direction: 15 minutes along the Sturt Highway from Mildura West. At Irymple, take Campbell Avenue turnoff.
Phone: (050) 24 6800
Fax: (050) 24 6605
Established: 1971
Winemaker: Bob Shields
Principal varieties grown: Chardonnay, semillon, riesling, colombard, sauvignon blanc, merlot, shiraz, chambourcin, cabernet sauvignon, mourvedre.
Ha under vine: 623

Principal wines & brands	Cellar potential
Salisbury Estate	2-3 years
Milburn Park	3 years
Castle Crossing	1-2 years
Tennyson Vineyards	2-3 years
Kasbah Vineyard (export only)	1-3 years
Singing Creek (export only)	1-2 years
Barrier Reef (export only)	2-3 years

Public & trade tours: No
Cellar door sales: Yes
Hours open to public: 10 am-4 pm Mon-Sat.
Points of interest: Scientifically advanced winemaking facilities.
Retail distribution: All states & internationally

Best's St Andrews, Lake Boga

The pioneer winery of the Swan Hill district, St Andrew's was established in 1930 by Frederick Thomson and his sons, Eric and Bill.

The Winery is five kilometres from the town of Lake Boga, off the Murray Valley highway. Of the 150 acre property, almost half is under vine. Yields are high and the quality of fruit is consistently excellent. Table wines are vintaged at St Andrews' then transferred to Concongella, Great Western, for subsequent maturation, blending and bottling. Viv Thomson and Simon Clayfield are the current winemakers.

Best's St. Andrews wines, sold under "Best's Victoria" label, reflect the considerable skills of both men. This is most evident in the quality of the chenin blanc and the exemplary cabernet sauvignon. Similarly, the St. Andrews Liqueur Muscat is a wine of great character and is most reasonably priced. Wines from Best's St. Andrews vineyard are most certainly a fine addition to the company's range and represent excellent value for money.

BEST'S ST ANDREWS VINEYARD, LAKE BOGA
Address: St Andrews, Lake Boga Vic. 3584
Direction: Winery Road, 5 km from Lake Boga
Phone: (050) 37 2154
Fax: (053) 56 2430
Established: 1930
Owner: The Thomson family
Winemaker: Viv Thomson & Simon Clayfield
Principal varieties grown: Shiraz, cabernet sauvignon, colombard, chenin blanc, riesling
Average annual crush: 400 tonnes

Principal wines & brands	Cellar potential
Victoria Shiraz	1-6 years
Victoria Cabernet Sauvignon	1-6 years
Victoria Chenin Blanc	2-5 years
Spaetlese Lexia	2-5 years
Vintage Port	10 years +

Conducted public & trade tours: Mon-Fri 11 am and 3 pm; other days by appointment
Cellar door sales: Yes
Hours open to public: 9 am-5 pm Mon-Fri; 9 am-4 pm Sat & public holidays; 12-4 pm Sun. of holiday periods only
Points of interest: Picnic area, pot-still highlight of tour, home of Best's fortified wines, brandy & Victoria table wines.
Retail distribution: Agents in State capitals with exception of Northern Territory and Western Australia.

Wingara Wine Group

WINGARA WINE GROUP
Address: Kulkyne Way, via Red Cliffs Vic.
Direction: South out of Red Cliffs on Calder Hwy,
turn left at Kulkyne Way then 20 kms on the right
Phone: (050) 29 1666
Fax:(050) 24 3316
Year of Establishment::1980
Winemaker: Mark Zeppel
Principal varieties grown: Chardonnay,
sauvignon blanc, riesling, traminer, semillon,
colombard, gordo, cabernet sauvignon, shiraz,
ruby cabernet, merlot
Ha under vine: 300
Average no. cases produced: 150,000

Principal wines & brands	Cellar potential
Sunnycliff	
Chardonnay	2-5 years
Cabernet Sauvignon	5-10 years
Colombard Chardonnay	2-5 years
Sauvignon Blanc	2-5 years
Deakin Estate	
Cabernet Sauvignon	5-10 years
Chardonnay	2-5 years
Colombard	2-5 years
Sauvignon Blanc	2-5 years
Sparkling Wine	2-5 years

Public & trade tours: By appointment only
Hours open to public: By appointment only
Retail distribution: Inchcape Liquor Marketing

The Sunnycliff vineyards were first planted from 1973 with the winery being commissioned in 1980. Initially all fruit processed at the winery was sold to other wineries as juice or wine. In 1989 the Sunnycliff range of wines was released. The company has undergone rapid expansion in recent years and in 1995 released its Deakin Estate range.

Today, with the application of new technology in viticulture and winemaking, Wingara Wine Group is at the forefront of value-for-money quality wine in Australia. In both the vineyards and the winery, every effort is directed to maximising the quality of the fruit and wine by preserving fruit flavours and having total control of all stages of production.

Tisdall

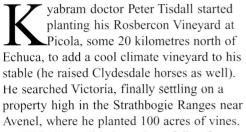

Kyabram doctor Peter Tisdall started planting his Rosbercon Vineyard at Picola, some 20 kilometres north of Echuca, to add a cool climate vineyard to his stable (he raised Clydesdale horses as well). He searched Victoria, finally settling on a property high in the Strathbogie Ranges near Avenel, where he planted 100 acres of vines.

With this well-balanced portfolio of vineyards and varieties Mount Helen Vineyard was a complete success. The Tisdall's turned their cheese factory at Echuca into a winery and with a stroke of genius secured the services of John Ellis who had put Rosemount wines on the map. Within a very short time, John was crushing more than 1,000 tonnes at the winery and Tisdall had become one of the biggest premium wine producers in Victoria.

In the late 1980s the Tisdall's purchased a large old brick warehouse building on the banks of the river at Echuca and spent a small fortune setting up a hospitality centre with a restaurant, large function area, a gallery with arts and crafts and a huge tasting area.The recession hit them with a real bite and eventually Tisdall was sold including Mount Ida artist, Leonard French's

highly regarded vineyard and wine label at Heathcote.

After several years, a little in the wilderness, Tisdall has risen once again through its purchase by Mildara Blass in late 1993. Already the increased resources and good management of Mildara Blass have seen marked improvements in the winery and wines. The Tisdall wines from Rosbercon are always lively and fresh, excellent value for money, whilst the Mount Helen wines have concentrated flavours and power from their cool climate growing conditions.The Mount Ida Red is always aromatic and full-bodied with great staying power. Tisdall is back on the rails.

Trentham Estate

One of the best located and prettiest wineries in Australia sits on the elevated banks on a perfect bend of the Murray River. Trentham Estate winery has a large glassed-in cafe-style restaurant affording panoramic views of the river in both directions over the sweeping lawns.

In front of the winery is a landing where each Thursday the historic paddle steamer Rothbury, built in 1881, pulls in after leaving Mildura at 10.30 am. After a leisurely lunch at the winery, you disembark at Mildura at 3.30 pm.

The trip includes a guided tour of the winery by winemaker Anthony Murphy whose family owns the property where they first planted vines back in 1909. Anthony worked at Mildara for some 11 years and while he makes the wine his brother Pat manages the 33 hectares of premium grape varieties. The wines are truly of international class. Aside from table wines, they produce both sparkling and fortified wines. I was particularly impressed by the chardonnay, the shiraz and the vintage port.

TRENTHAM ESTATE
Address: Sturt Highway, Trentham Cliffs NSW 2378
Direction: 15 km from Mildura on NSW side of Murray River
Phone: (050) 24 8888
Fax: (050) 24 8800
Year of Establishment: 1988
Winemaker: Anthony Murphy
Principal varieties grown: Chardonnay, colombard, sauvignon blanc, taminga, pinot noir, merlot, cabernet sauvignon, shiraz
Ha under vine: 33
Average annual crush: 350 tonnes
Average no. cases produced: 22,000

Principal wines & brands	Cellar potential
Chardonnay	2-5 years
Colombard Chardonnay	1-3 years
Noble Taminga	2-5 years
Merlot	5-10 years
Cabernet Sauvignon Merlot	5-10 years
Shiraz	5-10 years

Public & trade tours: By appointment only
Cellar door & mail order sales: Yes
Hours open to public: 9.00am-5.00pm Mon-Fri;
10 am-5 pm Sat-Sun.
Points of interest: Restaurant & vineyards
Retail distribution: All capital cities in Australia.

Stanley Wines Buronga

Just over the river into New South Wales lies the Stanley Buronga Winery, one of the largest wineries in NSW, with a capacity of some 50,000 tonnes.

This winery supplies wine for the always reliable and top class Stanley and Buronga Hill wine casks.

The winery also has a large, well set up, tasting and hospitality area. Although this is a massive winery it is aesthetically and neatly put together and making good quality and good value wines. It's well worth a visit while you are in the region.

STANLEY WINES
Address: Silver City Highway, Buronga NSW 2648
Phone: (050) 23 4341
Fax: (050) 23 4344
Owner: BRL Hardy Wine Company
Winemaker: Neil Lindsay

Principal wines & brands
Stanley 4lt Casks
Stanley 2lt Casks
Buronga 4lt Casks

Public & trade tours: By appointment only
Hours open to public: 10 am-4 pm Mon-Fri; 10.30 am-4 pm Sat; 12-4 pm Sun.

Like other Victorian wine-producing areas, Rutherglen's fortunes have fluctuated over the years. Rutherglen has seen so many natural and economic changes throughout its history that one must admire both the courage of the families who continued to persevere with the industry, and the strength and quality of the wines that enabled them to carry on.

The Rutherglen region was first settled by Lindsay Brown, who purchased the large Gooramadda property in 1839. Several of his farm-workers were from Germany and had brought vine cuttings with them, which were duly planted. Under pressure from these workers, Brown was encouraged to plant his own vines, which were also highly successful.

The discovery of gold in Rutherglen in 1860 was an event which greatly increased the local population. Within 10 years, however, the ore had become scarce and people turned to vines to make their fortune. By 1870 a number of large winemaking enterprises were in operation throughout the district. Some of these properties were built on a grand scale and included such magnificent homesteads as Camille Reau's, 'Tuilleries' and Alexander Caughey's 'Mt Prior'. Many family companies were established at this time, some of which are still in existence.

Development of the wine industry continued to expand towards the turn of the century, with further companies constructing imposing mansions and wineries. A grand castle was erected by the Sutherland Smith family's company, All Saints, and the Morris family also built a magnificent mansion at Fairfield, with enormous cellars capable of storing three million litres of wine. The burgeoning popularity of fortified wines was crucial to these developments, particularly as Rutherglen had ideal conditions for the production of Australia's best fortified wines.

Unfortunately the threat of phylloxera became a reality in 1899, when it was identified in the area, temporarily halting the growth of Rutherglen's wine industry. Many vineyards were destroyed but others were replanted with vines of a more resistant nature. This was encouraged by the government, which subsidised the price of the new vines. Some vignerons were unable to meet the costs of replanting, however, and by the outbreak of the First World War, these companies had faded from existence. Export of fortified wines to the United Kingdom sustained many companies throughout this time until the market collapsed during the Depression. Wine prices slumped and the government was forced to ration beer supplies to assist the ailing wine industry.

Fortified wines again became locally popular and Rutherglen experienced a period of relative growth and prosperity. Public tastes were also veering toward table wines and several companies, including Campbells, Bullers, All Saints and the Morris family developed new ranges of wines. For the most part red wines were produced but recent years have seen the production of high quality white wines in the area. Both semillon and chardonnay grapes are now proving to be very successful and Mount Prior, St Leonards and Campbells have excellent examples showing the potential of these varieties.

The liqueur muscats, tokays and frontignacs of the Rutherglen area are, without doubt, the best in Australia and are quite probably the best in the world. These wines are truly unique to Australia and are saluted by critics the world over.

Following the success of Rutherglen's table wines and a resurgence of interest in its fortifieds, many local winemakers have renovated, new wineries have been built and old ones re-opened. The restoration of the beautiful old All Saints 'Castle' Winery by the Brown family who purchased it several years ago is fabulous - the gardens and the restaurant function area are truly world-class. Chris Pfeiffer, formerly with Lindemans, has done an excellent job restoring and setting up, with his wife Robyn, an excellent winery in the old Seppelts distillery at Wahgunyah. Campbell's Winery, which has a fine reputation for the wines of four generations, is beautifully presented and provides visitors with the opportunity of walking through their 125 year old winery.

Rutherglen was the first region in Victoria to run a wine festival. These became legendary events during the 1970s. The region now has a number of successful wine events. In March, the Labour Day weekend hosts the Tastes of Rutherglen when the finest restaurants in the region bring their gourmet treasures to the wineries.

The Gourmet Getaway follows on the next week, (which is a long weekend in Canberra). The Queen's Birthday weekend in June sees the famous Winery Walkabout, with food and entertainment featuring at all the wineries. Winner of many tourism awards, something for all the family, Rutherglen is back with a vengeance.

Rutherglen

Rutherglen - Vic

1 All Saints Estate/Le Bistro Restaurant
2 Anderson Winery
3 R.I. Buller (Calliope Vineyard
4 Campbell's Rutherglen Winery
5 Chamber's Rosewood
6 Cofield Wines
7 Fairfield Vineyards
8 Gerhig's Winery
9 Jones Winery
10 Morris Wines
11 Mount Prior
12 Pfeiffer Wines
13 St Leonards
14 Stanton & Killeen
15 G Sutherland Smith & Sons

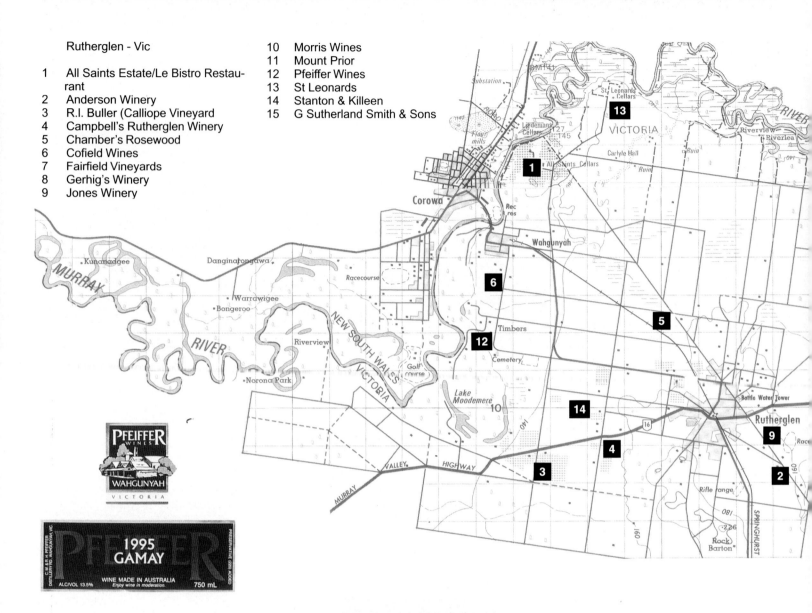

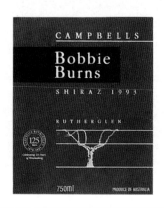

All Saints

All Saints must vie for the title of one of Australia's most imposing and impressive wineries. Its faded glory has been restored and enhanced to a breathtaking degree by the Brown family of Milawa who purchased the run-down winery and vineyards in 1993. They have created a hospitality centre beautifully and sensitively blended it into this classic, Scottish-castle-inspired winery.

The history of All Saints goes back to 1862 when George Sutherland Smith and his brother-in-law John Banks purchased a 520 hectare property at Wahgunyah on the Murray River. Sutherland Smith had been a tradesman at the castle of Mey in Caithness in Scotland and the winery was built to resemble this building and named after its Scottish location in the parish of All Saints.

All Saints is one of the premier producers of old fortified dessert wines. Its Museum releases contain predominantly 50-60-year-old wines aged in the old oak casks which fill the winery's huge Barrel Hall.

Winemaker, Neil Jericho, has had long experience with north-east Victorian wines. The table wines, particularly, have benefited from his input and state of the art winemaking equipment.

In a separate cellar building which overlooks the splendid formal gardens, there is a special North East Victoria Winemakers Hall of Fame which certainly has more living history and past glory than any other Australian wine region. The indoor/outdoor Terrace Restaurant has an innovative menu featuring local produce and The Great Hall is a wonderful venue for that special large function. A plan is currently being prepared to construct some accommodation cottages in the vineyards looking towards the Murray River.

ALL SAINTS ESTATE
Address: All Saints Road, Wahgunyah, Rutherglen Vic. 3687
Phone: (060) 33 1922
Fax: (060) 33 3515
Established: 1864
Owner: Brown Brothers
Winemaker: Neil Jericho
Principal varieties grown: Cabernet, shiraz, chenin blanc, chardonnay, semillon, marsanne, tokay, muscat, orange muscat, riesling
Ha under vine: 68
Average annual crush: 284 tonnes
Average no. cases produced: 30,000

Principal wines & brands	Cellar potential
'Classic Release'	
Shiraz	5-10 years
Cabernet Sauvignon	5-10 years
L.H. Semillon	5-10 years
N.V. Sparkling Cabernet	2-5 years
Chenin Blanc	2-5 years
Chardonnay	2-5 years
Vintage Port	10+ years
Muscat	5-10 years
Tokay	5-10 years

Public & trade tours: Yes
Cellar door & mail order sales: Yes
Hours open to public: All Saints 9 am-5 pm seven days a week (excl. Good Friday & Christmas Day); St Leonards 10 am-3 pm Sat-Sun (excl. Good Friday & Christmas Day)
Points of interest: Terrace Restaurant, picnic baskets, playground, Le Bistro at St. Leonards, Chinese Hut, self-guided tours, keg factory co-operage (demonstration and sales), Winemakers' Hall of Fame
Retail distribution: Victoria, NSW, ACT, Tasmania, south-east Queensland

R M Buller and Son Vineyard

Lieutenant Commander Reginald Buller purchased his vineyard, 5 km west of Rutherglen, in 1921 after returning from active service in the 1914-18 war. He named the vineyard 'Calliope' after the indomitable British warship which was the hero of A.B. (Banjo) Patterson's ballad.

The 24 hectare vineyard still includes the original plantings from which Reginald Buller made his fortified wines. In 1947 Reginald Buller was joined by his son Richard (Dick) who, having graduated from Roseworthy College was now qualified to assist in the family business. Four years later, in 1951, Reginald left his son in charge at Calliope and moved to Beverford, 16 km north of Swan Hill on the Murray River, where he established a new winery, distillery and vineyard. This winery now produces its own range of wines under the R.L. Buller & Son label. Dick's youngest son Andrew, also a Roseworthy College graduate, currently supervises Bullers' Calliope vineyard and winery. Rutherglen's variable rainfall means that this non-irrigated vineyard often has very low yields. The compensating factor is the concentrated flavour of the grapes.

The Buller range of fortified wines under the Black Label are among the best in the district, and include a vintage port as well as the Rutherglen Muscat and Tokay. The limited release Museum range Muscat and Tokay have been awarded medals and trophies both in Australia and overseas. Bullers also produce some excellent table wines. Their Wooded Semillon is complex and flavoursome, whilst their Calliope Shiraz has also been very successful on the show circuit. The reds are in the big, rich Rutherglen style.

Fine wines are not the only attraction at Calliope. Val Buller has created a fascinating bird park, which is open to the public featuring many rare native species.

R M Buller and Son Vineyard
Address: Head Office and Winery – Three Chain Road, Rutherglen Vic 3685
Phone: (060) 32 9660
Fax: (060) 32 8005
Winery: Murray Valley Highway Beverford Vic 3590
Phone: (050) 37 6305
Fax: (050) 37 6803
Cellar door & mail order sales: Yes (Rutherglen)
Hours open to public: Monday to Saturday, Sundays School Holidays and long weekends (Beverford) Closed Christmas Day, Good Friday Anzac day (morning)

Dick Buller

Campbells

In 1995, the Campbell clan were busy celebrating their 125th vintage, a significant achievement because the winery, one of the oldest in Australia, has been owned by the Campbell family from the planting of its first vine.

Scotsman John Campbell arrived in Australia in 1858 and immediately set out for the Beechworth goldfields. This stay was shortlived, for a short time later he married and moved to the 'Bobbie Burns' diggings at Rutherglen. When the gold supplies decreased, Campbell decided to stay in Rutherglen and establish a farm. He chose a 75 acre parcel of land adjacent to the gold diggings which he aptly called 'Bobbie Burns', and the following year he was granted a further 120 acres by the government.

Campbell concentrated mainly on grain crops but planted 2-1/2 acres of vines for himself, his family and friends. By 1885, this had increased to 38 acres. This growing concern saw the construction of a winery and the venture into the market place where the wines were very successful, both in sales figures and on the show circuit. In 1898, the vineyard was devastated by the vine louse phylloxera and by the time John Campbell died, 11 years later, wine production at Bobbie Burns was in a slump. Campbell's son David, determined to reverse the decline of the family wine interests, restored the cellar and replanted vines on resistant rootstock to ensure protection from phylloxera. In turn, his son Allen carried the business through the difficult years of the Depression.

One of the problems faced at this time was the build-up of wine stocks due to lack of sales. In an attempt to alleviate this situation the Campbells began the new practice of selling surplus wine at the cellar door; a stop-gap measure that enabled the continuity of the winery. Gradually the economic climate improved, eventually creating the conditions whereby the Campbells were able to purchase more land for expansion.

Allen's sons, Malcolm and Colin, currently run the business. Malcolm handles the rural side and the vineyard while Colin, a Roseworthy graduate, manages the winemaking and winery. Colin has proved beyond doubt that the Rutherglen area is capable of not only producing world class fortifieds and red wines, but can also produce excellent white wines. The successful release in 1995 of the Bobbie Burns Chardonnay adds to the already impressive reputation for whites that Campbell's continue to enjoy. The Bobbie Burns Shiraz has developed a cult following and the recently released super premium, Barkly Durif looks set to go the same way. Campbells fortifieds including ports, tokays and muscats are marvellous world-renowned wines, demonstrating the incredible style and standard achieved by the very best Rutherglen producers.

Campbell family members are all heavily involved in the business; Mrs Isabel Campbell, Malcolm and his wife Jenny, plus Colin and Prue - even Muscat the cat can't stay out of the picture. The winery is a picture of beautifully maintained history as can be seen on the self guided tour and in the wines to be enjoyed in the impressive yet friendly tasting room. The Campbell's are proud of their past and dedicated to the future.

CAMPBELLS RUTHERGLEN WINES
Address: Murray Valley Highway, Rutherglen Vic. 3685
Direction: 3 km west of Rutherglen on Murray Valley Highway
Phone: (060) 32 9458
Fax: (060) 32 9870
Established: 1870
Owner: Campbell family
Winemaker: Colin Campbell
Principal varieties grown: Shiraz, muscat, durif, cabernet sauvignon, riesling, chardonnay, semillon
Ha under vine: 60
Average annual crush: 750 tonnes
Average no. cases produced: 50,000

Principal wines & brands	Cellar potential
Bobbie Burns Shiraz	10+ years
The Barkly Durif	10+ years
Cabernet Merlot	5-10 years
Bobbie Burns Chardonnay	5 years
Silverburn	2-5 years
Semillon Chardonnay	2-5 years
Liqueur Muscat	
Liqueur Tokay	
Rutherglen Muscat	
Liquid Gold	
Merchant Prince Muscat	
Isabella Tokay	

Guided public & trade tours: By appointment only
Cellar door & mail order sales: Yes
Hours open to public: 9 am-5 pm Mon-Sat; 10 am-5 pm Sun.
Points of interest: Self-guided tour, including explanation of wine-making process
Retail distribution: National Distribution, Inchcape Liquor Marketing.

Morris of Rutherglen

In 1859, George Morris purchased a 222 acre property at Browns Plains, which he called 'Fairfield'. Following the success of his first 39 acres of vines, Morris expanded his vineyard so that by 1872 he had 617 acres under vine.

During the 1880s Morris' good fortune led to the building of the imposing Fairfield mansion, which became one of the showpieces of the area. More than half of Fairfield's output was exported to the United Kingdom where it became very successful on the international show circuit. In fact George Morris had such a reputation that in 1886 he was appointed Wine Commissioner at the Indian Colonial Exhibition in London.

By the 1890s George Morris was in charge of Australia's largest winery. Seeking also to make a name for himself, George's son, Charles Morris, purchased his own property three kilometres east of Fairfield at Mia Mia in 1887 and also planted vines. The resultant fruit was sold to and processed at Fairfield.

The Fairfield vineyards were attacked suddenly by phylloxera at the turn of the century. Wine production rapidly declined and following the founder's death the company ceased production altogether, and was eventually sold. However, at Mia Mia, after the devastation wrought by the vine louse, Charles Morris replanted and continued to make fortified wines.

Today the winery is run by its founder's great-grandson, David. David carries on the family tradition producing a range of red table wines including Durif which is a wine of great body and character. Likewise his chardonnay is great with both excellent fruit and strong varietal character.

The Morris fortifieds need little introduction as, like those of the region, they are made skilfully and compare favourably with the best in the world. Morris Wines was sold to Orlando in 1970 but fortunately Mick Morris (company winemaker, wine industry legend - and David's father) was retained as consultant after his retirement. David, as current winemaker and production manager is following in his father, Mick's footsteps by carrying on the fine family tradition of more than a century.

Pfeiffer Wines

Chris Pfeiffer was fortified winemaker for Lindemans Wines, his last position being just across the Murray River from Rutherglen, in Corowa. In 1984 he and his wife Robyn purchased the grand old Seppelt's Distillery in Wahgunyah, and renovated the 19th Century Winery.

The tasting area is full of character, and the scenic picnic area and old timber bridge provide an idyllic location for enjoying Pfeiffer's gourmet lunch hampers.

The original 10 ha vineyard was planted in 1963, and since 1984 this has been expanded to 22 ha. Chris has a small planting of the elusive grape variety Gamay, which he crafts into an early drinking style of spicy wild berry flavours. The old low yeilding pinot noir vines produce a red of great character. Since 1984 Chris has had some cabernet sauvignon, riesling and shiraz vines grown in the cool Kiewa Valley, near Mt. Beauty. The lifted aromatics of these grapes enhance the elegance of style and balance for which Pfeiffer Wines are renowned. The delicate dry riesling in particular benefits from this influence.

The Auslese Tokay is a beautiful dessert wine, and an impressive selection of fortified wines - muscat, tokay, vintage port and a tawny port containing 26 varieties - complete the range.

PFEIFFER WINES
Address: Distillery Road, Wahgunyah, Vic 3687
Direction: Off Wahgunyah-Rutherglen Road, between Wahgunyah & Rutherglen
Phone: (060) 332805
Fax: (060) 333158
Established: 1984
Winemaker: Christopher Pfeiffer
Principal varieties grown: Chardonnay, pinot noir, gamay, cabernet sauvignon, merlot, shiraz, rutherglen muscat, rutherglen tokay, touriga
Ha under vine: 22
Average no. cases produced: 13,000

Principal wines & brands	Cellar potential
Chardonnay	5-10 years
Riesling	2-5 years
Chardonnay-Semillon	2-5 years
Cabernet Sauvignon	5-10 years
Shiraz	2-5 years
Old Distillery Port	Average
Old Distillery Tokay	Age
Old Distillery Muscat	Now

Hours open to public: 9 am-5 pm Mon-Sat; 11 am-4 pm Sun
Points of interest: Picnic hampers available (ordering essential). River/lake cruises available for groups, booking necessary.

Stanton & Killeen

Timothy Stanton and his son John Lewis Stanton came to Victoria in 1855 from Suffolk in England, in search of gold. They finally settled in Rutherglen where they planted vines on their farm, making their first wine in 1875.

The vineyard, known as 'Park View,' was destroyed by phylloxera around the turn of the century. The vineyard was replanted but succumbed again to the depression of the 1930s. Timothy's grandson, John Richard, became a successful vigneron in his own right and in 1921 presented his son, John Charles (Jack) Stanton with 30 hectares of land which became known as 'Gracerray'. While still working for his father Jack planted his own winery and his first vintage was in 1925.

Norm Killeen arrived in Rutherglen in 1940 as a young graduate in agricultural science to work at the Research Institute. In 1948, he married Jack Stanton's daughter, Joan, and joined Jack at the winery in 1953, becoming winemaker in 1967. The business became known as Stanton & Killeen. Jack died in 1990 at 95 years of age. I well remember photographing him in the new tasting area in 1986.

Norm's son, Chris Killeen, now makes the wines. A new vineyard specialising in red was planted at Moodemere in 1968 and another 6 hectares in 1978 called 'Quandong', the property's name before Gracerray. The Stanton & Killeen fortifieds which include tokay, muscat and vintage port are outstanding, as are their big Rutherglen reds. Chris also makes some very respectable whites.

Winemaker: Chris Killen

STANTON & KILLEEN WINES
Address: Jacks Road, Rutherglen, Vic. 3685
Direction: 3 km west of Rutherglen
Phone: (060) 32 9457
Fax: (060) 32 8018
Established: 1875
Winemaker: Chris Killeen
Principal varieties grown: Shiraz, cabernet sauvignon, durif, merlot, muscat, muscadelle, chardonnay, touriga
Ha under vine: 30
Average annual crush: 100 tonnes
Average no. cases produced: 10,000

Principal wines & brands	Cellar potential
1992 Shiraz	6-10 years
1992 Durif	8-12 years
1992 Cabernet	5-10 years
1990 Vintage Port	15-20 years
Liqueur Muscat	
Liqueur Tokay	
Liqueur Port	

Trade tours: Yes
Hours open to public: 9 am-5 pm Mon-Sat; 10 am-5 pm Sun.

An introduction to Western Victoria

O wing to the dispersed nature of viticulture throughout Victoria and the enormous distances encountered from region to region, this chapter will include the smaller inland areas of Great Western, Pyrenees, Ballarat and Drumborg near the coast.

The best-known area is Great Western, 218 kilometres west of Melbourne. Centred around a small town of the same name, the district is hilly, of poor soils and is at the mercy of extreme climates, including frosts. Fruit yields are therefore low but, due to the slow ripening period which creates high grape sugar levels, these yields are of excellent quality.

Since its inception out of the gold rush, the Great Western district has produced long living, high quality wines. Vines were planted in the 1860s by two Frenchmen, Jean Trouette and Emile Blampied and the Best family. In time, the former property faded from existence, leaving the Best family's Great Western and Concongella wineries and vineyards to prosper and expand. Following the death of Joseph Best, the Great Western concern was sold to Hans Irvine who emphasised champagne production. B Seppelt and Sons bought Great Western in 1918.

Of the 44 district vine growers of 1893, only two, Seppelt Great Western along with the Thomson family, at what was formerly Best's Concongella Vineyard, survive today. Nowadays the Great Western district is part of the region known as Grampians with the two pioneer wineries joined by a number of new ventures, led by Mount Langi Ghiran Vineyards in 1969.

During the 1960s Seppelt decided to expand their operations in Victoria and began a search for suitable land. Owing to quarantine regulations it was not possible to take cuttings from South Australia. As the company wished to continue producing fruit from cool climate areas, an alternative site in Victoria was required. Karl Seppelt purchased property at Drumborg outside Portland, which he first planted to vines in 1964. The coastal climate is milder than at Great Western and, since Seppelt's successful establishment at Drumborg, others have been encouraged to plant in this area.

The Pyrenees winemaking district, includes Avoca, Moonambel and Redbank. Located north-west of Ballarat in the Pyrenees range, the undulating landscape

provides ideal conditions for the manufacture of a wide range of wines. Vines were first planted in the 1840s by Adams on Mountain Creek, closely followed by a Mr Mackereth in 1848. The Mackereth concern was sold and dismantled in 1929, and Mountain Creek closed operations in 1947.

In 1963, John Robb arrived at Avoca and planted extensive vineyards for a consortium of the Remy Martin Company from France and an Australian wine merchant, Nathan and Wyeth. Altnough initially established for brandy production, Chateau Remy has changed direction, specialising in fine sparkling wines. During the early 1970s other vineyards were established in the Pyrenees, including Taltarni, Warrenmang and Dalwhinnie. In 1973 Neill and Sally Robb established the Redbank Winery and

have since acquired an outstanding reputation for their red wines.

Wine-makers of the Pyrenees region are highly sucdessful at producing a large selection of wine styles, ranging from the excellent sparkling wines of Taltarni and Chateau Remy to the minty reds produced by Redbank and others. Local conditions have contributed to their prosperity. Although fruit yields tend to be low and the climate is cold and rainfall moderate, the grapes are first-rate.

A smaller winegrowing area centers around Ballarat. Again, like many Victorian "Born Again" wine districts, the area supported a flourishing wine industry in the 1800s. Ian Home pioneered the new resurgence in 1976 when he established Yellowglen.

Climate and topography vary throughout Western Victoria. So too do the wines produced in each region. For instance, Great Western, although famed for its sparkling wine, is also the origin of highly acclaimed table wines. The Drumborg and Ballarat areas produce cool climate wines of classic style, whilst the Pyrenees seems able to produce any variety of wine desired. While each district is diverse in style and direction, they all share a commitment to the Winemaking Industry of Victoria and, as a result, produce wines of distinction. Many wineries have hospitality facilities adding to the pleasure of visiting these regions.

Western Victoria

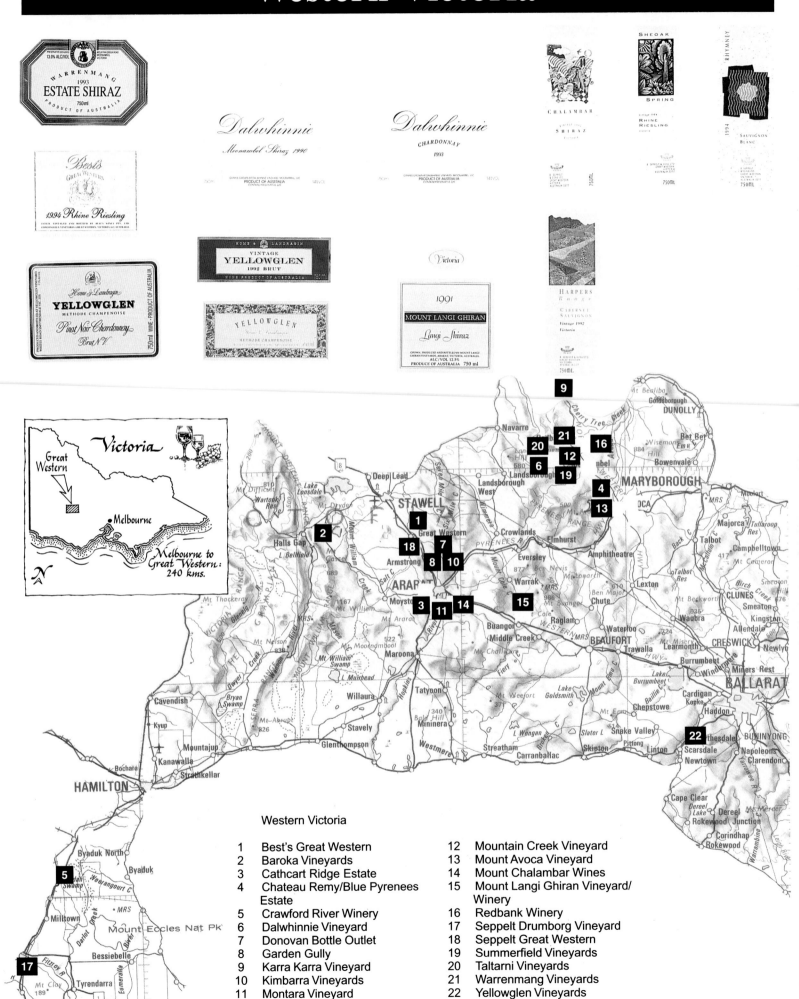

Western Victoria

1	Best's Great Western	12	Mountain Creek Vineyard
2	Baroka Vineyards	13	Mount Avoca Vineyard
3	Cathcart Ridge Estate	14	Mount Chalambar Wines
4	Chateau Remy/Blue Pyrenees Estate	15	Mount Langi Ghiran Vineyard/ Winery
5	Crawford River Winery	16	Redbank Winery
6	Dalwhinnie Vineyard	17	Seppelt Drumborg Vineyard
7	Donovan Bottle Outlet	18	Seppelt Great Western
8	Garden Gully	19	Summerfield Vineyards
9	Karra Karra Vineyard	20	Taltarni Vineyards
10	Kimbarra Vineyards	21	Warrenmang Vineyards
11	Montara Vineyard	22	Yellowglen Vineyards

Mount Langi Ghiran

Langi is aboriginal for 'home of' and Ghiran is the yellow-tailed black cockatoo. Langi is also the home of two of the best red wines in Australia. The Langi shiraz, with its pepper, mulberry and cedar cigar box character, and the cassis and cedar wood cabernet sauvignon are as awesome as the spectacular vineyard location spread across the valley between Mount Langi Ghiran and Mount Cole. This cool isolated location was originally apple country, back in the gold rush days of the 1850s. Vines were first planted in 1880, but saw their demise around 1920, like much of Victoria's other vineyards.

Trevor Mast graduated from the Geisenheim University of winemaking in Germany in the 1970s and on returning to Australia in 1975 he became winemaker at Best's Great Western. In 1980 he began planting a vineyard at Mount Chalambar and in 1987 bought the Langi Ghiran Vineyard from the Fratin Brothers. Trevor's financial partner in the venture is Ian Menzies, nephew of the late Sir Robert.

The Mount Chalambar Rhine Riesling is always top class, showing plenty of spice, perhaps due to Trevor's German training. I have been very impressed with the Mount Chalambar Chardonnay, as well. Also recommended is the Mount Langi Sauvignon Blanc, a superb gold medal standard wine at the tropical fruit end of the flavour spectrum.

MOUNT LANGI GHIRAN VINEYARDS PTY LTD
Address: Warrak Road, Buangor, Vic. 3375
Direction: Western Highway at Buangor (26 km east of Ararat)
Phone: (053) 54 3207
Fax: (053) 54 3277
Established: 1968
Owner: I. Menzies/T. Mast
Winemaker: Trevor Mast
Principal varieties grown: Shiraz, cabernet sauvignon, riesling, pinot gris
Ha under vine: 45
Average no. cases produced: 10,000

Principal wines & brands	Cellar potential
Langi Shiraz	5-10 years
Langi Cab. Sauvignon/Merlot	5-10 years
Langi Riesling	2-5 years
Langi Pinot Gris	0-2 years

Public & trade tours: By appointment
Cellar door & mail order sales: Yes
Hours open to public: 9 am-5 pm Mon-Fri; 12-5 pm Sat-Sun.
Points of interest: BBQ, spectacular views of mountains and forest
Retail distribution: Fesq Dorado, Victoria, NSW, Qld, WA; Porter & Co, SA; David Johnstone, Tasmania

of Salinger and some of the other special limited releases, including the marvellous Show Sparkling Burgundies. The wine is then disgorged (that is dead yeast or lees removed) using the transfer method for some products and the traditional method (i.e. methode champenoise) for more premium styles. The new complex at Great Western can process a total of 20 million-plus bottles, a volume that, going by current sales figures, is necessary to meet popular demand. The winemaking at Seppelt is in the capable hands of Ian McKenzie and his team, both for sparkling, still whites and reds. The recently released Seppelt Victorian Portfolio wines with their distinctive classy labels have been a big success - the 1991 Harpers Range Red,

in fact, won the Jimmy Watson Memorial Trophy for best first year red wine in 1992.

The background of many of the early settlers in the region, including Hans Irvine, was French, which I am sure had much to do with the sparkling wine focus. The cool climate is ideal, both for the special kind of viticulture needed for sparkling wine grapes and the making and ageing of the wines.

Over the years, Seppelt Great Western, as well as enjoying a fine reputation for both sparkling wines and still table wines, has been blessed with some extraordinary winemakers. Skilled and talented, these men of vision have greatly contributed to the Australian wine scene. The heritage left by

Joseph Best from the early days of the 1860's, through to Hans Irvine and Seppelt's first manager, Reginald Mowatt, paved the way for the great Colin Preece who, having taken over from Reginald Mowatt in 1932, gave Australia such classic wines as Moyston Claret, Chalambar Burgundy, Rhymney Chablis and Arawatta Riesling. Colin's enormous talents contributed largely to Great Western's establishment as a major winemaking force and this tradition of excellence is today being continued by a professional team of winemakers who are developing exciting wines that will bring credit to the Australian wine industry.

Yellowglen

What has become one of Australia's most successful wine ventures was originally established in 1971 as a hobby vineyard by Ballarat businessman and gastronome, Ian Home. The Yellowglen Vineyard at Smythesdale, 18 kilometres south-west of Ballarat, was planted with eight hectares of mainly red grape varieties.

When the vines reached maturity, some of the fruit was processed under the supervision of Gary Farr at Bannockburn vineyard, north-east of Geelong. A number of red and white wines were released under the Yellowglen label. The remainder of fruit was made into sparkling wines by the talented Neill Robb.

In 1982 Ian Home went into partnership with Dominique Landragin, previous sparkling winemaker for Seppelt. Born in the Champagne district of France, Dominique trained at Beaune in Burgundy, working for several major champagne houses before leaving for Australia. The two men decided to concentrate their efforts on the creation of a superior range of methode champenoise wines.

Two years later the classic yellow-labelled Yellowglen Brut Non Vintage was released, followed by Australia's first rose methode champenoise, and a brut cremant a year later. Cremant sparkling champagne contains approximately half the gas of other

champagne and spends a longer time on yeast lees, creating a classic 'creamy' style. Such was the success of this range that Yellowglen was able to develop from a small concern to one of Australia's leading premium sparkling wine suppliers in little more than a decade.

Needless to say, when Mildara purchased the company in 1984 it was worth millions. Home and Landragin stayed on for a time, but today this hugely successful business is run by the extremely competent Mildara team. Yellowglen's meteoric rise in the wine industry has proved beyond a doubt that Australians are not only fond of champagne, but are also appreciative of fine quality.

Chateau Remy - Blue Pyrenes Estate

A renaissance in viticultural activity in the Pyrenees region occurred in the early 1960s when the French Cognac giant, Remy Martin, teamed with the Australian wine and spirit merchants, Nathan & Wyeth, to form Chateau Remy.

Sited on the open alluvial soils which had attracted thousands of goldseekers a century before and with access to a permanent unlimited water supply the company had chosen perhaps the best and most versatile cool climate location within Australia to conduct its winemaking activities.

Although the focus of operation in the early years was on brandy production the company quickly realised the potential this vineyard site had for the production of premium table and sparkling wines and quickly the Chateau Remy label established itself as a leading Australian brand of methode champenoise.

During the 1980s the French parent company took total control of the Chateau Remy operations and consolidated its Australian holdings at this prime Avoca site. Change came quickly with massive vineyard expansion, the erection of a totally new winery, the construction of vast underground cellars and the appointment of a new manager/winemaker, Vincent Gere. With outstanding winemaking qualifications, and coming from a French wine family rich in pedigree, Vincent embarked on establishing

a marque that was generic in concept yet was reflective of the characteristics of this unique Pyrenees location. It was to be called Blue Pyrenees Estate.

To meet this Estate appellation, only sections of the vineyard were used where fruit consistently met strict flavour criteria. This fruit was used as the basis for the original 'Blue Pyrenees' - a Bordeaux style red, the Reserve Chardonnay and the exquisite Reserve Brut Methode Tranditionelle which now also appears under this distinctive label.

The Blue Pyrenees Estate range of wines undoubtedly represents the pinnacle of winemaking achievement so far in the evolution of this Estate. Their high quality is a reflection of both the nature of the Estate grown cool climate fruit, and the care and expertise with which it has been handled. The beautifully fresh and delicate, 1991 Reserve Brut '*methode traditionelle*', into which Vincent and his team have blended more than 50 different cuvees of Estate grown pinot noir, chardonnay and pinot meunier, has already established a niche for itself in the quality end of the market.

Chateau Remy/Blue Pyrenees Estate will have more than 200 ha under vine by the end of 1997 and it promises to be one of the most exciting viticultural developments in Australia. Moreover, with its picturesque location, nearby waterfalls and lookout, and extensive garden surroundings, its visitors centre is also destined

to become an increasingly popular visitor and tourist destination.

Vincent Gere

CHATEAU REMY - BLUE PYRENEES ESTATE
Address: Vinoca Road, Avoca Vic. 3467
Direction: On Sunraysia Highway, 66 km from Ballarat
Phone: (054) 65 3202
Fax: (054) 65 3529
Established: 1963
Owner: Remy Martin
Winemaker: Vincent Gere/Kim Hart
Principal varieties grown: Chardonnay, pinot noir, pinot meunier, cabernet sauvignon, cabernet franc, merlot, shiraz, sauvignon blanc, semillon
Ha under vine: 152
Average annual crush: 1,000 tonnes
Average no. cases produced: 72,000

Principal wines & brands	Cellar potential
Blue Pyrenees	
Brut Reserve	3-7 years
Estate Red	8-10 years
Estate Chardonnay	3-7 years
Chateau Remy	
Chardonnay-Pinot N.V.	2-5 years
Fiddlers Creek	
Pinot Noir	2-5 years
Sauvignon Blanc	2-5 years
Chardonnay	2-5 years
Cabernet/Shiraz	5-10 years
Semillon	3-7 years

Public & trade tours: Yes
Cellar door & mail order sales: Yes
Hours open to public: 10 am-5 pm seven days a week
Points of interest: Restaurant on weekends, cooperage museum, underground cellars, petanque club, Remy Martin Portfolio Exhibition, BBQ facilities, art displays, lookout, waterfalls

Redbank

Neill Robb worked at various wineries in South Australia before taking a position as Champagne-maker at Chateau Remy in 1970. In 1973 Neill left Chateau Remy to develop his own vineyard and winery at Redbank, in the Pyrenees region of western Victoria, at the same time consulting on the development of Yellowglen and Bannockburn.

Neill and his wife, Sally, planted eighteen hectares of vines and, using local century-old red bricks, built their steep-gabled winery and colonial-style home. Redbank, named after the small town three kilometres to the north, is a credit to the Robb's, being both elegant and distinctly Australian.

Redbank processes other high quality fruit, brought in from growers around central and western Victoria. It is Neill's policy to process each load of fruit separately. The most well-known Redbank wine from their own grapes is the blend of cabernet sauvignon, shiraz, malbec, merlot and cabernet franc named 'Sally's Paddock.' This is an extremely well-structured red wine, with intense colour, flavour and adequate, but soft, tannins which ages extremely well. Several years ago, Neill and Sally introduced a range of wines under the Redbank 'Long Paddock' label, sourced from cool regions of south-eastern Australia. These wines represent excellent value for money and solve the shortage of saleable wine, often a difficulty for the Robb's and provides a valuable export wine alternative.

REDBANK WINERY

Address: Redbank, Vic. 3478
Direction: 200 km north-west of Melbourne on Sunraysia Highway
Phone: (054) 67 7255
Fax: (054) 67 7248
Established: 1973
Winemaker: Neill Robb
Principal varieties grown: Cabernet sauvignon, shiraz, cabernet franc, malbec, merlot, pinot noir
Ha under vine: 20
Average no. cases produced: 35,000

Principal wines & brands	Cellar potential
Sally's Paddock	10+ years
Hard Hill Cabernet	5-10 years
Pinot Noir	2-5 years
Long Paddock Shiraz	5-10 years
Long Paddock Chardonnay	2-5 years
'Emily' NV Brut	

Public tours: By appointment only
Cellar door & mail order sales: Yes
Hours open to public: 9 am-5 pm Mon-Sat; 10 am-5 pm Sun.
Points of interest: BBQ facilities, picnic areas
Retail distribution: Australia-wide.

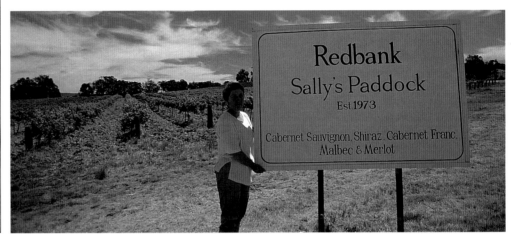

Warrenmang Vineyard Resort

The vineyard was planted in 1974 but it was not until the mid-1980s under the dynamic drive of restaurateurs, Luigi and Athalie Bazzani, that things really began to happen. Warrenmang's Restaurant is now one of Victoria's most celebrated dining locations, set high on a hill, overlooking the vineyards and valleys of the Pyrenees. Rated American Express Best Country Restaurant in 1994/5 and awarded 2 Hats in the Age newspaper Good Food Guide. There is outdoor dining in summer and roaring log fires in winter.

When Luigi created the restaurant in 1989 he knew that guests would find it hard to leave the warm inviting atmosphere and the wonderful surrounds, so he built a little village of cottages and chalets where guests could retire after savouring the pleasures of his table.

Today the Resort has four different styles of accommodation, two bedroom chalets, the romantic Rose Cottage, the six unit Lodge and The Grange with five suites plus a penthouse, all featuring stylish decor, outdoor balconies and private facilities.

Warrenmang also has a separate, fully equipped conference centre for 100 delegates with two tennis courts, swimming pool, an indoor/outdoor heated hot tub in a unique location overlooking the vines and a large barbecue pavilion.

The Warrenmang wines are led by the Grand Pyrenees, a huge opulent red wine but the multi award winning Shiraz has gained much acclaim Australia wide. The late harvest traminer and new 'Bazzani' label wines incuding a vintage port are all popular regional styles. Visitors can enjoy complimentary wine tours and tastings daily with the added bonus for house guests of 20% discount off wine purchases.

WARRENMANG VINEYARD RESORT

Address: Mountain Creek Road, Moonambel, Vic. 3478
Direction: 80 km north-west of Ballarat - just off the Sunraysia Highway
Phone: (054) 67 2233
Fax: (054) 67 2309
Established: 1974
Owner: Luigi & Athalie Bazzani
Winemaker: Roland Kaval
Principal varieties grown: Shiraz, cabernet sauvignon, merlot, cabernet franc, chardonnay traminer, dolcetto
Ha under vine: 12.9
Average no. cases produced: 7,000

Principal wines & brands	Cellar potential
Warrenmang Grand Pyrenees	8-10 years
Warrenmang Estate Shiraz	5-10 years
Warrenmang Late Harvest Traminer	1-5 years
Warrenmang Chardonnay	1-5 years
Bazzani Chard. Chenin Blanc	2-5 years
Bazzani Cab. Shiraz Dolcetto	2-5 years
Bazzani Vintage Port	10+ years

Public & trade tours: Daily or by appointment
Cellar door & mail order sales: Yes
Hours open to public: 9 am-5 pm seven days a week; restaurant - lunch & dinner daily
Points of interest: Luxury chalet style accom. for 85 guests, award winning restaurant (2 hats - Age Good Food Guide, American Express Best Country Restaurant 1994/5) featuring vintage Pyrenees wines, pool, heated spa, tennis courts, Conference Centre, house guests receive 20% disc. off wine purchases.
Retail distribution: Melbourne & Ballarat, most outlets. Direct mail or phone, Sydney & Queensland distribution available late 1995.

An introduction to the Yarra Valley

The history of wine in Australia has an amazing way of repeating itself. Fashions in taste change, economic conditions and the scourges of nature take their toll, but the truly great wines and vineyards that bear them will always re-emerge. Such is the history of the Yarra Valley in Victoria. The district is situated around the towns of Lilydale, Yarra Glen and Healesville with some vineyards in the outer suburbs of Melbourne.

Vines were first planted in the Yarra Valley around 1840 by William Ryrie, a farmer who came south from New South Wales in search of good land. This district, however, blossomed with the Swiss settlers who were encouraged to emigrate to Victoria by Sophie, wife of the first Governor of Victoria, Charles La Trobe. Sophie was the daughter of the Swiss Counsellor of State and was well-connected, mixing in circles which included the brothers Hubert and Paul de Castella, ancestors of our famous marathon runner, Robert de Castella. Hubert founded St. Hubert's Winery in 1854 and another of his countrymen, Baron de Pury, founded Yerinberg in 1862.

These Swiss pioneers were well versed in winemaking and viticulture and had a great influence on the growth and success of the area as a wine producing district. St. Hubert's Winery won the German Emperor's Grand Prize for the Best Australian Wine Exhibitor in the Great Melbourne Exhibition in 1880, for which the grand Exhibition Buildings in Melbourne were built. The prize reflected the ideal wine-growing conditions of the area.

Vineyard areas in the Yarra Valley expanded rapidly and by the late 1860s they covered around 150 hectares. By 1890, Victoria produced almost 60 per cent of Australia's wine - more than all the other states combined.

Unfortunately, around this time, tastes changed and fortified wines became the fashion. The lack of knowledge about bacterial spoilage meant, too, that bad wines abounded, as fortification became the norm. Cool climate, low-yielding areas that produced fine table wines, such as the Yarra Valley, died out and by the early part of the 20th century most vineyards in the Yarra had ceased operating. The last vintage was at Yeringberg in 1921.

It is often thought that the vine louse, phylloxera, was responsible for the demise of the Yarra Valley, but surprisingly it was one of the few areas in Victoria not attacked and decimated by this disease. The re-birth of the Yarra Valley came more than 40 years after

that last vintage in 1921.

There is a certain rivalry between the new pioneers as to who was actually the first in the renaissance. However, I feel the honour should be shared. In 1963, Reg Egan, a Melbourne solicitor, set up residence and started a small vineyard of several hectares in the outer Melbourne suburb of Wantirna South. Now he crushes about 15 tonnes each vintage. Although a little south of the Yarra

region proper, I feel this is rightly classified as a Yarra Valley vineyard. A little north of Wantirna Estate is Kellybrook in the suburb of Wonga Park. Darren Kelly founded his enterprise in 1962 and made both still and sparkling wines from apples grown in his orchard; today the vines vastly outnumber the apple trees.

The true renaissance started in the Yarra Valley in 1968/9 when St. Hubert's Yarra

1991
yarra
cabernet merlot

1993
yarra
chardonnay

1993
yarra
gold

1991
yarra
pinot noir

Yering, Fergussons and Yeringberg all got underway with planting. They were followed closely by Chateau Yarrinya (now De Bortoli's) and Seville Estate in 1971 and more lately by Yarra Burn and Warramate in 1976. Many other ventures have been successfully launched since. Chief among them is Domaine Chandon, the offshoot of the French Möet and Chandon champagne company.

Wine tourism has gripped the Yarra, the annual Grape Grazing in March sees this at its zenith with wine, food and music pumping out. Many excellent restaurants and cellar door hospitality areas each week attract thousands of keen wine drinkers, from all corners of the world. The Yarra Valley is once again a wine mecca.

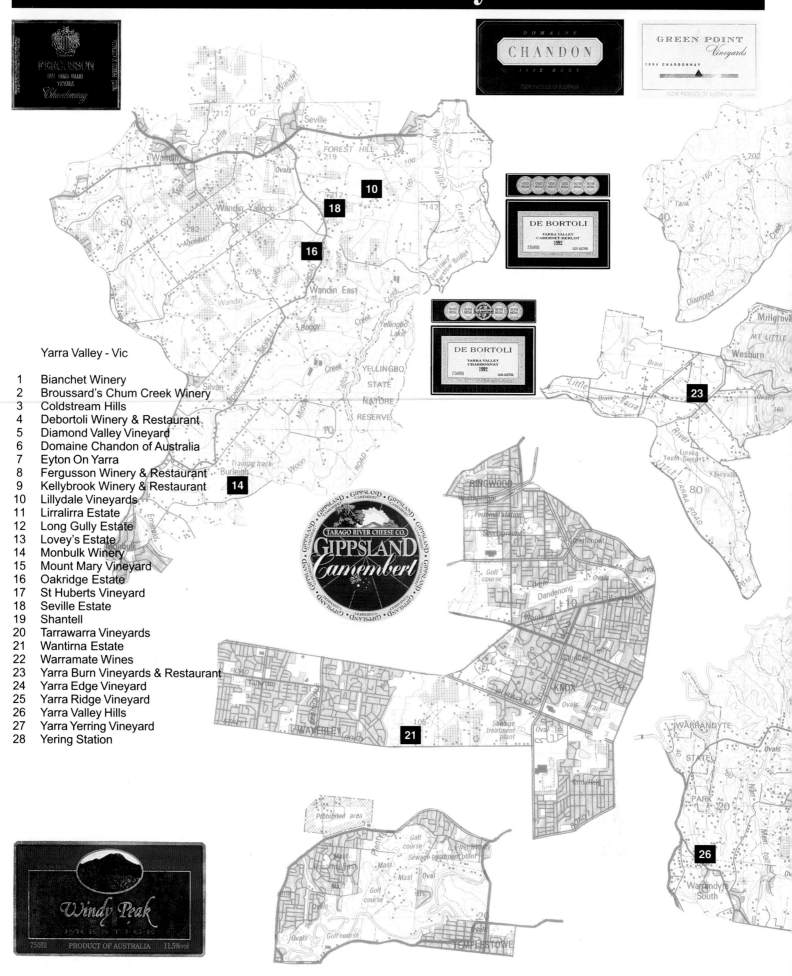

Yarra Valley - Vic

1   Bianchet Winery
2   Broussard's Chum Creek Winery
3   Coldstream Hills
4   Debortoli Winery & Restaurant
5   Diamond Valley Vineyard
6   Domaine Chandon of Australia
7   Eyton On Yarra
8   Fergusson Winery & Restaurant
9   Kellybrook Winery & Restaurant
10 Lillydale Vineyards
11 Lirralirra Estate
12 Long Gully Estate
13 Lovey's Estate
14 Monbulk Winery
15 Mount Mary Vineyard
16 Oakridge Estate
17 St Huberts Vineyard
18 Seville Estate
19 Shantell
20 Tarrawarra Vineyards
21 Wantirna Estate
22 Warramate Wines
23 Yarra Burn Vineyards & Restaurant
24 Yarra Edge Vineyard
25 Yarra Ridge Vineyard
26 Yarra Valley Hills
27 Yarra Yerring Vineyard
28 Yering Station

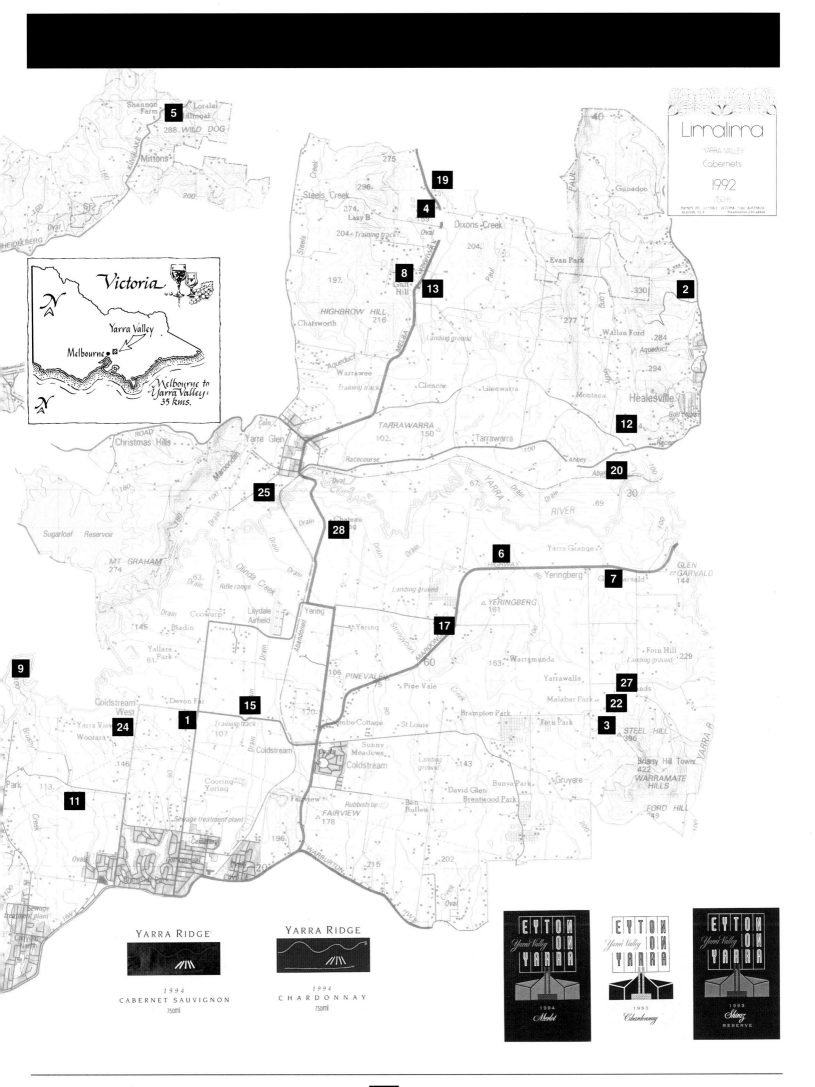

YARRA RIDGE

1994
CABERNET SAUVIGNON
750ml

YARRA RIDGE

1994
CHARDONNAY
750ml

De Bortoli - Yarra Valley

One of the largest and most successful family wine businesses in Australia is De Bortoli. It has risen from virtual obscurity to a prominent respected position in the premium wine industry in less than a decade.

The company's foundation goes back to 1928, four years after Vittorio De Bortoli arrived in the Riverina area of New South

Wales from his homeland in northern Italy. Vittorio and his hard working wife, Giuseppina, established a 22 hectare vineyard at Bilbul and eight years later were making 550,000 litres of wine per year. The original vats and winery are now housed inside the giant complex at Bilbul. De Bortoli really arrived on the wine map when winemaking dynamo Darren,

Vittorio's grandson, made a botrytised semillon sauternes-style dessert wine in 1982. It took the wine world by storm, becoming one of the most awarded wines in Australia's history. The 'Noble One' is a sensational wine each year. After a long search for a contrasting cool climate vineyard and winery, the family purchased Miller's Chateau Yarrinya vineyard and

winemaking is in the capable hands of Steve Webber, who worked for a time at Rouge Homme in Coonawarra. Steve is married to chief executive Deen De Bortoli's daughter Leanne, who runs the showpiece restaurant and hospitality centre on the hill above the winery. The restaurant is large and extremely professionally run, with the feel of a Tuscan bistro and very warm and friendly service. The restaurant also enjoys sweeping panoramic views over the vineyards and the mountain ranges in the distance.

The first crush in 1987 was only 30 tonnes; in 1995 this was elevated to 1,500 tonnes and future growth is planned. The winery produces three ranges of wine. The domain-grown De Bortoli Yarra Valley wines with classic, elegant, yet solid labels, feature a chardonnay, pinot noir, shiraz, cabernet sauvignon and cabernet merlot. The Windy Peak range is a Victorian selection from vineyards around the state and includes a methode champenoise made from pinot noir, labelled 'Prestige'. The third range is 'Montage', where the wines are built from components from the south-eastern winegrowing regions of Australia; its colourful, artistic label is itself a montage.

De Bortoli is a well-founded, professional family business which does credit to the Yarra Valley and demands a visit.

turreted winery in 1987. Although not large, Chateau Yarrinya had leapt into prominence by winning a Jimmy Watson Memorial Trophy.

The vineyards have been dramatically expanded by De Bortoli, as has the winery which is partially underground. A separate winery building was constructed in 1995 and the vineyard expansion continues. The

---

DE BORTOLI YARRA VALLEY

Address: Pinnacle Lane, Dixons Creek, Vic 3775
Phone: (059) 65 221
Fax: (059) 65 2464
Established: 1987
Owner: De Bortoli family
Winemaker: Stephen Webber/David Slingsby-Smith
Principal varieties grown: Cabernet sauvignon, shiraz, pinot noir, cabernet franc, merlot, chardonnay, riesling, sauvignon blanc, semillon, traminer
Ha under vine: 100
Average annual crush: 1,200 tonnes
Average no. cases produced: 70,000

Principal wines & brands	Cellar potential
Yarra Valley	
Cabernet Sauvignon	5-15 years
Shiraz	5-10 years
Pinot Noir	5-10 years
Cabernet Merlot	5-10 years
Chardonnay	2-5 years
Windy Peak	
Prestige (Sparkling)	1-3 years
Chardonnay	2-5 years
Rhine Riesling	2-5 years
Cabernet Sauvignon Merlot	5-10 years
Pinot Noir	5-10 years

Public & trade tours: By appointment only
Cellar door & mail order sales: Yes
Hours open to public: 10 am-5 pm daily.
Points of interest: Restaurant overlooking vineyard, featuring northern Italian inspired cuisine.
Retail distribution: Available through most fine wine outlets.

Domaine Chandon

The world's largest champagne house, Moët et Chandon, is no stranger to the New World of wine. It set up a superb champagne cellar and restaurant complex in the Napa Valley back in 1973 and has made forays into other countries.

John Wright, who was president of the Californian operation and involved in its establishment, came to Australia several times in the early 1980s. He was accompanied on some visits by the charming French winemaker, Edmund Maudiere, who bears an uncanny resemblance to the great monk, Dom Perignon himself, who discovered the champagne making process back in the early 1600s quite by accident.

Careful perfectionists in all they do, Moët chose top flight oenologist Dr. Tony Jordan to head up its Australian venture. Tony, at the time, was running the renowned oenological consultancy service Oenotec. As soon as the sites in the Yarra Valley was chosen, vines were planted, but Tony had already made sparkling wine base material in 1986 at wineries using Oenotec Services, such as Mitchelton and Katnook. The resulting sparkling wines were already lying on tirage at Seppelts Great Western, as the contract for the Yarra Valley property was being signed - forethought and planning are a big part of champagne making.

The beautiful buildings housing the winery, sparkling wine tirage cellars and the stunning tasting and hospitality area were completed in December 1990. The first wine, a 1986, was released to celebrate the occasion and to start the necessary cash flow. Moët at first saw only the local market as of interest and planned a total production of 50,000 cases.

Export (under the Green Point Vineyards label) is mainly to Europe and now accounts for 25 per cent of the production and 70,000 cases is not far away. I am sure the future will see even bigger production.

Even in the days of modern machinery and technology, methode champenoise production is an art form, a mosaic bringing together an enormous number of pieces like a giant jigsaw, which takes time and a great deal of human skill and effort. Apart from its own extensive Yarra Valley and Strathbogie Ranges vineyards, Domaine Chandon has a network of growers under contract, mainly in the cool regions of southern Victoria and also sources grapes from as far away as Hobart - Tasmania and Fonty's Farm Vineyard near Pemberton in south-west Western Australia.

The base wines are all made separately, then comes the assemblage, pulling the base wines together to form the cuvees for the secondary fermentation. For this exacting task, an absolutely tranquil environment is needed. The architects (Allen Jack & Cottier of Sydney) designed this assemblage room in a tower above the winery, absolutely isolated, where the winemaking team Tony Jordan, Wayne Donaldson, Maryann Egan, Kelly Healey and Richard Geoffroy (oenologist from Moet et Chandon) can concentrate 100 per cent on their work to find the perfect matches for the master cuvee for each of the various Domaine Chandon blends.

Needless to say, the finished product celebrates the skill and experience of centuries of champagne-making, combined with the innovation and skill of our Australian winemakers, not forgetting the great grapes that form the base of it all.

When you visit Domaine Chandon, you can sit in the vaulted tasting area with its world class view over the vineyards and mountains, and for a small fee, enjoy a crystal flute of any of the Domaine Chandon range with a delicious gourmet platter. What better way to celebrate a visit to the Yarra Valley?

Green Point

reen Point is the name of the Moet et Chandon property Domaine Chandon in the heart of the Yarra Valley, only 50 minutes drive south east from the centre of Melbourne. Planning of the 40 hectare vineyard began in 1987 and the vineyard is now a picture of ordered manicured vines forming a mosaic of colour and texture over the rolling hills that typify the valley.

Aside from making sparkling wines of world class quality and international repute, Domaine Chandon make a range of table wines under the Green Point Vineyards label which includes two chardonnays, one a powerful complex style, the other a crystal clean style that is very much made in the French Chablis style.

The Green Point name also carries over to the magnificent tasting and high-ceilinged hospitality room. The full-length windows frame a spectacular view over the vines, the winery lake and the mountains with their deep blue hues giving a regal solidarity to the whole scene. A sunset in autumn with the full moon rising into the rosy sky is a memory Milan and I will never forget. Green Point is a truly magic place that lifts Australian wine to another dimension.

Make your way to Moet's Australian gem and take in one of the many art, music and fun happenings it is becoming famous for.

Eyton on Yarra

The Eyton on Yarra Winery and Restaurant is situated on Maroondah Highway, Coldstream in the Yarra Valley.

The winery, cellar door, restaurant and surrounding acres of vines are the realisation of the vision of Yarra Valley grazier, Mr Newell Cowan and is considered one of the premier winery and restaurant complexes in the country.

The winery takes its name from Mr Cowna's "Eyton on Yarra" property, which was originally established by the Syme family - of publishing fame - in the 1800s when land was first taken up in the Yarra Valley. Mr Cowan purchased the property in 1977, initially for cattle and general grazing.

In the late 1980s he saw an opportunity to plant vines on the land, and, not a man to do things by halves, subsequently acquired the nearby Coldstream Winery. At this point, shortly after his 80th birthday, he decided to take the grape growing process one step further and produce the wine as well.

It is on the original Eyton property that most of the grapes are grown for the Eyton on Yarra wines. Grapes from 120 acres of vines grown on the two properties go to make the stylish Eyton on Yarra wines.

The Eyton on Yarra wines are produced from premium fruit grown on the property with the unique and distinctive regional fruit character of the Yarra Valley. They comprise a pinot chardonnay methode champenoise, a chardonnay, a cabernet merlot, a reserve shiraz, a sauvignon blanc and pinot noir.

The Eyton on Yarra Winery and Restaurant is a visitor-oriented winery offering fine food and premium wines in a relaxed and inviting environment. A spiral staircase rises from the centre of the open plan restaurant to a platform giving viewing access over the working winery and Eyton tower which provides magnificent views across the vineyards and the Yarra Valley.

Newell Cowan's vision for the future of Eyton on Yarra is to create quality wine and surroundings in which wine and food can be enjoyed. At 83 years of age, he can stand back and look on, happy in the knowledge that his vision has been realised.

It is an absolute must to visit this Rolls Royce winery. The no expenses spared wines are also top class. Newell's daughter Deidre is equally as energetic and hard working. The sky is obviously the limit for this well thought out winery, adding yet another fine dimension to this exciting wine region.

EYTON ON YARRA

Address: Lot 7 Maroondah Highway, Coldstream, Vic 3770
Direction: Corner of Maroondah Highway & Hill Road, Coldstream, Vic 3770
Phone: (059) 62 2119
Fax: (059) 62 5319
Established: 1993
Winemaker: Justin McNamee
Principal varieties grown: Sauvignon blanc, chardonnay, cabernet sauvignon, merlot, pinot, shiraz
Ha under vine: 47
Average annual crush: 400 tonnes

Principal wines & brands	Cellar potential
Chardonnay	2-5 years
Cabernet/Merlot	5-10 years
Merlot	5-10 years
Shiraz	5-10 years
Pinot/Chardonnay Sparkling	5-10 years

Cellar door & mail order sales: Yes
Hours open to public: 10.30 am-4.30 pm seven days a week
Points of interest: Restaurant - specialising in dishes made from local produce
Retail distribution: Rutherglen Wine & Spirits Co, Melbourne.

Fergusson Winery

Peter Fergusson planted vines on his property near Yarra Glen in 1968. The business has since become one of the most popular wineries in the Yarra Valley, with much to offer the visitor.

Fergusson is owned and managed by Peter Fergusson and his wife Louise. The excellent restaurant is housed in an attractive colonial-style building and features innovative country cuisine devised and prepared by Louise, a gold medallist at the Culinary Olympics and a graduate of La Varenne in Paris. In fact, she has just released a superb cook book "The Beginning & End of Cooking" featuring Yarra Valley cuisine and wines of the region which is available in the winery's Australiana shop and selected local wineries and book shops. Fergusson's menu includes fresh home-grown herbs and vegetables, local yabbies, mountain trout and farm cheeses which are made by Louise. The Fergusson's had a disastrous fire some years ago, and the entire restaurant area was destroyed only to be immediately rebuilt bigger and better. The hard work involved in establishing this award-winning tourist attraction has been carried over into the vineyard and winery.

The vineyard was initially planted to a

majority of red grape varieties but expanded to include chardonnay and sauvignon blanc. Fergusson's have both a black label Estate range and the more affordable Tartan range plus a unique product called 'Winter Warmer'. Peter's training as an industrial chemist has helped him to be an innovative and successful winemaker.

During the months from November to May hot air balloon rides leave the winery in the early morning. The Fergusson Restaurant is constructed with solid native timbers. The antique spit in the huge fireplace does not remain idle and Peter Fergusson is a deft hand with the carving knife. The cathedral ceilings and refectory furniture add atmosphere to the many functions held at the winery and entertainment is often at hand.

You can also stay overnight in the charming 'Cabernet Cottage'.

FERGUSSON WINERY
Address: Wills Road, Yarra Glen, Vic 3775
Direction: Wills Road, Yarra Glen Vic 3775
Phone: (059) 65 2237
Fax: (059) 65 2405
Established: 1968
Owner: Fergusson Family
Winemaker: Chris Keyes
Principal varieties grown: Chardonnay, shiraz, cabernet sauvignon, cabernet franc, merlot, pinot noir, sauvignon blanc
Ha under vine: 10
Average annual crush: 65 tonnes
Average no. cases produced: 5,000

Principal wines & brands	Cellar potential
Victoria Chardonnay	2-5 years
Jeremy Shiraz	5-10 years
Benjamyn Cabernet Sauvignon	5-10 years
Tartan Chardonnay	2-5 years
Tartan Sauvignon Blanc	2-5 years
Tartan Shiraz	5-10 years
Winter Warmer	0-1 years

Public & trade tours: By appointment only
Cellar door sales: Yes
Hours open to public: 11 am-5 pm seven days a week
Points of interest: Restaurant - daily, Australiana Shop, overnight accommodation, hot air ballooning
Retail distribution: Westwood Wine Agencies, Victoria only; export, UK & New Zealand.

Lirralirra Estate

Lirralirra is an aboriginal word for 'small bird.' The name was chosen by Alan Smith and his wife for their idyllic property near Lilydale, after the blue wrens that made their home in the garden-like setting of the vineyard.

That was back in 1981. The conditions appeared to be ideal for producing a top class botrytised wine akin to the great French sauternes. With this in mind, Alan planted 2.1 hectares of classic sauterne varieties - semillon, sauvignon blanc and muscadelle. Unfortunately the botrytis usually comes a little late in May and the risk of rot in the grapes was high. Alan decided to make dry white wines with the semillon and sauvignon blanc, while most of the muscadelle have been grafted over to the bordeaux red varieties of cabernet sauvignon, cabernet franc and merlot. Four-fifths of a hectare of pinot noir were added later.

The vines of Lirralirra average some 80 metres above sea level and are planted on north-east facing slopes. Alan's wines have been consistent winners at the Lilydale show. The sauvignon blanc is deliciously fruit driven, while the semillon is fresh and fruity when young it develops magnificently in the bottle. Lirralirra's pinot noir emulates well

the silky Burgundian mouth feel. The Bordeaux style red is 75 per cent cabernet sauvignon with the added complexity of merlot and cabernet franc.

Production of Lirralirra wines is restricted to 400-500 cases and they are available only from the cellar door, through the mailing list

or at selected restaurants in the Yarra Valley. The cellar door is open on weekends and public holidays and every day during January. But Alan and Jocelyn are usually on the property at other times and assure me they welcome visitors by chance!

LIRRALIRRA ESTATE
Address: Paynes Road, Chirnside Park, Vic 3116
Direction: North into Edward Road at Chirnside Park ShoppingCentre then west into Paynes road
Phone: (03) 9735 0224
Established: 1981
Owner: A.G. & J.M. Smith
Winemaker: Alan Smith
Principal varieties grown: Pinot noir, semillon, sauvignon blanc, cabernet sauvignon cabernet franc, Merlot
Ha under vine: 2.2
Average no. cases produced: 500

Principal wines & brands	Cellar potential
Cabernet	2-5 years
Pinot Noir	5-10 years
Semillon (Wooded)	2-5 years
Semillon	2-5 years
Sauvignon Blanc	2-5 years

Public tours: Yes
Cellar door & mail order sales: Yes
Hours open to public: 10 am-6 pm w/e and PH or by chance
Points of interest: Small hands-on operation
Retail distribution: Cellar door only

Lillydale Vineyards

Alex White was in the second wave of vinous pioneers when he started planting his Lillydale Vineyard in the southern part of the Yarra Valley, just off the Warburton Highway at Seville. The soil in this part of the valley is a rich red colour, formed by ancient volcanic action. Pinot noir and chardonnay seem to thrive in a cool climate and this soil type.

The first white wines from Alex, a trained chemist, really made an impact in the early 1980s. An aromatic spicy gewurztraminer and a floral intense riesling became eagerly sought after. This was followed by a classic chardonnay of the finer-boned structure -melons and tropical fruit with a subtle almond nuttiness and a vanilla bean character, enhanced by judicious ageing in French oak. The pinot noir and the cabernet sauvignon with a touch of merlot were equally as impressive.

The quality and style of Lillydale's wines and its beautiful outlook on the Warburton Ranges did not escape the notice of the McWilliam's family wine company, anxious to expand into premium cool regions. In 1994 McWilliam's bought Lillydale Vineyards. Alex White has

stayed on for a period as consultant winemaker working with Max McWilliam and the Lillydale wines are, if it is possible, getting even better with the maturing vineyards and the capital input of McWilliam's. The latest sauvignon blanc is a stunner and Lillydale also makes an outstanding botrytised noble riesling.

When on your travels through the Yarra, you must drop in and try these exciting wines.

Long Gully Estate

Reiner Klapp had an extremely successful electronics business. When colour television first came to the Australian market in the early 1970s, Reiner was at the forefront with the top selling German Brands, then the market leaders.

At the same time he bought a beautiful property in the Yarra Valley near Healesville at the apex of 'Long Gully', which runs between the Warburton Ranges and a smaller range of hills which divides it off from the main part of the Yarra Valley. Reiner and his delightful wife Irma, built a lovely weekend home in amongst a grove of trees. They run a few horses and hereford cattle, but Reiner is not an idle person and he had heard of the vineyard revolution that was sweeping the valley, so it wasn't long before he planted vines.

The first vintage was in 1982 with a riesling. Today Long Gully Estate is like a well-oiled German motor car. The vineyards are lush with substantial vines, but neatly trimmed. The winery is spotless, even during vintage, and a pretty German-Alsatian Cottage forms an ideal tasting and entertaining area.

Long Gully Estate has been extremely successful in international wine shows. In 1993 they pulled off an incredible 'Coup' at Intervin, the New York/Toronto massive wine show held annually. The Long Gully Estate wines entered, were their 1990 Merlot and 1990 Cabernet Sauvignon. The 12,000 entries were fined down to 800 odd finalists. After rewarding several hundred gold, silver and bronze medals, five only trophies were issued. From this world's best selection, Long Gully Estate won two of the five, an incredible achievement!

Long Gully Estate make extremely good whites, including a chardonnay, semillon and a sauvignon blanc. Some years a sauvignon blanc/semillon blend is also made. The reds include an award-winning pinot noir, shiraz, merlot and cabernet sauvignon. All the wines have very refined, almost European characters to them. The tannins in the reds are very fine.

Long Gully Estate is a class winery that is well worth seeking out. Look out for the newly released Irma's Cabernet, which has received five gold medal – it's great.

Mount Mary Vineyard

MOUNT MARY VINEYARD
Address: Coldstream West Road, Lilydale Vic.
3140, PO Box 626, Lilydale Vic 3140
Phone: (03) 9 739 1761
Fax: (03) 9 739 0137
Established: 1971
Winemaker: John Middleton/Mario Marson/Peter
Draper
Principal varieties grown: Chardonnay,
sauvignon blanc, semillon, muscadelle, pinot noir,
cabernet sauvignon, cabernet franc, merlot,
malbec, petit verdot
Ha under vine: 12
Average annual crush: 40-45 tonnes
Average no. cases produced: 3,000

Principal wines & brands	Cellar potential
Quintet, Red Blend	Up to 20 years
Triolet, White Blend	Up to 15 years
Chardonnay	Up to 15 years
Pinot Noir	Up to 20 years

Mail order sales: Yes
Retail distribution: Various shops, restaurants,
free mailing list.

An early pioneer in the Yarra Valley was Lilydale doctor John Middleton. On leave from the Royal Australian Air Force during the Second World War, he met great Australian winemaker Colin Preece of Great Western. It became a lifelong friendship.

With Colin's inspiration, John and his wife Marli planted a small vineyard in the Yarra Valley in 1957, the first vineyard in the region since the 1920s. In 1971, they purchased 71 hectares which now includes their vineyards, winery and home. John's is a first-class operation, hand-crafting wines allocated once a year to eagerly waiting mailing list customers. Mount Mary pioneered the term 'cabernets', used for the cabernet sauvignon, merlot, malbec, cabernet franc and petit verdot blend from the vineyard. Mount Mary also make a sauvignon blanc/semillon/ muscadelle blend, another Bordeaux classic. The chardonnay and pinot noir are also top class.

Seville Estate

Seville Estate was one of the earliest vineyards to be established during the viticultural rebirth of the Yarra Valley. Owned and operated by Peter and Margaret McMahon, planting began in 1972 on a beautiful ridge of old volcanic soils overlooking the Upper Yarra Valley. The compact high-tech vineyard of 4.1 hectares is planted with cabernet sauvignon, cabernet franc, merlot, pinot noir, chardonnay and the renowned shiraz..

SEVILLE ESTATE
Address: Linwood Road, Seville, Vic. 3139
Phone: (059) 64 4556
Fax: (059) 64 3585
Established: 1972
Owner: P.G. & M.L. McMahon
Winemaker: Peter McMahon and Alastair Butt
Viticulturalist: Alastair Butt
Principal varieties grown: Cabernet sauvignon,
cabernet franc, merlot, pinot noir, shiraz,
chardonnay
Ha under vine: 4.1
Average annual crush: 24 tonnes
Average no. cases produced: 1,500

Principal wines & brands	Cellar potential
Seville Estate	
Cabernet	5-10 years
Pinot Noir	5-10 years
Shiraz	5-10 years
Chardonnay	2-5 years

Mail order sales: Yes
Hours open to public: Last weekend November;
first weekend December
Retail distribution: Select Vineyards, 56 Clarke
Street, South Melbourne, Victoria. Various shops
and restaurants.

Peter also pioneered botrytis affected rieslings with spectacular results, producing some of Australia's most luscious "stickies".

The empasis at Seville Estate is on fruit character. The wines are not over extracted or commercially structured, but reflect the rich variety of fruit flavours which the Seville "terroir" can produce. In recent years the peppery shiraz has proved most successful, winning numerous show awards and trophies.

Careful cellaring of the cabernets will be rewarded with a rich, elegant, and valuable wine. The chardonnay is a lively food wine showing integrated melon, citrus and oak characters. It develops beautifully with age into honeyed richness. Pinot noir has the spice and mouthfeel of the top burgundies and shows the variety's suitablity to Seville soils.

The wines of Seville Estate are serious contenders in the Australian Industry, taking pride of place on tables and in cellars throughout the country.

Yarra Ridge

Recently Yarra Ridge was acquired by the astute Mildara Blass Company. This winery has had a meteoric rise to fame since its inception in 1988 by Louis Bialkower, a founding partner of the Melbourne firm Clayton-Utz, who for a number of years worked side by side with celebrated wine writer and fellow Yarra Valley vigneron James Halliday.

In 1982 Louis purchased land in the Yarra Valley in the foothills of the Christmas Hills, often referred to as the 'Yarra Ridge'. In the following year he planted five hectares to cabernet sauvignon, pinot noir and chardonnay and with further plantings the area had grown to 20 hectares by 1994. New varieties included merlot, cabernet franc and sauvignon blanc. In 1993, Lois entered a joint venture arrangement with Mildara Wines which has seen even more dynamic growth in Yarra Ridge sales and a huge amount of capital growth starting in the vineyard.

Yarra Ridge purchased 40 hectares of land near the Yarra Glen Racecourse in 1994 which by 1995 has been entirely planted. A huge dam has been constructed to aid in the establishment of this substantial vineyard. The soils on all the Yarra Valley vineyards are the grey alluvial podsolic loams so eagerly sought after by 19th century vignerons such as Hubert-Francois de Costello.

Winemaking is in the hands of affable giant winemaker Rob Dolan, a former league

Louis Bialkower

with a beautiful leafy cassis and black currant-styled cabernet sauvignon with a touch of merlot and cabernet franc, very reminiscent of the best of Bordeaux. The Bordeaux theme continues with the botrytis semillon with lemon, honey and apricot lusciousness.

The elevated tasting and hospitality area is in an elevated position and has panoramic views over the valley. Yarra Ridge's enviable show record of 14 trophies and more than 200 medals in Australian wine shows in only six years of exhibiting has been well earned. Why not treat yourself to a taste of Yarra Ridge and discover the exciting flavours that have given this winery such an outstanding name?

YARRA RIDGE VINEYARD
Address: Glenview Road, Yarra Glen Vic. 3775
Phone: (03) 730 1022
Fax: (03) 730 1131
Established: 1988
Owner: Mildara Blass
Winemaker: Rob Dolan
Principal varieties grown: Chardonnay, sauvignon blanc, pinot noir, cabernet sauvignon, merlot, shiraz, botrytis semillon
Ha under vine: 50
Average annual crush: 1,000 tonnes
Average no. cases produced: 65,000

Principal wines & brands	Cellar potential
Yarra Ridge	
Chardonnay	2-10 years
Sauvignon Blanc	2-5 years
Pinot Noir	2-5 years
Cabernet Sauvignon	5-10 years
Botrytis Semillon	2-5 years
Merlot	2-5 years
Reserve Shiraz	5-10 years
Reserve Pinot Noir	5-10 years

Public & trade tours: By appointment only
Cellar door & mail order sales: Yes
Hours open to public: 10 am-5 pm Mon-Fri; 10 am-5.30 pm w/e and PH

---

footballer whose winemaking career began at Rouge Homme in 1991/82 under the winemaking legend John Vickery. When we visited, Rob was preparing 1,600 imported oak barriques ready for vintage.

The owners of Yarra Ridge believe strongly that quality improvements will come from the vineyard and have invested heavily in modern viticultural techniques such as the 'Scott Henry', 'Te Kauwhata two tier', the 'Geneva Double Curtain' and 'U' System trellises aimed at extra fruit and leaf exposure and keeping an air flow through the vines.

The Yarra Ridge Chardonnay has had unparalleled success on the Australian circuit. Up until the 1993 vintage, the 1989, 90, 91, 92 and 93 had all won not only gold medals, but trophies as the best chardonnay in the shows. I am sure this success will continue. The Yarra Ridge Sauvignon Blanc, with its lifted herbal and gooseberry aromas and flavours, has quickly become a market leader, as has the spicy pinot noir with its plum and cherry fruit flavours. The range is rounded off

Tarrawarra Vineyard

Tarrawarra Vineyard is one of Australia's most picturesque wine Estate's. One enters via a tree lined circular driveway mounting the steep knoll on which a winery of distinctive modern lines is located, above lawns and vines running down to a lake.

Owner Marc Besen established Tarrawarra Vineyard in 1983 with the vision of creating world class pinot noir and chardonnays. The Vineyard's reputation for wines of classic magnitude was established beyond doubt when the 1991 Tarrawarra Pinot Noir won Best Dry Red in the Open Classes at the 1993 Royal Melbourne Wine Show - an unprecedented success for a pinot noir. The chardonnay is also in the rich, complex mould, with state-of-the-art equipment in the winery and top class oak being used innovatively and to perfection.

The fact that Tarrawarra concentrates solely on these two classic Burgundian varieties contributes to their success in producing benchmark examples of Yarra Valley pinot noir and chardonnay - rated amongst the finest wines in Australia.

TARRAWARRA VINEYARD
Address: Healesville-Yarra Glen Road, Yarra Glen, Vic. 3775
Phone: (059) 62 3311
Fax: (059) 62 3887
Established: 1983
Owner: Marc Besen
Winemakers: Michael Kluczko/Alex Kahl
Principal varieties grown: Chardonnay, pinot noir,
Ha under vine: 11
Average annual crush: 150 tonnes
Average no. cases produced: 10,500

Principal wines & brands	Cellar potential
Tarrawarra	
Chardonnay	2-5 years
Pinot Noir	5-10 years
Tunnel Hill	
Chardonnay	2-5 years
Pinot Noir	5-10 years

Public & trade tours: By appointment only
Cellar door & mail order sales: Yes
Hours open to public: 10.30 am-4.30 pm Mon-Fri
Retail distribution: The Wine Co, Victoria, NSW.

An introduction to Western Australia

The first settlers of the new colony of Western Australia arrived in 1829 on the ship Parmelia, five years before the settlement of Victoria and South Australia.

Even before the official settlement of Perth, vine cuttings were planted near Fremantle and on Garden Island, but none survived. It was Charles McFaull who planted 300 cuttings at Hamilton Hill and became the state's first successful viticulturist.

In 1834, George Fletcher Moore planted the first vines in the Swan Valley, cuttings obtained from the Cape of Good Hope in South Africa. The oldest winery in Australia, Olive Farm, just near Perth's airport, was established in 1830 and is still going strong today. Olive Farm's founder, Thomas Waters, became the first person to commercially market wine in Western Australia, but was closely followed by fellow Parmelia passenger, John Septimus Roe, the colony's first surveyor general, who founded Sandalford wines in 1840.

Many other areas of the south-west corner of the state were planted with vines in those early years, but commercially only the Swan Valley survived. The Swan Valley industry thrived and by the 1960s Western Australia was second only to South Australia in the number of wineries in the state. It was not, however, until the 1970s when the development boom in the Western Australian wine industry began.

This development was preceded by a report on the viticultural potential of a number of regions in the south west of the state by agricultural scientist, Dr John Gladstones. He highlighted a number of regions with great potential, Margaret River and Mount Barker amongst them.

A new experimental vineyard was planted by the Department of Agriculture at Forest Hill near Mount Barker in 1965. I well remember tasting two red wines made by Jack Mann at Houghton from the vineyard. That was back in 1972, the wines were several years old and Jack was most enthusiastic about the region's potential. They were certainly memorable wines.

Western Australia has seen the greatest growth in wine regions in Australia over the last two decades with six major regions now boasting many vignerons. The Swan Valley has been joined by Margaret River, the Great Southern Region around Mount Barker, the Pemberton/Warren Valley area, the South West Coastal Plains and the Darling Ranges and Perth Hills.

The quality of Western Australian wines and the range of styles is extraordinary and although Western Australia produces less than two per cent of Australian wine production, it accounts for around 20 per cent of the nation's premium bottled wines above $12 per bottle. Houghton is a huge Australian premium producer, but others, including Evans & Tate, Sandalford, Vasse Felix, Leeuwin Estate and Goundrey are significant Australian premium producers.

Wine tourism in Western Australia is a credit to the state, with the Margaret River region having a number of world class winery restaurants and galleries. A wine adventure around Western Australia is a rich experience, indeed. It makes the journey to the West a most worthwhile one.

1 Baldivis Estate
2 Blackwood Crest Wines
3 Capel Vale Wines
4 Killerby Vineyards
5 Leschenault Vineyard
6 Peel Estate
7 Thomas Wines

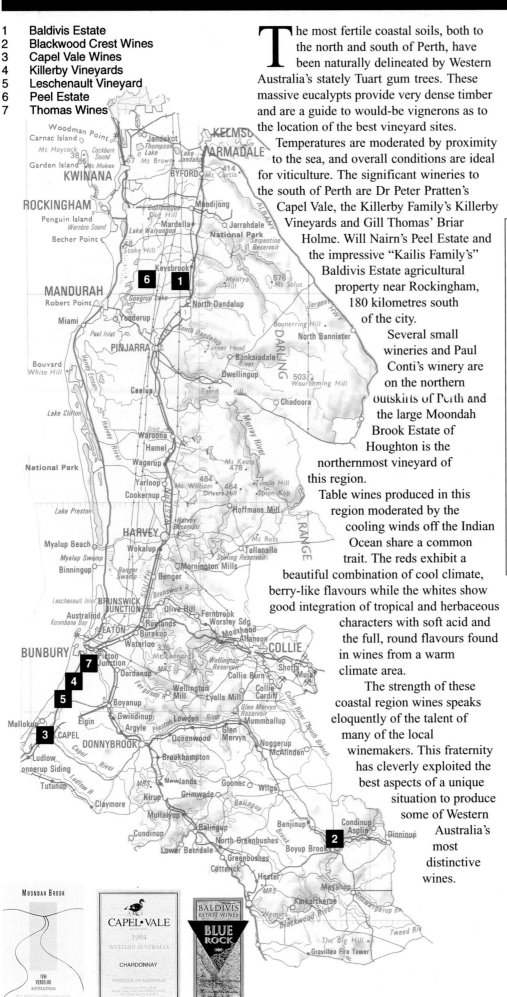

Coastal Plains:
19 kms. north
of Perth, to
220 kms. south.

Western Australia

Coastal Plains

Perth

The most fertile coastal soils, both to the north and south of Perth, have been naturally delineated by Western Australia's stately Tuart gum trees. These massive eucalypts provide very dense timber and are a guide to would-be vignerons as to the location of the best vineyard sites.

Temperatures are moderated by proximity to the sea, and overall conditions are ideal for viticulture. The significant wineries to the south of Perth are Dr Peter Pratten's Capel Vale, the Killerby Family's Killerby Vineyards and Gill Thomas' Briar Holme. Will Nairn's Peel Estate and the impressive "Kailis Family's" Baldivis Estate agricultural property near Rockingham, 180 kilometres south of the city.

Several small wineries and Paul Conti's winery are on the northern outskirts of Perth and the large Moondah Brook Estate of Houghton is the northernmost vineyard of this region.

Table wines produced in this region moderated by the cooling winds off the Indian Ocean share a common trait. The reds exhibit a beautiful combination of cool climate, berry-like flavours while the whites show good integration of tropical and herbaceous characters with soft acid and the full, round flavours found in wines from a warm climate area.

The strength of these coastal region wines speaks eloquently of the talent of many of the local winemakers. This fraternity has cleverly exploited the best aspects of a unique situation to produce some of Western Australia's most distinctive wines.

DARLINGTON ESTATE

Address: Lot 39 Nelson Road, Darlington WA 6070
Phone: (09) 299 6268
Fax: (09) 299 7107
Established: 1983
Owner: Balt & Francesca Van Der Meer
Winemaker: Balt Van Der Meer
Principal varieties grown: Chardonnay, semillon, sauvignon blanc, cabernet sauvignon, shiraz, merlot
Ha under Vine: 7
Average annual crush: 30-40 tonnes
Average no. cases produced: 2,500

Principal wines & brands	Cellar potential
Cabernet Sauvignon	5-10 years
Chardonnay	2-5 years
Semillon/Sauvignon Blanc	2-5 years
Cabernet/Merlot	5-10 years
Shiraz	5-10 years
Blanc De Noir	2-5 years

Public tours: By appointment only
Cellar door & mail order sales: Yes
Hours open to public: 12-5 pm Thurs-Sun
Points of interest: Brasserie style restaurant, functions, weddings
Retail distribution: Cellar door, mail order, liquor stores and restaurants

THE KILLERBY FAMILY'S KILLERBY VINEYARDS

Address: Via Lakes Road, Stratham WA 6230
Direction: via Lakes Road, Stratham
Phone: (097) 95 7222 or 1800 655 722
Fax: (097) 95 7835
Established: 1973
Owner: Elizabeth Killerby
Winemaker: Matt Aldridge & Anna Killerby
Principal varieties grown: Cabernet, shiraz, chardonnay, semillon
Ha under vine: 16
Average annual crush: 100 tonnes
Average no. cases produced: 8,000

Principal wines & brands	Cellar potential
Cabernet Sauvignon	5-10 years
Shiraz	5-10 years
Semillon	2-5 years
Chardonnay	2-5 years
April Classic White	0-2 years
April Classic Red	0-2 years
Vintage Port	

Public & trade tours: By appointment only
Cellar door & mail order sales: Yes
Hours open to public: 10 am-5 pm seven days
Points of interest: Picnic lunch and tours are welcome (by appointment), BBQ & picnic area, Cheeseboards available. Awarded 15 trophies since 1991. Official for the Festival of Perth.
Retail distribution: Perth, Western Australian outlets and NSW and Victoria. Direct mail enquiries welcome.

Baldivis Estate

Some 60 kilometres south of Perth on the coastal plains near Rockingham lies the impressive horticultural estate of the Kailis family, the most important part of which is devoted to the family's favourite pursuit, winemaking.

Peter Kailis has overseen the small family business started by his father George, who sold fresh fish, door to door, growing into Australia's largest seafood business. Not content with this, he has been involved in the establishment of the large food chains, Pizza Hut and Red Rooster. His entrepreneurial flair has spilt over into many other industries, including timber, packaging and construction.

Peter's parents arrived during the First World War from the tiny Greek Island of Kastellorizo, and through hard work set the foundations for their family's future in their adopted land.

The thirsty black-grey soils of the Serpentine River plains gives good drainage and the cooling sea breezes provides an ideal disease-free environment where fruit and varietal flavours shine through. The vineyard's soils are supplemented by an organic cocktail of chicken manure and mulch and are partly irrigated during the summer months.

The Baldivis wines have performed particularly well in local and interstate wine shows and the chardonnay has been placed

in the top 100 wines in the Sydney International Winemakers Competition. Baldivis Wines are also flourishing on the overseas market. The United Kingdom is the largest market for their cabernet merlot and wooded chardonnay. The recently arrived winemaker is Jane Gilham who founded the small Tasmanian vineyard and winery d'Entrecasteaux with her family in 1985. Jane's winemaking experience also includes two years in the Clare Valley in South Australia and four years in France.

On our visit to the family Estate, we were treated to a cornucopic harvest feast in the vineyard with the Kailis family and the estate's management team. Mark Kailis is a trained and extremely competent chef - it was quite a day. I was so impressed with Mark's culinary efforts, producing the simple classic Mediterranean dishes, Italian from his mother's side and Greek from his father's

The estate also has a large entertainment and hospitality area where many functions are held, enjoying of course the fine wine, produce and cuisine of the talented Kailis family. The Baldivis wines all have beautiful clean fresh fruit flavours, and comprise a semillon, a semillon/sauvignon blanc, chardonnay, a fruit-driven cabernet/merlot and an excellent light fruity pinot noir called 'Blue Rock' which can be served chilled in summer in the European tradition. Some of

the wines carry the 'Lake Kathryn' label, named after Peter's mother and daughter. When you are in Perth, why not take a run down to Baldivis to share in its bountiful produce?

BALDIVIS ESTATE

Address: 165 River Road, Baldivis WA 6171
Direction: 60 km south of Perth
Phone: (09) 525 2066
Fax: (09) 52 52411
Established: 1982
Owner: Kailis Consolidated
Winemaker: Jane Gilham
Principal varieties grown: Chardonnay, cabernet merlot, sauvignon blanc, semillon, merlot
Ha under vine: 10
Average annual crush: 100 tonnes
Average no. cases produced: 6,000

Principal wines & brands	Cellar Potential
Chardonnay	2-5 years
Unwooded Chardonnay	2-5 years
Cabernet Merlot	5-10 years
Classic (Sauvignon Blanc Semillon Chardonnay)	2-5 years
Semillon	2-5 years
Blue Rock Pinot/Cabernet	2-5 years

Public & trade tours: By appointment only
Cellar door & mail order sales: Yes
Hours open to public: 10 am-4 pm Mon-Fri; 11 am-5 pm w/e & holidays
Points of interest: Enclosed function area with seating for 150 people; gas barbecues. Catering can be arranged - choice of menus upon request. Cellar door area features estate-grown produce such as avocados, olives and limes, pickles, jams etc.
Retail distribution: National Liquor, WA; Estate Wine Distributors, NSW. Overseas agents and other information on retail available on request.

Moondah Brook

In the late 1960s Houghton managing director Ian Smith began searching for a vineyard site capable of producing grapes for the very successful Houghton White Burgundy, later to become Australia's biggest selling bottled table wine.

Mr. J.M. Clayton, the then co-ordinator of agricultural industries, pointed out a site, ideal because of its soil type and the natural spring on the property supplying the Moondah Brook with water at the rate of three million gallons a day, every day of the year.

The property had formerly been held on option by Penfold Wines under the advice of the late, great winemaker Max Schubert, but Penfold favoured development in the Upper Hunter and let the option drop.

Despite being north of the Swan Valley, its slightly elevated position and the effect of the cooling afternoon sea breezes means its climate is somewhat cooler. The soils are fertile, deep red loams.

Moondah Brook is one of the healthiest and largest vineyards in the state. The vineyard supplied some of Australia's first varietal verdelho, chenin blanc and chardonnay in the mid 1970's. The verdelho with its crisp tropical fruit flavours and silky texture is one of Australia's finest examples of its style.

Today the range consists of verdelho, chenin blanc, chardonnay and cabernet sauvignon. The growth of the verdelho and chenin blanc have been extraordinary especially with the increased interest in Asian cuisine and as an alternative to chardonnay.

Moondah Brook

Address: Dale Road, Middle Swan WA 6056
Phone: (09) 274 5100
Fax: (09) 274 5372Owner: BRL Hardy Wine Company
Winemaker: Paul Lapsley
Principal varieties grown: Verdelho, chenin blanc, chardonnay, cabernet sauvignon

Principal wines & brands/Cellar potential
Moondah Brook

Verdelho	2-5 years
Chenin Blanc	2-5 years
Chardonnay	2-5 years
Cabernet Sauvignon	5-10 years

Public tours: By appointment only
Cellar door & mail order sales: Yes
Hours open to public: 10 am-5 pm seven days
Retail distribution: National

Rob Brown

Perhaps the staggering number of medical practitioners actively involved in the wine industry says something of the beneficial effects of wine in moderation.

Dr. Peter Pratten is a member of this fraternity. In addition to his medical practices he has, with his wife Elizabeth, made the time to establish and manage the Capel Vale Winery and Vineyard.

Capel Vale was founded in 1975 and is located on the banks of the Capel River. Vines produce excellent fruit with high yields. Fruit flavour is maximised by the use of unusual U-shaped trellises which provide excellent leaf and fruit exposure. During the 1980s the Prattens established two other vineyards, one just upstream on the Capel River from their winery and Stirling Estate. They have called this new vineyard Capel Wellington Estate. They also established their Whispering Hill, between Mt. Barker and the Porongurups in the Great Southern Region.

In 1995 a further 40 hectares was planted in the Lefroy Valley, between Manjimup and Pemberton, in the high country of the south of Western Australia.

During the late 1980s Capel Vale made a real coup in securing the talented Rob Bowen, who had been making wines for Plantagenet in the Great Southern. Their excellent range of wines has been joined by a super premium red, 'Baudin.' This classic Bordeaux blend recognises the French explorer Nicholas Baudin, who named Geographe Bay just downstream from the winery.

In 1993 Krister Jonsson joined the team as winemaker. His fine attention to detail and technique combined with Rob Bowen's expertise has added depth and complexity to all the wine styles in the range.

CAPEL VALE

Address: Lot 5, Stirling Estate, Mallokup Road, Capel WA 6271
Direction: 1 km west of Capel Town, 250 km south of Perth
Phone: (097) 271986
Fax: (097) 27 1904
Established: 1974
Owner: Dr P Pratten
Winemaker: Rob Bowen & Krister Jonsson
Principal varieties grown: Chardonnay, riesling, sauvignon blanc, semillon, merlot, shiraz, cabernet sauvignon
Ha under vine: 100

Principal wines & brands	Cellar potential
Capel Vale	
Chardonnay	5-10 years
Riesling	2-5 years
Sauvignon Blanc/Semillon	2-5 years
Shiraz	5-10 years
Merlot	5-10 years
Cabernet Sauvignon	5-10 years
Baudin (Optimal Bordeaux Red)	5-10 years
Frederick (Optimal Chardonnay)	5-10 years
C.V. Classic Red	5-10 years
C.V. Gold Label Chardonnay	2-5 years
C.V. Gold Label Pinot Noir	5-10 years

Trade tours: By appointment only
Cellar door & mail order sales: Yes
Hours open to public: 9 am-4.30 pm seven days a week
Points of interest: Picnics by appointment
Retail distribution: Throughout Australasia, UK, Germany, Holland, Switzerland, Hong Kong, Japan, Taiwan, some USA

PAUL CONTI WINES

Address: 529 Wanneroo Road, Woodvale WA 6026
Phone: (09) 409 9160
Fax: (09) 309 1634
Established: 1958
Owner: Paul A Conti
Winemaker: Paul and Jason Conti
Principal varieties grown: Shiraz, chardonnay, cabernet sauvignon, chenin blanc, sauvignon blanc, muscat alexandria
Ha under vine: 17
Average no. cases produced: 8,000

Principal wines & brands	Cellar potential
Cabernet Sauvignon	10+ years
Hermitage	10+ years
Chardonnay (Wooded)	5-10 years
Chenin Blanc	5-10 years
Sauvignon Blanc	5-10 years
Late Picked Frontignac	2-5 years

Public & trade tours: By appointment only
Cellar door sales: Yes
Hours open to public: 9.30 am-5 pm Mon-Sat
Points of interest: Restaurant
Retail distribution: Perth, W.A, M.G.M; Sydney, Premier Vineyards; Throughouy Australia, UK and Japan

Margaret River

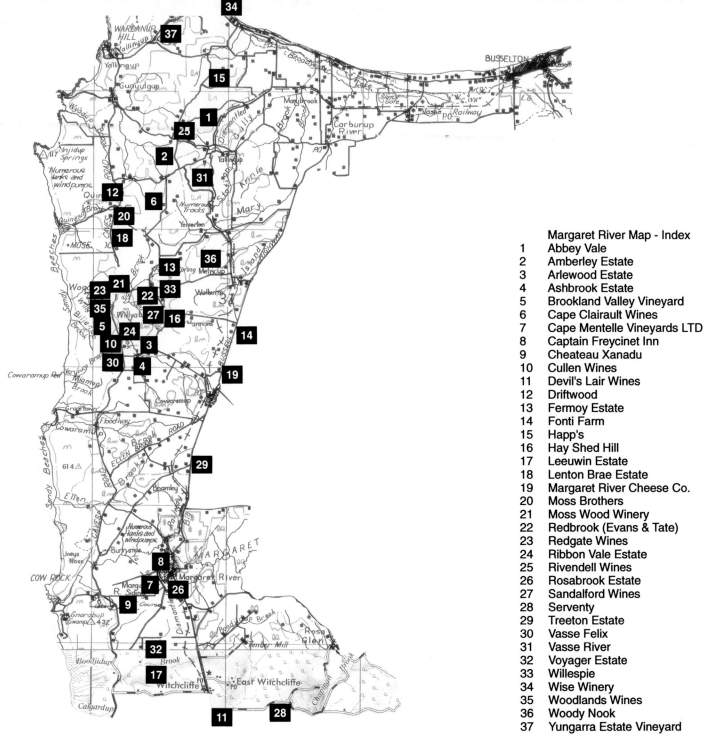

Margaret River Map - Index

1   Abbey Vale
2   Amberley Estate
3   Arlewood Estate
4   Ashbrook Estate
5   Brookland Valley Vineyard
6   Cape Clairault Wines
7   Cape Mentelle Vineyards LTD
8   Captain Freycinet Inn
9   Cheateau Xanadu
10 Cullen Wines
11 Devil's Lair Wines
12 Driftwood
13 Fermoy Estate
14 Fonti Farm
15 Happ's
16 Hay Shed Hill
17 Leeuwin Estate
18 Lenton Brae Estate
19 Margaret River Cheese Co.
20 Moss Brothers
21 Moss Wood Winery
22 Redbrook (Evans & Tate)
23 Redgate Wines
24 Ribbon Vale Estate
25 Rivendell Wines
26 Rosabrook Estate
27 Sandalford Wines
28 Serventy
29 Treeton Estate
30 Vasse Felix
31 Vasse River
32 Voyager Estate
33 Willespie
34 Wise Winery
35 Woodlands Wines
36 Woody Nook
37 Yungarra Estate Vineyard

DEVIL'S LAIR
Margaret River
1993
PINOT NOIR

CULLEN
MARGARET RIVER
Classic Dry White
1994
PRODUCED & BOTTLED BY CULLEN WINES
CAVES ROAD COWARAMUP W.A.
750ml PRESERVATIVE (220) ADDED 13.5% ALC/VOL
PRODUCT OF AUSTRALIA

DEVIL'S LAIR
Margaret River
1992
CABERNET MERLOT

1991 Cabernet Sauvignon
Merlot
Cabernet Franc
BROOKLAND
VALLEY
vineyard

Margaret River

Evans&Tate
1993
MARGARET RIVER
CABERNET SAUVIGNON
PRODUCE OF AUSTRALIA
750ml

SANDALFORD
1840
COLLECTION
1994
CLASSIC DRY WHITE
Margaret River
Mount Barker

MARGARET RIVER
BRIE
BATCH   g NET
PRODUCT OF AUSTRALIA

LEEUWIN ESTATE
1994
Margaret River
Rhine Riesling
PRODUCE OF WESTERN AUSTRALIA

VOYAGER
ESTATE
MARGARET RIVER
1992
CABERNET
SAUVIGNON
MERLOT
Produce of Australia 750ml

MOSS WOOD
MARGARET RIVER
CABERNET SAUVIGNON
1993
75cl
GROWN VINTAGED & BOTTLED AT DOMAINE MOSS WOOD
P.O. BOX 12, BUSSELTON, WESTERN AUSTRALIA, 6280
Alcohol 13.0% by Volume

CAPE MENTELLE
CABERNET MERLOT 1993
'Trinders Vineyard'

REDGATE
of
MARGARET RIVER
Classic Dry White
1994
Redgate Wines Pty. Ltd. Boodjidup Road
Margaret River, Western Australia
Preservative (220) added   12.7%
750ml PRODUCE OF AUSTRALIA ALC/VOL

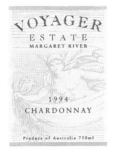

VOYAGER
ESTATE
MARGARET RIVER
1994
CHARDONNAY
Produce of Australia 750ml

AMBERLEY
MARGARET RIVER
CABERNET MERLOT
1992

CABERNET
SAUVIGNON
1993
XANADU
750ml

BROOKLAND
VALLEY
Vineyard
1993
Chardonnay
MARGARET RIVER
PRODUCT OF AUSTRALIA
13.8% Alc/Vol 750ml

1994 Sauvignon Blanc
BROOKLAND
VALLEY
vineyard

Margaret River

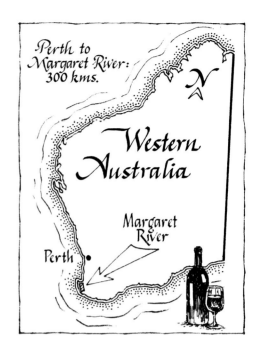

Perth to
Margaret River:
300 kms.
N
Western
Australia
Margaret
River
Perth

REDGATE
of
MARGARET RIVER
Cabernet Sauvignon
1992
Redgate Wines Pty. Ltd. Boodjidup Road
Margaret River, Western Australia
Preservative (220) added   12.5%
750ml PRODUCE OF AUSTRALIA ALC/VOL

BUSSELTON
RESEARCH RED
1992
PRODUCED & BOTTLED BY CULLEN WINES
CAVES ROAD COWARAMUP W.A.

LENTON BRAE
1993 MARGARET RIVER
CHARDONNAY
ESTATE BOTTLED PRODUCE OF LENTON BRAE
MARGARET RIVER WESTERN AUSTRALIA
750 ml   14.0% alc/vol

LEEUWIN ESTATE
1991
Margaret River
Cabernet Sauvignon
PRODUCE OF WESTERN AUSTRALIA

AMBERLEY
1994
CHENIN

SECESSION
1·9·9·4
XANADU
MARGARET
RIVER

An introduction to Margaret River

The Margaret River region is centred around the town of Margaret River, south of Bunbury, on a large peninsula. The climate is temperate and rainfall high. Long, dry summers and high rainfall, a yearly average of more than 1,100 mm, ensure crops ripen well in soils ideally suited to viticulture. These are well-drained sandy loams over water retentive clay subsoils.

Irrigation throughout the area therefore is largely unnecessary. Even the State's largest vineyard of 140 hectares operates successfully without any need for irrigation. This vineyard belongs to Sandalford and contributes to the total area of 500 hectares under vine for the region.

As with other Australian wine-producing areas, Margaret River's wine industry is well represented by the medical profession. The initial development of the region for viticulture was recommended by a report written by Dr. John Gladstones in 1965. Margaret River's first vines were planted by Dr. Tom Cullity of Vasse Felix two years later. Several other medical men followed suit, including Dr. Bill Pannell of Moss Wood and Dr. Kevin Cullen of Cullen's.

Red wines from Margaret River have proved very successful; the best of these have been made by various wineries from cabernet sauvignon grapes, as well as cabernet franc and merlot. Shiraz is not widely grown but has achieved good results, and pinot noir has also produced excellent wines.

Of the white grape varieties, semillon and sauvignon blanc have shown consistently brilliant results, producing fine wines of fresh, crisp styles with pronounced herbaceous and capsicum/asparagus flavours. The palates are rich and mouth-filling, with a frequent hint of tropical fruit, unlike some wines of this type from other regions which can tend towards a flat palate. Semillon particularly shows lifted tropical and herbaceous characters seldom seen elsewhere, with chardonnay and verdelho grapes having produced excellent wines for the region. Riesling however, proved to be less than successful when first introduced, but early problems with the variety now seem to have been overcome. The 1985 Leeuwin Estate Rhine Riesling amply demonstrates the variety's potential, while some of the late-picked rieslings are also very good. The 1984 Auslese Riesling produced by Sandalford has been awarded trophies, and continues to score close to full marks in masked tastings.

Aware of the potential and beauty of their district, the inhabitants of Margaret River have established a series of fine restaurants and accommodation houses. The cuisine of many cultures can be found in the town of Margaret River and the hotel of the same name has much to offer its guests. Similarly, the Captain Freycinet Motel offers luxurious accommodation and an excellent restaurant at reasonable prices. A number of wineries, both large and small, have constructed restaurants, art galleries and other art and craft establishments. A trip to 'Flutes' at Brookland Valley is an absolute must - visitors can sit on the decking overlooking the lake and splendid vineyard, and enjoy some sensational cuisine in a truly special atmosphere. Other large restaurants exist at Amberley, Leeuwin Estate and Vasse Felix. Cullens and many of the smaller wineries also have great casual eateries, many with exceptional views in this truly beautiful region.

Fishing, surfing and bushwalking add an extra dimension to Margaret River, which now certainly vies for the title of the premier wine tourism region in Australia. During the early 1980s, Leeuwin Estate inaugurated outdoor concerts at dusk, featuring such extraordinary performers as the London Philharmonic Orchestra, Kiri Te Kanawa and James Galway. Around 7,000 delighted attendees enjoy those magnificent events, many more clamour for tickets but just can't get in. The stature and value of these events for Margaret River are inestimable. Margaret River is a vinous paradise, virtually without equal in the world, and its wines are indeed truly world class.

Amberley Estate

Amberley Estate has fast become one of the largest and most important wineries in Margaret River. Since the first planting in 1986 on the Thornton Road property and the first vintage in 1990 Amberley has established itself as a producer of characteristic Margaret River wines.

Amberley is blessed with one of the prettiest locations in Australia, a sheltered gully resplendent with stands of imperious red gums. The elegant white winery building is surrounded by manicured gardens and lawns which sweep down to a pond and the vineyards beyond - it looks like they were always supposed to be there and, like the wine, the staff are bright and bubbly.

A considerable area of vineyard is planted with chenin blanc. This truly underrated variety with its lifted apple and quince like flavours has performed marvels under the expert winemaking and guidance of Eddie Price, a native Western Australian, who in 1982 became dux of the Roseworthy oenology course winning the major course prizes.

Although being commercially tempted to vary, the philosophy of the Amberley label is to remain a producer of wine from the fruit grown solely in the Margaret River Appellation. The belief of the owners and management is that a steady growth pattern utilising produce from arguably one of the best growing areas in Australia will be far outweighed by the short term gains of outside blending.

The 1995 vintage will be long remembered in Margaret River for the very dry growing season, the extremely hot and bird-plagued start to the harvest and resultant worry over fruit quality, but most of all for the quality of the wines. The white wines are at least the equal of 1994. The red wine quality is simply superb. In fact, the reds probably represent that one year in ten when everything goes exactly right. The quality and depth of flavour is astounding so look out for the 1995's.

The top selling chenin is accompanied by an excellent sauvignon blanc, semillon, semillon/sauvignon blanc - the Margaret River specialty - and a classic. The Nouveau, can be chilled a little and makes an ideal accompaniment to a delicious lazy lunch under the verandah of the winery. Don't forget to try the rich, wild berry flavoured cabernet merlot with its lifted aromatic characters which typify this top class wine maker.

Inset: Winemaker, Eddie Price

AMBERLEY ESTATE
Address: Thornton Road, Yallingup WA 6282
Phone: (097) 55 2288
Fax: (097) 55 2171
Established: 1986
Winemaker: Eddie Price
Principal varieties grown: Semillon, sauvignon blanc, chenin blanc, chardonnay, merlot, cabernet franc, cabernet sauvignon
Ha under vine: 40
Average no. cases produced: 20,000
Public & trade tours: By appointment only
Cellar door & mail order sales: Yes
Hours open to public: 11 am-4.30 pm seven days
Points of interest: Light lunches available

Brookland Valley

Malcolm Jones is a visionary person and his vision is certainly not of the petty variety. Brookland Valley is not just pretty, it is a vinous paradise with every detail, materially and aesthetically, perfectly in place.

In fact it is Peter Pan who calls the tune as he plays his flute, happily gazing over the Willyabrup Brook. This beautiful symbol of eternal youth and optimism was one of the last of the wax-moulded bronze cast studies crafted back in 1893. Malcolm and his wife Deirdre discovered him one day in an antique shop in Sydney. He has now found an idyllic home at Brookland Valley Vineyard.

Malcolm graduated from Lincoln University in New Zealand in 1963 with a degree in agricultural science. A successful career as a farm management consultant and business executive followed until some 20 years later, when Malcolm's love of the land

and desire to change his life-style led to the search for a rural retreat. In fact, their purchase at Brookland was in no way associated with the thought of a commercial venture. After building their home on the property, they decided a life of total relaxation was not for them. It was following discussions with the then owner of Vasse Felix Winery, David Gregg, a former cheesemaker, about their plans to build a cheese factory that they decided wine was more their style.

Perhaps it was his many years of consulting that led Malcolm to seek expert advice, starting with wine industry guru, Brian Croser, then managing Oenotech Services. This led on to involvement by Brian's then partner, Dr. Tony Jordan, on the wine side and Garry Crittenden on the vineyard side. Nowadays Gary Baldwin, who purchased Oenotech Services advises on the winemaking for Brookland Valley, conducted by Vasse Felix.

South Australia's highly respected viticultural consultant, Di Davidson, helps with the vineyard, but Malcolm's training and experience in agriculture has certainly been put to good use. The 50 acre vineyard of close-planted manicured vines surrounding the lake are a real showpiece and produce first-rate fruit. The wines are all individually styled - the sauvignon blanc is at the tropical fruit end of the flavour spectrum, with a touch of herbaceousness, whilst the chardonnay has subtle melon and grapefruit flavours complemented by toasty hazelnut-like oak from fine French oak barriques. The cabernet/merlot/cabernet franc red is rich with cherry and plum overtones and spends considerable time in new oak. It's a wine which I am sure will age very well indeed.

Malcolm and Deirdre's daughter Liza is in the dynamic mould of her parents. In 1989 she graduated as the dux of the diploma course in

hospitality and tourism at Perth's Bentley College and she also received the honour of 'Student of the Year' as the best of the entire college course students.

Her first project was to create the superb 'Flutes' restaurant, gallery and function facility with her parents at Brookland Valley. Cantilevered over the lake, it overlooks the picture book valley and vineyards. Natural colours and materials such as the superbly scented Zamia Palm fronds covering the pergolas, and the floor to ceiling windows inviting the beauty of nature into the classy casual interior, rival any winery restaurant, world wide. This class carries through to the innovative cuisine, both creative and of great value. Liza operated this hospitality centre for 2-1/2 years before travelling overseas where she worked in London for a leading wine merchant. Liza is now back in Australia and in charge of marketing both the Brookland

Valley wines and the Flutes complex. It would be wrong to say any job is easy, but with what Liza and her family have created, it certainly gives her a head start.

Since 1993 John and Pat Poynton purchased a fifty percent interest with Dee and Malcolm to further develop Brookland Valley's future project of 12 beautiful villas in 95 acres of wildeness bushland surrounding the Willyabrup Brook as it winds down to the Indian Ocean. Bushwalking tracks through to the hilltops are now in place. This development is sensitively and beautifully blended into the natural environment and each complex is available for sale and can be leased back to Brookland Valley to be rented to visitors for short-term stays. I can't imagine a more idyllic week, or so, than a break at Brookland Valley, it would certainly beat keeping up with the Joneses!

BROOKLAND VALLEY VINEYARD
Address: Caves Road, Willyabrup WA 6284
Phone: (097) 55 6250
Fax: (097) 55 6214
Established: 1984
Winemaker: Garry Baldwin
Principal varieties grown: Chardonnay, sauvignon blanc, cabernet sauvignon, merlot, cabernet franc
Ha under vine: 20
Average no. cases produced: 7,000

Principal wines & brands	Cellar potential
Chardonnay	5-10 years
Sauvignon Blanc	2-5 years
Cabernet Merlot	5-10 years

Public & trade tours: By appointment
Cellar door & mail order sales: Yes
Hours open to public: 11 am-4.30 pm Tues-Sun
Points of interest: Flutes Cafe, an award-winning restaurant; Preludes Gallery, wine & food, art and objects for living well with food and wine.
Retail distribution: Negociants Australia National distributors.

Cape Mentelle

David Hohnen, 'the squire of Cape Mentelle,' has expanded the breadth of his squiredom quite considerably in the last decade.

David began his quite remarkable career in the wine industry back in 1968 at Stonyfell Winery in South Australia where he decided winemaking was for him. David completed his oenology studies at the Fresno University in California and on returning to Australia in 1972 he, along with brother Mark, planted vines on the family's investment land at Margaret River. David then went to Victoria where he worked with Dominique Portet, establishing the Taltarni Vineyards.

When he came back to Western Australia in 1976, the vineyard needed rehabilitation. Cape Mentelle came under the spotlight when they won the Jimmy Watson Memorial Trophy with their 1982 Cabernet Sauvignon. To prove it was no fluke, David repeated the feat the following year with his 1983 wine. These awards did much to promote the Margaret River region. In 1985, David established Cloudy Bay in New Zealand and produced some extraordinary sauvignon blancs. Cloudy Bay now produces a range of

wines, including a fine methode champenoise, 'Pelorus.'

In 1990 Veuve Clicquot Ponsardin, the massive French champagne house, obtained a major share in Cape Mentelle, putting an indelible stamp of approval on David Hohnen's enterprises.

The Cape Mentelle range includes a shiraz and cabernet merlot, as well as the cabernet sauvignon. David also produces one of Australia's few zinfandels, a variety grown in California. This makes a huge,

black, spicy red - a wine for heroes. The two Mentelle whites are the region's first semillon/sauvignon blanc blend - and a full-bodied chardonnay.

CAPE MENTELLE VINEYARDS
Address: Wallcliffe Road, Margaret River, WA 6285
Direction: 4 km west of Margaret River
Phone: (097) 57 3266
Fax: (097) 57 3233
Established: 1976
Owner: David Hohnen & Veuve Clicquot Ponsardin
Winemaker: John Durham
Principal varieties grown: Chardonnay, cabernet sauvignon, shiraz, semillon, sauvignon blanc, zinfandel, merlot
Ha under vine: 80
Average annual crush: 700 tonnes
Average no. cases produced: 50,000

Principal wines & brands	Cellar potential
Cabernet Sauvignon	10+ years
Semillon Sauvignon	3 years
Shiraz	5-10 years
Cabernet Merlot	2-5 years
Chardonnay	2-5 years
Zinfandel	10+ years

Tours: By appointment only
Cellar door & mail order sales: Yes
Hours open to public: 10 am-4.30 pm daily
Points of interest: Rammed earth winery, set in beautiful native gardens
Retail distribution: Tucker Seabrook, NSW & Qld, Fesq Dorado Vic. & Tas; Tucker Seabrook Classic Wines, SA; West Coast Wine Cellars WA; Negociants, NZ

Chateau Xanadu

The Chateau Xanadu vineyard was established in 1977, by Irish doctors John and Eithne Lagan. As the winery's name suggests, this operation is more than a mere business. John and Eithne share a passion for art and literature, in addition to their love of wine. Their home houses one of the world's most extensive collections of early books and printed works and the name 'Xanadu' is taken from the epic poem by Samuel T. Coleridge.

The winery has been constructed from local stone and boasts beautiful stained glass windows. A love of beauty has been carried over into the vineyard at Chateau Xanadu. There are 50 acres of the 400 acre property under vine and varieties are semillon, sauvignon blanc, chardonnay, cabernet sauvignon, merlot and cabernet franc.

The first wines were made at Xanadu in 1981 and some excellent wines were produced right from the beginning. I well remember tasting the 1985 semillon during a visit to the winery in 1986. Its huge gooseberry flavour and complexity were a knock-out. Today most of the semillon finds its way into the excellent 'Secession,' a great Bordeaux-style dry white.

Winemaker since 1990 has been the

innovative Swiss, Jurg Muggli. One of his recent additions has been 'Featherwhite', a dry rose, barrel-fermented cabernet sauvignon, drained first and kept cool in the barrels for three months. It is lively, dry and with the complexity often lacking in this style. The Chateau Xanadu Cabernet Sauvignon with a little merlot and cabernet franc is impressive. Of a deep blue mauve colour, the wine displays fresh floral and mint aromas with cassis, fruit flavours. These are well integrated with oak.

The focus today at Xanadu is firmly on innovative quality winemaking and grapegrowing with the passionate and talented duo of Conor Lagan and Jurg Muggli who are pushing the frontiers of premium winemaking with outstanding results.

CHATEAU XANADU
Address: Terry Road, Margaret River WA 6285
Direction: 4 km southwest of Margaret River township
Phone: (097) 57 2581
Fax: (097) 57 3389
Established: 1977
Owner: Drs J & E Lagan
Winemaker: Jurg Muggli
Principal varieties grown: Semillon, chardonnay, cabernet sauvignon, sauvignon blanc, merlot, cabernet franc
Ha under Vine: 16.5
Average Annual Crush: 250 tonnes
Average No. Cases Produced: 15,000

Principal Wines & Brands/Cellar Potential	
Cabernet Sauvignon Reserve	10+ years
Cabernet Sauvignon	5-10 years
Chardonnay	2-5 years
Semillon	2-5 years
Secession (Semillon/ Sauvignon Blanc)	2-5 years
Featherwhite (Rose)	2-5 years
Noble Semillon	5-10 years

Public & trade tours: By appointment only
Cellar door & mail order sales: Yes
Hours open to public: 10 am-5 pm seven days
Points of interest: A unique range of hand-painted wine bottles individually crafted by artist-in-residence, Robert Lawson. Also 'Vine Candelabras' and other displays of art.
Retail distribution: (National) Sydney, Melbourne, Canberra, Brisbane, Adelaide, Perth, WA.

Above: Conor Lagan (left) and Jurg Muggli

Captain Freycinet

Right in the heart of the township of Margaret River is the impressive Captain Freycinet Motor Inn, named after the French explorer who first charted the coastline. The aesthetically pleasing buildings in earth-toned bricks blend in perfectly with their setting and the rooms in the cottage-type units at the rear open out onto the forest.

Everything in this wine-oriented establishment is spacious, and vaulted ceilings certainly give it an air of grandeur. The dining and other hospitality areas all have open fires burning in winter, providing an ideal atmosphere for a private getaway, or a group or business conference visit to the region. The chef and catering staff are keen about their work and have produced their own recipe book which is available at reception.

Max Oldfield, mine host and manager, is an old hand in the hospitality business and promotes a friendly, casual but professional attitude among the staff. The Captain

Freycinet is one of Australia's better wine-themed Inns and excellent value for money. Why not book in for a few days, it's right in the centre of this magnificent wine mecca of Margaret River.

Evans & Tate - Redbrook

John and Toni Tate had been great fans of the early wines of Margaret River, and friends of the pioneer vigneron, Tom Cullity. In 1974, two years after establishing their Evans & Tate headquarters in the Swan Valley, they purchased 28 hectares of land in Margaret River, planting vines the following year.

At present the vineyard comprises semillon, sauvignon blanc, chardonnay, shiraz, cabernet

sauvignon, cabernet franc and merlot which supply a major portion of their grape requirements. In 1994 they purchased a further 100 hectares of land at Jindong in the north of the region and established "Lionel's Vineyard" a 40 hectare development named after John Tate's late father, the first Tate to enjoy wine in Australia.

I have been particularly impressed by the Evans & Tate Margaret River Semillon, with its honey and lemon highlights and clean

herbaceous flavours, it has been a most successful wine on the show circuit. The Western Australia Classic formerly known as Margaret River Classic, a semillon/sauvignon blanc launched in 1987, has become one of Western Australia's best selling wines and is excellent value. But it is the cabernet sauvignon that has grabbed the limelight; the 1991 in particular had the critics swooning. The delightful cottage with its gorgeous gardens in the middle of the

REDBROOK ESTATE
Address: Cnr Caves and Metricup road, Willyabrup WA 6280
Direction: 250 kms suth west of Perth
Phone: (097) 55 6244
Fax: (097) 55 6283
Established: 1974
Owner: Tate Family
Winemaker: Brian Fletcher
Principal varieties grown: Cabernet sauvignon, merlot, shiraz, chardonnay, sauvignon blanc, semillon
Ha under vine: 19
Average annual crush: 1,100 tones
Average no. cases produced: 85,000

Principal wines & brands	Cellar Potential
Margaret River Chardonnay	5-10 years
Margaret River Sauvignon Blanc	5-10 years
Margaret River Merlot	5-10 years
Margaret River Shiraz	5-10 years
Margaret River Semillon	1-5 years
Western Australia Classic	0-1 years
Gnangara Shiraz	1-5 years
Two Vineyards Chardonnay	1-5 years
Western Australia Sav. Blanc	1-5 years
Barrique 61 Cab. Merlot	1-5 years

Public tours: By appointment only
Cellar door & mail order sales: Yes
Hours open to public: 10.30 am-4.30 pm seven days
Points of interest: Wine tasting, picnic grounds
Retail distribution: Evans & Tate WA and NSW. Wholesale outlets in other states.

vineyard is a pretty place to drop off for a top-class tasting if you are in the region.

Cullens Winery

flavours with nutty overtones and the cabernet/merlot/cabernet franc blend contains 65% cabernet sauvignon grapes and integrates superb cassis flavours with distinct floral aromas.

Unfortunately Kevin recently passed on, but Di has started a special memorial fund in Kevin's memory to help his medical pioneering project, The Busselton Research Foundation. Di, along with her suppliers, have created a red wine, the 'Busselton Research Red,' and all proceeds go to the Foundation.

The Cullens' professional approach to winemaking has paid off. Their wines are distinctive and of consistently high quality. Cullens delightful winery has much to offer the visitor, including a warm and friendly welcome. Their company is a valuable contributor to Western Australia's wine industry.

Winemaker, Vanya Cullen

D r. Kevin Cullen and his wife Diana planted the first vines on their property south of Willyabrup in 1971. Their first wines were made three years later and proved very successful. Expansion and development continued and vines now cover more than 28 hectares.

The winery consists of two buildings and was constructed from the local red stone by the Cullens and neighbouring farmers. One of these buildings houses the up-to-date equipment and a laboratory, while the other provides storage space for wines maturing in their oak casks. The latter building also includes a delightful tasting area and kitchen which provides imaginative food for visitors. This aspect of the business is capably managed by the Cullens' daughter Shelley.

Di is the seemingly tireless manager.

Another daughter, Vanya, is the winemaker and is the holder of both a science degree and a diploma of oenology. Di has remained in touch with the most contemporary winemaking and viticultural practices. Her considerable knowledge has no doubt been augmented by Vanya's wide experience which includes some time spent at the famous Robert Mondavi Winery in California and Drouhins of Burgundy.

It is not surprising that as a result of such expertise Cullens wines are consistently excellent. Their semillon sauvignon blanc is of an elegant, grassy, herbaceous style which renders it highly compatible with seafood. Cullens chardonnay is a complex combination of almond, melon and apricot flavours with a hint of smoky oak. The pinot noir exhibits delicious strawberry and cherry

---

CULLEN WINES
Address: Caves Road, Cowaramup WA 6284
Phone: (097) 55 5277
Fax: (097) 55 5550
Established: 1971
Winemaker: Vanya Cullen
Principal varieties grown: Cabernet sauvignon, merlot, cabernet franc, pinot noir, chardonnay sauvignon blanc, semillon, rhine riesling
Ha under vine: 28
Average annual crush: 150-200 tonnes
Average no. cases produced: 10,000 - 12,000

Principal wines & brands	Cellar potential
Cabernet merlot	5-10 years
Sauvignon Blanc	2-5 years
Chardonnay	2-5 years
Classic Dry White	2-5 years

Trade tours: By appointment only
Cellar door & mail order sales: Yes
Hours open to public: 10 am-4 pm seven days
Points of interest: Light lunches, coffees and teas
Retail distribution: Fine Wine Specialist, Sydney; Barrique, Queensland; Sutherlands, Melbourne; Tuckers, WA; and cellar door sales.

Busselton Red

B ack in 1966, about the time the first Margaret River vineyards were being contemplated, a unique medical research project was begun by the late Dr. Kevin Cullen, founder of Cullen's Wines, and colleagues Professors Tim Welborn, Michael McCall, David Curnow and Norman Stenhouse.

The project, a world first, was a widely-based community health survey, where thousands of residents of Busselton received free, periodic, complete health checks and

preventative medical advice, with the results being tabulated.

In fact, Busselton residents' life expectancy is now the longest in Australia, and among the longest in the world. The project was threatened with termination through lack of Government funding, so Di Cullen in her husband's memory, has launched 'The Busselton Red' to raise funds and awareness of the project. Di's suppliers Anthony Smith (corks and caps), Ashley Jones (label designs), Label World (printers)

and Visyboard, have all donated 100% of their products and services, along with Cullen's Wines in this admirable venture.

The wine, a Margaret River cabernet sauvignon, is an excellent full-bodied red and at $90 for a box of six bottles, freight-free to anywhere in Australia, it's a bargain. Just sent a cheque along with delivery instructions to Cullen's Wines and drink to your own health and the memory of a great wine man.

Devil's Lair

Phil Sexton is a very focussed individual, making seriously good wines. This extraordinarily talented man of great vision has been bewilderingly successful in a number of areas in the hospitality industry.

Phil, in fact, began his career as a trainee brewer at Perth's Swan Brewery in a bid to earn the money to attend the oenology course at the Charles Sturt University in Wagga Wagga. His qualifications as a science graduate, majoring in bio-chemistry, stood him in good stead. Through Swan, he went to Birmingham University in England, where he completed a masters degree. Phil then travelled through Europe where he hatched the idea of a boutique brewery. He later established the remarkably successful Matilda Bay Brewing Co. and purchased a number of hotels and bars, all creatively themed.

His successful hospitality and brewing endeavours allowed him to amass the capital necessary to become a serious vigneron, his long cherished dream. His thoroughness and vision is powerful, indeed. He didn't want just any sort of vineyard. He sought a gravelly site where the vines would have to dig deep for sustenance and moisture. In this struggle, as is the case with the world's greatest vineyards, they would produce top quality complex grapes. A particular site appealed to him. He had visited there as an anthropology student in his university days to study the ancient lair of a larger version of today's Tasmanian Devil, now extinct on the mainland. In 1981 Phil purchased the property next door to the devil's lair, which had partly been used as a gravel pit, supplying ballast for the Western Australian railways. The location, some 20 kilometres south of Margaret River and slightly elevated, is definitely cooler than the northerly part of the region and picking occurs some several weeks later. The cabernet sauvignon is often not picked until late April.

The 85 acres of vines are mostly planted on the steep slopes surrounding a massive lake with a surface area of 35 acres. In 1993, the winery was commissioned and will be crushing 250 tonnes by 1996. Previous vintages were made at Plantagenet in Mount Barker. The first red from the property was a 1990 cabernet sauvignon which also contained a small percentage of merlot and cabernet franc. This wine was instantly successful at the annual SGIO Wine Awards in Perth, where it won the champion prize and a trip to California for Phil and his wife, Allison, with $2,000 in their pockets. He repeated this feat, winning the S.G.I.O.

Championship award in 1994 with his 1993 Pinot Noir, winning a trip to France.

I am sure that these honours were appreciated as a vindication of Phil's persistence with his long-held dream of becoming one of Australia's great vignerons. In many ways, he is already there. The unique Devil's Lair label is as individual as his rich and characterful wines.

DEVIL'S LAIR
Address: Rocky Road, Forrest Grove via Margaret River WA 6285
Adminstration and Trade Enquiries: 42 Henry Street, Freemantle WA 6160
Phone: (09) 336 3262
Fax: (09) 336 3263
Established: 1980
Owner: Philip & Allison Sexton
Winemaker: Janice McDonald
Principal varieties grown: Chardonnay, pinot noir, cabernet sauvignon, cabernet franc, merlot
Ha under vine: 35
Average annual crush: 215 tonnes
Average no. cases produced: 15,000

Principal wines & brands	Cellar potential
Chardonnay	2-5 years
Cabernet Merlot	5-10 years
Pinot Noir	5-10years

Trade tours: By appointment only, Cellar door targeted to open summer 1995/96
Mail order sales: Yes
Hours open to public: By appointment only
Retail distribution: Restricted in Australia although good restaurant distribution. 50 per cent of production goes overseas

Lenton Brae

In 1990 his 1988 cabernet won the SGIO trophy and a free trip to California and Bordeaux. Lenton Brae's other wines, a chardonnay and a semillon/sauvignon blanc, are also award winners - the 1992 Chardonnay winning 3 trophies at the Perth Royal Wine Show, including the inaugural Wine Press Club award for the top White Wine of any category.

The tasting room integrated into the winery, with the afternoon sun streaming in through the stained glass windows, is a must to visit in Margaret River. Lenton Brae sits astride a small hill (hence theword 'brae') directly alongside and overlooking Mosswood.

Bruce Tomlinson's many years as an architect, much of the time designing buildings for the harsh climate of the mining towns in the north of Western Australia, gave him a good grasp of the necessities and aesthetics for rural architecture. He has designed and constructed a modern winery and home at Lenton Brae that blends beautifully into its environment and yet is practical and very pleasing to the eye.

Bruce and his wife, Jeanette, have just moved down to the property to oversee its operations more closely and their son Edward, a Roseworthy graduate, is now in charge of the winemaking, aided by the expert advice of Gary Baldwin from Oenotech.

LENTON BRAE ESTATE
Address: Caves Road, Willyabrup WA 6280
Phone: (097) 55 6255
Fax: (097) 55 6268
Established: 1982
Winemaker: Edward Tomlinson B.Ap.Sc.(Adel)
Principal varieties grown: Semillon, chardonnay sauvignon blanc, merlot, cabernet sauvignon
Ha under vine: 11
Average annual crush: 95 tonnes

Cellar door & mail order sales: Yes
Hours open to public: 10 am-6 pm daily
Retail distribution: Fine Wine Wholesales, WA; Harbury, Vic.

Moss Wood

Moss Wood was established by Dr. Bill Pannell and his wife, Sandra, in 1969. The first grapes planted on the 10 hectare Willyabrup property were cabernet sauvignon. These have since been followed by pinot noir, semillon and chardonnay. Great care was taken both in choosing the site for the vineyard and the vines to be planted. As a result, fruit has been of very high quality.

The first wine, a cabernet sauvignon, was made in 1973. Later wines were made with the assistance of Roseworthy graduate Keith Mugford. The pinot noir of Moss Wood almost defies description with its complex rich flavours, silky texture and long finish combining to make this one of the best wines of this variety in Australia. Part of the procedure employed to create this magnificent wine involves a considerable sacrifice on the part of the Mugfords in that they thin the bunches before the grapes ripen, to lower the crop and increase the intensity of flavour in the grapes.

The other red release from Moss Wood is their cabernet sauvignon. This intense wine consistently rates as one of Australia's top ten reds, integrating deep flavours of mint and herbs. The last three releases have been outstanding, showing a floral lift in the bouquet. In recent years, the Moss Wood white wines have shown considerable development. The unwooded semillon shows toasty complex flavours echoed by the chardonnay. The latter wine is more complex, however, as a result of varietal differences and the careful wood ageing of half of the wine, prior to blending with the remainder.

Keith Mugford

The reputation established by Bill and Sandra Pannell at Moss Wood has been carried on and enhanced by the hard work and winemaking skill of the Mugfords. Both families have made considerable contributions to the Margaret River region and the best of Moss Wood's wines are comparable to any in the world.

MOSS WOOD WINERY
Address: Metricup Road, Willyabrup WA 6280
Phone: (097) 55 6266
Fax: (097) 55 6303
Established: 1969
Winemaker: Keith Mugford
Principal varieties grown: Cabernet sauvignon, pinot noir, chardonnay, semillon, petit verdot, cabernet franc, merlot
Ha under vine: 8.5
Average annual crush: 75 tonnes
Average no. cases produced: 4,500

Principal wines & brands	Cellar potential
Cabernet Sauvignon	15-20 years
Chardonnay	10-15 years
Pinot Noir	10-15 years
Semillon	10-15 years

Public & trade tours: By appointment only
Cellar door & mail order sales: Yes
Hours open to public: 10 am-4 pm Mon-Sat.
Retail distribution: Tucker Seabrook, WA; Fesq Dorado & Co, NSW; Porter & Co, SA; Sutherland Cellars, Vic; Barrique Wines, Qld.

Leeuwin Estate

As one of Australia's leading producers of high quality varietal wines, Leeuwin has 91 hectares of immaculately tended vines and a state-of-the-art winery.

The guiding philosophy of Leeuwin, since its inception in 1974 has been to produce wines of distinctive character and supreme quality. That this philosophy has been successful is apparent in the recognition and acclaim which Leeuwin has received from experts both in Australia and Overseas.

As one of the five founding wineries in the Margaret River region, the property was identified by eminent American winemaker, Robert Mondavi, as being ideal for the production of premium quality wine. With Mondavi as mentor, the Horgan family set about transforming their cattle farm into a boutique vineyard and winery. A nursery was planted in 1974 and the vineyards were planted over a five year period from 1975. The first trial vintage was in 1978.

The mild, frost free winters, warm summers, and rich soil of the Leeuwin vineyard are ideal for the production of sauvignon blanc, chardonnay, riesling, cabernet sauvignon and pinot noir.

Broadly following the French style of handling, Leeuwin has concentrated on achieving complexity, balance and longevity in its wines through a blend of traditional and modern techniques.

Leeuwin's finest wines are known as the *"Art Series"* range. Paintings are commissioned from leading contemporary Australian artists to adorn the labels of these wines.

The *"Art Series"* wines have received much international attention and critical acclaim, with authoritative publications ranking the wines with the top 150 in the world and the top 20 in the *"New World"*. In particular, Leeuwin's Art Series Chardonnays have twice been awarded gold medals in *"Wine International Challenges"*, sponsored by the British publication *"Wine Magazine"*, which awarded the Leeuwin 1986 Chardonnay the overall trophy for best Chardonnay in 1992. The wines have also received *"Decanter"* Magazine's highest recommendation.

International demand for Leeuwin wines has resulted in exports to numerous countries and the wines being carried in the first class compartments of many international airlines.

Just as the pursuit of excellence manifests itself in the quality of Leeuwin wines, so too is it expressed in the aesthetic beauty of the winery, which overlooks a meadow, surrounded by a majestic forest of karri trees. Although the building is primarily a modern winery, master architects have created a highly original and uniquely Australian structure that blends harmoniously with its natural environment. The building itself has won a Civic Design Award.

Leeuwin is famous for its annual alfresco concerts, which are performed in the natural amphitheatre in front of the winery. The tradition of the Leeuwin concerts began in 1985 when the London Philharmonic Orchestra travelled 17,000 kms, with ten tonnes of luggage, to perform alongside the kookaburras in this unique bushland setting. Since then the concerts have featured several international orchestras and leading performers, including Dame Kiri Te Kanawa, James Galway, Ray Charles, Dionne Warwick, Diana Ross, Tom Jones, international soprano star Julia Migenes and tenors, Perrin Allen and George Benson. The success of these concerts has resulted in an additional annual concert which features Australian talent.

Working on the principle that fine wines, food and the arts are highly complementary, Leeuwin Estate has evolved into a significant tourist attraction. The staging of the concerts has resulted in tourism awards for "Major Tourist Attraction" and recognition as best "Significant Local Event" along with a citation for its contribution to the arts.

Housed within the winery is Leeuwin's award winning restaurant. Adorning the restaurant walls is the collection of contemporary Australian art used on the labels featuring paintings from more than thirty prominent Australian artists including Sir Sidney Nolan, Lloyd Rees, John Olsen, Robert Juniper and Arthur Boyd. The restaurant has been a recipient of a Gold Plate Award and has attracted guest appearances from some of Australia's leading chefs.

The Leeuwin Estate is the venue for many art and photographic exhibitions and the various splendidly appointed hospitality areas provide an ideal setting for these very successful events.

Leeuwin Estate is truly a vision splendid and it is a moving experience to see everything carried out with such personal care and attention to detail.

As they say in the classics, Leeuwin Estate "have really got their act together".

LEEUWIN ESTATE WINERY
Address: Stevens Road, Margaret River WA 6285
Phone: (09)430 4099 & (09) 576 253 (winery)
Fax: (09) 430 5687
Established: 1974
Owner: Rural Developments Pty Ltd
Winemaker: Robert Cartwright
Principal varieties grown: Riesling, chardonnay, sauvignon blanc, pinot noir, cabernet sauvignon
Ha under vine: 92
Average annual crush: 500 tonnes
Public & trade tours: Daily
Cellar door & mail order sales: Yes
Hours open to public: 10 am-4.30 pm seven days
Retail distribution:Fesq Dorado, NSW & Qld; Nelson Wine Co., Victoria; Michael Hartley, SA

Redgate

One of the most extraordinary and pleasurable experiences in compiling this book occurred on Anzac Day, 1995. Milan and I were taking some early morning photos at Redgate, making the most of the sunrise, when who should appear on the doorstep of the winery but founder, Bill Ullinger, on his way to the Anzac Day ceremony in Margaret River.

In chatting with Bill, he reminisced on his last bombing raid as a 21 year old pilot in charge of a massive Lancaster bomber, 50 years earlier, in 1945. Fifty years to the day it was, on Anzac Day 1945. When we asked to take his photo he said, 'Do you want me to put my medals on?' I replied, 'We won't take your photo without them.'

As we took Bill's photo, with the Australian flag flying above the winery's outdoor tank farm, up walked our old friend Andrew Forsell with whom we spent many happy days in California.

Andrew was a winemaker for many years for the high profile Sonoma Winery, Ironhorse. Bill's son, Paul, was next to appear on the scene. He and Andrew then took us through the wines, from the 1995 vintage just completed, Andrew's first vintage working with Paul. The wines were truly superb and I am sure will win many accolades before they are all consumed, although given their enormous fruit flavours and great balance, you'd better get in quick!

Bill Ullinger established Redgate in 1976 at an age when many would be contemplating retirement. The property's purchase came after a long search of several hundred kilometres of Western Australia's coastline. Early teething difficulties and the first wine tax imposition in 1984 had the Ullingers on the verge of closing the winery's doors. Then came their victory at the 1984 Adelaide Wine Show, winning the prestigious Montgomery Trophy with their 1982 Cabernet Sauvignon.

The winery doesn't have the high flying profile of its neighbours, Leeuwin Estate and Cape Mentelle, but I have a distinct feeling that's all about to change and Bill Ullinger's 'red gate' is about to open and drop a few bombs to shake up the premium wine market. Watch out!

REDGATE WINES

Address: Boodjidup Road, Margaret River WA 6285
Phone: (097) 57 6488
Fax: (097) 57 6308
Established: 1977
Winemaker: Andrew Forsell
Principal varieties grown: Cabernet sauvignon, sauvignon blanc, semillon, chenin blanc
Ha under vine: 20
Average annual crush: 110 tonnes
Average no. cases produced: 12,000

Principal wines & brands	Cellar potential
Cabernet Sauvignon	5-10 years
Sauvignon Blanc Reserve	3-5 years
Cabernet Franc	3-5 years
Classic Dry White	0-4 years
Chenin Blanc	0-3 years
Chardonnay	2-5 years

Public & trade tours: By appointment only
Cellar door & mail order sales: Yes
Hours open to public: 10 am-5 pm seven days
Points of interest: BBQ facilities
Retail distribution: Perth, Melbourne, Sydney.

The largest vineyard in Western Australia is the 115 hectares of vines owned and operated by Sandalford Wines at Willyabrup. The vineyard is beautifully situated at the base of a small circular valley. This protected site prevents damage to vines by harsh onshore winds, yet allows fruit ample exposure to the sun.

Planting commenced in 1972 under supervision of the then managing director, John Roe. The current vineyard manager is the young and enthusiastic Ian Davies and he has overseen a transformation of the property. Retrellising, computer controlled irrigation and the implementation of a strict vineyard regeneration program has given rise to fantastic improvements to both quality and yield.

Davies came to Sandalford in 1993 after five years with Tarrawarra in Victoria's Yarra Valley. Before this he had experience in the Upper Hunter Valley after graduating in viticulture from Charles Sturt University in Wagga Wagga. This mixed experience in warm and cool climates and vastly different rainfall patterns prepared him well for his role at Margaret River.

All grapes are machine harvested at night and, to avoid deterioration in the transport to the company's Swan Valley winery, the white grapes are crushed, drained and chilled and the resulting grape 'must' transferred to the Swan. The red grapes are picked and transported in the cool of the night.

Late in 1985 a delightful new rammed earth tasting and cellar door area was constructed. The interior is furnished with polished jarrah (the local timber), and the area offers magnificent views over the vineyard. Sandalford's premium range is available, consisting of wines made from grapes grown in the Margaret River, Mount Barker and Pemberton regions. These are the Margaret River/Mount Barker Riesling, Mount Barker/Margaret River/Pemberton Chardonnay, Margaret River Verdelho, Margaret River/Mount Barker Shiraz and Margaret River Cabernet Sauvignon. These wines represent excellent value for the consumer; their quality is consistently high and the prices are very reasonable.

SANDALFORD WINES - CAVERSHAM VINEYARD & MARGARET RIVER VINEYARD
Address: 3210 West Swan Road, Caversham WA 6055 and Metricup Road, Cowaramup WA 6284
Phone: (09) 274 5922
Fax: (09) 274 2154
Established: 1840
Winemaker: Bill Crappsley
Principal varieties grown: Chardonnay, Rhine Riesling, Verdelho, Cabernet Sauvignon, Shiraz, Semillon, Chenin Blanc, Sauvignon Blanc
Ha under vine: 190
Average annual crush: 900 tonnes
Average no. cases produced: 75,000

Principal wines & brands	Cellar potential
Pemberton Chardonnay	2-5 years
Verdelho	2-5 years
Rhine Riesling	2-5 years
1840 Collection Classic Chardonnay	2-5 years
1840 Collection Classic Dry White	2-5 years
1840 Collection Classic Dry Red	2-5 years

Public & trade tours: Yes
Cellar door & mail order sales: Yes
Hours open to public: 10 am-5 pm seven days (Caversham); 10.30 am-5 pm seven days (Margaret River)
Points of interest: Plans underway for redevelopments including brasserie, emporium and function centre
Retail distribution: Australia-wide through hotels, restaurants and liquor stores; WA /NT, Sandalford Wines; NSW/ACT - Hill International Wines; Vic/ Tas, Rutherglen Wine & Spirit Co; SA, Richard Mackie Fine Wines; Qld, Wine Partners.

Voyager

VOYAGER ESTATE
Address: Stevens Road, Margaret River WA 6285
Phone: (09) 385 3133
Fax: (09) 383 4029
Established: 1978
Owner: Michael Wright
Winemaker: Stuart Pym
Principal varieties grown: cabernet sauvignon, chardonnay, chenin blanc, semillon, sauvignon blanc, merlot
Ha under vine: 27
Average annual crush: 200 tonnes
Average no. cases produced: 13,000

Principal wines & brands	Cellar potential
Chardonnay	2-5 years
Cabernet Sauvignon/Merlot	5-10 years
Semillon	5-10 years
Classic (Sauvignon Blanc/ Semillon blend)	2-5 years
Chenin Blanc	2-5 years

Public & trade tours: By appointment only
Cellar door & mail order sales: Yes
Hours open to public: Cellar sales due to open to public mid-1996
Retail distribution: Selected bottle shops and restaurants

In a region with some of Australia's most beautiful wineries, none quite match the stunning symmetry and fresh clean lines of Voyager with its 'Cape Dutch' design, reminiscent of the great wineries in the Cape Province of South Africa. This is all the more fitting as the first vines planted in Margaret River, some 100 years ago, were from South Africa. Voyager also makes an excellent chenin blanc, the grape made famous in South Africa under the name Steen.

In 1991 Michael Wright bought the Freycinet Winery from the Gherardi family, who had named it after the French sea captain who explored the coast of the region. Faced with a legal challenge from the Spanish 'Frexinet' methode champenoise makers, and confusion with the small Tasmanian winery of the same name, Wright named the property 'Voyager' based on his family company name.

Michael's father became involved in mining as a partner to Lang Hancock in their massive Pilbara iron mines in northern Western Australia. Michael Wright was looking for a fresh rural challenge and although a teetotaller himself, decided wine was for him.

His Voyager property includes a substantial 750 acres, of which 400 are suitable for vines. The vineyard covers 60 acres at present and is aided by a 120,000 cubic metre dam capable of supplying supplementary irrigation to 140 acres. New plantings of 30 acres are planned, comprising semillon and cabernet sauvignon, and by the turn of the century a production of 25,000 - 30,000 cases of premium wines are anticipated. The showpiece tasting and hospitality complex in its stunning garden setting is to open in 1996, and a sense of excitement in the region awaits this significant event.

Already the Voyager wines have made a mark for themselves. Australia's leading wine industry magazine 'Winestate' has regularly awarded the wines four and three star ratings, putting them amongst Australia's best. The range includes a complex barrel fermented chardonnay, a varietal semillon with great palate length, which includes about 10% sauvignon blanc to give it a tropical and herbaceous lift. A third of this wine is also barrel fermented, certainly it will age well. The other whites are a fresh unwooded 'Classic', 75% sauvignon blanc and 25% semillon, and finally, the fresh fruit-driven chenin blanc. The only red at present is the cabernet sauvignon with a touch of merlot blended in for softness. A super premium red is planned, but the varietal make-up and style is yet to be determined.

Voyager has not rushed any of the necessary moves needed to make it a leading Australian wine company. I am sure the future will prove the huge investment involved has been worthwhile.

Fonti Margaret River Cheeses

The Margaret River Region is not onlygreat wine country but harbours some of the best dairy land in Western Australia. The natural alliance between cheese and wine goes back into time immemorial. A great full-bodied red with a sharp vintage cheddar, a rich sweet botrytis with a ripe french-style brie - what more noble combination could one wish for?

The cheese industry over the last 15 years has undergone the same sort of enormous growth and development that began with wine a decade before.

European-style cheeses, the soft bries and camemberts, the Swiss sweeter styles, the many Italian farm styles including ricotta and the English inspired vintage cheddars are all produced in this region. The Margaret River Cheese Company makes excellent soft ripened cheeses. After a long association with Fonti Dairies, just up the Bussell Highway at Metricup, the two companies have merged. Fonti make the Swiss and Italian styles along with ricotta and Australia's best pot set yoghurts.

Managing Director, Phil Ellingworth and his team of cheesemakers under Terry

Scott do an excellent job. Both dairies are open for visitors with tasting and sales areas. The larger Fonti factory has a display of old cheesemaking equipment and a viewing window into the production area. Fonti's magnigficent cream milk shakes are hard to beat.

If you are looking for a change after visiting some of the 12 wineries within 10 kilometres of these cheesemakers, drop in. If you've got the kids with you, it makes an educational and enjoyable change for them. Then it's back to the wines.

An introduction to Great Southern

Some 400 km south of Perth, near the Great Southern Ocean, is a wine region of world potential which is already producing some exciting wines.

Geographically it is the largest wine producing area in Australia, spread between the towns of Albany, Denmark, Mt.Barker and Frankland, forming a square of some 2,500 kilometres. That's around 625,000 acres, which could provide three times the current Australian wine grape harvest if it were all planted to vines. This, of course would not be possible, but it does show the area's potential.

The climate is perfect, cool with dry summers and wet winters; some supplementary irrigation is necessary, but the country lends itself to the construction of dams. In the east, the Stirling and Porongurup Ranges provide an awesome beauty unrivalled by any other Australian wine region. Its isolation adds to this feeling of grandeur.

The southern coastline is stunning and the stands of eucalypts in the west are breathtaking. Yields are low, but quality is outstanding. The five sub-regions - Albany, Stirling Ranges, Porongurup, Mt.Barker, Denmark and Frankland - support more than 20 producers, all established within the last 25 years. The first winery in the region, Plantagenet, was commissioned in time for the 1975 vintage, with the area's first vineyards being established less than 30 years ago.

During the late 1950s the relieving horticultural advisor to the region was Bill Jamieson, later to become Western Australia's Great Southern government viticulturist. He was struck by the orchard region's potential for wine and followed this through over the decades. The great Maurice O'Shea from the Hunter Valley was adamant, if he had his time as a winemaker again, it would be near Albany in Western Australia.

The first vines, an experimental vineyard under Bill Jamieson's control at the Pearse family's Forest Hill property at Mt. Barker, was planted in 1965. This was followed by plantings a couple of years later by ex-Adelaide Lord Mayor John Roche at his Frankland River property. I tasted the first wine made from the region's grapes at the Houghton Winery Cafe in 1972. A 1972 cabernet sauvignon made by Jack Mann, enjoyed straight from the barrel, it was certainly impressive.

Rieslings from the Great Southern led the way with their limey intense flavours. Pinot noir has been a real star, as has chardonnay. I am sure this could be a great region for methode champenoise. Cabernet sauvignon does well, as does shiraz and even sauvignon blanc. There are so many micro-climates and soil types, I am sure that great wines of all varieties are possible. From a wine tourist's point of view this region of natural beauty, freshness and great wines, is well worth the effort to discover. I know I always look forward to my visits there.

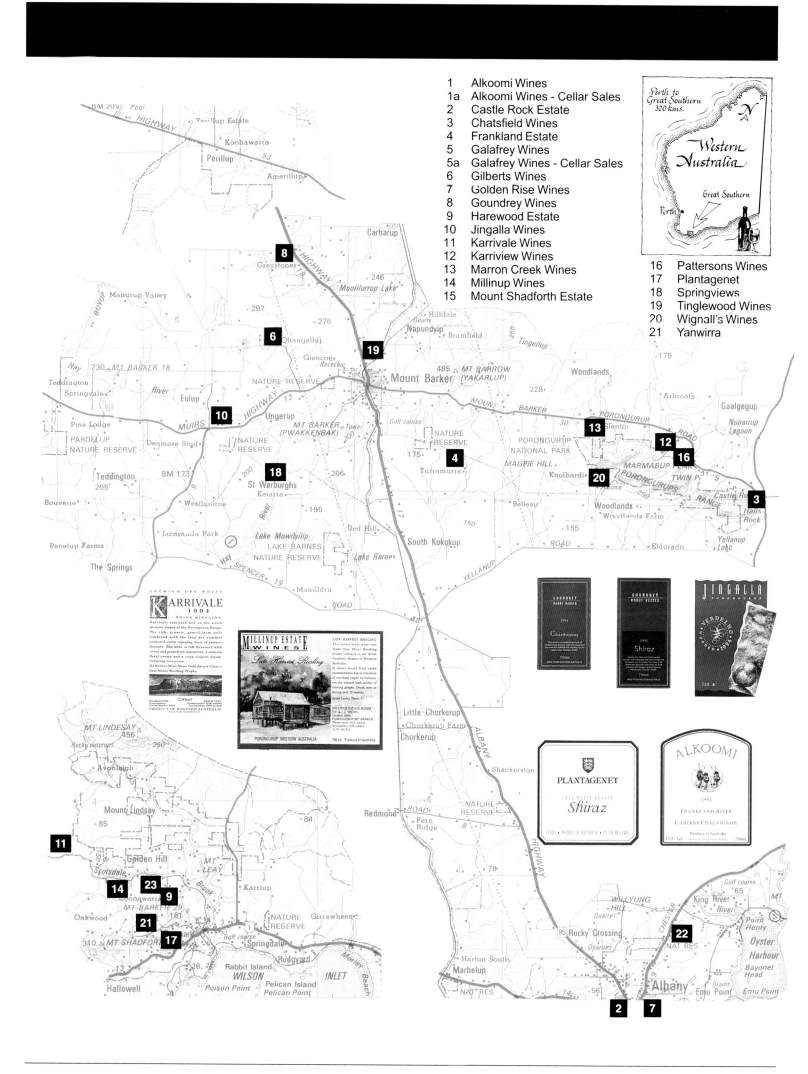

1   Alkoomi Wines
1a Alkoomi Wines - Cellar Sales
2   Castle Rock Estate
3   Chatsfield Wines
4   Frankland Estate
5   Galafrey Wines
5a Galafrey Wines - Cellar Sales
6   Gilberts Wines
7   Golden Rise Wines
8   Goundrey Wines
9   Harewood Estate
10 Jingalla Wines
11 Karrivale Wines
12 Karriview Wines
13 Marron Creek Wines
14 Millinup Wines
15 Mount Shadforth Estate

16 Pattersons Wines
17 Plantagenet
18 Springviews
19 Tinglewood Wines
20 Wignall's Wines
21 Yanwirra

Perth to Great Southern 320 kms.

Western Australia

Alkoomi

Judy and Merv Lange have one of Australia's most isolated vineyards and wineries, near Frankland in the Great Southern. They are affable, hardworking people of the land and produce outstanding wines in a no-fuss manner and market them at great value prices.

Merv's family purchased the 6,250 acre property in the 1920s and ran a mixed farming operation, concentrating on wool. The late 1960s saw wool prices tumble and Merv decided to experiment with vines, inspired by John Roche up the road and the successful plantings at the Pearse's Forest Hill farm.

In 1970, he planted a couple of acres of cabernet which were totally decimated by frost. Not to be daunted and somewhat taunted by his neighbours, he was determined to succeed; ploughing in the dead vines, he commenced again. Today, more than 100 acres of healthy premium vineyards under the care of Judy and Merv's son, Wayne, supply an ever-increasing market for the Alkoomi (the name is an aboriginal word meaning 'watering place') wines.

Alkoomi's blended classic red (shiraz/cabernet/merlot/malbec) is excellent value. The biggest seller is their aromatic, limey

rhine riesling, while the cabernet sauvignon is a regal style. Top-priced wine is a rich 100% Malbec, unusual for Australia; it needs a year or two to soften. Deserved success came to Alkoomi in 1989 as their sauvignon blanc of that year won them a $5,000 overseas wine trip at the annual Western Australian SGIO Wine Awards.

ALKOOMI WINES

Address: Wingebellup Road, Frankland WA 6396 & 225 Lower Stirling Terrace, Albany WA 6330
Direction: 11 km west of Frankland
Phone: (098) 55 2229
Fax: (098) 55 2284
Established: 1971
Owner: Merv & Judy Lange
Winemaker: Michael Staniford
Principal varieties grown: Cabernet, shiraz, riesling, sauvignon blanc, chardonnay, malbec.
Ha under vine: 42
Average annual crush: 400 tonnes
Average no. cases produced: 28,000

Principal wines & brands	Cellar potential
Chardonnay	5-10 years
Cabernet Sauvignon	10+ years
Malbec	10+ years
Classic Red	5-8 years
Sparkling Red (Burgundy)	10+ years
Sauvignon Blanc	2-5 years
Riesling	5-10 years
Classic White	3-5 years

Public & trade tours: By appointment only
Cellar door & mail order sales: Yes
Hours open to public: 10.30 am-5 pm daily
Points of interest: Functions by appointment, BBQ facilities
Retail distribution: Fine Wine Wholesalers WA; Haviland Wine Co, NSW; National Wine Merchants, Vic; Barrique, Qld; Tasmanian Fine Wines, Tas; S. & V. Wine Merchants, SA; Tim Seats Ltd, NT; Capital Fine Wines, ACT.

Plantagenet

PLANTAGENET WINES

Address: Lot 45 Albany Highway, Mount Barker WA 6324
Phone: (098) 51 2150
Fax: (098) 51 1839
Established: 1974
Winemaker: Gavin Berry
Principal varieties grown: Cabernet sauvignon, shiraz, pinot noir, chenin blanc, chardonnay, riesling, muscat
Ha under vine: 20
Average annual crush: 320 tonnes
Average no. cases produced: 20,000

Principal wines & brands	Cellar potential
Omrah Chardonnay (Unoaked)	0-3 years
Mount Barker Chardonnay	0-5 years
Riesling	0-5 years
Chenin Blanc/Sauvignon Blanc	0-5 years
Frontignac	0-3 years
Cabernet Sauvignon	5-10 years
Shiraz	5-10 years
Pinot Noir	0-5 years
Sparkling	0-3 years

Public & trade tours: Yes
Cellar door & mail order sales: Yes
Hours open to public: 9 am-5 pm Mon-Fri; 10 am-4 pm w/e
Points of interest: Free gas barbecue, catering organised by appointment, shady picnic grounds, children's swings. Hosts Mount Barker Wine Festival - second weekend January (annually)
Retail distribution: All states

Despite the establishment of an experimental vineyard at the Forest Hill Vineyard in 1965, Tony Smith's 'Plantagenet' was the first commercial vineyard in the Mount Barker area.

Tony and several partners founded the Bouverie Vineyard at Denbarker in the late 1960s. Plantings followed at Wyjup in 1971 and three years later an old apple-packing shed in Mount Barker was purchased. This has since been converted into a functional, well-equipped winery which processes, bottles and provides storage space for a number of local vineyards in addition to Plantagenet.

The first Plantagenet wines were made by David McNamara in 1974. Four years later, Roseworthy graduate Robert Bowen was hired as winemaker. The skills and innovative ability of this young Victorian brought great success on the show circuit.

Rob has now moved on to Capel Vale and was replaced by the high profile winemaker John Wade who had been in charge of the wines at Wynns Coonawarra for many years. John added further lustre to the Plantagenet wines and further expanded the contract winemaking.

The introduction of the 'Omrah'

unwooded chardonnay in 1989 proved to be a stroke of genius. It has become one of the biggest selling Western Australian whites, and appeals to those who prefer the more fruit-driven styles which generally taste better with food.

Plantagenet, under John's former assistant and successor, Gavin Berry, are concentrating more on their own wines with less contract activity now.

Goundrey

From small beginnings, the Goundrey Wines enterprise has become not only by far the largest in the Great Southern region, but also ranks in the top four wineries in the state in terms of size, being bigger than any of the wine producers in the better-known Margaret River wine region.

In the early 1970's a small five acre vineyard of cabernet sauvignon and riesling was planted at the original Windy Hill vineyard, just south west of Mt Barker. The first vintage was produced in 1976 and in 1988 the company Goundrey Wines Limited, was formed, which allowed for the purchase of the Langton property. This magnificent 200 hectare river valley property, is now home to the main vineyard of 83 hectares including a large and modern winery which was completed in time for the 1989 vintage. The imposing winery is situated high on the valley slopes, and beside it lies the historic homestead which houses the cellar door sales.

The combination of a cool climate and fertile soils, plus modern and effective viticultural techniques produce a high concentration of aromas and flavours. Two ranges of wine are now being produced under the quality 'Goundrey' label, and a small volume under the premium 'Reserve' label.

The 1995 vintage saw a record 980 tonne crush at Goundrey's. With the vision and quality to succeed, Goundrey Wines looks set to be a dynamic presence in the Western Australian wine industry in the future.

GOUNDREY WINES
Address: Langton, Muir Highway, Mount Barker WA 6324
Direction: 10 km from Mount Barker
Phone: (098) 51 1777
Fax: (098) 51 1997
Established: 1971
Owner: Goundrey Wines Ltd
Winemaker: Brenden Smith
Principal varieties grown: Cabernet, shiraz, riesling, sauvignon blanc, chardonnay
Ha under vine: 67
Average annual crush: 800-1,000 tonnes
Average no. cases produced: 40,000

Principal wines & brands	Cellar potential
Goundrey Reserve Shiraz	5-10 years
Goundrey Reserve Riesling	5-6 years
Goundrey Reserve Sauvignon Blanc	3-4 years
Goundrey Reserve Chardonnay	6-8 years
Goundrey Reserve Cabernet	5-10 years
Goundrey Unwooded Chardonnay	2-5 years
Goundrey Chenin Blanc	2-5 years
Goundrey Classic White Semillon/Sauvignon Blanc	2-5 years
Goundrey Cabernet Merlot	2-5 years

Public & trade tours: By appointment only
Cellar door & mail order sales: Yes
Hours open to public: 10 am-4.30 pm Mon-Sat 11 am-4.30 pm Sun

Points of interest: Winetasting in the lovely old homestead. picnic in the gardens.
Retail distribution: Negociants Australia distribute to retail/restaurant in Queensland, New South Wales, ACT, Victoria, South Australia & Western Australia

Millinup Estate Wines

Peter Thorn is steeped in wine history. His ancestors arrived in Australia in 1850 and settled in the Barossa Valley at Angaston. Peter's father, Lindsay, was a vigneron in the Swan Valley and represented the region for some years in the West Australian parliament as the member for Toodyay and for six years was Minister for Lands.

Ironically, Peter's career took him into real estate, again in the wine regions of the Perth Hills and Swan Valley. He and his late wife, Lesley, were drawn to the beauty of the Porongurups and in 1988 purchased a property complete with a small vineyard.

Whilst Lesley was busy painting (her canvases can be seen in the tasting area and on the wine labels of the estate), Peter was busy building, firstly renovating an old cottage near the entrance to the property, then a delightful new accommodation unit alongside the tasting room. Together with the old Pioneer Cottage this is available for short or long stays at exceptionally good value prices. Many guests have come back a number of times, and I don't blame them - the views and the peace are wonderful.

Peter's riesling and late harvest riesling are great and the spicy cabernet franc is a

lovely lunchtime red, with the fuller-bodied cabernet sauvignon, cabernet franc and merlot blend just the shot with dinner in your cottage.

Jingalla

Jingalla was planted in 1979. Its location is truly beautiful, nestled under Twin Peaks on the northern slopes adjacent to Devil's Slide and Nancy's Peak in the Porongurup National Park.

Geoff Clarke, a former shearer, and his wife Nita, began the project on the 240 acre property of Nita's family, the Coads. Geoff and Nita were later joined by Barry Coad, Nita's brother, and his wife Shelley. At first the vineyard was established to sell the grapes, but when the first crop came along, the challenge of winemaking became too strong.

Jingalla have had considerable success in wine shows, particularly with their reds. The 1986 cabernet sauvignon was the first wine from the Porongurups to win a trophy when it was named best Western Australian red of the show. I was particularly impressed by their semillon, which sees about two weeks in wood, following the barrel fermenting of the verdelho, a family favourite. Both wines had delicious honeysuckle and pineapple overtones and plenty of mouthfilling flavour.

The riesling, like all I saw in the region, was exceptional, with pineapple, lime and passionfruit leaping out of the glass. Jingalla also make a Great Southern blended white, which is no slouch either. The reds were impressive as well, particularly the shiraz - cherries and raspberries with freshly-ground nutmeg and cinnamon. Superb! The tasting area and winery are full of rustic charm and make for a great visit.

JINGALLA WINES
Address: Bolganup Dam Road, Porongurup WA 6324
Phone: (098) 53 1023
Fax: (098) 53 1023
Established: 1979
Owner: Geoff & Nita Clarke, Barry & Shelley Coad
Winemaker: Brendan Smith/Geoff Clarke
Principal varieties grown: Verdelho, semillon, rhine & Geisenheim riesling, cabernet sauvignon, shiraz
Ha under vine: 8
Average annual crush: 43 tonnes
Average no. cases produced: 2,500

Principal wines & brands	Cellar potential
Verdelho-Barrel Fermented	2-5 years
Shiraz	5-10 years
Cabernet Sauvignon	5-10 years
Semillon-Wooded	2-5 years
Rhine Riesling	2-5 years
Great Southern White	2-5 years
Great Southern Red	2-5 years
Cabernet Rouge	2-5 years

Public & trade tours: By appointment only
Cellar door & mail order sales: Yes
Hours open to public: 10.30 am-5 pm seven days
Points of interest: Catered-for meals (by booking only); children's playground, Porongurup Wine Festivals
Retail distribution: WA, Jingalla Wines; Vic, Dennis Carstairs, Sutherland Cellars; Queensland, Harbottle Brown

Karrivale

Under the awesomely beautiful Gibraltar Rock, on the slopes of the picturesque Porongurup Range, lie the panoramic Karrivale vineyards and wine cellar of Campbell and Annette McGready, stalwarts of the region. At their very attractive cellar door visitors are always extended a warm welcome.

A big mountain of a man, Campbell took over the 500 acre dairy farm after his father's death in 1956, but it was not until 1979 that they planted vines. Inspiration for this move came from friend and modern day wine pioneer, Tony Smith, of Plantagenet. The first plantings, 2.5 acres of riesling, came from Tony's Wyjup Vineyard. In 1982 a further 2.5 acres of riesling were planted, followed by five acres of chardonnay and four of shiraz. The rieslings of Karrivale are particularly impressive. On visiting, I tasted the 1990, 91, 92, and 93 as well as the 94 Late Harvest Style. All have fresh citrus blossom characters; the 1994s are some of the best rieslings I've ever tasted.

Campbell is a builder at heart and built the cellar and the gallery tasting room, constructed of stone from the Porongurup, the world's oldest mountain range. The calligraphic exhibition with a real wine flavour, by Valda Talbot, certainly contains a few pearls of wisdom which Campbell and Annette have heeded well.

KARRIVALE WINES
Address: Woodlands Road, Porongurup, WA 6324
PO Box, 146 Mount Barker, WA 6324
Phone: (098) 53 1009
Fax: (098) 53 1129
Established: 1979
Owner: Campbell McGready
Winemaker: Gavin Berry by contract with Plantagenet Wines
Principal varieties grown: rhine riesling, chardonnay, shiraz, cabernet sauvignon
Ha under vine: 6.5
Average annual crush: 20 tonnes
Average no. cases produced: 1,000

Principal wines & brands	Cellar potential
Rhine Riesling	up to 14 years
Late Harvest Style	2-5 years

Cellar door sales: Yes
Hours open to public: 10 am-5 pm Wed-Sun & Public Holidays or by appointment
Points of interest: Panoramic views, calligraphy exhibition, picnic area, crafts, bush walk
Retail distribution: Cellar sales and mail order Perth, Sydney, Brisbane

The viticultural region known as the Swan Valley includes the Perth suburbs of Guildford, Bassendean and Midland and extends 15 kilometres to the north along the Swan River.

The first vines were planted by Thomas Waters at Olive Farm in 1829, the same year that settlers arrived in the state.

Western Australia's first commercial vineyard was Sandalford, planted in the Swan Valley by John Septimus Roe in 1840. Houghton, however, was to become the region's most significant wine producer. The company was established when Dr John Ferguson planted vines in 1859.

Following the First World War, the small number of the area's winemaking fraternity was suddenly boosted by the arrival of many Yugoslav and other European immigrants. As a result, hundreds of small family winemaking operations came into existence. Most families sold their wine in bulk from their cellar doors, while some winemakers had become more serious about commercial marketing and packaging.

In addition to the mainly traditional winemakers, and the area's larger concerns of Sandalford and Houghton, the Swan Valley now also hosts a group of winemakers growing in importance. These include Evans and Tate, famous for their red wines and challenging to become the state's second largest vigneron. Another worthy winery is the Jane Brook Estate of Beverley and David Atkinson, which also boasts a casual vineyard

cafe. The Lamont Winery of Jack Mann's daughter, Corin, also makes traditional full bodied Swan Valley styles along with having a first class restaurant run by Corin's daughter, Kate. Westfield Wines, owned and operated by John Kosovich, makes consistently fine reds, whites and fortifieds, including an excellent vintage port.

Without doubt the most significant influence on the wine industry of the Swan Valley was the indomitable and idiosyncratic Jack Mann. Jack began his winemaking career at Houghton in 1922. Fifty one vintages later, in 1972, he retired having made legendary innovations to Australia's wine industry.

In 1937, Jack produced the first vintage of Houghton's White Burgundy. The popular taste of the day was for fortified wines, but the full-bodied flavour of the White Burgundy saw it become Australia's first widely accepted table wine.

The wine has continued to be made, and its great success owes much to Jack's winemaking philosophy and technical developments. The introduction of ideas such as cooling during fermentation and picking fruit only when completely ripe, contributed to the creation of Houghton's full-bodied wines. Jack also retained grape skins in fermenting wines to further strengthen flavours.

Another of Jack's developments arose when attempting to crush the shrivelled grapes used in making fortified wines. An

ingenious 'Mincer' was created to crush these raisined grapes, and proved very successful in the production of Jack's excellent sherries, muscats and tokays.

Jack unfortunately passed on at the age of 83 years in 1989, but his wines still live on somewhere deep in my cellar.

The Swan Valley of today has much to offer the visitor. A very pleasant way to visit the larger wineries is to take a river cruise up the Swan River on either the Miss Sandalford or the Lady Houghton. These vessels are delightfully furnished, and depart from Perth's Barrack Street Pier at 10 am. The trip is completed by 4 pm.

On tours to either the Sandalford or Houghton wineries and vineyards wines are available for tasting and served with lunch.

The highlight of the year for the Swan Valley is the Annual "Spring in the Valley" festival held in October. This celebration of fine wines, superb food, music, art and theatre involves many of the leading wineries, who all feature at least three different attractions at their premises. You can enjoy classical, jazz or popular music from live bands, watch magicians and street theatre, participate with potters and painters, see wood carving, tour historic buildings and participate in many other interesting activities, all of course, accompanied by the fine wines and foods of the region. Many wineries choose this time to release their new vintages and some even offer the visitor a taste of wines yet to be released.

Swan Valley

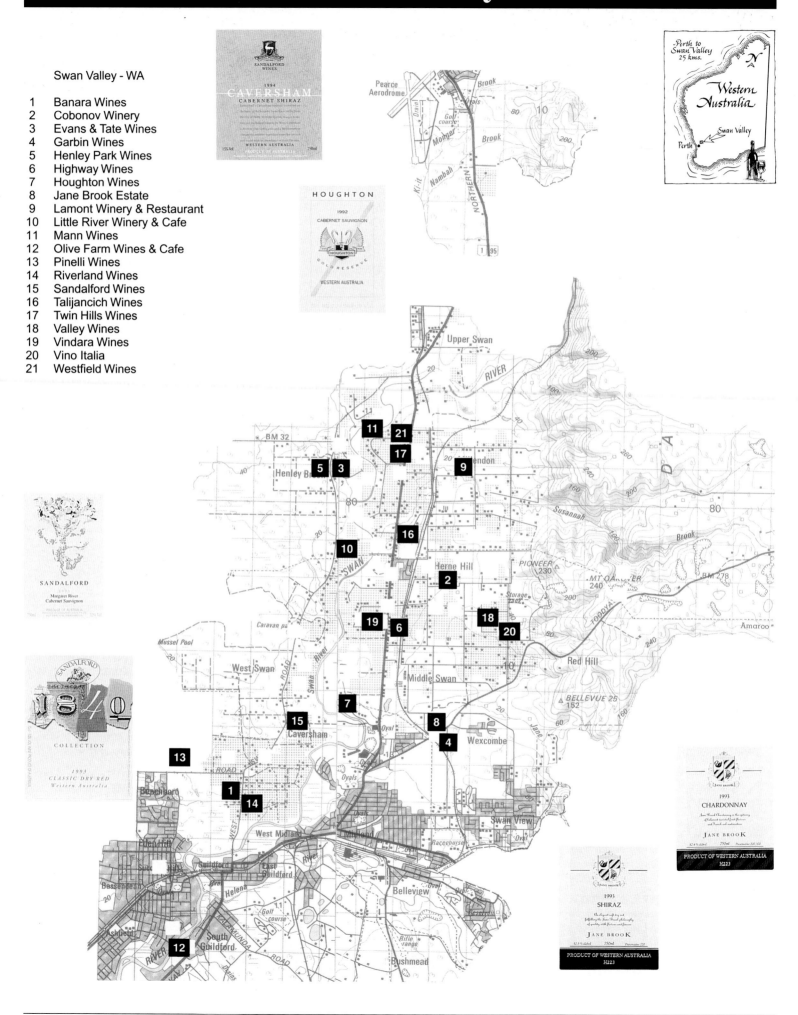

Swan Valley - WA

1. Banara Wines
2. Cobonov Winery
3. Evans & Tate Wines
4. Garbin Wines
5. Henley Park Wines
6. Highway Wines
7. Houghton Wines
8. Jane Brook Estate
9. Lamont Winery & Restaurant
10. Little River Winery & Cafe
11. Mann Wines
12. Olive Farm Wines & Cafe
13. Pinelli Wines
14. Riverland Wines
15. Sandalford Wines
16. Talijancich Wines
17. Twin Hills Wines
18. Valley Wines
19. Vindara Wines
20. Vino Italia
21. Westfield Wines

Houghton

Houghton was established in 1859 by colonial surgeon, Dr. John Ferguson. The vineyard was planted at Middle Swan and further developed by the founder's second son, Charles Ferguson.

By the time the property was purchased by the Emu Wine Company in 1950 the company had grown to a considerable size. The Emu Wine Company had already purchased the large Valencia Vineyard at Caversham and the addition of Houghton created Western Australia's largest wine company. Staff remaining with the company after the takeover included winemaker Jack Mann. His white burgundy, together with the cabernet sauvignon and fortified wines, were very popular on the Australian market. Much of Houghton's other output was exported and was highly successful on the overseas market.

Unfortunately, despite the company's financial success, Emu Wines did not re-channel profits into the company, but preferred to maintain a distance with the industry. The ingenuity of general manager Ian Smith and winemakers Jack Mann and Charlie Kelly at Valencia was tested to the limit. With little but the bare necessities, excellent wine continued to be made at Houghton.

Great changes occurred, however, four years after Jack's retirement in 1972. In 1976, the Emu Wine Company was purchased by Thomas Hardy & Sons, who immediately began work on updating winemaking equipment. Bill Hardy and, later, Jon Reynolds were appointed as the new

winemakers. Having graduated as dux of the Diploma D'Oenologique course from the University of Bordeaux in France, and having made several vintages at Hardy's McLaren Vale, Bill was more than qualified to take on this new position. Jon, originally from the Hunter Valley, had made wines at Reynella and came over to make the Houghton.

Without altering the award-winning style of the famous Houghton White Burgundy, Bill and Jon freshened the wine by employing up-to-date winemaking techniques. The Show Reserve Houghton White Burgundies with a blue label, released when fully matured, have shown just how good this Australian classic is. The standard white burgundies are bottle-aged and released under this Show Reserve label; all have won many gold medals and trophies in wine shows.

Currently the popular line range of wines that includes the Houghton White Burgundy also features - Semillon Sauvignon Blanc, Frankland River Rhine Riesling, Cabernet Sauvignon, Chablis and Cygnet. The Gold Reserve range is the flagship wines and includes a Cabernet Sauvignon, Chardonnay and Verdelho.

In addition to the company's wines, packaging also received a facelift under Hardy's management at Houghton. The new labels are simple yet elegant and the white burgundy has retained its distinctive blue stripe. The classic old cellars at Houghton and Dr. Ferguson's original home have also received some attention. Both have been beautifully restored and additions to the

cellars have been tastefully handled. The Middle Swan Winery is a joy to visit and exudes an air of history.

Houghton wines are popular throughout Western Australia and most releases are marketed Australia-wide. Over the years, the company has done much to further Western Australia's wine industry, particularly in its development of regions outside the Swan Valley.

Like several other medium-sized wine companies, (e.g. Wolf Blass, Wyndham Estate and Brown Brothers), Houghton have become one of Australia's success stories. As a result of innovative management, the company obtains good financial returns in exchange for its large investments. Houghton was involved in the merger that formed BRL Hardy in 1992.

The winery has benefited even further from the capital injection this merger provided. In 1994 new vineyards at Pemberton and Mount Barker were added to the collection and fruit from these properties will further enhance the premium end of the portfolio with additional wines.

Houghton White Burgundy still continues to be one of Australia's favourite whites and the 1997 vintage will be the 60th consecutive release for this famous wine.

Winemaker since 1985, Peter Dawson has now become chief winemaker for BRL Hardy based in Adelaide and was succeeded in 1993 by Paul Lapsley. Houghton continues to add lustre to the Western Australian wine industry like a star footballer in a champion team.

Jane Brook Estate

Beverley and David are very focused on their beloved Jane Brook Estate, situated at the base of the Darling Range in the beautiful Swan Valley, less than 30 minutes from Perth.

David discovered his passion for wine through a book on Australian wine he came across on his beat in the wheatlands, north of Perth, as marketing manager for an oil company. David and Beverley, as newlyweds in 1972, purchased the property known as "Vignacourt Wines". In 1984, after a decade of replanting the vineyad to premium varieties and re-equipping the winery for quality wine production, the Atkinson's changed the winery name to Jane Brook, the name of the brook which runs through the property. The Jane Brook was named by John Septimus Roe, the first Surveyor General of the Swan River colony, during his initial exploration of the upper reaches of the Swan River in September 1829. It was named in honour of Jane Currie, the wife of Capt. Mark Currie, the first Harbour Master of Fremantle.

Beverley and David have continued developing the vineyard and property into a show piece .... a tribute to hard work and commitment. The tasting and sales cellars are situated within this traditional rustic winery and there is an attractive vine covered courtyard and timber decking overlooking Jane Brook where lunches are served daily.

Lunch comprises a splendid vineyard platter of cheeses, pates, fruit and salads and is a perfect accompaniment to a glass of Jane Brook premium table wine. The welcoming and knowledgable staff at Jane Brook will make any visit a memorable one.

The domain of sales, marketing and export belongs to Beverley, whose energy and enthusiasm is boundless. During recent years she has learnt to speak Japanese to compliment their well funded and researched push into the Japanese market. The Atkinson's are now assisting the Western Australian wine industry to develop a Japanese wine export campaign, a challenge that they find fascinating.

Jane Brook make a classic range of varietal wines specialising in whites, wood aged chenin blanc, sauvignon blanc, chardonnay and an excellent Mount Barker Rhine Riesling. The cabernet merlot is full bodied with soft tannins. New winemaker, Lyndon Crockett, (ex Penfolds and Lindemans) has reintroduced a superb dry red shiraz style to the stable. Two excellent sparkling wines made by the traditional "methode champenoise" have been produced in the last three years. The 1993 Elizabeth Jane Chardonnay and Cabernet Merlot B.D.R. named after the Atkinson's daughter, Elizabeth Jane, and son, Benjamin David Robert, have both been scored highly at the last three Sheraton Wine Awards in Perth.

JANE BROOK ESTATE WINES
Address: 229 Toodyay Road, Middle Swan WA 6056
Direction: Situated on Toodyay Road between Roe Highway & Farrell Road
Phone: (09) 274 1432
Fax: (09) 274 1211
Email: janewine@highway1.com.au (Onaustralia go word: janewine)
Established: 1972
Owner: David & Beverley Atkinson
Winemaker: David Atkinson (senior)
Principal varieties grown: Chenin blanc, chardonnay, sauvignon blanc, cabernet sauvignon, merlot, shiraz
Ha under vine: 12.5
Average annual crush: 94 tonnes (plus contract growers)
Average no. cases produced: 7,000

Principal wines & brands	Cellar potential
Wood Aged Chenin Blanc	2-5 years
Chardonnay	2-5 years
Sauvignon Blanc	2-5 years
"Methode Champenoise" Chardonnay	5-10 years
"Methode Champenoise" Cabernet Merlot	5-10 years
Cabernet Merlot	5-10 years
Shiraz	5-10 years

Trade tours: By appointment only
Cellar door & mail order sales: Yes
Hours open to public: 7 days a week 12 am-5 pm including public holidays
Points of interest: Tasting and sales cellar are situated in a traditional working winery. Al fresco lunches served daily in the cellar by a log fire or in the garden courtyard overlooking Jane Brook.
Retail distribution: Distributed in Western Australia through liquor stores, hotels & restaurants direct from the cellar to liquor stores in Melbourne & Sydney, export to Japan & India.

Sandalford – Caversham Estate

Sandalford was established by one of the founding fathers of Western Australia - John Septimus Roe, the state's first Surveyor General.

Septimus Roe arrived on board the Parmelia in 1829 and quickly set about establishing the site for the beautiful city of Perth. After some ten years he was rewarded for his services with the granting of a tract of land on the banks of the upper reaches of the Swan Valley. The property was named "Sandalford" after the priory in Berkshire at which his father was rector.

Vines were planted on the property but they were made only for family consumption. The Roe family began commercial production of wines, during the 1940's and in 1971 the founders great grandson, John, replanted the vineyards and reorganised the business so that Sandalford became a private company.

The original site is now home to Sandalford's winery and Caversham vineyard which has 15 hectares planted to chenin blanc, verdelho, semillon, shiraz and cabernet sauvignon. There are two table and two fortified wines produced, the chenin verdelho and cabernet shiraz and the enormously popular Sandalera and Founders Reserve Liqueur Port.

In late 1992 the complexion of the company changed dramatically. After a brief period of overseas ownership a group of Western Australian business interests - determined to return the label to its former glory - combined to "buy back the farm".

Under the tutelage of renowned winemaker Bill Crappsley, formerly of Evans and Tate, and Ted Avery, ex General Manager of the Houghton Wine Company, the winery and vineyard was transformed. Vines were re-trained to the Scott Henry trellising system, new stainless steel tanks installed and winery's cooling system overhauled. Old oak was culled mercilessly and the wines improved dramatically.

On my recent visit to Sandalford I was most impressed with the improvements Bill and his team have worked hard to achieve but, above all, I was very impressed with the wines themselves - Sandalford is in good hands, indeed. There is a riverboat that brings visitors to Sandalford's Caversham vineyard and winery every day from Peth's Barrack Street Jetty. If travelling from Perth it's only a leisurely half hours drive.

Sandalford is again a rising star in the Western Australian wine scene - to the benefit of all wine lovers.

SANDALFORD WINES - CAVERSHAM VINEYARD & MARGARET RIVER VINEYARD

Address: 3210 West Swan Road, Caversham WA 6055; Metricup Road, Cowaramup WA 6284
Phone: (09) 274 5922
Fax: (09) 274 2154
Established: 1840
Winemaker: Bill Crappsley
Principal varieties grown: Chardonnay, riesling, verdelho, cabernet sauvignon, shiraz, semillon, chenin blanc, sauvignon blanc
Ha under vine: 190
Average annual crush: 900 tonnes
Average no. cases produced: 75,000

Principal wines & brands	Cellar potential
Pemberton Chardonnay	2-5 years
Verdelho	2-5 years
Rhine Riesling	2-5 years
1840 Collection Chardonnay	2-5 years
1840 Collection Semillion Blanc	2-5 years
1840 Collection Cabernet Shiraz Malbec	2-5 years

Public & trade tours: Yes
Cellar door & mail order sales: Yes
Hours open to public: 10 am-5 pm seven days (Caversham); 10.30 am-5 pm seven days (Margaret River)
Points of interest: Plans underway for redevelopments including brasserie, emporium and function centre
Retail distribution: Australia-wide through hotels, restaurants and liquor stores, Western Australia/Northern Territory, FOQ (WA) Pty Ltd; NSW/ACT, Hill International Wines; Vic/Tas, Rutherglen Wine & Spirit Co; SA, Richard Mackie Fine Wines, Qld, Wine Partners

An introduction to Pemberton

In virtually no time at all, an important new wine region, now supporting some 20 winemakers and a number of large vineyards of the Goliaths of the wine industry, has sprung to life. Deep in the karri, jarrah and redgum country, home of the tallest trees in Australia, lies one of the most exciting and beautiful Australian wine regions.

In the 1930s a small amount of wine was made at Middlesex in the heart of the region. Its real birth as a wine region however, came with the urging of Tony Devitt, agricultural and viticultural expert, who proposed vineyard and winemaking trials be undertaken.

It was the recommendation by Dr Gladstones in his viticultural report in the 1960s, that the area was well suited to early ripening vines such as chardonnay and pinot noir, that prompted this move. The results came through a decade later in 1987 with flying colours. Today, BRL Hardy through Houghton have a large investment in what will become one of the state's largest vineyards; no doubt Sir James Methode Champenoise is in focus for the fruit.

Domaine Chandon are sourcing fruit from a large vineyard at Manjimup. Salitage, the winery of John Horgan, is a splendid operation whose restaurant and planned winery should make it one of Australia's best large boutiques of the next century. Already its wines are world class. Gloucester Ridge have a great little winery near the extraordinary Gloucester Tree park and many other exciting developments such as Eastbrook Wines give this region huge potential to become an important part of the premium Australian wine scene.

Gloucester Ridge

It's a good thing the massive Gloucester tree does not topple over, as it would certainly add a different meaning to crushing at the pretty little winery in its shadow. At least 250,000 visitors climb this extraordinary Karri tree each year.

Don Hancock's uncle was the well-known Clare winemaker, Mick Knappstein, but Don and his wife, Sue, ran a cattle farm in the Margaret River region, ironically surrounded by vineyards. They eventually searched for a vineyard site and in 1981, bought at Pemberton. Vines didn't come until four years later and only a small area was planted.

The results were excellent, so the vineyard has been expanded to 15 acres and there are plans to double this. Slowly, the tourists began to drop in and the pretty little cellar door is being expanded to incorporate a bistro area. In the meantime, a hoard of school buses lurk behind the winery, providing Don and Susan with their daily bread as they operate this service in the area.

The Hancock's son, Michael, is vineyard manager and John Wade is the contract winemaker. Quite a large range of wines are made, including a couple of semi-sweet wines that have proven most successful with the tourists pouring through each day. The two chardonnays I tried, the Reserve and the unwooded version, would be gold medal winners in my book. Gloucester Ridge is obviously serious about its wines and is not just relying on its unique location.

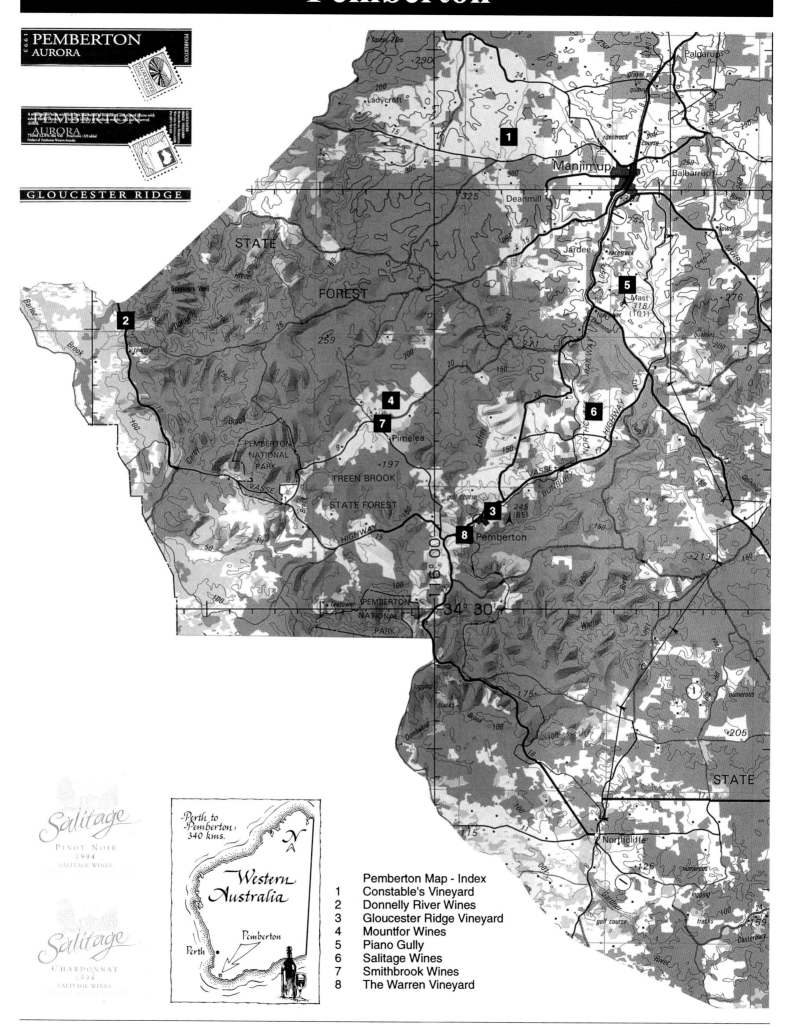

Pemberton Map - Index
1 Constable's Vineyard
2 Donnelly River Wines
3 Gloucester Ridge Vineyard
4 Mountfor Wines
5 Piano Gully
6 Salitage Wines
7 Smithbrook Wines
8 The Warren Vineyard

Perth to Pemberton: 340 kms.

Western Australia

Perth

Pemberton

Salitage

John Horgan is a perfectionist who never settles for second best. During the 1970s he set up Leeuwin Estate with his brother Denis, who purchased John's share in 1980. During this time, John developed a strong friendship with, and respect for, the great Robert Mondavi of California.

John also had a long-time love affair with the wines of Burgundy. In fact, along with a group of Australians, including two Burgundian enthusiasts, David Clarke and Ross Grant of Sydney, they purchased a French Burgundian Domain, La Pousse d'Or. Pousse in French is a noun meaning to shoot or grow, but also the verb means to drive somebody to do. D'or of course is gold.

John was driven to find somewhere in his homeland where he could grow the chardonnay and pinot noir vines to make truly Burgundian style wines. He found this land and climate at Pemberton, on the most elevated ridge of the region; the gravelly soil over ironstone provides the wines with a spine, and a distinct flinty character.

John and Jenny Horgan chose the name, a combination of the first two letters of the names of their four children, Sarah, Lisa, Tamara and Gerard.

The winery at Salitage is magnificent, vaulted and at the moment a little cavernous, as it has been designed to suit the needs of the future. Considering the already evident greatness of the wines, it was a move of considerable vision.

The wines all see some absolutely top class French oak barriques and they are at once rich and yet complex. So far, the range includes a fresh sauvignon blanc, more at the tropical fruit end of the flavour spectrum, a chardonnay rich with lemon and grapefruit flavours and toasty hazelnut overtones with some pineapple and banana tropical flavours - a real mouthful. The gamey, racy pinot noir has dark cherries bursting out. It's certainly in the best few examples of the variety in Australia. A cabernet blend has just been released and I was most impressed by both the 1993 and 1994 that I tried at the winery.

Winemaker is Patrick Coutts, a Roseworthy dux, who has made wine in the south of France at Limoux, in Germany's Rhinephalz, and at Paso Robles in California, as well as the high profile Australian wineries of Brokenwood and Domaine Chandon. The winery sports a large open restaurant area and a superb dining hall upstairs. Lunches, simple and classy, are served daily and are superb. Michael Bewsher, John Horgan's son-in-law, is the capable and energetic manager of the property. We will hear a lot more about this impressive winery and I'm sure it will all be good news.

Following the development of a wine industry in New South Wales, the next state to establish viticulture was Tasmania. The state's first commercial vineyard was planted by Bartholomew Broughton in 1823, near New Town, north of Hobart. Other landowners followed suit, developing vineyards around the state, but sadly the industry was short-lived. By the 1890s Tasmania's first involvement with winemaking was over.

A re-birth of the industry occurred during the late 1950s. The first commercial vineyard was established by Claudio Alcorso in 1958, on a beautiful peninsula in the Derwent River. The property is still in existence and is now known as Moorilla Estate. Encouraged by Alcorso's success, other vignerons began to plant vines and there are now four wine-producing regions. These are the Pipers River area north-east of Launceston, the Tamar Valley north of Launceston, the East Coast and finally Southern Tasmania - the area around Hobart - comprising the Derwent Valley, Coal Valley and the Huon - d'Entrecasteau Valleys. A large percentage of the production comes from the Pipers River region.

Although the State's production is relatively small, there are more than 50 wine producers and many more vineyards, and the industry is growing fast with the guidance and assistance of a very supportive State Government. The quality of Tasmanian wine has been of such a standard that mainland winemakers have had to take notice. Some wines have been exceptional.

It has been widely assumed that Tasmania's cool wet climate would prevent viticulture. This is far from the truth, as many areas of the State experience a mild climate, comparable with some parts of the mainland. Grapes tend to ripen slowly, but ripening is not often a problem to winemakers. All Tasmanian regions can be quite warm in some years, and surprisingly, in some seasons can experience drought conditions. Tasmanian wine styles are many, but the methode champenoise wines are absolutely outstanding, and many mainland wineries are either sourcing grapes or wines in Tasmania to use in their sparkling wine blends. Although Tasmania's winemakers cannot hope to compete with the volume of wine produced on the mainland, their wines are certainly capable of taking on the best in quality terms.

An introduction to Northern Tasmania

There are now two main regions in the north of Tasmania that have vineyards and make wine. The chief of these is the Pipers River region, some 35 kilometres north-east of Launceston. The climate in all Tasmanian wine regions is ideal for viticulture. The soils are generally rich and red, but also drain very well. The country is generally quite hilly and the easterly-facing slopes can be planted to give a better aspect to the sun and protect the vines from at times severe westerly winds.

Many of the vineyards have windbreaks of poplars which provide good growing season protection and add to the magnificent autumn kaleidoscope of colour this region enjoys. The red soils, the green, yellow and amber tones of the vine leaves, the deep blue skies and the fluffy white clouds are truly spectacular.

The region is by far the biggest producer in Tasmania, accounting for about 70 per cent of wine production. One of the first vineyard-wineries established was Heemskerk, back in 1975, a venture between Graham Wiltshire and the Fesq family wine business in Sydney. For a time the French Champagne house of Louis Roederer was involved, but today dynamic and visionary Tasmanian businessman, Joe Chromy, holds the reins.

Dr Andrew Pirie, who has a PhD in viticulture, established Pipers Brook Wines in 1974. Other large players are the Clover Hill vineyards of Dominique Portet's Taltarni Vineyard in Victoria and Rochecombe, Heemskerk's sister winery. Other smaller boutique producers such as Dalrymple make up the balance. In all, around eight wine producers cover the region.

Probably the prettiest viticultural area in Australia, and perhaps the world, is that surrounding the Tamar Estuary. The vineyards generally are planted on the relatively steep slopes of the eastern shores of this estuary which varies from several kilometres to several hundred metres in width. Many of these wineries have hospitality operations with restaurants and even accommodation. The active bird-life requires netting of the vines (or very active deterrents) to guard the valuable crop. The grapes in this region have a very long ripening period and often achieve high degrees of sugar combined with good acid levels, the winemaker's dream.

Wineries such as Marion's and Strathlynn make the most of their locations. Being less than half an hour from Launceston make a visit essential. The Lake Barrington Vineyard is the first in north-western Tasmania (really more north-centred). This beautiful vineyard and cute winery and tasting room overlooks the large Lake Barrington. With mountains all around, it's like being in the Swiss Alps. Of the northern Tasmanian wines, chardonnay, pinot noir and methode champenoise stand out but good riesling, sauvignon blanc, shiraz, merlot and cabernet sauvignon can be produced in the various microclimates that the region possesses.

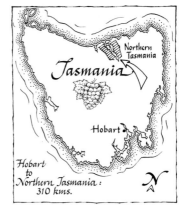

1	Bellingham Vineyard
3	Brook Eden Vineyard
4	Clover Hill Vineyard
8	Delrymple Vineyard
9	Delamere Vineyard
16	Heemskerk Vineyard
17	Holm Oak Vineyard
19	King Island Cheese
21	Lactos Master Cheesemakers
22	Lake Barrington Estate
23	Lalla Gully Vineyard
24	La Provence
25	Marions Vineyard
31	Pipers Brook Vineyard
33	Rochecombe Vineyard
34	Rotherhythe Vineyard
35	Rowella Vineyard
36	St Matthias Rosevears
38	Strathlynn Wine Centre

Clover Hill

CLOVER HILL
Address: Clover Hill Road, Lebrina, Tas 7254
Direction: Less than 1 km north-east through Lebrina, at top of hill on left
Phone: (003) 95 6114
Fax: (003) 95 6257
Established: 1986
Owner: Mr John Goelet
Winemakers: Dominique Portet & Shane Clohesy
Principal varieties grown: Chardonnay, pinot noir, pinot meunier
Ha under vine: 20
Average annual crush: 100 tonnes
Average no. cases produced: 3,000

Principal wines & brands	Cellar potential
Clover Hill	0-2 years

Public & trade tours: By appointment only
Cellar door & mail order sales: Yes
Hours open to public: All visits only by appointment
Points of interest: Vineyard and winemaking facility at present, visitor centre planned for December 1995
Retail distribution: Available in all States of Australia including ACT and Northern Territory, exported to the UK, Denmark & USA

The quest for superior quality fruit to produce a super premium Australian sparkling wine lead Taltarni Victorian winemaker, Dominique Portet, to Tasmania. In 1986, after a two year study, he purchased a prime hillside site on rich red volcanic soils, known as Clover Hill.

Located at Lebrina, in the Pipers River region of north east Tasmania, Clover Hill is a 75 hectare property, with 20 hectares so far planted to the three premium grape varieties chardonnay, pinot noir and pinot meunier. An on-site winery facility processes the grapes into still base wines, the conversion to sparkling wine being completed at Taltarni in Victoria. There are plans for the construction of a complete winery and visitor centre from December 1995. The three classic varieties will eventually comprise the finished blend, but the first two vintages are 100% chardonnay, the 1991 (Grand Championship Trophy at the Inaugural Cairns Wine Show) and the 1992 (Gold Medal - Hobart, Trophy - Perth and Trophy - Adelaide) providing evidence that Clover Hill is on its way to becoming one of the very finest Australian sparkling wines.

Dalrymple Vineyard

At first sight this impressive vineyard reminded me of a Roman amphitheatre. The rows of vines are in perfect symmetry and the vines are like soldiers standing guard over the developing winery and home of cancer specialist, Dr. Bertel Sundstrup and his wife, Anne.

DALRYMPLE VINEYARDS
Address: Pipers Brook Road, Pipers Brook, Tas. 7254
Phone: (003) 82 7222
Fax: (003) 82 7222
Established: 1987
Owner: Dr & Mrs (Anne) Bertel Sundstrup
Winemaker: Nicholas Butler
Principal varieties grown: Chardonnay, pinot noir, sauvignon blanc
Ha under vine: 10
Average annual crush: 45 tonnes

Principal wines & brands	Cellar potential
Chardonnay (wooded)	2-6 years
Chardonnay (unwooded)	1-4 years
Pinot Noir	5-10 years
Sauvignon Blanc (unwooded)	1-4 years

Trade tours: By appointment only
Cellar door & mail order sales: Yes
Hours open to public: 10 am-4 pm Mon-Fri; 10 am-5 pm w/e
Points of interest: Superb view of vineyards from new spacious cellar door tasting area. Visitors welcome to inspect vineyards.
Retail distribution: Aberfeldy Cellars, Hobart; Larters, Launceston.

Recently the Sundstrups have been joined in the business by the very knowledgeable and wise, Jill Mitchell, who for many years produced the outstanding Melbourne radio program of Ross Campbell.

Stretched across several hundred metres at the peak of this beautifully balanced hill of vines is a long sign on shadecloth that clearly reads, from the road many hundred metres below, 'Dalrymple Vineyard.' It is impressive indeed.

The establishment of the vineyard, close to the two biggest vineyards in Tasmania, Heemskerk and Pipers Brook, began in 1987 and the plantings include pinot noir, chardonnay and sauvignon blanc. The first vintage releases were in 1991 and all wines have won medals in Tasmania or mainland wine shows. The pinot noir and sauvignon have been made by Nicholas Butler at Holm Oak Winery on the Tamar, and the chardonnays at Heemskerk, although from 1995 all wines are now being made by Nicolas Butler. A winery has been constructed at Dalrymple and is in the process of being equipped. I predict great wines from this well organised venture.

Holm Oak Vineyards

Nicholas Butler has a splendid little winery and a gorgeous vineyard on the northern reaches of the Tamar Estuary, near Rowella. The name is taken from an evergreen oak tree just near the winery. Many other oaks line the driveways and the winery and vineyard entrance off the main road is one of the prettiest in Australia.

Nick had a brush with fame, so to speak, when Prime Minister, Paul Keating, who is not a big wine-drinker, took a shine to his 1992 Cabernet during an ALP conference in Hobart. The PM was attending a birthday party for journalists, Peter Harvey and Paul Bongiorno, when the Holm Oak Cabernet captured his palate. Not long afterwards an official order arrived from Canberra and Holm Oak is now a regular visitor at The Lodge for official functions.

Nick is a keen, enthusiastic and creative winemaker and makes wines for Dalrymple Vineyard also. If you want to see a charming small winery at work, in a beautiful location, visit Holm Oak. You could also take a leaf out of the Prime Minister's book and have Holm Oak at home.

HOLM OAK VINEYARDS
Address: RSD 256, Rowella Tas. 7270
Phone: (003) 94 7577
Fax: (003) 94 7350
Established: 1983
Winemaker: Nicholas Butler
Principal varieties grown: Pinot noir, cabernet sauvignon, riesling
Ha under vine: 6
Average annual crush: 52 tonnes
Average no. cases produced: 3,000

Principal wines & brands	Cellar potential
Cabernet Sauvignon	5-10 years
Pinot Noir/Chardonnay	2-5 years
Pinot Noir	2-5 years

Public & trade tours: By appointment only
Cellar door & mail order sales: Yes
Hours open to public: 12-5 pm seven days a week
Retail distribution: Australian Liquor Marketers in Tasmania only or contact the vineyard.

Marion's Vineyard

One could call Marion's Vineyard a small piece of paradise. The vineyard is located in a natural, north-east facing amphitheatre which overlooks the Tamar Estuary. Mark and Marion fell in love with this beautiful valley and its wine growing potential while visiting Tasmania in 1979. The following year they sold their California home and business and moved the family to Deviot.

They began clearing their 10 ha "jungle bush rock heap" and immediately planted 2 ha from a nursery a local had established for them before they left America. Vines grew rapidly and they crushed their first 5.5 tonnes in 1983. They opened Tasmania's first cellar door in October of that year.

Recently, a new stone winery with stained glass windows was built and the Semmens' original home is now self-contained accommodation, available for the wine traveller.

Above the winery is a restaurant and reception centre which can cater for up to 300 people. The tireless Marion is a talented chef and oversees all the catering, which is excellent. If you want something more casual, the BBQ facilities are very good and the view sensational.

In 1986 I was 'blown away' by the rich style and superb quality of Marion's pinot noir and chardonnay and have been a contented client ever since.

The Semmens also grow and produce an outstanding mullerthurgau, a German hybrid which produces great riesling styles in cool climates like theirs. The Deviot microclimate also helps Marion's produce a deep-coloured, robust cabernet sauvignon.

If you ever have the chance, come to a Marion's concert in the natural outdoor amphitheatre - it is a memorable experience.

MARION'S VINEYARD
Address: 51 Foreshore Drive, Deviot Tas. 7275
Phone: (003) 94 7434
Fax: (003) 94 7434
Established: 1980
Winemaker: Mark & Marion Semmens
Principal varieties grown: Pinot noir, chardonnay, cabernet sauvignon, muller-thurgau, pinot-gris, zinfandel
Ha under vine: 8
Average annual crush: 40 tonnes
Average no. cases produced: 2,500

Principal wines & brands	Cellar potential
Cabernet Sauvignon	5-10 years
Pinot Noir	5-10 years
Chardonnay	2-5 years
Muller-Thurgau	2-5 years
Afterglow-Pinot Noir Blush	2-5 years

Cellar door & mail order: Yes
Public & trade tours: Yes
Hours open to public: 10 am-5 pm seven days a week
Points of interest: Outdoor functions, weddings, deli, outdoor restaurant, wine and cheese tastings. All group functions. Accommodation (1 self contained unit) - more to be built in the near future
Retail distribution: Cellar door, mail order, shops and restaurants in Tasmania

Heemskerk

Established in the early 1970's, Heemskerk has become one of Tasmania's largest and better known wine producers. The vineyard is located in the heart of the Pipers River region, on rich red soils. The winery has a definite seafaring style with its high pitched roof and baltic timbers reminiscent of a stately galleon sailing through a sea of vines. Suitably, the venture was named "Heemskerk" after the ship of Tasmania's discoverer, Abel Tasman.

The climate of north east Tasmania is midway between that of Burgundy and Champagne in France. In warmer years this allows Heemskerk to produce rich, soft pinot noir wines, akin to the best of Burgundy, and every year, to produce chardonnay and pinot noir ideal for the splendid 'Jansz' Methode Champenoise Cuvee.

Of the table wines, the cabernet sauvignon, in particular, is extremely well regarded, setting the tone for the cool climate styles eagerly sought after by discerning wine consumers. With its hints of tobacco leaves, green tea and mulberry-like fruit, it has exceptional quality and flavour.

In collaboration with "Roederer", the prestigious Champagne House of France, one of Australia's best premium sparkling wines has evolved. The '89 cuvee took the wine world by storm, carrying the name 'Jansz' after the skipper of Tasman's smaller companion ship on his voyage of discovery. Normally Jansz has a base wine of 50 per cent chardonnay and 50 per cent pinot noir, but recent plantings of pinot meunier will add an extra complexity to the cuvee. Jansz spends approximately two and a half years ageing on yeast lees in the bottle. Shortly, a late disgorged version with five years tirage ageing will be added to the range. The development of the Jansz style is now in the hands of specialist sparkling winemaker Gary Ford, who has the experience of 12 vintages in Australia and France.

The Heemskerk vineyard has been extended by 43,000 vines and at 41 hectares will be, when fully planted, the largest in Tasmania. Heemskerk Wines, under the watchful eye of chief winemaker, Steve Goodwin, formerly of Baileys, continues to be among Australia's best producer of cool-climate table wines and increasingly, sparkling wines.

Heemskerk wines seem to me to have a natural affinity with the seafoods, cheeses and game meats for which Tasmania is justifiably renowned. The pristine environment gives clean, fresh and untainted, long-living flavours to the wines.

HEEMSKERK
Address: Pipers Brook Road, Pipers Brook Tas. 7254
Phone: (003) 82 7133
Fax: (003) 82 7242
Established: 1976
Owner: Tamar Valley Wines
Winemaker: Steve Goodwin and Garry Ford
Principal varieties grown: Pinot noir, chardonnay, riesling
Average annual crush: 114 tonnes
Average no. cases produced: 10,000

Principal wines & brands	Cellar potential
Jansz Sparkling	5-10 years
Chardonnay	2-5 years
Pinot Noir	5-10 years
Riesling	2-5 years
Cabernet Merlot	5-10 years

Public & trade tours: Yes
Cellar door & mail order sales: Yes
Hours open to public: 9 am-5 pm seven days a week (weekdays only during winter)
Retail distribution: Fesq Dorado & Company, national

Rochecombe Vineyard

Rochecombe Vineyard is a picture of beauty and order, with close vines trimmed in tall hedge-like rows which seem to spread forever over the gently rolling hills just south of the town of Pipers River. The vineyard runs down to the river and if you're very quiet you may be lucky enough to spot a platypus (the symbol on the Rochecombe label) playfully cavorting in the stream.

The winery is in its 10th year of operation and is very well equipped with a multitude of small tanks, with the ability to make many separate batches of wine. The future has been well catered for in this large impressive building. A very good restaurant adjoins the winery on a slight rise at the end of a beautiful driveway lined with splendid European trees, which were wearing their colourful autumn cloaks on our visit. This superbly-designed building features split levels and cleverly designed areas to create a cosy feel, but also gives panoramic views over the vineyards. Tastings can also be enjoyed, accompanied by a platter of fine Tasmanian cheeses and Blue Ribbon smallgoods.

The whole feel of Rochecombe is European, which is not surprising as it was founded by Swiss winemakers, Bernard and Brigitte Rochaix. Joe Chromy's JAC Group purchased the vineyard and winery complex recently and are investing heavily in an expansion program. I am sure the mainland and export wine markets will see more of the excellent Rochecombe Wines.

Chief winemaker for the JAC Group, Steve Goodwin, bases himself at Rochecombe and puts in a monumental amount of work to make sure the wines are truly world class. The vineyard reminds me a lot of Burgundy, with the vine training, red soils and undulating slopes. The Burgundian varieties of chardonnay and pinot noir dominate the vineyard, and, as well as producing fine table wines, contribute towards the creation of the sensational Janz Methode Champenoise. The vineyard also grows chenin blanc, riesling, sauvignon blanc and the cabernet-related Bordeaux varieties. A delicious pinot rose is also produced. Rochecombe is a credit to the Tasmanian wine industry, a vinous paradise.

ROCHECOMBE

Address: Baxters Road, Pipers River, Tasmania 7252
Phone: (003) 82 7122
Fax: (003) 82 7231
Established: 1983
Owner: Tamar Valley Wines
Winemaker: Steve Goodwin and Garry Ford
Principal varieties grown: Pinot noir, chardonnay, sauvignon blanc, cabernet merlot
Average annual crush: 138 tonnes

Principal wines & brands	Cellar potential
Chardonnay	2-5 years
Pinot Noir	5-10 years
Cabernet Sauvignon	5-10 years
Sauvignon Blanc	5-10 years

Public & trade tours: Yes
Cellar door & mail order sales: Yes
Hours open to public: 10 am-5 pm seven days a week
Points of interest: Restaurant
Retail distribution: Being set up - call vineyard for details

Pipers Brook

Dr. Andrew Pirie is generally acknowledged as Australia's most learned viticulturist, and is the country's first holder of a PhD in that subject. Before establishing his own vineyard, Andrew conducted an exhaustive Australia-wide search for the site most suited to producing European-style wines. He decided on Pipers Brook, to the north-east of Launceston, in 1974.

The wisdom of this decision is quickly evident when sampling any Pipers Brook wines. The demand for these wines is strong, so they are often hard to find. Andrew's prime objective has been to produce high quality, long-ageing wines, using viticultural techniques and site locations similar to those in the great French areas of Bordeaux, Burgundy and Alsace. Pipers Brook has five estates with the following vineyard locations:

Pipers River Region
Pipers Brook Vineyard   16.3ha (Pipers Brook)
Ninth Island Vineyard   12.9ha (Pipers Brook)
Pellion Vineyard   13.2ha (Weymouth)

West Tamar Region
Strathlynn Vineyard   20.4ha (Rosevears)
The Pier Vineyard   6.0ha (Rosevears)

The winemaking techniques are modern with state of the art equipment, using fine French oak for some of the wines.

Two labels are marketed: Pipers Brook Vineyard includes two chardonnays; the 'Summit,' from 21-year-old vines growing on the stony summit of Pipers Brook vineyard and only appearing in the best years, a flinty French Alsace-style riesling for which the vineyard became famous; 'Opimian,' a Bordeaux blend of cabernet/merlot/cabernet franc; and the 'Pellion' pinot

noir. There is also the Ninth Island label, comprising six wines. Dr Pirie is working on a methode champenoise at present, and knowing his exciting and demanding nature, it will be a stunner.

PIPERS BROOK VINEYARD LTD
THE WINERY
Address: Pipers Brook, via Lebrina, Tas. 7254
Direction: Highway B82, 40 minutes north-east of Launceston
Phone: (003) 82 7197
Fax: (003) 82 7226
Established: 1974
Winemaker: Dr Andrew Pirie
Ha under vine: 68.8
Average annual crush: 500 tonnes

Principal wines & brands	Cellar potential
Ninth Island Chardonnay	2-5 years
Ninth Island Straits Dry White	2-5 years
Pipers Brook Vineyard Chard.	5-10 years
Ninth Island Pinot Noir	2-5 years
Pipers Brook Vineyard Riesling	5-15 years
Ninth Island Tamar Cabernets	5-10 years
Pipers Brook Vineyard Pellion	5-10 years

Public & trade tours: Yes
Cellar door & mail order sales: Yes
Hours open to public: 10 am-4 pm Mon-Fri; 11 am-5 pm Sat-Sun (1 November to 30 April only)
Points of interest: Lunches served during summer months only
Retail distribution: All States except Tasmania, S. Smith & Son Pty Ltd; Tasmania, David Johnstone & Assoc.

Lactos Master Cheesemakers

Back in 1955 when Milan Vyhnalek arrived as a Czech refugee in Tasmania, with 300 years of cheesemaking in his family, he could think of only one word to describe Australian cheese - 'cheddar.' At that time, with our traditional Anglo Saxon based cuisine, very few varieties of cheese were made.

So when Milan began the Lactos factory at Burnie on the north-west coast of Tasmania it became Australia's first specialty cheese company making a range of European-style cheeses. Perhaps I should explain a little about the use of the words 'farmhouse' and 'specialty.' In cheesemaking they are in fact a little like the words we use in wine. Farmhouse cheese comes from only one farm and dairy herd. One could compare it to a boutique winery which produces a domain-sourced wine i.e. from its own vineyards only, although several varieties could be produced, such as a chardonnay and a cabernet sauvignon. Specialty cheeses on the other hand are like a regional varietal wine i.e. the Heritage True Blue of Lactos which is made from milk of the Burnie Region only.

Lactos is the biggest specialty cheesemaker in Australia. During the peak production period in the summer 320,000 litres of milk are made into cheese each day. When you consider that it takes about seven litres of milk to produce one kilogram of cheese, this is still a lot of cheese.

The cheesemaker is middle European Janos Kaldy, a youthful looking vibrant man who surprised me when he said he began working at Lactos back in 1972. Since then he has had a number of years working in America, his last job as cheesemaker at a large family factory in Illinois.

In 1981 Lactos was purchased by Bongrain, a large French Agro Alimentaire (food and beverage) company. Janos is a very thorough man and he took us on a full tour of the factory. Visitors must first don sterilised rubber boots, a hair net, a special coat and gloves. No bacteria can be permitted in a good cheese factory. Visitors then walk through a shallow bath of chlorinated water to sterilise their boots, again these baths are at every doorway. First port of call is the pasteurisation room where the milk is pasteurised overnight.

On day two the milk is inoculated with a culture to start the transformation of the milk sugar into lactic acid, a little like wine fermenting. The milk is now about 12-14 deg.C. The milk also has a coagulant added. The temperature of the milk is raised and it is stirred and 'cut' to a special recipe for each different cheese type. By now quite firm cheese in small cubes is put in various moulds and enters the drying room where it spends 24 hours on drying and draining trays. It is acid-adjusted to a pH degree of 5.1 which is pleasant to the human palate. The cheese then enters a brine bath; after this it is another day in the drying room. The various cheese styles then age for different lengths of time in curing rooms where the temperature and humidity are strictly controlled.

Lactos have just spent $1.75 million on a new ultra-filtration plant which can concentrate the strength of the milk by removing water from it without heating it or changing its character at all. I was fascinated by the machinery used to 'spike' the Heritage True Blue, inoculating it with lines of the blue penicillin mould which gives it its character. It is unique to Lactos and looks like an ancient torture chamber. Lactos have just changed the name of their best-selling range of soft ripened cheeses to Heritage, from Tasmania. The word Tasmanian, though, still appears on the label. Camembert, Brie and the famous 'True Blue,' a soft-ripened blue, are the styles.

Then there is the 'Domaine' range - larger, rich soft-ripened cheeses. The Sunrise Camembert has a little sun-ripened tomato and mild red pepper, finely chopped, and the Domaine Red Square, soft ripened with an orange rind, is a little

earthy and pungent. I love it when it is just starting to run inside. There is also the Domaine Deep Blue. Lactos make a Swiss style called St. Claire, at least the counterpart to Jarlsberg, and also an edam style - the Lady Nelson 'Cannonball' in dark wax looking just like a cannonball - and a gouda style, 'FolEpi,' with its unique wheatsheaf styled wax. (FolEpi is French for 'foolish

head of what' which refers to the errant wheat stalk which always (they say) falls from the stack). The Lady Nelson range takes its name from an old square rigger being restored as a youth training vessel. Lactos donate a royalty from every 'round' sold in a generous gesture supporting this project.

The final range of Lactos is their matured Club cheddar styles under the name 'Mersey

Valley.' Some edam and gouda styles are blended back with the ageing cheddar giving a bitey, crumbly but creamy texture. It is hard to explain but they are superb. Try some soon - in fact, make sure you always have some of the excellent Lactos cheese styles on hand for when you pull the cork on a bottle of good wine.

King Island Cheese Company

King Island is like an emerald jewel in a sea of changing colours and moods; this tiny island in Bass Strait, just off the coast of north-western Tasmania is one of the few regions in Australia which stays green all year around and in fact one of the few regions in the world where the dairy herds are able to feed all year on fresh green pastures.

Milan and I were determined to photograph a few head of cattle near the rocky coastline of this island where the cows far outnumber the 1,500 or so inhabitants. Our wish was about to be granted a hundred times over. Rod Banks, who manages the two farms of the King Island Dairy and 2,800 head of cows, took us out towards the coastline where a herd of year-old cows were supposedly grazing. We approached cautiously, because Rod had told us that if they saw us they would probably surround us, looking for feed over the last few months. They had become accustomed to being moved on to new grass pasture feed. Milan was happily snapping the odd few heifers grazing below when suddenly the others saw us. Within minutes 753 heifers were surrounding us - not quite a stampede but it gave Milan's camera some exciting minutes and I became, along with Rod's dog, a cattle-herding cowboy without a horse.

The light changes every moment on this island and the feel of nature is all around. Sea birds of all descriptions, people gathering the kelp for a thousand products, the fishing boats everywhere, the fresh clean breezes cleansed by thousands of miles of oceans - it is one of the purest environments in the world. This is critical when you're making a product gathered by cows from the grasses and then concentrated. Any impurity is magnified many times over.

Then it was on to the dairy where we met the cheesemaster, Frank Beaurain, who hails from Normandy in France, the home of camembert. Frank's cheesemaking career began as a young lad making cheese for his grandmother.

Cheesemaking in a small way began on the island in 1902, but it was not until 1939 that a cooperative for dairy products was formed. In the mid-1980s former manager, David Brewster, made King Island's first brie, a recipe totally conceived on the island.

The Co-op was struggling and in 1988 was taken over by The Island Food Company, a Melbourne-based rural company which also owns Butterfields, a leading Australian gourmet food distributor. The dynamic handling and ability to produce new-style soft ripened cheeses and blue cheeses of world class to fill this growing market niche has seen King Island Dairy go from strength to strength.

The King Island cheese range is led by the Cape Wickham Double Brie, a soft generous white mould cheese, made by old-fashioned methods. The sister cheese is the Phogues Cove Camembert, a little milder and whiter and

firmer in texture than a brie. Both match well with firm, full-bodied red wines or higher acid white styles. When you cut these cheeses seal and store the rest in the original wrapper to let it breathe a little. Cheese, like wine, is a living substance. Blue and strong cheeses should be wrapped in foil.

The Surprise Bay cheddar comes in two versions, one aged for 12 months; the other with slightly more 'bite' is aged for 18 months.

Cheese, like wine, is one of the few foods that improve with careful ageing. The recently released King Island's new range of blue cheeses including Endeavour Blue (gorgonzola style), Bass Strait Blue, Roaring Forties, Admirably Blue (stilton style) and Lighthouse Blue Brie, are all favourites of mine. They say many of the grasses on King Island come from the seeds of straw in

mattresses washed ashore from the hundreds of shipwrecks along the island's coast. Certainly their variety adds to the complexity of the soft full flavours of these truly world-class cheeses.

An introduction to Southern Tasmania

Southern Tasmanian wine regions surround Hobart. The first vineyard in Tasmania was planted by fabric baron, Claudio Alcorso, at Berriedale on the banks of the Derwent River, in a northern suburb of Hobart. Further up the Derwent Valley are several vineyards and wineries, including Meadowbank.

The next area planted was the Coal Valley, east of the Derwent, near Richmond and Campania. The fine Domaine A Stoney Vineyard is here and the Victorian Domaine Chandon's expanding Tolpuddle Vineyards, along with several other small wine ventures. The other Southern Region is the Huon and d'Entrecasteau Valleys, some 30 kilometres south of Hobart on the peninsula between the Huon River and Bruny Island.

Microclimates in these very cold viticultural regions - by world standards - is critical. Long sunshine hours in the summer help the equally long growing season, but the aspect of the slope and protection from the howling westerly winds is essential. The moderating effect of the many estuaries also plays an important role, helping produce some great wines - not without the viticulturist losing a little sleep. A number of wineries now have hospitality adjuncts helping make a visit a complete experience.

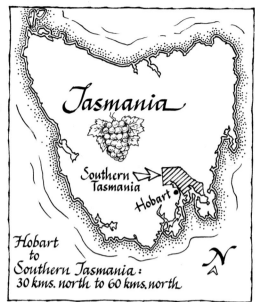

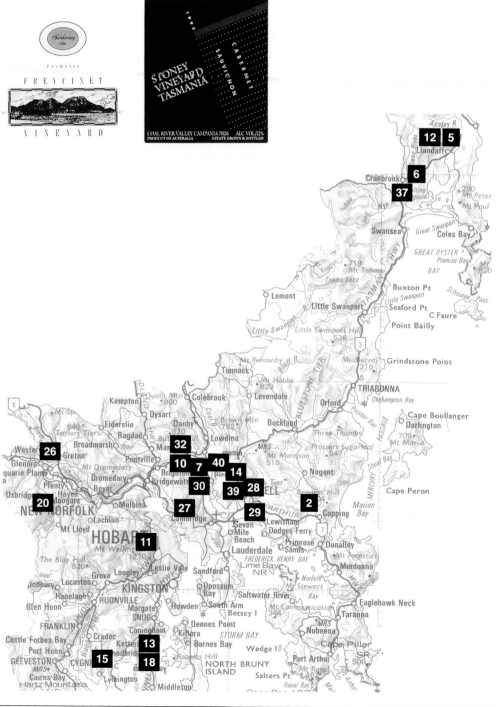

	Map - Index
2	Bream Creek Vineyard
5	Coombend Estate
6	Craigie Knowe Vineyard
7	Crosswinds Vineyard
10	Domaine A Stoney Vineyard
11	Elsewhere Vineyard
12	Freycinet Vineyard
13	Geddington Vineyard
14	Glenayr Vineyard
15	Hartzveiw Vineyard
18	Jollymont Vineyard
20	Kinvarra Estate
26	Meadowbank Vineyard
27	Milford Vineyard
28	Morningside Vineyard
29	Orani Vineyard
30	Palmara Vineyard
32	Richmond Park Vineyard
37	Spring Vale Vineyard
39	Tolpuddle Vineyards
40	Woodlands Vineyard

Domaine 'A' Stoney Vineyard

Stoney Vineyard began its life as the property of George and Priscilla Park in 1973. In 1988 Ruth and Peter Althaus tasted the wines at a comparative tasting on a trip from their native Switzerland. They fell in love with them and Tasmania. When they heard the property was on the market a year later they did not hesitate.

Peter was a senior executive with IBM in charge of the customer engineering department in Zurich. Peter is a great fan of Bordeaux wines and 70 per cent of the property is planted to red Bordeaux varieties - cabernet sauvignon, merlot, cabernet franc and petit verdot. A further 20 per cent is pinot noir with only 10 per cent in sauvignon blanc.

The soils are stony and well-drained with a thin layer of rich black clay. The low rainfall means some supplementary irrigation is necessary. The dry conditions with loads of sunshine and the north and east-facing slopes produce outstanding fruit. Peter is a fastidious winemaker and his wines are fantastic. A new winery is being built with an entertaining area to extend the superb cellars which are built into the Cool River Tier behind the vineyard.

DOMAINE A / STONEY VINEYARD
Address: Tea Tree Road, Campania Tas. 7026
Direction: between Richmond and Campania
Phone: (03) 62 604 174
Fax: (03) 62 604 390
Established: 1973
Owner: Peter & Ruth Althaus
Winemaker: Peter Althaus
Principal varieties grown: Cabernet sauvignon, pinot noir, sauvignon blanc
Ha under vine: 10
Average annual crush: 80 tonnes
Average no. cases produced: 5,000

Principal wines & brands	Cellar potential
Domaine A Cabernet Sauvignon	10+ years
Domaine A Pinot Noir	5-10 years
Stoney Cabernet Sauvignon	5-10 years
Stoney Pinot Noir	3-5 years
Stoney Sauvignon Blanc	2-5 years
Stoney Aurora	2-4 years

Public & trade tours: By appointment only
Mail order sales: Yes
Hours open to public: By appointment

Freycinet Vineyard

Geoff Bull is an individualist who has had a most interesting life. His first career was as an award-winning photo-journalist. Then a desire for the great outdoors led him to become an abalone diver off the east coast of Tasmania.

In 1980 he began planting vines on the steep slopes of his property at Bicheno on Tasmania's east coast. In a step by step process he established a small winery and vineyards which grew gradually under the large cypress trees at the foot of the steep slopes.

The two winery buildings include a splendid cafe-style tasting area. Geoff and Susan's daughter Lindy, studied winemaking. He has a degree from the famous Roseworthy College as does Lindy's husband, Claudio Radenti.

Riesling and muller thurgau were early varieties planted and make a concentrated dramatic floral style whilst the chardonnay, pinot noir and cabernet sauvignon are also excellent. The Freycinet Vineyard overlooks the spectacular Freycinet National Park area and coastline. Situated on the 42 degree latitudinal line, Freycinet Vineyard enjoys a unique micro-climate. The long growing season can sometimes extend into May and even June, combining very high sunshine hours with 1250 degree days (amongst the coolest climate summations for any vineyard in the world).

New winemaking equipment and top class French oak barriques in the skillful hands of the two young winemakers are making the most of superb grapes from Geoff's extremely well managed vineyards. Cabernet franc and merlot have come into bearing in recent years adding yet another dimension to their fine cabernet sauvignon.

FREYCINET VINEYARD
Address: Tasman Highway, Bicheno Tas. 7215
Direction: 18 km to the south of Bicheno
Phone: (002) 57 8384
Fax: (002) 57 8454
Established: 1980
Owner: Geoff & Sue Bull
Winemaker: Claudio Radenti
Principal varieties grown: Chardonnay, cabernet sauvignon, merlot, pinot noir, riesling, muller thurgau
Ha under vine: 4

Principal wines & brands	Cellar potential
Chardonnay	2-5 years
Riesling Muller Thurgau	0-1 years
Pinot Noir	5-10 years
Cabernet Sauvignon	5-10 years

Public & trade tours: Yes
Hours open to public: 9 am-5 pm Mon-Fri; 10 am-4.30 pm Sat-Sun
Points of interest: BBQ facilities, picnic area, light snacks served in summer. Jazz concert Easter Sunday - food, wine and music
Retail distribution: Selected bottle shops & restaurants

An introduction to Queensland

Wine production first began on a commercial level in Queensland in the unlikely location of Roma, almost 450 kilometres to the north-east of Brisbane. This venture was founded by Samuel Bassett in 1863. Vine cuttings were provided by Bassett's uncle who had an established vineyard in the Hunter Valley.

By the time Samuel's son, William, took control of the company in 1912, 'Romavilla' was a thriving business, with more than 180 hectares under vine. William Bassett had received winemaking tuition from the great Leo Buring, and his wines were highly sought-after. Romavilla has remained constantly in production. This seemed in doubt after William's death in 1973, but a group of Sydney businessmen purchased the property two years later, and production has continued.

While Romavilla is Queensland's longest operating winery, the vast majority of the state's industry is situated around the towns of Stanthorpe and Ballandean, near the border of New South Wales. The region is known as the 'Granite Belt', owing to its location on a small elevated plateau in the Great Dividing Range. Altitudes vary from 800 to 940 metres above sea level, making the area one of the highest wine-producing districts in Australia. Generally therefore, the climate is cool and not dissimilar to that experienced by the Margaret River region of Western Australia. Distance from the sea can result in harsh winters, and even occasional snow. The average maximum temperature during summer months is only 26 degrees centigrade and soils are decomposed granite varieties.

From a small bulk wine industry, began by the early European settlers, wine has now become a fully fledged industry, with larger vineyards and wineries being established.

The industry has expanded considerably and the Granite Belt now boasts more than 15 commercial wine-producing companies. Winemakers of the region are united in their desire to exploit the unique Queensland climate. Many innovative techniques are being employed and wines released so far show successful evidence of these efforts. In 1985, a light dry red wine was released onto the market by several local vignerons, with favourable results. Called 'Ballandean Nouveau', the wine is delightful served chilled and ideal for the Queensland market.

Every year on the first and second weekend of October the industry has its "Spring Wine Festival" attracting many wine and food enthusiasts to the region. This is followed on the third weekend by the "Australian Small Winemakers Show", attracting 550-600 entries involving every State in Australia.

The first Sunday in May boasts the extremely successful "Opera At Sunset", attracting over 1000 opera wine lovers to the wineries.

The Granite Belt region is a unique contributor to Australia's wine industry. Vignerons are highly motivated and justifiably proud of their region. I believe that the wines produced are of exceptional quality and are sure to become widely respected in the near future.

Queensland

1 Bald Mountain Vineyards
2 Ballandean Estate Winery
3 Bassetts Romavilla Winery Pty Ltd
4 Bungawarra Wines
5 Castle Glen

6 Felsberg Winery & Vineyards
7 Golden Grove Winery
8 Granite Cellars
9 Heritage
10 Inigo Granite Country Estate
11 Kominos Wines
12 Mount Magnus
13 Mountview Wines
14 Old Caves Winery
15 Robinsons Family Vineyards
16 Rumbalara Vineyards
17 Stone Ridge Vineyards
18 Winewood

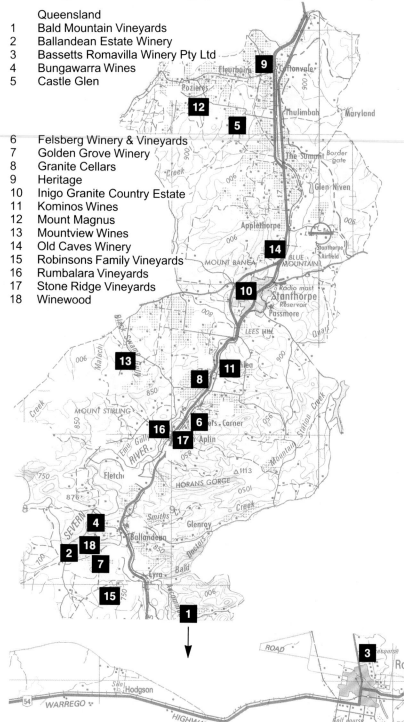

BALLANDEAN ESTATE
Address: Sundown road, Ballandean, Qld 4382
Direction: 4 km west of Ballandean
Phone: (076) 84 1226
Fax: (076) 84 1288
Established: 1968
Owner: Angelo & Mary Puglisi
Winemaker: Angelo Puglisi & Adam Chapman
Principal varieties grown: Shiraz, cabernet sauvignon, sylvaner, sauvignon blanc, muscat, semillon
Ha under vine: 18
Average annual crush: 80-120 tonnes
Average no. cases produced: 6,000

Principal wines & brands	Cellar potential
Ballandean Estate	
Print Label Shiraz	5-10 years
Cabernet/Malbec/Merlot	5-10 years
Semillon/Sauvignon Blanc	0-3 years
Late Harvest Sylvaner	5-10 years

Public & trade tours: Yes
Cellar door & mail order sales: Yes
Hours open to public: 9 am - 5 pm 7 days a week (except Good Friday & Christmas Day)
Points of interest: Cafe open most weekends. Group bookings for meals, any time by appointment, winery tours.
Retail distribution: Tucker & Co. Pty., Ltd. Brisbane & Sydney

KOMINOS WINES
Address: New England Highway, Severnlea Qld 4352
Phone: (076) 83 4311
Fax: (076) 83 4291
Established: 1976
Owner: Tony Comino
Winemaker: Tony Comino
Principal varieties grown: Riesling, semillon, chardonnay, shiraz, pinot noir, cabernet sauvignon, chenin blanc
Ha under vine: 6
Public & trade tours: Yes
Cellar door & mail order sales: Yes
Hours open to public: 9 am-4.30 pm seven days a week

MOUNT MAGNUS
Address: Donnelly's Castle Road, Pozieres via Stanthorpe, Qld 4352
Phone: (076) 85 3313
Fax: (076) 85 3313
Established: 1933
Principal varieties grown: Shiraz, cabernet, muscat, chardonnay
Ha under vine: 5
Average annual crush: 50 tonnes

Principal wines & brands	Cellar potential
Cabernet Shiraz	5-10 years
Semillon	5-10 years
Semillon Chardonnay	2-5 years
Pioneer Port	
Cabernet	5-10 years
Shiraz	5-10 years

Cellar door & mail order sales: Yes
Hours open to public: 9 am-5 pm Mon-Fri.
Points of interest: Bushwalks, Australia's highest altitude winery.

Chateau Hornsby – Northern Territory

Australia's most unusual viticultural location is that of Chateau Hornsby. You'll find it at Alice Springs in the Red Centre of Australia, not far from the world's largest monolith, Ayers Rock, the mysterious Olga's Range and Stanley Chasm.

Understandably, Alice Springs pharmacist, Denis Hornsby, and his wife, Miranda, were reluctant to leave this stunning landscape when they felt the urge to become vignerons, during the early 1970s. Against all odds and much well meant advice, the Hornsby's planted a small vineyard of three hectares in 1974. Grape varieties planted were mainly shiraz, cabernet sauvignon, semillon and riesling. The wines produced from the estate are very good indeed, a testimony to Denis' persistence.

One of the most unusual events at Chateau Hornsby occurred in 1984 with the semillon grapes. As is customary, grapes were harvested in early January. However, owing to the constant heat of the Central Australian climate, vines produced another ripe grape crop by December of the same year. Thus 1984 saw two grape harvests from the same vines. The climate also tends to confuse the vine. During one visit in May of 1986, I noticed new leaf shoots on vines that were still shedding their autumn-toned leaves. Denis explained that they had just received some rain after a dry spell and the vines were indeed confused. It goes without saying that irrigation is absolutely necessary at Chateau Hornsby for all but six weeks of the year. Water is pumped from a bore by submersible pump and delivered to the vineyard by trickle irrigation.

In 1994, Denis leased the retail, restaurant and tourism side of the business to the operator of "Spinifex Balloons" so Denis could spend more time in the vineyard and cellar (working). The restaurant, wine-tasting, wine sales, tourism part of the business now trades as "The Winery". Telephone (089) 555 133 or Fax (089) 555 532, open 7 days a week.

A restaurant is being established to provide both indoor and outdoor seating. An entertainment area has been constructed, and a regular performer is 'Foster-phone' virtuoso, Ted Egan.

The general atmosphere at the Chateau is worth crossing the desert for. The beauty of the location, the quality of the wines and delightful facilities ensure that the Hornsby's have many visitors. This unusual venture is bringing them well-deserved success.

CHATEAU HORNSBY

Address: Petrick Road, Alice Springs NT 0870
Direction: 10 km south-east of Alice Springs
Phone: (089) 52 6704
Fax: (089) 52 9558
Established: 1974
Winemaker: Denis Hornsby, Gordon Cook
Principal varieties grown: Shiraz, cabernet sauvignon, chardonnay, rhine riesling, semillon
Ha under vine: 3
Average annual crush: 15 tonnes
Average no. cases produced: 1,000 dozen

Principal wines & brands	Cellar potential
Hornsby Estate	
Shiraz	2-5 years
Chardonnay	2-5 years
Riesling/Semillon	2-5 years

Public & trade tours: By appointment only Ph 555 133 "The Winery", Fax 555 532
Cellar door & mail order sales: Yes
Hours open to public: 9 am-5 pm seven days a week
Points of interest: Restaurant (inside), bush restaurant (outside), hot air ballooning, music sundays
Retail distribution: Alice Springs only

An introduction to Classic Blends

One of the most complex skills acquired by Australia's most talented winemakers has been the art of blending wine. Among the great blenders in the history of Australia's wine industry I would include the late Maurice O'Shea from Mount Pleasant in the Hunter Valley (now owned by McWilliam's); Colin Preece from Seppelt at Great Western; Colin Haselgrove and Roger Warren from Thomas Hardy & Sons; Penfolds' great Max Schubert; Yalumba's Rudi Kronberger; and of course, the irrepressible Wolf Blass.

These men and others from today's top winemaking fraternity such as Brian Croser, John Duval, Brian Walsh and Peter Dawson all have in common the ability to recognise compatibility between two or more wines and blend them in the appropriate proportions, so that the end result is superior to any of the single components. Similarly, these winemakers share the responsibility of deciding the regional origin of fruit used. Blending possibilities are therefore virtually infinite and great winemaking skill is required to be successful in this regard.

During the varietal table wine boom of the 1970s, the blending of wines was often frowned upon. The phenomenal success of Wolf Blass must be attributed then both to his winemaking brilliance and marketing genius.

Fortunately, attitudes have now broadened and Australia's great blends are once again receiving the attention they deserve. The great classic Hunter Valley/McLaren Vale and Hunter/Barossa Valley blends have almost vanished. They are being replaced by exciting blends such as Nagambie (Victoria)/Coonawarra, Coonawarra/Barossa Valley, Coonawarra/Clare, and Coonawarrra/McLaren Vale. Fruit from South Australia's Langhorne Creek remains popular with blenders of red wines. Australia's blended wines are among the best in the world and add a fascinating dimension to the country's output.

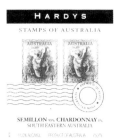

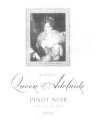

Queen Adelaide

Queen Adelaide is a regal name from which the beautifully situated and planned city of Adelaide took its name in 1836. This celebrated Queen of England features on one of Australia's most famous wine labels, which has been part of the Australian wine scene for many decades, and could be considered perhaps the best-known of the classic Australian blends.

The original Woodley's Winery was situated at Glen Osmond, a suburb of Adelaide on the Hills face some six or seven kilometres from the GPO, and made wine for many years before succumbing to the urban sprawl of Adelaide. Woodley's Queen Adelaide brand became famous for its quality and value for money, the chief varieties being a claret and a riesling.

In the 1980s the company was acquired by Seppelt who added a chardonnay to the Queen Adelaide stable. It proved an instant success, giving extremely good quality at a very reasonable price. Seppelt of course later became part of the giant Southcorp wine conglomerate which produces great wines at often unbelievably low prices. Today, Queen Adelaide is Australia's largest selling range of table wines.

I recently tried the new Queen Adelaide Pinot Noir selling for well under $10 and was very impressed. The expanding range of Queen Adelaide wines gives the wine-lover a regal choice at a price all her subjects can afford. Why not lift your glass and toast her Royal Highness?

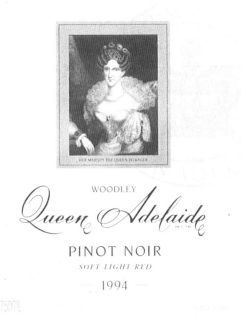

Wolf Blass Foundation

On July 1, 1995 the Wolf Blass Foundation was officially formed. On his 60th birthday in August the previous year, Wolf decided to form a foundation for the betterment of the Australian wine industry to reward achievement in all fields - viticulture, winemaking, wine marketing, media promotion and education involving wine.

Wolf's generosity in putting $A1 million into this foundation is to be heartily applauded; his foresight is not letting him down. The aim of the Foundation is not only to reward, but also to provide funds for the award winners to carry out further work and research in their respective fields for the benefit of the Australian wine industry. Wolf has always had the earnest desire to share good wine and the wealth it creates in every way with the industry he loves and the everyday person he relates to as well.

He has brought many people to the enjoyment of premium Australian wine through his unceasing and enthusiastic promotion of quality wine and the lifestyle culture it brings.

Fellow board member Guenter Prass A.M. brought about the revolution in sparkling and white wines with his technology in the 1950s, while Wolf revolutionised Australian red wines with his unique handling and barrel ageing in the 1970s, leading to his unsurpassed triple-winning Jimmy Watson wines and refocusing Australians on our great red wines.

Wolf Blass arrived in Australia in 1961 after making the fortunate choice between a sparkling winemaking offer in Venezuela or our own fair country. He took part in the sparkling wine revolution started by Guenter Prass but at the Kaiser Stuhl Winery. Wolf's flair and style became quickly obvious when, during an early Kaiser Stuhl pearl wine promotion, he poured sparkling wine out of a petrol pump - I don't know how that would go down in our heavily protective society today, but Wolf made his mark to the industry's benefit.

Wolf had a strong family background of wine in his East Germany homeland and as a youngster he worked in his grandfather's vineyard before going to the Wurzburg University where he became the youngest-ever graduate of the Kellermeister Diploma. Ever active and searching for a challenge after three years at Kaiser Stuhl, he became Australia's first freelance winemaker since

the great Leo Buring in 1919. For $2.50 per hour and 7 days a week, he travelled in his old Volkswagen beetle from winery to winery around South Australia; his results were legendary. He even sold wine as a consultant broker for 3-5 cents a gallon; his fortune was a long way off at this stage.

After consulting to TST Tollana, he was wooed to take on the permanent winemaking role for this new brand. Wolf did a fine job with the quality, style and of course promotion. In 1973, with a $2,000 overdraft, Wolf Blass wines began. The first vintage release was a 1966 which Wolf had tucked away. The old army shed on 2-1/2 acres of land at Nuriootpa became his headquarters, which he proceeded to get into ship-shape order. His policy right up until merging with Mildara some 15 years later was to crush at

the wineries selected in each region, bring the juice to his own winery which was superbly set up with many different tank sizes, and make the wines, nurturing them in his own way. He is, as many people say, a master blender, but he is much more - he is a master winemaker in every way. In 1991, the year he merged with Mildara, Wolf was honoured by his peers by being named 'International Winemaker of the Year' and received the revered Robert Mondavi Trophy. His role as a director and deputy chairman of Mildara Blass is maintaining style and quality of the wines and overseas promotion which he tackles in his usual no-effort-spared basis.

Wolf's vision for the Foundation is also to assist an interchange of a promising student from Adelaide University's Oenology

Course with a student from his old university at Wurzburg in Germany.

The Wolf Blass Foundation is seen by Wolf not as a means of self-promotion, but an opportunity for all companies in the industry, large and small, to participate and make the Foundation even stronger and more powerful. To this end, he will be focusing on gaining financial support as a top priority. Wolf has a wonderful way with people; he's straight to the point, but I've always found he knows what the point is and more than anything, he is willing to share things with his fellow human beings. Ein Prosit Wolfgang!

Cockatoo Ridge

In 1989, outgoing wine personality Geoff Merrill launched a brand in the competitive varietal price bracket. Geoff had a picturesque dam full of birdlife below his historic Mount Hurtle Winery.

Strolling around the water's edge one day, Geoff stumbled on a very large egg. Curious, he took it up to the laboratory, wrapped it in a blanket and placed it under a lamp to keep warm. A couple of days later, out popped 'Bruce the Goose'. Geoff returned him to the dam with a flock of wood ducks who welcomed him into the fold.

This ugly duckling story also has a happy ending - it was indeed 'the goose that laid the golden egg'. Geoff launched the brand name 'Wood Duck Dam', selling several thousand dozen wines in the first year. Most winemakers would be happy with that, but Geoff had other ideas; he wanted something uniquely Australian and tied in with wine history. This time it was his wife Janet who stepped in. Each dawn and dusk is heralded at Mt. Hurtle by the noisy corella cockatoos living in the large gums on the ridge behind the winery, where the vineyard and old crusher which used fed the gravity flow operation used to be. Coincidentally, corella comes from Latin and means 'to dig and burrow,' exactly what the corellas do in the vineyard.

'Cockatoo Ridge' was born in 1991 and in a few short years, the yearly sales of Cockatoo Ridge have soared so that the wine is on allocation to the trade each month. The chardonnay has led the way, but a red blend and a methode champenoise are selling like hot cakes too.

Overseas demand is strong and there just isn't enough wine to go around at present. However, Geoff is rightly not about to let the quality suffer to keep up supply. Cockatoo Ridge wines are attractively styled, priced and promoted, a winning combination. Geoff Merill was certainly no goose when he picked up the egg that hatched 'Bruce the Goose' and began the saga that launched Cockatoo Ridge.

COCKATOO RIDGE PTY LTD
Address: Mount Hurtle Winery, Pimpala Road, Reynella SA 5171
Phone: (08) 381 6877
Fax: (08) 322 2244
Established: 1991
Winemaker: Geoff Merrill
Principal varieties grown: Chardonnay, cabernet sauvignon, merlot, pinot noir, semillon

Principal wines & brands Cockatoo Ridge	Cellar potential
Chardonnay	2-5 years
Brut N.V.	
Cabernet Merlot	2-5 years

Trade tours: By appointment only
Cellar door & mail order sales: Yes
Hours open to public: 9 am-5 pm Mon-Fri; 12-5 pm Sun.
Points of interest: Fully-equipped commercial kitchen capable of catering for up to 100 people (by appointment)
Retail distribution: Distributed nationally through Tucker & Co. (Aust) Pty Ltd.

COCKATOO RIDGE

1994
South Eastern Australia
Chardonnay

Index

An introduction to New South Wales 7
An introduction to the Lower Hunter Valley 8
Hunter Valley Wine Society 12
Drayton's Bellvue 12
Lake's Folly 12
Allanmere 13
Briar Ridge 13
Brokenwood 14
Hungerford Hill 14
Calais Estates 15
Petersons 15
Little's Winery 16
Allandale 16
McWilliam's Mount Pleasant Winery 17
Lindemans Hunter Valley Winery 18
Simon Whitlam 20
Pendarves Estate 20
Sutherland Wines 21
Brian McGuigan 22
McGuigan Hunter Village 24
Hunter Valley Cheese Company 25
Vineyard Resort 26
Tamburlaine 27
Terrace Vale 27
J. Y. Tulloch and Sons 28
Tyrrell's Vineyard 29
Wyndham Estate 30

An introduction to the Upper Hunter Valley 32
Upper Hunter Valley 33
Arrowfield 34
Horseshoe Vineyard 35
Simon Gilbert 35
Rosemount Estate 36
Cruickshank Callatoota Estate 38
Reynolds Yarraman 39
Serenella Estate 39
Richmond Grove - Upper Hunter 40

An introduction to Mudgee 41
Mudgee 42
Botobolar Vineyard 43
Dumbrae Wines 43
Pieter van Gent 44
Huntington Estate 44
Craigmoor 45
Montrose 46
Stein's 47
Thistle Hill 47

An introduction to the Riverina 48
Riverina 49
West End Wines 50
Casella 50
The Cranswick Estate 51
De Bortoli Wines 52
McWilliam's Hanwood Winery 53
Lillypilly Estate 54
Miranda 55
Riverina Wines 56
Toorak Wines 57
Rossetto Wines 57

An introduction to Cowra 58
Richmond Grove - Cowra 59
Cowra Estate 59

An introduction to other wine producing areas of NSW 61
McWilliam's Barwang 64
Cassegrain 65
Charles Sturt University Winery 66
Cobbitty Wines (Cogno Brothers) 66
Grevillea Estate 67
Glenfinlass Wines 67

An introduction to South Australia 68
An introduction to the Adelaide Plains and Environs 70
Barossa Valley Estates 70
Adelaide Hills and Eden Valley 72
Gumeracha Cellars - Chain of Ponds Wines 73

Adelaide Hills 74
Hillstowe 76
Petaluma 77
Bridgewater Mill 78
Irvine 78
Mountadam 79
Tollana Woodbury Vineyard 80
Henschke - Eden Valley/Keyneton 81
Henschke - Lenswood 81
Penfolds Magill Estate 82
Hill Smith Estate 85
Heggies Vineyard 85
Pewsey Vale 85

An introduction to the Barossa Valley 86
Barossa Valley 88
Bethany Wines 90
Burge Family Winemakers 90
Charles Cimicky 91
Charles Melton 91
Chateau Yaldara 92
Kies Estate - Lyndoch Hills Cellars 93
Chateau Yaldara Motor Inn 94
Chateau Dorrien 95
Twin Valley Wines 96
Grant Burge Wines 97
Dorrien Estate - Cellarmaster Wines 98
Leo Buring 99
Basedow 99
Jenke Vineyards 99
Jacobs Creek 100
Krondorf 102
Kaesler Wines 104
Peter Lehmann 105
Richmond Grove - Barossa 106
Rockford 108
Miranda Rovalley Wines 109
Seppeltsfield 110
Wolf Blass 112
St Hallett Wines 114
Yalumba 115

An introduction to the Clare Valley 116
Clare Valley 117
Black Opal 118
Clare Central Inn and Treloars Restaurant 120
Penfolds Clare Estate 120
Jim Barry 121
Mitchell Wines 121
Duncan Estate 121
Leasingham 122
Crabtree of Watervale 123
Pikes Polish Hill River Estate 124
Taylors Wines 125
Wakefield Wines 126
Skillogalee Wines 126
The Wilson Vineyard 127
Tim Knappstein 128

An introduction to Coonawarra 129
Coonawarra 130
Balnaves of Coonawarra 132
Bowen Estate 132
Brand's Laira Wines 133
Chardonnay Lodge 134
Haselgrove Wines Coonawarra 135
Highbank 135
Hollick Wines 136
Leconfield 136
Mildara - Jamieson's Run Winery 137
Katnook Estate and Riddoch Winery 138
Rouge Homme 139
Lindemans - St George 140
Majella 140
Parker Coonawarra Estate 141
Rosemount - Coonawarra 141
Penley Estate 142
Redman's Redbank Winery 143
Wynns Coonawarra Estate 144
The Ridge Vineyard 146
Rymill Coonawarra 146
Robertson's Well 147

An introduction to Padthaway/Keppoch 148
Lindemans Padthaway 150
Browns' of Padthaway 150

An introduction to Langhorne Creek 151
Bleasdale 153
Bremerton Lodge 153
Lake Breeze 154
Temple Bruer 154

McLaren Vale - South Australia 155
Dennis of McLaren Vale 159
Kay Brothers - Amery Vineyard 159
Noons Wines 159
Merrivale Wines 160
Tinlins 160
Pertaringa Vineyards 161
Andrew Garrett Wines 163
The Barn Restaurant and Gallery 164
Hugo Winery 164
Haselgrove Wines 165
Stevens Cambrai 165
Hillstowe 166
The Salopian Inn 166
Richard Hamilton Wines 167
Crestview 168
Dyson Wines 168
Chapel Hill 169
Tatachilla 170
Wirilda Creek 171
St Francis Winery 171
Woodstock 172
McLaren Vale Olive Groves 173
Shottesbrooke 174
Maxwell Wines 174

Index

Coriole 175
Seaview 176
Scarpantoni 178
Wirra Wirra 179
Chateau Reynella 180
d'Arenberg 183
Fern Hill 184
Ingoldby 185
Hardy's Tintara 186
Maglieri 188
Manning Park 189
Marienberg 190
McLarens On The Lake 191
Middlebrook 192
Mount Hurtle - Geoff Merrill 193
Normans 194
Pirramimma 195
Ryecroft - Rosemount 196

An introduction to the Riverland 197
S.A. Riverland 198
Angove's 200
Angove's – St. Agnes Brandy 202
Kingston Estate 204
Renmano 206
Berri Estates 207

**An introduction to Currency Creek/
    Middleton Beach** 208
Currency Creek Winery 209
Middleton Estate Winery 210

An introduction to Victoria 211
Bendigo Region 212

An introduction to Bendigo 214
Mount Ida 214
Balgownie 215

An introduction to the Macedon Ranges 216
Cleveland 218
Knight Granite Hills 218
Cope-Williams – Romsey 219
The Hanging Rock Winery 220

An introduction to Sunbury 221
Goona Warra 222
Mount Aitken Estates 223
Wildwood 223

An introduction to East Gippsland 224
Lyre Bird Hill 226
Tarago River Cheese Company 226

An introduction to the Mornington Peninsula 227
Arthur's Restaurant 229
Elgee Park 229
Dromana Estate 230
Glynt by the Sea 232
Hanns Creek 233
Main Ridge Estate 233
Red Hill Estate 234
Tanglewood Downs 234
Stonier's Winery 235
Tuck's Ridge 236
T'Gallant 237

An introduction to Geelong 238
Idyll Vineyard 239

An introduction to Goulburn Valley 240
Chateau Tahbilk 242
Mitchelton Winery 244
Delatite 246

An introduction to Milawa/Glenrowan 247
Brown Brothers 248
Milawa Cheese Company 248

An introduction to Mildura/Swan Hill 249
Mildura - Swan Hill 250
Best's St Andrews, Lake Boga 252
Alambie Wine Co Ltd 252
Tisdall 253
Wingara Wine Group 253
Stanley Wines Buronga 254
Trentham Estate 254

An introduction to Rutherglen 255
Rutherglen 257
All Saints 258
R M Buller and Son Vineyard 258
Campbells 259
Morris of Rutherglen 260
Stanton & Killeen 261
Pfeiffers Wines 261

An introduction to Western Victoria 262
Western Victoria 264
Mount Langi Ghiran 266
Dalwhinnie 267
Best's Great Western 268
Fiddler's Creek 269
Taltarni 269
Seppelt Great Western 270
Yellowglen 272
Chateau Remy - Blue Pyrenes Estate 274
Warrenmang Vineyard Resort 275
Redbank 275

An introduction to the Yarra Valley 276
Yarra Valley 278
De Bortoli - Yarra Valley 280
Domaine Chandon 282
Green Point 284
Eyton on Yarra 285
Fergusson Winery 286
Lirralirra Estate 286
Lillydale Vineyards 287
Long Gully Estate 288
Seville Estate 289
Mount Mary Vineyard 289
Yarra Ridge 290
Tarrawarra Vineyard 292

An introduction to Western Australia 293
An introduction to the Coastal Plains of WA . 294
Darlington Estate 294
Killerby Vineyards 294
Baldivis Estate 295
Moondah Brook 296
Capel Vale 297
Paul Conti Wines 297
Margaret River 298

An introduction to Margaret River 300
Amberley Estate 301
Brookland Valley 302
Cape Mentelle 304
Chateau Xanadu 304
Captain Freycinet 305
Evans & Tate - Redbrook 305
Cullens Winery 306
Busselton Red 306
Devil's Lair 308
Moss Wood 309
Lenton Brae 309
Leeuwin Estate 310
Redgate 312
Sandalford - Margaret River Vineyard 313
Voyager 314
Fonti Margaret River Cheeses 315

An introduction to Great Southern 316
Great Southern 317
Alkoomi 318
Plantagenet 318
Goundrey 319
Millinup Estate Wines 319
Jingalla 320
Karrivale 320

An introduction to the Swan Valley 321
Swan Valley 322
Houghton 323
Jane Brook Estate 324
Sandalford – Caversham Estate 325
Gloucester Ridge 326

An introduction to Pemberton 326
Pemberton 327
Salitage 328

An introduction to Tasmania 330
An introduction to Northern Tasmania 332
Clover Hill 333
Dalrymple Vineyard 333
Holm Oak Vineyards 334
Marion's Vineyard 334
Heemskerk 335
Rochecombe Vineyard 336
Pipers Brook 337
Lactos Master Cheesemakers 338
King Island Cheese Company 340
An introduction to Southern Tasmania 342
Moorilla Estate 342
Domaine 'A' Stoney Vineyard 343
Freycinet Vinyard 343

An introduction to Queensland 344
Ballendean Estate 345
Kominos Wines 345
Mount Magnus 345

Chateau Hornsby – Northern Territory 346

An introduction to Classic Blends 347
Queen Adelaide 347
Wolf Blass Foundation 348
Cockatoo Ridge 350